Paralegals and Tribunal Practice and Procedure

Third Edition

Irv Ash

SCHOOL OF LEGAL AND PUBLIC ADMINISTRATION
Seneca College

Captus Press

Paralegals and Tribunal Practice and Procedure, Third Edition

© 2016 by Irv Ash and Captus Press Inc.

The publisher and the editor gratefully acknowledge the authors, publishers, and organizations for their permission to reproduce their work in this book. Care has been taken to trace ownership of copyright material contained in this book. The publisher will gladly take any information that will enable the rectification of any reference or credit in subsequent editions and apologizes for any errors or omissions.

Captus Press Inc.
Mail: Units 14 & 15, 1600 Steeles Avenue West
         Concord, Ontario Canada L4K 4M2
Telephone: (416) 736–5537
Fax: (416) 736–5793
Email: info@captus.com
Internet: http://www.captus.com

Library and Archives Canada Cataloguing in Publication

Ash, Irv
    Paralegals and tribunal practice and procedure / Irv Ash. — Third edition.

Includes partially annotated version of the Ontario Statutory Powers
    Procedure Act.
Includes bibliographical references.
ISBN 978-1-55322-297-2 (paperback).

    1. Administrative procedure—Ontario.   2. Administrative courts—Ontario.   3. Ontario. Statutory Powers Procedure Act.   4. Administrative courts—Canada.   I. Ontario.   Abandoned Orchards Act.   II. Title.

KEO891.A84 2016   342.713'0664   C2016-904285-5
KF5417.A84 2016

 Funded by the Government of Canada / Financé par le gouvernement du Canada | Canada

0 9 8 7 6 5 4
Printed in Canada

Contents

Part I
General Principles

3

Part II
Selected Ontario Agencies

4   Social Benefits Tribunal.   195

7 The Licence Appeal Tribunal — AABS

Part III
Selected Federal Agency

Dedication and Acknowledgements

This book is dedicated to my wonderful and lovely wife Irene — for just being her.

I acknowledge everyone at Captus Press who assisted in the production of this book, especially Pauline Lai. I appreciate all the help received from various people in many Ontario agencies, with contents provided and suggestions made, as well as various members of SOAR. Further, a nod to my colleagues at Seneca College, who were helpful to my growth as a communicator. I also wish to thank my friend, the late Pat Goodman, for her typing services when needed, and my brother, Mel Ash.

For this new edition, I want to also acknowledge many of my students at Seneca College, who used the first and second edition and enthusiastically pointed out errors and typos, which have been corrected in this edition. Any still existing errors and typos in this third edition are strictly the fault of the author.

Preface

It has been five years since this third edition was completed; but as always, the law is constantly in flux, so the author had to make even more changes. To assist the reader, especially one who has access to either of the previous editions, the new additions shall be broadly discussed in relation to each chapter; and before looking at each chapter, three major changes to the book will be elaborated on.

First, in many of the chapters, especially in the preamble to Part II, with a number of new pages and some appended material, the clustering of many Ontario's tribunals is expounded upon. This development has been quite dramatic in Ontario, with 17 already clustered in three groups. There have also been attempts by Ontario tribunal management to proselytize on the value of clustering; although other jurisdictions have used mergers to achieve similar ends, Ontario for now seems to be the one jurisdiction to use clustering.

Second, Chapter 7 in the two previous editions was on the Financial Services Tribunal. The author has deleted the chapter because the tribunal, which at the time the book was originally written, had just changed its jurisdiction over representatives, who are now likely paralegals licensed by the Law Society of Upper Canada. It is now unlikely that any paralegal would represent a client before the FST as the matters before it would be mostly minor with little compensation available. As the book is written primarily for paralegals, it seems wasteful to have a chapter on a tribunal not likely to be involved with paralegals.

Third, the chapter on the FSCO Dispute Resolution Group ("DRG") — the previous Chapter 8 — has been deleted, and a new chapter on the License Appeal Tribunal ("LAT") has replaced it due to changes in the *Insurance Act*, R.S.O. 1990, c. I.8. This Act shifted the process of resolving disputes about Statutory Accident Benefits arising from motor vehicle accidents in Ontario from the DRG to the LAT as of

April 1, 2016. As of the time of writing, the Automobile Accident Benefits Service ("AABS") has just begun accepting applications. Regulations and rules are in place but not practice directions. There are no decisions available yet to be examined. The information currently available only allows for the best educated guess as to how the procedures will be applied.

In respect to changes in the text, every chapter has some minor rewording and changes caused by re-reading the material. Chapter 1 has a reworded paragraph on clustering of Ontario tribunals. Chapters 2 and 3 have minimal changes. The preamble to Part II, as noted above, has a number of new pages regarding clustering, as well as some documents included in the appendix to the preamble. Chapter 4, Social Benefits Tribunal, has extra material on clustering and a discussion of recent changes to the SBT procedure, mostly due to the new Rules effective January 1, 2016 and the publishing of SBT decisions on CanLII. Chapter 5, Assessment Review Board, has clustering information as well as a table comparing similar provisions of the *Municipal Act* and the *City of Toronto Act*. Additionally, many changes are required due to the new ARB Rules that became effective April 2, 2013, as well as new forms, information sheets and changes to the explanatory literature. Chapter 6, Human Rights Tribunal of Ontario, has the cluster information, discussions of new amendments to the *Human Rights Code* regarding gender identity and gender expression, as well as new forms and practice directions, as reflected in the appendix to that chapter. Chapter 7 (a new chapter for this edition) discusses the Licence Appeal Tribunal, with a focus on the AABS branch. Finally, Chapter 8 (formerly Chapter 9), on the Canadian Human Rights Tribunal (CHRT), only required minor changes and rewording.

The author believes that major changes like those that occurred in the last five years need to be addressed to keep this book current and as useful as possible to the reader.

Please note that the text has continued with the old version of statute and case citation even though the *Canadian Guide to Uniform Legal Citation*, 8th ed. (Toronto: Carswell, 2014), a.k.a. the McGill Guide, has updated citations by deleting most periods.

Part I

General Principles

Basic Concepts of Administrative Law

1

LEARNING OBJECTIVES

After reading this chapter, the reader should be able to:

- define administrative law
- differentiate between the three branches or functions of government
- elaborate on various concepts of public policy
- explain the reasons for, the types of, and the functions of agencies
- compare and contrast agencies and courts
- identify specific rules and procedures for a specific agency
- assess the relevant provisions of the *Statutory Powers Procedure Act* as they relate to the rules and procedure of Ontario agencies
- document how various sections of the *Charter of Rights and Freedoms* have been applied to agency proceedings
- illustrate and discuss principles that flow from the duty to act fairly
- distinguish between the remedies of reconsideration, appeal, and judicial review that may be available in respect of an agency proceeding
- outline various concerns in respect of appealing an agency proceeding
- summarize the various remedies available from an agency proceeding pursuant to judicial review

INTRODUCTION

In the past 30 years, the number of court cases involving administrative law has increased tremendously. The reason for the increase is tied to both the unprecedented growth of government in Canada and the definition of administrative law. The definition involves government and governmental delegates, the legal restrictions imposed on the government when implementing public policy, and the remedies available to persons "harmed" by the misuse of governmental power. This chapter will attempt, in varying detail, to deal with each component of this definition.

The courts have been given **jurisdiction**, both **inherent** and **statutory**, to oversee and remedy many governmental actions. This jurisdiction, or power, derives in common law from the *Magna Carta* in 1215 and has been strengthened over the years by various statutes as well as by case law. Furthermore, in Canada, greater jurisdiction has been given to the courts by the constitutional documents that instituted and regulate the country, and by the federal–provincial split of jurisdictional powers. Before delving into various aspects of administrative law, it is necessary to review some aspects of government and the Canadian Constitution and to further discuss the concept of public policy and how it is legislated and enforced in the Canadian legal system.

BRANCHES OF GOVERNMENT

Canada has three branches (or functions) of government. The legislative (or parliamentary) branch includes elected Members of Parliament, both federal and provincial, and the federally appointed Senate. The major task of this branch is to introduce, debate, and institute new legislation, and to amend and/or repeal existing legislation. Once the legislation is enacted and **proclaimed in force**, it is the main duty of the executive branch (consisting of the Cabinets, both federal and provincial, and the attendant civil servants) to ensure compliance with each statute by means of governmental policy instruments (regulations and orders-in-council) that may be in force. This is achieved through the work of government ministries, departments, and agencies, as well as through boards, commissions, and tribunals. The third branch of government, the judicial branch (consisting of the persons in the legal system, i.e., judges, lawyers, and court administration staff), has basic obligations to interpret the legislation in specific cases in order to resolve disputes. If no relevant legislation is specified, the judicial branch must also determine the law to be applied. In addition to this basic obligation to interpret the legislation put before them, the courts' powers also include a review component. The courts oversee not only the appropriate exercise of substantive powers of government (constitutional law) but also the exercise of government's procedural powers (administrative law).

PUBLIC POLICY

It should be noted that almost all legislation is initiated by the governing party. By starting the legislative process, and then shepherding it to its conclusion, the governing party is putting into law parts of its governmental or public policy. This is just one facet of public policy that can be defined as a "conscious choice [of government or governmental authority] that leads to deliberate action — the passage of a law, the spending of money, an official speech or gesture, or some observable act — or inaction" (Stephen Brooks, *Public Policy in Canada: An Introduction* at 12). If it is conceded that the function of government is to govern, then any action taken by government in governing is public policy.

MECHANICS OF PUBLIC POLICY

Many different paths can be taken to achieve what the government of the day perceives as its objectives. A great deal of policy is developed internally in the caucus of the elected members of the governing party and through consultation with their advisors (sometimes their constituents) and the civil service. Policy is also derived from the party platform prior to elections; it can originate in various ways allowed by that party's internal constitution, and is developed in response to current issues. For example, policy actions can follow from senior ministers floating "trial balloons" at speaking engagements and in media interviews, from public hearings before standing committees of the legislature, or from reports from royal commissions appointed to investigate certain issues. Having determined the substance of the proposed public policy in a specific area, the government makes it governmental policy or law in a variety of ways that include (a) primary legislation (statutes), and (b) subordinate legislation (regulations and orders-in-council) properly published in statute books or in the **gazette**, respectively.

After the legislative function has been carried out, the next step is to enforce the legislation. If the legislation is regulatory — that is, it involves control of public and/or private sector operations in the "public interest", mechanisms will be found to achieve the desired ends. This is also the case for legislation that is operational in nature, such as legislation in respect of delivery of goods and/or services, review and/or advice, the use and conservation of resources, or legislation for disciplinary or other purposes.

Governments continue to enact and enforce more and more regulatory legislation. The main function of the executive branch of government is concerned with enforcing these laws. That function is often achieved by civil servants working for various ministries in the government, usually in specialized regulatory bodies. It should be noted that under constitutional law, the government can delegate its powers to legislate and enforce laws to bodies it creates. Such bodies shall, for the purposes of this chapter, be called agencies (including boards, commissions, authorities, committees, and tribunals). Although administrative law can, and does, deal with actions of Cabinet ministers and/or other elected members of government, it mostly involves judicial review and/or appeals (to be discussed below) by agencies.

AGENCIES

There are various reasons a government would appoint an agency to deal with a specific area, including, but not limited to, the following:

1. Specific expertise can be developed and applied.
2. The magnitude and complexity of government and its attendant workload requires a shift in responsibilities from elected members to such experts.
3. It is more timely and cost efficient to use an agency to deal with recurrent matters.
4. It offers a more precise, yet flexible and timely, way to deal with specific situations than going through the more cumbersome elected bodies.
5. It is a way to distance the government from the public effect of certain decisions or actions.
6. It allows future unforeseen events to be dealt with more efficiently.

Because there are many and diverse reasons agencies are created, there are many agencies in existence. In 1990, there were 485 government agencies in Ontario. By 1994, that number had grown to 716 (*Guide to Agencies, Boards and Commissions of the Government of Ontario* 1994 (Toronto, Ont.: Queen's Printer, 1995) at 3).

There are three main types of agencies:

• Advisory — provide information to government that will assist in developing policy or the ongoing delivery of programs. Some examples of Ontario advisory agencies are the Ontario Advisory

Council on Senior Citizens and the Ontario Advisory Council for Disabled Persons.

- Operational — deliver goods and/or services necessary to implement approved government policy or programs. Operational agencies in Ontario include the Workplace Safety and Insurance Board and Criminal Injuries Compensation Board.

- Regulatory (which also includes adjudicative bodies) — decision-making bodies that control public- or private-sector operations as authorized by their enabling legislation or the exercise of a licence-review function or an appeal function, with respect to both government and third-party decisions. The Canadian Radio and Telecommunications Commission (CRTC) and the Human Rights Tribunal of Ontario are examples of regulatory bodies.

Agencies may, if empowered, exercise legislative, executive, and judicial (adjudicative) functions. As will be discussed, the legislative function includes the ability to make rules and regulations according to the procedure to be followed by the agency. The executive function includes research and advice on government policy, and its administration and enforcement. An agency may have any or all of the above-mentioned powers, which must be specifically delegated by the legislation that established the particular agency.

An agency is established by legislation enacted by the government. That **enabling legislation** will have provisions that may delegate power to the agency in order to carry out certain stated objectives. Such legislation will usually set out general procedures of the agency, such as who has the right to appear before such agency and the jurisdiction and powers of the agency. Furthermore, the agency may, under the legislation, be empowered to make rules and regulations regarding its own procedures. Finally, the legislation will authorize the staffing of the agency and determine who may be eligible to be employed there.

AGENCIES COMPARED TO COURTS — ADJUDICATIVE FUNCTION

One function of agencies can be adjudicative. Agencies may determine rights, privileges, and/or obligations of persons in relation to another person, or to a group or society. An agency acting under such powers has been seen as having a **judicial or quasi-judicial function** that would seem to encroach on the judicial branch of government, i.e., the court system.

EXHIBIT 1.1
A Comparison between Courts and Agencies

COURTS	AGENCIES
• interpret and apply the law	• formulate (by regulation), interpret, and apply the law
• *stare decisis* applied (inflexible)	• no *stare decisis*, although attempts to be relatively consistent (flexible)
• formal — specific rules and procedures to be followed	• more informal — there may or may not be specific rules and procedures to be followed, but more procedural latitude is allowed
• make decisions based strictly on law; no policy or public interest concerns	• make many decisions based on public policy
• no relationship with parties before them, either before or after hearing	• likely to have many relationships with parties, both before and after adjudication
• unlikely to have expertise in decision-making area	• usually have expertise in decision-making area

---

There is considerable case law on the difference between the courts and agencies. Some agencies are similar to courts, in that both interpret legislation and apply it to specific cases. However, there are differences between the two bodies (see Exhibit 1.1).

One of the most contentious issues in the court–agency comparison is how far the judiciary should go in recognizing agencies' obligations to make decisions based on public interest (or the collective good of society). Public interest is foreign to the courts, which have always looked to individual rights, first and foremost. This tension can be observed in the greater or lesser control that the courts have exercised over agencies during the past 50 years (discussed later in this chapter).

STEPS TO DETERMINE RULES OF AGENCIES

We shall next examine the legal restrictions imposed on agencies. To determine the specific rules and procedures, or legal restrictions, followed by a specific agency, the following should be reviewed:

1. Enabling statute creating the agency
2. Regulations pursuant to the enabling statute

3. If applicable, general legislation that details rules and procedures applicable to certain agencies
4. *Canadian Charter of Rights and Freedoms* (Part I of the *Constitution Act 1982*, R.S.C. 1985, Appendix II, No. 44 (the
   Charter))
5. Rules, guidelines, and/or directives formulated by the agency
6. Rules set out in notices issued generally and/or for a particular
   proceeding
7. An overall common law requirement to "act fairly", and rules
   derived therefrom

Each of these steps will be discussed at some length to clarify how
such rules and procedures are found.

Enabling Statute

As we saw above, agencies must be created by government statute
that sets up an agency to advise on, operate in, and/or regulate a
legislated area. Usually, such an enabling statute will detail the com-
position of the agency, its powers and jurisdiction, and, occasionally,
rules and procedures. An agency that is set up under a specific
enabling Act may also be named as the relevant agency to hear
appeals of issues under different legislation. For example, the Social
Benefits Tribunal (SBT) was created under section 60(1) of the
Ontario Works Act, 1997, S.O. 1997, c. 25, Sched. A, as amended
(*OWA*), which also gave it some of its powers and jurisdiction. The
SBT was also given additional powers and jurisdiction under another
empowering statute, the *Ontario Disability Support Program Act,
1997*, S.O. 1997, c. 25, Sched. B, as amended (*ODSPA*).

Regulations Pursuant to the Enabling Statute

Enabling statutes will have provisions that allow regulations to be
made governing the rules and procedures to be applied by the agencies. Powers to develop and **promulgate** regulations are often
granted to the Governor General in Council (federal Cabinet) or the
Lieutenant Governor in Council (provincial Cabinet), depending on
whether the enabling Act is federal or provincial. The procedures in
respect of the SBT, for example, are prescribed in regulations by the
Ontario Lieutenant Governor in Council. Such regulations will usually
give details regarding documentation to be provided in a hearing,
time limits with which there must be compliance, and other hearing
procedures. Many agencies have rules and procedures detailed not in
regulations but, rather, in other ways.

Legislation That Establishes Rules for Many Boards

Some provincial jurisdictions (currently Alberta and Ontario) have provisions that govern procedures of numerous agencies set out in one statute. In Ontario, the statute is entitled the *Statutory Powers Procedure Act*, R.S.O. 1990, c. S.22, as amended (*SPPA*). Originally enacted in the 1970s to provide "minimum rules for proceedings of certain tribunals", the *SPPA* was an attempt by the Ontario government to codify the rules and procedures that the court system had developed for administrative agencies over the years, through the common law "duty to act fairly" and its predecessor concept, the "*rules of natural justice*". It was felt that there should be somewhat common rules and procedures for those agencies required to hold a hearing — that is, to exercise a "statutory power of decision".

It is important to note that the *SPPA* applies to all Ontario agencies exercising a statutory power of decision unless they are explicitly excluded by the provisions of the *SPPA* or another statute.

As initially conceived and enacted, the *SPPA* dealt with such matters as

1. determination of the parties to a proceeding;
2. notice provisions to advise of the case to be met and provision of time to prepare;
3. requirement of a public hearing unless there are reasons for a private hearing;
4. appropriate representation of parties at hearings, including examination and possibly cross-examination of witnesses;
5. powers of agencies to compel evidence;
6. rules regarding admissibility of evidence;
7. written decisions to be provided to all participants after the hearing; and
8. requirement of agencies to compile a record of the proceedings.

All of these matters are part of the common law "duty to act fairly", to be discussed later in this chapter.

Certain amendments were made in 1994 to the *SPPA*, under the *Statute Law Amendment Act (Government Management and Services)*, S.O. 1994, c. 27, that allow agencies that fall within the *SPPA* to have more cost-effective and efficient proceedings. Some of the amendments include (a) a general provision allowing any agency under the *SPPA* to make its own rules and procedures, and to promulgate them in the form of regulations; (b) a recognition of the value, where appropriate, of both written hearings and, especially, electronic hearings by amending the previous rules to allow such hearings; and (c) a provision permitting agencies to have pre-hearing conferences, determine more questions about admissibility of evidence, make interim orders, and have the power to review and vary a decision. More recent amendments to the *SPPA* in 1999 made certain changes, especially, but not limited to, inserting provisions for the appointment, with the consent of all the parties, of mediators, conciliators, and negotiators to facilitate resolution of a matter before a tribunal. This alternative dispute resolution system mirrors similar programs instituted in the civil court system to try to resolve matters without requiring the time, expense, and hard feelings of a court hearing. A further, more complete discussion of the *SPPA* appears in Chapter 2.

Charter of Rights and Freedoms

There are many general statements made in the *Charter* in terms of individual rights and freedoms. The judiciary has been given the power under the *Charter* to determine if a person's freedoms or rights have been infringed upon by some governmental law or action (including actions of agencies, as they are creations of governmental law). The judiciary has used various sections of the *Charter* to review the rules and procedures and, ultimately, the decisions of agencies.

Section 7 of the *Charter* states, "Everyone has the *right to life, liberty and security of the person* and the right not to be deprived thereof, except in accordance with the *principles of fundamental justice*" (italics added). Through a series of decisions, the Supreme Court of Canada (SCC) has read into those italicized words principles of procedural fairness. Although such principles existed in the common law concept of the rules of natural justice, the *Charter* has entrenched those principles as part of the basic constitutional law of Canada.

After analyzing the decisions at the SCC, two leading authors on administrative law summarized the principles as follows:

> These [principles] include the rights to notice, and a hearing, and unbiased decision-making and all the other related, procedural rights. One must then ask whether any particular procedural right should be afforded in the specific case. Several limiting factors should be examined. First, the purpose of the impugned legislation should be considered and a balance should be struck between the demands of fairness and efficiency. The competing interests of the state and the individual must be balanced. Second, in extradition matters at least (and perhaps more generally), the Court may ask whether denying the remedy would "shock" the conscience of Canadians or violate the standards of the international community. Third, the nature of the decision-making function will be analyzed. Depending upon where the function resides [or] the continuum of administrative

decision-making, a higher or lower degree of procedural fairness will be required. The closer the decision-maker is to the legislative (or policy) end of the spectrum, the lower the standard of procedural fundamental justice which is required. A higher degree of fairness is required as the decision-maker moves along the spectrum toward judicial or quasi-judicial deliberations. (David Jones & Anne de Villars, *Principles of Administrative Law* 2d ed. (Toronto, Ont.: Carswell, 1994) at 57–58)

Agencies have powers to force the production of documents or evidence by summons and/or subpoena, or to permit entry of premises to conduct searches by search warrants. They must comply with section 8 of the *Charter*, which states that such seizures or searches must be reasonable. Various decisions in the courts have determined that individuals must have some sort of sliding scale in their right to privacy. The reasonableness of privacy is dependent on the circumstances, such as the purposes of the search and other related factors. Furthermore, certain procedural safeguards must usually be maintained, e.g., a decision-maker authorizing such search or seizure must be impartial and must base it on reasonable evidence being supplied.

Section 13 of the *Charter* states, "A witness who testifies in any proceeding has the right not to have any incriminating evidence so given used to incriminate that witness in any other proceedings, except in a prosecution for perjury or for the giving of contradictory evidence." This section is not the same as the American Fifth Amendment, which allows a person to not give any evidence that would tend to incriminate him or her. Instead, evidence given by a person may not be used to incriminate that person in a subsequent or other proceeding.

Section 14 of the *Charter* states, "A party or witness in any proceeding who does not understand or speak the language in which the proceedings are conducted or who is deaf has the right to the assistance of an interpreter." Furthermore, the interpreter must translate word for word and not summarize the information being translated. Notice that the *Charter* makes no reference as to who pays for the interpreter, making such issue open for discussion.

Rules, Guidelines, and Directives Formulated by the Agency

Some enabling statues, such as the Ontario *Workplace Safety and Insurance Act, 1997*, S.O. 1997, c. 16, Sched. A, as amended, under subsection 159(1) for the Workplace Safety and Insurance Board

(WSIB) and subsection 173(1) for the Workplace Safety and Insurance Tribunal (WSIAT), give specific power to agencies to determine their own practice and procedure. Depending on the statute, the rules made by the agency, in respect of practice and procedure, may have the force and effect of a regulation. The regulation, however, must be approved by the appropriate Cabinet, and the guidelines to promulgate such rules as regulations must be followed. If, however, the agency has made its rules in a non-statutory form, as described in the next paragraph, such rules must be followed if they are mandatory.

Rules Set Out in Notice Generally or for a Particular Proceeding

For reasons of flexibility, agencies usually have some latitude in determining which rules should apply generally, and in a particular proceeding, provided that the overriding concern of fairness is met. This concern is also addressed when determining whether the specific rules are mandatory (must be followed) or directory (may be followed). Although consistency in rules is preferable, it is not necessary to follow all rules if there is a risk of unfair treatment. It is recognized that in these situations agencies have the power to broadly interpret, and even change, rules as long as no party is prejudiced. On the other hand, if some or all of the parties have acted in reliance upon a specific rule, it would not be correct to amend such a rule.

Common Law Requirement to "Act Fairly" and the Rules Derived Therefrom

The steps to determine the rules of any agency discussed above should be observed through the lens of the court-developed "duty to act fairly" and its predecessor concept, the "rules of natural justice". The rules of natural justice have largely been supplanted by the duty of fairness and, therefore, are not very relevant here. The courts have used the obligation to require any decision-making body to act fairly as a means to determine a person's rights and obligations. A successful attack by way of judicial review, as discussed later, has been decried by some opponents as interference with agencies' freedom to act in determining the public interest. The reply to this position notes that the courts will only interfere where a party is treated unfairly and where the decisions have a sufficiently serious effect on the party. This suggests that the more adverse the effect on the party, the greater the duty to act fairly, as shown by an increase in the procedural protections. But in an emergency, an agency may be entitled to have more flexibility in its procedural protections, at least initially. Therefore, it can be argued that there is a sliding scale of procedural protections mandated on an agency, depending on certain factors that sometimes are recognized by the courts.

Notwithstanding any other requirements, before an agency can make a decision adverse to a person's interest, at a minimum a person should be

- told of the case to be met; and
- given an opportunity to respond.

Both "notice of the case" and "right to respond" can range, depending on the circumstances, from verbal advice to written notice to provision of documentary evidence in the former situation, and from written to electronic hearing or, most likely, oral hearing in the latter situation. These minimum requirements can be observed in rules adopted by most agencies to be fair to the parties because the courts would likely impose them anyway. However, even if no rules are prescribed for an agency to follow, the duty to act fairly will impose a number of rules on the agency, as outlined in the next paragraphs.

Status

One of the most important preliminary matters to be decided by an agency is who has the status to appear before it. A person who should appear before an agency but is denied an opportunity to appear would be considered unfairly treated. The most likely person to have status as a **party to the proceeding** is a person who may be seriously affected by the outcome of the proceeding. Factors used to determine whether a person is seriously affected include the subject matter of the proceeding, the person's interest in the subject matter, and the effect that the decision might have on that interest. Using the concept of "serious effect" allows not only persons directly affected, such as a named party or the complainant in a disciplinary proceeding, to appear before it, but also members of the public who may have the status of an **intervenor**. This is especially important in an agency environment, where the public interest is so compelling and the effect of a decision might be far-reaching.

Notice

The general principle here states that except for emergencies, advance notice advising of a proceeding where a decision may be made must be given to all persons who would be affected by the decision. Such notice should be explicit and state the time and place of the proceeding, in order that those persons affected may take action to protect their position. Whether service is verbal, written, or even by newspaper advertisement, it must be effective: the notice must reach the person and be timely enough to enable the person to adequately prepare.

Disclosure

In order for the person affected by the possible decision to have an opportunity to make appropriate submissions, the person should be informed of the case to be met. That includes disclosure of (a) all relevant information that the agency may take into account when rendering a decision, (b) the issues as presented to the agency, and (c) the penalties that could be imposed on the person. A party to a proceeding may very well be entitled to more disclosure than an intervenor. In some limited circumstances, only partial or even no disclosure is permissible when it involves confidential information or information that would cause harm if released. Disclosure of information must be timely and should be given as soon as reasonably possible in the circumstances.

Adjournments (or Stays)

Even where there is no provision in the enabling statute to allow it, agencies have inherent discretionary jurisdiction to adjourn proceedings to ensure fairness. An agency would likely grant a stay in the following situations: (a) a party received insufficient notice, (b) a party received late or improper disclosure, (c) a new issue is raised in the hearing, requiring time for a party to prepare, and (d) a related matter is being heard in another agency or in court. In determining whether to grant a discretionary adjournment, an agency will usually review such factors as complexity of the proceedings, previous stays, if any, interest of the persons affected, and costs of the stay. If a stay is granted, the agency will likely fix the time and place for the resumption of the proceedings.

Effective Participation (Especially the Right to Representation)

In order for a party to properly deal with a hearing, such party must be present at the hearing. That means the agency should only carry on with a hearing if all parties are present, unless it is shown that such missing party or parties had effective notice of the hearing but decided not to attend. In almost all circumstances, any person who has a right to appear in a hearing has the right to be represented by a representative who can present the case for the person. An agency may have some discretion, under its enabling Act, to allow for a representative and to take into account the ability of the parties involved to represent themselves, the nature and complexity of the proceedings (the more complex or serious the matter, the more likely that a representative will be allowed), and the possible consequences of the proceedings. If an agency denies the use of a representative, it must state its reasons for doing so. Unless the legislation requires it, the representative does not have to be a lawyer, and, in fact, almost all agencies in Ontario will allow licensed paralegals or laypersons with some specialized knowledge to represent parties in a hearing.

Public or Private (in Camera) Hearings

The general rule for most hearings, whether in court or before an agency, states that they should be public, for reasons of fairness and as a safeguard against covert actions. However, especially for hearings before an agency, there is discretion to have *in camera* hearings for national security reasons or if a person, such as a party or even a witness, could be harmed by a public hearing. In some situations, such as a hearing before the Workplace Safety and Insurance Appeals Tribunal, the hearing is private unless the parties to the hearing unanimously agree to allow the public to be present. This situation likely has to do with a possibility of embarrassment if evidence as to the worker's physical condition and health became public knowledge.

Evidence

In order to reach a decision, an agency must base all findings of fact upon the relevant evidence. On the whole, the rules of evidence, which are formal and usually strictly applied in court, are much less formal when applied by an agency. Therefore, types of uncertain evidence, such as hearsay, and unqualified "expert" evidence will likely be admitted, although in determining whether to admit the evidence the agency must also determine the relevance. Even if the evidence is admissible, the agency must also determine the evidence's weight (probative value) and its credibility. If the evidence does not have much value or is not believable, possibly because of contradictions, the agency will likely gloss over the evidence. An agency also has the right to take notice of commonly accepted facts (judicial notice) without the need for evidence to prove those facts.

Witnesses

Witnesses before an agency can give evidence in written or oral form, depending on the circumstances and the provisions of relevant legislation. Oral evidence is usually adduced by questions posed by the party calling the witness, or by members of the agency itself, who often participate in an active way, unlike most court proceedings. The difficult issue for most agencies to determine is when a party has the right to cross-examine a witness, which can be done whether the initial submission is in a written or oral form. Although certain Acts require cross-examination, an agency has discretionary power to grant it. The party must convince the agency that the party should be given the opportunity to correct or controvert any relevant and prejudicial statement made by the witness. More specifically, cross-examination will be allowed if it is the only means to reveal or test the evidence that goes to the heart of the hearing, if there is conflicting and/or contradictory evidence, and if cross-examination provides the best way to assess the credibility of the witness.

Proof and Non-suit Motions

Parties who bring an application to appear before an agency usually carry the burden of proving their case. However, the standard used to determine if the burden has been met is not the **"beyond a reasonable doubt" test** used in criminal court proceedings but, rather, the **"balance of probabilities" test** used in civil court proceedings. In making a finding of fact and the eventual decision, the agency should be reasonably satisfied that the facts occurred, which depends on such factors as the nature of the facts to be proven and the consequences that would flow from the finding of fact. Once the party with the burden or onus to prove the case has finished her/his submissions, the other party has the ability to make a motion for a non-suit (dismissal) without making any submissions. In determining whether to grant the motion, the agency must determine whether the first party made a *prima facie* case. The *prima facie* test has less of a burden of proof than the balance of probability test and is used by the agency in making its decision on the motion. It requires looking at the evidence in the light most favourable to the party who presented it. Even if the evidence is weak and not very credible, if there is any evidence at all to support the contentions of the party presenting the case, the agency should not grant a motion of non-suit.

Evidence by Compulsion

Pursuant to legislation, many agencies are granted powers to obtain relevant evidence in the following ways:

1. exercise of search and/or seizure powers;
2. use of inspection powers; and
3. use of subpoena and/or summons powers.

All of these are subject to section 8 of the *Charter*.

With respect to search and/or seizure, an authorized person is permitted to pay a surprise visit to search for and/or seize evidence. Prior authorization is given by a person who should not have an interest in the proceeding and should be satisfied on reasonable and probable grounds, provided under oath, that it is reasonable to grant a search and/or seizure warrant. Such person is usually not a member of the agency, but it is not necessarily a judge either. The search should not be a general search but should be a search of a specific situation and anything relevant to it.

As allowed under the enabling Act, inspection orders permit inspectors to view premises for spot audits and to regulate businesses. The usual purpose of the inspection is to protect the public interest, and it is likely to be carried on during reasonable hours.

Documents and/or witnesses can be subpoenaed to require production and/or attendance, respectively. If there is non-compliance, contempt proceedings can be initiated before the appropriate court. If non-compliance is proven beyond a reasonable doubt, the offender can be imprisoned. Certain documents cannot be compelled — most commonly those that are privileged, such as solicitor–client communications for the purposes of obtaining legal advice, and Cabinet or ministerial communications where disclosure would prejudice the public interest. Summonses will be granted to compel a witness to appear if the party requesting it can show that such witness is reluctant to appear, that the evidence likely to be obtained is relevant, and that it is unlikely to be obtained in any fashion other than by a summons.

Orders and Decisions

Unless required by the appropriate legislation to be in writing, in theory an oral final order or decision is acceptable. However, there is much case law from the SCC that requires most decisions to be in writing and to include reasons. The decision should be given as expeditiously as possible, and some enabling Acts even have a specific time limit for a decision to be handed down. Although reasons may not be required, agencies usually give reasons for the decision, especially if the decision might be raised in court on appeal or by way of judicial review (discussed below). The following are some of the problems that can arise if the reasons for the decision are not included:

1. Lack of reasons may undermine confidence in the agency.
2. The court will disregard the agency's expertise if it is not demonstrated by stated reasons for the decision.
3. The court can derive adverse inferences if there are no reasons to review.

4. A disturbing impression of injustice may be left with those reading the decision.
5. The parties do not know why the decision was made, or if there are any grounds for appeal or judicial review.

Further, if the enabling Act requires reasons to be given, and there are none, the decision is likely null and void. The reasons, as given, should adequately explain how the agency reached its conclusions, whether based on fact, law, or public policy.

Over and above the rules or procedures to be followed by agencies with respect to the duty to act fairly, three other principles derived originally from the rules of natural justice are important: (i) the impartiality of the decision-maker (no bias), (ii) the decision-maker's not fettering his or her discretion, and (iii) the agency's acting within its jurisdiction. If any of these principles are not followed, an application for judicial review will likely be successful.

The next three items — Bias, Improperly Fettering Discretion, and Jurisdiction — are not part of the duty to act fairly; however, the author included them here because all three, like the duty to act fairly, are derived from common law and, if there is non-compliance, will allow for the remedy of judicial review.

Bias

If, in the exercise of its powers, an agency is found to lack neutrality or impartiality and/or to have had personal interest in mind, the decision of the agency will likely be null and void. If a member of an agency is found to be biased, that member will be disqualified from hearing the case. Indicators of bias of a member of the adjudicating agency include the following:

- Pecuniary interest in the proceeding
- A friend, business associate, or relative as a party or a witness, unless the connection is a past and/or distant one
- Improper conduct at the hearing, such as flippant or derogatory language, expressed feelings of hostility or antagonism, or repeated interference in the proceedings
- Private meetings with one party to the exclusion of others
- Social meetings with parties or witnesses prior to or during the hearing
- A predetermined view of the issues (although a tentative prior view is acceptable as long as there is an opening for persuasion)

It is important to remember that an appearance of bias, or a reasonable apprehension of bias (where a reasonable person would suspect that a member may be influenced by improper considerations to favour one party over another), will likely be sufficient for the court to find bias. Therefore, if a member of an agency hearing a case believes there may be a bias situation, it is best if the member abstains from the decision or, possibly, disqualifies or recuses herself or himself from the proceeding. Once that is done, an unbiased member or unbiased panel can be put in place. It should also be noted that certain agencies are, under statute, biased, such as labour arbitration boards with members drawn from management and labour. Please also note that not only can there be actual adjudicator bias or reasonable apprehension of adjudicator bias, there can also be actual institutional bias and reasonable apprehension of institutional bias where actual or likely bias is systemic in the agency.

Improperly Fettering Discretion

Agencies are given wide discretion in such areas as the responsibility to apply rules to each situation as it arises, as long as the agency is fair. Other areas of discretion include determining whether a specific situation is covered by the legislation, which action is warranted, and consideration of public policy applied to specific situations. An agency must observe the obligation to promote the objects of its enabling legislation. If an agency exercises its discretion arbitrarily or dishonestly, a court may rule that the agency is acting in bad faith and, therefore, that its actions are reviewable. Bad faith, however, must be proven. Discriminating against and treating a specific person differently, or making a decision based on an improper purpose or irrelevant consideration, are indicators of bad faith.

The most likely example of improper fettering of discretion is the application by an agency of **stare decisis**, or standing by precedent. Most agencies keep copies of decisions accessible, and it is quite common for appropriate and, sometimes, inappropriate prior decisions to be submitted to an agency. If the agency bases its decision solely or predominately on a prior decision without proper regard to the actual case before it, a court would likely determine that there has been improper fettering of its discretion. Although consistency is desirable, it is not an all-encompassing obligation for an agency to follow, as it would have been in the judicial branch of government. Further, there are ways to make a decision without making it obvious that *stare decisis* was used.

Not only is it inappropriate to improperly fetter discretion, it is also wrong to not exercise discretion that is conferred on an agency. In the right circumstances, as discussed in the section on judicial review (p. 25), an agency can be compelled to exercise its discretion.

Jurisdiction

The agency can exercise only the power given to it by its enabling or empowering legislation. If the agency acts outside its jurisdiction, say by giving remedies it is not empowered to give under the legislation, that would be outside its jurisdiction and could be challenged on judicial review. Another situation likely calling for judicial review occurs when an agency has the authority to hear a matter but refuses, which is usually referred to as "declining jurisdiction".

REMEDIES AVAILABLE IF A DECISION OF AN AGENCY IS NOT SATISFACTORY

Once an agency has made a decision, the parties should comply. There are legal mechanisms available to try to ensure compliance. However, depending on certain circumstances, especially when permitted to do so by legislation, a party may be able to have the decision

- reconsidered,
- appealed, or
- judicially reviewed.

by making an appropriate application. Reconsideration involves an agency's revisiting a case, after making a decision, in order to look at it again because of a request to do so. An appeal is requested to allow an appellate body, either an appellate agency or a court, to look at the result on the merits of a case because the decision may be "wrong". An application for judicial review is made because there is some question not of the results, but of the rules and procedures used to achieve those results. To better understand options or alternatives that can be exercised, each shall be discussed in turn.

Reconsideration

Under either an enabling Act or other general legislation, such as the *SPPA*, some agencies are given the power to review or reconsider the decision made and to change it, if appropriate. An example of a reconsideration involving an agency would be the case of an applicant for some type of financial assistance benefits, who has applied for a hearing with the Social Benefits Tribunal (SBT). If the SBT has made a decision to refuse benefits, the party who was denied has the option to request reconsideration by the SBT, to appeal the decision to court, or to apply for judicial review. In choosing the appropriate option, it is important for the party to assess the reasons for his or her attempt to have the decision reversed. If the party does not like the decision but does not have any new evidence, or cannot point to errors made by an agency (other than the SBT), the party should not take any action. However, if he or she has evidence of errors by the SBT, such as relevant evidence not considered, bias, unfair treatment by non-adherence to appropriate procedures, or mistakes of law or fact, the party can apply for reconsideration by the SBT. If a ground such as new evidence exists, it would be best for the party in this example to request reconsideration. This may be the best option if the expeditiousness and cost of a reconsideration overwhelmingly favour the party over either of the other options. In other words, reconsideration will happen much sooner and cost much less. The appropriate legislation will state the scope of reconsideration, if any. Note that the grounds for reconsideration of a decision of the SBT are unusually broad and do not consist solely of new evidence.

Appeal

The second option available to the party in the above example would be to appeal the decision. With respect to a decision of the SBT, the appeal is made to Ontario Divisional Court. In order to determine if any appeal rights exist against the decision of any agency, either the enabling Act or other appropriate legislation must be consulted. If no appeal rights are explicitly granted in any agency's decision in the legislation, no appeal can be made. Note that the legislation could designate a court, as in the example, or another agency to hear the appeal. For example, decisions from the Workplace Safety and Insurance Board are appealed to the Workplace Safety and Insurance Appeals Tribunal. The following are important matters in respect of appeals.

Status (Who May Appeal)

As will be seen in most of the discussion of appeals, one must first and always look at the legislation to determine who can appeal. If the Act states that only a "party" may appeal or it is silent on the matter, then only a party to a proceeding can appeal. However, the legislation could be broader and give status to appeal to such persons as intervenors or even some members of the general public. This can be achieved by the use of such phrases as "adversely affected", "aggrieved person", or even "interested party". The appellate body has the right to determine if the "appellant" is allowed to appeal under the words of the legislation. Although somewhat unusual because of the possible appearance of bias, some Acts allow the agency to be an appellant.

Scope of Appeal

The scope of an appeal, or the grounds upon which an appeal can be heard, is set out in the statute. Such grounds can be that the agency made errors on questions of jurisdiction, law, or fact, or some combination of such grounds. In brief, the following points are raised:

- A question of jurisdiction relates to whether the agency did not have the power to hear the case or, if initially having such power, commits some act to lose or exceed such power (Actions taken outside jurisdiction are **ultra vires** (outside the power) and may be rendered null and void.)

- A question of law relates to the interpretation and application of the law to the facts of a specific case (Although this appears to be a clear position, there has been much disagreement as to whether a suggested error is a question of law, fact, or jurisdiction.)

- A question of fact relates to the facts as found or determined by the adjudicator, usually after the perusal of the submissions of witnesses and physical and documentary evidence

Some case law suggests it is an error of jurisdiction to make a decision where there is a total lack of evidence. Usually issues related to evidence are considered questions of fact. However, if necessary (where an appellate body wants to have the right to grant an appeal even though the Act limits appeals to questions of jurisdiction), it has been decided in some cases to call it an error of jurisdiction. The question of alleged errors and their categorization is even more important for judicial review and shall be discussed further below.

Type of Appeal

Depending on the statute, the appellate body could hear the appeal in a number of ways:

- A hearing *de novo* (a new hearing), where the appellate body would act as a new adjudicator and rehear the matter without any reference to the decision appealed (The parties would be able to submit any and all evidence to support their positions.)

- A new hearing where the appellate body has the right to look at and, even, refer somewhat to the decision appealed from

- A review of a record of the agency that arrived at the decision, without oral hearing of arguments by the party or parties, regarding errors made by the agency that appear on the record (This method is most often used in appeals from a court decision.)

Furthermore, the error must be appealable pursuant to the statute granting the appeal rights. In this way of appeal, the agency is required to produce a record that will usually include the following documents: (a) the specific decision under appeal, (b) any interlocutory or interim orders, (c) the reasons for the decision, (d) the notice for the original adjudication from which the decision arose, (e) all documentary evidence, and (f) the transcript of the proceedings, if any. The first means of appeal is the broadest and, in effect, puts the appellate body in the position of a body hearing the matter for the first time.

The method of appeal will have a direct relationship to the powers of the appellate body to make a decision. If hearing *de novo* is the type required by statute, the appellate body's decision will replace that of the original agency decision-maker. However, other modes of appeal, especially by reviews of the record, will likely mean a return to the agency for a new hearing, although before a new adjudicator or panel. To ensure that the new adjudicator does not make the same mistakes, the appellate body may be able to provide directions along with the order for a new hearing.

General Concerns Regarding Appeals

Items such as notice of appeal, leave to appeal (where required), and stay of an agency decision during the process of appeal are all detailed in the enabling Act or other relevant legislation. Normally, rules about the time to file and where to file an appeal are strictly enforced. There is, however, the ability in most circumstances to exercise discretion to extend the time where it would be fair to do so. If leave to appeal is required, a *prima facie* case must be made by the possible appellant of the substance of the arguments supporting the requested appeal. The general position on stays (or holding in abeyance) is that an application for a stay before the appellate body must be granted if the decision has been appealed. Normally, the agency's decision is effective immediately, even if an appeal has been launched; but the appellate body, if granted such power, can order a stay until the decision is made on the appeal.

Two further points should be made about appeals and how they relate to applications for judicial review. First, it is usually better, if the grounds allow it, to launch an appeal rather than make application for judicial review. The powers of the appellate body to possibly hear the case anew and consider the merits of the decision are almost always wider than the reviewing court's power. Second, if the application for judicial review is made while appeal rights exist but have not been explored, the court will almost invariably refuse to hear the application until all appeal rights have been exhausted.

Judicial Review

The third way that a decision of an agency can be challenged is by an application for judicial review. Such application was formerly by the mechanism of a prerogative writ. This method is still available, but other mechanisms now exist to provide similar review. This method shall be considered in detail, including (i) specific remedies available (i.e., prerogative writs, statutory applications, and remedies under private law), (ii) the grounds for the types of review, (iii) privative clauses (statutory provisions to try to limit or even prevent review), and (iv) other specific concerns.

Prerogative Writs

Prerogative writs are mechanisms developed over the centuries by English common law to control arbitrary government action. Initially, they were orders issued by the Crown to oversee and direct the actions of its underlings. Over time, issuance of these writs was transferred to superior courts and became part of their inherent jurisdiction to supervise governmental decisions.

As these writs can be granted on a discretionary basis (similar to equitable remedies), there are certain situations where the court will usually refuse to grant this remedy. As previously discussed, if there is another valid remedy available, such as appeal, the court will likely not grant the application. Another reason to exercise the discretion not to grant a writ is that the grant would be ineffective because it would be academic or useless. Other situations where the writ may be refused relate to the actions of the party who objects and brings the application:

1. If the party has waived or acquiesced knowingly in the agency's error;
2. If the party has taken too long to seek this remedy (*laches*); or
3. If the party has, by his or her conduct, such as bad faith, become disentitled to review (**clean hands doctrine**).

Generally, the court requires that the applicant for a writ be a person who has a sufficient interest in the proceeding. The application is brought against an agency who, depending on circumstances, may be able to participate actively in the court review or may only be a neutral friend to the court.

The five prerogative writs still in use, to varying degrees, are *certiorari*, prohibition*, mandamus*, *quo warranto*, and *habeas corpus*.

CERTIORARI

This writ allows the court to quash (basically, stop or nullify) a final decision of an agency on certain grounds, usually errors of jurisdiction made by the agency. Originally part of the superior court's inherent jurisdiction to supervise inferior courts, it was extended over the years to include certain supervisory powers over agencies. It can be applied only after the agency has made the improper decision, and not before that time. Historically, *certiorari* was available if an agency acted judicially or quasi-judicially; however, more recent cases have decided that it can also be used to quash decisions of agencies acting administratively. Limitations to the use of this writ include its non-applicability to legislative decisions, or delegated legislation, or the Crown itself (except for certain situations). However, it does apply to public bodies whose power is granted by legislation.

PROHIBITION

Prohibition is essentially the same as *certiorari* in terms of its history and limitations, except that it can be applied for at any stage prior to the making of the final decision. It is used, therefore, to try to prevent something from being done before the ultimate order or award is made.

MANDAMUS

An application for mandamus, if granted, will result in an order by the court to compel an agency to perform a statutory duty where the agency has refused to do its duty. If the power an agency is refusing to exercise is discretionary, *mandamus* would likely ensue — but only to require such agency to exercise the discretion, not to dictate the way it must be exercised. In order to use this writ the following circumstances must exist:

- The applicant must have status to apply; in this situation, there must be a public duty to act owed by an agency to the applicant.
- An explicit demand has been made to the agency that it must act, and there has been a refusal to do so.
- As with all prerogative writs, it does not apply against the Crown or its agents when not acting under a statutory duty.

QUO WARRANTO

Rarely applied for, this writ, if granted, will state that a person has the right to hold a public office. It is of little relevance to agency proceedings.

HABEAS CORPUS

This writ, which is centuries old, is used to quash an illegal detention of the applicant. Only the detained persons or someone acting on their behalf can make application. The grounds for granting the writ relate to errors of law or jurisdiction.

Statutory Applications in the Nature of Judicial Review

PROVINCIAL (ONTARIO AND ALBERTA)

Most provinces have legislation to provide potential applicants with an alternative to requesting one of the prerogative writs against provincial agencies. In fact, some of the provinces, including Ontario, have, in effect, abolished some of the prerogative writs. The Ontario statute that accomplishes that task is the *Judicial Review Procedure Act*, R.S.O. 1990, c. J.1, as amended (*JRPA*), specifically section 7, which turns applications for *mandamus*, prohibition, and *certiorari* into applications under the *JRPA*. The intent of the legislation was to make such applications a summary proceeding with fairly consistent procedures to be heard by the Ontario Divisional Court. Under section 2(1)1, an application is made by way of an originating notice to request an order in the nature of *mandamus*, prohibition, and *certiorari*. That provision means that all the laws developed under those three specified remedies are still important. Section 2(1)2 of the *JRPA* also puts into summary form two kinds of private law remedies (discussed below) historically available to applicants. Under that section, the applicant can request a declaration or an injunction, or both remedies, in relation to the exercise or purported exercise of a statutory power of decision. "Statutory power of decision" is defined as the power conferred on an agency by a statute to make a decision affecting the rights, duties, or powers of any person, or the eligibility of a person to receive a licence or benefit. Note that the application in replacement of the three prerogative writs is not restricted to the exercise of statutory power. Detailed rules of procedure with respect to the *JRPA* are set out in the Ontario *Rules of Civil Procedure*. Also note that the definition of "party" includes some groups that are not persons at law and, therefore, likely did not previously have standing to bring an application for a prerogative writ. Alberta has legislation very similar to the Ontario legislation discussed in this paragraph.

FEDERAL

In making application for any of the prerogative writs against an agency under federal jurisdiction, the *Federal Court Act*, R.S.C. 1985, c F-7, as amended (*FCA*), states that the Federal Court — Trial Division has exclusive jurisdiction over all such applications. An exception to this provision provides that the Federal Court of Appeal has the exclusive jurisdictions over applications in 15 specified federal agencies. The application for judicial review, so called, is made pursuant to the rules and procedures of section 18.1 of the *FCA*. As in the *JRPA*, such applications are meant to be heard in a summary fashion. The section also gives extensive powers to the court to order all the types of relief that could be granted under the prerogative writs, if any of the enumerated errors exist. When the *FCA* was first enacted, certain wordings allowed for an application for judicial review only if the agency was acting in a judicial or quasi-judicial manner. This led to many cases where the issue was not whether there was an error that could be reviewed, but whether the agency was exercising a judicial or quasi-judicial jurisdiction. Recognizing this problem, the legislators amended the *FCA*, effective in 1992, to remove the distinction between judicial and quasi-judicial jurisdiction.

Remedies under Private Law

Relief may also exist pursuant to common law and/or equitable remedies awarded through an ordinary lawsuit. Specifically, one could simply sue the agency in tort, likely for some form of negligence, although some intentional torts could also support the action. In this situation, the claimant alleges that an agency has either committed an intentionally improper conduct that interferes with that person (intentional tort), or is careless in performing some action that causes damage to the person to whom such agency owes a duty of care (negligence). In order for an action in tort to succeed, the conduct complained of must be illegal or *ultra vires*. A review of the case law indicates that the court will likely find agencies liable if the elements of the specific tort can be proven. However, the courts have also recognized the need for flexibility for agencies to effectively function. It should also be noted that, historically, there was a limit to the parties one could sue: In the past, "Crown immunity" had basically prevented a person from bringing a tort action against the Crown in an official capacity. Federal and provincial legislation has effectively brought Crown immunity to an end — although strict time limits have been imposed to restrict the right of action. There is much more material to be discussed about tortious actions that can be brought against agencies, but that is outside the scope of this chapter; however, the relief that can be granted in consequence of a successful action in tort are discussed below.

DECLARATORY RELIEF

This discretionary relief (also known as declaratory judgment or declaration) is a non-coercive judgment of the court setting out the legal positions of the parties and/or the law applicable to them. Although not binding, since there is no legal way to enforce such a judgment, declarations have become an accepted way for a person to have a court determine whether an agency had the power to take certain actions. It is also a very flexible remedy, with few technical requirements to be followed, and can be used in a number of ways. The courts have normally issued declarations against agencies as part of their supervisory function with respect to the legality of certain governmental actions. Remember that a declaration can be obtained in summary fashion under the *FCA* and, with limitations, as an exercise of statutory power under the *JRPA*.

INJUNCTION

An injunction is a discretionary equitable remedy by which the court can order a party to act or refrain from acting in a certain way, and if there is non-compliance a party would be liable for contempt of court. There are two main types of injunctions, both of which have been used against agencies after a successful tort action. One type is a mandatory injunction, similar to *mandamus*, to compel an agency to act in a lawful manner. The other type is a prohibitory injunction, similar to prohibition, to restrain an agency that acts, or even threatens to act, in an illegal fashion.

Furthermore, injunctions are available on an interim basis, without a full-blown trial and, possibly, without initial notice to the other side. An interim injunction will enjoin an agency until such time as the cause of action is tried and, possibly, a permanent injunction is granted. Standing to bring an action for an injunction, along with Crown immunity issues, must be addressed before an injunction can be successfully obtained. Also, in a similar way to declaratory relief, injunction relief can be granted under both the *FCA*, for federal agencies, and under the *JRPA*, for Ontario agencies.

DAMAGES

In any successful action for tort, the court has the obligation to award the common law remedy of damages to compensate the victim for certain types of loss or injury suffered as a result of the tort. Once the amount (or quantum) of damages is proven on the balance of probabilities to the court's satisfaction, the court will order the **tortfeasor** to pay such damages. Not only will the innocent party be compensated for losses suffered through no fault of such party, but liability for damages may act as a deterrence to the wrongdoer. The potential for deterrence can clearly be seen in the ability of the court to award punitive or exemplary damages in circumstances where an agency has acted maliciously. These principles dealing with damages have been accepted where a tort action has been successful against an agency. One issue still open for resolution is whether a purely economic loss is compensable. As in the other two private remedies examined above, items such as standing and Crown immunity may be relevant. There is no provision for a summary award of damages under either the *FCA* or the *JRPA*.

Although in some jurisdictions it is possible to apply for one or more prerogative writs, to apply for statutory judicial review, and to commence a private law action for one or more of the private law remedies, most persons will likely make application only under the appropriate statute. Application is made in a summary fashion and is, therefore, less costly and more expedient and provides grounds, in most circumstances, at least as broad as the other remedies. Although a discussion of grounds for judicial review can be overwhelming, the following are some concepts to remember.

Grounds for Judicial Review

As previously mentioned, the grounds for most appeals of agency decisions usually relate to the merits or the result of the decision by questioning the findings of fact by the adjudicator. Typically, the grounds for judicial review relate to how the result was achieved and are likely determined by looking for jurisdictional or legal errors. It is possible that a resourceful court can make what appears to be a possible question of fact into a question of law; however, the grounds for judicial review tend to be very narrow. A vast amount of case law exists on the sole issue of whether an alleged error of an agency is reviewable, but an analysis of the law is beyond the scope of this chapter. However, certain principles can be canvassed.

The major focus of determining proper grounds for judicial review revolves around the statutory power of an agency to take a particular action. Usually the court must determine if the statutory power exists, or, if it does exist, whether an agency has exceeded or has somehow lost its statutory power. This is a search to discover the jurisdiction of the agency. It can also be classified as a question of law, because if an agency took an action without the statutory power or the jurisdiction to do so, such action would be declared illegal. Determining jurisdiction often requires the reviewing court to interpret appropriate legislation to determine exactly what an agency's jurisdiction is.

As an agency is a creation of its enabling Act and other relevant legislation, understanding the words of all of such legislation is usually the first step the court takes to determine whether an agency has acquired the appropriate jurisdiction. Other initial issues may include whether there has been compliance with all preliminary matters, such as proper notice. Any or all of these issues may be examined in order for the court to determine if the agency has acquired jurisdiction.

If the jurisdiction is properly acquired, an agency's actions can still be reviewed if it exceeds or loses its jurisdiction. Broadly speaking, an agency can exceed or lose jurisdiction in three ways: (i) abuse of discretion, (ii) no compliance with the duty to be fair, and (iii) bias. (Refer to material detailed earlier, pp. 13–21, in this chapter for a more comprehensive discussion.) Certain concepts regarding each of the three ways jurisdiction can be lost are discussed below.

Abuse of discretion can include the following actions: (i) exercising a discretionary power in bad faith for improper or irrelevant considerations; (ii) making a decision with no evidence whatsoever or by ignoring relevant information; (iii) using discretion to obtain an improper result because it is discriminatory or unreasonable, or it is made due to a misunderstanding of the law; and (iv) improperly fettering discretion. Notice how an evidentiary problem, which is normally a question of fact, can become an abuse of discretion issue. A reviewing court can find that because there is no evidence to support the exercise of discretion, an agency can lose its jurisdiction; therefore, the decision is reviewable.

The origins of procedural fairness, or the duty of any agency to be fair to parties before it, are derived from the rules of natural justice. These rules of natural justice, developed over the centuries to try to ensure that a party was treated fairly, were initially reserved for agencies acting in a judicial or quasi-judicial manner. The need to characterize the function of an agency was all-important because if an agency was acting in a legislative or executive manner, the rules of natural justice were likely not applicable. However, in most but not all situations, it is no longer relevant to characterize function, since an agency is required to act fairly in most of its functions. The determination of whether an agency has acted fairly is based upon whether the rules following the duty to act fairly, as stated earlier in this chapter, have been followed. Such rules of natural justice are basically that any such rule must be dependent on fairness to the persons involved in the proceeding.

The loss of jurisdiction due to the bias of an agency is also derived from the duty to be fair. Various types of bias by agencies are discussed elsewhere in this chapter. It is important to note the problem of whether bias should be judged by the strict objective test used in courts or by a more subjective standard, because agencies need to consider public policy in their decision making. Such public policy obligations may make an agency's actions appear biased to a party. Many agency members have criticized the courts in going too far to make agency proceedings appear like court proceedings. Different considerations often apply for agencies and courts.

A further ground for review — specifically, for an application for an order of, or in the nature of, *certiorari* — is an error on the face of the record. These are not jurisdictional errors; they are errors of law that are clear from looking at the record of the proceeding. They allow the court to quash a decision of an agency. An example of an error of law is an agency's incorrectly interpreting and/or applying a statutory provision other than its own enabling legislation. Numerous recent cases have tried to place limitations on which errors of law, on the face of the record, are quashable by positing tests to be followed.

These tests arose to try to deal with "privative clauses", discussed below. The most important test suggests that errors of law that are "patently unreasonable" are errors of jurisdiction and, therefore, reviewable even with a privative clause. This test has been used, and possibly misused, in numerous court decisions to try to determine the ambit of judicial review by way of *certiorari*. Such cases have made it difficult to state a consistent principle to be applied, other than that the test is important in this area as a way around a privative clause.

Privative Clauses

A privative clause is a statutory provision intended to prevent, or at least limit, the right of the judiciary to hear appeals or judicial review applications. The legislature's intent in using such a clause stems from a concern that the courts have intervened too readily and in areas better left to an agency's expertise and streamlined procedure. No matter what the specific wording of a privative clause is, it will not prevent a court from reviewing an agency's action based on a jurisdictional error. Therefore, a privative clause will only be of use where there is an error of law on the face of the record. The three common general types of privative clauses in use are as follows:

1. A final and binding clause, or similar wording, that means there is no appeal of an agency's decision but that still allows the court to determine whether any jurisdictional errors exist if the decision is unreasonable.
2. An exclusive jurisdiction clause to the effect that only an agency has exclusive jurisdiction to determine certain matters. This clause has the same basic effect as in item 1.
3. A clause that prevents any application for any prerogative writ or declaration. Again, this clause has the same basic effect as item 1.

There has been much discussion about whether an agency's decision should be reviewable by the courts and, if so, what the appropriate limits are, if any, to such review. This is yet another issue that threatens to go unanswered in the near, and possibly distant, future, although the 2008 SCC case of *Dunsmuir v. New Brunswick*, 2008 SCC 9 (the *Dunsmuir* case) has addressed some of the issues by positing a two-part test regarding the standard of review. If the decision is clearly based upon the agency's expertise, the standard is whether the decision was based on *reasonableness*, thereby having the court defer to such expertise. If, on the other hand, the agency made a decision not in its expertise, such as statutory interpretation, the decision must be *correct*. There are still other concerns that are usually considered under judicial review.

Other Concerns in Judicial Review

There are usually time limits within which to apply for judicial review. Such time limits often are strictly enforced, although there is usually some discretion, based on fairness, to extend the time. The time limit is usually found in the enabling legislation or any rules pursuant to it. A stay of an agency decision is not automatically in place upon making an application for judicial review. It must be specifically and separately applied for to the appropriate court, which must be convinced of the efficacy of granting a stay. The hearing is a review, not a new hearing, which is why the record, as discussed previously, is so important. This is an absolute necessity where the review application is based on an error of fact on the record. Problems occur in this area where the agency does not have much in the way of transcripts. Usually the successful party in an application for judicial review will have costs awarded in his or her favour.

POSSIBLE TRENDS IN ADMINISTRATIVE LAW IN CANADA

There is a fair amount of tension between those who believe that agencies should have comparative freedom from the courts and those who want agencies to follow rules and procedures as overseen by courts. On the one hand, there is the obligation by agencies to follow and even develop public policy, which is or may be foreign to the court's perspective of individual rights. On the other hand, there is the court's traditional role to ensure justice is done and seen to be done. There is a need for the expertise and cost-effectiveness of agencies, but should these be at the expense of fairness to a specific person? There have been relatively recent examples of methods to try to find new ways to resolve issues even before they get to an agency hearing, let alone to court. One example is the use of mediation in some situations before the WSIB. There have been attempts to have a different forum for review than the court, as in the use in a number of provinces of an ombudsperson. This governmental, yet independent, official has the power to scrutinize governmental abuses affecting members of the public. Such investigation includes not only how the result was achieved, but the merits of the result. In England, a Council of Tribunals was created to review and approve all rules and procedures adopted by agencies. This comprehensive and considered approach to ensure fair rules may result in less need for parties to appear before the court to argue an unfair rule. However, even if some or all of the steps discussed in this paragraph are taken, court cases will still be forthcoming. There are just too many concerns still debated to foresee an early end to the tensions.

A situation with the possibility of becoming trend-setting has recently occurred in Ontario — that is, the creation of tribunal clusters. Under the *Adjudicative Tribunals Accountability, Governance and Appointments Act, 2009*, the Ontario government is allowed to create clusters of tribunals, which is the grouping of a number of existing tribunals into a group, in the hope that it will allow for more common rules and procedures, meaning more interplay between members of each agency and therefore higher efficiency and effectiveness. This may also lead to more uniformity and possibly economies of scale and easier secondment to other agencies in the cluster. Under O. Reg. 126/10, as am. by O. Reg. 59/15, the following clusters have been created since 2010: the Environment and Land Tribunals Ontario, consisting of five existing tribunals; the Social Justice Tribunals Ontario, consisting of eight existing tribunals; and the Safety, Licencing Appeals and Standards Tribunals Ontario, consisting of five existing tribunals. As of this third edition being written, few other jurisdictions have used clustering. However, civil servants in Ontario, such as Michael Gottheil and Doug Ewart — as detailed in their paper "Improving Access to Justice through International Dialogue: Lessons for and from Ontario's Cluster Approach to Tribunal Efficiency and Effectiveness" found on the Social Justice Tribunals Ontario website — are trying to proselytize on behalf of clusters. Clustering of agencies in Ontario is discussed in greater detail in the preamble to Part II.

CHAPTER SUMMARY

In this chapter, the reader discovered a definition of administrative law that led into a discussion of the three branches of government. After a summary review of public policy, the essential characteristics of agencies were introduced. Specifically, agencies are seen as creations of government that, if empowered to do so, can exercise many of the same functions of any or all of the three branches of government. Various types of agencies, and a comparison between agencies and the courts, were discussed.

After the concept and uses of agencies were explored, there was a lengthy discussion of the ways to determine what specific rules and procedures are applicable to a specific agency. This discussion included an exploration of such factors in the Ontario *Statutory Powers Procedure Act*; sections 7, 8, 13, and 14 of the *Charter of Rights and Freedoms*; and the "duty to act fairly". The duty to act fairly was first defined and then broken down into some of its component parts to allow the reader to discover how the common law provides at least some procedural protections to parties involved in an agency proceeding. Other common law principles — no bias and no fettering the discretion or the jurisdiction of the decision-maker — were also introduced.

Remedies available if there is a complaint or concern regarding an agency proceeding were then discussed. The remedies are (a) reconsideration by the same agency; (b) appeal to another agency, or to court, or both; or (c) judicial review by the courts. Substantial details regarding the requirements, procedure, scope, and type of appeal were discussed. Also reviewed were the remedies available under judicial review: (a) prerogative writs; (b) statutory applications, both federally and in Ontario; and (c) private law remedies of tort, declaratory relief, injunction, and damages.

Finally, there was a discussion of possible future trends in administrative law in Canada.

GLOSSARY OF NEW TERMS AND KEY CONCEPTS

balance of probabilities test The standard used by the trier of fact in a civil proceeding (the judge or the jury, where appropriate) to determine whether the plaintiff or the defendant has won the case. If the evidence is more in favour of one party, even if just barely, then that party should be awarded the decision in the case.

beyond a reasonable doubt test The standard used by the trier of fact in a criminal proceeding (judge or the jury, where appropriate) to determine whether the accused is found guilty or not guilty. If there is any reasonable doubt that the accused did not commit the offence charged, there must be a finding of not guilty.

clean hands doctrine A principle of the law of equity that requires someone seeking to invoke an equitable rule to have conducted himself or herself fairly and honourably in the events leading up to and during the proceeding, and in the proceeding itself.

enabling legislation (act, statute) A law that permits a person (which for most purposes includes an individual, a corporation, and an agency) to do something that, prior to the law, the person was not permitted to do.

gazette The name of a publication issued by both the federal and provincial governments in Canada on a regular basis, containing official notices and announcements, and in which regulations made under the authority of a statute are first published.

judicial or quasi-judicial (function, manner, jurisdiction) The authority or power of a court or a body similar to a court (that is, a body with the power to decide a person's rights) to decide matters before it. The rules of natural justice were historically applied to these bodies, as well as to court proceedings. These bodies were different from agencies, whose decisions applying administrative juris-diction were not subject to the rules of natural justice.

inherent jurisdiction (also statutory jurisdiction)   A power or right that is vested in an authority (agency or court) intrinsically. (*Statutory jurisdiction* is a power or right that is vested in an author-ity derived from legislation.)

intervenor   A person who is given status to participate in a pro-ceeding even though the person is not a party to the proceeding.

proclaimed in force   A bill does not come into force (or become a statute) automatically when it is passed; it must first be proclaimed in force, that is, officially recognized as a statute.

promulgate   To publish a law.

stare decisis   Latin, "following precedent"; a legal doctrine that says that if a prior case is decided in a higher court in the same jurisdiction and on similar facts, then that prior case decision must be followed by subsequent courts.

tortfeasor   A person who commits a tort (a civil wrong excluding an action in contract).

ultra vires   Latin, "outside (or beyond) the power"; an action or a statute that is determined by the courts to be outside the powers assigned to the legislature that enacted it.

REVIEW QUESTIONS

1. What are the three branches of government in Canada?
2. Describe how public policy becomes law in Canada.
3. Where would you find how an agency was created, and the powers granted to it?
4. Discuss at least five reasons an agency may be created.
5. Detail the three types of agencies that can exist.
6. Set out five differences between an agency and a court.
7. What are the seven steps to determine which rules and proce-dures apply to a specific agency?
8. How does the *Statutory Powers Procedure Act* determine rules and procedures to be applied to an Ontario agency?
9. Discuss how four sections of the *Charter of Rights and Free-doms* are used to imply rules to be used in an agency pro-ceeding.
10. What are the two main components or principles that are derived from the "duty to act fairly"?

11. List and explain the three remedies available if there is a problem or concern arising from an agency proceeding.
12. Set out three types of appeal, and the scope of each.
13. What are the remedies available when it is determined that judicial review will be allowed?
14. Discuss the grounds that must exist before judicial review may be awarded.
15. What is a privative clause, and how is it used to avoid judicial review?
16. List and discuss three methods in which public policy is derived or developed.
17. In order for notice to meet the requirement of the duty to act fairly, how may it be given in order to achieve its ends?
18. What is the usual burden of proof used by agencies to determine whether a case has been proven?
19. How does an agency deal with "hearsay" evidence before it at a hearing?
20. List three ways in which most agencies can obtain evidence by compulsion.
21. List three types of relief available if a person successfully sues an agency under tort law.

DISCUSSION QUESTIONS

1. Agencies are a better way to determine a person's rights than are the courts. Discuss.
2. If an agency is meant to deal with matters in an expeditious and cost-effective manner and if the expertise is developed in the agency, is it worthwhile or even appropriate to allow a court to interfere with an agency's decision?
3. Have the various statutory and common law protections imposed on an agency's proceedings placed enough or too many rules on an agency's proceedings?
4. Should there be so many remedies available to a person who is concerned with an agency proceeding?
5. What changes would you make in Canadian administrative law? Why?
6. Why do the philosophies of some incoming governments lead to an expansion of the number and powers of agencies, and those of others lead to a contraction of the numbers and powers of agencies?
7. Discuss the current and future effects of the *Charter of Rights and Freedoms* on agencies.

8. List four indicators of bias in an agency and/or an adjudicating member.

SUGGESTED READINGS AND WEB RESOURCES

Blake, Sara. *Administrative Law in Canada*, 5th ed. (Toronto, Ont.: LexisNexis Canada, 2011).

Brooks, Stephen. *Public Policy in Canada: An Introduction*, 6th ed. (Toronto, Ont.: Oxford University Press, 2012).

Finkelstein, Neil, & Brian M. Rogers (eds.), *Recent Developments in Administrative Law* (Toronto, Ont.: Carswell, 1987).

Jones, David & Anne de Villars. *Principles of Administrative Law*, 6th ed. (Toronto, Ont.: Carswell, 2014).

Law Society of Upper Canada. *Administrative Law: Principles, Practice and Pluralism* (Scarborough, Ont.: Carswell, 1993).

———. *Recent Developments in Administrative Law* (Toronto, Ont.: Department of Continuing Legal Education, 1995).

Macaulay, Robert W., & James L.H. Sprague, *Hearings before Administrative Tribunals* (Toronto, Ont.: Carswell, 2010).

Moskoff, Franklin R., ed. *Administrative Tribunals: A Practice Handbook for Legal Counsel* (Aurora, Ont.: Canada Law Book Inc., 1989).

WEBSITES

The Canadian Legal Information Institute (CanLII) website for legislation and cases:
   <http://www.canlii.org/en/index.html>

Irwin Law, Canadian Legal Dictionary: <http://www.irwinlaw.com/cold>

The *Statutory Powers Procedure Act* in General

2

LEARNING OBJECTIVES

After reading this chapter, the reader should be able to:

- elaborate on the principle of statute annotation
- appreciate how minimum standards of acting fairly are imposed by statute on most Ontario agencies
- summarize key provisions of the *SPPA*
- identify how cases and/or decisions assist in the interpretation of statutory provisions
- illustrate and discuss how minimum standards of the duty to act fairly are applied in Ontario agencies
- distinguish between lawyers, licensed paralegals, and lay representatives as dealt with under the *SPPA*
- document the importance of public hearings in administrative law and the exceptions to this principle under Ontario law
- explain the importance of costs in relation to Ontario agencies, as well as how awarding of costs in agencies matters has been viewed as a "strategic lawsuit against public participation"

INTRODUCTION

The Ontario statute, the *Statutory Powers Procedure Act*, R.S.O. 1990, c. S.22, as amended (*SPPA*), can be called a statute of general application as it applies to most Ontario agencies. As noted in the previous chapter, this statute was to set out "minimum" rules of fair procedure that should apply to tribunals (as defined under the Act). It is basically a codification, as extended, of the case law developed under the rules of natural justice, more currently called the duty to act fairly or the duty of procedural fairness. See the previous chapter for a brief discussion of the history of the *SPPA*, both in its original form and after the major amendments to it made in 1994 and 1999.

This chapter will examine specific and important provisions of the *SPPA* and, where appropriate, briefly discuss court cases and/or agency decisions that have examined such specific sections of the Act (called "annotating"). It is hoped that upon reviewing this chapter, the reader will have a better idea of (i) the relevance of the *SPPA*, either directly or indirectly, to Ontario agencies, and (ii) how procedures need to be followed to make sure a person has a fair hearing.

THE *SPPA* CLAUSES

Section 1 — Interpretation

Subsection (1) has definitions of 10 words or phrases, and three are important to the reader:

- "Representative" means a person authorized under the *Law Society Act* to represent a person in a proceeding. (This is the definition, in addition to ss. 10 and 23(3) of the *SPPA*, that allows those licensed by the Law Society of Upper Canada, including lawyers and paralegals, to represent a person before a tribunal.)

- "Statutory power of decision" means the power to make a decision, given by or under a statute, affecting a person's legal rights, powers, privileges, immunities, duties or liabilities, or the eligibility of a person to receive or continue a benefit or licence. (This broad definition is needed to differentiate those agencies who have a statutory power of decision and therefore to whom the *SPPA* may apply under s. 3 and those agencies which do not exercise a statutory power of decision and to whom the *SPPA* does not apply.)

- "Tribunal" means one or more persons upon whom a statutory power of decision is conferred by or under a statute (Even agencies not specifically named as tribunals would be covered by the

THE *SPPA* CLAUSES | **41**

definition and are referred to as such under the *SPPA* as long as it exercises a statutory power of decision.)

Also defined are various types of hearings.

The definition of "statutory power of decision" was examined in the Ontario Divisional Court (Div. Ct.) case of *Lerew v. St Lawrence College of Applied Arts and Technology*, [2005] O.J. No. 1436, 196 O.A.C. 363, 138 A.C.W.S. (3d) 591 (the *Lerew* case), involving an application for judicial review of a decision of a student appeals committee. The court, in deciding whether the procedural fairness provisions of the *SPPA* applied, looked at whether that Act was applicable and to do so looked at the definition of "statutory power of decision". It considered the definition in subsection 1(1) and the applicability provision in subsection 3(1) and stated that the "[c]ommittee here does not exercise a statutory power of decision, as it is not exercising a specific power or right conferred by statute to make a decision".

Subsection (2) extends the meaning of the word "person" as used in the Act.

Section 2 — Liberal Construction of the Act and Rules

The *SPPA* and any rules made under sections 17.1(4) and 25.1 are to be "liberally construed to secure the just, most expeditious and cost-effective determination of every proceeding on its merits". This gives authority to the tribunal to interpret the provisions of the Act or the rules made pursuant to it in a broad fashion to achieve a just, fast, and inexpensive result.

Section 3 — Application of the Act

Subsection (1) states that, subject to subsection (2), the *SPPA* applies to a proceeding by a tribunal in the exercise of a statutory power of decision where the tribunal is required by or under a statute or otherwise by law to hold, or afford parties to a proceeding an opportunity for, a hearing before making a decision. This means that any tribunal making a decision affecting a person's rights is bound by this Act to give the parties the opportunity for a hearing, except where subsection (2) applies or where the enabling legislation states that the *SPPA* does not apply.

Subsection (2) sets out specific proceedings where the *SPPA* does not apply, including the various Ontario courts and situations where specific other rules and procedures apply, such as the coroner, arbitrators, and those persons who investigate and make a report that is not determinative of the final decision.

The Div. Ct. case of *Harrison v. Orillia Soldiers' Memorial Hospital*, [2006] O.J. No. 3973, 56 Admin. L.R. (4th) 198, 153 A.C.W.S. (3d) 993 (the *Harrison* case) examined subsections 3(1) and 3(2) to determine if the decision of the hospital board to revoke privileges fell within the applicability provision of the *SPPA*. The court determined that under subsection 3(1), for the Act to be applicable, the tribunal was required by or under legislation or "otherwise by law" to hold a hearing. Specifically, it stated as follows:

> While the Board owes a duty of procedural fairness to a physician when it decides to revoke or suspend an appointment, a full and formal hearing is not required at common law. The fact that the Hospital, in its by-laws, chose to provide certain procedural safeguards for the affected individual does not trigger the full application of the *SPPA* to its proceedings.

Section 4 — Waiver

Subsection (1) states that any procedural requirement of the *SPPA* or other legislation applying to "a proceeding may be waived with the consent of the parties and the tribunal". Subsection (2) allows for a waiver of rules made under the *SPPA*, also by consent. These provisions allow for the waiver of any procedural requirements or rules as long as all the parties and the tribunal consent, thereby allowing for flexibility, if needed, and not enforcing rules by rote.

Section 4.1 — Disposition without Hearing

Unless the enabling legislation requires a hearing, the tribunal can make a decision without a hearing if the parties consent. This provides flexibility where all agree a hearing is not needed.

Section 4.2 — Panels Related to Certain Matters

Subsection (1) allows the chair of a tribunal to assign one or more members to a panel to hear and determine a procedural or interlocutory matter. The Div. Ct. case of *Lennon v. Ontario (Superintendent of Financial Services)* (2007), 87 O.R. 736, 231 O.A.C. 83, 161 A.C.W.S. (3d) 805 (the *Lennon* case) examined subsection 4.2(1) in relation to an appeal of an FST decision. The court declined to interfere with the Superintendent of Financial Services' decision of consenting to the merger of two pension plans. The appeal alleged that the FST denied procedural fairness to the appellants in a number of ways, including the specific situation set out in the court's decision:

The appellant objected to these affidavits being filed without requiring the affiants to testify in person. This issue was raised in a pre-hearing conference with the Tribunal Chair, who afforded all sides an opportunity to be heard. The appellant did not object to this pre-hearing procedure at the time, before the full panel of the Tribunal, or before us. The appellant does not challenge the jurisdiction of a single member of the Tribunal to make this ruling prior to the hearing. (Such a procedure is authorized by s. 4.2(1) of the *SPPA*.)

In assigning members to such a panel, subsection (2) states that the chair shall take into consideration any requirement imposed by other applicable legislation "that the tribunal be representative of specific interests".

Section 4.2.1 — Panel of One
Subsection (1) allows the chair of a tribunal to decide that a panel of one can hear a proceeding unless there is a statutory requirement of more than one person on the panel, and subsection (2) permits a panel of less than what is statutorily required if all the parties consent. The intent is to spread a fixed number of adjudicators over more hearings if possible and if needed.

Section 4.3 — Expiry of Term
If the term of office of a tribunal member participating in a hearing where the decision is not yet given expires, the term shall be deemed to continue for the purpose of participating in the decision. As one of the requirements of the duty to act fairly is that the person who heard the case should make the decision, this provision tries to remove the impediment of an expiring term to such a principle.

The Sup. Ct. J. case of *Conway v. Darby* (2008), 174 A.C.W.S. (3d) 353 (the *Darby* case) discussed section 4.3 in respect of a submission made to the effect that the adjudicator who heard the original matter was no longer a member of the Consent and Capacity Board and, therefore, could not hear new submissions regarding costs. The appeal on that matter, however, was withdrawn since the adjudicator could hear the new matter, as stated in the case:

> Mr. Nemetz, the Board member who initially heard the matter, was no longer a member of the Board so the costs of the initial hearing would be wasted as a hearing *de novo* would be required. Respondent's counsel advised that Mr. Nemetz would be able to continue the hearing pursuant to section 4.3 of the *Statutory Powers Procedure Act*, R.S.O. 1990, c. S.22.

Section 4.4 — Incapacity of Member

Subsection (1) states that if a tribunal member, "who has participated in a hearing, becomes unable, for any reason, to complete the hearing or to participate in the decision, the remaining member or members may complete the hearing and give a decision" subject to subsection (2), which says that subsection (1) does not apply if other legislation deals with the issue. Section 4.4 allows a hearing to proceed even if one member of a panel of adjudicators cannot continue due to incapacity.

Section 4.5 — Decision Not to Process
Commencement of Proceeding

Subsection (1) permits the tribunal or its administrative staff to decide not to process the documents relating to the commencement of a proceeding if (i) the documents are incomplete or are received after the time required to commence has elapsed, or the fee required is not paid, or there is some other technical defect, and (ii) the decision not to process is made in compliance with subsection (3), which requires the tribunal to make rules under section 25.1 respecting the making of such decision. As well, any of the grounds for refusing to process and the requirement for the processing to be resumed must be set out in the notice prescribed in subsection (2). The intent here is to allow the tribunal or its staff to not process documents if there are defects, on the conditions that there are rules in place and there is some possibility for the party to correct such defects.

Section 4.6 — Dismissal of Proceeding without Hearing

Subsection (1) states that, subject to the requirements of (i) subsection (5), giving notice and considering submissions; and (ii) subsection (6), setting rules, in accordance with section 25.1, for early dismissal of a proceeding,

> a tribunal may dismiss a proceeding without a hearing if
> (a) the proceeding is frivolous, vexatious or is commenced in bad faith;
> (b) the proceeding relates to matters that are outside the jurisdiction of the tribunal; or
> (c) some aspect of the statutory requirements for bringing the proceeding has not been met.

This provision is intended to prevent abuses of the process and to have matters that should not be heard by the tribunal dismissed early on in the process without wasting undue time and money.

The arbitration decision under the Financial Services Commission of Ontario auspices in *Luskin v. Personal Insurance Co. of Canada* (2007-10-01), FSCO 1943, FSCO A06-001216 (the *Luskin* decision), involved whether the arbitration should be dismissed based on the non-performance of obligations imposed on the insured and his counsel in pre-hearings, as well as their non-attendance at pre-hearings. The arbitrator dismissed the arbitration with the following explanation:

> It is unusual to dismiss an arbitration prior to a full hearing on the merits, absent the consent of both parties to a dismissal. There are, however, rare instances when the circumstances suggest that a matter should not be forced to proceed through the system to a formal arbitration hearing, such as when the outcome is a foregone conclusion and there is absolutely no possibility of success.
>
> The easy, uncontroversial route to take is to let this arbitration proceed, unopposed, to the final hearing, with the opposing party accumulating costs all the way. In this matter, I think such an approach is inappropriate, a waste of resources, and potentially unfair to both parties.
>
> On the face of it, it would be a travesty of justice and waste of resources if there was no way to terminate an arbitration in circumstances where there was no possibility of success at a hearing. Certainly, if a party bringing the arbitration is unwilling to participate in the process, and providing instructions to counsel, let alone appearing for pre-hearings, motions, and hearings as required, such would likely be the case.
>
> An early dismissal of an arbitration relies on more than just an interpretation of the general principles of the arbitration system. At least three potential bases for an early decision dismissing an arbitration are found in the *Statutory Powers Procedure Act* (*SPPA*), a law which applies to all arbitrations.

The arbitrator then made reference to sections 4.6(1), 4.6(2), and 7(1) and then examined the word "vexatious" as used in subsection 4.6(1)(a), which relates to an abuse of process or bringing "the administration of justice and the arbitration system into disrepute".

Before there is an early dismissal under subsection (1), subsection (2) requires that the tribunal shall give notice of its intent to dismiss to all parties if the proceeding is being dismissed on grounds of matters that are outside the jurisdiction of the tribunal or to the party commencing the proceeding for any other grounds. The notice of intent to dismiss must comply with subsection (3) — that is, (i) providing the reasons for dismissal; (ii) the right of the parties to make submission with respect to the dismissal to the tribunal; and

(iii) the amount of time the parties have to make the submissions. Written submissions by a party who receives a notice of early dismissal may be made in accordance with subsection (4), which must be considered by the tribunal under subsection (5).

Section 4.7 — Classifying Proceedings

> A tribunal may make rules under section 25.1 classifying the types of proceedings that come before it and setting guidelines as to the procedural steps or processes (such as preliminary motions, pre-hearing conferences, alternative dispute resolution mechanisms, expedited hearings) that apply to each type of proceeding and the circumstances in which other procedures may apply.

This is one of a number of sections that gives a tribunal authority to deal with certain matters if the tribunal makes such rules under section 25.1.

Section 4.8 — Alternative Dispute Resolution

Under subsection (1), the tribunal may direct parties in a proceeding to participate in an alternative dispute resolution (ADR) mechanism (defined in subsection (2) as including "mediation, conciliation, negotiation, or any other means of facilitating the resolution of issues in dispute") if (i) the tribunal has made rules under section 25.1 concerning the use of ADR (and containing procedural guidelines as outlined in subsection (3)); and (ii) all parties consent to participating in it. The ADR may be used to resolve the whole proceeding or issue(s) arisen from the proceeding. As in the court system, there is a move toward resolving disputes in agencies by ADR. The rules of the tribunal made under section 25.1 can also require mandatory ADR in all or specific circumstances pursuant to subsection (4). Note also that subsection (5) states that the rules may provide that the person appointed to conduct the ADR be independent of the tribunal or a member of the tribunal; but if a member is so appointed, then such member cannot subsequently hear the matter unless the parties consent.

Section 4.9 — Person Conducting ADR Not Compellable and Notes Kept May Not Be Used As Evidence

Subsection (1) states that no person appointed to conduct the ADR "shall be compelled to give testimony or produce documents in a proceeding before the tribunal or in a civil proceeding with respect to matters that come to his or her knowledge in the course of exercising his or her duties under this or any other Act", and no notes or records kept by such a person are admissible in a civil proceeding under subsection (2). This is to ensure that the parties participating know that anything said in the ADR process cannot be used in a subsequent proceeding and, therefore, the parties may be more forthcoming.

Section 5 — Parties

> The parties to a proceeding shall be the persons specified as parties by or under the statute under which the proceeding arises or, if not so specified, persons entitled by law to be parties to the proceeding.

If the enabling legislation does not specify who the parties are, such determination would be done in accordance with case law.

The Div. Ct. case of *McFadyen v. Ontario (Mining and Lands Commission)*, [2007] O.J. No. 4875, 232 O.A.C. 239, 162 A.C.W.S. (3d) 873 (the *McFadyen* case), involved an application for judicial review of an order of the Mining and Lands Commissioner, partly on the basis that the applicants submitted that they were not added as parties to the proceedings that led to the order. The court examined section 5 of the *SPPA* regarding identities of the parties to a matter before a tribunal. In looking at the facts, the court stated that the Commissioner had allowed the applicants to make a submission and file affidavit material supporting their request to be added as parties as well as granted them an oral hearing. The court held that the Commissioner applied the correct approach in determining party status:

> The tribunal is not restricted to the test that is applicable to court proceedings, but may consider other matters, including the subject-matter of the decision-making power, the nature of the issue to be decided at the hearing and the object of the governing legislation.

Section 5.1 — Written Hearings

Written hearings, as defined in subsection 1(1), may be held if the tribunal's rules made under section 25.1 deal with it. The tribunal shall not hold a written hearing if a party satisfies the tribunal that there is good reason for not doing so under subsection (2), but this does not apply under subsection (2.1) if the hearing is dealing with procedural matters. In other words, if the rules allow written hearings, they can be used for procedural matters and for any other matter unless a party shows there are good reasons not to use a written hearing. Note also that subsection (3) states, "[i]n a written hearing, all the parties are entitled to receive every document that the tribunal receives in the proceeding."

An example of the use of a written hearing is illustrated in the Human Rights Tribunal of Ontario's (HRTO) decision of *Domingues v. Fortino*, 2007 HRTO 7 (CanLII) (the *Domingues* decision). The HRTO first noted the power of the Tribunal to hold a written hearing under section 5.1 of the *SPPA* and then cited a previous decision:

> In *Sanford v. Koop*, 2005 HRTO 28 (CanLII), the Tribunal held that it had the authority to hold a written hearing in appropriate circumstances. While not purporting to enumerate all cases where a written hearing would be appropriate, the Tribunal specifically found that where a respondent chooses not to participate in the Tribunal's legal processes and the Commission or Complainant requests a written hearing, it would be rare for the Tribunal to schedule an oral hearing (*Sanford, supra*, at paras. 19 and 21).

In *Sanford*, the HRTO also discussed, at paragraphs 30 and 31 of its decision, the nature of evidence that would normally be required at a written hearing:

> Again, case law suggests that mere pleadings will not be sufficient to establish an evidentiary basis for findings of fact and remedial orders, where a hearing is required to be held (*Re City of Windsor, supra*). The Tribunal finds however that affidavits or statutory declarations by persons who would otherwise have provided *viva voce* evidence had the hearing been held as an oral hearing would be a proper form of evidence. These could contain statements based on personal knowledge, or information and belief (as long as the basis for the information and belief was set out in the affidavit). Also, business records and medical reports which would normally be admissible before the Tribunal without the necessity of calling the maker of the document, would generally be admitted. The Tribunal would retain the power to question an affiant, or rule or place conditions upon the admissibility of a document.
>
> The Tribunal notes that it is always to be open to parties to make submissions as to the appropriate form of evidence in a written hearing in a particular case. The comments above set out what the Tribunal considers appropriate in the normal course, and in circumstances where a respondent chooses not to participate in a hearing.

Section 5.2 — Electronic Hearings

Electronic hearings, as defined in subsection 1(1), may be held if the tribunal's rules made under section 25.1 deal with it. The tribunal shall not hold an electronic hearing if a party satisfies the tribunal that it is likely to cause the party significant prejudice under subsection (2), but this does not apply under subsection (3) if the hearing is dealing with procedural matters. In other words, if the rules allow electronic hearings, they can be used for procedural matters and for any other matter unless a party shows it is likely to cause the party significant prejudice. Note also that subsection (4) states, "[in an] electronic hearing, all the parties and the members of the tribunal participating in the hearing must be able to hear one another and any witnesses throughout the hearing." The electronic set up must allow all persons involved to hear each other, which, in theory, allows both telephone conference calls and video-conferencing.

Section 5.2.1 — Combination of Hearings

> A tribunal may, in a proceeding, hold any combination of written, electronic and oral hearings.

Section 5.3 — Pre-hearing Conferences

Subsection (1) mandates that, subject to any other applicable legislation pursuant to subsection (1.1), if pre-hearing conferences are covered in rules made pursuant to section 25.1, tribunals may direct the parties to participate in a pre-hearing conference to consider the following:

(a) the settlement of any or all of the issues;
(b) the simplification of the issues;
(c) facts or evidence that may be agreed upon;
(d) the dates by which any steps in the proceeding are to be taken or begun;
(e) the estimated duration of the hearing; and
(f) any other matter that may assist in the just and most expeditious disposition of the proceeding.

The subsection allows for a broad type of pre-hearing conference, which can be used to achieve multiple purposes and is aimed at making the ultimate resolution of the matter faster and cheaper to obtain. In the Ontario Municipal Board (OMB) decision of *Re the City of Burlington Official Plan Amendment No. 3* (2006), 54 O.M.B.R. 340, 2006 CLB 13469 (the *Burlington* decision), a motion was brought to determine the validity of an order made by the OMB in a pre-hearing procedure. The OMB dismissed the motion, referring to, *inter alia*, powers given to it to deal with such situations, including section 5.3 of the *SPPA*:

> [S]ection 5.3(1) of the *SPPA* ... permits the Board, in the context of pre-hearing conferences, to make orders that may "assist in the just and most expeditious disposition of the proceeding".

Under subsection (2), the chair can designate anyone, even a member of the tribunal, to preside over the pre-hearing conference, and a member so designated may make orders considered necessary or advisable with respect to the conduct of the proceeding pursuant to subsection (3). However, if such member presides at the pre-hearing in which the parties attempt to settle issues, that member cannot also preside at the hearing unless the parties consent under subsection (4). This disqualification is to attempt to have the adjudicator not hear matters before the hearing that might affect the decision. Please note subsection (5) may allow for pre-hearing conferences to be done electronically, which are done by many agencies.

Section 5.4 — Disclosure

Subsection (1) mandates that, subject to any other applicable legislation pursuant to subsection (1.1), if there are rules in this area made pursuant to section 25.1,

> the tribunal may, at any stage of the proceeding before all hearings are complete, make orders for,
> (a) the exchange of documents;
> (b) the oral or written examination of a party;
> (c) the exchange of witness statements and reports of expert witnesses;
> (d) the provision of particulars;
> (e) any other form of disclosure.

This provision allows disclosure in agencies, which may not be as formal or detailed as in the court system but is absolutely essential for fair hearings. Note that subsection (2) states that subsection (1) does not authorize the disclosure of privileged information.

The Div. Ct. case of *York Region District School Board v. Ontario College of Teachers* (2007), 154 A.C.W.S. (3d) 804, 2007 CLB 8617, 56 Admin. L.R. (4th) 313, 221 O.A.C. 55 (the *York Region* case), deals with an application for the judicial review of a decision made by the Discipline Committee of the Ontario College of Teachers (the Discipline Committee). The application was based on solicitor–client privilege and inadvertent disclosure of documents. In the case, the judge noted the relevant section of the *SPPA*:

> Section 5.4(2) of the *Statutory Powers Procedure Act* makes an order for disclosure subject to the same exception for privileged information.

Section 6 — Notice of Hearing

Subsection (1) states that the "parties to a proceeding shall be given reasonable notice of the hearing by the tribunal", and such notice, pursuant to subsection (2), shall include a reference to the statutory authority under which the hearing will be held. The purpose of the provision is to ensure the parties have sufficient time and explanation of the hearing in order to properly prepare for it. Specific details of what is to be included in a notice of oral hearing, written hearing, and electronic hearing are enumerated in subsections (3), (4), and (5), respectively. These subsections provide a guide for the tribunal as to the minimum contents of the notice, depending on the format of hearing involved.

Toronto Transit Commission v. A.T.U., Local 113 (2007), 164 A.C.W.S. (3d) 810, 2007 CLB 13690, [2007] OLRBREP.SEPT/OCT 982, 233 O.A.C. 14 (the *TTC* case) is a Div. Ct. case that involves an application for judicial review of two decisions of the Ontario Labour Relations Board (the OLRB). The application was litigated on the basis of a telephone conference call setting up a hearing with limitations on the presentation of evidence. The court summarized the situation as follows:

> [The appellant] took the position that the Board had exceeded its jurisdiction by conducting the hearings as "expedited hearings"; the first, on short notice and without the Union's participation; and the second, with unfairly limited presentation time. As a result, it complained it had not been afforded full opportunity to present evidence and make submissions. This was alleged to be a natural justice denial of procedural fairness and required the setting aside of both orders.

One of the arguments raised was that section 6 of the *SPPA* "also requires a notice of hearing, sets out the content of the notice and gives the parties a similar right to demonstrate that significant prejudice will likely be caused by an electronic hearing". The court held that section 6 of the *SPPA*, as well as the Rules of Procedure of the OLRB and its enabling legislation, allowed the OLRB to act as it did, and therefore there was no denial of natural justice.

Section 7 — Effect of Non-attendance at Hearing After Due Notice

Where notice of an oral hearing under subsection (1), a written hearing under subsection (2), or an electronic hearing under subsection (3) is given to a party, the tribunal may proceed with the hearing in the absence or without the participation of that party and that party is not entitled to any further notice in the proceeding. This, however, does not apply to the party who acted in accordance with subsection 6(4)(b)or 6(5)(c) and succeeded in convincing the tribunal not to hold the written or electronic hearing prescribed in the notice. The intent of this provision is to make the process fair to all parties by allowing the hearing to proceed even if a party is absent or not participating, as long as proper notice has been given.

In the appeal order of *McCormack v. Aviva Canada Inc.* (2008-03-03), FSCO 2120, Appeal P06-00024 (the *McCormack* decision), conducted under the auspices of the Financial Services Commission of Ontario (FSCO), the FSCO dismissed the appeal of the representative of the insured of the arbitration order, which required that representative to personally pay expenses of the insurance company.

In examining the matter, the Director's Delegate discussed the ramifications of section 7:

> You seem to suggest that, since Mr. McCormack has not responded, he can be noted in default and your appeal can succeed automatically. However, that is not how matters proceed at tribunals. The *Statutory Powers Procedure Act*, R.S.O. 1990, c. S.22, only provides that, where a party does not attend at a hearing despite receiving notice, "the tribunal may proceed in the absence of the party and the party is not entitled to any further notice in the proceeding." [s. 7(1)]
>
> You must still proceed with the appeal if you wish to reverse the arbitrator's decision. As for Mr. Isabella seeking arbitration expenses after he asked for a withdrawal without expenses, I remind you that the same expenses provisions — that a representative may be liable for advancing a frivolous or vexatious claim — apply on appeal as at arbitration.

Section 8 — Where Character of the Party Is At Issue

> Where the good character, propriety of conduct or competence of a party is an issue in a proceeding, the party is entitled to be furnished prior to the hearing with reasonable information of any allegations with respect thereto.

This provision gives the party notice and information of such issue, allowing for better preparation.

In the Div. Ct. case of *Yar v. College of Physicians and Surgeons of Ontario* (2009), 174 A.C.W.S. (3d) 1199, 2009 CLB 1240 (the *Yar* case), Dr. Yar appealed the finding of professional misconduct by a panel of the Discipline Committee of the College of Physicians and Surgeons of Ontario (the Discipline Committee). In determining the appeal, the court looked at the adequacy of notice given to the person subjected to disciplinary proceedings:

> Adequacy of notice is a fundamental principle inherent in the duty of procedural fairness in disciplinary proceedings. This has been codified in section 8 of the *Statutory Powers Procedure Act*, R.S.O. 1990, c. S.22 which provides the notice requirements in the context of a disciplinary proceeding.

Section 9 — Public and Private Hearings and Maintenance of Order

Oral hearings are to be public under subsection (1) except

> where the tribunal is of the opinion that,
> (a) matters involving public security may be disclosed; or
> (b) intimate financial or personal matters or other matters may be disclosed at the hearing of such a nature, having regard to the circumstances, that the desirability of avoiding disclosure thereof in the interests of any person affected or in the public interest outweighs the desirability of adhering to the principle that hearings be open to the public,
> in which case the tribunal may hold the hearing in the absence of the public.

Similarly, members of the public are to have reasonable access to the documents submitted in a written hearing under subsection (1.1) unless, in the opinion of the tribunal, the two grounds in subsection (1) apply; electronic hearings are to be open to the public under subsection (1.2) unless, in the opinion of the tribunal, the grounds in subsection (1) apply or it is not practical to do so. Although the public should be invited to attend any hearing, there has to be a balance between the rights of public security and the rights of privacy of persons not to have intimate financial or personal matters widely known. Subsection (2) authorizes the tribunal to make such orders and give such directions as it considers necessary for the maintenance of order at the hearing; and if such order or direction is disobeyed, the tribunal may call for the assistance of any peace officer to enforce such order or direction, taking such action as necessary. This allows the tribunal to obtain assistance to maintain order, which may not be initially available, unlike in the case of a court.

The Div. Ct. case of *Lifford Wine Agencies Ltd. v. Ontario (Alcohol and Gaming Commission)*, [2003] O.J. No. 4972, 179 O.A.C. 76, 127 A.C.W.S. (3d) 1 (the *Lifford Wine* case) involved a hearing before the Alcohol and Gaming Commission of Ontario, ordered to be held *in camera*. The court made the following statement regarding open hearings:

> Section 9(1) of the *Statutory Powers Procedure Act* and the common law both strongly favour open hearings, particularly when involving a hearing before a public body such as in this case. There are strong public policy reasons for this. A quote from the judgment of Doherty J.A. in *Her Majesty the Queen v. Toronto Star Newspapers et al.*, [2003] O.J. No. 4006:
>
> > [4] "A publication ban should only be ordered when:
> > (a) such an order is necessary in order to prevent a serious risk to the proper administration of justice because reasonably alternative measures will not prevent the risk, and
> > (b) the salutary effects of the publication ban outweigh the deleterious effects on the rights and interests of the parties and the public, including the effects on the right to free expression, the right of the accused to a fair and public trial, and the efficacy of the administration of justice."
>
> That quote deals with a publication ban, however the same practical test applies in the instant case.

Section 9.1 — Proceedings Involving Similar Questions

Unless the *Consolidated Hearings Act*, as set out in subsection (2), applies or the provisions of subsections (3) or (4) apply, subsection (1) states that

> If "two or more proceedings before a tribunal involve the same or similar questions of fact, law or policy, the tribunal may,
> (a) combine the proceedings or any part of them, with the consent of the parties;
> (b) hear the proceedings at the same time, with the consent of the parties;
> (c) hear the proceedings one immediately after the other; or
> (d) stay one or more of the proceedings until after the determination of another one of them.

It is hoped that similar matters can be dealt with more expeditiously and more economically by giving the tribunal various alternative mechanisms. The Ontario Municipal Board's 2007 joint decision (No. 0489) in *Lee-Mar Investments Ltd. v. Toronto (City)*, File No. LC060012 and *Maple Leaf Firelog Products Company v. Toronto (City)*, File No. LC060026 (jointly called the *Lee-Mar/Maple Leaf* decision), is an example of such a consolidation. Furthermore, under subsection (5), if "the parties to the second-named proceeding consent, the tribunal may treat evidence that is admitted in a proceeding as if it were also admitted in another proceeding that is heard at the same time" under subsection 9.1(1)(b).

Section 10 — Right to Representation

> A party to a proceeding may be represented by a representative.

This section, along with the definition of representative in subsection 1(1) and the details of subsection 23(3), allows paralegals licensed by the Law Society of Upper Canada to represent persons at an agency without being excluded by the tribunal on the grounds of incompetence: See *Romanchook v. Garda Ontario*, [2009] HRTO 1077, an interim decision of the HRTO where this matter was discussed (the *Romanchook* decision).

The Federal Court of Appeal, in the case of *Law Society of Upper Canada v. Canada (Minister of Citizenship and Immigration)* (2008), 295 D.L.R. (4th) 488, 2008 CLB 5684, 168 A.C.W.S. (3d) 152, 2008 FCA 243, 72 Imm. L.R. (3d) 26, 383 N.R. 200 (the *LSUC* case), looked at representation by non-lawyers in different jurisdictions in Canada:

> Representation by non-lawyers is a common feature of administrative adjudication: see, for example, Ontario's general administrative procedural code, the *Statutory Powers Procedure Act*, R.S.O. 1990, c. S.22, section 10.

Section 10.1 — Examination of Witnesses

> A party to a proceeding may, at an oral or electronic hearing,
> (a) call and examine witnesses and present evidence and submissions; and
> (b) conduct cross-examinations of witnesses at the hearing reasonably required for a full and fair disclosure of all matters relevant to the issues in the proceeding.

This provision allows a party to adduce evidence and question the other side's evidence to ideally permit the fairest hearing possible.

The Sup. Ct. J. case of *Conway v. Ontario* (2008), 172 A.C.W.S. (3d) 503, 2008 CLB 12281 (the *Conway* case), involves an appeal of a decision of the Consent and Capacity Board on various grounds, including that the appellant was not permitted to cross-examine a witness. In looking at such ground, the court stated the following:

> Section 10.1(b) of the *Statutory Powers Procedure Act*, R.S.O. 1990, c. S.22, provides that a party to a proceeding may conduct cross-examinations of witnesses "reasonably required for a full and fair disclosure of all matters relevant to the issues in the proceeding."

Section 11 — Rights of Witnesses to Representation

Under subsection (1), a witness at an oral or electronic hearing is entitled to be advised by a representative as to his or her rights. Such representative can take no other part in the hearing except with leave of the tribunal. Further pursuant to subsection (2) where the hearing is closed to the public, the witness's representative is not entitled to be present except when that witness is giving evidence. Under this provision, witnesses are entitled to independent advice as needed.

Section 12 — Summonses

Subsections (1)–(3.1) in this section relate to (i) the ability of the tribunal to issue summonses to require any person, including parties, to give evidence under oath/affirmation and to produce documents and things in evidence; (ii) the form and service of summons; and (iii) fees and allowances allowed for such summons. Subsections (4)–(7) detail the ability of a judge of the Superior Court of Justice to issue a bench warrant against a person based upon proving certain facts under subsections (5)–(7). Such a warrant is to be in prescribed form and is directed to any police officer for apprehension of the person to be brought before the tribunal in accordance with subsection (4.1). If there is a concern that a witness will not appear, the mechanism of asking for a summons, which ultimately leads to the issuance of a bench warrant, may ensure the appearance where possible, and that is helpful as the hearing will likely be adjourned pending the appearance of the witness. Without the service of a summons, the tribunal will be unlikely to adjourn the hearing pending the arrival of the recalcitrant witness.

In the arbitration pre-hearing decision in *Kuan v. Kingsway General Insurance Co.* (2008-03-28), FSCO 1742, FSCO A07-002341 (the

Kuan decision), conducted under the auspices of the FSCO, there was an order for production of documents. The arbitrator of the case justified its decision with a reference to the *SPPA*:

> Section 12(1) of the *Statutory Powers Procedure Act*, R.S.O. 1990, c. S.22 ("*SPPA*") also grants extensive powers to tribunals, including arbitrators, to order the production of relevant evidence in matters before them.

Section 13 — Contempt Proceedings

Subsection (1) states that if a witness summoned under section 12, without lawful excuse, fails to attend the hearing (s. 13(1)(a)) or does not perform acts legally required by the tribunal (s. 13(1)(b)), or if a person does any other thing that would be considered contempt of court, "the tribunal may, of its own motion or on the motion of a party to the proceeding, state a case to the Divisional Court setting out the facts and that court may inquire into the matter and, after hearing any witnesses who may be produced against or on behalf of that person and after hearing any statement that may be offered in defence, punish or take steps for the punishment of that person in like manner as if he or she had been guilty of contempt of the court." Subsection (2) states that subsection (1) applies if a person who, without lawful excuse, (i) fails to participate in the oral or electronic hearing that replaces the written hearing objected to by this person under subsection 6(4)(b); or (ii) fails to attend a pre-hearing conference required by the tribunal. Although tribunals do not have the court's inherent jurisdiction to directly manage its process up to and including putting the offender into custody, they can use this section to have a court take whatever steps are necessary to manage the hearing against unlawful disruptions.

In the case of *Petsinis v. Escalhorda*, [2000] O.J. No. 3324, [2000] O.T.C. 570, 99 A.C.W.S. (3d) 486 (the *Petsinis* case), the Superior Court of Justice dealt with an application for leave to appeal a contempt order arising out of a proceeding under the *Tenant Protection Act*. In looking at the issue of contempt, the court noted that the *SPPA* "does not authorize a tribunal to make a finding of contempt itself. It simply allows the tribunal to state a case to the divisional court for it to make a finding of contempt."

Section 14 — Protection for Witnesses

Subsection (1) protects witnesses giving evidence in two ways as follows:

> A witness at an oral or electronic hearing shall be deemed to have objected to answer any question asked him or her upon the ground that the answer may tend to criminate him or her or may tend to establish his or her liability to civil proceedings at the instance of the Crown, or of any person, and no answer given by a witness at a hearing shall be used or be receivable in evidence against the witness in any trial or other proceeding against him or her thereafter taking place, other than a prosecution for perjury in giving such evidence.

Although Canadian law does not give a right not to answer questions on the basis that the answers would lead to self-incrimination, the protection in this section, similar to giving evidence in a court setting, means that evidence given is not admissible in any other proceeding taking place afterward except for prosecution for perjury.

Section 14 was discussed in the Ontario Municipal Board decision of *Kimvar Enterprises Inc. v. Simcoe (County)* (2007), 57 O.M.B.R. 493, 2007 CLB 13145, 37 M.P.L.R. (4th) 294 (the *Kimvar* decision). The case involves a motion to adjourn. One of the grounds for the motion is expressed below:

> The Moving Parties submit that Kimvar has launched a number of lawsuits against members of the IDA and related individuals. Accordingly, their ability to make their case before the Board is impaired as key witnesses find themselves intimidated to publicly oppose the development.

In looking at the submission, the OMB stated the following:

> The Board finds that the existence of these lawsuits cannot possibly be a basis for an adjournment. As Mr. Miller submitted, intimidation is a defined tort and it is simply not enough to come before the Board and say I am afraid to give evidence because I will get sued. The Board is subject to the requirements of the *Statutory Powers Procedure Act*, R.S.O. 1990, c. S.22 (SPPA). Witnesses who appear before the Board are subject to the protection set out in section 14 of the SPPA.

Section 15 — Evidence

Subsection (1) states that the tribunal may admit as evidence, whether sworn or admissible in court, any oral testimony, document, or thing "relevant to the subject-matter of the proceeding and may act on such evidence, but the tribunal may exclude anything unduly repetitious". Subsections (2) and (3) set out the specific situations where evidence is inadmissible at a hearing: (i) evidence considered privileged under the law (ss. (2)(a)), (ii) evidence designated as inadmissible by the enabling or other statute (ss. (2)(b)), and (iii) oral testimony, documents, or things for which the extent or purpose of its use as evidence is expressly limited by an Act (ss. (3)). Instead of the extensive rules of evidence with the countless exceptions used in court, tribunals are allowed to admit any evidence, with certain exceptions, that is relevant and not unduly repetitious. Copies of a document or other thing may be admitted as evidence if the tribunal is satisfied as to its authenticity under subsection (4), and copies of documents certified by a member of the tribunal are admissible as evidence in a proceeding in which the document is admissible as evidence of the document under subsection (6). Subsection (5) allows, if the tribunal gives leave and authorizes it, for a photocopy of the document to be filed as evidence. The original document can either be released or photocopied and certified by a member of the tribunal to be given instead.

The Div. Ct. case of *Ontario Racing Commission v. Hudon*, 2008 CLB 14037, (2008), 173 A.C.W.S. (3d) 666 (the *Ontario Racing* case), looked at the admissibility of evidence in dealing with an application for judicial review. The court made the following observations:

> The wording of s. 15(1) is permissive. It grants a tribunal the discretion to accept or reject evidence that is not admissible in a court. Depending on the circumstances, a tribunal may reasonably decide that evidence inadmissible at common law should not be admitted before it.

Section 15.1 — Use of Previously Admitted Evidence

Previously admitted evidence, as defined in subsection (2), means that evidence already admitted in another court or tribunal proceeding may be treated as evidence admitted by the tribunal in its proceeding if the parties consent (ss. (1)). This power of allowing the use of previously admitted evidence, pursuant to subsection (3), is in addition to the power of the tribunal to admit evidence under section 15. With the parties' consent, this additional power to admit evidence allows the tribunal to circumvent the formal rules regarding admitting evidence, leading to a faster and less costly proceeding.

An example of a decision that discussed the use of previously admitted evidence can be found in *F.(D.) v. Wawanesa Insurance Co.* (2007-08-13), FSCO 779, FSCO A05-000779 (the *F.(D.)* decision), an arbitration pre-hearing decision conducted under the auspices of the FSCO. The arbitrator of the case was requested to order that the insurer pay for the transcript of the evidence of a previous arbitration between the parties. The arbitrator ruled against the request because section 15.1 requires the consent of both parties to the use of previously admitted evidence, and the insurer did not consent in this case. In other words, in this case there was no jurisdiction for the arbitrator to order it.

Section 15.2 — Witness Panels

> A tribunal may receive evidence from panels of witnesses composed of two or more persons, if the parties have first had an opportunity to make submissions in that regard.

If such a situation occurs, this power should reduce the time needed for the proceeding, as a panel can give the evidence at the same time instead of calling separate witnesses.

Section 16 — Notice of Facts and Opinions

This section allows the tribunal, in making its decision, to take notice of (i) facts judicially noticed (i.e., things that are commonly known or readily verifiable) and (ii) "any generally recognized scientific or technical facts, information or opinions within its scientific or specialized knowledge". This power allows for a faster hearing as this information can be taken notice of without the need for a party to adduce evidence to prove it. The adjudicator who takes notice in this way should state what was taken notice of in the decision so that the parties are aware of it.

Section 16.1 — Interim Decisions and Orders

Under this section, a tribunal may make interim decisions and orders (ss. (1)) without giving reasons (ss. (3)). The tribunal, under subsection (2), may also impose conditions on an interim decision or order. There are many situations where the tribunal hears an issue, often raised by motion, which must be decided prior to hearing the whole matter, and the power given to a tribunal under this section allows tribunals to make decisions on such preliminary or specific matters.

The Div. Ct. case of *Franklin v. College of Physicians and Surgeons of Ontario* (2007), 161 A.C.W.S. (3d) 496, 2007 CLB 9849, 230 O.A.C. 206 (the *Franklin* case), looked at the specific issue of awarding costs on the interim order of an adjournment, which was brought before the court on judicial review. The court stated the following on the issue:

> The Discipline Committee has no jurisdiction to order costs as a condition of an interim decision to adjourn a hearing, pursuant to s. 16.1(2) of the *Statutory Powers Procedure Act*, R.S.O. 1990, c. S.22.

There are numerous decisions of this and other courts holding that express statutory authority is required for an administrative tribunal to order costs (see, for example, *Birnbaum v. Institute of Chartered Accountants of Ontario*, [1991] O.J. No. 330 (Div. Ct.) at 3; *Persaud v. Society of Management Accountants of Ontario* (1997), 144 D.L.R. (4th) 375 (Div. Ct.) at 384).

The cases relied on by the College suggesting a power to award costs deal with this issue in *obiter* (see *Howatt v. College of Physicians and Surgeons of Ontario*, [2003] O.J. No. 138 (Div. Ct.) at paragraph 32 and *Re Morgan v. Association of Ontario Land Surveyors* (1980), 28 O.R. (2d) 19 (Div. Ct.) at 22).

Section 16.2 — Time Frames

A tribunal shall establish guidelines setting out the usual time frame for completing proceedings that come before the tribunal and for completing the procedural steps within those proceedings.

This power allows tribunals to set up guidelines and time frames to ensure that matters proceed at a proper pace.

Section 17 — Decision; Interest

Subsection (1) states that a decision must be given in writing and written reasons must be provided if requested:

A tribunal shall give its final decision and order, if any, in any proceeding in writing and shall give reasons in writing therefor if requested by a party.

Although this provision is permissive, tribunals will give reasons for almost any decision due to the increasing court decisions requiring tribunals to provide reasons for their decisions. In the Div. Ct. case of *Ontario (Alcohol and Gaming Commission Registrar) v. Arena Entertainment Inc.* (2008), 167 A.C.W.S. (3d) 131, 2008 CLB 4390, 235 O.A.C. 195 (the *Arena* case), the court looked at the issue of giving reasons:

Section 17(1) of the *Statutory Powers Procedure Act*, R.S.O. 1990, c. S.22, requires the Board to give its final decision and order in writing and give reasons in writing therefor.

The purpose of providing adequate reasons is to explain to the parties the basis of the decision and to permit appellate courts to properly review the decision. The appellant is correct that reasons must reflect consideration of the main relevant factors and must reveal the reasoning process (see *Gray v. Ontario (Disability Support Program, Director)* (2002), 59 O.R. (3d) 364 (Ont. C.A.) at page 374 citing *VIA Rail Canada Inc. v. Canada (National Transportation Agency)* (2001), 193 D.L.R. (4th) 357 (F.C.A.) citing *Baker v. Canada (Minister of Citizenship and Immigration)*, [1999] 2 S.C.R. 817 and *Northwestern Utilities et al v. Edmonton (City)*, [1978] 1 S.C.R. 684).

Subsection (2) allows the tribunal to award interest as follows:

> A tribunal that makes an order for the payment of money shall set out in the order the principal sum, and if interest is payable, the rate of interest and the date from which it is to be calculated.

This provision gives tribunals the power to award interest where appropriate and not necessarily on a fixed scale set out in the enabling legislation and its rules and practice directions.

Section 17.1 — Costs

This section imports the Canadian court's power to award costs in the Agency setting so that tribunals can effectively punish those parties that act in a reprehensible manner. The tribunal, under subsection (1), may order a party to pay all or part of another party's costs in a proceeding if (i) that party's behaviour is considered to be "unreasonable, frivolous or vexatious" or that party "has acted in bad faith" (as described in subsection (2)); and (ii) the tribunal has made specific cost rules pertaining to the ordering of costs, the circumstances in which costs may be ordered, and the amount of costs or the manner in which the cost is to be determined (as allowed in subsection (4)). Subsection (5) states that subsections 25.1(3)–(6) apply to rules made under subsection (4). (The amendments were enacted on June 22, 2006.)

In the case of *Ontario (Environmental Protection Act, Director) v. Becker Milk Co.*, [2005] 78 O.R. (3d) 556, O.J. No. 4514 (the *Becker Milk* case), the Superior Court of Justice dealt with an appeal by the Director against an order of the Environmental Review Tribunal (ERT) awarding costs of an appeal to the respondents. The Director appealed the order on the grounds that the ERT had no jurisdiction to award costs. The position of the ERT was that it had jurisdiction pursuant to section 17.1 of the *SPPA* as it made rules pursuant to section 25.1 of the *SPPA* dealing with costs. The court reviewed the ERT's Rules of Practice and identified rules that deal with costs as follows:

COSTS

73. In a proceeding in which the Tribunal has statutory authority to award costs, parties are required to make every effort to negotiate a costs settlement. Applications for a costs award can be submitted to the Tribunal only when a negotiated settlement cannot be reached. Negotiated settlements do not require Tribunal review or approval.

74. A costs application may be filed with the Tribunal at any time prior to the conclusion of the Hearing, or no later than within 30 days from the date of the issuance of the decision and reasons therefor, or final order.

The court disagreed with the ERT and stated its finding as follows:

It is evident from a reading of these rules that they do not meet the requirements of section 17.1(2)(b) of the *SPPA*. Accordingly, it is our respectful view that the rules of the Tribunal were insufficient to enable the Tribunal to acquire authority to award costs pursuant to section 17.1(2)(b) of the *SPPA*.

Although the Tribunal has adopted Guidelines on Costs Awards in addition to guidelines on various other matters, guidelines are not rules and do not serve to substitute for the rules required by section 17.1(2)(b) of the *SPPA*. The distinction between rules and guidelines is recognized by section 27 of the *SPPA* which reads as follows:

Rules, etc., available to public
27. A tribunal shall make any rules or guidelines established under this or any other Act available for examination by the public. 1999, c. 12, Sched. B, s. 16(9).

Nor has the Tribunal provided, as in the previous version of its rules, that its rules require compliance with the guidelines, thereby perhaps effectively incorporating the guidelines into the rules.

In the decision *Kimvar Enterprises Inc.* (Kimvar) *v. Nextnine Limited et al.* (Nextnine) (2009), OMB PL050290, the OMB was asked to award Kimvar costs of approximately $3,200,000 against various losing parties of the OMB proceeding known as the "the Big Bay Point" hearing. These costs were sought on a partial indemnity basis for legal and consulting costs incurred by and on behalf of Kimvar and others. To determine the result, the OMB looked at the following issues:

The application requires determination of whether the conduct of Nextnine and Gilberts during the Big Bay Point proceeding warrants an award of costs. When distilled, three main issues emerge from Kimvar's application. First, can the Board, as a matter of law, award costs against Gilberts, the law firm that represented Nextnine during the hearing. Second, was the conduct of Nextnine (and Gilberts, if the answer to the first issue is yes) unreasonable, frivolous or vexatious or in bad faith such that an award of costs should be made in favour of Kimvar. Third, should an award of costs be denied on the basis that Kimvar's application has been brought for improper purposes and, as a matter of public policy, should costs be awarded in any event. Prior to responding to the issues, a brief summary of the applicable law is set out below.

The Board first stated that the statutory jurisdiction to award costs is found in both s. 97(1) of the *Ontario Municipal Board Act* and s. 17.1 of the *SPPA*, which allows for the awarding of costs if rules have been made in accordance with subsection 17.1(2) and 17.1(4). In this case the rules exist in Rules 102–104, which make awarding of costs against a party dependent on the party's conduct being "unreasonable, frivolous or vexatious" or whether "the party has acted in bad faith".

The OMB found that the conduct complained of against Nextnine should not attract costs.

In looking at the issue regarding an award of costs against the law firm representing Nextnine, the following was found:

> Section 97(2) of the OMB Act does not specify "by whom" or "to whom" costs are to be paid. The Board is given discretion. By analogy to section 131 of the CJA a reasonable interpretation is that it means "by which parties"; however, there is no direction from the court in this regard. Nevertheless, the Board's Rules are clear on costs. The Board has stated clearly that where one party believes that another party has acted unreasonably or there is bad faith, that party can ask for costs. The Board is the master of its own practice and procedure. The Board has made a policy choice that in the event costs are at issue, it is for a party to seek costs against another party. The Board rejects the argument that because the Board's Rules do not preclude costs being sought against counsel resort must be had to the Rules of Civil Procedure. The opposite is true. The Rules are structured to provide clear direction on costs and need not be augmented.

Finally, Kimvar argued that if costs cannot be awarded against a non-party (e.g. legal counsel), the Board would lose its ability to control its own process. The Board disagrees and there is no reason to believe that unreasonable conduct will escape scrutiny. First, parties will always remain liable for conduct that attracts an award of costs and each case is considered on its own merits. The Board notes that distinguishing improper conduct as between a party and its counsel is in any event not always easy. Kimvar was clear at the outset that it could not actually know the degree of responsibility for improper conduct before and at the hearing, which should respectively be borne by Nextnine and Gilberts. Second, under the SPPA any tribunal, including the Board, can prevent abuses of process. The standard is high (see *Volfson v. Royal & Sun Alliance Insurance Co. of Canada*, 2005 CarswellOnt 5232 (Ont.Div.Ct.)). Abuse of process was not the foundation of the claim against Gilberts.

Finally, the OMB looked at the issue of whether the application for costs had been brought for improper purposes. For example, if the cost claim was brought for the purpose of silencing public opposition, it constitutes an improper purpose. The OMB found that if an award of costs is made in this situation, it would create a "chilling effect" and discourage public participation in its process.

The resulting finding of the OMB clarified the awarding of costs in OMB hearings and also dealt with the concept of a "strategic lawsuit against public participation (SLAPP)" as follows:

The decision in this matter is intended to reinforce and reiterate the Board's practice that costs are not awarded lightly nor are they awarded routinely. Awards of costs are rare, especially proportionate to the number of cases decided by the Board. Potential parties and the public should not be fearful of participating in Board proceedings, a sentiment that has been expressed in decision after decision. Costs should never be used as a threat or a reason to dissuade public participation. The Board has the statutory jurisdiction to award costs for the purpose of controlling its process. Costs before the Board have never been intended to follow "the cause" nor are they intended in any way to indemnify a successful party. Each application for costs is decided on its own merit, based on an assessment of conduct.

Section 18 — Notice of Decision

Subsection 1 states that the "tribunal shall send each party who participated in the proceeding, or the party's representative, a copy of its final decision or order, including the reasons if any have been given", by regular lettermail (with deemed delivery by such method per subsection (2)), by electronic or telephone transmission (with deemed delivery by such method per subsection (3)), and by some other method that allows proof of receipt if the tribunal has made rules under section 25.1 that deal with the matter and the deemed delivery by such method (per subsection (4)). This section not only gives the tribunal flexibility in sending out the decision; by stating the deemed delivery of the decision, it also sets the clock in terms of the timeline to take the next step, if any. The specified deemed delivery days, as set out in subsections (2)–(4), do not apply under subsection (5) if "a party that acts in good faith does not, through absence, accident, illness or other cause beyond the party's control, receive the copy until a later date than the deemed date of delivery".

In the appeal of the criminal case, *R. v. Devgan* (2007), 226 C.C.C. (3d) 312, 2007 CLB 23, 76 W.C.B. (2d) 122, 53 C.R. (6th) 104 (the *Devgan* case), heard in the Superior Court of Justice, one of the issues raised was the duty under the *SPPA* to provide notice of the decision. The court had to determine the impact of section 18 on the case before it, and it stated the following:

> The notice requirement in s. 18 of the *SPPA* requires a "tribunal" to send each party who participated in a proceeding, a copy of its final decision or order.

The case then discussed whether the particular Registrar had a "statutory power of decision" as defined by section 1. The court found the Registrar had no such power, and the notice of revocation was simply an administrative practice and "not, in itself, the exercise of a statutory power of decision".

Section 19 — Enforcement of Orders

Subsection (1) states that "[a] certified copy of a tribunal's decision or order in a proceeding may be filed in the Superior Court of Justice by the tribunal or by a party and on filing shall be deemed to be an order of that court and is enforceable as such." Under subsection (2), a party who files an order under this section shall notify the tribunal within 10 days after filing. In accordance with subsection (3), the sheriff shall enforce the order as if it were an execution issued by the Superior Court of Justice upon the receipt of a certified copy of such order for the payment of money. It is important to note that the tribunal's decision or order, once filed in the Superior Court of Justice, is treated as a court order and enforceable as such.

The arbitration decision of *Peters v. Aviva Canada Inc.* (2007-01-10), FSCO 2629, FSCO A05-000196 and A05-000197 (the

Peters decision), conducted under the auspices of the FSCO, is an example of a decision that discussed the enforcement of orders. In the case, the arbitrator made an order regarding the expenses and interest awarded in winning the arbitration. The arbitrator made the following finding:

> While the alternative might be to apply the post-judgement interest provisions of the *Courts of Justice Act*, these provisions relate specifically to court judgements, not arbitral orders. While section 19(1) of the *Statutory Powers Procedure Act* provides for a certified copy of a tribunal's decision or order in a proceeding to be filed in the Superior Court of Justice, the result is that such an order is enforceable as an order of the Superior Court, not that the provisions of the *Courts of Justice Act* are imported *holus bolus* into the administrative forum.

Section 20 — Record of Proceeding

> A tribunal shall compile a record of any proceeding in which a hearing has been held which shall include,
> (a) any application, complaint, reference or other document, if any, by which the proceeding was commenced;
> (b) the notice of any hearing;
> (c) any interlocutory orders made by the tribunal;
> (d) all documentary evidence filed with the tribunal, subject to any limitation expressly imposed by any other Act on the extent to or the purposes for which any such documents may be used in evidence in any proceeding;
> (e) the transcript, if any, of the oral evidence given at the hearing; and
> (f) the decision of the tribunal and the reasons therefor, where reasons have been given.

This section sets out what is to be contained in a record of a tribunal's proceeding. Note that a transcript of the hearing is only included if it exists, and most tribunals do not have transcripts produced.

Section 21 — Adjournments

This section allows a hearing to be adjourned by a tribunal on its own motion or where it is shown to the tribunal's satisfaction "that the adjournment is required to permit an adequate hearing to be held", recognizing the need for adjournments where necessary.

Section 21.1 — Correction of Errors

This section allows for clear minor errors to be corrected by the tribunal as follows:

> A tribunal may at any time correct a typographical error, error of calculation or similar error made in its decision or order.

In *Ramalingam v. State Farm Mutual Automobile Insurance Co.* (2008-02-15), FSCO 2813, Appeal P05-00026 (the *Ramalingam* decision), conducted under the auspices of the FSCO, the appeal involved an arbitration order regarding expenses. In examining the matter, the Director's Delegate discussed the use of section 21.1 as follows:

> I note, however, that subsequent to Arbitrator Feldman's decision, the arbitration expense order and other portions of the *Dwumaah* decision were amended on December 6, 2007 as a calculation error in accordance with Rule 65.5 of the [*Dispute Resolution Practice Code*] and section 21.1 of the *Statutory Powers Procedure Act*, R.S.O. 1990, c. S.22.

Similar amendments to correct minor errors can be found in *Chung v. Unifund* (2010-05-31), FSCO 669, FSCO A09-000198, and *Thevaranjan v. Personal Insurance* (2011-05-20), FSCO 3443, FSCO P09-00015V.

Section 21.2 — Power of Review

The power of review or reconsideration, as it is more commonly called, is given to the tribunal under subsection (1) as follows:

> A tribunal may, if it considers it advisable and if its rules made under section 25.1 deal with the matter, review all or part of its own decision or order, and may confirm, vary, suspend or cancel the decision or order

provided the review shall take place within a reasonable time after the decision or order is made under subsection (2). Further to subsection (3), if there is a conflict between this section and any other Act, the other Act prevails. This mechanism, if used in the right situation, is faster and cheaper than appeal or judicial review.

In the Ontario Labour Relations Board decision of *6377289 Canada Inc. v. Tang* (2007), 57 Employment Practices Branch File No. 48001421, Docket No. 3373-06-ES (the *Tang* decision), section 21.2 was discussed. The case involved a reconsideration of a decision. Although the issue of whether to grant reconsideration is specific to its enabling legislation, it is useful to see what factors are to be taken into account when deciding whether to reconsider:

The Board's power to reconsider decisions under the *Employment Standards Act, 2000*, S.O. 2000, c. 41, as amended (the "Act") arises from section 21.2(1) of the *Statutory Powers Procedure Act*. The test applied by the Board is the same as it applies to requests for reconsideration under the *Labour Relations Act*. In order to provide parties before the Board with a substantial degree of certainty, the Board generally treats its decisions as final. Thus, the Board will not permit a party to attempt to reargue its case under the guise of a request for reconsideration. The Board will not normally reconsider a decision unless:

(a) A party wishes to make representations or objections not already considered by the Board that it had no opportunity to raise previously;

(b) A party wishes to adduce evidence which could not previously have been obtained with reasonable diligence and which would be practically conclusive of the issue or make a substantial difference to the outcome of the case; or

(c) The request raises significant and important issues of Board policy which the Board is convinced were decided wrongly in the first instance.

The Board may also consider such factors as the motives for the request for reconsideration in light of a party's conduct, and the resulting prejudice to another party if the case is reopened. See generally *Cineplex Odeon Corp.*, [1996] OLRB Rep. Nov./Dec. 922 and the cases cited therein.

Section 22 — Administration of Oaths

A member of a tribunal has power to administer oaths and affirmations for the purpose of any of its proceedings and the tribunal may require evidence before it is to be given under oath or affirmation.

It is fairly common for most tribunals currently to give an affirmation rather than an oath as an oath may require a number of holy books to be available, depending on the belief of the person so swearing, which may not be easily available, especially if the hearing is in a temporary location.

Section 23 — Powers re Control of Proceedings

In addition to the contempt powers set out in section 13, tribunals should have a sufficient arsenal of powers to prevent abuse of the process. Under subsection (1), the tribunal is given broad powers to prevent abuse of its process: "A tribunal may make such orders or give such directions in proceedings before it as it considers proper to prevent abuse of its processes". Such orders or directions include (i) the power to "reasonably limit further examination or cross-examination of a witness where what was done was sufficient to disclose fully and fairly all matters relevant" (per subsection (2)) and (ii) the power to exclude those incompetent to work in the process, granted under subsection (3), as follows:

> A tribunal may exclude from a hearing anyone, other than a person licensed under the *Law Society Act*, appearing on behalf of a party or as an adviser to a witness if it finds that such person is not competent properly to represent or to advise the party or witness, or does not understand and comply at the hearing with the duties and responsibilities of an advocate or adviser.

The OMB decision of *Re Mississauga (City) Official Plan Amendment No. 25* (2008), OMB Case No. PL070625, 59 O.M.B.R. 80, 2008 CLB 3906, discussed subsection 23(3) as it relates to "lay" representation. The case involved the competence of a party's representative and discussed licensed paralegals and also "lay" representatives. The OMB laid out the issue and the facts as follows:

> The City challenges Mr. Dell's competence to represent the appellants before this tribunal. The basis of the challenge is that Mr. Dell, in appearing on behalf of other persons, would be tantamount to providing unauthorized legal services.
>
> The challenge arises from the recent amendments to a number of statutes, including the *Law Society Act*, R.S.O. 1990, c. L.8, which has the effect of setting forth a more rigorous regime dealing with the question of the provision of paralegal services. Motivated by the protection of the public, the provision of legal services in some areas of the law under the Act is limited or prohibited depending [on] whether the persons are holders of licences, exempted by Statute or exempted by By-law.
>
> The City argued that pursuant to Section 1(5) of the *Law Society Act*, if a person engages in conduct that involves the application of legal principles, and judgements, he will be providing legal services. Section 1(6) of the Act provides for an expansive definition and in subparagraph 3 of this subsection, the meaning of "provision of service" is to include representation of a person in a proceeding before an Adjudicative Body. "Adjudicative Body" is defined to include a tribunal established

under an Act of Parliament or the Legislature of the Province of Ontario.

Based on what was presented, it seems that if a person is to represent someone before the Board in matters requiring the application of legal principles and making legal judgements, he may fall within the ambit of providing legal services.

The OMB then considered specifically subsection 23(3):

Lay representations before the Board is a feature of life that has been flourishing since its inception. The instances where difficulties arise are few and far between. For this Board, it is not a problem and certainly not a problem in need of a solution. Whether representatives are legal, lay or combined, the Board has always been able to conduct our hearings in a manner befitting a tribunal functioning under the *Statutory Powers Procedure Act*, R.S.O. 1990, c. S.22, and complying with the rules of natural justice. These include cases where there are multi-parties with multifarious concerns and poly-technical issues. The Municipal Bar, to its credit, has never taken on an officious air or elitist stance towards unrepresented parties or lay representatives. Over the decades, our adjudication has evolved to a stage where coexistence with lay representatives or unrepresented parties is a norm rather than an exception. To upset this delicate but seamlessly workable balance, the Board would require far more persuasive arguments than what have been presented by Mr. Minkowski.

What Mr. Minkowski has not done, whether by design or inadvertence, is to refer to and engage in an in-depth analysis in relation to Section 23(3) of the *Statutory Powers Procedure Act*, R.S.O. 1990, c. S.22.

After quoting subsection 23(3), the OMB asked the following questions and makes a finding:

Does this provision suggest that the Board has some discretion to allow persons with competence that are neither licensed nor exempted from the *Law Society Act* to represent others at our hearings? If the Board is obligated *ab initio*, as suggested by the City to exclude representatives other than those persons authorized under the *Law Society Act*, why does this provision seem to provide an escape? Does this provision not point to a direction that is overlooked: namely, the administrative tribunals can use the yardstick of competence as the test whether a lay representative, other than those authorized, can appear? Does representation of hearings inevitably require the application of legal principles and legal judgements? If not, does it not make sense for this Board at least, to deal with matters on a case-by-case basis, or does the *Law Society Act* mandate a different approach?

These and some other ramifications are required to be addressed and addressed fully before the Board would make a *carte blanche* prohibition.

The City has not presented any evidence indicating that Mr. Dell is not competent to represent others. Nor has it turned to the relevant provision as indicated above and make a fulsome submission in this regard. Additionally, the Board has misgivings whether Mr. Dell is appreciative whether he might be in an exempted category.

Accordingly, the Board will not exclude Mr. Dell from representing others for reasons enumerated above.

This decision notes that lawyers and licensed paralegals are to be treated in the same fashion under subsection 23(3). Also see the *Romanchook* decision cited in Section 10 above. Note that before an amendment in 2006, this provision would allow a tribunal to exclude an incompetent paralegal; but as the amendment classifies a paralegal licensed by the LSUC as a representative, such exclusion cannot occur. However, it is possible that someone could make a complaint to the LSUC about a particular paralegal. Furthermore, while lawyers or licenced paralegals may not be excluded under subsection 23(3), tribunals can make an order to prevent a lawyer or a paralegal from appearing on any basis other than competence, including conflicts: see *Romanchook v. Garda Ontario*, 2009 HRTO 1077.

Section 24 — Notice
Subsection (1) allows the tribunal, where the tribunal is of the opinion that it is impractical to give notice of the hearing or to send the decision itself to all or any of the parties individually, to give notice to such parties either by public advertisement or by otherwise as the tribunal directs. If a notice of a decision is to be given, subsection (2) requires that the notice shall inform the parties where to obtain copies of the decision and the reasons, if reasons were given. This again gives flexibility to the agency on how parties can be informed of a hearing or sent the actual decision.

Section 25 — Appeal Operates As a Stay, Exception
Subsection (1) says that an appeal from a decision of a tribunal to a court or other appellate body operates as a stay in the matter unless

(i) another piece of legislation that applies to the proceeding expressly provides to the contrary; or (ii) the tribunal, or the court, or other appellate body orders otherwise. It is, however, stated in subsection (2) that an application for judicial review or proceedings enumerated under subsection 2(1) of the *Judicial Review Procedure Act* is deemed not an appeal. This provision, when applicable, obviates the need to request a stay and therefore reduces paperwork.

In the appeal order of *I.(N.) v. Allstate Insurance Co. of Canada* (2008-03-07), FSCO 2358, Appeal P07-00024 (the *N.I.* decision), conducted under the auspices of the FSCO, the appeal requesting a stay of an arbitration order was dismissed. The Director's Delegate first quoted section 25(1) and then stated the following:

> Subsection 283(6) of the *Insurance Act*, R.S.O. 1990, c. I.8 (as amended) expressly provides that an appeal does not stay the order of an arbitrator, unless the Director decides otherwise. As stated by Delegate McMahon in *Guardian Insurance Company of Canada and Armstrong*, (FSCO P00-00037, July 20, 2000), a stay from an order of an arbitrator at the Financial Services Commission of Ontario ("FSCO") is the exception, rather than the rule.
>
> As noted in prior cases, the stay as an exception on appeal also differs from the *Ontario Rules of Civil Procedure*, R.R.O. 1990, Regulation 194, which provide, at Rule 63.01(1), that the delivery of a notice of appeal from an interlocutory or final order stays, until the disposition of the appeal, any provision of the order for the payment of money, except a provision that awards support or enforces a support order.
>
> Given that arbitration orders, in significant measure, reimburse expenditures arising from a motor vehicle accident or replace lost income, services or possessions, the same considerations regarding support orders exist, including the need for timely payment. Further, subsection 283(6) of the *Insurance Act* is consistent with subsection 283(1) (which limits appeals of the order of an arbitrator to a question of law), both provisions showing deference to arbitration decisions.
>
> Delegate McMahon, in determining whether a stay should be granted in *Armstrong*, adopted Delegate Richardson's criteria in *Canadian Home Assurance Company and Scavuzzo* (OIC P-000626, May 18, 1992), namely:
> 1. the *bona fides* of the appeal;
> 2. the substance of the grounds for appeal; and,
> 3. the hardship to the respective parties if the stay is granted or refused.

Section 25.0.1 — Control of Process

The section again gives the tribunal the power to control its process:

> A tribunal has the power to determine its own procedures and practices and may for that purpose,
> (a) make orders with respect to the procedures and practices that apply in any particular proceeding; and
> (b) establish rules under section 25.1.

To take advantage of the extra powers available under this statute, many agencies make their own rules pursuant to section 25.1 and/or make appropriate practice directions.

In the Div. Ct. case of *Ontario Kraft Canada Inc. v. Menkes Lakeshore Ltd.* (2007), 159 A.C.W.S. (3d) 7, 2007 CLB 5197, 228 O.A.C. 1, 56 O.M.B.R. 391, 37 M.P.L.R. (4th) 42 (the *Ontario Kraft* case), Kraft Canada Inc. sought leave to appeal an OMB decision on the basis that "the decision of the OMB is incorrect in law, that the Board breached principles of natural justice and that Kraft was denied a fair hearing." In its decision, the court looked at the question: Did the OMB violate the rules of natural justice by refusing to allow Kraft Canada Inc. to lead evidence? The court considered the issue of control of the process and offered the following view:

> Under the *Statutory Powers Procedure Act*, R.S.O. 1990, c. S.22 (SPPA), s. 25.0.1, the Board, as an administrative tribunal exercising a statutory power of authority, maintains absolute jurisdiction and control over its own procedure.

Section 25.1 — Rules

As noted in many sections above, a tribunal can make its own rules governing the practice and procedure before it, pursuant to subsection (1). Subsections (2)–(4) set out the conditions on this rule-making authority: (i) rules may be of general or particular application; (ii) rules shall be consistent with the *SPPA* and with other applicable Acts; and (iii) rules are to be made available to the public in English and French. According to subsection (5), tribunal rules made under subsection (1) are not regulations as defined in Part III (Regulations) of the *Legislation Act, 2006*; therefore, they are effective once made and require no further authorization. As stated in subsection (6), this rule-making authority does not take away but is an addition to "any power to adopt rules that the tribunal may have under another Act".

In *Hadley v. J.A.C.S. Cartage*, 2010 HRTO 226, one of the bases that the respondents used in their request for the early dismissal of the application was "3. that the Application should be dismissed as frivolous, vexatious or as having been commenced in bad faith pursuant to s. 4.6(1)(a) of the Statutory Powers Procedure Act, R.S.O. 1990, c. S.22, as amended ('SPPA')". The HRTO, in its interim decision, denied this request, citing section 25.1:

> [7] Section 4.6(1)(a) of the SPPA does allow Tribunals to dismiss applications on the basis that they are frivolous, vexatious or have been commenced in bad faith, but only if the Tribunal has made a Rule to that effect pursuant to section 25.1 of the SPPA. The Tribunal has not made such a Rule. Accordingly, I find that the Tribunal does not currently have the power to dismiss an Application as "frivolous, vexatious or [as having been] commenced in bad faith" pursuant to s. 4.6(1)(a) of the SPPA.

> [8] I note further that the provisions of the Code as it read prior to June 30, 2008, allowed the Ontario Human Rights Commission to decide not to deal with complaints if they were "frivolous, vexatious, or made in bad faith." However, the Code was amended, effective July 1, 2008, enabling applicants to file their Applications directly with the Tribunal. The new Code does not contain a provision which allows the Tribunal to dismiss or otherwise refuse to deal with Applications on the basis that they are frivolous, vexatious or as having been commenced in bad faith.

Section 26 — Regulations

This section allows for the making of regulations for a specific purpose: "prescribing forms for the purpose of section 12".

Section 27 — Rules, etc., Available to the Public

> A tribunal shall make any rules or guidelines established under this or any other Act available for examination by the public.

As a result of the mandate, the rules are currently easily available by downloading them from an agency's website.

See *Becker Milk* case under section 17.1, above.

Section 28 — Substantial Compliance

This provides for less strict formality by allowing for substantial compliance as follows:

> Substantial compliance with requirements respecting the content of forms, notices or documents under this Act or any rule made under this or any other Act is sufficient.

Section 32 — Conflict

This provision is meant to make this statute prevail over other legislation if there is a conflict, unless the other legislation expressly stated that its provisions and regulations override those in the *SPPA*:

> Unless it is expressly provided in any other Act that its provisions and regulations, rules or by-laws made under it apply despite anything in this Act, the provisions of this Act prevail over the provisions of such other Act and over regulations, rules or by-laws made under such other Act which conflict therewith.

The *Human Rights Code*, R.S.O. 1990, c. H.19, is an example of a legislation that contains such expressly stated provision overriding the SPPA: "Despite section 32 of the *Statutory Powers Procedure Act*, this Act, the regulations and the Tribunal rules prevail over the provisions of that Act with which they conflict."

CHAPTER SUMMARY

This chapter examined most of the sections of the *SPPA* through excerpts of the Act, with explanation of their significance where warranted. Further, if possible, a case or a decision that discussed the provision was also cited and reviewed in order to assist the reader to better understand the importance of various provisions of the legislation, which provides the "minimum rules of fair procedures" applicable to most Ontario agencies. The cases and decisions reviewed in this chapter also throw light on how specific Ontario agencies, including some agencies discussed in succeeding chapters, discuss this important legislation.

REVIEW QUESTIONS

1. What is an annotated statute?
2. What is a "statutory power" of decision, and why is it important in Ontario administrative law?
3. In what situations does the *SPPA* apply to Ontario agencies, and in what situation does it not apply?
4. What circumstance will allow the term of a tribunal member to continue past expiry?
5. In what circumstances can a matter before a tribunal be dismissed without a hearing under both statute and case law?

6. What requirements and benefits are imposed upon an Ontario tribunal wishing to allow the parties to use Alternative Dispute Resolution?

7. How are the parties to a matter before an Ontario agency determined?

8. What are the various formats of hearing allowed by the *SPPA*, and how can an Ontario agency allow the parties to choose a particular format?

9. What are the requirements for each type of format of hearing?

10. What can occur if a party does not attend a hearing of which that party received proper notice?

11. What provisions of the *SPPA* allow an Ontario agency to control its own process?

12. When is evidence admissible in a hearing of an Ontario agency?

13. Are written reasons for a decision by an Ontario agency required, and if so, when?

14. What is reconsideration, and when can it be utilized?

15. Do the rules of an Ontario agency have to be available to the public, and if so, how are they made available?

DISCUSSION QUESTIONS

1. Due to the 2006 amendments to legislation allowing licensed paralegals to act for parties before Ontario agencies, is there now a distinction between lawyers and licensed paralegals on one side and lay representatives on the other? If so, is this appropriate, or should the consumer have greater choices to obtain representation?

2. In the Canadian system of law, one of the factors used in the court system to encourage settlement is the award of costs to the winning side: from approximately one-third to a virtual indemnity of the winner's expenses to be paid by the losing side. It seems that this concept is starting to appear in agency hearings. Is this a good turn of events, considering that agencies were historically meant to be cheaper, faster, and more efficient than the courts?

Appendix 2.1
The *Statutory Powers Procedure Act*
R.S.O. 1990, C. S.22
(As of April 30, 2016)

INTERPRETATION

1.(1) In this Act,

"electronic hearing" means a hearing held by conference telephone or some other form of electronic technology allowing persons to hear one another;

"hearing" means a hearing in any proceeding;

"licence" includes any permit, certificate, approval, registration or similar form of permission required by law;

"municipality" has the same meaning as in the *Municipal Affairs Act*;

"oral hearing" means a hearing at which the parties or their representatives attend before the tribunal in person;

"proceeding" means a proceeding to which this Act applies;

"representative" means, in respect of a proceeding to which this Act applies, a person authorized under the *Law Society Act* to represent a person in that proceeding;

"statutory power of decision" means a power or right, conferred by or under a statute, to make a decision deciding or prescribing,
  (a) the legal rights, powers, privileges, immunities, duties or liabilities of any person or party, or
  (b) the eligibility of any person or party to receive, or to the continuation of, a benefit or licence, whether the person is legally entitled thereto or not;

"tribunal" means one or more persons, whether or not incorporated and however described, upon which a statutory power of decision is conferred by or under a statute;

"written hearing" means a hearing held by means of the exchange of documents, whether in written form or by electronic means.

Meaning of "person" extended

(2) A municipality, an unincorporated association of employers, a trade union or council of trade unions who may be a party to a proceeding in the exercise of a statutory power of decision under the statute conferring the power shall be deemed to be a person for the purpose of any provision of this Act or of any rule made under this Act that applies to parties.

LIBERAL CONSTRUCTION OF ACT AND RULES

2. This Act, and any rule made by a tribunal under subsection 17.1(4) or section 25.1, shall be liberally construed to secure the just, most expeditious and cost-effective determination of every proceeding on its merits.

APPLICATION OF ACT

3.(1) Subject to subsection (2), this Act applies to a proceeding by a tribunal in the exercise of a statutory power of decision conferred by or under an Act of the Legislature, where the tribunal is required by or under such Act or otherwise by law to hold or to afford to the parties to the proceeding an opportunity for a hearing before making a decision.

Where Act does not apply

(2) This Act does not apply to a proceeding,

(a) before the Assembly or any committee of the Assembly;

(b) in or before,
(i) the Court of Appeal,
(ii) the Superior Court of Justice,
(iii) the Ontario Court of Justice,
(iv) the Family Court of the Superior Court of Justice,
(v) the Small Claims Court, or
(vi) a justice of the peace;

(c) to which the Rules of Civil Procedure apply;

(d) before an arbitrator to which the *Arbitrations Act* or the *Labour Relations Act* applies;

(e) at a coroner's inquest;

(f) of a commission appointed under the *Public Inquiries Act, 2009*;

(g) of one or more persons required to make an investigation and to make a report, with or without recommendations, where the report is for the information or advice of the person to whom it is made and does not in any way legally bind or limit that person in any decision he or she may have power to make; or

(h) of a tribunal empowered to make regulations, rules or by-laws in so far as its power to make regulations, rules or by-laws is concerned.

WAIVER

Waiver of procedural requirement

4.(1) Any procedural requirement of this Act, or of another Act or a regulation that applies to a proceeding, may be waived with the consent of the parties and the tribunal.

Same, rules

(2) Any provision of a tribunal's rules made under section 25.1 may be waived in accordance with the rules.

DISPOSITION WITHOUT HEARING

4.1 If the parties consent, a proceeding may be disposed of by a decision of the tribunal given without a hearing, unless another Act or a regulation that applies to the proceeding provides otherwise.

PANELS, CERTAIN MATTERS

4.2(1) A procedural or interlocutory matter in a proceeding may be heard and determined by a panel consisting of one or more members of the tribunal, as assigned by the chair of the tribunal.

Assignments

(2) In assigning members of the tribunal to a panel, the chair shall take into consideration any requirement imposed by another Act or a regulation that applies to the proceeding that the tribunal be representative of specific interests.

Decision of panel

(3) The decision of a majority of the members of a panel, or their unanimous decision in the case of a two-member panel, is the tribunal's decision.

PANEL OF ONE, REDUCED PANEL

Panel of one

4.2.1(1) The chair of a tribunal may decide that a proceeding be heard by a panel of one person and assign the person to hear the proceeding unless there is a statutory requirement in another Act that the proceeding be heard by a panel of more than one person.

Reduction in number of panel members

(2) Where there is a statutory requirement in another Act that a proceeding be heard by a panel of a specified number of persons, the chair of the tribunal may assign to the panel one person or any lesser number of persons than the number specified in the other Act if all parties to the proceeding consent.

EXPIRY OF TERM

4.3 If the term of office of a member of a tribunal who has participated in a hearing expires before a decision is given, the term shall be deemed to continue, but only for the purpose of participating in the decision and for no other purpose.

INCAPACITY OF MEMBER

4.4(1) If a member of a tribunal who has participated in a hearing becomes unable, for any reason, to complete the hearing or to participate in the decision, the remaining member or members may complete the hearing and give a decision.

Other Acts and regulations

(2) Subsection (1) does not apply if another Act or a regulation specifically deals with the issue of what takes place in the circumstances described in subsection (1).

DECISION NOT TO PROCESS COMMENCEMENT OF PROCEEDING

4.5(1) Subject to subsection (3), upon receiving documents relating to the commencement of a proceeding, a tribunal or its administrative staff may decide not to process the documents relating to the commencement of the proceeding if,

(a) the documents are incomplete;
(b) the documents are received after the time required for commencing the proceeding has elapsed;
(c) the fee required for commencing the proceeding is not paid; or
(d) there is some other technical defect in the commencement of the proceeding.

Notice

(2) A tribunal or its administrative staff shall give the party who commences a proceeding notice of its decision under subsection (1) and shall set out in the notice the reasons for the decision and the requirements for resuming the processing of the documents.

Rules under s. 25.1

(3) A tribunal or its administrative staff shall not make a decision under subsection (1) unless the tribunal has made rules under section 25.1 respecting the making of such decisions and those rules shall set out,

(a) any of the grounds referred to in subsection (1) upon which the tribunal or its administrative staff may decide not to process the documents relating to the commencement of a proceeding; and
(b) the requirements for the processing of the documents to be resumed.

Continuance of provisions in other statutes

(4) Despite section 32, nothing in this section shall prevent a tribunal or its administrative staff from deciding not to process documents relating to the commencement of a proceeding on grounds that differ from those referred to in subsection (1) or without complying with subsection (2) or (3) if the tribunal or its staff does so in accordance with the provisions of an Act that are in force on the day this section comes into force.

DISMISSAL OF PROCEEDING WITHOUT HEARING

4.6(1) Subject to subsections (5) and (6), a tribunal may dismiss a proceeding without a hearing if,

(a) the proceeding is frivolous, vexatious or is commenced in bad faith;

(b) the proceeding relates to matters that are outside the jurisdiction of the tribunal; or

(c) some aspect of the statutory requirements for bringing the proceeding has not been met.

Notice

(2) Before dismissing a proceeding under this section, a tribunal shall give notice of its intention to dismiss the proceeding to,

(a) all parties to the proceeding if the proceeding is being dismissed for reasons referred to in clause (1)(b); or

(b) the party who commences the proceeding if the proceeding is being dismissed for any other reason.

Same

(3) The notice of intention to dismiss a proceeding shall set out the reasons for the dismissal and inform the parties of their right to make written submissions to the tribunal with respect to the dismissal within the time specified in the notice.

Right to make submissions

(4) A party who receives a notice under subsection (2) may make written submissions to the tribunal with respect to the dismissal within the time specified in the notice.

Dismissal

(5) A tribunal shall not dismiss a proceeding under this section until it has given notice under subsection (2) and considered any submissions made under subsection (4).

Rules

(6) A tribunal shall not dismiss a proceeding under this section unless it has made rules under section 25.1 respecting the early dismissal of proceedings and those rules shall include,

(a) any of the grounds referred to in subsection (1) upon which a proceeding may be dismissed;

(b) the right of the parties who are entitled to receive notice under subsection (2) to make submissions with respect to the dismissal; and

(c) the time within which the submissions must be made.

Continuance of provisions in other statutes

(7) Despite section 32, nothing in this section shall prevent a tribunal from dismissing a proceeding on grounds other than those referred to in subsection (1) or without complying with subsections (2) to (6) if the tribunal dismisses the proceeding in accordance with the provisions of an Act that are in force on the day this section comes into force.

CLASSIFYING PROCEEDINGS

4.7 A tribunal may make rules under section 25.1 classifying the types of proceedings that come before it and setting guidelines as to the procedural steps or processes (such as preliminary motions, pre-hearing conferences, alternative dispute resolution mechanisms, expedited hearings) that apply to each type of proceeding and the circumstances in which other procedures may apply.

ALTERNATIVE DISPUTE RESOLUTION

4.8(1) A tribunal may direct the parties to a proceeding to participate in an alternative dispute resolution mechanism for the purposes of resolving the proceeding or an issue arising in the proceeding if,

(a) it has made rules under section 25.1 respecting the use of alternative dispute resolution mechanisms; and

(b) all parties consent to participating in the alternative dispute resolution mechanism.

Definition

(2) In this section,

"alternative dispute resolution mechanism" includes mediation, conciliation, negotiation or any other means of facilitating the resolution of issues in dispute.

Rules

(3) A rule under section 25.1 respecting the use of alternative dispute resolution mechanisms shall include procedural guidelines to deal with the following:

1. The circumstances in which a settlement achieved by means of an alternative dispute resolution mechanism must be reviewed and approved by the tribunal.

2. Any requirement, statutory or otherwise, that there be an order by the tribunal.

Mandatory alternative dispute resolution

(4) A rule under subsection (3) may provide that participation in an alternative dispute resolution mechanism is mandatory or that it is mandatory in certain specified circumstances.

Person appointed to mediate, etc.

(5) A rule under subsection (3) may provide that a person appointed to mediate, conciliate, negotiate or help resolve a matter by means of an alternative dispute resolution mechanism be a member of the tribunal or a person independent of the tribunal. However, a member of the tribunal who is so appointed with respect to a matter in a proceeding shall not subsequently hear the matter if it comes before the tribunal unless the parties consent.

Continuance of provisions in other statutes

(6) Despite section 32, nothing in this section shall prevent a tribunal from directing parties to a proceeding to participate in an alternative dispute resolution mechanism even though the requirements of subsections (1) to (5) have not been met if the tribunal does so in accordance with the provisions of an Act that are in force on the day this section comes into force.

MEDIATORS, ETC.: NOT COMPELLABLE, NOTES NOT EVIDENCE

Mediators, etc., not compellable

4.9(1) No person employed as a mediator, conciliator or negotiator or otherwise appointed to facilitate the resolution of a matter before a tribunal by means of an alternative dispute resolution mechanism shall be compelled to give testimony or produce documents in a proceeding before the tribunal or in a civil proceeding with respect to matters that come to his or her knowledge in the course of exercising his or her duties under this or any other Act.

Evidence in civil proceedings

(2) No notes or records kept by a mediator, conciliator or negotiator or by any other person appointed to facilitate the resolution of a matter before a tribunal by means of an alternative dispute resolution mechanism under this or any other Act are admissible in a civil proceeding.

PARTIES

5. The parties to a proceeding shall be the persons specified as parties by or under the statute under which the proceeding arises or, if not so specified, persons entitled by law to be parties to the proceeding.

WRITTEN HEARINGS

5.1(1) A tribunal whose rules made under section 25.1 deal with written hearings may hold a written hearing in a proceeding.

Exception

(2) The tribunal shall not hold a written hearing if a party satisfies the tribunal that there is good reason for not doing so.

Same

(2.1) Subsection (2) does not apply if the only purpose of the hearing is to deal with procedural matters.

Documents

(3) In a written hearing, all the parties are entitled to receive every document that the tribunal receives in the proceeding.

ELECTRONIC HEARINGS

5.2(1) A tribunal whose rules made under section 25.1 deal with electronic hearings may hold an electronic hearing in a proceeding.

Exception

(2) The tribunal shall not hold an electronic hearing if a party satisfies the tribunal that holding an electronic rather than an oral hearing is likely to cause the party significant prejudice.

Same

(3) Subsection (2) does not apply if the only purpose of the hearing is to deal with procedural matters.

Participants to be able to hear one another

(4) In an electronic hearing, all the parties and the members of the tribunal participating in the hearing must be able to hear one another and any witnesses throughout the hearing.

DIFFERENT KINDS OF HEARINGS IN ONE PROCEEDING

5.2.1 A tribunal may, in a proceeding, hold any combination of written, electronic and oral hearings.

PRE-HEARING CONFERENCES

5.3(1) If the tribunal's rules made under section 25.1 deal with pre-hearing conferences, the tribunal may direct the parties to participate in a pre-hearing conference to consider,

(a) the settlement of any or all of the issues;
(b) the simplification of the issues;
(c) facts or evidence that may be agreed upon;
(d) the dates by which any steps in the proceeding are to be taken or begun;
(e) the estimated duration of the hearing; and
(f) any other matter that may assist in the just and most expeditious disposition of the proceeding.

Other Acts and regulations

(1.1) The tribunal's power to direct the parties to participate in a pre-hearing conference is subject to any other Act or regulation that applies to the proceeding.

Who presides

(2) The chair of the tribunal may designate a member of the tribunal or any other person to preside at the pre-hearing conference.

Orders

(3) A member who presides at a pre-hearing conference may make such orders as he or she considers necessary or advisable with respect to the conduct of the proceeding, including adding parties.

Disqualification

(4) A member who presides at a pre-hearing conference at which the parties attempt to settle issues shall not preside at the hearing of the proceeding unless the parties consent.

Application of s. 5.2

(5) Section 5.2 applies to a pre-hearing conference, with necessary modifications.

DISCLOSURE

5.4(1) If the tribunal's rules made under section 25.1 deal with disclosure, the tribunal may, at any stage of the proceeding before all hearings are complete, make orders for,

(a) the exchange of documents;
(b) the oral or written examination of a party;
(c) the exchange of witness statements and reports of expert witnesses;
(d) the provision of particulars;
(e) any other form of disclosure.

Other Acts and regulations
   (1.1) The tribunal's power to make orders for disclosure is subject to any other Act or regulation that applies to the proceeding.

Exception, privileged information
   (2) Subsection (1) does not authorize the making of an order requiring disclosure of privileged information.

NOTICE OF HEARING

6.(1) The parties to a proceeding shall be given reasonable notice of the hearing by the tribunal.

Statutory authority
   (2) A notice of a hearing shall include a reference to the statutory authority under which the hearing will be held.

Oral hearing
   (3) A notice of an oral hearing shall include,
(a) a statement of the time, place and purpose of the hearing; and
(b) a statement that if the party notified does not attend at the hearing, the tribunal may proceed in the party's absence and the party will not be entitled to any further notice in the proceeding.

Written hearing
   (4) A notice of a written hearing shall include,
(a) a statement of the date and purpose of the hearing, and details about the manner in which the hearing will be held;
(b) a statement that the hearing shall not be held as a written hearing if the party satisfies the tribunal that there is good reason for not holding a written hearing (in which case the tribunal is required to hold it as an electronic or oral hearing) and an indication of the procedure to be followed for that purpose;
(c) a statement that if the party notified neither acts under clause (b) nor participates in the hearing in accordance with the notice, the tribunal may proceed without the party's participation and the party will not be entitled to any further notice in the proceeding.

Electronic hearing

(5) A notice of an electronic hearing shall include,

(a) a statement of the time and purpose of the hearing, and details about the manner in which the hearing will be held;

(b) a statement that the only purpose of the hearing is to deal with procedural matters, if that is the case;

(c) if clause (b) does not apply, a statement that the party notified may, by satisfying the tribunal that holding the hearing as an electronic hearing is likely to cause the party significant prejudice, require the tribunal to hold the hearing as an oral hearing, and an indication of the procedure to be followed for that purpose; and

(d) a statement that if the party notified neither acts under clause (c), if applicable, nor participates in the hearing in accordance with the notice, the tribunal may proceed without the party's participation and the party will not be entitled to any further notice in the proceeding.

EFFECT OF NON-ATTENDANCE AT HEARING AFTER DUE NOTICE

7.(1) Where notice of an oral hearing has been given to a party to a proceeding in accordance with this Act and the party does not attend at the hearing, the tribunal may proceed in the absence of the party and the party is not entitled to any further notice in the proceeding.

Same, written hearings

(2) Where notice of a written hearing has been given to a party to a proceeding in accordance with this Act and the party neither acts under clause 6(4)(b) nor participates in the hearing in accordance with the notice, the tribunal may proceed without the party's participation and the party is not entitled to any further notice in the proceeding.

Same, electronic hearings

(3) Where notice of an electronic hearing has been given to a party to a proceeding in accordance with this Act and the party neither acts under clause 6(5)(c), if applicable, nor participates in the hearing in accordance with the notice, the tribunal may proceed without the party's participation and the party is not entitled to any further notice in the proceeding.

WHERE CHARACTER, ETC., OF A PARTY IS IN ISSUE

8. Where the good character, propriety of conduct or competence of a party is an issue in a proceeding, the party is entitled to be furnished prior to the hearing with reasonable information of any allegations with respect thereto.

HEARINGS TO BE PUBLIC; MAINTENANCE OF ORDER

Hearings to be public, exceptions

9.(1) An oral hearing shall be open to the public except where the tribunal is of the opinion that,

(a) matters involving public security may be disclosed; or

(b) intimate financial or personal matters or other matters may be disclosed at the hearing of such a nature, having regard to the circumstances, that the desirability of avoiding disclosure thereof in the interests of any person affected or in the public interest outweighs the desirability of adhering to the principle that hearings be open to the public,

in which case the tribunal may hold the hearing in the absence of the public.

Written hearings

(1.1) In a written hearing, members of the public are entitled to reasonable access to the documents submitted, unless the tribunal is of the opinion that clause (1)(a) or (b) applies.

Electronic hearings

(1.2) An electronic hearing shall be open to the public unless the tribunal is of the opinion that,

(a) it is not practical to hold the hearing in a manner that is open to the public; or

(b) clause (1)(a) or (b) applies.

Maintenance of order at hearings

(2) A tribunal may make such orders or give such directions at an oral or electronic hearing as it considers necessary for the maintenance of order at the hearing, and, if any person disobeys or fails to comply with any such order or direction, the tribunal or a member thereof may call for the assistance of any peace officer to enforce the order or direction, and every peace officer so called upon shall take such action as is necessary to enforce the order or direction and may use such force as is reasonably required for that purpose.

PROCEEDINGS INVOLVING SIMILAR QUESTIONS

9.1(1) If two or more proceedings before a tribunal involve the same or similar questions of fact, law or policy, the tribunal may,

(a) combine the proceedings or any part of them, with the consent of the parties;

(b) hear the proceedings at the same time, with the consent of the parties;

(c) hear the proceedings one immediately after the other; or

(d) stay one or more of the proceedings until after the determination of another one of them.

Exception

(2) Subsection (1) does not apply to proceedings to which the *Consolidated Hearings Act* applies.

Same

(3) Clauses (1)(a) and (b) do not apply to a proceeding if,

(a) any other Act or regulation that applies to the proceeding requires that it be heard in private;

(b) the tribunal is of the opinion that clause 9(1)(a) or (b) applies to the proceeding.

Conflict, consent requirements

(4) The consent requirements of clauses (1)(a) and (b) do not apply if another Act or a regulation that applies to the proceedings allows the tribunal to combine them or hear them at the same time without the consent of the parties.

Use of same evidence

(5) If the parties to the second-named proceeding consent, the tribunal may treat evidence that is admitted in a proceeding as if it were also admitted in another proceeding that is heard at the same time under clause (1)(b).

RIGHT TO REPRESENTATION

10. A party to a proceeding may be represented by a representative.

EXAMINATION OF WITNESSES

10.1 A party to a proceeding may, at an oral or electronic hearing,

(a) call and examine witnesses and present evidence and submissions; and

(b) conduct cross-examinations of witnesses at the hearing reasonably required for a full and fair disclosure of all matters relevant to the issues in the proceeding.

RIGHTS OF WITNESSES TO REPRESENTATION

11.(1) A witness at an oral or electronic hearing is entitled to be advised by a representative as to his or her rights, but such representative may take no other part in the hearing without leave of the tribunal.

Idem

(2) Where an oral hearing is closed to the public, the witness's representative is not entitled to be present except when that witness is giving evidence.

SUMMONSES

12.(1) A tribunal may require any person, including a party, by summons,

(a) to give evidence on oath or affirmation at an oral or electronic hearing; and

(b) to produce in evidence at an oral or electronic hearing documents and things specified by the tribunal,

relevant to the subject-matter of the proceeding and admissible at a hearing.

Form and service of summons

(2) A summons issued under subsection (1) shall be in the prescribed form (in English or French) and,

(a) where the tribunal consists of one person, shall be signed by him or her;

(b) where the tribunal consists of more than one person, shall be signed by the chair of the tribunal or in such other manner as documents on behalf of the tribunal may be signed under the statute constituting the tribunal.

Same

(3) The summons shall be served personally on the person summoned.

Fees and allowances

(3.1) The person summoned is entitled to receive the same fees or allowances for attending at or otherwise participating in the hearing as are paid to a person summoned to attend before the Superior Court of Justice.

Bench warrant

(4) A judge of the Superior Court of Justice may issue a warrant against a person if the judge is satisfied that,

(a) a summons was served on the person under this section;

(b) the person has failed to attend or to remain in attendance at the hearing (in the case of an oral hearing) or has failed otherwise to participate in the hearing (in the case of an electronic hearing) in accordance with the summons; and

(c) the person's attendance or participation is material to the ends of justice.

Same

(4.1) The warrant shall be in the prescribed form (in English or French), directed to any police officer, and shall require the person to be apprehended anywhere within Ontario, brought before the tribunal forthwith and,

(a) detained in custody as the judge may order until the person's presence as a witness is no longer required; or

(b) in the judge's discretion, released on a recognizance, with or without sureties, conditioned for attendance or participation to give evidence.

Proof of service

(5) Service of a summons may be proved by affidavit in an application to have a warrant issued under subsection (4).

Certificate of facts

(6) Where an application to have a warrant issued is made on behalf of a tribunal, the person constituting the tribunal or, if the tribunal consists of more than one person, the chair of the tribunal may certify to the judge the facts relied on to establish that the attendance or other participation of the person summoned is material to the ends of justice, and the judge may accept the certificate as proof of the facts.

Same

(7) Where the application is made by a party to the proceeding, the facts relied on to establish that the attendance or other participation of the person is material to the ends of justice may be proved by the party's affidavit.

CONTEMPT PROCEEDINGS

13.(1) Where any person without lawful excuse,

(a) on being duly summoned under section 12 as a witness at a hearing makes default in attending at the hearing; or

(b) being in attendance as a witness at an oral hearing or otherwise participating as a witness at an electronic hearing, refuses to take an oath or to make an affirmation legally required by the tribunal to be taken or made, or to produce any document or thing in his or her power or control legally required by the tribunal to be produced by him or her or to answer any question to which the tribunal may legally require an answer; or

(c) does any other thing that would, if the tribunal had been a court of law having power to commit for contempt, have been contempt of that court,

the tribunal may, of its own motion or on the motion of a party to the proceeding, state a case to the Divisional Court setting out the facts and that court may inquire into the matter and, after hearing any witnesses who may be produced against or on behalf of that person and after hearing any statement that may be offered in defence, punish or take steps for the punishment of that person in like manner as if he or she had been guilty of contempt of the court.

Same

(2) Subsection (1) also applies to a person who,

(a) having objected under clause 6(4)(b) to a hearing being held as a written hearing, fails without lawful excuse to participate in the oral or electronic hearing of the matter; or

(b) being a party, fails without lawful excuse to attend a pre-hearing conference when so directed by the tribunal.

PROTECTION FOR WITNESSES

14.(1) A witness at an oral or electronic hearing shall be deemed to have objected to answer any question asked him or her upon the ground that the answer may tend to criminate him or her or may tend to establish his or her liability to civil proceedings at the instance of the Crown, or of any person, and no answer given by a witness at a hearing shall be used or be receivable in evidence against the witness in any trial or other proceeding against him or her thereafter taking place, other than a prosecution for perjury in giving such evidence.

(2) Repealed.

EVIDENCE

What is admissible in evidence at a hearing

15.(1) Subject to subsections (2) and (3), a tribunal may admit as evidence at a hearing, whether or not given or proven under oath or affirmation or admissible as evidence in a court,

(a) any oral testimony; and

(b) any document or other thing,

relevant to the subject-matter of the proceeding and may act on such evidence, but the tribunal may exclude anything unduly repetitious.

What is inadmissible in evidence at a hearing
   (2) Nothing is admissible in evidence at a hearing,

(a)   that would be inadmissible in a court by reason of any privilege under the law of evidence; or

(b)   that is inadmissible by the statute under which the proceeding arises or any other statute.

Conflicts
   (3) Nothing in subsection (1) overrides the provisions of any Act expressly limiting the extent to or purposes for which any oral testimony, documents or things may be admitted or used in evidence in any proceeding.

Copies
   (4) Where a tribunal is satisfied as to its authenticity, a copy of a document or other thing may be admitted as evidence at a hearing.

Photocopies
   (5) Where a document has been filed in evidence at a hearing, the tribunal may, or the person producing it or entitled to it may with the leave of the tribunal, cause the document to be photocopied and the tribunal may authorize the photocopy to be filed in evidence in the place of the document filed and release the document filed, or may furnish to the person producing it or the person entitled to it a photocopy of the document filed certified by a member of the tribunal.

Certified copy admissible in evidence
   (6) A document purporting to be a copy of a document filed in evidence at a hearing, certified to be a copy thereof by a member of the tribunal, is admissible in evidence in proceedings in which the document is admissible as evidence of the document.

USE OF PREVIOUSLY ADMITTED EVIDENCE

15.1(1) The tribunal may treat previously admitted evidence as if it had been admitted in a proceeding before the tribunal, if the parties to the proceeding consent.

Definition
   (2) In subsection (1),

"previously admitted evidence" means evidence that was admitted, before the hearing of the proceeding referred to in that subsection, in any other proceeding before a court or tribunal, whether in or outside Ontario.

Additional power

(3) This power conferred by this section is in addition to the tribunal's power to admit evidence under section 15.

WITNESS PANELS

15.2 A tribunal may receive evidence from panels of witnesses composed of two or more persons, if the parties have first had an opportunity to make submissions in that regard.

NOTICE OF FACTS AND OPINIONS

16. A tribunal may, in making its decision in any proceeding,

(a) take notice of facts that may be judicially noticed; and
(b) take notice of any generally recognized scientific or technical facts, information or opinions within its scientific or specialized knowledge.

INTERIM DECISIONS AND ORDERS

16.1(1) A tribunal may make interim decisions and orders.

Conditions

(2) A tribunal may impose conditions on an interim decision or order.

Reasons

(3) An interim decision or order need not be accompanied by reasons.

TIME FRAMES

16.2 A tribunal shall establish guidelines setting out the usual time frame for completing proceedings that come before the tribunal and for completing the procedural steps within those proceedings.

DECISION; INTEREST

Decision

17.(1) A tribunal shall give its final decision and order, if any, in any proceeding in writing and shall give reasons in writing therefor if requested by a party.

Interest

(2) A tribunal that makes an order for the payment of money shall set out in the order the principal sum, and if interest is payable, the rate of interest and the date from which it is to be calculated.

COSTS

17.1(1) Subject to subsection (2), a tribunal may, in the circumstances set out in rules made under subsection (4), order a party to pay all or part of another party's costs in a proceeding.

Exception

(2) A tribunal shall not make an order to pay costs under this section unless,

(a) the conduct or course of conduct of a party has been unreasonable, frivolous or vexatious or a party has acted in bad faith; and

(b) the tribunal has made rules under subsection (4).

Amount of costs

(3) The amount of the costs ordered under this section shall be determined in accordance with the rules made under subsection (4).

Rules

(4) A tribunal may make rules with respect to,

(a) the ordering of costs;

(b) the circumstances in which costs may be ordered; and

(c) the amount of costs or the manner in which the amount of costs is to be determined.

Same

(5) Subsections 25.1(3), (4), (5) and (6) apply with respect to rules made under subsection (4).

Continuance of provisions in other statutes

(6) Despite section 32, nothing in this section shall prevent a tribunal from ordering a party to pay all or part of another party's costs in a proceeding in circumstances other than those set out in, and without complying with, subsections (1) to (3) if the tribunal makes the order in accordance with the provisions of an Act that are in force on February 14, 2000.

Submissions must be in writing

(7) Despite sections 5.1, 5.2 and 5.2.1, submissions for a costs order, whether under subsection (1) or under an authority referred to in subsection (6), shall be made by way of written or electronic docu-

ments, unless a party satisfies the tribunal that to do so is likely to cause the party significant prejudice.

(8), (9) Repealed.

NOTICE OF DECISION

18.(1) The tribunal shall send each party who participated in the proceeding, or the party's representative, a copy of its final decision or order, including the reasons if any have been given,

(a) by regular lettermail;
(b) by electronic transmission;
(c) by telephone transmission of a facsimile; or
(d) by some other method that allows proof of receipt, if the tribunal's rules made under section 25.1 deal with the matter.

Use of mail
(2) If the copy is sent by regular lettermail, it shall be sent to the most recent addresses known to the tribunal and shall be deemed to be received by the party on the fifth day after the day it is mailed.

Use of electronic or telephone transmission
(3) If the copy is sent by electronic transmission or by telephone transmission of a facsimile, it shall be deemed to be received on the day after it was sent, unless that day is a holiday, in which case the copy shall be deemed to be received on the next day that is not a holiday.

Use of other method
(4) If the copy is sent by a method referred to in clause (1)(d), the tribunal's rules made under section 25.1 govern its deemed day of receipt.

Failure to receive copy
(5) If a party that acts in good faith does not, through absence, accident, illness or other cause beyond the party's control, receive the copy until a later date than the deemed day of receipt, subsection (2), (3) or (4), as the case may be, does not apply.

ENFORCEMENT OF ORDERS

19.(1) A certified copy of a tribunal's decision or order in a proceeding may be filed in the Superior Court of Justice by the tribunal or by a party and on filing shall be deemed to be an order of that court and is enforceable as such.

Notice of filing

(2) A party who files an order under subsection (1) shall notify the tribunal within 10 days after the filing.

Order for payment of money

(3) On receiving a certified copy of a tribunal's order for the payment of money, the sheriff shall enforce the order as if it were an execution issued by the Superior Court of Justice.

RECORD OF PROCEEDING

20. A tribunal shall compile a record of any proceeding in which a hearing has been held which shall include,

(a) any application, complaint, reference or other document, if any, by which the proceeding was commenced;

(b) the notice of any hearing;

(c) any interlocutory orders made by the tribunal;

(d) all documentary evidence filed with the tribunal, subject to any limitation expressly imposed by any other Act on the extent to or the purposes for which any such documents may be used in evidence in any proceeding;

(e) the transcript, if any, of the oral evidence given at the hearing; and

(f) the decision of the tribunal and the reasons therefor, where reasons have been given.

ADJOURNMENTS

21. A hearing may be adjourned from time to time by a tribunal of its own motion or where it is shown to the satisfaction of the tribunal that the adjournment is required to permit an adequate hearing to be held.

CORRECTION OF ERRORS

21.1 A tribunal may at any time correct a typographical error, error of calculation or similar error made in its decision or order.

POWER TO REVIEW

21.2(1) A tribunal may, if it considers it advisable and if its rules made under section 25.1 deal with the matter, review all or part of its own decision or order, and may confirm, vary, suspend or cancel the decision or order.

Time for review

(2) The review shall take place within a reasonable time after the decision or order is made.

Conflict

(3) In the event of a conflict between this section and any other Act, the other Act prevails.

ADMINISTRATION OF OATHS

22. A member of a tribunal has power to administer oaths and affirmations for the purpose of any of its proceedings and the tribunal may require evidence before it to be given under oath or affirmation.

POWERS RE CONTROL OF PROCEEDINGS

Abuse of processes

23.(1) A tribunal may make such orders or give such directions in proceedings before it as it considers proper to prevent abuse of its processes.

Limitation on examination

(2) A tribunal may reasonably limit further examination or cross-examination of a witness where it is satisfied that the examination or cross-examination has been sufficient to disclose fully and fairly all matters relevant to the issues in the proceeding.

Exclusion of representatives

(3) A tribunal may exclude from a hearing anyone, other than a person licensed under the *Law Society Act*, appearing on behalf of a party or as an adviser to a witness if it finds that such person is not competent properly to represent or to advise the party or witness, or does not understand and comply at the hearing with the duties and responsibilities of an advocate or adviser.

NOTICE, ETC.

24.(1) Where a tribunal is of the opinion that because the parties to any proceeding before it are so numerous or for any other reason, it is impracticable,

(a) to give notice of the hearing; or
(b) to send its decision and the material mentioned in section 18,

to all or any of the parties individually, the tribunal may, instead of doing so, cause reasonable notice of the hearing or of its decision to be given to such parties by public advertisement or otherwise as the tribunal may direct.

Contents of notice

(2) A notice of a decision given by a tribunal under clause (1)(b) shall inform the parties of the place where copies of the decision and the reasons therefor, if reasons were given, may be obtained.

APPEAL OPERATES AS STAY, EXCEPTION

25.(1) An appeal from a decision of a tribunal to a court or other appellate body operates as a stay in the matter unless,

(a) another Act or a regulation that applies to the proceeding expressly provides to the contrary; or
(b) the tribunal or the court or other appellate body orders otherwise.

Idem

(2) An application for judicial review under the *Judicial Review Procedure Act*, or the bringing of proceedings specified in subsection 2(1) of that Act is not an appeal within the meaning of subsection (1).

CONTROL OF PROCESS

25.0.1 A tribunal has the power to determine its own procedures and practices and may for that purpose,

(a) make orders with respect to the procedures and practices that apply in any particular proceeding; and
(b) establish rules under section 25.1.

RULES

25.1(1) A tribunal may make rules governing the practice and procedure before it.

Application

(2) The rules may be of general or particular application.

Consistency with Acts

(3) The rules shall be consistent with this Act and with the other Acts to which they relate.

Public access

(4) The tribunal shall make the rules available to the public in English and in French.

Legislation Act, 2006, Part III
(5) Rules adopted under this section are not regulations as defined in Part III (Regulations) of the *Legislation Act, 2006*.

Additional power
(6) The power conferred by this section is in addition to any power to adopt rules that the tribunal may have under another Act.

REGULATIONS

26. The Lieutenant Governor in Council may make regulations prescribing forms for the purpose of section 12.

RULES, ETC., AVAILABLE TO PUBLIC

27. A tribunal shall make any rules or guidelines established under this or any other Act available for examination by the public.

SUBSTANTIAL COMPLIANCE

28. Substantial compliance with requirements respecting the content of forms, notices or documents under this Act or any rule made under this or any other Act is sufficient.

29.–31. Repealed.

CONFLICT

32. Unless it is expressly provided in any other Act that its provisions and regulations, rules or by-laws made under it apply despite anything in this Act, the provisions of this Act prevail over the provisions of such other Act and over regulations, rules or by-laws made under such other Act which conflict therewith.

33., 34. Repealed.

FORMS 1, 2 Repealed.

Advocacy before Administrative Agencies

3

LEARNING OBJECTIVES

After reading this chapter, the reader should be able to:

- appreciate the importance of good advocacy to the legal system and the parties involved
- elaborate on key principles in being a good advocate
- distinguish between being a good advocate in court and being a good advocate in an agency setting, if applicable
- detail the various ways a good advocate prepares for a hearing
- compare and contrast tips suggested for appearing before the Assessment Review Board with those for appearing before the Human Rights Tribunal of Ontario
- differentiate between introducing evidence in an agency hearing and in a court trial
- understand the importance of updating legal knowledge for being a good advocate
- detail the need for appropriate behaviour when dealing with an agency in order to achieve the best result for a client
- demonstrate the key concepts of good advocacy

INTRODUCTION

In order to provide the best service possible to a client involved in a matter before an administrative agency, an Ontario paralegal has "a duty to provide legal services and discharge all responsibilities to clients, tribunals, the public and other licensees honourably and with integrity" (R. 1.03(a) of the *Paralegal Rules of Conduct*), meaning that although the paralegal must be zealous in representing the client's position and interests, the representative must do so within the *Paralegal Rules of Conduct* as published by the Law Society of Upper Canada.

Advocacy before administrative agencies is much like advocacy before the courts and requires similar preparation and strategies. In practice, however, some subtle differences need to be observed. The bottom line, nevertheless, is that being a good advocate in any setting requires thorough preparation of the client's case by looking through the lens of the setting in which you are appearing. Rather than having the author jot down points to remember in order to become an effective advocate, the reader is best served by hearing directly from decision-makers as to what techniques are best used when advocating for a client before an administrative agency. The author requested a list of hints, or do's and don'ts, from an educational committee of an agency, a current and a former vice-chair of an agency, and a current justice of the peace. These hints are set out below, with little editing, so that the reader has direct advice, unfiltered by the author. Although there is a fair amount of duplication, that duplication should indicate important commonalities and stress that such advice is very useful to the reader.

TIPS FOR PARTIES APPEARING BEFORE THE ASSESSMENT REVIEW BOARD

Offered by the ARB Members' Education Committee
Rick Stephenson (Chair of the Board),
Susan Mather (Vice-Chair and Chair of the Education Committee),
Marcie Bourassa and Bob Butterworth (Vice-Chairs),
Bernie Cowan, Joe Wyger, Don Whitehurst, Janet Walker,
Sandra Driesel, and Peter Andrews (Members)

1. Know the relevant legislation and regulations — review relevant Board decisions.

2. Be familiar with Board Rules of Practice and Procedure (available on the Board's website).

3. Check the ARB's website for other helpful information.

4. Learn about the ARB's process. Proceedings can vary among tribunals.

5. Provide disclosure in advance. Send copies of your exhibits to the other parties in advance of the hearing date (often required by the rules) even if not required, and ask for copies of their material.

6. Meet with other parties in advance of the hearing date.
   (a) Settlements are encouraged.
   (b) If you are unable to resolve by settlement, try to narrow issues.
   (c) An agreed statement of facts and/or description of the property saves everyone a lot of time and effort and reduces the risk.

7. Check the meeting location in advance and arrive early for the hearing. The board meets in municipalities across Ontario; some locations are difficult to find. Hearings generally proceed on a "first come, first served" basis.

8. Turn cell phones off.

9. Address the tribunal, not the other parties.

10. Be sure the adjudicator's note-taking is finished before moving on to your next point. Most board meetings are not recorded. Members rely heavily upon their note-taking.

11. Have extra copies of exhibits available.

12. Advise your client that exhibits remain with the board for at least six months and are returned only upon request.

13. Be courteous and always respectful, not argumentative.

14. Be brief, but keep in mind you only have one opportunity to present your case.

15. Focus your oral arguments and evidence.

16. Remember that case law is not evidence. It should be held for final submissions.

17. When submitting written briefs, highlight the important passages, and direct the board to those passages during the hearing. Never assume that the board will read passages after a hearing. Direct the adjudicator to key points in your written material.

18. Be aware that photos on cell phones and video equipment cannot be received as exhibits.

TEN TIPS FOR ADVOCACY BEFORE TRIBUNALS

Courtesy of David A. Wright,
Acting Chair, Human Rights Tribunal of Ontario

1. **Learn About the Tribunal**

   Be sure to know as much as possible about the tribunal you will be appearing before. If you have not done so before, start by reading the relevant legislation, the tribunal rules, and some of its case law. Learn about the tribunal's culture by talking to colleagues and tribunal staff. Remember that tribunals' approaches to dispute resolution are often different from each other and from those of the courts.

2. **Be Prepared**

   Start your preparation well in advance of the hearing to avoid making last-minute requests or amendments. Know the facts and your theory of the case throughout the litigation process. Make any preliminary or interim requests as soon as possible. Remember that mediation requires preparation, too!

3. **Listen To and Educate Your Client**

   Listen to your client's full story; do not be too quick to dismiss aspects of what he or she tells you as irrelevant. Understand your client's point of view and concerns — remember you are there to represent his or her interests. Tell your client what to expect at the hearing or mediation, and give him or her a realistic assessment of the possible end result prior to the outcome.

4. **Have a Mediation Strategy**

   Think about various possible options for settlement, and about how the other side will approach the issues and what their concerns are. Explore your client's bottom line before the mediation commences.

5. **Write Carefully**

   Well-written letters and submissions are of the utmost importance. Write in a short, clear, and straightforward manner. Use plain language, not "legalese".

6. **Focus Your Oral and Written Arguments**

   Be sure you have fully thought out how your facts relate to the statute, rules, and any relevant cases. Explain this to the decision maker in a concise manner. Use summaries and introductions, and explain the structure of your arguments at the outset.

7. **Make Concessions When Appropriate**

It is rarely better, from a strategic point of view, to make an argument that will almost certainly lose than to concede. Being fair to the other side helps give the tribunal confidence in you. Making appropriate agreements with the other side before the hearing will save time, effort, and possibly your client's money.

8. **Look at the Issues from the Adjudicator's Perspective**

Remember that you have to convince the adjudicator, who has different concerns from your client's. These include making the right decision, being consistent with other tribunal members, having the hearing run smoothly and efficiently, being fair to all parties, and getting to the heart of the issues in dispute. The adjudicator is always thinking about how he or she will write the decision.

9. **Listen Carefully to the Adjudicator's Questions**

Adjudicators generally ask questions to understand or test your position, not to trip you up or throw you off your game plan. Questions show what is concerning the adjudicator. When you answer them, consider carefully why the adjudicator is asking them and how you can allay his or her concerns.

10. **Be Courteous**

Always treat the tribunal and the opposing party or representative with respect and courtesy. Being aggressive or impolite will not help your client.

DOs AND DON'Ts FOR PARALEGALS APPEARING BEFORE ADMINISTRATIVE AGENCIES

Courtesy of Her Worship Mary A. Ross Hendriks,
Justice of the Peace, Toronto Region, Ontario Court of Justice
(formerly Vice-chair, Human Rights Tribunal of Ontario)

Please be mindful of the fact that the *Statutory Powers Procedure Act* (*SPPA*) applies to most hearings conducted by Ontario boards. This has some real significance to you as a representative. First, the *SPPA* empowers boards to create their own Rules of Practice. Please ensure that you are aware of the latest rules and forms used by the boards before which you appear, since they are often amended every few years to keep pace with change. You can find these rules and forms on various board websites. You must use these rules and forms. Please be mindful of any deadlines set within these rules, so that you are able to map out a schedule for your pre-hearing preparations.

The *SPPA* also allows for a real relaxation of the rules of evidence. Sections 2 and 15 of the *SPPA* allow virtually anything to be admitted and permit the adjudicator to decide what weight, if any, to give it. That being the case, while documents that would normally be hearsay may be admitted into evidence, you have merely proven to the tribunal that a document exists, not the truth of its contents. The rules of evidence apply in criminal proceedings and in provincial offence cases. You should read a few leading textbooks on evidence, even in the administrative context, to understand fully how these rules apply or are modified by the *SPPA*, since this is critical knowledge for you as representatives.

Adjudicators find it very helpful if representatives provide them with a bound book of case law upon which they rely, which should include a cover page that sets out each case, its citation, and a cross-reference to the tab in the brief. The cover page should set out the title of proceeding, and your name and Law Society number in the bottom right-hand corner. It is also very helpful to provide adjudicators with a copy of your final submissions in a written form, even if you make final submissions orally. A cover page should also be included here, with the title of proceeding, the words "Final Submissions", and your name and Law Society number in the bottom right-hand corner. It is very professional to do this, and it helps supplement the notes that the adjudicators make for themselves.

Most board hearings are not recorded officially, unlike court proceedings, and so it is impossible to order a transcript. If your case is of extremely grave importance, please discuss with your client whether you are able to hire an official court reporter to prepare transcripts, which will be an official record of the proceeding. Determine this prior to the commencement of the hearing, and then approach the Registrar of the board to seek the adjudicator's permission to create an official record. As a matter of courtesy, you should offer to share copies of this record with all participants and the adjudicator. You may be able to do some cost-sharing with the opposing side, but the board will not contribute to the cost of these transcripts, which may be very high. The notes of an adjudicator or a member of the bench are normally held at common law to be beyond production, so if you cannot have an official record created, then it is up to you to bring a colleague with you to make detailed notes while you present your case. Your colleague may use pen and paper or a laptop to do so. If you are short-staffed, you may need to make your own notes.

In terms of expert witnesses, most boards have rules that deal with the amount of notice required for the opposing side. Typically, representatives provide the opposing side with a "willsay" of what the expert will say in evidence, and a copy of his or her résumé. Experts must be qualified by the board before they begin testifying. Please ensure that you are aware of how to qualify an expert witness, and how an expert's qualifications may be challenged by the other side.

Once you know who will be adjudicating your case, you may wish to read some of their prior decisions in cases related to your case. You should also read the decisions of their colleagues in related matters, particularly recent ones. You can access <www.canlii.org> from any computer (although that site only has decisions of selected boards) and obtain case law for free, and then note them up online. You may also enter the adjudicator's name, to read his or her decisions. In order to prepare fully, I urge you to obtain a private publisher's annotated copy of the statute that you are using (if it exists), read all the key cases listed, and note them up. The results of your legal research will help you craft your key arguments in advance and provide the analysis you will need for your final submissions.

Many legal publications, including *The Law Times* and the *Lawyers Weekly*, for example, are available on a subscription basis. I urge you to subscribe to a broadly based publication in newspaper format, which is relatively inexpensive, plus any specialized law journals or periodicals in the areas in which you practise so that you are able to keep up with changes to the law. If this is a financial burden, please regularly visit law and government libraries, such as the excellent one on labour, pay equity and human rights law housed with the Ontario Labour Relations Board (on different floors), and avail yourself of the journals and periodicals there. In addition, please attend continuing legal education lectures offered by a number of providers on a regular basis in order to increase your knowledge base. If you miss a lecture, you may be able to purchase it on CD or watch a re-broadcast of it. The practitioners who speak at these lectures and who provide papers spend a great deal of time and energy preparing, and their materials may help you see issues in a new light.

Finally, encourage your clients to avail themselves of any mediation opportunities that may be provided by the board for free, or even arrange for the services of a privately appointed mediator, chosen by both representatives. Mediation is an excellent tool and, for most cases, is a more efficient way of dealing with litigious matters. If your client's case is not a leading case that is going to change the law, then a confidential mediation session is something that should be pursued.

ANALYSIS OF HINTS AND LISTS

All the points listed and discussed above should be taken to heart by the practitioner, but there are three points that should be stressed, as follows.

- Preparation is essential to the advocate and takes many forms. Understanding your client's case and the law applicable to it as well as the other side's positions, being familiar with the evidence likely to be adduced and the witnesses that will be called, and knowing the procedures to be followed in the proceedings before the agency are just some of the items that need work. As noted above, being knowledgeable about the appropriate legislation and rules of the specific agency will go a long way in preparing to represent your client.

- Closely related to preparation is the necessity to update your knowledge of the appropriate law, including the enabling legislation and any other relevant statutes and regulations. These can change constantly (especially regulations), and you will not engender confidence with the adjudicator if you reference items no longer in force. Updating your knowledge of the case law (i.e., court judgments) relevant to the agency and your matter is important as a Court of Appeal decision you may be relying on may have been overturned at the Supreme Court of Canada in the meantime. Alternatively, a new decision at variance with or in support of what you believe is an important case may have occurred. You should also update your knowledge of decisions of the agency, as key points in your matter may have recently been determined that may have an impact on your matter. Although agencies are not bound by *stare decisis*, they do try to be consistent, if possible, so having the latest decisions will be useful to the advocate.

- Being courteous may seem to be a small point, but it can have huge impact on the confidence the adjudicator has in the representative. As well, it can also affect one's reputation, especially if the representative is discourteous to the adjudicator, to the other side, or to witnesses, not to mention how it might impact on the adjudicator in hearing the case and making a decision. After all, the adjudicator is human.

Numerous pages of this book could be filled with advice on how to be a great advocate; however, it is probably best to read a variety of the large number of texts written on advocacy as well as to observe good advocates in person. Most important, though, is one's use of such information to practise good advocacy in your matters. With experience, a representative will improve; and by following the hints above and desiring to be excellent in the work that is entailed, the representative will quickly become a reliable, trustworthy, and effective advocate.

CHAPTER SUMMARY

This chapter provided a review of tips offered by three "inside" sources of good advocacy skills needed to best present a client's case. It was felt that persons on the front lines hearing advocates would provide the best practical advice on how to succeed. By setting out each source's tips or comments in full, it is hoped that the reader can compare and contrast and, by dint of repetition, focus on the key concepts of good advocacy.

REVIEW QUESTIONS

1. What tip(s) are mentioned in all three sources quoted in the chapter?
2. What should a good advocate do before a hearing?
3. What should a good advocate do during a hearing?
4. What should a good advocate do after a hearing?
5. How can an advocate enhance her/his reputation with (a) the client, (b) the agency, and (c) her/his peers?
6. List five actions that would be viewed as bad advocacy.

EXERCISE

After reviewing the chapter, demonstrate good advocacy skills in presenting an argument before an adjudicator (a student posing) based upon the *Barker v. Famous Players, A Division of Viacom Canada Inc.*, 2004 HRTO 10 interim decision (the *Barker* decision), specifically the issue of reprisal discussed in that decision and briefed in Chapter 6.

SUGGESTED READINGS

Adair, Geoffrey. *On Trial: Advocacy Skills Law and Practice*, 2d ed. (Markham, Ont.: LexisNexis Butterworths, 2004).

Blatt, Arlene, & JoAnn Kurtz. *Advocacy for Paralegals* (Toronto, Ont.: Emond Montgomery Publications, 2009).

Cromwell, Thomas (compiled by). *Effective Written Advocacy* (Aurora, Ont.: Canada Law Book, a division of The Cartwright Group Ltd., 2008).

Finlay, Bryan, & Cromwell, Thomas. *Witness Preparation Manual*, 2d ed. (Aurora, Ont.: Canada Law Book Inc., 1999).

Noble, Cinnie, L. Leslie Dizgun, & D. Paul Emond. *Mediation Advocacy: Effective Client Representation in Mediation Process* (Toronto, Ont.: Emond Montgomery Publications, 1998).

Salhany, Roger. *Cross-Examination: The Art of the Advocate*, 3d ed. (Markham, Ont.: LexisNexis Butterworths, 2006).

White, Robert. *The Art of Trial* (Aurora, Ont.: Canada Law Book Inc., 1993).

Stuesser, Lee. *An Advocacy Primer*, 4th ed. (Toronto, Ont.: Carswell, 2015).

McEwan J. Kenneth, *Sopinka on the Trial of an Action*, 3d ed. (Toronto, Ont.: LexisNexis, 2016).

Part II

Selected Ontario Agencies

How to Deal with Selected Ontario Agencies and Clustering of Agencies

This part of the text discusses selected Ontario tribunals, boards, and commissions under the following topics:

- Overview and background
- Enabling legislation, including statute(s) and any appropriate regulation(s)
- Relevant regulation(s), if any (in addition to those discussed in enabling legislation)
- Tribunal procedures:
  - Rules
  - Practice directions
  - Forms
- Policies
- Explanatory literature from the Tribunal
- Relevant cases and/or decisions

Selected tribunals and boards applicable to paralegals representing clients at those agencies will be discussed. The objective of Part II is to provide guidelines for paralegals who represent a client in these Ontario tribunals. The material included and discussed will primarily be drawn from an individual tribunal's own website, which will be referenced extensively, as well as from the websites of the appropriate government departments that deal with these tribunals. Ontario tribunals that fall under the *Statutory Powers Procedure Act* (*SPPA*), in whole or in part, will be noted in the section dealing with tribunal procedures. The cases and decisions mentioned in the Relevant Cases and/or Decisions section can be found on the tribunal's website or from research into cases and decisions online or at most law libraries. Although paralegals are not lawyers, to be a good advocate and to best represent a client it is necessary for them to find, understand, and use appropriate cases and/or decisions in their work. Further research over and above that supplied in this book must always be done by the paralegal in preparing to appear before any tribunal.

The review of websites and the research for this edition of the book were done in early 2016. Since the law constantly changes, paralegals should continue to verify information provided here to ensure its currency and validity. By applying a systematic review of the website of a tribunal that is not explored in this book, paralegals can learn the practice and procedure of any tribunal before which they may appear.

Before dealing with specific Ontario agencies in their individual chapters, it is important to expand on the reference in Chapter 1 about the recent trend in Ontario toward the clustering of agencies. Although this topic will also be briefly addressed for specific agencies in their individual chapters, it is useful to have a more detailed overview of clusters in this preamble to Part II of this textbook.

The Ontario government decided on a policy of clustering in the late 2000s, as evidenced by the following statute: *Adjudicative Tribunals Accountability, Governance and Appointments Act, 2009*, S.O. 2009, c. 33 ("*ATAGAA*"). Pursuant to this Act, the purpose of the legislation, as set out in s. 1, was "to ensure that adjudicative tribunals are accountable, transparent and efficient in their operations while remaining independent in their decision-making". Clustering of agencies was mandated in s. 15, to be done by regulation under this Act "if, in the opinion of the Lieutenant Governor in Council, the matters that the tribunals deal with are such that they can operate more effectively and efficiently as part of a cluster than alone." In respect of the governing of an adjudicative tribunal included in a cluster, if a provision of another Act or regulation is in conflict with section 16 or 17 of the *ATAGAA*, section 16 or 17 of the *ATAGAA* prevails, as stated in section 19.

Ontario Regulation 126/10 was passed in 2011 to institute clustering, and it has been amended a few times, the last amendment being O. Reg. 59/15 to create three clusters:

1. **Cluster of environment and land tribunals** (the "ELTO"):
   - **Assessment Review Board** (Chapter 5 of text)
   - Board of Negotiation continued under subsection 27(1) of the *Expropriations Act*
   - Conservation Review Board
   - Environmental Review Tribunal
   - Ontario Municipal Board

2. **Cluster of social justice tribunals** (the "SJTO"):
   - Child and Family Services Review Board
   - Criminal Injuries Compensation Board
   - Custody Review Board
   - **Human Rights Tribunal of Ontario** (Chapter 6 of text)
   - Landlord and Tenant Board

- Ontario Special Education Tribunal (English)
- Ontario Special Education Tribunal (French)
- **Social Benefits Tribunal** (Chapter 4 of text)

3. **Cluster of safety, standards and licensing tribunals** (the "SLASTO"):
   - Animal Care Review Board
   - Fire Safety Commission
   - **Licence Appeal Tribunal** (Chapter 7 of text)
   - Ontario Civilian Police Commission
   - Ontario Parole Board

SLASTO

SLASTO launched its website, <www.slasto.gov.on.ca>, in April 2013. As of May 2016, the SLASTO website was still being developed, and there is very little information or resources available other than links to each of the clusters' agency websites and information on updating the Auto Insurance Dispute Resolution System (AIDRS), now the Automobile Accident Benefits Service (AABS), which will be part of the License Appeal Tribunal functions as of April 1, 2016. SLASTO will be discussed further in Chapter 7 on the LAT. In order to understand the reason for and the possible directions of clustering in Ontario, we will conduct a quick review of the other two clusters' websites.

ELTO

On the ELTO website, <www.elto.gov.on.ca>, the Presentations Web page, under "Mandate, Mission, Core Values", embeds various presentations made by Ontario agency experts to various groups to explain the implementation and the hopes for the first cluster in Ontario, the ELTO. The first presentation listed on the page is "Notes for Remarks to the Municipal Law Section of the Ontario Bar Association" made by Michael Gottheil, Executive Chair Environment and Land Tribunals Ontario on September 16, 2010. In it he states:

> We have developed new position descriptions for the Associate Chairs, Vice-chairs and Members. These are uniform across ELTO, and include important features such as making it clear that the Associate Chairs are responsible for participating in the overall management of ELTO, rather than merely being delegated heads of individual tribunals. The position descriptions also include references to ongoing professional development, ethical standards, decision review processes, working in teams as appropriate, respecting diversity, facilitating access to

justice and other aspects of a modern tribunal committed to excellence and accessibility.

Mr. Gottheil then advised his listeners of some of the following initiatives that had been commenced or were in the process of starting:

> **Enhancing adjudicative expertise, capacity and excellence.** We are focusing on professional development through a pan-ELTO committee which will bring a planed [*sic*] and structured approach to this important area. ELTO's training plan will feature ELTO-wide programs offered to members of all tribunals. Where, as appropriate, tribunal-specific programs are also offered, they will be priorized, developed and coordinated through the pan-ELTO training committee.
>
> **Better use of the skills of staff** to enhance the dispute resolution process as part of tribunal teams, with adjudicators, committed to responsiveness to users and adjudicative excellence.
>
> **Cross appointments**: we will explore this carefully and strategically. There won't be a wholesale approach to cross-appointments, but we will look for ways to strengthen the skill sets available to those making case assignments within a tribunal. This flows from the view I have often expressed that the expertise of a tribunal vests in its members as a group, not necessarily in each individual member. When you broaden the skill sets within a tribunal, you strengthen its collective expertise, and its ability to deploy that expertise to serve the tribunal's users and the public interest. ...
>
> **Joint Board rules**. These are, by definition, complex and important proceedings which raise issues within the jurisdiction of two Boards. I think we can do better than forcing them into one or other of a tribunal's set of rules built for matters within its jurisdiction alone. Instead, we should think carefully about the issues that are dealt with in these joint board proceedings, and design a stand-alone set of rules to ensure that they can be dealt with in an accessible, just and expeditious fashion.
>
> **Mediation:** One theme I have heard in many discussions is the desire for more mediation services. I fully agree, and want to work with those inside and outside ELTO to build on what we have already developed in this area. As you will all know, this requires training and, sometimes, recruitment, and must be advanced carefully and well if it is to gain the support and acceptance it needs to become a more regular way to resolve matters before ELTO tribunals.

The last presentation on that ELTO Web page is a presentation for the 2010 Australian Conference of Planning and Environmental Courts and Tribunals entitled "Improving Access to Justice through International Dialogue: Lessons for and from Ontario's Cluster Approach to Tribunal Efficiency and Effectiveness", by Michael Gottheil and Doug Ewart, and a copy is attached as Appendix II.1 to this preamble. Gottheil and Ewart state that the ELTO cluster "was created to demonstrate that clustered tribunals can be more efficient than the same tribunals operating alone and that the matters they deal with can be addressed more effectively, and access to justice and the quality of tribunal services can be significantly improved, when they operate as part of a cluster". Later they state: "Importantly, the legislated rationale for a cluster is not limited to improvements in efficiency, which we might equate with procedure and administration, but equally includes improved effectiveness in how the subject matters within the cluster are dealt with. There are two key concepts here: i) effectiveness, not just efficiency; and ii) effectiveness in relation to substance (subject matter), not just process." Wrapping up the discussion of why Ontario created the ELTO cluster, Gottheil and Ewart state the following: "Overall, it would seem that these provisions evince an intention by the Legislature to develop clusters of tribunals for purposes that go beyond administrative efficiencies and coordination. After all, such goals could be achieved by appointing outside efficiency experts and by encouraging the tribunals to work together. Referring to subject matter effectiveness and appointing a single chair for a number of tribunals send a stronger message about coordination and signal a more serious desire for change. They suggest a need to interpret and apply a cluster mandate in a way which gives effect to this integrative legislative intention, subject only to respecting the unchanged statutory mandates of the constituent tribunals."

A comprehensive discussion of the key features of the ELTO cluster follows on pp. 7–8 of the paper, after which, on p. 9, Gottheil and Ewart detail how "Ontario's cluster has many of the features common to amalgamations or mergers"; concerns that are foreseen about clusters are set out on pp. 10–11. The paper then discusses challenges for the future.

SJTO

On the SJTO website <www.sjto.gov.on.ca>, the key items to note are on the Reports, Plans and Standards Web page, which has the annual reports for the years 2010–11 to 2013–14 for the SJTO. The report starts with an informative Executive Chair's message as well as annual reports of each of the individual agencies that make up the cluster. Selected portions of the 2013–14 Annual Report are attached as Appendix II.2 to the preamble.

The SJTO published a set of Common Rules as well as two Practice Directions, which are grounded in the core adjudicative values and principles of the SJTO that govern the work of the cluster. The Common Rules and the two Practice Directions provide a consistent overarching framework of procedures that will continue to evolve.

Following are summaries of the Common Rules and the two Practice Directions, which are common to all agencies in the SJTO cluster, including the SBT and HRTO.

SJTO Common Rules

As a preamble to the Common Rules, there is a provision entitled "Introduction" and another entitled "How to Use the Rules". The "Introduction" basically states that it applies to all the agencies in the cluster and is meant to "provide a consistent overarching framework of common procedures that will continue to evolve." The other provision lists the agencies in the cluster and states that the Common Rules, listed under "Part A — Adjudicative Values and Interpretive Principles", form part of the rules and procedures of each agency. These rules are summarized below:

"Rule A1: Application" states that the Common Rules apply to each of the SJTO tribunals.

"Rule A2: Definitions" defines "rules and procedures" and "tribunals".

"Rule A3: Interpretation" makes it clear that the rules shall be applied liberally and purposely interpreted (i) to promote fair, just, and expeditious resolution of disputes; (ii) to allow parties to participate effectively in the process with or without representation; and (iii) to ensure that procedures, orders, and directions are proportionate to the importance and complexity of the issues. Further, the rules are to be applied in a manner consistent with the *Human Rights Code*.

"Rule A4: Tribunal Powers" states that the tribunal may exercise any of its powers, except where otherwise provided, and may waive or vary the application of any rule or procedure except where doing so is prohibited by legislation or a specific rule.

"Rule A5: Accommodation of a Human Rights Code-Related Need" states that participants, as defined by the rule, to the proceedings are entitled to accommodation, and a request for accommodation should be made to the tribunal as soon as possible.

"Rule A6: Language" allows that written materials may be provided to the tribunal in either English or French and that individuals may participate in tribunal proceedings in either French, English, or American or Quebec Sign Language. Further, a person appearing before the tribunal may use an interpreter, and such services will be provided upon request in accordance with tribunal policy.

"Rule A7: Courtesy and Respect" states all "persons participating in proceedings before or communicating with the tribunal must act in good faith and in a manner that is courteous and respectful of the tribunal and other participants in the proceeding."

"Rule A8: Abuse of Process" allows the tribunal to make such orders or "directions in proceedings before it as it considers proper to prevent abuse of its processes." Further, the tribunal has the power (i) to find a person to be a vexatious litigant and dismiss a matter for that reason, and (ii) to require a person who is found to be a vexatious litigant to obtain permission from the tribunal to commence further proceedings or to take further steps in a proceeding.

"Rule A9 Representatives" sets out rules regarding representatives to parties:

> A9.1 states that "[p]arties may be self-represented, represented by a person licensed by the Law Society of Upper Canada or by an unlicensed person where permitted by the *Law Society Act* and its regulations and by-laws."

> A9.2 states the various duties and obligations that representatives owe to the tribunal and to the party being represented.

> A9.3 states the responsibilities of the representative and the rights of the tribunal when a party ceases to act for a client.

> A9.4 allows the tribunal to disqualify any representative from appearing in front of it "where the representative's continued appearance would lead to an abuse of process."

"Rule A10 Litigation Guardians" sets out (i) numerous rules regarding the naming and removing, as well as the responsibilities of a Litigation Guardian needed for a party who is either a minor or lacking mental capacity to participate in the tribunal proceedings; and (ii) the form and content of the declaration needed for such appointment.

Practice Direction on Litigation Guardians before Social Justice Tribunals Ontario

This Practice Direction discusses at length how a person who does not have legal capacity can be a party to a case before an SJTO tribunal through a litigation guardian. It relates to Rule A10 of the SJTO Common Rules. Those persons include minors and parties with mental capacity issues, and the Practice Direction defines each situation and sets out the declaration required of and the responsibility of the litigation guardian, and the naming and removing of such person. Persons interested in litigation guardians should look at the Practice Direction in more detail.

Practice Direction on Representation before Social Justice Tribunals Ontario

This Practice Direction, which should be read in conjunction with Rule A9 of the Common Rules, discusses who can represent a party before the agencies in the SJTO cluster. A support person can attend a hearing or mediation to assist the person but is not considered a representative. A party can also self-represent. A party can choose a representative who may be a lawyer or paralegal licensed by the LSUC or an unlicensed person if that person falls within the category of persons the LSUC has exempted from its licensing requirements. The Practice Direction sets out a partial list of the current exemptions to permit unlicensed persons to be representatives and provides a link to the LSUC website for the complete list. A discussion of the responsibilities imposed upon the representative occurs at the end of the Practice Direction.

The SJTO Common Rules and the two Practice Directions are included as appendices to this introductory chapter.

Also included as an appendix to this chapter is the speech, with the accompanying paper entitled "Ontario's Tribunal Clusters: 'Many attend, few understand' (with apologies to Leo Durocher)", given by Michael Gottheil, Chair of Social Justice Tribunals Ontario, in March 2014 at the LSUC's Six-Minute Administrative Lawyer meeting. The paper provides a broad overview of clustering and how the SJTO cluster had functioned for the first three years since its designation as a cluster in early 2011.

To wrap up the subject of clustering in Ontario, it is no longer sufficient for the reader to go to the website of an individual agency. If an agency is part of a cluster, there is also a need to look at the cluster website. The need to recognize the common rules and procedures within a cluster is likely be one of the important results of clustering.

Appendix II.1
An ELTO Presentation[†]

Improving Access to Justice through International Dialogue: Lessons for and from Ontario's Cluster Approach to Tribunal Efficiency and Effectiveness

Michael Gottheil and Doug Ewart[1]

INTRODUCTION

Presenting this paper as part of an international overview of "Jurisdiction, Structure and Civil Practice and Procedure" at the 2010 Australian Conference of Planning and Environmental Courts and Tribunals provides a unique opportunity to open and encourage a dialogue with some of the only jurisdictions in the world to have joined land and environment issues in a tribunal similar to Ontario's[2] new Environment and Land Tribunals (ELTO) cluster[3]. As well, it supports an exchange of ideas and experience with jurisdictions which for some years have been leaders in tribunal reform more generally, and which accordingly offer a rich source of inspiration and guidance for Ontario's clustering initiative.

At the same time, Ontario has something to contribute to a two-way learning process: our initial research[4] suggests that Ontario's clustering model, while new, addresses several of the concerns which have been raised in academic and law reform discussions of tribunal mergers, amalgamations or clusters. And, it is hoped that some of the analysis in this paper on linkages between tribunal processes and access to justice may advance the sharing of experience and ideas in that area as well.

This paper seeks to foster these exchanges by providing core information on Ontario's cluster, and by putting forward for debate and consideration some perspectives on how structure, process and procedure can be designed to facilitate, in practical and tangible ways, the pre-eminent goal of access to justice, particularly in the context of clustered or amalgamated tribunals. Through discussion at the conference, and inclusion in its published proceedings, this paper will reach a much wider audience than could otherwise be hoped for. If the resulting cross-jurisdictional dialogue, comparative research and broad-based information sharing are similarly increased, the paper will have served its purposes.

[†] Source: <http://www.elto.gov.on.ca/stellent/groups/public/@abcs/@www/@elto/documents/webasset/ec083413.doc>. Also available: SJTO website, Speeches and Papers.

The paper is structured in three parts. Part I provides an overview and preliminary analysis of Ontario's recent tribunal clustering initiative. Part II moves to the more general discussion of how tribunal practices and procedures can be designed to improve access to justice, and sketches the role which clustering or amalgamation can play in that regard. Part III then expands on two of the themes from Part II by exploring at greater length the expert and active-collaborative[5] approaches to adjudication, with particular reference to three recent developments in Canada which may be of interest to those administering or studying tribunals elsewhere, and on which international commentary will be instructive as related and further developments are considered in Canada.

PART I: CLUSTERING

A. The Concept

The core rationales for directing the resolution of disputes to tribunals rather than to courts lie in the focused expertise and greater accessibility of tribunals. For the first of these reasons, and because tribunals developed gradually as acceptance of them moved out from the initial forays, and generally in response to issues faced by particular ministries or departments, tribunals have tended to be created to adjudicate disputes in a single area, and have been closely associated with their host ministry or department.

While the resulting silos promote and preserve specialization, they can lead to the inefficient use of infrastructure resources, as well as to tribunals which can become insular and self-referential. They may offer little caseload variety or professional development for adjudicators and can be prone to capture by one or more stakeholder groups or the host department or ministry. And, where its caseload is small, a tribunal may simply lack the resources to support an effective and sophisticated administrative justice organization despite its best efforts to achieve that goal.

Structural responses to these issues have come relatively recently, and have ranged from full amalgamation (unification), to amalgamation with distinct lists or groups of adjudicators for defined subject areas, to creating oversight bodies or secretariats which coordinate some aspects of the work of otherwise distinct tribunals.

Clustering is situated toward the middle of this spectrum. It can be defined[6] as a grouping of a subset of a jurisdiction's tribunals under one adjudicative leader, with each tribunal maintaining its own statutory jurisdiction[7], subject matter expertise, stakeholder relationships and (apart from the overall Chair) its distinct membership.[8]

There are few examples of clustering around the world, and none in North America, which bring together ELTO's particular group of high profile, high-impact tribunals[9]. However, the Victorian Civil and Administrative Tribunal's creative development and use of lists within an amalgamated structure, and the New South Wales Land and Environment Court's 30 years of experience with a subject matter jurisdiction which closely parallels ELTO's overall jurisdiction, provide particularly significant experiential bases to support further comparative analyses.

B.   The Ontario Model

1.   *The Legislation: A Focus on Linkages and Synergies*

Ontario's first cluster of tribunals[10], ELTO, is at the heart of Ontario's ongoing administrative justice reforms. It was created to demonstrate that clustered tribunals can be more efficient than the same tribunals operating alone and that the matters they deal with can be addressed more effectively, and access to justice and the quality of tribunal services can be significantly improved, when they operate as part of a cluster. It is widely seen as a key indicator of Ontario's commitment to improve and modernize administrative justice overall.

Clustering in Ontario started informally, with the five tribunals which constitute ELTO[11] being brought to one location and placed under one ministry[12], and with the administrative infrastructure for all being amalgamated[13]. This process was accelerated with the appointment in November, 2009 of one Executive Chair to lead all of the clustered tribunals, and with the introduction and passage that Fall of legislation to create the legal structure for clustering.

That *Act*, the *Administrative Tribunals Accountability, Governance and Accountability Act, 2009*[14], (the *Tribunals Act*) provides a broad framework for the governance of all adjudicative[15] tribunals in Ontario. It deals with matters such as requirements to prepare and publish documents outlining core structural elements of tribunals (their missions, mandates, qualifications for members, service standards, complaints policies, ethics plans, etc[16]) and requires that appointments of members of a tribunal be made on the recommendation of its tribunal chair following a merit-based competition[17]. In the *Tribunals Act*, the government is also given the power to designate two or more tribunals "as a cluster" if the matters they deal with are such that "they can operate more effectively and efficiently as part of a cluster than alone"[18].

The particular way in which the provision governing clustering was drafted appears to send some important messages as to the Legislative intention behind this concept. Pursuant to the *Act*, in order to cluster two or more tribunals the government is to have looked at the subject matters they deal with and determined that there is something about those subject matters that can be better dealt with in a clustered structure. In the Ontario approach to clustering, the rationale for a cluster accordingly lies in the subject matters of the constituent tribunals. And, once the government uses its clustering power, the tribunals are designated "as a cluster"[19]. This gives tangibility to the concept of a cluster — a cluster is more than a label: once constituted, it becomes an entity recognized by statute with its own identity and purpose.

Importantly, the legislated rationale for a cluster is not limited to improvements in efficiency, which we might equate with procedure and administration, but equally includes improved effectiveness in how the subject matters within the cluster are dealt with. There are two key concepts here: i) effectiveness, not just efficiency; and ii) effectiveness in relation to substance (subject mater [*sic*]), not just process.

The Act goes on to say that the accountability and governance documents which all tribunals in Ontario are required to have must, in the case of a cluster, be jointly developed and entered into[20]. As noted above, these documents include, among others, a mission statement and a description of the skills and attributes required of tribunal members. The fact that the tribunals in a cluster must jointly develop a mission, and a joint statement of the members' attributes and qualifications, indicates again that we are directed to look at a cluster as more than an administrative home for a collection of tribunals.

Once a cluster is created, the government may appoint an Executive Chair to oversee and manage all the tribunals in the cluster. That Executive Chair then, by statute, has all of the powers and duties assigned to the chair of each of the constituent tribunals by any statute, regulation, order-in-council or directive[21]. This choice to vest all of the previous chairs' powers and duties in just one chair signals an intention to go beyond a coordinating chair model to create an integrating chair.

Overall, it would seem that these provisions evince an intention by the Legislature to develop clusters of tribunals for purposes that go beyond administrative efficiencies and coordination. After all, such goals could be achieved by appointing outside efficiency experts and by encouraging the tribunals to work together. Referring to subject matter effectiveness and appointing a single chair for a number of tribunals send a stronger message about coordination and signal a more serious desire for change. They suggest a need to interpret and apply a cluster mandate in a way which gives effect to this integrative legislative intention, subject only to respecting the unchanged statutory mandates of the constituent tribunals.

2. *Synopsis of Key Features*

Seen from the international perspective, the following key elements of Ontario's clustering model may be of particular interest[22]:

- Tribunals are grouped into a cluster in part because of a discerned linkage among the subject matters over which each of them has jurisdiction. This differs from approaches which group tribunals by reference to the kinds of powers they exercise or matters they deal with (for example, reviews of governmental action vs. disputes between parties, or purely private matters vs. matters also involving the public interest); or by the kinds of adjudicative models they employ (for example, the "full" adversarial approach vs. an active, inquiring adjudicative model); or by the users of the services of the clustered tribunals (for example homeowners re: property tax and renovation issues, or businesses re: licensing and regulatory matters).

- Each clustered tribunal has a distinct legal jurisdiction, even though the subjects within a tribunal's jurisdiction (for example, a wetland) may also, for other purposes, fall within the jurisdiction of another tribunal. As a corollary, each tribunal is likely to maintain a distinct set of stakeholders.

- Each clustered tribunal has a complement of adjudicators appointed specifically to it, with exclusive jurisdiction over the matters coming before that tribunal. This feature may be of particular relevance to those who are concerned about the dilution of subject matter expertise in amalgamated models, as it ensures both initial expertise[23] in the matters before a tribunal and increases the likelihood that there will be a sufficient diet of that work to maintain that expertise among its members.

- Although containing these features of distinctiveness, the cluster must give effect to the legislative intent behind it by using the fact of being clustered to improve the effectiveness with which each constituent tribunal discharges its specific statutory mandate. This appears to call for efforts to enrich the jurisprudence of each tribunal by bringing a broader range of knowledge, experience and perspectives to bear on the matters that come before it, and by fostering an enhanced ability to see and respond appropriately to areas of subject matter connectedness.

- Through selective cross-appointments, extensive cross-training[24] and co-location, the experiential and knowledge bases of adjudicators are broadened. This not only promotes the subject matter synergies referred to immediately above, but as well recognizes the importance of common, high standards of accessible adjudicative practices across a cluster. At the same time, it should provide increased job satisfaction and career mobility for adjudicators.

- The leadership structure of the tribunal need not be established by strict adherence to the previous governance hierarchies of the constituent tribunals. The *Act* contemplates an Executive Chair with all of the powers and duties of the previous chair of each tribunal. Beyond that, it permits, but does not require, the appointment of an Associate Chair for each tribunal. While that appears to be the direction the government is taking for ELTO, there is nothing to prevent having no Associate Chairs, or having Associate Chairs who are responsible for more than one tribunal, or, perhaps, appointing them on a non-tribunal basis, such as, for example, by cluster function such as mediation services, professional development, adjudication practices, expedited matters, and so on. Even where Associate Chairs are appointed on a tribunal-specific basis, the job descriptions for those Associates can make it clear that their key responsibilities are to the governance and development of the cluster as a whole[25]. In addition, the Act permits the Associate Chairs to be appointed as Alternate Executive Chairs of the cluster as a whole, further reinforcing their corporate role.

- While the back office functions of all five tribunals have been amalgamated into a single administrative service for matters like finance and communications, tribunal-specific staff are being retained for the case-processing functions of the constituent tribunals. This reflects the view that adjudicators and all others in the tribunal who process cases should be seen as a team who together serve the members of the public bringing disputes forward for resolution. Having staff with a sophisticated knowledge of the caselaw, stakeholders and procedures of each tribunal is essential to building and fostering that capacity, and [to] the reciprocal respect and trust it calls for between adjudicators and staff.

- The five ELTO tribunals now operate under a common mission and mandate statement and a common set of core values[26]; an ELTO-wide conflict of interest policy and code of conduct are nearing completion as this is being written.

- The five tribunals were co-located as a step prepatory [sic] to the appointment of an Executive Chair and the legislative recognition of the cluster. They operate on four floors of an office building in central Toronto. While initially each tribunal had more or less distinct space in that building, steps are underway to redesign the premises so that all adjudicators are on the same floor, the senior management group is housed together, tribunal counsel are co-located, and so on.

In addition to these unique — at least viewed collectively — attributes, Ontario's cluster has many of the features common to amalgamations or mergers. These include:

- The exponentiation of the reach of a single leadership team, and hence the ability to modernize the operations of a number of tribunals (increased professional development, effective use of decision-quality mechanisms, a user focus, more active adjudication, etc) in a consistent, expedited and harmonious way.

- Finding opportunities to provide processes tailored to users whose interests may cross tribunal boundaries, for example, homeowners seeking a minor variance (dealt with by the OMB) or appealing a property assessment (dealt with by the ARB). As is the case in amalgamations, a cluster may be able to create de facto cross-tribunal "lists" within the cluster through cross-appointments and unified codes of procedures for classes of cases which fall within the jurisdiction of more than one of the clustered tribunals, but particularly affect the same specific parts of the province's population.

- Using the expertise and experience of a broad pool of adjudicators and staff to develop improved approaches to common adjudicative issues such as the use of expert evidence or managing complex cases.

- Increasing the quality of decisions because of the multi-tribunal pool of expertise.

- Offering, in addition to the specific benefits of having a larger pool of staff and adjudicators noted immediately above, the ability to better ensure diversity more generally, with the consequential benefit that the cluster as a whole is more reflective of the face and perspectives of the entire province.

- Making it easier to maintain a pool of adjudicators competent to conduct proceedings in more than one language.

- Improving the geographic reach of the tribunals where members reside across the province and are qualified for cross-appointment within the cluster.

- Providing, through cross-appointments, an enhanced ability to rely upon full-time members.

3. *Some Current Issues*

The above matters all speak to the potential benefits of the ELTO cluster. However, compelling as the theory of clustering may be, and despite the encouragement offered by some of the experience elsewhere, there are a myriad of small and large management and leadership challenges involved in converting a very bare bones statutory framework into a functioning cluster which is respected both internally and externally. Highlights among them are the following:

- Protection of subject matter expertise, and public confidence in that expertise, while also encouraging broad professional development and improving subject matter cross-fertilization[27] (maximizing subject matter synergies);

- Issues around cross-appointments (integrative value vs. potential loss of tribunal-specific expertise and collegiality, or the appearance of such loss leading to concerns from tribunal members and stakeholders if such appointments are not selective and strategic);

- Conflict of interest issues across the cluster, particularly for part time members with active practices in areas dealt with by the cluster[28];

- Providing subject matter leadership within each tribunal without Balkanizing them;

- Building an integrated leadership cadre and culture for the cluster as a whole given the varying cultures and ways of doing business which may have developed in the clustered tribunals over time, and perhaps particularly given the practical reality of the work involved in overseeing the day to day operations of several busy tribunals while also leading the overall strategic development and management of the cluster. And, more generally, managing the amount of time required to operationalize a cluster at the administrative level in a way which also permits a modernization agenda to be advanced.

- Preserving innovative adjudicative techniques which may be challenged if a tribunal using them is clustered with a number of more traditional tribunals;

- Getting the benefit of a richer base for decision-reviews and finding opportunities to leverage training, without raising concerns that one subject area or tribunal is being preferred or without diluting expertise;
- Creating integrative office environments without losing the benefits of close collaboration at specific tribunals.

Conclusion

Despite the above-noted challenges, it seems clear that when properly conceived and resourced clustering can provide a mechanism to obtain efficiencies in infrastructure usage and to develop and implement modern tribunal practices. It also offers the potential to be built in a way which increases the effectiveness with which each clustered tribunal applies expertise[29] to discharge its particular statutory jurisdiction, and, as Part II of this paper will suggest, which increases access to justice.

PART II: DESIGNING STRUCTURE, PROCESS AND PROCEDURE TO ACHIEVE ACCESS TO JUSTICE

Before exploring ways in which tribunals — and clustering — can increase access to justice, it is important to unbundle that term and to give equal weight to both elements of the phrase 'access to justice'. Although so frequently used that it trips off the tongue or pen as a single concept, two important and analytically distinct thoughts are contained within it. The first, access, is a means; the second, justice, is an end. Thus while access primarily involves the ability to be meaningfully and equitably heard by a decision maker, justice adds the very important dimension of a principled and fair result, based on the merits, and unaffected by differing resources or individual or systemic disadvantage. Seen in this way access to justice might colloquially be phrased as 'getting to a good place in a good way'.

This Part will first outline a wide range of ways in which tribunals can actively promote access to justice for all tribunal users or potential users. It will focus on matters which many or most tribunals can achieve within existing budgets and statutory powers, or with only modest adjustments to them. In particular, broader access concepts such as intervener funding or enhanced legal aid, and institutional justice concepts such as tenure and the level of remuneration for adjudicators, are not the focus of this paper. Similarly, although access to justice is often considered in relation to other important matters such as plain language, practical guides, clear forms, and accessible hearing rooms, this paper's focus is on [] how the structures, policies and procedures a tribunal uses in <u>adjudication</u> can be tailored to advance access to justice[30].

While the procedural and structural initiatives discussed in this Part are not particularly novel, it is perhaps novel — and instructive — to view them through an access to justice lens. This not only provides a unifying theme to make coherent the implementation of a series of otherwise discrete and sometimes controversial reforms, but as well provides a theme which is very likely to engender significant public support to counter the more entrenched views which otherwise may dominate conversations about these kinds of reforms. Part II will end with a brief analysis of how a clustered or amalgamated approach to tribunals can facilitate the adoption of these measures, and hence may itself be a means to advance access to justice.

The access to justice initiatives canvassed in Part II run the gamut from the atmosphere which prevails throughout a tribunal, through to its internal review mechanisms. Several of them cover territory which is often a central part of the debate about the respective merits of the adversarial and inquisitorial systems of adjudication. It is accordingly important to stress at the outset that this paper does not situate its discussion of access to justice within that debate[31]. The issue for this paper is not whether tribunals should move towards a new adjudicative model, but rather it is to outline reforms that alone, or especially in combination, may increase access to justice wherever the underlying system or starting-point.

This approach reflects the view that 'first-principles' debates about which total system is preferable can not only impede making any significant change, but can also obscure the ways in which sound practices from varying systems can be integrated into a number of models. For example, some of the elements of the active-collaborative model discussed in this paper are quite consistent with elements found within adversarial systems, especially, but not only, in pre-trial matters. In any event, the paper suggests that the possible reforms be considered on their individual and collective merits, and not through the often ideological lens of a total-system debate.

Setting that debate aside, this section of the paper will explore, <u>from a user perspective</u>, what kinds of changes to, or extrapolations from, existing structures, processes and policies have the potential to significantly increase access to justice at tribunals. It suggests that there is indeed a very wide range of areas in which initiatives can be brought forward by tribunals to achieve that objective. These ideas can be 'mixed and matched' in various jurisdictions at various times and for varying subjects and user groups. A seismic shift from one model of adjudication to another is not needed to draw upon these initiatives to meaningfully improve access to justice at any given tribunal or grouping of tribunals.

Illustrative Access Initiatives

The following initiatives are put forward in brief outline form to illustrate the many mechanisms open to tribunals which have the potential to improve access to justice. While in some instances initial reflections are offered on how an initiative might best be put into practice, each would still require context-specific analysis and fleshing-out, ideally in close collaboration with stake-holders, before being added to a tribunal's procedural repertoire.

As well, each needs to be considered not only from the perspective of those who now find it difficult or impossible to equitably use tribunal services, important as that perspective is, but as well from two additional perspectives. The first is that of those who, with varying degrees of ease, already effectively navigate tribunal services. They too can benefit from reduced costs and delays when modern adjudicative practices are used, and perhaps as well when the credibility of the processes they use, and the decisions they seek to rely on, are enhanced through broader access. The second is the perspective of the public at large, and indeed the public interest, which also benefit when tribunal decisions can be based on a full spectrum of relevant perspectives.

1. Commensurate Proceedings

Where proceedings are managed to ensure that they are commensurate with the core issues needed to decide a case, proceedings are neither longer nor more complex than they have to be to fairly decide the determinative issues. As a result, a significant deterrent is removed for those who are less able to afford the cost in money or time of longer processes, or who are less adept or comfortable in complex and protracted matters. Even for those who may have sufficient resources to engage in more costly or lengthy litigation, there is neither private benefit nor a public interest in having cases go on longer than needed to reach a fair outcome on the merits.

Indeed, a purely economic analysis would conclude that, apart from those who work in the legal field, no party benefits from protracted and costly litigation, except perhaps by being able to outlast the other parties through dint of resources. Assuming that this is not a strategy a tribunal would want to endorse, the notion that there is value in having litigation last longer than needed to determine the core issues falls away. So too does the argument that procedural fairness requires that parties have the right to solely determine the course of the litigation. Parties have the right to be heard, not to litigate.[32]

In this connection, it is also appropriate to take into account the reality that limited public resources are dedicated to the justice system, and perhaps particularly to its administrative justice arm. The misuse, or unnecessary use, of those precious resources by one set of litigants automatically reduces the capacity of the system as a whole to meet the needs of others in a timely and effective way[33]. When that is allowed to happen, access to justice is undermined.

Even where the work of ensuring that proceedings are commensurate to the nature of the matter requires as much additional adjudicator time outside the hearing, to shape the proceeding, as it saves in hearing time, and thus does not enlarge the capacity of the tribunal to hear more matters, it can significantly enhance access to, and the experience of, justice at tribunals.

2. *Standing and Participation*

Rules of standing and participation can be designed to validate the relevance of a broad range of interests and to bring additional voices to the table. This approach can improve the range, and the contextual analysis of, the information available to the decision-maker and can facilitate a breadth of participation which promotes the credibility of the process and the quality and legitimacy of its outcomes[34]. In a virtuous circle this can then further encourage people who have an interest in the matter, and who have relevant information, to come forward to add their information and analysis to the record on which a decision will be made.

As with certain other matters discussed here, these considerations can be particularly important where tribunal decisions must reflect the public interest, and not just resolve a *lis* between the parties. In these circumstances, more open processes can help ensure that the adjudicator has the information needed to make the required decision in a way which reflects the community's shared, long-term interest in a good outcome, rather than just the information needed to declare a winner.

3. *Welcoming Public Participation*

An open door will not alone bring a broader set of views to a tribunal. At least two "attitudinal" approaches are also necessary. First, tribunals must ensure an atmosphere at counters and in hearing/mediation rooms that is supportive of and welcoming to those who are not regular users of the tribunal, and that avoids creating the impression of a club[35] composed of insiders. As with other issues, a "whole of tribunal" approach is required, in which staff at all levels, as well as adjudicators, are committed to creating, and have the training and support to create, an atmosphere which is experienced as inclusive by all.

Second, tribunals must, through their actions and in their decisions, demonstrate that they have a serious interest in all relevant views being put forward. Although perhaps initially counterintuitive, this can mean being relatively strict about requiring those who wish to participate to explain how they have a relevant point to make, and, having done so, that they provide a focused presentation on that point. Simply indulging those who want to say something to a tribunal can all too easily lead to proceedings being conducted in a way which creates the impression, and sometimes reflects the reality, that the non-traditional participants are being pandered to, and that their views were never intended to get serious consideration. Enhancing access to justice means facilitating "informed participation", which ensures not only that the hearing will be conducted efficiently but as well that participation is effective.

Similarly, where there has been broader participation, adjudicators should take care to give it reasoned consideration in their decisions. This should go beyond an isolated recitation of the fact of participation or the points made, to instead demonstrate that the perspective has been considered and integrated throughout the adjudicator's reasoning wherever it is relevant.

4. Effective Participation by the Self-represented

Much has been written about how adjudicators can assist those without representation to participate in legal processes in a meaningful way[36]. This paper will not attempt to summarize that literature. For our purposes, what is important is that tribunal processes be reconsidered with a view to how they can be adjusted to facilitate the reality, where that is the case, that a significant number of tribunal users will not be represented.

This is a fundamentally different approach than taking traditional procedures as a given, and then bolting-on various accessories and ancillary aids to try to make those procedures less daunting for those without representation. It calls for looking at processes through the eyes of those without representation, and more generally, through the eyes of the parties, rather than their representatives. Truly accessible processes will be those which are understandable and navigable by parties, whether or not they are represented. In much the same way as with modern approaches to accessibility and accommodation for persons with disabilities, the focus should not be on accommodating "special needs", but rather on working to incorporate universal design features.

But, care should be taken to identify these issues, and possible responses to them, with users of tribunal services, including those who have been, or can speak for, unrepresented participants. When this is done, a different perspective may emerge, such as the expectation of process or formality which many individuals may bring to a hearing based on movies or television programs. For some, an untraditional process, or informality itself, may be taken as a signal that their claim is not seen as significant because it has not been granted the grandness of a traditional, formal, court-like approach. For the purposes of this paper, what matters is not the specifics of how processes are made understandable and accessible, but rather the inclusive re-examination of adjudicative systems to improve access to justice[,] to tribunal processes, and to a just outcome, for all participants, whether or not they are represented.

5. Expert Adjudicators

Increased use of expert adjudicators can reduce the need for technical and expert evidence[37]. It can also permit adjudicators to confidently reduce the issues in play and the amount of evidence heard overall, based on an expert appreciation of what is required to fairly decide the matter. And, where a tribunal through its recruitment, training and retention policies, and its adjudication practices, is well-known for its expertise, parties will have confidence in these rulings and will be inclined to respect rather than challenge them.

The resulting shorter, better-focused proceedings will help ensure that outcomes are based on the relevant evidence and issues, rather than on the resources of the respective parties. This will provide confidence among all potential tribunal users that they can participate in a cost-effective way, and that their evidence and submissions will be properly understood and fairly evaluated, and in these ways will encourage participation in tribunal proceedings.

Of the above matters, managing expert evidence will likely provide the greatest challenge to a tribunal. Depending on the nature and complexity of the matters dealt with by a tribunal, expert adjudicators alone[38] will not routinely eliminate the need for parties to retain experts and present expert evidence. Highly complex and technical matters will often require expert evidence. And unless a tribunal employs an investigatory approach, and is properly resourced to fully canvass and bring forward the needed technical evidence, it will be the parties' responsibility to do so. In those circumstances, even though expert adjudicators will lead to efficiencies in a number of ways, including in how expert evidence is managed and heard, their use will not eliminate the need for the parties to bring forward expert evidence, or any inequalities in their respective resources to do so.

6. *Active-Collaborative Adjudication*[39]

For our purposes, the active-collaborative style of adjudication is one in which expert adjudicators take an active role in narrowing and focusing issues both before and during hearings, and in eliciting and testing evidence at hearings, to help keep proceedings commensurate, accessible, and navigable for all parties and participants. It will usually be supported by rules which direct the parties to provide the kind of information a tribunal needs to be active in an effective manner. For example, rules can ensure that the adjudicator who will hear a matter receives and is expected to review detailed application and response questionnaires, documents to be relied on and statements of witnesses intended to be called well in advance of the hearing (or any pre-hearing conference dealing with the shape of the hearing) and is informed as early as possible of the positions the parties will be taking and the outcomes they are seeking to achieve.

These kinds of rules not only permit the early and effective focusing of a case and management of the parties' participation, but as well allow the adjudicator to identify areas on which additional evidence is needed from the parties[40]. Such rules may also make it clear that the proceeding is to start with a clear definition from the adjudicator, after hearing from the parties, of what is really in dispute, and what the tribunal must determine to resolve that dispute. They may also give the adjudicator express powers to elicit evidence in chief from witnesses called by the parties, and to both control and conduct cross examination to help ensure equitable access to, and a balanced record[41] for, the tribunal's decision-making[42].

This approach is referred to as collaborative as well as active because the parties remain responsible for adducing evidence, and because it requires the adjudicator to review with the parties, either at a pre-hearing conference or at the commencement of the hearing, or both, what issues remain in dispute and what additional evidence, beyond the record already filed, is needed to fairly determine the matter. In some kinds of matters, this can take the form of a "consultation" in which determinations can be made as to the matters on which *viva voce* evidence is necessary.[43]

The distinction between this approach and pre-hearings or pre-trials in traditional adjudicative models, is that if no consensus is reached, the adjudicator, after hearing the parties, can determine the issues to be addressed, and what evidence is required to determine the matter.

Overall, in an active-collaborative adjudication model the adjudicator's sophisticated knowledge of the subject area and procedures is deployed to the benefit of all parties, and to advance the public interest in an efficient proceeding, and a just outcome consistent with applicable laws, precedents and policies. The model can help to ensure that a party's inadequate knowledge of the issues or jurisprudence, or their inability to appreciate what needs to be proven or to see gaps in the record, or to effectively lead evidence or test the evidence from other parties, do not impede a fair and just outcome. In these ways, both access and justice can be advanced.

As noted, to support this approach, detailed rules of practice are highly desirable. Such rules enhance "informed participation" by signalling to parties the types of information that will be required, or expected by the tribunal, in the adjudication of the case. In addition, they enhance "informed access" by clearly setting out shared expectations of the respective responsibilities of the parties and the tribunal, and of the process.

As well, detailed rules promote consistency in approach across a tribunal as all adjudicators are working from a clear set of standards[44]. Such rules can also provide a clear, integrated framework for the exercise of a more active style, and thus may help a reviewing court understand the context in which a particular ruling was made[45]. And, where the rules are developed in consultation with stakeholders, significant issues and potential pitfalls can be identified early and addressed appropriately, myths and misunderstandings can be put to rest in an informal setting, and a consensus around new approaches can be nurtured.

7. *Controlling the Use of Expert Evidence*

Tribunals can shape their proceedings to better define the role for experts, limiting the advantage enjoyed by those who can afford more, more senior, or better prepared, experts. Tribunals can also use techniques such as joint experts, panels of experts or tribunal-appointed experts to help ensure neutral information and level the playing field. And, as a minimum, they can work to avoid creating a culture in which expert testimony, whether or not strictly opinion evidence, is seen to be privileged over non-expert evidence.

8. Decision Quality/Framework Decisions

By putting in place processes to ensure high-quality, consistent decisions, a tribunal can enhance public confidence in having recourse to it, and thus encourage individuals, regardless of their resources, to make use of its services, and to accept the tribunal's decisions as final. Where these goals are achieved, the final resolution of matters is expedited and, as well, the tribunal's decisions will provide clear guidance for the future and thereby reduce the need for litigation and advance the interests of justice.

Particularly where the review of government action is involved, decisions can be expressly crafted to provide clear guidelines for government decision-makers, thus promoting consistency "on the ground" and further reducing the need for often-costly litigation. Indeed, the Land and Environment Court in New South Wales appears to go beyond issuing framework decisions:

> The Court extrapolates principles from the cases and publishes them. The principles can be used by agencies in future decision-making.[46]

In these ways, a tribunal can provide ongoing access to justice without further recourse to the tribunal. This allows tribunal resources to be used to increase access for others by reducing delays in getting to their matters.

9. Reconsideration

Reconsideration of its decisions by a tribunal can reduce the need for costly and often complex appellate proceedings, which can be outside the reach of some participants whether as initiators or respondents. At the same time, however, its use requires considerable caution to avoid having tribunal decisions seen as "just first drafts". Properly used, reconsideration serves simply as a backstop for effective decision quality assurance mechanisms in a tribunal.

10. Engagement of Non-traditional Stakeholders

Broad and inclusive stakeholder engagement can advance access to justice by including and demonstrably valuing the views and perspectives of all categories of users of a tribunal, including those who are not traditionally seen as stakeholders. For many tribunals, stakeholders tend to be defined as the bar which practices before them and perhaps representatives of the significant repeat participants. This not only narrows the perspectives being offered to the tribunal, but as well it further reinforces the impression that other perspectives (or even classes of users or potential users of tribunal services) are not as welcome or valued, even in the context of a hearing.

Making the not-inconsiderable effort to meaningfully include more disparate interests will encourage a wider cross-section of users to feel fully welcome at the tribunal in all that it does. It will also ensure that the tribunal's processes are informed by all categories of potential users. And at the same time, getting out to[] and engaging with the wider community can help ensure that the tribunal has a better context for understanding the practical application of its mandate, and for designing its processes and procedures, including through a better appreciation of the real-life experiences of those who are not regular users of the tribunal.

11. Recruitment and Professional Development

Finally, access to justice is also advanced through recruitment processes and professional development initiatives which attract, develop and retain very high quality adjudicators and staff members. The resulting culture of excellence will not only itself attract increasingly strong candidates to the tribunal, but as well will inspire confidence in tribunal users that serious and thoughtful presentations are worth the time and effort they entail, thus simultaneously advancing both access and justice.

Clustering and Amalgamations as Potential Accelerants

Whether and how to integrate any or all of the above initiatives into the structure, procedures and policies of any given tribunal can be a daunting matter to contemplate. Each issue may have to be debated, each stakeholder group consulted, and each potential public relations issue dealt with, often in a context where the caseload, or the sensitivity of the issues, or limited tribunal policy and engagement capacity, make the effort not practical even where the benefits are seen to be great. The impediments to proceeding will be even greater where the stakeholder group that may benefit is simply too small or diffuse to effectively counter entrenched interests in any public dialogue.

But in several ways the context of a clustered or amalgamated tribunal can assist in achieving access to justice. First, at least in the early days, the creation of a new structure, for some or all of a jurisdiction's tribunals, creates an expectation of change. While the prospect of change may not always be welcomed, both internally and[] externally, amongst those who have found ways to make the system work to advance their interests, when governments propose tribunal amalgamation or clustering it is generally as part of an effort to improve the quality of administrative justice. Hence, change will be seen, or at least can be presented as, a positive step. And second, creating a new structure designed to improve overall effectiveness and efficiency will necessarily lead to a need to reflect upon existing tribunal process, procedures and policies, and thus provide a context for proposed changes.

As well, there is an economy of scale in bringing an access to justice initiative to a group of tribunals. Much of the policy development, consultation, rules drafting and communications planning can be unified, especially where tribunals with related subject matter jurisdictions are involved. Similarly, only one leadership team is needed to advance and manage the change agenda. And, for both of these reasons, conflicting approaches and messaging in rolling out access initiatives for a number of tribunals can be avoided, creating a climate in which the changes can be considered on their merits, without the small differences creating undue distractions.

At the level of the tribunals themselves, a clustered or amalgamated group of tribunals is likely to contain a larger pool of adjudicators and staff to draw upon for creativity and ideas as access initiatives are being developed. And, as access initiatives are rolled out, the potential to develop a critical mass of those who know how to use them effectively is much greater than in a single tribunal. Further efficiencies, and greater consistency, can also flow when a larger cadre of adjudicators and staff can be trained together on new approaches, ideas and understandings, and can support each other in using them.[47]

Finally, the scale of change can itself be a driving factor. Particularly if the involved tribunals are a large proportion of a jurisdiction's tribunals[48], or contain a significant number of its more respected ones, the ability to counter the sometimes stultifying inertia of the status quo can be dramatically increased. Change, even fundamental change, can become a mainstream endeavour rather than an isolated one.

PART III. THREE CANADIAN EXAMPLES OF THE ACTIVE-COLLABORATIVE APPROACH TO ADJUDICATION

In this Part the paper will outline three recent Canadian examples of what we are calling the active-collaborative adjudication model. One arose from a legislative reform initiative; the second was developed outside a legislated base, and then, with some refinements, was incorporated into Canada's largest class action settlement; and the third was developed in a tribunal's rules without any change in the legislation governing its procedural powers.

The purpose here is not to explore these models in depth, but only to draw from them ideas and approaches which may be of interest elsewhere, and on which comment from a broad international perspective will be highly informative on whether and how they should be further adopted and expanded in the Canadian context.

1.   The Human Rights Tribunal of Ontario

Through amendments brought forward in 2006, Ontario's *Human Rights Code*[49] is now a Canadian high-water mark for a legislated framework establishing an expert and active-collaborative[50] model of adjudication.

The amendments were brought forward as part of a move to a direct access model of human rights protection[51]. They give Ontario's Human Rights Tribunal the express legislative authority to adopt non-traditional, non-adversarial approaches to adjudication, and a specific direction to use the procedures and practices which in its opinion "offer the best opportunity for a fair, just and expeditious resolution of the merits"[52]. Most importantly, however, those powers and that duty were clearly anchored in a comprehensive legislated framework that evinces a clear legislative intention to permit a fundamentally different approach to adjudicating human rights matters.

The *Code* left most of the design of the new direct access adjudication system to be done by the Tribunal through its rules[53]. However, in both the express language used, and the specific powers granted, the legislation is clear that non-adversarial procedures[54] are fully intended and supported, and that Tribunal rules to that effect prevail over Ontario's quite traditional, adversarial-based legislated code of procedures for tribunals[55].

Specifically, the legislation authorizes the Tribunal to make rules which permit its adjudicators to[56]:

(i) define or narrow the issues required to dispose of an application and limit the evidence and submissions of the parties on such issues;

(ii) determine the order in which the issues and evidence in a proceeding will be presented;

(iii) conduct examinations in chief or cross-examinations of a witness;

(iv) prescribe the stages of its processes at which preliminary, procedural or interlocutory matters will be determined;

(v) make or cause to be made such examinations of records and such other inquiries as it considers necessary in the circumstances; and

(vi) require a party to a proceeding or another person to produce any document, information or thing; provide a statement or oral or affidavit evidence; or in the case of a party to the proceeding, adduce evidence or produce witnesses who are reasonably within the party's control[57].

In these provisions, the Legislature has given the Tribunal the power to shape and control the hearing, and to provide for matters even more clearly anathema to the adversarial system such as conducting, as opposed to just limiting, cross-examination. Importantly, it specifically framed this grant of authority as permitting approaches that are alternatives to <u>adversarial</u> procedures, and not just to the less specific-concept of alternatives to <u>traditional adjudicative</u> procedures. Reinforcing this authorization to apply alternative hearing approaches, the *Code* provides[58] that both the Tribunal's rules and the *Code* itself:

> shall be liberally construed to permit the Tribunal to adopt practices and procedures, including alternatives to traditional adjudicative or adversarial procedures that, in the opinion of the Tribunal, will facilitate fair, just and expeditious resolutions of the merits of the matters before it[59].

Importantly, the Legislature enacted these changes as part of a coherent package of reforms governing how the Tribunal is to operate. The *Act* was the first legislation in Canada to require open, competitive, merit based appointments of members. The requirements include[60]:

(i) experience, knowledge or training with respect to human rights law and issues;
(ii) aptitude for impartial adjudication; and
(iii) aptitude for applying the alternative adjudicative practices and procedures that may be set out in the Tribunal rules.

These requirements accomplish two key things. First, they establish a legislated link between the concepts of an active adjudication model, and an expert cohort of adjudicators. This link is fundamental to both the workability and credibility of active approaches to adjudication in a legal landscape dominated by a more adversarial model. And, second, persons seeking appointment to the tribunal are put on notice that they must bring to the Tribunal an aptitude for working, and a willingness to work, outside the adversarial paradigm.

After going on to provide for the specific new powers set out above, the *Code* then addresses the opposite end of the process, and reinforces the Tribunal's ability to employ an active adjudicative approach, by creating a special standard to be applied if the exercise of discretion under the Tribunal's rules is challenged. This special standard is in addition to the general privative clause found in the *Code*, which insulates the Tribunal from reversal unless a decision is found to be patently unreasonable[61]. It provides that a decision cannot be set aside because of the way discretion was exercised under the rules unless the exercise of discretion "caused a substantial wrong which affected the final disposition of the matter"[62].

This provision would appear to establish three important principles. First, dissonance with traditional modes of procedure is not a reason to reverse a Tribunal decision: only substantial wrongs may be considered on review. Second, even a substantial wrong is not sufficient to reverse a proceeding unless the result has been affected. And, flowing from the second matter above, it would appear that exercises of discretion under the rules cannot be challenged until the proceeding is concluded, meaning that even those who are wedded to traditional adversarial practices will nonetheless have to conduct proceedings under the Tribunal's non-adversarial model rather than bringing pre-emptive strikes to try to prevent new approaches from even being tried out.

Overall we see in this Ontario initiative a unified framework which calls for a tribunal to be staffed by expert adjudicators, with an aptitude for alternative adjudicative practices, and then permits them to be given extensive non-traditional and non-adversarial powers. It goes on to require that this grant of authority and rules made pursuant to it be interpreted broadly to permit these alternatives, and that the tribunal use procedures which offer the best opportunity for justice and expedition. It then insulates the exercise of discretion under the rules from being overturned unless it has caused a substantial wrong which affected the outcome. In the result, it appears that the new powers, which might be more easily challenged without this coherent legislative context, are substantially protected by being enveloped in a comprehensive legislative regime.

2. The Indian Residential School (IRS) Dispute Resolution Model

This out of court adjudication model[63], now known as the Independent Assessment Process (IAP), is being used to resolve over 20,000 claims of sexual and serious physical abuse arising from Canada's Indian Residential Schools. Two matters relevant to this paper's discussion of the active-collaborative adjudication model are found in the IAP's blending of the adversarial and inquisitorial systems. They are the conduct of examinations in chief and cross examinations exclusively by neutral adjudicators, and the use of neutral expert witnesses selected and instructed by the adjudicator.

The IRS dispute resolution model was initially developed by Canada's federal government through consultations with former students, counsel who represent former students, and representatives of the four denominations which operated the various schools. Published as a detailed procedural code, it was then offered to former students on an opt-in basis, whether or not they had previously commenced a civil action, and without prejudice to their right to pursue an action in the courts if they were dissatisfied with the result of the adjudication.

As of 2005, about three thousand former students had come forward to use the model, at which point it became subsumed in class action negotiations to resolve all of the issues arising from the operation of the schools[64]. Those negotiations, led by the Hon. Frank Iacobucci, a former Justice of the Supreme Court of Canada, included as one key element the adoption of an adjudication model to address individual claims of sexual and serious physical abuse. With some enlargements to its scope, the pre-existing IRS dispute resolution procedural code was essentially adopted for that part of that settlement. All elements of the settlement, which at some $4 billion represents Canada's largest class action settlement to date, were then approved as fair and reasonable by superior courts in nine different Canadian jurisdictions[65].

The IRS model was designed to replicate, as closely as possible, the levels of damages awarded by the courts in sexual and physical abuse lawsuits. In the voluntary opt-in phase, awards could and did exceed $200,000. When, pursuant to the class action settlement, the model became essentially the only avenue to resolve claims, higher awards, up to just over $500,000, became possible within the model[66]. In the result, the unique features of the model should be considered in light of the fact that it has been adopted by the federal government, plaintiffs' counsel, the former students, and the churches, and approved by the Courts, to determine very serious matters involving very serious amounts of compensation.

For our purposes, only two elements of the model will be reviewed[67]. The first is that the model permits only the neutral[68] adjudicator to question or cross-examine any witness other than an expert witness. While having its genesis in the desire to assure sexual and physical abuse claimants that they would not be subject to inappropriate cross-examinations, the model was also based on the expertise which specially-trained[69] adjudicators could bring to determining and then eliciting the evidence they needed to resolve a given case[70].

Given that serious issues and significant sums, as well as personal and institutional reputations[,] were at stake, the adoption of inquisitorial model techniques for the eliciting[71] and testing of testimony, other than from experts, is particularly significant, as it does not permit counsel for the claimant, government or church to examine or cross-examine most witnesses.

As this departs dramatically from the approach which is familiar to most civil litigation counsel, and to at least their institutional clients, some recognition of the adversarial system was required to obtain agreement to the model. In the end, a unique blending of the two systems on this point was developed. Pursuant to that blend, where counsel are not permitted to question a witness (which is the case for the vast majority of witnesses in these matters), they can require the adjudicator to put any desired line of questioning to the witness. This can be done before the hearing, along with an identification of areas counsel believe need particular scrutiny at the hearing[72], or at the hearing itself. With only limited discretion over whether the issue will be pursued, but full control over the actual questions, the adjudicator must act as requested[73]. And, counsel can require the adjudicator to hear any witness with relevant evidence, except an expert witness (see below).[74]

Although this degree of party involvement is incorporated in the model, the model makes it clear to the adjudicators that they must take the lead in eliciting and testing testimony from the parties' witnesses. Their role at a hearing is not to wait for questions to be proposed by counsel, but rather to lead and test the evidence[75]. The hearing is not counsel-driven; the process simply permits counsel to intervene where matters, in their view, are being or may be missed.

Consistent with the distinction between investigative processes and inquiring ones, the model does not permit the adjudicators to call their own evidence. The adversarial concept of party control thus applies to the evidence to be called, as well to insistence on lines of questioning. These significant roles for counsel respect the view that they may often know their case, and often the case they have to meet, better than an adjudicator. That knowledge leads to their being able to assess what evidence is needed, as well as to an awareness during the proceeding of issues that are not being fully developed in the evidence, or are not being properly tested. In part for these reasons (see below), the model also permits counsel to question expert witnesses.

A second aspect of the IRS process which is relevant to the active-collaborative adjudication model is the way it structures the provision of expert evidence. The approach taken here was again to blend adjudicator control with party input. Adjudicator control comes from the core rule that expert evidence is to come from a neutral expert, chosen and instructed by the adjudicator. Party involvement comes from the rule that the expert has to be chosen from a list approved in advance by representatives of the four stakeholders[76] and, as noted above, from counsel being allowed to directly question an expert witness.

The lists of experts are standing lists, selected by representatives of the institutional parties as being broadly acceptable to all. A fresh list is not developed for each case. This not only expedites the selection process in individual cases, but as well removes from it the strategic considerations counsel might otherwise try to bring to the generation of the list.

Once an adjudicator selects an expert from the list, it is for the adjudicator to instruct the expert on what the live issues are and to arrange for them to give evidence. The adjudicator provides the expert with a transcript of the hearing, and any relevant records that have been filed. The adjudicator then briefs the expert on the adjudicator's preliminary findings so that, to the greatest extent possible, their opinion can be based on the facts that are likely to be found[77]. This removes a common source of complexity where expert evidence is given. The expert's report is tabled with the parties, who may then require that the expert give oral evidence, and may question the expert at a resumed hearing[78].

In the result, the selection of an expert, and the obtaining of their opinion, are greatly expedited. The generic acceptability of each potential expert has been pre-determined, taking into account the interests of all stakeholder groups. The adjudicator then chooses the expert for a particular case and briefs them on the facts that are likely to be found, and on the exact issue on which their opinion is needed. This removes partisan tactics from what is supposed to be a process of providing the adjudicator with information needed to decide a particular case, and at the same time removes the difficulties often caused by injecting conflicting expert opinions into the adjudicative process.

Overall, in both of the ways outlined in this discussion, the IRS model demonstrates how a move to an active adjudication approach, even to the extent of barring party-examination and cross-examination of witnesses and having the adjudicator select and brief expert witnesses, can be made palatable where a strong rationale can be demonstrated, and where certain of the core interests and values of the adversarial system are respected.

3. The Environmental Review Tribunal's Rules for Green Energy Appeals

The green energy rules published in July, 2010 by Ontario's Environmental Review Tribunal (ERT) are of interest as they show how a tribunal, without any new legislated authority in relation to its procedures, can adopt a more active or collaborative style of adjudication to respond to a new substantive mandate. The mandate at issue here, recently given to the ERT, is to determine appeals which any resident of the province may bring against government approvals of green energy projects[79].

These appeals are expected to be complex because of the reactions which projects like wind farms sometimes engender, and because of the test which the Tribunal must apply in determining them:

(a)   serious harm to human health; or

(b)   serious and irreversible harm to plant life, animal life or the natural environment[80].

Under the legislation providing for those approvals and the appeals against them, the Tribunal must issue its decision within six months of the appeal being filed with the Tribunal; if it fails to do so, the approvals are in most circumstances deemed to have been upheld[81]. For this reason, and because of the potential complexity of the issues and the number of parties or participants, a more active approach to determining these appeals was needed.

At the same time, the Tribunal remained bound by Ontario's *Statutory Powers Procedure Act*[82] (SPPA), which is generally structured to support a traditional adversarial approach to adjudication. Working within this context, the Tribunal adopted four key amendments to its rules.

First, it added to its rules a generic schedule for all of the events required to deal with these appeals, whether involving steps by the parties such as disclosure, or hearing events before the Tribunal. Pursuant to this schedule, the parties are informed before an appeal is launched that the hearing will start 8 weeks after the last date for filing an appeal. Within that eight-week period, several other events, including two preliminary hearings to address procedural matters, and a potential mediation, are provided for at pre-set intervals. The rules then provide only an extremely narrow opportunity for any of those dates to be changed[83].

When an appeal is filed, the Tribunal completes the template schedule with the actual dates for each event, and provides it to the parties within 8 days of the expiry of the time for filing an appeal. The schedule is then provided to other parties and participants in the proceeding as they are added. In the result, everyone involved in a matter knows from the earliest possible time not only the steps required to ready the matter for a hearing and to have it heard, but as well the exact dates on which those events will occur. This offers a good example of managing the expectations of potential parties and participants from the outset, rather than having to impose tight deadlines on individuals who expected to have much more time to develop and present their case. Delays which flow from wrangling over dates are also largely avoided in this process.

Second, the Tribunal brought into its rules a number of provisions to provide for a more active approach. Although largely drawn from the SPPA, the inclusion of these provisions in the Rules collects in one place the powers the Tribunal has to be more active. As such, the Rules signal to the parties that the Tribunal intends to be active, and also, for the reasons discussed above[84], provide an accessible, consistent code to guide adjudicators and those appearing in front of them in the application of those powers. The rules are as follows[85]:

> The Tribunal may require that, no later than seven days before the main Hearing, the Parties provide to the Tribunal a list of facts and issues that remain in dispute.
>
> The Tribunal may identify, define or narrow the issues to be determined and the evidence to be heard in the proceeding and may direct the order in which issues and evidence will be considered.
>
> The Tribunal may reasonably limit further examination or cross-examination of a witness where the Tribunal is satisfied that the examination or cross-examination has been sufficient to disclose fully and fairly all matters relevant to the issues in the proceeding.
>
> The Tribunal may allocate the time permitted for the making of submissions.
>
> The Tribunal may question Parties, Participants, Presenters, witnesses or representatives on their behalf and advise when additional evidence, witnesses or submissions might assist the Tribunal.

Third, to support the role it will play in defining and managing the hearing, the Tribunal's rules require the parties to provide more information in their initial filings than it requires in other matters: in particular, they must provide at a very early date statements of the issues and the material facts they will rely on[86].

Fourth, the Rules require the parties to provide disclosure not only to each other, but as well to the Tribunal, before the first preliminary hearing. This disclosure includes all existing documents and lists of witnesses and a summary of intended evidence and, for respondents, their response to the appellant's issues. Further disclosure requirements arise after the preliminary hearing[87].

These latter two provisions critically underpin the more active approach, as they equip the Tribunal, at an early date, with the information it needs to apply its own expertise to determining what issues are seriously in play, and what evidence it needs to determine those issues.

While seemingly modest steps, the new rules, taken as a whole, reflect the core values of the active collaborative model: party responsibility for the evidence to be heard; early sharing of detailed information with the tribunal; an active tribunal role in shaping the hearing, after hearing from the parties, and the potential for the tribunal to question witnesses and counsel at the hearing to elicit information needed to resolve the case. As such, the ERT's green energy rules represent a significant new direction for the Tribunal.

Conclusion

Building a modern adjudicative tribunal requires attention to a host of considerations: the purposes behind the establishment of the tribunal; the nature of the disputes and parties that may come before the tribunal; the potential for tribunal "structures, practices and procedures" to advance or impede access; and the recruitment, training and retention of highly qualified staff and adjudicators.

In all they do, tribunals should be user-centred, and maintain their focus on core values of integrity, transparency, accessibility and fairness. Tribunals must understand that they play a critical role within the justice system, and in many ways, are the real face of justice for a community.

This paper has reviewed the issues of access, structures and process from that perspective and within the context of Ontario's recent clustering initiative and recent Canadian experience with the active-collaborative model of adjudication. It is hoped the paper will serve to spark analysis and commentary to advance the international sharing of ideas and experience which increasingly plays a central role in helping all who work in tribunals better serve their users and communities.

NOTES

1. Michael Gottheil is Executive Chair of Environment and Land Tribunals Ontario, and Chair of each of its constituent tribunals. He was Chair of the Human Rights Tribunal of Ontario from 2005 to 2009, following some 20 years in the private practice of administrative, human rights and labour law. Doug Ewart is Senior Advisor, Administrative Justice Reform Project, Environment and Land Tribunals Ontario. He has over 30 years experience in justice policy development for both the Ontario and Canadian governments in fields including civil, family, administrative, criminal, aboriginal and human rights law, and equality rights issues. The views in this paper are those of the authors and do not represent the views of the Government of Ontario.
2. With a population of just over 13 million, Ontario is Canada's largest province. It has 37 provincially-appointed adjudicative tribunals, along with two levels of provincially-established trial courts and a Court of Appeal. Reflecting Canada's constitutional structure, a federal trial court and appellate court also operate in Ontario, dealing with, among other matters, reviews of the decisions of federally appointed (as opposed to provincially-appointed) tribunals. The final level of appeal in Canada is the Supreme Court of Canada.
3. To date, the closest analogy we have found to ELTO's collective jurisdiction is one of the hosts of the conference, the Land and Environment Court of New

South Wales (NSW). The subject matters dealt with by the two bodies are uncannily similar, although the NSW Court has a much broader environmental jurisdiction. The fact that the NSW Court has operated for three decades in a field which Ontario has just entered is an example of why sharing information and ideas at this conference is of key importance to Ontario.

4. Part I of [t]his paper has benefited from the research, analysis and insights of Jamie Baxter, a 2010 graduate of the University of Toronto Law school who prepared a very useful background paper on clustering while serving as a summer student at ELTO under the general supervision of Dean Lorne Sossin of the Osgoode Hall Law School of York University.

5. See n. 31, *infra*.

6. While the term is not widely used, it has been used in this context with a different meaning than the one employed here — see the New Zealand Law Commission, which uses 'clustering' to describe bringing tribunals together in a much more unified way ("fewer and larger" tribunals "integrated within a single entity") than the above definition suggests: *Determining Justice for All, A Vision for New Zealand's Courts and Tribunals*, March 2004. at page 288).

7. In comparing the effectiveness of groupings of tribunals internationally, it is important to be aware of whether those groupings have been established in a context where statutory reforms amalgamated or merged the jurisdictions of the constituent tribunals or, more fundamentally, sought to rationalize laws and policies governing the issues which come before the grouped tribunals. In the case of Ontario, for example, neither was done, and clustering will play out in the absence of any other reforms related to the jurisdiction of the clustered tribunals or the legislative and policy context within which they work in their often overlapping areas of operation.

8. In the cluster context, cross-appointments do not diminish the reality that each member of a tribunal has been specifically appointed to it, and has jurisdiction only over matters before the specific tribunal(s) to which they have been appointed. This is reinforced in Ontario, where to be cross-appointed within a cluster it would appear that an adjudicator must meet the statutory criteria for appointment to any tribunal, which include "experience, knowledge or training in the subject matter and legal issues dealt with by the tribunal" to which they are to be appointed. See s. 14 of the *Adjudicative Tribunals Accountability, Governance and Accountability Act, 2009*, S.O. 2009, Ch. 33, Sch. 5. With the exception of its provisions regarding clustering, the *Act* has not yet been proclaimed.

9. A somewhat similar, smaller-scale initiative is found in Washington State's development of its Environment and Land Use Hearings Office. While this will bring together boards which hear planning as well as environmental matters, it would appear that the integration this involves is primarily at the administrative rather than the adjudicative level.

10. In August of 2010 the Ontario government indicated that it was proceeding with a second cluster comprised of "social justice" tribunals, and initiated a competition for its Executive Chair.

11. The tribunals which comprise Environment and Land Tribunals Ontario are:

    The **Assessment Review Board**, which hears property assessment appeals to ensure that properties are assessed and classified in accordance with the provisions of the *Assessment Act*. The Board also operates under a variety of other legislation and hears appeals on property tax matters.

    The **Board of Negotiation,** which conducts voluntary mediation in the event of a dispute over the value of land expropriated by a public authority. If no settlement is reached, the matter may be appealed to the Ontario Municipal Board.

The **Conservation Review Board,** which conducts proceedings where there are disputes concerning properties that may demonstrate cultural heritage value or interest, or disputes surrounding archaeological licensing. After determining a matter, the Board then makes recommendations to the final decision-making authority in the particular case, either a local municipal council or the Minister of Culture.

The **Environmental Review Tribunal**, which hears applications and appeals under numerous environmental and planning statutes including the *Environmental Bill of Rights, 1993*, the *Environmental Protection Act*, the *Ontario Water Resources Act* and the *Safe Drinking Water Act, 2002*. The Tribunal also functions as the Niagara Escarpment Hearing Office to hear development permit appeals and Niagara Escarpment Plan amendment applications for this protected World Biosphere Reserve, and serves as the Office of Consolidated Hearings to hear applications for joint hearings where separate hearings before more than one tribunal would otherwise be required.

The **Ontario Municipal Board,** which hears applications and appeals in relation to a range of municipal planning, financial and land matters including official plans, zoning by-laws, subdivision plans, consents and minor variances, land compensation, development charges, electoral ward boundaries, municipal finance, aggregate resources and other issues assigned to the Board by numerous Ontario statutes.

12. The two ELTO tribunals which were not already under the jurisdiction of the Ministry of the Attorney General were moved to that Ministry. This was seen as reflecting the role administrative tribunals play in the broader justice system[;] it was also seen as an indication that tribunals are justice agencies, independent from line ministries, as opposed to bodies delivering government programs.

13. The establishment of this cluster followed an extensive consultation process and analysis undertaken in 2005–2006 by the then Chair of the Ontario Labour Relations Board, Kevin Whitaker (now the Hon. Mr. Justice Whitaker of the Superior Court of Justice). See the *Interim Report of the Agency Cluster Facilitator for the Municipal, Environment and Land Planning Tribunals*, January 31, 2007 and the *Final Report*, August 22, 2007.

14. *Supra*, n. 8.

15. In Ontario, the term adjudicative tribunal means a tribunal prescribed as such under the *Tribunals Act*. There is no legislated definition of the term. See O. Reg. 126/10 for the current list of adjudicative tribunals.

16. The *Tribunals Act, supra*, n. 8, sections 3–8.

17. *Ibid.*, section 14. Note that the government may make exceptions to this: see ss. 23(e).

18. *Ibid.*, section 15. This provision has been proclaimed in force.

19. See O. Reg. 126/10 which formally constitutes the ELTO cluster. See also ss. 16(3) of the *Tribunals Act, supra* n. 8 which provides for the appointment of alternate chairs "of the cluster".

20. *Ibid.*, section 18.

21. *Ibid.*, section 17. Note that the government has the power to exempt by regulation some of the duties which might otherwise flow to an Executive Chair under this provision: see ss. 23(f).

22. As noted above, the ELTO cluster was created, and is being built, without any underlying rationalization of the constituting statutes for the five tribunals, nor of the more than 100 statutes and policies which define and shape their jurisdiction. This is an important distinction from other tribunal reorganizations or

amalgamations, and must be kept in mind when international comparisons are made.

23. See n. 8, *supra*.

24. For example, ELTO's training plan will feature ELTO-wide programs offered to members of all tribunals. Although, as appropriate, tribunal-specific programs will also be offered, they will be priorized, developed and coordinated through the pan-ELTO training committee.

25. Pursuant to the current ELTO position description, an Associate Chair "is a member of ELTO's senior management team and assists in building and leading the ELTO cluster of tribunals" in addition to providing jurisprudential leadership for and day-to-day oversight [but not being the delegated head] of one or more of ELTO's constituent tribunals.

26. These and other ELTO documents may be found at www.elto.gov.on.ca.

27. See, for example, the observation of Justice Brian J. Preston that "[a] one-stop shop also facilitates better quality and innovative decision-making in both substance and procedure by cross-fertilization between different classes of jurisdiction", in "Operating an Environmental Court: the Experience of the Land and Environmental Court of New South Wales", a paper delivered as the Environmental Commission of Trinidad and Tobago Inaugural Distinguished Lecture on Environmental Law, (at page 26 of the text): also published in (2008) 25 EPLJ 385.

28. See *Grand River Conservation Authority v Her Majesty the Queen in Right of Ontario (Ministry of Transportation)*, Ontario Municipal Board, unreported, April 23, 2010.

29. In a cluster, this expertise can be seen as including the experience and knowledge of all adjudicators in the cluster, just as within a single tribunal expertise can (and should) be seen as being that of the tribunal institutionally rather than only that of any given tribunal member who presides over a case. Indeed, the doctrine of deference to tribunal expertise makes little sense unless that expertise is seen as inhering in the tribunal's historical and collective experience in the field rather than in each appointee to it, however new to the tribunal or whatever their background.

30. Although processes such as mediation, conciliation and arbitration can also advance access to justice, they represent well-trod ground, and also will not be explored here.

31. To the extent that readers are driven to view some of the concepts in this section through the lens of an inquisitorial approach, a brief comment on that term is required. For the purposes of this paper, a key distinction must be drawn between the civil concepts of an investigating magistrate and an inquisitorial adjudicator. Confusion can result when the term inquisitorial is applied to both. Readers will better appreciate this paper if they exclude the investigative model from their conceptualization of the inquisitorial approach, and hence do not think of it here in terms of a tribunal conducting its own investigation and calling its own evidence. To help draw this distinction, this paper will avoid the term inquisitorial as much as possible, and will primarily use the term 'active-collaborative' adjudication to describe the suite of practices which a tribunal may use to i) obtain early disclosure to the tribunal (including through detailed application and response forms and by suggesting, without directing, additional areas to be covered or witnesses who might be called); ii) focus the issues for determination using the information supplied by the parties and its own expertise; and iii) manage, direct and sometimes conduct the eliciting and testing of the parties' evidence at a hearing.

32. See, Michael Gottheil, *A Case for Alternative Adjudicative Models: Enhancing Access to Justice in Administrative Law Proceedings*; Regulatory Boards and Administrative Law Litigation Journal (2009), Vol. X, No. 2 (Federated Press).

33. Of particular interest in this regard is the provision of the New South Wales *Civil Procedure Act, 2005*, which requires the Court to manage proceedings having regard to a number of objects, including "the timely disposal of the proceedings, and all other proceedings in the court, at a cost affordable by the respective parties" [s. 57(1) emphasis added].

34. Although it was posted just as this paper was being finalized, and hence could not be fully reflected in the analysis herein, a very recent comparative analysis of two Australian Courts dealing with the reviews of development approvals seems to provide strong support for this proposition. See Andrew Edgar, "Participation and Responsiveness in Merits Review of Polycentric Decisions: A Comparison of Development Assessment Appeals", July, 2010, (http://ssrn.com/abstract=1650387), also published at (2010), 27 E.P.L.J. 36.

35. See Justice Kevin Bell: "[Tribunal members, advocates and witnesses [perhaps especially experts]] all seem to know the rules and procedures, and may even demonstrate personal familiarity with each other. But the new advocate in the Tribunal, the self-represented party, and the family and community members looking on may only experience anxiety, uncertainty, a sense of exclusion and even, in some cases, humiliation. Presentation by a tribunal to the uninitiated of being a club is entirely unintended but has very negative consequences ... [including] a profound sense of disempowerment ... [that] is felt at the personal level and experienced as disrespect for the dignity of the individual", in "The role of VCAT in a changing world: the President's review of VCAT", Speech delivered to the Law Institute of Victoria, September 4, 2008, at 17–18.

36. See, as just one example, the Canadian Judicial Council's 2006 "Statement of Principles on Self-Represented Litigants and Accused Persons", at www.cjc-ccm.gc.ca. It can be noted that some of the concerns in the literature about an adjudicator appearing biased when they intervene to help an unrepresented party cope with the process are addressed in the active-collaborative model of adjudication discussed *infra*. In that model, an adjudicator plays an active role in relation to all parties, such that their interventions are not seen favouring the self-represented parties.

37. "A court can address inequality of alms between the parties. Specialization and the availability of technical experts (commissioners) in the Court address in part inequality of resources and access to expert assistance and evidence": per Justice Brian J. Preston, *supra*, n. 27.

38. See point 7, *infra*.

39. The authors acknowledge with appreciation the research into active adjudication models undertaken by ELTO summer student, Samantha Green, a first year student of the University of Toronto Law School, under the general supervision of Dean Lorne Sossin of the Osgoode Hall Law School of York University.

40. See n. 31, *supra*, re the distinction between this approach and common conceptions of the inquisitorial model. It must be recognized (and confronted) that within this approach, while the adjudicator takes an active role in shaping the hearing and identifying relevant issues and evidence, the tribunal does not become responsible for developing a full record. Care must be taken to make clear to parties, particularly self-represented parties, that it is not the tribunal's responsibility to make out their case. Further, expert adjudicators and active-collaborative adjudicative approaches cannot turn a complex legal issue into a simple non-legal matter.

41. In its practice direction on expert and technical evidence, para. 8, the Environmental Review Tribunal provides as follows: "The decisions that the Tribunal must make involve the public interest and may have serious and far-reaching environmental consequences. These decisions must be based on a balanced record, composed of accurate and reliable technical information and professional opinions. All Parties and their representatives and witnesses have a responsibility to contribute to such a balanced record to assist the Tribunal to fulfill its duty." See the Tribunal's July 9, 2010 Rules of Practice and Practice Directions; http://www.ert.gov.on.ca/stellent/groups/public/@abcs/@www/@ert/documents/webasset/ec082677.doc.

42. See the expanded discussion in Part III, *infra*.

43. The Ontario Labour Relations Board's 'consultation' process permits the Board to determine that no *vive voce* evidence is needed. That process was developed by the Board to deal with certain classes of cases which require very expeditious processing to avoid becoming moot. The legislative anchor for this is a provision identifying a defined subset of the Board's jurisdiction, and providing that no hearing at all is required to determine those matters. This provision was then used by the Board to support rules which permit Board members to determine whether to hear evidence, or simply have the parties elaborate or make submissions on their written materials. The process, and court decisions upholding it, are very helpfully set out in a recent article by OLRB Vice Chair Jack Slaughter: *A Review of the Interim Order Powers and Consultation Processes of the Ontario Labour Relations Board*, The Advocate's Quarterly, Vol. 37 at 87.

44. While generally desirable, this approach is key where novel approaches are being brought forward in an area which contains many legal and public relations landmines, and where reviews are likely to be taken to more traditionally-oriented courts. In these circumstances, extemporizing by well-meaning adjudicators can lead to controversy and reversals, potentially setting back a significant part of a modernization agenda.

45. The legislative framework for Ontario's Human Rights tribunal, discussed in Part III, below, is an excellent example of how an integrated set of provisions, running from the qualifications of adjudicators through to specific limits on review by the courts, can provide a solid foundation for tribunal rules which establish a more active adjudication model.

46. Justice Preston, *supra* n. 27 at 30.

47. Note, however, the potential to drown innovation if traditional, adversary bodies are merged with ones which are attempting to develop more innovative and active approaches; especially in a lawyer dominated situation inertia will inevitably favour tradition-bound approaches.

48. While the economies of scale outlined above argue for large scale amalgamations, there can also be similar benefits in smaller scale clusters, provided there is some inherent logic to the grouping. Where that is the case, having regard to the subject matters dealt with by the grouped tribunals, and most particularly to their amenability to the same access initiatives (and especially with regard to the style and pace of adjudication), support for change may be generated even in smaller communities of interest.

49. R.S.O. 1990 c. H-19, as amended.

50. See n. 31, *supra*, for an overview of how these terms are used in this paper.

51. Before the amendments, Ontario's human rights system required that complaints of human rights violations be filed with the Human Rights Commission. That body investigated complaints and tried to resolve them through mediation. If that did not succeed, and the Commission felt it was appropriate to do so, the Com-

mission could refer the matter to the Human Rights Tribunal for adjudication. In such proceedings, the Commission had carriage of the complaint. About 150 matters were referred to the Tribunal annually, out of about 2400 complaints filed with the Commission each year. In the new system, claimants have direct access to the tribunal, which receives their complaints and adjudicates them. Over 3,000 claims are now received annually by the Tribunal.

52. *Supra*, n. 49, s. 40.
53. As the legislation was proceeding through the Ontario Legislature, the authors worked together in developing, through extensive consultations with a wide range of stakeholders, the Tribunal's new model for receiving and resolving human rights claims.
54. *Supra*, n. 40, ss. 43(3)(a). See also s. 41.
55. *Ibid.*, ss. 42(2).
56. *Ibid.*, ss. 43(3).
57. The Tribunal also has the power to appoint a person to make an inquiry into a matter and report back to the Tribunal and the parties (s. 44). The Tribunal's Rules suggest that this power is not likely to be used with any great frequency: see Rule 20.2.
58. *Supra*, n. 40, s. 41.
59. *Ibid.*, s. 41. This provision is significant because the existing Ontario interpretative rules already required that the Act be given a [fairly] large and liberal interpretation: s. 61 of the *Legislation Act, 2006*, S.O. 2006, c. 21, Sch. F, and so the inclusion of this further, specific provision in relation to non-adversarial approaches has particular salience.
60. *Ibid.*, ss. 32(3). Note that this anticipated by some two years the new requirements of the *Tribunals Act*, *supra*, n. 7.
61. *Ibid.*, ss. 45.8.
62. *Ibid.*, ss. 43(8).
63. Doug Ewart led the federal government's development, with former students, their counsel and the churches, of the opt-in model discussed below, and, under the direction of the federal negotiator, headed up the negotiations of this element of the class-action resolution of the IRS matter.
64. In addition to the abuse claims, the negotiations involved compensation for the fact of attendance at the schools, a truth and reconciliation process and enhancements to healing programs.
65. See for example, *Baxter et al v. Canada (Attorney General)* (2006), 83 O.R.(3d) 481 at para. 85. For examples of approving decisions which specifically adverted to the inquisitorial nature of the claims resolution model, see *Ammaq et al v. Canada (Attorney General)*, [2006] N.U.C.J. 24 at 26, and *Semple et al v. Canada* (2006), 213 Man. R. 220, para. 15.
66. From 2007 to July, 2010, over $600 million has been paid out pursuant to the IAP process for the first 5,000 claims. Another 15,000 are anticipated. See information on the website of the Indian Residential Schools Adjudication Secretariat at irsad-sapi.gc.ca.
67. For the purposes of this paper, references will be to the Independent Assessment Process adopted in the class action proceedings, although the key issues discussed here are largely unchanged from the earlier opt-in model. That document can be found in Schedule D to the IRS Settlement Agreement, which is posted on the website noted immediately above.
68. Both when the model was offered by Canada, and under the court-approved settlement, all adjudicators are recruited through an open, competitive process and are appointed on the joint recommendation of representatives of four groups: the

former students; counsel for former students; the churches; and the federal government. Each of these groups has a veto over each appointment, so that in every proceeding all participants, and perhaps particularly the former students bringing their claims forward, can be assured that the adjudicator is neutral.

69. In addition to adjudicative practices and the details of the model, this training included the history of the residential school system and perspectives of former students on a number of key issues. See in this regard the decision of the Federal Court of Appeal in an unrelated matter concerning the use of an inquisitorial approach in immigration matters. In *Thamotharem v. Canada (Minister of Citizenship and Immigration)*, [2008] 1 F.C.R. 385, the Court upheld a guideline which provided that a claimant would first be questioned by an official rather than by his or her counsel, noting in part that the immigration adjudicators had received training in questioning refugee claimants: see para. 38.

70. This role is facilitated by the requirement that claimants provide detailed information to the Secretariat before their claim can advance for adjudication.

71. But not the gathering: see IAP, *supra*, III(e)(iv). "The [adjudicator's] role is inquisitorial, not investigative. This means that while the adjudicator must bring out and test the evidence of witnesses, only the parties may call witnesses or produce evidence, other than expert evidence.

72. IAP, *supra*, III(d)(ii).

73. IAP, *supra*, III(e)(ix). Where counsel attend hearings, they may meet with the adjudicator at intervals to suggest questions or lines of inquiry. The adjudicator must explore the proposed lines of inquiry unless he or she rules them to be irrelevant to credibility, liability or compensation in the IAP, but the adjudicator retains discretion on the wording of the questions put to a witness.

74. IAP, *supra*, III(e)(x).

75. IAP, *supra*, III(e)(ii). In this inquisitorial model, the adjudicator is responsible for managing the hearing, questioning all witnesses (other than experts retained by the adjudicator) and preparing a decision with his or her conclusions and reasons; and III(e)(iii): The adjudicator's questioning must both draw out the full story from witnesses (leading questions are permitted where required to do this), and test the evidence that is given (questioning in the form of cross examination is permitted where required to do this).

76. IAP, *supra*, III(f)(v).

77. IAP, *supra*, III(f)(v).

78. While to some extent this role for counsel reflects the fact that experts do not routinely feel intimidated in the adversarial process, it primarily flows from the selection and briefing role played by the adjudicator and from the general recognition of the role of counsel in the IAP.

79. See s. 142.1 of the *Environmental Protection Act*, R.S.O. 1990, c. E-19, as amended.

80. *Ibid.*, ss. 142.1(3).

81. *Ibid.*, ss. 145.2(6). And see Rule 37, *Rules of Practice* and *Practice Directions of the Environmental Review Tribunal*, July 9, 2010. The Rules may be found at http://www.ert.gov.on.ca/english/guides/index.htm .

82. R.S.O. 1990, c. S.22, as amended.

83. *Supra*, n. 81, Rule 32, and Appendix A.

84. See n. 44, *supra*, and the accompanying text.

85. *Ibid.*, Rules 179–185.

86. *Ibid.*, Rules 29 and 34.

87. *Ibid.*, Appendix A.

Appendix II.2
Selected Excerpts of the Annual Report of the SJTO[†]

Social Justice Tribunals Ontario
Providing fair and accessible justice

Social Justice Tribunals Ontario
2013-14 Annual Report

Child and Family Services Review Board
Custody Review Board
Human Rights Tribunal of Ontario
Landlord and Tenant Board
Ontario Special Education (English) Tribunal
Ontario Special Education (French) Tribunal
Social Benefits Tribunal

Disponible en français

[†] Reproduced from SJTO website: "Reports, Plans and Standards" <http://www.sjto.gov.on.ca/documents/sjto/2013-14%20Annual%20Report.html>. © Queen's Printer for Ontario.

MANDATE, MISSION AND VALUE STATEMENT

Our Mandate

Social Justice Tribunals Ontario is a cluster of seven adjudicative tribunals with a mandate to resolve applications and appeals brought under eight statutes relating to child and family services oversight, youth justice, human rights, residential tenancies, disability support and other social assistance, and special education.

Our Mission

Social Justice Tribunals Ontario (SJTO) and its constituent tribunals will:

- provide fair, effective, timely and accessible dispute resolution
- promote consistency in the application of the legislation and its processes while remaining responsive to differing cases, party needs and to an evolving understanding of the law
- maintain the highest standards of professionalism, integrity and quality of work and
- be leaders in the administrative justice community.

Our Value

The core values inform how the SJTO and its constituent tribunals approach their mandate. They set the foundation for rules and policies, how those rules and policies will be applied, and how we deliver service to the public. The Core Values are:

- Accessibility
  - We will strive to enhance full and informed participation of parties in the process, whether or not they have legal representation.
  - We are committed to diversity and inclusiveness.
  - We will provide dispute resolution processes that are proportionate and appropriate to the issues in dispute.
- Fairness and Independence
  - SJTO and its constituent tribunals must be, and be seen to be, impartial and independent in their decision making functions.
  - Our decisions will be based on the evidence and the applicable law, and will be supported by clear, concise and coherent reasons.
- Timeliness
  - We are committed to providing timely dispute resolution services and issuing decisions within a reasonable timeframe after a hearing.
- Transparency
  - Our processes, procedures and policies will be clear, understandable and consistently applied.

- Professionalism and Public Service
  - Members and staff will exhibit the highest standards of public service, integrity and professionalism.
  - We will be responsive to stakeholder needs by engaging in meaningful outreach and consultation.

SOCIAL JUSTICE TRIBUNALS ONTARIO

Message from Michael Gottheil, Executive Chair
Social Justice Tribunals Ontario

I am proud of the accomplishments of SJTO, and its role in the administration of justice in Ontario. We provide fair, accessible dispute resolution to thousands of Ontarians each year. In 2013–14 alone, our tribunals received and resolved more than 100,000 cases. Over the past year we also focused on boosting capacity and expertise, looking for ways to work more efficiently, and collaborating with our justice sector partners.

Because of the breadth of our jurisdiction and the nature of the disputes we deal with, our users are extremely varied. We resolve disputes between landlords and tenants, hear appeals from people seeking social assistance and complaints from those who feel the service they received from children's aid societies has been unfair. We deal with applications about human rights and the rights of children and families relating to education. These are important issues that touch the lives of families and individuals in fundamental ways. The public and the parties who appear before the SJTO tribunals have a right to fair, impartial and expert dispute resolution, and that is our primary commitment.

A high percentage of our users are people with disabilities, individuals who face literacy, language and communication barriers, and persons who experience social and economic disadvantage. Overwhelmingly, the parties who appear before the SJTO tribunals are self-represented. This means our processes, procedures and the way we resolve disputes must be sensitive to the needs of the people who seek our services.

We continue to work on ways to improve access to information and to our services. In 2014–15 we will launch a new website. The site will provide users with information that is easy to find and easy to understand. People who use screen readers will also find the new site easier to navigate. Also, following recommendations made by Andrew Pinto in his Report of the Human Rights Review 2012, we have modified the information and forms of the Human Rights Tribunal of Ontario to make them easier to use.

Looking ahead, we will be introducing e-filing at the Landlord and Tenant Board. E-filing will allow users to file anytime from anywhere and provide guided steps for both landlords and tenants. Also at the Landlord and Tenant Board, we are beginning to develop an online wizard which will help users find answers they need more easily. Referrals to existing legal and community resources are being built into the tool.

SJTO has also developed a policy which lays out how we will provide accommodation for persons with disabilities. One of our commitments is to publish information on the accessibility features at each SJTO hearing location so that people can research what is available ahead of their hearing. The policy also establishes accommodation co-ordinators for each tribunal — staff who have training in accommodation, and can be a single, knowledgeable point of contact for users who require accommodation. Watch for that information to appear on our website later in 2014–15.

To uphold the highest standards of integrity and quality of adjudication, we continue to develop our professional development program. Our annual educational event, called "The Institute"[,] was last held in May 2013 and covered topics like evidence, decision writing, early resolution, mediation and communication in the hearing room. The Institute is also an opportunity for SJTO members and mediators to share their skills, experiences, and perspectives, and to enrich their expertise. In 2014, our professional development unit also created and delivered a training module on human rights to all tribunals.

As I mentioned, the SJTO is a part of the justice system in Ontario, and we have a responsibility to respond to the challenges the sector faces. This past year saw the release of a number of important reports on Access to Justice, including the National Action Committee Report on Access to Civil and Family Justice and the Canadian Bar Association's report: Reaching Equal Justice. Both reports highlight the challenges we face in access to justice, and provide recommendations.

At SJTO, we have been working with justice sector partners to meet these challenges. For example, we have begun to work on a project with legal clinics and the Ministry of Community and Social Services to streamline the process for social assistance appeals. Also at the Social Benefits Tribunal, we are discussing ways to facilitate limited retainers and unbundled legal services. This allows legal clinics to serve more people and make more strategic decisions about how to allocate limited resources.

At the Landlord and Tenant Board, we are working with social housing providers to develop approaches to dispute resolution which better fit the needs of social housing landlords and their tenants by enhancing access to mediation and including community support workers in the mediation and resolution process. At the Child and Family Services Review Board, we are borrowing from the aboriginal community to introduce restorative justice techniques. This approach has obvious benefit for our aboriginal users, but has been received with excitement and promise from non-aboriginal users, as the nature of family disputes and disputes with children's aid societies lend themselves to more collaborative and restorative approaches.

While these initiatives are exciting, we know that ultimately, their success depends upon whether they are truly effective and responsive to user needs. As a result, we have launched a project to develop an evaluation framework which will help us assess our organizational strength against common justice sector benchmarks and also seek feedback from our users. Lilian Ma, Landlord and Tenant Board Associate Chair, has been assigned to this important project, and we expect an evaluation framework later this year.

Finally, I have a few announcements about the SJTO team. First, I am very pleased to announce that Yola Grant joined SJTO as the Associate Chair for the Human Rights Tribunal of Ontario on April 16, 2014. Yola was a labour, employment and human rights lawyer with Grant & Bernhardt and held a number of policy and legal positions in the public sector including counsel at the Pay Equity and Employment Equity tribunals, and the predecessor to the HRTO, the Board of Inquiry. I have to thank Naomi Overend who did an outstanding job acting as Associate Chair of the tribunal during the recruitment period.

I also want to warmly thank Kim Bugby, who has taken on the role of Coordinating Vice Chair of the Landlord and Tenant Board, while the board's Associate Chair, Lillian Ma, leads our evaluation framework project.

Finally, I want to thank all the adjudicators on each of our tribunals for their professionalism and dedication to fair, accessible dispute resolution. I am proud to work with all of you.

Michael Gottheil, Executive Chair
Social Justice Tribunals Ontario

Message from Ellen Wexler, Executive Lead
Social Justice Tribunals Ontario

I am proud to submit this annual report. It reminds me of how much we have accomplished at SJTO this year and I'm excited about what's in store in the year ahead. Service excellence is a priority for Social Justice Tribunals Ontario. To that end, on April 1, 2012, we introduced service standards which tell people how long they can expect it will take for their hearing or mediation to be scheduled and heard in each of SJTO's seven tribunals. The standards keep us focused on providing our clients with fair, effective, timely dispute resolution, even as we adapt to legislative change and adopt new technologies. This year, we reported on how we are doing in meeting those standards. In most instances we met or exceeded the standards but in some cases, we fell short. Having standards in place means that we know when and where we need to improve so we can start finding solutions. You can review the service standards results under each of the tribunal headings in this report and on our website.

We are committed to the active offer of French language services for Francophones across Ontario. SJTO's new policy on French language services means that clients seeking services in French know what they can expect from any SJTO tribunal. The policy promises that our frontline services and documents like publications, forms, notices and rules will be available in French. We also commit to providing bilingual adjudicators and mediators on request, or, in cases where one is not available, an interpreter.

Accessibility, diversity and inclusion are core values of SJTO. This year we demonstrated our commitment through a number of initiatives that are outlined in the report, including new policies, improved information and training. Another priority for the SJTO is co-location. In June of 2013, we announced that we would be moving our downtown Toronto offices to 25 Grosvenor St. in Toronto. The relocation will begin in early 2016 and I look forward to having our tribunals under one roof. It will allow us to truly realize the benefits of clustering by sharing knowledge, expertise, space and equipment.

On the human resources front, we replaced three directors of case management with an SJTO Director of Operations, who ensures a coordinated approach to operations across the cluster. Each tribunal also has a registrar and front line managers, who provide leadership on case-management, administration and day-to-day operations.

There are a lot of innovative things going on in SJTO tribunals. To improve service delivery and reduce costs, tribunals shared hearing space and used video technology for more mediations and hearings. We have put a renewed focus on alternative dispute resolution methods including mediation. You'll find more about these initiatives in the operational highlights section of each tribunal.

I would like to extend a special thank you to all of the staff and members at SJTO. Every year, we resolve over 100,000 disputes. The professionals across our organization — in administration, customer service, mediation, finance, HR, IT, and adjudication — are the primary reason for our success.

Ellen Wexler, Executive Lead
Social Justice Tribunals Ontario

LEGISLATIVE AUTHORITY: SJTO

Social Justice Tribunals Ontario (SJTO) is established under the authority of the *Adjudicative Tribunals Accountability, Governance and Appointments Act, 2009* (ATAGAA). The creation of SJTO is part of the government's ongoing efforts to ensure adjudicative tribunals[] best serve the public by being accountable, transparent and efficient in their operations, and independent in their decision making functions. Section 15 of the ATAGAA states that the government may designate a cluster when *"the matters that the tribunals deal with are such that they can operate more effectively and efficiently as part of a cluster than alone."*

OPERATIONAL HIGHLIGHTS: SJTO

2013–2014 was the second year of SJTO's three-year operational plan. This year, the senior leadership team reviewed and updated the plan to ensure that SJTO remains on track to deliver high-quality dispute resolution to Ontarians.

The plan identifies four strategic priorities to guide SJTO's work: dispute resolution, external service delivery, tribunal modernization and internal transformation.

Dispute Resolution

Cross-appointments: One of the benefits of clustering is the ability to cross-appoint members to more than one of the cluster's tribunals. While each tribunal deals with cases under specific legislation, there are overlaps in the subject areas, the nature of the disputes and the parties who appear before SJTO tribunals. Cross appointments enhance members' skills and knowledge which builds adjudicative capacity and expertise across the cluster. They also give the tribunals more flexibility in scheduling hearings, making dispute resolution more timely and accessible. The SJTO now has 20 cross-appointed members.

While there are many benefits to cross-appointments, ensuring and enhancing expertise remain priorities. Thus all cross appointed members are required to meet the competencies set for each tribunal to which they are appointed.

Recruitment: The process for recruitment of adjudicators under ATAGAA[] supports SJTO's ability to attract individuals with superior knowledge, skills and expertise. Each vacancy is filled through an open, competitive, merit-based process, in which candidates are screened and interviewed by an SJTO panel, after which candidates are recommended to the Attorney General.

Mediation and dispute resolution: SJTO has also been building the capacity of mediation and early dispute resolution programs, in part by training members and staff mediators through SJTO's annual Professional Development Institute and other professional development components.

Professional development: SJTO held its third annual Professional Development Institute event, bringing together all members, staff mediators and senior managers for intensive education and training on topics such as decision writing, mediation, evidentiary issues, communication in the hearing room, and accommodating participants who have mental health challenges.

Common Rules of Procedure: Developed after extensive stakeholder consultation, SJTO's Common Rules of Procedure took effect on October 1, 2013. The Common Rules apply to all SJTO tribunals and provide a consistent framework in areas such as timeliness and accessibility, as well as providing authority to appoint litigation guardians and control abuse of process.

External Service Delivery

Hearing rooms: To improve service delivery and reduce costs, tribunals shared hearing space and used video technology during more mediations and hearings. Performance standards: Service excellence is a priority for SJTO. For the second year, SJTO measured its performance against service standards and published the results on the SJTO website.

Overall, the numbers are fairly positive and we are moving in the right direction. SJTO is serious about meeting these standards and if they are not being met, we examine why. Action plans to help meet these standards include increasing the number of hearings, the use of early resolution sessions and streamlining business processes. These initiatives are helping us achieve our targets.

French language services: SJTO's new policy on French language services establishes a consistent standard for tribunals across the cluster so that clients seeking services in French know what they can expect to receive. The policy will be implemented in summer 2014.

Web communications: SJTO is creating a new website. The new site will replace the individual tribunal sites, giving the public access to all SJTO and tribunal information and services in one location. The site is expected to launch in winter 2015.

Consultations: SJTO consults with stakeholders and the public on process, procedure, service and accessibility. When new or amended rules or policies are proposed, SJTO has committed to posting the revisions on the SJTO website for a minimum of two weeks.

Tribunal Modernization

Evaluation: SJTO began developing an evaluation framework. The framework will help us assess our performance and develop evidence-based plans to address gaps and respond to the evolving needs of the communities we serve.

Internal Transformation

Management structure: SJTO introduced a new management structure to support more effective and efficient business processes. A Director of Operations position was established to ensure a coordinated approach to operations across the cluster. To support the Director of Operations, three Registrar positions have been put in place. These positions are responsible for overseeing case management as well as day-to-day operations at the SJTO tribunals.

Co-location: SJTO continues to work on co-locating a number of its Toronto offices. Co-location will lead to increased accessibility, capacity and expertise for the cluster. The project plan has SJTO co-locating most Toronto offices in early 2016.

Virtual staff meetings: SJTO began holding regular staff meetings via video conference. The meetings support the alignment of the cluster's tribunals by keeping staff across the province up-to-date on changes happening across SJTO. Holding the meetings virtually offers flexibility in staff scheduling, ensuring services to the public are not disrupted.

Tribunal Initiatives

In addition to these corporate (cluster-level) activities, each of the tribunals led initiatives that support the strategic priorities. These projects are highlighted in the sections of the report for each tribunal.

ACCESSIBILITY AND DIVERSITY AT SJTO

Access to justice, diversity and inclusion are core values of SJTO. We are committed to an inclusive work environment that reflects Ontario's diversity and to designing barrier-free policies, processes and services.

Accessibility

In 2013–14, SJTO developed a cross cluster *Accessibility and Accommodation Policy* that outlines our commitment to treating all people with dignity and respect and supports their independence. The policy is accompanied by a *Multi-Year Accessibility and Accommodation Plan* which is focused on identifying and removing barriers so that all members of the public have equitable access to our services.

In 2013–14, SJTO improved access in the following ways:

- Established common rules for our tribunals to achieve more consistent access
- Developed and published a plain language "Guide to Mediation at the HRTO"

- Implemented digital recording of Social Benefits Tribunal hearings. Recordings have been requested by persons with cognitive and/or mental health issues to help recall what happened during the hearing.
- Used more telephone and video conferencing at the Social Benefits Tribunal. These hearing formats meant that parties who have a disability that makes travel difficult or who live far from the hearing site, did not have to travel.
- Trained staff on the Integrated Accessibility Standards Regulation and the Ontario *Human Rights Code* related obligations
- Established an Accommodation Coordinators Working Group to provide an opportunity for our tribunals to share best practices and develop in-house training programs
- Participated in a consultation session with persons with disabilities and the organizations that represent them to help SJTO establish its own practices.

Diversity

The Multi-Year Accessibility and Accommodation Plan is linked to the Multi-Year Diversity Plan which has commitments in four categories: people, processes, services and results.

These are some of the SJTO initiatives that supported diversity:

- Established a committee that supported diversity, inclusion and accessibility in the organization.
- Posted a statement of commitment to diversity and inclusion, and the three-year diversity plan, on SJTO's public website
- Sponsored "Day of Pink" activities across the cluster to raise awareness of the negative impacts of bullying
- Hosted "Positive Space" training for interested employees in Toronto, and
- Conducted a staff/member survey on diversity and inclusion to identify areas of focus for the plan.

Commitments to accessibility and inclusion are also found in SJTO's mission and core values, our Code of Conduct and our business plan.

HUMAN RIGHTS TRIBUNAL OF ONTARIO

LEGISLATIVE AUTHORITY: HRTO

The Human Rights Tribunal of Ontario (HRTO) is established under the Ontario *Human Rights Code*. Since June 2008, all claims of discrimination under the *Code* have been dealt with through applications filed with the HRTO. The HRTO's primary role is to provide an expeditious and accessible process for resolving those applications through voluntary mediation or, where the dispute is not resolved through mediation, a hearing and an enforceable decision.

OPERATIONAL HIGHLIGHTS: HRTO

HRTO focused on tribunal modernization and external service delivery. The tribunal continued to reduce its active caseload. HRTO is also working closely with stakeholders to address recommendations of the Pinto Report.

Tribunal Modernization

The "Pinto Report" reviewing Ontario's human rights system reforms was released in November 2012. Although the report was generally positive about the new system, it contained a number of recommendations specific to the HRTO. In response to the recommendations, the HRTO has changed processes, modified forms and, in April 2014, will be introducing new practice directions for parties. Practice directions give practical advice on how to interpret tribunal rules. Work to revise the application and response forms to reduce duplication and length and increase accessibility continues. The HRTO also posted more accessible Word versions of the application forms to its website.

External Service Delivery

HRTO is working with the Human Rights Commission and the Human Rights Legal Support Centre to further improve the effectiveness and efficiency of the human rights system in Ontario.

SERVICE STANDARDS: HRTO

The first mediation date offered to parties will be scheduled to take place within 150 calendar days from the date the parties agree to mediation 80% of the time.
Result: 88%

The first hearing date offered to parties will be scheduled to take place within 180 calendar days from the date the application is ready to proceed to all hearings 80% of the time.
Result: 37%
The average number of days for this standard was 194

Decisions for hearing[s] which take three days or less will be issued within 90 calendar days 80% of the time.
Result: 71%
The average number of days for this standard was 83

Decisions for hearings which take longer than three days will be issued within 180 calendar days 80% of the time.
Result: 54%
The average number of days for this standard was 169

STATISTICS AND COMMENTARY: HRTO

Caseload

The HRTO reduced its caseload in 2013–2014. There were 3,061 open applications at the start of the fiscal year. By year-end, that number had been reduced by 67 cases to 2,994 (with 421 of these remaining cases deferred pending the outcome of some other proceeding outside the HRTO). This was accomplished in spite of an increase of 405 applications over last fiscal year.

	2013–2014	2012–2013	2011–2012
Applications received	3,242	2,837	2,740
Cases reactivated	31	27	40
Cases closed	3,341	3,105	3,364
Active cases at year-end	2,994	3,061	3,302

Of the cases closed in fiscal 2013–14 where the application was accepted, 1,601 (64 per cent) were closed within one year. The average time from application acceptance to closure was 363 days, with a median of 263 days.

A geographical breakdown of applications based on the applicant's postal code.

	2013–2014	2012–2013	2011–2012
Eastern (K)	13%	12%	11%
Central (L)	38%	37%	37%
Toronto (M)	24%	24%	25%
Western (N)	17%	19%	18%
Northern (P)	6%	6%	6%
Other	2%	3%	2%

Percentage of applications based on each of the five social areas covered by the Code. Note that while most applications only allege discrimination in respect of one social area, some are based on more than one, so the total exceeds 100 per cent by a small amount.

SOCIAL AREA	2013–2014	2012–2013	2011–2012
Employment	74%	77%	76%
Goods, Services and Facilities	22%	21%	21%
Housing	6%	6%	5%
Contracts	1%	1%	1%
Membership in a Vocation Ass'n	1%	1%	1%
No Social Area	2%	2%	1%

Percentage of applications in which each prohibited ground under the Code is raised. Because many applications claim discrimination based on more than one ground, the totals in the chart far exceed 100%.

Ground	2013–2014	2012–2013	2011–2012
Disability	54%	57%	54%
Reprisal	27%	25%	25%
Sex, Pregnancy and Gender Identity	25%	22%	25%
Race	22%	22%	19%
Colour	16%	15%	13%
Age	13%	15%	14%
Ethnic Origin	17%	15%	15%
Place of Origin	15%	13%	13%
Family Status	13%	10%	8%
Ancestry	13%	11%	9%
Sexual Solicitation or Advances	8%	6%	5%
Creed	8%	6%	7%
Marital Status	8%	5%	8%
Sexual Orientation	8%	4%	4%
Association	5%	4%	3%
Citizenship	6%	4%	4%
Record of Offences	3%	4%	3%
Gender identity*	7%	2%	
Gender expression*	5%	1%	
Receipt of Public Assistance	2%	2%	1%
No grounds	4%	2%	3%

* Bill 33, *An Act to amend the Human Rights Code with respect to gender identity and gender expression*, came into force on June 19, 2012, adding these two grounds. The HRTO application form was amended to reflect these new grounds in late June 2012.

Mediation

Ground	2013–2014	2012–2013	2011–2012
Mediations held	1,562	1,283	1,635
Settled at the mediation	59%	60%	62%
Applicant representation	63%	50%	42%
• Lawyer / paralegal	3%	3%	4%
• Other representative	34%	47%	55%
• Self-represented			
Respondent representation	85%	85%	84%
• Lawyer / paralegal	2%	2%	2%
• Other representative	13%	13%	14%
• Self-represented			

Hearings and Decisions

Type of Decision	2013–2014	2012–2013	2011–2012
Final decision on the merits	143	134	95
Discrimination found	56	47	40
Discrimination not found	87	87	55
Dismissal on a preliminary basis (including following summary hearings)	871	699	786
Deferrals	191	252	229
*Other procedural issues	525	424	358
Reconsideration	151	142	140
Breach of settlement decision	24	5	12

* Includes instances such as jurisdictional issues, where the matter was dealt with by another court, the granting or denying of adjournments or no response was filed.

The HRTO also issued 1,794 Case Assessment Directions dealing with various procedural issues.

Transitional Applications and Commission Referred Complaints

June 2008 amendments to the *Code* established the new human rights system and included a mechanism for dealing with complaints still pending at the Ontario Human Rights Commission. For a period of one year, the complainant could bring the complaint to the HRTO by filing an application under section 53 of the *Code*. The HRTO received almost 2,000 such applications. As well, the Commission continued to refer complaints to the HRTO until December 31, 2008.

Most of the Transition Applications and Commission Referred Complaints have been resolved. At the end of fiscal 2013–2014, the open caseload was:

Transitional Applications

16 open cases:

- 2 were pending final decision
- 12 were deferred pending the outcome of some other process
- 1 was at the hearing stage
- 1 was combined with s.34 applications

Commission Referred Complaints

2 open cases:

- 1 for monitoring
- 1 group of cases being case managed for outstanding issues (special diet files processed as one case)

. . . .

SOCIAL BENEFITS TRIBUNAL

LEGISLATIVE AUTHORITY: SBT

The Social Benefits Tribunal (SBT) was established in 1998 under Part IV of the *Ontario Works Act*, 1997. Appeals are heard under that act and the *Ontario Disability Support Program Act*, 1997. The SBT considers appeals by individuals who have been refused social assistance and recipients of social assistance who disagree with a decision that affects the amount of, or their eligibility for, social assistance.

The SBT conducts hearings throughout Ontario. Because of the sensitive personal information involved in these cases, the legislation requires that all hearings must be held in private.

OPERATIONAL HIGHLIGHTS: SBT

SBT focused in the areas of tribunal modernization, dispute resolution and external service delivery. The SBT enhanced the Interim Assistance process and prioritized the use of the Early Resolution Program while maintaining strong relationships with stakeholders through the establishment of several new working groups.

Tribunal Modernization

Digital recording of hearings was implemented across SBT in early 2014. These recordings give all parties access to an accurate record of the hearing.

Dispute Resolution

SBT continues to review and improve the Early Resolution Program (ERP) which is an important tool in achieving efficient and effective dispute resolution. The ERP is held via telephone and includes the two parties and a SBT staff member, who seeks ways to resolve the appeal without a full hearing. Criteria have been developed to ensure that appropriate cases are selected for ERP. This year, SBT scheduled over 1,525 ERP sessions, an increase of 41% from the previous year. This year's settlement rate was 30%, an improvement from the previous year's 21%.

External Service Delivery

Interim assistance may be available to those who are experiencing financial hardship while waiting for a hearing before the SBT. A team produced revised guidelines which were introduced in November 2013 and are proving to be a valuable resource for staff. The new guidelines establish a more consistent process and allow staff to process requests more quickly.

Building on its ongoing communication with stakeholders, a new working group with membership from SBT, Ministry of Community and Social Services and legal aid clinics was formed to make recommendations to the Practice Advisory Committee (PAC). The working group is also developing a new case streaming strategy that would identify problems with appeals early in the process, notify the applicants of the problems and, where possible, resolve the appeal prior to scheduling a hearing.

SERVICE STANDARDS: SBT

Appeals will be scheduled with a notice of hearing sent out no later than 30 calendar days after receipt of the appeal that sets a hearing date 180 calendar days after the notice of hearing 80% of the time.
Result: 70%

Legislated timeframe for this standard is 60 days. The actual average number of days for this standard was 37 days after receipt of the appeal that sets a hearing date of 186 calendar days after the notice of hearing.

Decisions will be issued within 30 calendar days 80% of the time.
Result: 71%

Legislated timeframe for this standard is 60 days. The actual average number of days for this standard was 24.

STATISTICS/COMMENTARY: SBT

The SBT completed 14,225 appeals in 2013–14, an increase of 900 from the previous year but due to a substantial number of incoming appeals the number of outstanding appeals still increased by more than 500 cases. The overall average case processing time increased slightly from 8.7 months to 8.9 months.

	2013–2014	2012–2013	2011–2012
Appeals Received	14,768	15,430	13,435
Completed	14,225	13,325	12,816
Pending	11,898	11,355	9,250
Case Processing Time (Months)	8.9	8.7	9.2

Appeals Completed With or Without a Hearing

	2013–2014	2012–2013	2011–2012
Completed Without a Hearing*	4,936 (35%)	4,952 (37%)	4,940 (39%)
Completed With a Hearing**	9,289 (65%)	8,373 (63%)	7,876 (61%)

* Completed without a hearing includes the following: appeal resolved before a hearing due to respondent's consent or appellant's withdrawal (e.g. — after early resolution process), reconsideration request not granted, no contact from appellant, no jurisdiction, other administrative reasons.
** Completed with a hearing includes decisions released following a reconsideration hearing.

Appeals by Program

	2013–2014	2012–2013	2011–2012
Ontario Disability Support Program	13,732 (93%)	14,317 (93%)	12,329 (92%)
Ontario Works	1,036 (7%)	1,113 (7%)	1,106 (8%)
Total	14,768	15,430	13,435

Ontario Disability Support Program (ODSP) Appeals by Category

ODSP	2013–2014	2012–2013	2011–2012
Refusal	12,613 (92%)	13,307 (93%)	11,163 (91%)
Cancellation & Suspension	353 (2%)	282 (2%)	321 (2%)
Amount & Reduction	659 (5%)	628 (4%)	736 (6%)
Other	107 (1%)	100 (1%)	109 (1%)
Total	13,732	14,317	12,329

Ontario Works (OW) Appeals by Category

OW	2013–2014	2012–2013	2011–2012
Refusal	229 (22%)	280 (25%)	336 (30%)
Cancellation & Suspension	393 (38%)	397 (36%)	363 (33%)
Amount & Reduction	383 (37%)	409 (37%)	387 (35%)
Other	31 (3%)	27 (2%)	20 (2%)
Total	1,036	1,113	1,106

Tribunal Decisions by Outcome

ODSP	2013–2014	2012–2013	2011–2012
Granted	4,789 (54%)	3,961 (50%)	3,600 (50%)
Denied	2,436 (28%)	2,434 (31%)	2,172 (30%)
Denied in Absentia*	1,163 (13%)	941 (12%)	910 (12%)
Other**	443 (5%)	531 (7%)	550 (8%)
Total	8,831	7,867	7,232

OW	2013–2014	2012–2013	2011–2012
Granted	57 (12%)	48 (9%)	84 (13%)
Denied	186 (41%)	192 (38%)	243 (38%)
Denied in Absentia*	155 (34%)	151 (30%)	197 (30%)
Other**	60 (13%)	115 (23%)	120 (19%)
Total	458	506	644

* Cases denied in absentia — appellant was not present for the hearing.
** Other decisions include the following: consent order, no appeal before the tribunal, appeal out of time, no jurisdiction, matter resolved or withdrawn, or cases referred back to the Director or Administrator to reconsider the original decision in accordance with the directions given by the tribunal.

. . . .

SJTO MEMBERS*
(AS OF MARCH 31, 2014)

SJTO EXECUTIVE CHAIR AND ALTERNATE

Adjudicator	First Appointed	Term Ends
Michael Gottheil (Executive Chair)	March 2011	March 2016
Dr. Lilian Yan Yan Ma (Alternate Executive Chair)	March 2011	March 2016

The Executive Chair and the Alternate Chair are members of each of the adjudicative tribunals that are included in the cluster.

* In this and following sections, indicates member is cross-appointed to other tribunals

. . . .

HUMAN RIGHTS TRIBUNAL OF ONTARIO

Adjudicator	First Appointed	Term Ends
Paul Aterman (Vice-Chair)	October 2012	October 2014
Kenneth Bhattacharjee (Vice-Chair)	September 2008	September 2018
Catherine Bickley	January 2011	January 2016
Keith Brennenstuhl* (Vice-Chair)	September 2007	September 2017
Ruth Carey*	August 2012	December 2016
Ena Chadha (Vice-Chair)	September 2007	September 2017
Kevin Cleghorn	January 2011	January 2016
Brian Cook (Vice-Chair)	September 2008	September 2018
Genevieve Debane (Vice-Chair)	June 2011	June 2016
Andrew Diamond	August 2008	August 2018
Maureen Doyle* (Vice-Chair)	August 2008	February 2016
Brian Eyolfson (Vice-Chair)	August 2007	August 2017
Michelle Flaherty*	October 2008	June 2014
Aida Gatfield	January 2013	January 2015
Suzanne Gilbert*	December 2012	March 2016
Maurice Green	January 2013	January 2015
Mark Handelman	August 2008	August 2018
Beverly Harris	December 2012	December 2014
Mark Hart (Vice-Chair)	September 2007	September 2017
Dale Hewat	September 2008	September 2018
Judith Hinchman	August 2008	August 2018
Kaye Joachim	December 2005	September 2015
Janice Diane Johnston	January 2011	January 2016
Judith Keene	November 2008	August 2015
Dawn Kershaw* (Vice-Chair)	October 2012	May 2015
Robert Lefebvre*	February 2014	February 2016
Michael Lerner	January 2011	January 2016
Ian Mackenzie	March 2011	March 2016

Adjudicator	First Appointed	Term Ends
John Manwaring	May 2009	May 2014
Kathleen Martin (Vice-Chair)	June 2006	September 2017
Yasmeena Mohamed	January 2011	January 2016
David Muir (Vice-Chair)	August 2008	August 2018
Eva Nichols*	February 2013	August 2016
Naomi Overend (A) Associate Chair	August 2013	April 2014
Jo-Anne Pickel (Vice-Chair)	October 2012	October 2014
Sheri Price (Vice-Chair)	September 2008	September 2018
Daniel Randazzo	December 2012	December 2014
Leslie Reaume (Vice-Chair)	June 2007	June 2017
Alison Renton (Vice-Chair)	October 2008	October 2018
Caroline Rowan	October 2005	October 2014
Douglas Sanderson (Vice-Chair)	January 2011	January 2016
Janice Sandomirsky	August 2008	August 2018
Jennifer A. Scott (Vice-Chair)	July 2006	September 2014
Jayashree (Jay) Sengupta* (Vice-Chair)	September 2008	September 2018
Brian Sheehan	August 2008	August 2018
Lorne Slotnick	September 2008	September 2018
Mary Truemner (Vice-Chair)	September 2008	September 2018
Rosemary Walden-Stephan*	December 2012	July 2016
Eric Whist	September 2008	September 2018
Ailsa Wiggins	August 2008	August 2018

. . . .

SOCIAL BENEFITS TRIBUNAL

Adjudicator	First Appointed	Term Ends
Elizabeth Beckett*	August 2012	April 2014
Terry Brouillet	June 2013	June 2015
Brian Brown	April 2004	May 2016
Jean Buie	October 2013	October 2015
Sylvie Charron* (Vice-Chair)	December 2009	October 2014
Dorte Deans	September 2005	October 2015
Harold Dolan	August 2013	August 2015
Patrick Doran*	June 1998	May 2017
Denise Dudley	March 2005	March 2015
Thomas F. Fagan	June 2013	June 2015
Nathan Ferguson	June 2006	June 2014
Lisa Freedman	August 2013	August 2015
Romona Gananathan	September 2013	September 2015
Kelly Gaon	August 2008	June 2015
Audrey Hummelen (Vice-Chair)	June 2007	October 2014
Anna Jurak*	May 2004	June 2016
Dawn Kershaw*	June 2006	June 2016
Jennifer Khurana	July 2013	July 2015

Adjudicator	First Appointed	Term Ends
Linda Lebourdais	February 2005	February 2015
Sandra Macchione*	November 2006	November 2016
Janice MacGuigan	May 2008	May 2018
Sherry MacIsaac	May 2013	May 2015
Roslynne Mains	January 2003	February 2015
Allan Matte	February 2014	February 2016
Carol Anne McDermott*	June 2007	June 2017
Frank Miclash	October 1999	November 2014
Beverly Moore (Associate Chair)	October 2006	September 2015
Robert Murray* (Vice-Chair)	May 2004	February 2016
William Murray	June 2008	November 2017
Marilyn Mushinski	June 2004	July 2016
Monica Purdy	March 2005	March 2015
Josephine Racioppo	September 2013	September 2015
Margaret Reynolds	April 2006	April 2014
Tony Riccio	October 2005	November 2015
Sherene Shaw	February 2005	February 2015
Richard Simpson	October 2005	October 2016
Holly Solomon	June 2013	June 2015
Rosemary Walden-Stephan*	February 2001	July 2016
Roy Wood	March 2005	March 2015

SJTO FINANCIAL INFORMATION

EXPENDITURES AND REVENUES

April 1, 2013–March 31, 2014

VOTE & ITEM 303-7 Residential Tenancy	2013–14 ($)	2012–13*** ($)	2011–12** ($)
Salaries	30,253,209	30,161,085	31,503,018
Benefits	4,389,513	3,915,122	4,064,677
Travel & Communications	2,281,703	2,426,156	2,578,866
Services	7,536,302	7,715,211	7,512,619
Part-Time Members per diem	1,791,418	1,751,894	1,607,339
Supplies & Equipment	609,028	691,431	722,803
Total	46,861,173	46,660,899	47,989,322
Fees*	12,017,104	12,110,484	12,079,147

Source: Draft Public Accounts

* Fees collected from the Landlord and Tenant Board for filing applications. They are deposited in the Consolidated Revenue Fund

** 2011–12 was the first year for SJTO

*** 2012–13 financial information has been updated to reflect final adjustments

Appendix II.3
SJTO's Common Rules[†]

INTRODUCTION

Social Justice Tribunals Ontario (SJTO) is a cluster of seven adjudicative tribunals with a mandate to resolve applications and appeals under eight statutes relating to child and family services oversight, youth justice, human rights, residential tenancies, disability support and other social assistance, and special education.

The SJTO is committed to providing quality dispute resolution across the cluster including ensuring that its procedures are transparent and understandable. Identifying common procedures and values across the SJTO and, where appropriate, harmonizing those procedures improves access to justice and fosters consistency in the application of fundamental principles of fairness.

These Common Rules are grounded in the core adjudicative values and principles of the SJTO which govern the work of the cluster. The Common Rules provide a consistent overarching framework of common procedures that will continue to evolve.

HOW TO USE THESE RULES

  a. The SJTO Common Rules apply to all cases in any SJTO tribunal and form part of the rules and procedures of each tribunal.
  b. For more specific rules please refer to the rules and procedures of:
    • Child and Family Services Review Board
    • Custody Review Board
    • Human Rights Tribunal
    • Landlord and Tenant Board
    • Ontario Special Education Tribunal — English
    • Ontario Special Education Tribunal — French
    • Social Benefits Tribunal

[†] Reproduced from SJTO website: "Rules of Procedure" <http://www.sjto.gov.on.ca/english/Resources/Commonrules/index.htm>. © Queen's Printer for Ontario.

PART A — ADJUDICATIVE VALUES AND INTERPRETIVE PRINCIPLES

A1   APPLICATION

The Common Rules apply to the proceedings of the SJTO. The Common Rules form part of the rules of each SJTO tribunal.

A2   DEFINITIONS

"rules and procedures" includes rules, practice directions, policies, guidelines and procedural directions;

"tribunal" means any SJTO tribunal or board.

A3   INTERPRETATION

A3.1   The rules and procedures of the tribunal shall be liberally and purposively interpreted and applied to:

   a.   promote the fair, just and expeditious resolution of disputes,

   b.   allow parties to participate effectively in the process, whether or not they have a representative,

   c.   ensure that procedures, orders and directions are proportionate to the importance and complexity of the issues in the proceeding.

A3.2   Rules and procedures are not to be interpreted in a technical manner.

A3.3   Rules and procedures will be interpreted and applied in a manner consistent with the *Human Rights Code*.

A4   TRIBUNAL POWERS

A4.1   The tribunal may exercise any of its powers at the request of a party, or on its own initiative, except where otherwise provided.

A4.2   The tribunal may vary or waive the application of any rule or procedure, on its own initiative or on the request of a party, except where to do so is prohibited by legislation or a specific rule.

A5   ACCOMMODATION OF *HUMAN RIGHTS CODE*-RELATED NEEDS

A5.1   A party, representative, witness or support person is entitled to accommodation of *Human Rights Code*-related needs by the tribunal and should notify the tribunal as soon as possible if accommodation is required.

A6   LANGUAGE

A6.1   Individuals may provide written materials to the tribunal in either English or French.

A6.2   Individuals may participate in tribunal proceedings in English, French, American Sign Language (ASL) or Quebec Sign Language (QSL).

A6.3   A person appearing before the tribunal may use an interpreter. Interpretation services will be provided, upon request, in accordance with tribunal policy.

A7   COURTESY AND RESPECT

A7.1   All persons participating in proceedings before or communicating with the tribunal must act in good faith and in a manner that is courteous and respectful of the tribunal and other participants in the proceeding.

A8   ABUSE OF PROCESS

A8.1   The tribunal may make such orders or give such directions in proceedings before it as it considers proper to prevent abuse of its processes.

A8.2   Where the tribunal finds that a person has persistently instituted vexatious proceedings or conducted a proceeding in a vexatious manner, the tribunal may find that person to be a vexatious litigant and dismiss the proceeding as an abuse of process for that reason. It may also require a person found to be a vexatious litigant to obtain permission from the tribunal to commence further proceedings or take further steps in a proceeding.

A9   REPRESENTATIVES

A9.1   Parties may be self-represented, represented by a person licensed by the Law Society of Upper Canada or by an unlicensed person where permitted by the *Law Society Act* and its regulations and by-laws.

A9.2   Individuals representing a party before a tribunal have duties to both the tribunal and the party they are representing. Representatives must provide contact information to the tribunal and be available to be contacted promptly. Representatives are responsible for conveying tribunal communications and directions to their client. Representatives should be familiar with tribunal rules and procedures, communicate the tribunal's expectations to their client, and provide timely responses to the other parties and the tribunal.

A9.3   Where a representative begins or ceases to act for a client, the representative must immediately advise the tribunal and the other parties in writing, and provide up-to-date contact information for the party and any new representative. Where a representative ceases to act for a client the tribunal may issue directions to ensure fairness to all parties and to prevent undue delay of proceedings.

A9.4   The tribunal may disqualify a representative from appearing before it where the representative's continued appearance would lead to an abuse of process.

A10   LITIGATION GUARDIANS

A10.1   This Rule applies where a person seeks to be a litigation guardian for a party. It does not apply where no litigation guardian is required as a result of the nature of the proceeding.

A10.2   Persons are presumed to have the mental capacity to manage and conduct their case and to appoint and instruct a representative.

Litigation Guardian Declarations

A10.3   A litigation guardian for a minor under the age of 18 is required to file a signed declaration in the form designated by the tribunal, confirming:

    a. the litigation guardian's consent to serve in this role;

    b. the minor's date of birth;

    c. the nature of the relationship to the minor;

    d. that any other person with custody or legal guardianship of the minor has been provided with a copy of the materials in the proceeding and a copy of the SJTO practice direction on litigation guardians;

    e. that the litigation guardian has no interest that conflicts with those of the person represented;

    f. an undertaking to act in accordance with the responsibilities of a litigation guardian as set out in Rule A10.8; and

    g. that the litigation guardian is at least 18 years of age and understands the nature of the proceeding.

A10.4   A litigation guardian for a person who lacks mental capacity to participate in the tribunal proceeding must file a signed declaration in the form designated by the tribunal, confirming:

    a. the litigation guardian's consent to serve in this role;

    b. the nature of the litigation guardian's relationship to the person represented;

    c. reasons for believing that the person is not mentally incapable of participating in the proceeding;

    d. the nature and extent of the disability causing the mental incapacity;

    e. that no other person has authority to be the person's litigation guardian in the proceeding;

    f. that any person who holds power of attorney or guardianship for the person for other matters has been provided with a copy of the materials in the proceeding and a copy of the SJTO practice direction on litigation guardians;

    g. that the litigation guardian has no interest that conflicts with the interests of the person represented;

    h. an undertaking to act in accordance with the responsibilities of a litigation guardian as set out in Rule A10.8; and

    i   that the litigation guardian is at least 18 years of age and understands the nature of the proceeding.

Naming and Removing a Litigation Guardian

A10.5   Upon the filing of a complete declaration as required by this Rule and unless refused or removed by the Tribunal, the person may act as litigation guardian for the party.

A10.6 The Tribunal will review the declaration and may direct submissions by the parties on whether the litigation guardian should be refused pursuant to Rule A10.7.

A10.7 Upon review of the declaration, or at any later time in the proceeding, the Tribunal may refuse or remove a litigation guardian on its own initiative or at the request of any person because:
  a. the litigation guardian has an interest that conflicts with the interests of the person represented;
  b. the appointment conflicts with the substitute decision making authority of another person;
  c. the person has capacity to conduct or continue the proceeding;
  d. the litigation guardian is unable or unwilling to continue in this role;
  e. a more appropriate person seeks to be litigation guardian; or
  f. no litigation guardian is needed to conduct the proceeding.

Responsibilities of Litigation Guardians

A10.8 A litigation guardian shall diligently attend to the interests of the person represented and shall take all steps necessary for the protection of those interests including:
  a. to the extent possible, informing and consulting with the person represented about the proceedings;
  b. considering the impact of the proceeding on the person represented;
  c. deciding whether to retain a representative and providing instructions to the representative; and
  d. assisting in gathering evidence to support the proceeding and putting forward the best possible case to the tribunal.

A10.9 No one may be compensated for serving as a litigation guardian unless provided for by law or a pre-existing agreement.

A10.10 When a minor who was represented by a litigation guardian turns 18, the role of the litigation guardian will automatically end.

Appendix II.4
Practice Direction on Representation before
Social Justice Tribunals Ontario[†]

Practice Directions support the Social Justice Tribunals Ontario (SJTO) Common Rules of Procedure and provide guidance about what the Tribunal expects of the parties and in turn what the parties can expect of the Tribunal. They assist in understanding and applying the rules.

PURPOSE

This Practice Direction discusses the representation of parties before the tribunals and boards of the Social Justice Tribunals Ontario ("tribunals"), including who can represent a party and the obligations of representatives. It relates to Rule A9 of the SJTO Common Rules.

SUPPORT PERSONS

A support person, such as a family member or friend, may attend a hearing or mediation with a party or witness to assist the person in participating in the proceeding, communicating with the Tribunal and making necessary decisions and may sit with the party during the hearing or mediation. Such a support person is not considered a representative, so long as they do not make submissions on the party's behalf.

SELF-REPRESENTED

A party may be self-represented and appear before the Tribunal and present his or her case. The SJTO's rules are interpreted and applied to allow parties to participate effectively in the process, whether or not they are represented by a lawyer or paralegal.

REPRESENTATIVES

A party may also choose to appoint another person to represent him or her in SJTO proceedings.

[†] Reproduced from SJTO website: "Rules of Procedure" <http://www.sjto.gov.on.ca/documents/sjto/Practice% 20Directions/Representation%20before%20SJTO.html>. © Queen's Printer for Ontario.

The representative may be:

- a lawyer, licensed by the Law Society of Upper Canada (LSUC),
- a paralegal, licensed by the LSUC, or
- an unlicensed person, if that person falls within a category of persons the LSUC has exempted from its licensing requirements.

A person who is not licensed, whose license is suspended or who is not in an exempted category will not be permitted to act as a representative in SJTO proceedings.

LICENSED REPRESENTATIVE

A licensed representative is a lawyer or paralegal licensed by the LSUC. A licensed representative must be in good standing with the LSUC and must provide his or her license number to the Tribunal.

There are Rules of Conduct for lawyers and for paralegals established by the LSUC.

UNLICENSED REPRESENTATIVE

An unlicensed person may represent a party in proceedings before the SJTO if that person falls within the specific licensing exemptions established by the LSUC.

A person who is not licensed may be asked by the SJTO to identify the LSUC exemption category to which he or she belongs.

The current exemptions permit the following unlicensed persons, among others, to act as a representative:

- an unpaid friend or neighbour who is not in the business of providing legal services, who does not receive compensation, and who provides legal services in no more than 3 matters in a year
- an unpaid family member who is not in the business of providing legal services and who does not receive compensation
- a member of Provincial Parliament (MPP) or the Constituency assistant working in the MPP's office
- an employee or volunteer from a trade union or appropriate organization
- students, volunteers and employees of legal clinics funded through Legal Aid Ontario
- individuals employed by a single employer, for example, a municipal prosecutor or employee of a corporation appearing on behalf of the corporation

A complete list of approved exemptions is on the LSUC's website.

A person who is not licensed and who is not exempt from licensing requirements will be not permitted to act as a representative in an SJTO proceeding. This would include:

- a friend, neighbour or family member who expects to/or receives compensation in return for acting as a representative
- an unpaid friend or neighbour who has already provided legal services in respect of three matters in that year
- subject to limited exceptions, a member of a board of directors of a corporation who is not an employee of the corporation

Representative's Responsibilities

Where a party is represented, the Tribunal will communicate with the party through its representative.

Representatives must treat all participants and the Tribunal with courtesy and respect. Both licensed and unlicensed representatives are expected to know and follow the Tribunal's rules and procedures and any directions or orders made during the proceeding. Acting on the client's behalf and instructions, a representative is responsible for all communications with the Tribunal and the other parties and for preparing and presenting the client's case to the Tribunal.

The Tribunal may exclude a representative from a hearing where necessary to prevent an abuse of process (for example, because the representative has a conflict of interest) or, in the case of unlicensed representatives, where the Tribunal finds the representative is not competent to properly represent or to advise the party or witness, or does not understand and comply at the hearing with the duties and responsibilities of a representative, *Hansen v. Toronto (City)*, 2010 HRTO 13.

The Tribunal recognizes that limited scope retainers exist. A representative on a limited scope retainer shall ensure the client understands the extent and scope of the services that will be provided and is responsible for advising the tribunal when no longer retained.

Effective as of October 1, 2013   sjto.ca

Appendix II.5
Practice Direction on Litigation Guardians before Social Justice Tribunals Ontario[†]

Practice Directions support the Social Justice Tribunals Ontario (SJTO) Common Rules of Procedure and provide guidance about what the Tribunal expects of the parties and in turn what the parties can expect of the Tribunal. They assist in understanding and applying the rules.

PURPOSE

This Practice Direction discusses how a person who does not have legal capacity can be a party to a case before the tribunals and boards of the Social Justice Tribunals Ontario ("tribunal") through a litigation guardian. It relates to Rule A10 of the SJTO Common Rules. The SJTO is committed to making its processes accessible and responsive to persons with disabilities, and in particular to persons with cognitive disabilities. Rule A10 is part of an ongoing effort to review tribunal processes to ensure that they are responsive to these needs.

Being legally incapable means that, under the law a person is unable to make certain decisions for himself or herself. A party may be legally incapable in a tribunal proceeding for one of two reasons: either they are a minor (under the age of 18) or they do not have the mental capacity to make decisions about the issues in the case.

GENERAL

Rule A10 only applies where another person wants to be a litigation guardian for a party in a case. The tribunal has no power to require the Public Guardian and Trustee or the Children's Lawyer to be a litigation guardian. For a discussion of tribunals' powers to appoint a litigation guardian, see *Yuill v. Canadian Union of Public Employees*, 2011 HRTO 126. This Practice Direction and Rule A10 do not address situations where one party believes that another party does not have capacity to conduct the proceeding. The relevant legal principles applicable to that situation are discussed in *Romanchook v. Garda Ontario*, 2009 HRTO 1077 and *Collier v. Freeland*, 2011 HRTO 399.

[†] Reproduced from SJTO website: "Rules of Procedure" <http://www.sjto.gov.on.ca/documents/sjto/ Practice% 20Directions/Litigation%20Guardians%20before%20SJTO.html>. © Queen's Printer for Ontario.

Rule A10 also does not apply where a litigation guardian is not needed.

Everyone 18 years of age and over is presumed, unless there is a reason to believe otherwise, to have legal capacity to make decisions. This includes the decisions to start a case before a tribunal and to decide what to do during the case. If someone does not have the capacity to bring or respond to a case then they may need a litigation guardian to do so for them.

As discussed below, the litigation guardian must file the appropriate tribunal form and provide the relevant supporting documents. Normally, this is done at the start of the case. However, if a case is already underway, it can be done later when the need for a litigation guardian is clear.

The litigation guardian must agree to take on this role. Litigation guardians must be at least 18 years of age and must understand the nature of the case before the tribunal.

MINORS

Depending on the type of case, a minor who is a party may require a litigation guardian. There are some situations where it is not necessary for a minor to have a litigation guardian. Applications at the Human Rights Tribunal of Ontario are the only cases at the SJTO where litigation guardians for minors are typically necessary and used.

A parent or a legal guardian will usually be a minor's litigation guardian. Others who may act as a litigation guardian for a minor include a person with legal custody of the minor, a court appointed guardian of the minor's property under the *Children's Law Reform Act*, R.S.O. 1990, c. C.12, or the Children's Lawyer. If this applies, the litigation guardian must file a document proving this.

A litigation guardian for a minor must file a signed form confirming the minor's date of birth, the nature of his or her relationship to the minor, and various declarations. The litigation guardian must send a copy of the documents in the case (for example, the application or appeal, and response if any) and a copy of this Practice Direction to any other person with custody or guardianship rights of the minor (for example, another parent with joint custody). Form 4A at the Human Rights Tribunal of Ontario should be used for the declaration. If you seek to become a litigation guardian for a minor in a proceeding before another tribunal, provide your declaration the form of a letter.

PARTIES WITH MENTAL CAPACITY ISSUES

If a party does not have the mental capacity to make decisions in the tribunal proceeding someone else (such as a friend, family member, or support worker) may be their litigation guardian and bring or defend a case for them.

The term "mental incapacity" in this context means someone who cannot understand information needed to make decisions about the case or cannot understand the consequences of such decisions.

There may already be someone with the power to be the litigation guardian in the tribunal process, for example, a substitute decision maker. A substitute decision maker is someone with a continuing power of attorney, or a court-appointed or statutory guardian of property under the *Substitute Decisions Act*, 1992. The authority of a substitute decision maker may cover different things. It is important to check whether a substitute decision maker has the power to be the litigation guardian in the litigation before the tribunal. If so, only the person who has this power can be the litigation guardian at the tribunal. A person who is already a litigation guardian usually does not need to file evidence about the disability with their declaration.

A litigation guardian for a person who lacks capacity to make decisions in a tribunal proceeding must file a signed form confirming the nature of his or her relationship to the person, why he or she believes that the person lacks the mental capacity to make decisions in the proceeding, a description of the disability causing the mental incapacity, and various declarations.

The forms for the declaration are:

- Human Rights Tribunal of Ontario: *Form 4B*
- Landlord and Tenant Board: *Request to be a Litigation Guardian: Mental Incapacity*
- Child and Family Services Review Board: *Application for Litigation Guardian: Mental Incapacity*

Forms have not been created for the other SJTO tribunals since litigation guardians are not typically necessary and used. If you seek to become a litigation guardian for a party with mental capacity issues in a proceeding before a tribunal without a form, provide your declaration in the form of a letter.

It is helpful to provide further evidence to show that the person cannot make the needed decisions. For example, a capacity assessment, medical or other evidence of the person's mental health or intellectual disabilities, or a statement from a trained community or support worker. If the litigation guardian already has the legal power to conduct legal proceedings, the document confirming this power is usually all that needs to be attached.

If there is someone who has the power to make decisions for the person, but this does not include the power to act in the tribunal case, the litigation guardian must send a copy of the materials (for example, the application or appeal, and any response) to this person together with a copy of this Practice Direction. A person cannot ask to be a litigation guardian if there is already some other person with legal power to be the litigation guardian, see Rule A10.4e.

DECLARATION AND RESPONSIBILITY OF
LITIGATION GUARDIANS

Litigation guardians must declare (promise) that they will fulfil the responsibilities set out in Rule A10.8.

Litigation guardians must make decisions in the interests of the party they represent. They must learn about the case and the tribunal's processes. Litigation guardians must diligently look out for the interests of the person they are representing. They must do everything needed to protect those interests. Before filing a case, the litigation guardian must consider the impact it would have on the person they are representing.

As much as possible, the litigation guardian must inform and consult the person when making decisions about the case. This will depend upon the person's understanding and ability.

The litigation guardian must decide whether to hire a lawyer or paralegal. The litigation guardian must provide instructions to the lawyer or paralegal, if there is one. To the extent possible, the represented person should also consult with the representative directly. The litigation guardian must assist in finding evidence to put forward the best possible case.

No one can be paid to be a litigation guardian unless this is provided for by law or in a pre-existing agreement. Litigation guardians cannot negotiate a settlement of a party's case that pays them for their work as litigation guardian. When a litigation guardian receives settlement monies, the money generally belongs to the person they are representing.

NAMING AND REMOVING A LITIGATION GUARDIAN

Once the completed form, including the declaration[,] is filed, the person is the litigation guardian. There is no need for the tribunal to make an order "appointing" the litigation guardian.

The tribunal will review the materials when they are filed, and if it has concerns that the litigation guardian is not appropriate, it may ask for submissions on whether the litigation guardian should be refused under Rule A10.7.

The tribunal can also, at any other time during the proceeding, decide whether a litigation guardian should be removed. The tribunal may do so on its own initiative, or on request of a party or other person, including the person who is represented by the litigation guardian.

The reasons a litigation guardian may be refused or removed include:

a. the litigation guardian has an interest that conflicts with the interests of the person represented;
b. the appointment conflicts with the substitute decision making authority of another person;

    c. the person has capacity to conduct or continue the proceeding;

    d. the litigation guardian is unable or unwilling to continue in this role;

    e. a more appropriate person seeks to be litigation guardian; or

       no litigation guardian is needed to conduct the proceeding.

Conflict of Interest

A litigation guardian cannot have a conflict of interest with the person he or she is representing. Where a person believes that a litigation guardian has a personal interest that conflicts with the interest of the person they are representing, then that person can file a request asking the tribunal to remove the litigation guardian.

For a further discussion of what it means to have a conflict of interest, please see *Gronnerud (Litigation Guardians of) v. Gronnerud Estate*, 2002 SCC 38 and *Yuill v. CUPE*, 2012 HRTO 366.

Conflict with Another Person's Decision Making Authority

The litigation guardian must declare that he or she has provided a copy of the materials in the proceeding to any other person who has substitute decision making authority, such as through a continuing power of attorney, court or tribunal order, or custody of a child. If allowing the litigation guardian to act would conflict with this other person's authority to make decisions for the represented person, then the tribunal may refuse or remove the litigation guardian. This may occur, for example, where a court or the Consent and Capacity Board has already appointed some other person as a litigation guardian for the party. Where another person believes they are the proper litigation guardian they can request that the tribunal appoint him or her instead.

Represented Person Has Capacity

When a minor turns 18, he or she will become the party in his or her own name and the role of the litigation guardian will automatically end. If a party who initially lacked mental capacity to participate becomes capable of making decisions in the proceeding, the litigation guardian will be removed or refused.

Since capacity can vary and fluctuate, it is important for a litigation guardian to think carefully about whether a party can represent him or herself. Persons with capacity issues may be able to participate in a tribunal proceeding by themselves with appropriate accommodations. The tribunal will accommodate parties' needs in accordance with the *Human Rights Code*, R.S.O. 1990, c. H.19, as amended ("*Human Rights Code*") and the tribunal's policies on accessibility and accommodation.

Tribunal processes facilitate the involvement of others who may support a person in making decisions or in representing himself or herself before the tribunal. An unpaid friend or family member may act as a representative, and may also appear as a support person: see the Practice Direction on Representation before Social Justice Tribunals Ontario.

Litigation Guardian Unable to Continue

A litigation guardian has to be able to make decisions about the case. If the litigation guardian cannot continue in this role, he or she may be removed.

A More Appropriate Person seeks to be Litigation Guardian

The tribunal may refuse or remove a litigation guardian if there is someone else who would be more appropriate. If someone (for example a parent or substitute decision maker) believes that he or she is a more appropriate person to act as a litigation guardian then a request can be made that the tribunal remove the current litigation guardian and appoint him or her.

No Litigation Guardian Required

In some cases a minor will not need a litigation guardian as they can participate directly in a tribunal proceeding as a party. In these cases the tribunal may refuse the litigation guardian because no litigation guardian is required due to the nature of the proceeding.

At the Child and Family Services Review Board and Custody Review Board, a child can participate in proceedings without a litigation guardian. These tribunals do not typically require or use litigation guardians for children and youth because of the statutory provisions governing their proceedings.

At the Social Benefits Tribunal a person who is under 18 years of age can participate in proceedings as a party without a litigation guardian. For example, minors may file an appeal of a decision regarding whether or not they are eligible for income assistance under the *Ontario Works Act*, 1997 because there are special circumstances that justify the assistance. A minor who has a dependent child may file an appeal of a decision regarding that minor's eligibility for assistance on behalf of his or her dependent child.

At the Human Rights Tribunal of Ontario a 16 or 17 year old who has withdrawn from parental control, and is making a claim of discrimination in housing, can file an application on his or her own behalf (see section 4(1) of the *Human Rights Code*). Similarly, at the Landlord and Tenant Board a person who is a 16 or 17 years old, who has withdrawn from parental control and who is a tenant, may file an application on his or her own behalf (see section 4(1) of the *Human Rights Code*).

The tribunal may also refuse or remove a litigation guardian where a litigation guardian is unnecessary because the person has a sufficient level of capacity to participate in the proceeding without one. At the HRTO, if a party has some capacity then he or she can be assisted in bringing an Application under s.34(5) of the *Human Rights Code*. This section of the *Code* allows persons to consent to have someone else file an application on their behalf and make decisions in the case for them (see Form 27 and the HRTO's Practice direction on filing applications on behalf of another person). In this way a friend, organization or family member can file an application on behalf of any person.

The HRTO has found that a person does not have to be able to make all decisions about the case to consent to an application being brought on their behalf under section 34(5) of the *Code*. Rather, it is sufficient that they understand what it means to file a human rights application, to give someone the power to make the decisions for them, and to end their case. For a discussion of section 34(5) of the *Code* please see *Kacan v. OPSEU*, 2010 HRTO 795 and the HRTO's Practice Direction on filing applications on behalf of another person.

If a litigation guardian has been removed, the tribunal may either order that the party will conduct the proceeding in his or her own name, substitute a new person as litigation guardian, or order that the proceeding cannot continue until someone else comes forward to be the litigation guardian.

Effective as of October 1, 2013   sjto.ca

Appendix II.6
A Presentation at the LSUC
2014 Six-Minute Administrative Lawyer Meeting

Ontario's Tribunal Clusters:
"Many Attend, Few Understand"
(with apologies to Leo Durocher)[†]

Michael Gottheil
Executive Chair Social Justice Tribunals Ontario

PART I: AN INTRODUCTION TO CLUSTERING

a) What is Clustering?

- Clustering brings together a specific group of adjudicative tribunals within a single organization, but maintains each tribunal's distinct statutory jurisdiction and membership

- Clustering follows a trend in a number of jurisdiction[s] globally (Québec, Australia, New Zealand, U.K.) which aims to restructure the administrative tribunal sector, but to date is an approach unique to Ontario

- Under the *Adjudicative Tribunals Accountability, Governance and Appointments Act, 2009* ("*ATAGAA*"), the government may designate a cluster when:

    "...the matters that the tribunals deal with are such that they can operate more effectively and efficiently as part of a cluster than alone." (s.15)

- Clusters are formed by Regulation under *ATAGAA*. The constituting statute of each constituent tribunal is not changed

- Pursuant to *ATAGAA* the government shall appoint an Executive Chair, who has all of the powers, duties and responsibilities of the Chairs of each constituent tribunal

- The government may appoint an Associate Chair for each of the constituent tribunals

---

[†] A Presentation at the Law Society of Upper Canada, 2014 Six-Minute Administrative Lawyer Meeting, March 20, 2014 Toronto, Ontario. Available at: SJTO website, "Speeches and Papers" <http://www.sjto.gov.on.ca/documents/sjto/The%20Six-Minute%20Administrative%20Lawyer%202014.pdf>. © Queen's Printer for Ontario.

- The Executive Chair may assign any of his or her responsibilities (except that of Ethics Executive) to any Associate Chair or Vice Chair

- Beyond this modest statutory framework, and the directive that the purpose of clustering is to enhance the "efficiency and effectiveness" of how subject matters are dealt with, there are no articulated legislative or policy objectives that set out how clusters are to be organized, or specific initiatives they should pursue. This has led some to see clustering as an evolutionary or organic transformation exercise, which allows each cluster to develop in ways that best respond to the needs of their respective user communities, and the mandates of their constituent tribunals. The uncertainties inherent in clustering can seem puzzling, or even daunting, but the model has the potential to support innovative approaches to the delivery of justice.

b) Clustering To Date

- Environment and Land Tribunals Ontario (ELTO)
  - Assessment Review Board
  - Board of Negotiation
  - Conservation Review Board
  - Environmental Review Tribunal
  - Ontario Municipal Board

- Social Justice Tribunals Ontario (SJTO)
  - Child and Family Services Review Board
  - Custody Review Board
  - Human Rights Tribunal of Ontario
  - Landlord and Tenant Board
  - Ontario Special Education Tribunals
  - Social Benefits Tribunal

- Safety, Licence Appeals and Standards Tribunals Ontario (SLASTO)
  - Animal Care Review Board
  - Fire Safety Commission
  - Licence Appeal Tribunal
  - Ontario Civilian Police Commission
  - Ontario Parole Board

All tribunals have been "migrated" to the Ministry of the Attorney General, and the clusters "report through" the Policy and Administrative Tribunal Division of MAG.

Combined, the 3 clusters administer over 140 statutes, and receive approximately 160,000 applications and appeals annually. By contrast, the Superior Court of Ontario receives 95,000 new matters and the Small Claims Court receives 45,000 matters each year.

c) Clustering as Justice Modernization

Why Cluster?
Principles and Possibilities

Individual Tribunals	Clusters	Amalgamation
Specialist	Inter-disciplinary	Generalist
Insular	Inter-connected	Loss of Identity
Close to Stakeholders	Balanced Relationships	Disconnected
Uneven Caseload	Strategic Assignments	Dilution
Uneven Resources	Strategic Allocation	Bureaucratic
Fragmentation	Coherence (?)	Goliath

d) Challenges

- Defining a vision that resonates — internally and externally
- Building confidence among users
- Getting everyone to stay on course, where there is no roadmap, and no set destination
- Capacity of government to deliver on Co-location and IT

PART II: SJTO: 3 YEARS ON

a) Introduction

- SJTO was designated as a cluster early in 2011
- When designated, SJTO had approximately:
  - Budget $48m
  - 360 staff, 90 full time and 100 part time adjudicators
  - 97,000 cases annually
  - 5 separate case management and administrative units, including 4 Directors and 5 Registrars

b) Efficiencies Achieved

- 5% reduction in budget allocation
- 10% reduction in FTEs
- 5% increase in caseload
- 0 backlog
- Initial co-location: 4 of 7 tribunals
- Sharing of hearing centres in Toronto, Hamilton, London, Ottawa
- Consolidation of management structure
- Reduction in number of Directors, Registrars, Case Management units
- Consolidation of legal and corporate services

c)   **Achievements to Date**

- Cluster-wide Professional Development Unit
  - Annual PD Institute for 200 full and part time adjudicators and mediators
  - Tribunal specific new member training modules, including core competencies
  - Development of training modules in human rights, decision writing, evidence, credibility assessment which can be delivered in-person and on-line
  - Also supports staff training, and training for specific initiatives
  - Strategic use of other professional development offerings such as SOAR, CCAT and[] OBA and CIAJ

- Cross-appointments
  - 10% of SJTO membership is currently cross-appointed
  - Specific, strategic and deliberate — to enhance expertise, not dilute it
  - A vehicle to support professional and career development, regional coverage, caseload fluctuation, the inter-disciplinary dimension of SJTO's collective mandate

- Legal
  - All tribunals now have access to expert, in-house legal unit
  - Assists in development of coherent body of jurisprudence, supports tribunals' expertise

- Communications
  - Consolidated website: facilitates access to information and services
  - Co-ordinated resources, policy and approach for: Issues Management, FOI/Privacy, Complaints, Accessibility and Accommodation
  - Consolidated Annual Report, business planning, fiscal management and reporting, operational planning and reporting

- Stakeholder Relations
  - Position of Executive Chair allows for active and transparent engagement with government, legal and community stakeholders
  - E.g. establishment of working group between SBT, MCSS and community clinics to develop procedural improvements in social assistance matters

- Capacity for Innovation
  - Efficiencies and economies of scale allow for development of support models for legal services, professional development, accountability and controllership, communications
  - Provides capacity for pilot and innovative projects. E.g.:
    i. Child and Youth Division
    ii. Expedited Scheduling at LTB

      iii. Pre-Hearing Conferences at LTB
      iv. Co-op Housing Disputes
      v. Medical Review pilot at SBT

d)   Lessons to Date: Do's and Don'ts

- Do's
  - Embrace Efficiency
  - Set a Vision
  - Co-locate
  - Build Capacity and Confidence
  - Focus on Outcomes — Mind what Matters

- Don'ts
  - Expect too much too soon

Social Benefits Tribunal

4

WHAT THIS CHAPTER OFFERS

- The background of the Social Benefits Tribunal (SBT)
- A discussion of the cluster of the Ontario social justice tribunals (SJTO) and its impact on the SBT
- Details and explanation of the enabling statutes and regulations relevant to the SBT
- Provisions of the *Statutory Powers Procedure Act* relevant to the SBT
- Concepts of public policy relevant to the SBT
- Specific rules and procedures for the SBT
- A walk-through of the SBT website
- Summaries of relevant cases and decisions highlighting legal principle or issue in question
- A flow chart summarizing the procedural stages of an appeal before the SBT

LEARNING OBJECTIVES

After reading this chapter, the reader should be able to:

- state the statutes and regulations that govern the operation of the SBT
- research the SBT website for important information needed to understand the agency's practices and procedures and to represent a client properly before the SBT
- compare and prioritize the various sources of practice and procedure of the SBT
- apply the specific rules and procedures in a proceeding before, during, and after a hearing of the SBT
- argue the law before the SBT using appropriate legislation and case law

INTRODUCTION

The Social Benefits Tribunal (SBT) is an Ontario adjudicative agency created and given power by legislation to hear appeals from decisions made by persons working in or through the Ontario Ministry of Community and Social Services regarding the amount of or eligibility for the benefits for social assistance, as set out on the SBT website, <www.sbt.gov.on.ca>.

OVERVIEW AND BACKGROUND

Basic social assistance is provided in Ontario by or through the Ministry of Community and Social Services to those in immediate financial need either due to lack of, or insufficiency in, employment or due to disabilities. Basic social assistance also supports children with severe disabilities. Before the creation of the SBT, its predecessor, the Social Assistance Review Board (SARB), considered appeals regarding social assistance under the now repealed *Family Benefits Act* and other statutes.

ENABLING LEGISLATION

The SBT was created on June 1, 1998, under subsection 60(1) of the *Ontario Works Act, 1997*, S.O. 1997, c. 25, Sched. A, as amended (the *OWA*), which also gave the SBT some of its powers and jurisdiction. The SBT was also given additional powers and jurisdiction under another empowering statute, the *Ontario Disability Support Program Act, 1997*, S.O. 1997, c. 25, Sched. B, as amended (the *ODSPA*). The sections of both Acts and the relevant regulations related to the SBT are set out below.

OWA and O. Reg. 134/98

Assistance under OWA

This statute was enacted to establish a program to, among other things, provide "temporary financial assistance to those in need while they satisfy obligations to become and stay employed" (ss. 1(b)) by providing both employment assistance (s. 4) and basic financial assistance (s. 5) to those persons who satisfy all conditions of eligibility under the Act and the regulations made under it (ss. 7(1)). The delivery of financial assistance is delegated to delivery agents by the Minister of Community and Social Services (ss. 38.(1)). Pursuant to subsection 39(1), there are 47 Consolidated Municipal Service Managers at the municipal level (in Northern Ontario, they are called

District Social Services Administration Boards) and 111 First Nations delivery agents (see Recommendations for an Ontario Income Security Review (May 2010), page 3, <http://www.mcss.gov.on.ca/documents/en/mcss/publications/social/sarac%20report/SARAC%20Report%20-%20FINAL.pdf>).

Decision of the Administrator and Internal Review

Every delivery agent appoints an administrator to oversee the administration under the Act (s. 43) and who, among other things, determines eligibility for employment assistance and basic financial assistance (s. 44). Once an administrator makes a decision regarding the eligibility for and the amount, if any, of assistance, "such administrator shall give notice to the applicant or recipient of a decision that may be appealed and the notice shall advise the applicant or recipient that he or she may request an internal review of the decision" (s. 24). The formalities and contents of the notice of decision are set out in O. Reg. 134/98, s. 67. According to subsection 26(1) of the Act, any decision by an administrator regarding eligibility for, or the amount of, basic financial assistance may be appealed to the SBT. Decisions set out in subsection 26(2) of the Act (including prescribed decisions defined in section 68 of O. Reg. 134/98) cannot be appealed to the Tribunal. **Before the appeal to the SBT of a decision can be commenced, there must be a request to do an internal review (s. 27(1)).** An internal review occurs when the applicant or recipient requests that the administrator consider the decision and whether or not to change it. The specifics about timing for the request for an internal review are set out in section 27 of the *OWA* and section 69 of O. Reg. 134/98. An internal review must be completed within 30 days from the day the request is submitted and must be done by someone who did not make the original decision (s. 70 of O. Reg. 134/98). Details regarding delivery of and the contents of the internal review are given in section 71 of O. Reg. 134/98. Under subsection 27(4) of the *OWA*, the *SPPA* does not apply to the internal review.

Appeal to the SBT

The specifics of appeal to the SBT are detailed in section 28 of the *OWA* and sections 72–79 of O. Reg. 134/98. The date to request an appeal is 30 days from the date the decision is final. (That time can be extended by the SBT under subsection 28(2) of the *OWA*.) The appeal shall commence no later than one year from the date of the decision and shall be done with a notice of appeal form approved by the Minister (s. 72 of O. Reg. 134/98). The notice of appeal shall set out the reasons for requesting the appeal (ss. 28(1)). The parties to the hearing before the SBT are the "administrator, the applicant or recipient who requested the hearing, and any other persons specified by the Tribunal" (ss. 28(4)), and the Director can be added to the proceeding by the SBT if requested by the Director (ss. 28(5)). A spouse can also be added as a party in a specific circumstance, but that spouse cannot launch an appeal of that determination (ss. 28(6–7)).

Upon receipt of the notice of appeal, the SBT shall send a copy of the notice to any other parties in the proceeding (O. Reg. 134/98, ss. 73(1)). Subsection 28(8) allows the administrator and the Director to make written submissions in place of, or in addition to, appearing at a hearing. The submissions, however, must be filed with the SBT within 30 days after the administrator has received a copy of the notice of appeal and shall then be provided to all other parties (O. Reg. 134/98, ss. 73(2–3)). Under subsection 28(10) of the *OWA*, the "parties to a hearing shall be given an opportunity before the hearing to examine any written or documentary evidence that a party proposes to introduce at the hearing". The SBT is required under section 74 of O. Reg. 134/98 to send, within 60 days of receipt of the notice of appeal, the notice of hearing, including whether it is to be an oral hearing (in which case to include date, place, and time of hearing) or "paper" (written), and the dates that the parties are to provide written submissions and documentary evidence to the SBT. **The SBT is required to give the parties at least 30 days' notice of the hearing. Under subsection 28(11) of the *OWA*, the onus is on the appellant to satisfy the SBT that the decision of the administrator is wrong.** Some of the procedures for the conduct of an oral hearing before the SBT are the following:

- The appellant shall present his or her case first at an oral hearing of an appeal before the SBT, unless the administrator agrees otherwise.

- The SBT shall ensure that the evidence at an oral hearing of an appeal is recorded by notes taken by an SBT member participating in the hearing or by a method from which a transcript can be produced.

These are set out in section 76 of O. Reg. 134/98 and should be referred to if there is an oral hearing of the appeal.

Interim Assistance

After the request for an appeal but before the SBT can make a decision, the SBT, under section 30 of the *OWA*, can direct the administrator to provide interim assistance "to an applicant or recipient if the Tribunal is satisfied that the person will suffer financial hardship during the period needed for the Tribunal to complete its review and give notice of its decision" up to a maximum, as set out in section 77 of O. Reg. 134/98. The *SPPA* does not apply to any proceeding of the SBT regarding interim assistance (ss. 30(3)).

Decision of the SBT

Within 60 days after it last receives evidence or submissions on the appeal (O. Reg. 134/98, ss. 78(1)), the SBT must deliver a written decision to the parties. Under section 31 of the *OWA*, the SBT's orders include (a) denying the appeal, (b) granting the appeal, (c) granting the appeal in part, or (d) referring the matter back to the administrator for reconsideration with any directions the SBT considers proper. Furthermore, the SBT decision must include reasons and takes effect when it is made and, if it is appealed, continues in effect until a decision of the Divisional Court is made on appeal. Appeals can be denied if the proceedings fall within the circumstances listed in section 34 of the *OWA*. The SBT's findings of fact shall be based exclusively on evidence admissible and facts of which notice may be taken under sections 15, 15.1, 15.2, and 16 of the *SPPA*, and the decision shall include the principal findings of fact and its conclusions based on those findings (O. Reg. 134/98, ss. 78(2–3)). Note that under section 33 of the *OWA*, the SBT "shall refuse to hear an appeal if it determines the appeal to be frivolous or vexatious".

Reconsideration of SBT Decision

Section 79 of O. Reg. 134/98 details timelines and procedural matters relating to requesting the SBT to reconsider its decision on the appeal. The ultimate deadline for reconsideration request is one year after the decision. "Under no circumstances can the SBT extend the time for requesting a reconsideration hearing beyond one year past the date of the SBT's decision."

Appeal of SBT Decision

There is no privative clause preventing an appeal of an SBT decision: subsection 36(1) of the *OWA* states that the "Director and any party to a hearing may appeal the Tribunal's decision to the Divisional Court on a question of law". Currently, the *Law Society Act* and the Paralegal Rules of Conduct do not allow paralegals to appear in Divisional Court, so we will skip the review of the procedures of the SBT under the *OWA* and its O. Reg. 134/98 and continue with a review of the appropriate sections of the enabling legislation for further information. However, if you are faced with a decision that should be appealed, note that under section 81 of O. Reg134/98, the appeal **must** be commenced by filing a notice of appeal with Divisional Court, usually within 30 days after receiving the decision of the SBT.

General Jurisdictional and Procedural Matters of the SBT

General provisions regarding the SBT are contained in Part IV of the *OWA*, specifically, sections 60–67. Section 64 envisions either one adjudicator or a panel made up of one presiding member and the rest of the panel. Sittings for hearings can occur anywhere in Ontario "and in the manner and at the times the Tribunal considers most convenient for the proper discharge and speedy dispatch of its business" (ss. 65(1)); alternately, the SBT may hold a paper hearing (ss. 65(2)). **Notwithstanding the *SPPA*, all hearings before the SBT are private (ss. 66(1)).** Also under subsection 66(2), no members hearing the matter shall have had any prior dealings with the matter or *ex parte* communication with any parties except as allowed under the subsection 66(3), where hearing members seek legal advice or have discussions with other members of the Tribunal. Pursuant to subsection 66(4), only the member who was present throughout the hearing and heard the evidence and argument of the parties can make a decision of that Tribunal hearing. A request can be made under subsection 66(5) to the SBT, and if it believes that there will be financial hardship to a party or witness attending the hearing, it may pay such party or witness travelling and living expenses, as necessary, to enable such attendance at the hearing. There are specific restrictions on the jurisdiction of the SBT to make a decision or to inquire into specific situations as set out in section 67.

ODSPA and O. Reg. 222/98

Assistance under ODSPA

The *ODSPA*, among other things, "provides income and employment support to eligible persons with disabilities" (ss. 1(a)). Under subsection 10(1), an application for income support shall be made to the Director of the Ontario Disability Support Program (the Director), using a form as required by the Director and containing information required by section 14 of O. Reg. 222/98.

Decision of the Director and Internal Review

The Director oversees the administration under the Act (ss. 37(1)) and, among other things, determines eligibility for income support (s. 38). Once the Director makes a decision regarding the eligibility for and the amount, if any, of income support, the "Director shall give notice to the applicant or recipient of a decision that may be appealed and the notice shall advise the applicant or recipient that he or she may request an internal review of the decision" (s. 19). The formalities and contents of the notice of decision are set out in O. Reg. 222/98, s. 56. According to subsection 21(1) of the *ODSPA*, any decision by the Director regarding eligibility for, or the amount of, income support may be appealed to the SBT other than decisions set out in subsection 21(2), decisions regarding employment support (ss. 21(3)), and those in section 57 of O. Reg. 222/98. **Before the appeal to the SBT of a decision can be commenced, there must be a request for an internal review (ss. 22(1)).** An internal review occurs when the applicant or recipient requests that the Director consider whether or not to change the decision. The specifics about timing for the request for an internal review are set out in section 22 of the *ODSPA* and section 58 of O. Reg. 222/98. An internal review must be completed within 30 days of the request to do it and must be done by someone who did not make the original decision (O. Reg. 222/98, s. 59). Details regarding delivery and contents of the internal review are detailed in section 60 of O. Reg. 222/98. Under subsection 22(4) of the *ODSPA*, the *SPPA* does not apply to the internal review.

Appeal to the SBT

The specifics of appeal to the SBT are detailed in section 23 of the *ODSPA* and sections 61–65 of O. Reg. 222/98. The date to request an appeal is 30 days from the date the decision is final (although that time can be extended under subsection 23(2) of the *ODSPA*). The appeal shall commence no later than one year from the date of the decision and shall be done using a notice of appeal form approved by the Minister (O. Reg. 222/98, s. 61). The notice of appeal shall set out the reasons for requesting the appeal (ss. 23(1)). The parties to the hearing before the SBT are the "Director, the applicant or recipient who requested the hearing and any other persons specified by the Tribunal" (ss. 23(4)). A spouse can also be added as a party in a specific circumstance, but that spouse cannot launch an appeal of that determination (ss. 23(5–6)). Upon receipt of the notice of appeal, the SBT shall send a copy of the notice to any other parties in the proceeding (O. Reg. 222/98, ss. 62(1)). Subsection 23(7) allows the Director to "make written submissions in place of or in addition to appearing at a hearing" to be filed with the SBT within 30 days after the Director has received a copy of the notice of appeal, and submissions shall then be provided to all other parties (O. Reg. 222/98, ss. 62(2–3)). Under subsection 23(9) of the *ODSPA*, the parties to a hearing are entitled to examine, before the hearing, any written or documentary evidence that a party proposes to introduce at the hearing. The SBT is required under section 63 of O. Reg. 222/98 to send, within 60 days of receipt of the notice of appeal, the notice of hearing, including whether it will be an oral hearing (in which case to include date, place, and time of hearing) or paper (written) hearing, and the dates by which the parties are to provide written submissions and documentary evidence to the SBT. The SBT is required to give the parties at least 30 days notice of the hearing. **Under subsection 23(10) of the *ODSPA*, the onus lies on the appellant to satisfy the SBT that the decision of the Director is wrong.** Some of the procedures for the conduct of an oral hearing before the SBT include the following:

- The appellant shall present his or her case first on an oral hearing of an appeal before the SBT, unless the Director agrees otherwise.

- The SBT shall ensure that the evidence at an oral hearing of an appeal is recorded by notes taken by an SBT member participating in the hearing or by a method from which a transcript can be produced.

These are set out in section 65 of O. Reg. 222/98 and should be referred to if there is an oral hearing of the appeal.

Interim Assistance

After the request for an appeal but before the SBT can make a decision, the SBT, under section 25 of the *ODSPA*, can direct the Director to provide interim assistance, up to a maximum as set out in section 66 of O. Reg. 222/98, to a recipient if the SBT is convinced that the person will suffer financial hardship during the period that the SBT needed to complete its review and give notice of its decision. The *SPPA* does not apply to any proceeding of the SBT regarding interim assistance (ss. 25(3)).

Decision of the SBT

Within 60 days after it last receives evidence or submissions on the appeal (O. Reg. 222/98, ss. 67(1)), the SBT must deliver a written decision to the parties. Under section 26 of the *ODSPA*, the SBT can (a) deny the appeal; (b) grant the appeal; (c) grant the appeal in part; or (d) refer the matter back to the Director for reconsideration, with any directions the SBT considers proper. Further, such decision must include reasons and takes effect when it is made and, if it is appealed, continues in effect until a decision of the Divisional Court is made on appeal. Appeals can also be denied if the proceedings fall within the circumstances listed in section 29 of the *ODSPA*. The SBT's findings of fact shall be based exclusively on evidence admissible and facts of which notice may be taken under sections 15, 15.1, 15.2, and 16 of the *SPPA*, and the decision shall include the principal findings of fact and its conclusions based on those findings (O. Reg. 222/ 98, ss. 67(2–3)). It is also important to note that, under section 28 of the *ODSPA*, the SBT "shall refuse to hear an appeal if it determines the appeal to be frivolous or vexatious".

Reconsideration of SBT Decision

Section 68 of O. Reg. 222/98 details the timelines and other procedural matters for requesting the SBT to reconsider its decision on the appeal. "No request for reconsideration may be made more than one year after the decision."

Appeal of SBT Decision

There is no privative clause preventing an appeal of the decision of the SBT: subsection 31(1) of the *ODSPA* states that the "[a]ny party to a hearing may appeal the Tribunal's decision to the Divisional Court on a question of law". Currently the *Law Society Act* and the Paralegal Rules of Conduct do not allow paralegals to appear in Divisional Court, so we will not review the procedures of the SBT under the *ODSPA* and its O. Reg. 222/98, but we will continue to review the appropriate sections of both Act and regulation for further information. However, if you are faced with a decision that should be appealed, note that under section 70 of O. Reg. 222/98, the appeal *must* be commenced by filing a notice of appeal with Divisional Court, usually within 30 days after receiving the SBT's decision.

General Jurisdictional and Procedural Matters of the SBT

General provisions regarding the SBT are contained in Part IV of the *OWA* — specifically, sections 60–67. As those general sections of the *OWA* set out features of the SBT, the *ODSPA*, which gives the SBT jurisdiction to hear appeals under its statute, takes the SBT as it finds it; therefore, those general provisions still apply to the SBT. The review of those general sections of the *OWA*, above, would be useful even if your case were under the *ODSPA*.

RELEVANT REGULATIONS

The review of the regulations relevant to the procedures of the SBT was done in the review of the enabling legislation above.

SOCIAL JUSTICE TRIBUNALS OF ONTARIO
(the tribunal cluster that includes the SBT)

As detailed in the preamble portion to this Part II, clusters of Ontario agencies started to occur in 2009, and the second cluster created was the SJTO, which included the SBT. On the SJTO website, there is a Web page entitled "Reports, Plans and Standards" containing the Annual Report 2013–14 (portions of this report appear as Appendix II.2), which includes a report of the SBT. In addition, there are the SJTO Common Rules and two Practice Directions, which apply to all agencies in the SJTO cluster and which are summarized in the preamble portion to Part II.

As the mandate for clusters is to rationalize procedures and resources within the cluster, it is likely that more such common practices will be developed for the SJTO, and the reader should continually review both the SBT and SJTO websites to keep up to date.

CHANGES TO PROCEDURES OF THE SBT

The Web page entitled "Latest News" on the SBT website home page states that as of December 1, 2015, new rules and forms have been instituted as of January 1, 2016, and states in summary form why the new rules and forms are important to appellants, respondents, and everyone dealing with the SBT, with a link to the new rules and forms.

Further, to provide better public access to SBT decisions, the SBT as of October 2012 has made "the majority of its decisions available to the public by posting them on the Canadian Legal Information Institute (CanLII) website, as is done by other SJTO tribunals. ... Publication of Tribunal decisions will occur after the decision has been issued to the parties and following the removal of personal information. All proceedings before the Tribunal are private and the Tribunal will ensure that decisions are anonymized before they are forwarded for publication." Also announced was the development of "a new format for its decisions — in part to meet the requirements of the publisher CanLII, and in part to improve quality standards and the readability of its decisions and in part to improve consistency within the SJTO cluster of tribunals. The new format includes such enhanced features as numbered paragraphs, increased spacing, standardized font styles and a running header that includes the appeal file number on each page of the decision." (Exhibit 4.1 shows an SBT decision in the new format found on the CanLII website.)

EXHIBIT 4.1
A Sample SBT Decision

 Social
Benefits
Tribunal
Ontario

APPELLANT
Appellant's Representative   Vicki Doidge

RESPONDENT   Director, Ontario Disability Support Program
Respondent's Representative   Linda Grainger

TRIBUNAL PANEL   Bittu George
                                               Beverly Moore

Hearing Date   August 28, 2013
SBT File No.   1203-03822
Citation   2013 ONSBT 5125

2013 ONSBT 5125 (CanLII)

DECISION

ISSUE

[1]   The Appellant disagrees with the Director's December 1, 2011 decision that she is not a person with a disability, as defined in section 4 of the *Ontario Disability Support Program Act, 1997* (the *Act*). The Director determined that the impairments were not substantial and also that there were no substantial restrictions in one or more of the activities of daily living listed in section 4(1) of the *Act*.

DECISION

[2]   The appeal is denied.

PRELIMINARY ISSUE

[3]   The Respondent's representative requested that the Tribunal dismiss the Appellant's appeal for lack of jurisdiction. Specifically, the Respondent's Representative stated that the Appellant had missed the deadline for filing the appeal application with the Tribunal. The Appellant was required to file her appeal by January 18, 2012, which is 30 days from the

Continues....

Exhibit 4.1 continued

SBT File Number 1203-03822

date of the Director's final decision letter (dated December 19, 2011). The Appellant filed her appeal application with the Tribunal on March 23, 2012. The Appellant stated that she filed the appeal at the suggestion of her Ontario Works caseworker. She had no explanation as to why she did not file it within the required 30 days and did not suggest any reason why the deadline for filing her appeal application should be extended.

REASONS

[4]   The Tribunal denied the Appellant's request for an extension of time. The Appellant was required to file her appeal within 30 days of the Director's final decision, pursuant to Section 23 of the *Ontario Disability Support Program Act* and Section 61 of *Ontario Regulation 222/98*. The Tribunal has the discretion to extend the time for filing an appeal, if there are apparent grounds to file the appeal, and if there are reasonable grounds for requesting an extension of time, pursuant to subsection 23(2) of the *Ontario Disability Support Program Act* and subsection 61(2) of *Ontario Regulation 222/98*. The Tribunal did not find the reasons for the delay provided by the Appellant to be reasonable grounds to grant an extension. The Appellant had received the Director's final decision letter of December 19, 2011. That letter specifically stated that the deadline for filing an appeal application with the Board was January 18, 2012. The Appellant did not provide a sufficient reason why she was unable to file the appeal by the January 18, 2012 deadline.

ORDER

[5]   The appeal is dismissed. The decision of the Director is affirmed.

2013 ONSBT 5125 (CanLII)

Signed by Bittu George	**Date issued** December 12, 2013
Signed by Beverly Moore	**Date issued** December 12, 2013

2

RULES

Part I of the Rules of Procedure for appeals to the Social Benefits Tribunal is the Social Justice Tribunals Ontario Common Rules, which apply to all other tribunals within the cluster. The Common Rules came into effect on October 1, 2013. Part II is SBT-specific rules that apply solely to the SBT and are effective as of January 1, 2016, and apply to appeals to the SBT from the appropriate government parties regarding eligibility for benefits under the appropriate legislation and for requests for Interim Assistance from such legislation. Immediately below is a summary of the key rules (you should not rely on the summary but rather read the Rules directly):

Part I — SJTO Common Rules

See the summary in the preamble to Part II.

Part II — Social Benefits Tribunal Specific Rules

"Rule 1 General Rules" makes reference to s. 25.1 of the *SPPA* and allows the Associate Chair of the SBT to make Practice Directions. There are 20 words or phrases defined in R. 1.3, with numerous powers given to the SBT to provide for "the fair, just and expeditious resolution of any matter before it". The rules regarding communicating with the SBT, especially for parties to the proceedings, are detailed in Rs. 1.9–1.14.

"Rule 2 Appeals" to SBT makes it clear that "[b]efore commencing an appeal to the SBT the appellant must file a written request for internal review within 30 days of receiving the Administrator/Director's decision or have been granted an extension of time to request an internal review" and that such request to extend time must be made to the Administrator/Director. What may be appealed and who the parties are to an appeal are set out in Rs. 2.3–2.4 for *OWA* decisions and in Rs. 2.5–2.6 for *ODSPA* decisions.

"Rule 3 Filing an Appeal" requires the filing of Form 1 with the SBT by certain dates, as set out in R. 3.1. The Form 1 "must include enough information and documents to enable the SBT to determine whether there is adequate information to process the appeal"; if the SBT determines that the Form 1 is insufficiently complete, it can proceed with actions set out in R. 3.2. Extensions of time requirements for filing Form 1 are set out in R. 3.3. The rules regarding interim assistance granted to an appellant due to financial hardship the appellant will suffer until the appeal is decided are set out in Rs. 3.4–3.10.

"Rule 4 Responding to an Appeal" states, in R. 4.1, that the SBT will deliver Form 1 to the respondent and any other party; and the respondent, under R. 4.2, must deliver to the appellant and file with the SBT a completed Form 3, including the information set out in the rule. Rules 4.3–4.5 detail what respondents must do when their position changes and the timelines for such changes. Rule 4.6 sets out what the SBT may do when there is non-compliance with Rule 4.

"Rule 5 Filing Documents with the SBT" sets out the *required* format and content in Rs. 5.1–5.3 and how to be filed in R. 5.4. There are specific rules as to when documents are to be filed for *OWA* appeals under R. 5.9 and for *ODSPA* appeals under Rs. 5.10–5.11. Rules 5.12–5.15 set out the consequences where there is failure to comply with these rules regarding filing; especially R. 5.14, which states that "[a] party may not present evidence or make submissions with respect to a fact or issue that was not raised in the Appeal (Form 1) or Response to Appeal or disclosed in accordance with the Rules unless the SBT is satisfied this would not cause substantial prejudice or undue delay to the proceedings."

"Rule 6 Delivery of Documents" contains various rules on the delivery of documents.

"Rule 7 SBT Proceedings" starts with various rules on confidentiality (Rs. 7.1–7.3), including that all hearings of the SBT are not open to the public. Hearing dates and locations are covered in Rs. 7.4–7.6, which also deal with the ability of a party or witness to get financial assistance to travel. Rules 7.7–7.10 deal with form of hearings, including what must be done when objecting to a particular form of hearing. What needs to be done if a respondent wants to appear at the hearing and what happens if an appellant fails to attend as required are described in Rs. 7.11–7.12, Attendance at the Hearing. Rules 7.13–7.15 deal with *Human Rights Code* claims. The rules governing requests to intervene and requests for a court reporter are Rs. 7.16–7.18 and Rs. 7.19–7.20, respectively. The need for prior disclosure of witnesses is covered under Rs. 7.21–7.23.

"Rule 8 Summons" details the provisions regarding issuance and service of summons upon witnesses (Rs. 8.1–8.3).

"Rule 9 Withdrawal of Appeal" sets out how it can happen.

"Rule 10 Request to Re-open" allows for a request to re-open an appeal that was closed without a hearing (Rs. 10.1–10.3).

"Rule 11 Dismissal of Appeal Outside Jurisdiction" details how the SBT may do so (Rs. 11.1–11.3).

"Rule 12 Summary Hearing" gives the SBT the power to hold a summary hearing on its own initiative or at the request of a party to determine if the appeal should be dismissed in whole or in part due to there being no reasonable prospect it will succeed. The provisions of how to do so are set out in Rs. 12.1–12.4.

"Rule 13 Requests to Reschedule or Adjourn Hearing" requires that such requests are in writing and follow the provisions of Rs. 13.1–13.5.

"Rule 14 Amending Clerical Errors" allows for the corrections of typographical errors in accordance with Rs. 14.1–14.2.

"Rule 15 Reconsideration" allows a party to request reconsideration of a final decision of the SBT by filing Form 2 within 30 days of receiving a decision (R. 15.1) or more than 30 days in accordance with R. 15.2, but not more than one year of the final decision (R. 15.3). Interim assistance orders are not final decisions in accordance with R. 15.4.

"Rule 16 Appeal to Divisional Court" allows any party to appeal the SBT decision to the Divisional Court on a question of law. The appeal must be made in accordance with Rs. 16.1–16.2.

PROCEDURES OF TRIBUNAL

The SBT, as of January 1, 2016, has rules detailing the procedures of the tribunal, as discussed above, and also uses the procedures set out by the enabling legislation discussed above, as well as "Practice Directions" published on the SBT website. The "Policy Directives" published on the Ministry of Community and Social Services website (<http://www.mcss.gov.on.ca/en/mcss/programs/social/directives/index.aspx>) are not binding on the SBT. As stated on the Ministry's website, in any conflict between the Policy Directives and the Practice Directions, the Practice Directions prevail. However, it might be useful to understand the Ministry's position on the items listed there. Following is a discussion of each.

PRACTICE DIRECTIONS OF THE SBT

The Practice Directions are not rules of the SBT specifically but, rather, are the intended guidelines for the procedures that the SBT would like everyone to follow when appearing before the SBT. The Practice Directions should be read as non-binding expansions of the Rules that took effect on January 1, 2016. Set out below are summaries, including quoted provisions of the Practice Directions, but the reader should review the whole text to obtain complete information on each.

Practice Direction — Interim Assistance

This direction discusses the ability of the SBT to award interim assistance while waiting for the hearing and the decision, if the SBT feels that the appellant will face financial hardship during such time. If the appellant loses at the hearing, any interim assistance will be an overpayment and subject to recovery. When assessing applications for interim assistance, the SBT must consider legislation as well as relevant court decisions. The determination of interim assistance is a separate decision-making process from the appeal, and the success or failure of an interim assistance application has no bearing on the end result of the appeal. The appellant must complete, as fully as possible, the tribunal's "Application for Interim Assistance", which is section 4 of the Appeal Form (to be discussed below) pursuant to R. 3.4. An application to extend the interim assistance must be made in accordance with R. 3.7. A party who objects to an interim assistance decision shall write to the Chair of the Social Benefits Tribunal, setting out detailed reasons why that decision should be reversed or amended, with a copy of the letter to the other party. The reasons for objecting will be assessed by the Tribunal, and a written response will be sent to both parties as quickly as possible.

Practice Direction — Reconsideration Requests

With the power of discretion, the SBT is able to discourage unnecessary requests and still allow for reconsideration hearings where a serious error or omission has occurred. In exercising its discretion to grant reconsideration hearings, the SBT needs to strike a balance between preserving the finality of Tribunal decisions and the need to address substantive problems in the tribunal's decisions without the need for a further appeal to court or judicial review. A request to reconsider a decision must be made in writing using the prescribed form "Application for Reconsideration" (to be discussed below) in accordance with R. 15. The SBT will take into account the following factors when deciding whether to grant a reconsideration hearing:

- Has the tribunal acted outside its jurisdictions?
- Has the tribunal violated the rules of natural justice or procedural fairness?
- Has the tribunal made a serious error of law?
- Could the new evidence that would have had a material effect on the decision have been obtained by reasonable diligence for the original hearing? (This includes evidence that has come into existence since the original hearing.)
- Is there any other substantial ground relevant to the decision?

If the request is granted, the SBT will send a Notice of Hearing providing the date, time, and place of the reconsideration hearing. Any member of the SBT can be assigned to hear the reconsideration other than the member who made the original decision, unless it is a limited reconsideration.

Practice Direction — Rules for Electronic Hearings

Noting that electronic hearings can be held pursuant to the *SPPA*, the direction allows the SBT to have telephone hearings if all the parties and the Tribunal members who participate in the hearing are able to hear one another and any witnesses throughout the hearing. Further, it is noted that a telephone hearing of the SBT is private and confidential; thus, the parties are required to make arrangements to ensure that the privacy and confidentiality of the hearing are maintained at their premises. A telephone hearing can be used for procedural issues and any other matter, unless a party objects and the SBT is convinced that such a hearing is likely to cause significant prejudice to that party. Factors that the SBT may consider in determining whether a telephone hearing should be held include the following:

- The nature of the appeal and whether it is suitable to hear the matter by telephone
- The type of evidence that may be required for the hearing and whether credibility is an issue
- The ability to conduct a fair and private hearing
- The number of persons that may be involved in the hearing, including parties, counsel, and witnesses
- The need to expedite certain types of appeals
- Convenience to the parties
- A party's request for a telephone hearing and the reasons for the request
- Estimated duration of the hearing
- The cost and efficiency of conducting a hearing by telephone
- Special circumstances, such as the unavailability of an interpreter

Also discussed in this Direction are (i) the contents of a notice of a telephone hearing; (ii) the condition for accepting the objection under R. 7.9 (i.e., to demonstrate that such hearing would likely cause the party significant prejudice); and (iii) the procedures that a party must follow in order to launch the objection. It is also noted that right to object is not applicable to electronic hearings that concern procedural matters only. If the person appealing fails without reasonable cause to be available for the hearing, the SBT may proceed in the absence of the party.

Practice Direction — Rescheduling of Hearings and Adjournments

The SBT wants a hearing to occur at the date, time, and place already set, unless it agrees to change it. The fact that a legal representative cannot attend an already scheduled hearing is not necessarily grounds to change the date. A request to change a date should be made as soon as it is known that there is a problem. Although the SBT will likely change a date only for exceptional circumstances, it can change the hearing date on its own motion to accommodate internal issues: (i) "A request for a new hearing date will be considered either as a request for administrative rescheduling or as a request for an adjournment" in accordance with R. 13.1. If the circumstances do not qualify for administrative rescheduling, the request to change the date or time of the hearing will be considered as a request for an adjournment, which must follow the procedure in R. 13.2, with objections to such request under R. 13.3.

The SBT will give the parties at least 30 days' notice of the hearing date, unless the parties give written consent to have a hearing at an earlier date. If a party requests a rescheduled date, it must be in writing and given to both the SBT and the other party. Reasons for a new date and a daytime telephone number to discuss the request must be included in the written request. Some of the factors the SBT will consider when there is a request to change the hearing date are (i) whether the change is necessary to ensure a fair and timely hearing, (ii) the existence of any previous changes, (iii) whether the request was made at the earliest opportunity, (iv) whether the party made reasonable efforts to avoid the need for a new date, (v) whether anyone would be prejudiced if the request was granted or denied, and (vi) whether there is a serious personal emergency or compassionate factor. An adjournment request can also be made at the commencement of the hearing, but the party requesting should be prepared to start the hearing if the request is refused.

Usually, the SBT will reschedule if all parties consent.

Practice Direction — Early Resolution Opportunities

This Early Resolution Program (ERP), although not mandatory, as it is on consent, provides the parties with "Early Resolution Opportunities" (EROs) — a variety of alternative dispute resolution processes — to resolve appeals prior to the formal tribunal hearing. The program will allow the SBT to identify and implement early opportunities to resolve cases, making the tribunal fair and efficient and thereby reducing backlogs and costs. In the event that the ERO did not fully resolve the issues, it will help the parties to narrow and clarify issues to make eventual hearings more timely and focused.

An ERO is a private and confidential dispute resolution process that includes "in-person or telephone pre-hearing conferences, in-person or telephone settlement discussions, negotiations, concilia-tions and mediations". An ERO session will *not* be rescheduled unless there are special circumstances to reschedule. A Notice of Early Resolution Opportunity Session will be sent to the parties after the filing of the appeal. What is to be included in such a notice is detailed in the Direction. The factors a party would consider to participate in such a session are discussed. Written submissions may be filed with the SBT and the other parties before the session. If a party objects to the session or fails to attend, the session will not proceed unless special circumstances exist to adjourn the session, and the appeal will continue. The possible outcomes of the session, other than resolving the issue(s) on a full and final basis, are listed in the Direction.

Practice Direction — Procedure for Human Rights Issues or Challenges

In *Tranchemontagne v. Ontario* (Director, Disability Support Pro-gram), 2006 SCC 14, the Supreme Court of Canada confirmed that the SBT has jurisdiction, which it cannot decline, to consider Ontario *Human Rights Code* ("*Code*") challenges to its governing legislation — the *Ontario Disability Support Program Act, 1997* and/or the *Ontario Works Act, 1997*. This case prompted the SBT to institute a two-stage procedure in this Practice Direction to deal with human right issues and challenges raised under the *Code*.

All human rights issues or challenges before the SBT will follow the two-stage procedure prescribed in this Direction: Stage 1 hearing looks at the merits of the appeal; Stage 2 hearing considers the *Code* challenge if the appeal is not denied in Stage 1.

The first step for a party raising a human rights issue or chal-lenge is to file a written Notice of the *Human Rights Code* Claim (Form 4) under R. 7.13 no later than 60 days prior to hearing the appeal with the SBT. The notice contains, among other things, par-ticulars of the challenge, the section(s) of the *Ontario Human Rights Code* (*Code*) relied upon, the desired remedy, and contact particu-lars of the party's representative. The SBT will write to the party to acknowledge receiving the Notice. If more information is needed, the SBT will direct the party to provide it within 30 days. The SBT will send the written notice to the other parties within 10 days of receipt. A party who wishes to reply to such written notice must notify the SBT and send a copy of its intent to the Ministry of Community and Social Services, the Attorney General of the Province of Ontario, and the other parties within 30 days of receiving the written notice forwarded by the SBT. Where a party does not send a written notice of its intention to reply in the proper time, the SBT will assume that such party will not be participating in the human rights issue or challenge. As a general rule, the SBT will hold a pre-hearing conference to determine the procedure for the hearing of the challenge. In most cases, the SBT will address the human rights challenge or issue only after the main issue on the appeal has been heard, and only if it is raised pursuant to these procedures. If the appeal of the main issue is granted, the human rights issue or challenge will not be dealt with.

If the SBT determines that, after receipt of a party's notice, the human rights issue or challenge is frivolous or vexatious, it may refuse to hear it; after notifying the party who raised it, the party must confirm whether the appeal on its merits should proceed.

Any person seeking status to intervene in an appeal must submit a written request according to Rs. 7.16–7.17.

Practice Direction — Recording Proceedings

The SBT hearings are held privately, and the contents of the proceedings, including the digital recording, are confidential. The transcript of the recording is treated the same as the member's notes of the hearing and will not be prepared and produced unless the SBT has been served with a Notice of Appeal. A copy of the transcript may be provided, at a fee of $5.00, to parties of the proceedings on the conditions that confidentiality will be respected and request is made to the Registrar within one year of the final decision.

Self-recording by parties to the hearing may be allowed if the SBT Member is satisfied that the conditions he/she imposed are met. This type of recordings, including its transcript, is not considered part of the SBT's record of proceedings and cannot be used in other proceedings. Permission to record the hearing may be withdrawn in accordance with the Direction.

Although rare, the SBT may grant a party's request in accordance with R. 7.19 to provide a court reporter if the request is (i) supported with details and (ii) made to the Registrar in writing at least a month before the hearing. With permission, a party can also pay to have a court reporter. If a transcript of the court reporter's recording is produced, a copy must be provided to the SBT, which will be included in the record of the proceeding.

Practice Direction — Pre-Hearing Conferences

The procedure used by the SBT for scheduling and conducting pre-hearing conferences is set out in Practice Direction 8. Pre-hearing conferences can be held at the request of a party or at the direction of the SBT (unless there are special or unusual circumstances to dispense). A pre-hearing conference request by a party must be made in writing, with reasons set out, and within 10 days of the filing of the appeal. Where an appeal raises a human rights issue or challenge, a pre-hearing conference is mandatory, and all parties must attend to discuss procedural matters prior to the hearing. For the purposes of this Practice Direction, a pre-hearing conference is a meeting with all the parties conducted by a SBT member by way of one or a combination of telephone, videoconferencing, oral in-person session, or in writing. The purposes of the pre-hearing conferences are those set out in the provisions of the Direction, and evidence is not to be presented. Once a pre-hearing conference is requested or directed, a Notice of Pre-Hearing Conference will be sent, as soon as practicable, to the parties, setting out the format(s) of the conference and its date, place, and time. Details about the choice of format are discussed in the Direction, and the matters that can be dealt with in the pre-hearing conference are set out the Direction. The various outcomes of the pre-hearing conference are detailed in the Direction.

Practice Direction — Representation before Social Justice Tribunals Ontario

See the summary in the preamble to Part II.

Practice Direction — Litigation Guardians before Social Justice Tribunals Ontario

See the summary in the preamble to Part II.

POLICY DIRECTIVES

The policy directives listed on the Web page "Social assistance policy directives" on the Ontario Ministry of Community and Social Services website, <www.mcss.gov.on.ca>, provide interpretation of the two Acts that govern Ontario's social assistance programs: the *OWA* and the *ODSPA*. The directives provide background on various relevant topics involving the SBT, such as the ones set out immediately below, but these directives are not legally binding.

Policy Directives Regarding the *OWA*

Recipients or applicants for social assistance have the right to appeal an administrator's decision. Information on the appeal procedure is provided in section 10 of the Ontario Works Policy Directives:

10.1 — Notice and Internal Review Process
(i) Sets out the requirement for a notice of decision (either in writing or in electronic format); and (ii) provides details — including form and content, timeliness for filing and extensions, and decision procedure — of the internal review process. **Note that a written internal review request is mandatory for any decision that may be appealed to the SBT.**

10.2 — Appeal Process
Provides an overview of the appeal process at the SBT (from filing an appeal to the SBT to requesting a reconsideration of the SBT decision, and to appealing to the Divisional Court). Obligations of the parties and the SBT are detailed in the directive.

10.3 — Recovery of Interim Assistance
Recovery occurs when an applicant or participant loses an appeal, withdraws an appeal, or fails to attend an SBT hearing after being issued Interim Assistance. The Interim Assistance payment(s) paid is considered an overpayment, and the amount to be recovered is dependent on whether the appeal was denied partially or in full. This directive outlines how to calculate an overpayment in interim assistance to determine the amount to recover.

Policy Directives Regarding the *ODSPA* — Income Support Directives

An ODSP recipient or applicant for Income Support who disagrees with the administrator's decision and wants to appeal the decision can refer to "13. Internal Reviews and Appeals" of this directive for information on the appeal procedure:

13.1. — Notice of Decision and Internal Review Process
Sets out the requirement for written notice of decisions and the Internal Review process. **Note that all decisions appealable to the SBT are subject to an internal review.**

13.2. — Appeals
Outlines processes, rules and responsibilities when dealing with appeals to the SBT and for subsequent appeals to Divisional Court.

13.3. — Recovery of Interim Assistance
Outlines how to calculate an overpayment in interim assistance to determine the amount to recover.

FORMS[1]

All the forms, except two, are available electronically on the "Forms and Filing" Web page.

Appeal Form (Form 1)

Now available online, this form must be used to appeal a decision under the enabling legislation of the SBT. **The form is set out in the Appendix to this chapter, but it is important to check for the most current form on the SBT website, as changes can occur often.** As mentioned earlier, to appeal an administrator's decision, an internal review request must first be made, within 30 days after receiving the decision. The timeline for filing the appeal form to the SBT will then be 30 calendar days from (i) the receipt of the internal review decision, or (ii) the elapse of the 30 calendar day period allowed for the completion of the internal review. If you do not file within the timelines, reasons for the late filing must be given.

Application for Reconsideration (Form 2)

Either party to the appeal — the applicant/recipient or the administrator — can request a reconsideration using the application form (now available online) set out in Appendix 4.3, by (i) providing the reasons why the request should be granted and (ii) filing with the SBT within 30 days after receiving the decision of the SBT. A reconsideration is a fresh hearing of the appeal, and the party requesting will receive a letter from the SBT, within 60 days after it receives the Application for Reconsideration, stating whether or not a reconsideration hearing will be granted.

Other forms mentioned on the Forms and Filing Web page are listed below:

- Response to Appeal (Form 3)
- Request to Extend Interim Assistance (There is no form for this request. To make a request, submit a letter.)
- Request for Adjournment (There is no form for this request. To make a request, submit a letter.)
- Notice of *Human Rights Code* Claim (Form 4)
- New Medical Information (Form 5)
- Request for Travel Assistance (Form 6)
- Statement of Delivery (Form 7)
- Request for Summons (Form 8)

---

[1] Forms 1 and 2 discussed in this section can be found in the Appendix to this chapter.

POLICIES

1. Ministry Policies

The Ministry of Community and Social Services has three policy directives for its social assistance programs. The Ontario Works Policy Directives and the Ontario Disability Support Program — Income Support Directives include the appeal procedure to the SBT. The relevant sections of the legislation are discussed earlier on pages 207–216.

2. Policies of the SBT

There are two named policies of the SBT. The first is entitled "Accessibility and Accommodation Policy" and is located on the Accessibility and Accountability Web page. This policy incorporates the standards set out in the Accessibility Standards for Customer Service passed under the *Accessibility for Ontarians with Disabilities Act, 2005*. The Policy reflects the core principles of dignity, independence, integration and equal opportunity for access to and use of services at the Tribunal. If appropriate to the reader, review the policy on the website.

The second policy is entitled "French Language Services Policy" and is found on the Language Services Web page. If appropriate, the reader should review the policy on the website.

EXPLANATORY LITERATURE FROM THE SBT

Appeal and Hearing Process Web Page

This Web page describes in layman's language each step in the process involving the SBT. The process has five steps: Step 1 — Before you file; Step 2 — Filing an appeal; Step 3 — Preparing for your appeal; Step 4 — At the appeal; and Step 5 — After the appeal. There is also a discussion of Early Resolution Opportunities and Interim Assistance.

Annual Report

Prior to being a part of the SJTO, the SBT furnished to the public, through its website, an annual report discussing important matters that arose in the fiscal year. **As part of the SJTO cluster, the SBT no longer offers its annual report on its website; rather, the report is included in the SJTO annual report. The discussion set out immediately below is based on the 2013–2014 Annual Report and is intended to give the reader an idea of the information that may be available in such annual reports, specifically the SBT part. Portions of such Annual Reports are to be found in Appendix II.2 starting on page 155.**

The SJTO executive chair's message commences the report, discussing important events in the SJTO over that year's period and new initiatives undertaken by the SJTO as a cluster.

The membership of the SBT is listed at the end of the report. As of February 2016, the most current Annual Report for the SJTO on its website was 2013–14. In it, after the material for the SJTO, each individual agency in the cluster has a brief annual report. The SBT portion starts with a broad review of the recent past and initiatives for the future, followed by statistical tables about appeals to the SBT.

FAQs

The FAQs has, as of February 2016, three commonly asked questions with answers. This Web page may provide further assistance. Alternatively, the SBT can be contacted directly with information on the Contact the SBT Web page.

RELEVANT CASES AND/OR DECISIONS

The cases and decisions discussed next are not meant to be exhaustive. They should not be relied upon as legal opinion but are, rather, the author's interpretation. An update of cases and decisions, and the reader's own research and briefing, must be done in any event.

Sixteen cases of Ontario Court of Appeal (C.A.) and Divisional Court (Div. Ct.), and before one judge of the Superior Court of Justice (Sup. Ct. J.), are reviewed and discussed in this section. The Supreme Court of Canada (SCC) case of *Tranchemontagne v. Ontario (Director, Disability Support Program)* (the SCC case of *Tranchemontagne*) is briefed due to its importance. The cases shall be discussed in chronological order, with the oldest one first.

As noted on the SBT website, the SBT started to publish its decisions in a specific format on the CanLII website, starting at the end of 2012. As of February 27, 2014, 6036 SBT decisions have been posted onto the CanLII website. This action has now allowed the public, including paralegals, to access decisions of the SBT. Because all published decisions include not only the judgment but also the reasons, the public are able to better understand the SBT's rulings. At the end of this section, an SBT decision, selected at random from the CanLII website, *1209-11614 (Re)*, is included.

Guy v. Northumberland (County) Administrator, Ontario Works

Guy v. Northumberland (County) Administrator, Ontario Works, [2001] O.J. No. 2166, 201 D.L.R. (4th) 752, 147 O.A.C. 261, 105

A.C.W.S. (3d) 1165 (the *Guy* case), is a 2001 Div. Ct. case that relates to the cancellation of social benefits to an applicant and her two minor sons under the *OWA*, and the decision was upheld by the SBT. The reason the administrator cancelled the social benefits was that the trust funds beneficially owned by the two sons, which were considered assets, were not disclosed by the applicant. Although the *OWA* did not define "assets", there was a policy directive that defined the term to include a beneficial interest in assets held in trust that can be readily converted to cash. In looking at the evidence before it, the SBT held that the beneficial interest was an asset, which was liquid and accessible, and confirmed the decision of the administrator.

In this appeal, the court first stated that the "standard of review for decisions of the Social Benefits Tribunal and its predecessor, the Social Assistance Review Board, is one of correctness". The court then looked at SBT's definition of "assets". "It is clear from the decision of the Tribunal ... that the concepts of liquidity and accessibility continue to play an important role in the Tribunal's attempt to define assets. In my view, the Tribunal's approach is correct. To do otherwise would make a mockery of the legislation." Upon agreeing with the SBT for applying liquidity and accessibility to define "assets", the court turned to determine whether the SBT was correct in finding the trust funds should be treated as assets. After reviewing previous cases on point and the terms of the trust and the intention of the testator, the court found that the funds were not accessible by the two sons and held that the SBT erred and that the trust funds were to be excluded as assets for the purposes of determining eligibility. (Check out the 2013 SBT decision, *1207-08651 (Re)*, where the appellant included this case to support her appeal and failed.)

Ontario (Director, Disability Support Program) v. Eluck

Ontario (Director, Disability Support Program) v. Eluck, [2001] O.J. No. 3764, 151 O.A.C. 369, 109 A.C.W.S. (3d) 172 (the *Eluck* case), is a 2001 Div. Ct. decision on whether the Director of the Disability Support Program "had authority to cancel, rather than suspend Mr. Eluck's income support in circumstances where he was incarcerated for a period in excess of one month". Eluck had been receiving social assistance because he was categorized as a "permanently unemployable person". The Director, upon learning that Eluck was in jail for five months, cancelled his assistance. "Mr. Eluck appealed that decision to the Social Benefits Tribunal, which determined that while the Director was correct in finding that the Appellant was ineligible for benefits while he was incarcerated, the Director had no authority to cancel Mr. Eluck's benefits due to his incarceration. The Tribunal found that Mr. Eluck remained eligible for benefits as a person with a disability and that his benefits were simply suspended for the period of his incarceration, and not cancelled." The Director appealed the decision of the SBT on the basis of a question of law. After looking at various sections of the enabling legislation, the court held that the *ODSPA* "is social welfare legislation that confers benefits and ought to be interpreted in a broad and generous manner, with any ambiguities resolved in favour of the benefit claimant". Furthermore, the court held that "the argument of the Director strains both the intent and the wording of the Act and the Regulation. Specifically, the Act permits the 'suspension' of income and that is specifically what sections 9, 26(2) and 35 of the Regulation comprehend. To accept the argument of the Director would mean that in every case of 'suspension' there would be an automatic 'cancellation', which would betray the specific power mandated by the Act." The decision of the SBT was, therefore, upheld.

McLaughlin v. Ontario (Director, Disability Support Program)

In *McLaughlin v. Ontario (Director, Disability Support Program)*, [2002] O.J. No. 1740 (the *McLaughlin* case), a 2002 Div. Ct. decision, the applicant appealed the decision of the Disability Support Program Director to the SBT that he did not suffer from substantial physical impairment. The SBT applied the test of "substantial physical impairment" under subsection 4(1)(a) of the *ODSPA* and agreed with the Director. The appellant submitted that the SBT had applied the wrong test, but the court held that the reasons for the decision demonstrate that the SBT applied the proper test. As to the argument that the SBT erred "by imputing the substantial-restriction-of-daily-activities concept of subsection 4(1)(b) into its 'substantial impairment' consideration", if that was an error, the court held that that was in applying the law to the facts, which is a matter of mixed fact and law, and not appealable. As noted in s. 31(1) of *ODSPA*, only questions of law are appealable to the Divisional Court.

Gray v. Ontario (Director, Disability Support Program)

The 2002 Ont. C.A. case of *Gray v. Ontario (Director, Disability Support Program)*, [2002] O.J. No. 1531 (the *Gray* case), deals with "the important issue of the appropriate determination of substantial impairment within the meaning of s. 4(1) of the *ODSPA*". The court starts with the proposition that "as social welfare legislation, any ambiguity in the interpretation of the *ODSPA* should be resolved in the claimant's favour". The discussion then examined the phrase "person with a disability" and the word "substantial" as follows:

> Compared with its predecessor and with similar federal legislation, it would appear that the current definition of "person with a disability" in the *ODSPA* was intended to encompass a

broader segment of society and to provide assistance to persons with significant but not severe long-term functional barriers.

With respect to the interpretation of the word "substantial" in s. 4(1)(a) of the *ODSPA*, I am of the view that the word should be given a flexible meaning related to the varying circumstances of each individual case in a manner consistent with the purposes of the Act.

Although we are dealing with a social assistance scheme as contrasted with the interpretation of legislation related to insurance, I believe that a useful analogy may be drawn from the exception provided in s. 266 of the *Insurance Act*, R.S.O. 1990, c. I.8. In this provision, personal injury litigation arising from automobile accidents is prohibited except for persons with "permanent serious impairment of an important bodily function". In *Meyer v. Bright* (1993), 15 O.R. (3d) 129 (C.A.), this court has interpreted this provision as follows at p. 142:

> An impairment of an important bodily function which is serious to one person may not necessarily be a serious one for someone else. The task of the court in each case will be to decide whether the impairment is serious to the particular injured person who is before the court. In performing that task the question will always be the detrimental effect which the impairment has upon the life of the particular injured person. It is impossible for this court to lay down general guidelines of the concept of seriousness in all cases. Each case must be decided upon its own facts.

The judgment then focuses on two things: (i) the SBT's decision against the appellant in terms of the evidence as found by the tribunal and (ii) whether the tribunal drew from previous cases as well as the enabling legislation, that is, "[t]he Tribunal's decision shall include the principal findings of fact and its conclusions based on those findings" (O. Reg. 222/98, ss. 67(3)). In looking at the SBT's decision, the court found the following:

> It is simply unclear what relevant evidence the Tribunal accepted and what it rejected. It is my view that the Tribunal has not fulfilled its responsibilities pursuant to section 67(3) of the *ODSPA* to set out the principal findings of fact and its conclusions based on those findings.
>
> There is little or no explanation of the reasoning process that led the Tribunal to conclude that "the Appellant is not a person with a disability within the meaning of section 4(1) of the *Ontario Disability Support Program Act*". It was incumbent

upon the Tribunal to make findings of fact concerning the appellant's testimony and the reports prepared by her doctor.

The Tribunal also appears to have asked itself the wrong question when it stated that "according to her testimony (the appellant) is able to cope on a day-to-day basis". The issue is, of course, not whether the appellant "can cope on a day-to-day basis" but whether she can function in the workplace, function in the community, or attend to her personal care. Both the appellant and her physician stated that she could not, and I repeat that the Tribunal emphasized that the appellant was a credible witness.

Both the errors made by the SBT as set out in the quoted passages above allowed the court to state that there was a question of law and an error. However, the judgment stated that "in light of s. 31(5) of the *ODSPA*, we are constrained in the relief we may grant. Thus, the matter is referred back to the Tribunal for reconsideration in accordance with the direction that this court is satisfied that the appellant is 'a person with a disability within s. 4(1) of the *Ontario Disability Support Program Act*'".

Gioris v. Ontario (Director, Disability Support Program)

Gioris v. Ontario (Director, Disability Support Program), [2002] O.J. No. 2416, 161 O.A.C. 277 (the *Gioris* case), was a 2002 Div. Ct. decision that dealt with judicial review. The appellant had a hearing before the SBT, where he raised numerous alleged instances of breaches of the rules of natural justice. The court broke down his arguments into five issues as follows:

1. Did the Tribunal breach its duty to proceed fairly and follow the principle of *audi alteram partem* when it expelled the applicant from the hearing?
2. Did the Tribunal make an error of law and exceed its jurisdiction by not accepting his actual childcare expenses as "necessary"?
3. Did the Tribunal make a reviewable error by failing to take notice of a final decision of the Social Assistance Review Board?
4. After inviting the Applicant to make submissions on tape-recording the hearing, did the Tribunal deal unfairly with the Applicant by refusing to hear his submissions at the beginning of the next day?
5. Did the Tribunal exceed its jurisdiction and deny the Applicant fairness by failing to provide 30 full days' notice of the hearing date as required by the regulations?

In its decision, the court focused on issues 1, 4, and 5:

1. With respect to the appellant being "expelled" from the hearing, the SBT has the right to control its own process, and the actions of the appellant were such that the SBT could properly exclude him and not be in breach of the rules of natural justice, especially as the appellant suffered no prejudice.
2. In terms of issue 4, the court held that the SBT was not required to tape-record its hearings under its enabling legislation and that the SBT was exercising its discretion not to tape the hearings.
3. With respect to the short notice (in this case 27 days, instead of the mandated 30 days for the 13th and 14th appeals, which raised the same issues as the first 12 appeals), the court held that it "was an efficient and sensible solution that created no unfairness to the applicant".

Finally, the court made its last finding that the appellant "has not shown any breach of the rules of natural justice [by the SBT]. If he had shown such a breach, we would have exercised our discretion to refuse him a re-hearing as we are all of the view that there was no miscarriage of justice".

Thomas v. Ontario (Director, Disability Support Program)

In a 2004 Div. Ct. decision, *Thomas v. Ontario (Director, Disability Support Program)*, [2004] O.J. No. 2702, 131 A.C.W.S. (3d) 1175 (the *Thomas* case), the appellant appealed the SBT decision on the basis that key evidence was not addressed in the reasons of the Tribunal in this case. The court held that the SBT "was obligated to address this evidence and make findings of fact" and concluded that there was an error in law. The case was sent back to the SBT for a new hearing before a differently constituted tribunal.

Sandiford v. Ontario (Director, Disability Support Program)

The issue of "person with a disability" was the focus of a 2005 Div. Ct. decision, *Sandiford v. Ontario (Director, Disability Support Program)*, [2005] O.J. No. 858, 195 O.A.C. 143, A.C.W.S. (3d) 857 (the *Sandiford* case). After reviewing the matter to date and the procedural elements set by the enabling legislation, the court focused on the evidence given at the SBT and the SBT's decision in finding that the appellant did not have a substantial physical or mental impairment as required by subsection 4(1) of the *ODSPA*.

In its decision, the court found the SBT erred in three areas.

First, the court held that the SBT erred in concluding that the medical and psychological evidence filed is insufficient to establish that the appellant's condition amounts to substantial. Quoting relevant passages of the *Gray* case, the court held that the word "substantial" had a flexible meaning, and the "Tribunal must then evaluate the whole of the evidence to assess whether the statutory test is met", which the SBT did not do.

Second, the court held that the SBT erred in drawing an adverse inference from the fact that the required "Activities of Daily Living Report" was completed by a nurse practitioner who was not a person involved in the appellant's treatment. "The nurse practitioner had known the appellant for two years. In light of demands made upon physicians' time and the shortage of general practitioners, resort to other persons with prescribed qualifications is not unreasonable. The nurse practitioner was authorized by the regulations to complete the form."

Finally, the court held that there was an error in applying the test for substantial impairment. The SBT's conclusion that there was a job which the appellant might be able to perform did not address the question of whether there was a substantial impairment. The fact that the Appellant is not precluded from one kind of employment does not mean that she did not suffer from a substantial impairment.

Based on the errors, the court dismissed the SBT decision. Further, because there was urgency to the matter, the court did not refer the matter back to the SBT. Rather, the court granted the appeal, pursuant to subsection 31(5)(b) of the *ODSPA*, and after concluding that the appellant's condition met the "substantial impairment" test ordered that "the Appellant is eligible for income support as a 'person with disability' under the *ODSPA*, effective April 1, 2001".

Rea v. Simcoe (County Administrator, Social Services Department)

Rea v. Simcoe (County Administrator, Social Services Department), [2005] O.J. No. 5543, 79 O.R. (3rd) 583, 205 O.A.C. 297, 144 A.C.W.S. (3d) 758 (the *Rea* case), is a 2005 Ont. C.A. decision regarding the effect of not providing information relating to changes in the appellant's circumstances in accordance with section 7 of the *OWA* and section 14 of O. Reg. 134/98. After looking at sections 14(1) and 35 of O. Reg. 134/98, the court held that the requirement of providing updated information was central to the entire scheme of the *OWA*; therefore, when the appellant's assistance was terminated, so was her dependent daughter's.

Dowswell v. Ontario (Disability Support Program, Director)

Dowswell v. Ontario (Disability Support Program, Director), [2006] O.J. No. 973, 265 D.L.R. (4th) 511, 208 O.A.C. 200, 146 A.C.W.S. (3d) 739 (the *Dowswell* case), is a 2006 Div. Ct. case that deals with the determination of the benefit unit and what should properly occur when there is a separation in the benefit unit in terms of retroactive payments. The court held that there was a question of law raised by the SBT's decision and that the standard for review as per the *Gray* case is correctness. As the Director knew of the parties' separation at the time of awarding retroactive benefits, it was not correct in law to provide a windfall to the non-separated spouse of the appellant's disability benefit. The court therefore held that the appellant should receive an equal share of the retroactive payment.

Ontario (Director, Disability Support Program) v. Crane

In *Ontario (Director, Disability Support Program) v. Crane*, [2006] O.J. No. 4564, 83 O.R. (3rd) 321, 278 D.L.R. (4th) 374, 217 O.A.C. 61, 153 A.C.W.S. (3d) 236 (the *Crane* case), a 2006 Ont. C.A. case, the key issue again was the definition of the term "person with a disability" as defined by subsection 4(1) of the *ODSPA*. After all the required proceedings had been utilized, an appeal went to the Divisional Court on the basis that the SBT erred in law in its interpretation of subsection 4(1) and also in its findings of the facts of "three years continuous part-time employment". A majority of the Divisional Court held that the SBT incorrectly interpreted subsection 4(1) and also made a palpable and overriding error. The Court of Appeal did not agree with the Divisional Court on its interpretation of subsection 4(1) and, rather, agreed with the interpretation by the SBT:

> In summary, s. 4(1) of the *ODSPA* presents three questions — substantial impairment, substantial restriction in certain activities, and verification. These are separate questions that require separate analysis and answers. The onus is on the claimant to establish all three factors. Accordingly, if the Tribunal concludes that the claimant has failed to establish one of the factors, it need not deal with the other factors. Finally, in some cases (but not all) there can be an overlap in the evidence relevant to the factors in paragraphs (a) and (b) of s. 4(1). That is because although the concept of impairment is anchored in medicine, the determination of whether an impairment is substantial will require consideration of the whole person, including a person's ability to function in the domains of personal care, community and workplace.

> The Divisional Court conflated or collapsed the analysis required under s. 4(1)(a) and (b) into a single inquiry. It erred in so doing.
>
> The Tribunal, on the other hand, framed its analysis in a proper fashion. With respect to s. 4(1)(a), it focused on the medical evidence relating to Ms. Crane's impairment, including the report and extensive clinical notes of the family doctor, and reports by a rheumatologist and a psychiatrist.

The Court of Appeal, however, did find, as the majority of the Divisional Court found, that the SBT made an error in its critical finding of fact that Ms. Crane worked continuously for three years part-time, when the evidence showed it was only four months:

> In my view, the majority was correct to conclude that this misapprehension of the evidence amounted to a palpable and overriding error. The Tribunal made the same error twice, so there can be no suggestion that the error was merely a typographical error. The error relates to a crucial part of the evidence, namely, Ms. Crane's work history. The error is a substantial one — there is a large difference between four months and three years continuous part-time work. Finally, as McMurtry C.J.O. emphasized in *Gray*, the *ODSPA* is remedial legislation. It follows from these points that Ms. Crane is entitled to have her claim assessed on the basis of an accurate understanding by the Tribunal of the crucial aspects of her current situation, including her employment history.

A new hearing before a different member of the SBT was ordered.

Omar v. Ontario (Director, Disability Support Program)

The issue of the alleged conflict between two sections of the regulation made under the *ODSPA* was the focus of the 2007 Div. Ct. decision, *Omar v. Ontario (Director, Disability Support Program)*, [2007] O.J. No. 1216, 156, A.C.W.S. (3d) 509 (the *Omar* case). The court ruled that there was no conflict between subsection 47(7) and subsection 64(1)(a) of O. Reg. 222/98 and that the SBT did not have the authority to hear new evidence of the appellant's condition in the period following the Director's decision. The court pointed out that the SBT could only conduct an appeal hearing in accordance with the regulations. If new evidence appears after the date of the Director's decision, the applicant could re-apply for support.

Lloyd v. Ontario (Director, Disability Support Program)

In *Lloyd v. Ontario (Director, Disability Support Program)*, [2007] O.J. No. 1452, 217 O.A.C. 385, 156 A.C.W.S. (3d) 1202 (the *Lloyd* case), a 2007 Div. Ct. case, the issue of "person with a disability" under subsection 4(1) of the *ODSPA* was explored again. In this case, both the Director and the SBT held that the appellant was not a person with a disability as her chronic pain was not substantial impairment based on the evidence. The court found that the SBT "erred in law by applying the wrong test in that it assessed the appellant's condition on her good days when she had a higher level of physical activity as opposed to assessing her condition during her recurrent bad days".

The court found the SBT also "failed to make findings respecting the frequency and unpredictability of bad days in its analysis of whether the appellant had a substantial impairment". Based on these errors, the court referred the matter back to the SBT for a fresh hearing before a different panel.

Wareham v. Ontario (Minister of Community and Social Services)

In the 2008 Sup. Ct. J. decision, *Wareham v. Ontario (Minister of Community and Social Services)*, [2008] O.J. No. 166 (the *Wareham* case), the court dealt with a motion to strike a statement of claim in a class action law suit making various claims against the administration of the *ODSPA*. Although the case does not deal with the SBT, it is useful in looking at the enabling legislation.

In striking out the claims, except for the claim under section 7 of the *Canadian Charter of Rights and Freedoms*, the court set out a useful summary of the substantive rules and procedures of the *ODSPA*, given as follows:

> The provisions of the *ODSPA* and of Regulation 222/98 (the "Regulation") made pursuant to it are complex and elaborate. Among other things, they provide for decisions to be made to grant, or refuse, support by a Director of the ODSP appointed by the Minister, the manner in which applications are to be made, the information they must contain, the persons who are to make determinations of disability, internal reviews of contested decisions, appeals to the Social Benefits Tribunal established under the OW, and appeals on questions of law to the Divisional Court. There are also extensive provisions for the recovery of amounts paid to persons who were not eligible, and overpayments, and for periodic reviews of determinations of disability. Time limits are imposed for completing applications,

for requests for internal reviews and for various steps involved in appeals to the Tribunal and requests for it to reconsider its decisions. There are also stipulated times within which internal reviews of the Director's decisions, and decisions of the Tribunal, must be completed. There is, however, no time limit for the Director's initial decision on an application.

The provisions for evaluating an applicant's assets and budgetary requirements and the calculation and payment of income support and other benefits are particularly elaborate and extend over more than 20 pages of the Regulation. Despite — or, perhaps, because of — the evident minute attention to detail that is reflected in the legislation, the Regulation and the more than 80 policy directives issued by the Ministry of Community and Social Services, the plaintiffs claim that the Crown has created and maintained an unnecessarily time-consuming and inefficient application process. They rely, in particular, on their plea that the overwhelming majority of applicants experience a delay of between six months to one year before receiving an initial response to their application.

The application process is in two parts. Financial eligibility must first be determined by applying through an OW, or an ODSPA [*sic*], office. If a favourable determination is made, the applicant will be provided with a disability determination package ("DDP") which must be completed and returned to the disability adjudication unit within 90 days. The DDP consists of a number of forms which include a health status report and an "Activities of Daily Living Index" that must be completed by a prescribed health care professional. The disability adjudication unit includes persons appointed by the Director under section 4(2) of the *ODSPA* to make determinations of disability.

The court then set out the position of the plaintiffs as follows:

The plaintiffs claim that the delays, and other alleged deficiencies of the ODSP, have resulted from the Crown's negligence; impaired the mental and physical health of class members and violated their human dignity and self-worth; discriminated against them on the basis of their disability; violated their right to security of the person; breached a fiduciary duty owed to them; and resulted in the Crown's unjust enrichment.

Smith v. Ontario (Director, Disability Support Program)

Smith v. Ontario (Director, Disability Support Program), [2008] O.J. No. 302 (the *Smith* case), is a 2008 Div. Ct. decision. Here, the appellant appealed the decision of the Director, and thereafter the

SBT, on the question of his entitlement to a retroactive payment for a special diet allowance, which was denied in both instances. His grounds for appealing the decision of the SBT were stated as follows:

(a) the Tribunal erred by fundamentally misapprehending the facts;

(b) the Tribunal erred in law by failing to interpret the applicable Regulation retroactively; and

(c) the Tribunal failed to comply with rules of natural justice by basing its decision on a lack of corroborative evidence without giving him notice that such evidence would be required.

After stating that the test used by the court to determine questions of law is one of correctness, the court said the first ground was not valid because it is not a question of law and the reasons given for the decision demonstrate that the SBT was alive to the evidence presented before it. With respect to the second ground, the court held that whether the regulation was retroactive or not, the evidence did not indicate that the appellant was entitled to the retroactive payment. As it was considered by the SBT, the SBT did not err in law. With respect to the ground of judicial review due to breaches in the rules of natural justice, the court held that since corroborative evidence would clearly be necessary, there was no duty on the SBT to give notice and therefore "[h]e has not been prejudiced in any way by the lack of notice".

Oliveira v. Ontario (Director, Disability Support Program)

Oliveira v. Ontario (Director, Disability Support Program), [2008] O.J. No. 622, 2008 ONCA 123 (the *Oliveira* case), is an Ont. C.A. case that had to determine the effect of joint custody on income support to the head of a benefit unit with dependent children. The appellant and her spouse had custody of three young children on an alternating week basis. The Director, based on the CRA's decision on the appellant's eligibility for Canada Child Tax Benefit, determined that the appellant was entitled to only one-half of the income support payments for her three dependent children. That decision was appealed to the SBT. The SBT held that, out of the three components of income support, the appellant was eligible for 100 percent of two: shelter and benefits. For the basic needs component, the SBT found that the entitlement for one-half of the payments was appropriate. The appellant appealed to the Divisional Court with respect to the decision on the basic needs allowance. The Divisional Court concluded that the SBT did not err in law and dismissed the appeal. The appellant further appealed to the Court of Appeal on a question of law: there is no authority under the enabling legislation for the SBT.

After looking at relevant cases, especially the SCC case of *Tranchemontagne*, the court determined that a tribunal can interpret its enabling legislation by going beyond it in the right circumstances. Specifically, the court stated the following:

> [A]dministrative bodies empowered to decide questions of law "may presumptively go beyond the bounds of their enabling statute and decide issues of common law or statutory interpretation that arise in the course of a case properly before them, subject to judicial review on the appropriate standard". See *Tranchemontagne v. Ontario (Director, Disability Support Program)*, [2006] 1 S.C.R. 513 at para. 24, *per* Bastarache J., upholding this court's decision on the issue of whether the Tribunal had jurisdiction to consider the Ontario *Human Rights Code*, R.S.O. 1990, c. H.19. Bastarache J. noted at para. 26, "[t]he presumption that a tribunal can go beyond its enabling statute ... exists because it is undesirable for a tribunal to limit itself to some of the law while shutting its eyes to the rest of the law."

Using that concept, the court found the following:

> In situations where a recipient of income support is a co-resident, is incarcerated or in hospital, the amount of income support paid is proportionately reduced. See O. Reg. 222/98, ss. 17, 35, 36. Thus, the intention of the legislation is to account for the realities of a given situation. The appellant submits, however, that the prescribed deductions are the only ones permitted by the Act and Regulation, and the Tribunal had no choice but to order payment of 100 per cent of basic needs throughout the year.
>
> I disagree with this view. Where the legislation in question does not expressly confer a power, gaps in legislation may be filled when doing so is necessary to the operation of the legislative scheme.

As the original legislation did not envision joint custody, the court held that a tribunal had the jurisdiction to make the order it did; and as there is a basis for the order, there was no error in law. The two other submissions of the appellant, that the finding ignored the evidence and that such a finding breached the *Ontario Human Rights Code*, were quickly held not applicable in the facts of the case, and the appeal was dismissed.

Bongard v. Ontario (Director, Disability Support Program)

Bongard v. Ontario (Director, Disability Support Program), [2008] O.J. No. 1461 (the *Bongard* case), is a 2008 decision of the Divisional Court. *Bongard* dealt with the definition of spouse under subsection 1(1)(a) of O. Reg. 222/98 under the *ODSPA*. The issue was whether a statutory declaration signed by the appellant and Ms. Bernier is a mutual declaration as required by the definition of spouse in the Regulation and whether the SBT erred in law by so finding. The court held as follows:

> The Tribunal found on the basis of the signed form and all the circumstances that the requirements of s. 1(1)(a) of the regulation had been satisfied. We are not persuaded that the Tribunal made an error of law. It was open to the Tribunal to take into account the surrounding circumstances to determine whether the statement made in the signed form constituted a declaration by both the appellant and Ms. Bernier.
>
> We are also satisfied that the Tribunal's reasons are adequate, as they make findings of fact, took into account competing arguments and explained how the decision was arrived at.

The court therefore dismissed the appeal.

1209-11614 (Re)

In *1209-11614 (Re)*, 2013 ONSBT 2093 (CanLII), the SBT dealt with an appeal of a decision by a Disability Adjudication Unit (DAU) to deny the appellant's application for income support as a "person with a disability". The DAU did not find that the appellant met the definition of "a person with a disability" under section 4(1) of the *ODSPA*. In the appeal, the SBT set out the *ODSPA* requirements for "a person with disability" consideration: verification of impairments, duration and restrictions, as well as substantial impairment and restrictions. After reviewing the evidence with respect to the issue of substantial impairment, citing both the *Crane* case and the *Gray* case for guidance, the SBT concluded that "the level of impairment did not meet the threshold of substantial as set out in section 4(1) of the *Act*, at the time of the Director's decision" and denied the appeal.

TRANCHEMONTAGNE: A CASE BRIEF

The SCC case of *Tranchemontagne* has changed the SBT's procedure, as mentioned in Practice Direction 6, discussed above. A detailed discussion of the case is presented, in a case brief, below.

PARTIES: T and W (the "Appellants")
Director, Ontario Disabilities Support Program (the "Respondent")
CHRC, OHRC, The SBT and others (the "Intervenors")

CASE CITATIONS: [2006] S.C.J. No. 14, [2006] A.C.S. No. 14, 2006 SCC 14, 2006 CSC 14, [2006] 1 S.C.R. 513, [2006] 1 R.C.S. 513, 266 D.L.R. (4th) 287, 347 N.R. 144, J.E. 2006-879, 210 O.A.C. 267, 42 Admin. L.R. (4th) 104, 2006 CarswellOnt 2350, 147 A.C.W.S. (3d) 326, EYB 2006-104056, 56 C.H.R.R. D/1

BACKGROUND (FACTS)

This matter arose as two separate applications by the Appellants to the Respondent for support pursuant to the *ODSPA* as being a person with a disability. The Respondent denied benefits, and after a request for internal review the Respondent denied again. The Appellants then appealed to the SBT. The SBT dismissed the Appellants' appeals due to subsection 5(2), which states that a person is not eligible for income support if the disability is alcoholism. The SBT also stated it did not have jurisdiction to consider the applicability of subsection 5(2) pursuant to the *Ontario Human Rights Code* (the *Code*). The Appellants' appeals were joined and taken to the Divisional Court, which agreed with the SBT that it had no jurisdiction to consider the *Code* and dismissed the appeal. After leave to appeal was granted, the Court of Appeal held that the SBT had the power to declare a provision of the *ODSPA* inapplicable due to its discriminatory nature but that the SBT was not the most appropriate forum for which a *Code* issue could be decided and, therefore, dismissed the appeal. The Appellants then appealed to the Supreme Court of Canada.

ISSUES

A majority of the court (a 4–3 split among the judges) determined there were two main issues in the case:

1. Does the SBT have the jurisdiction to consider the *Code* in rendering its decisions?
2. If the answer to the first question is "yes", should the SBT have declined to exercise its jurisdiction in the present cases?

DECISION

For reasons set out in the majority decision, the appeal was allowed. The case was remitted to the SBT so that it could rule on the applicability of subsection 5(2) of the *ODSPA*.

REASONS

To answer the jurisdiction issue, the majority first looked at relevant sections of both enabling statutes, specifically sections 1, 4, 5, 29(3) and 31(1) of the *ODSPA* and sections 1 and 67(2) of the *OWA*, as well as the Preamble and sections 1 and 47(1) and (2) of the *Code*. The majority looked at the legislative intent and scheme of both the *ODSPA* and the *OWA* and then noted that the jurisdiction of the SBT involves questions of law. The majority held the SBT had power to examine to go beyond its enabling statute:

> The presumption that a tribunal can go beyond its enabling statute — unlike the presumption that a tribunal can pronounce on constitutional validity — exists because it is undesirable for a tribunal to limit itself to some of the law while shutting its eyes to the rest of the law. The law is not so easily compartmentalized that all relevant sources on a given issue can be found in the provisions of a tribunal's enabling statute. Accordingly, to limit the tribunal's ability to consider the whole law is to increase the probability that a tribunal will come to a misinformed conclusion. In turn, misinformed conclusions lead to inefficient appeals or, more unfortunately, the denial of justice.

The majority then addressed the argument that the wording of subsection 67(2) of the *OWA* does not give the SBT the jurisdiction to look at subsection 5(2):

> That section provides that the SBT cannot determine the constitutional validity of a provision or regulation and cannot determine the legislative authority for making a regulation. ...
>
> The *Code* emanates from the Ontario legislature. As I will elaborate below, it is one thing to preclude a statutory tribunal from *invalidating* legislation enacted by the legislature that created it. It is completely different to preclude that body from *applying* legislation enacted by that legislature in order to resolve apparent conflicts between statutes. The former power — an act of defying legislative intent — is one that is clearly more offensive to the legislature; it should not be surprising, therefore, when the legislature eliminates it. Yet the latter power represents nothing more than an instantiation of legislative intent — a legislative intent, I should note, that includes the primacy of the *Code* and the concurrent jurisdiction of administrative bodies to apply it.
>
> Thus the argument based on s. 67(2) is defeated because the legislature could not possibly have intended that the *Code* be denied application by analogy to the Constitution. While it clearly prohibited the SBT from considering the constitutional validity of laws and regulations, it equally clearly chose not to invoke the same prohibition with respect to the *Code*.

The majority then looked at section 47 of the *Code* and stated the following:

> The importance of the *Code* is not merely an assertion of this Court. The Ontario legislature has seen fit to bind itself and all its agents through the *Code*: s. 47(1). Further, it has given the *Code* primacy over all other legislative enactments: s. 47(2). As a result of this primacy clause, where provisions of the *Code* conflict with provisions in another provincial law, it is the provisions of the *Code* that are to apply.

The majority then differentiated between the effect of the primacy provisions in the *Code* and section 52 of the *Constitution Act, 1982* and stated the following in answering the first issue:

> I therefore conclude that the SBT has jurisdiction to consider the *Code*. The *ODSPA* and *OWA* confirm that the SBT can decide questions of law. It follows that the SBT is presumed to have the jurisdiction to consider the whole law. More specifically, when it decides whether an applicant is eligible for income support, the SBT is presumed able to consider any legal source that might influence its decision on eligibility. In the present appeal, the *Code* is one such source.
>
> There is no indication that the legislature has sought to rebut this presumption. To the contrary, the legislature has announced the primacy of the *Code* and has given itself clear directions for how this primacy can be eliminated in particular circumstances. The legislature has indeed prohibited the SBT from considering the constitutional validity of enactments, or the *vires* of regulations, but it did nothing to suggest that the SBT could not consider the *Code*. I cannot impute to the legislature the intention that the SBT ignore the *Code* when the legislature did not even follow its own instructions for yielding this result.
>
> The *ODSPA* and *OWA* do evince a legislative intent to prevent the SBT from looking behind the statutory and regulatory scheme enacted by the legislature and its delegated actors. However, consideration of the *Code* is not analogous. Far from being used to look behind the legislative scheme, the *Code* forms part of the legislative scheme. It would be contrary to legislative intention to demand that the SBT ignore it.

In discussing the second issue, whether the SBT should have declined jurisdiction, the majority stated that once the SBT had the jurisdiction to hear the case, it could decline jurisdiction to look at the *Code* issue if the legislature gave it the power to so decline. After looking at the enabling legislation again, as well as how the legislature gave power to both the OHRC and the courts to decline jurisdiction, the majority stated the following:

> Since the SBT has not been granted the authority to decline jurisdiction, it cannot avoid considering the *Code* issues in the appellants' appeals. This is sufficient to decide the appeal.

In *obiter dicta* the court then looked at reasons why the SBT should look at *Code* issues, and the judge writing for the majority stated the following at the end of his decision:

> I conclude that the SBT is a highly appropriate forum in which to argue the applicability of s. 5(2) of the *ODSPA* under the *Code*. In general, encouraging administrative tribunals to exercise their jurisdiction to decide human rights issues fulfills the laudable goal of bringing justice closer to the people. But more crucial for the purposes of the present appeal is the fact that the legislature did not grant the SBT the power to defer to another forum when it is properly seized of an issue. Absent such authority, the SBT could not decline to deal with the *Code* issue on the basis that a more appropriate forum existed.

The minority decision also looked at the enabling legislation and the *Code* and determined that the SBT cannot invalidate a provision of the enabling legislation that defines its mandate; therefore, it lacked jurisdiction.

REVIEW QUESTIONS

1. What is the enabling legislation for the SBT?
2. Where would you find the practices and procedures of the SBT?
3. Pursuant to the enabling legislation, how does the *SPPA* apply to the SBT?
4. What does the privative clause of the enabling legislation related to the SBT prevent and allow, and under what circumstances?
5. What practices and procedures of the SBT deal with the procedures before the SBT in dealing with human rights issues? Briefly summarize those procedures.
6. What practices and procedures give discretion and flexibility to the SBT in applying the SBT Rules?
7. What forms are important with the SBT, and how are they utilized?

8. What is the appropriate procedure to have a motion dealt with by the SBT?
9. What jurisdiction is the SBT given to reconsider a decision under the various procedures and practices of the SBT?
10. How do the various procedures of the SBT deal with Alternative Dispute Resolution?

EXERCISE

Based upon the facts of the *Tranchemontagne* case briefed in the chapter, fill out form(s) to institute this matter currently before the SBT.

Appendix 4.1
Overview of Procedural Stages of a Matter Before the SBT

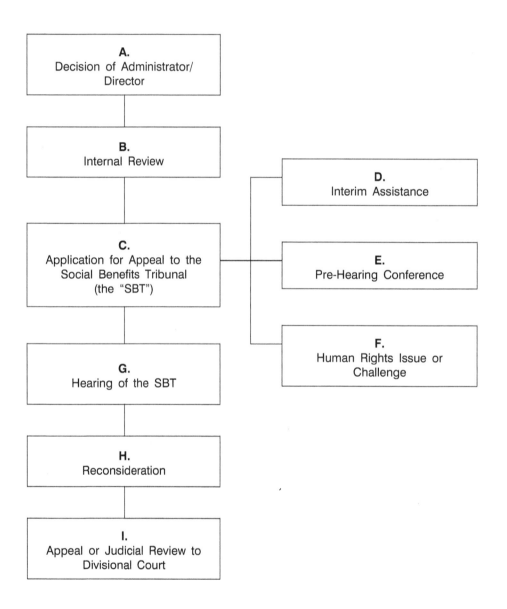

SUMMARY

A. Decision of Administrator/Director

If decision by

(a) Administrator
- *OWA*, s. 44 — Eligibility and amount of basic financial assistance;
- *OWA*, s. 24 — Notice of decision to applicant;
- O. Reg. 134/98, s. 67 — Formalities of contents of the notice of decision

(b) Director
- *ODSPA*, s. 38 — Eligibility and amount of income support;
- *ODSPA*, s. 19 — Notice of decision to applicant;
- O. Reg. 222/98, s. 56 — Formalities of contents of the notice of decision

Look at the following:
- Rule 2

B. Internal Review

OWA, ss. 27(1)
- Before the appeal to the SBT of a decision can be commenced, there must be a request to do an internal review;
- Timing and specifics of request for internal review in *OWA*, s. 27 and O. Reg. 134/98, s. 69;
- An internal review must be completed within 30 days of the request by someone who did not make the original decision, and details regarding delivery of and contents of the internal review are in sections 70–71 of O. Reg. 134/98;
- The *SPPA* does not apply to an internal review under subsection 27(4) of the *OWA*.

ODSPA, ss. 22(1)
- Before the appeal to the SBT of a decision can be commenced, there must be a request to do an internal review;
- Timing and specifics of request for internal review in *ODSPA*, s. 22 and O. Reg. 222/98, s. 58;
- An internal review must be completed within 30 days of the request by someone who did not make the original decision, and details regarding delivery of and contents of the internal review are in sections 59–60 of O. Reg. 222/98;
- The *SPPA* does not apply to an internal review under subsection 22(4) of the *ODSPA*.

Look at the following:
- FAQs on SBT website — Internal Review

C. Application for Appeal to the SBT

OWA, s. 28 and O. Reg. 134/98, ss. 72–79
- Detail specifics of an appeal to the SBT;
- Timeline for appeal is 30 days from date decision is final but can be extended (*OWA*, ss. 28(1,2)) with commencement no later than one year from decision date and appeal requested by submitting a notice of appeal form approved by the Minister (O. Reg. 134/98, s. 72);
- Notice of appeal shall set out reasons for appeal (*OWA*, ss. 28(1));
- Parties to appeal set out in *OWA*, ss. 28(4,7);
- Upon receipt, the SBT sends copy of notice to parties (O. Reg. 134/98, ss. 73(1));

- Format of hearings and disclosure discussed under *OWA*, ss. 28(8–10) and O. Reg. 134/98, ss. 73–74;
- Under subsection 28(11) of *OWA*, the onus is on the appellant to satisfy the SBT on the appeal that the decision of the administrator is wrong;
- According to subsection 26(1) of *OWA*, any decision by an administrator regarding eligibility for or the amount of basic financial assistance may be appealed to the SBT other than decisions set out in subsection 26(2) and section 68 of O. Reg. 134/98;
- Under section 33 of the *OWA*, the SBT "shall refuse to hear an appeal if it determines the appeal to be frivolous or vexatious".

ODSPA, s. 23 and O. Reg. 222/98, ss. 61–65
- Detail specifics of an appeal to the SBT;
- Timeline for appeal is 30 days from date decision is final but can be extended (*ODSPA*, ss. 23(1,2)) with commencement no later than one year from decision date and appeal requested by submitting notice of appeal form approved by the Minister (O. Reg. 222/98, s. 61);
- Notice of appeal shall set out reasons for appeal (*ODSPA*, ss. 23(1));
- Parties to appeal set out in *ODSPA*, ss. 23(4,6);
- Upon receipt, the SBT sends copy of notice to parties (O. Reg. 222/98, ss. 62(1));
- Format of hearings and disclosure discussed under *OWA*, ss. 28(7–9) and O. Reg. 222/98, ss. 62–63;
- Under subsection 23(10) of *ODSPA*, the onus is on the appellant to satisfy the SBT on the appeal that the decision of the director is wrong;
- According to subsection 21(1) of *ODSPA*, any decision by a director regarding eligibility for, or the amount of, income support may be appealed to the SBT with exceptions that are set out in subsection 21(2) and section 57 of O. Reg. 222/98;
- Under section 28 of the *ODSPA*, the SBT "shall refuse to hear an appeal if it determines the appeal to be frivolous or vexatious".

Look at the following:
- Rules 3–6
- Appeal and Hearing Process Web page on the SBT website — Steps 2 and 3
- SBT website — Forms — Appeal Form

D. Interim Assistance

OWA, s. 30: After the request for an appeal, but before the SBT can make a decision, the SBT can direct the administrator to provide interim assistance "to an applicant or recipient if the tribunal is satisfied that the person will suffer financial hardship during the period needed for the tribunal to complete its review and give notice of its decision", up to a maximum as set out in section 77 of O. Reg. 134/98.

The *SPPA* does not apply to any proceeding of the SBT regarding interim assistance (ss. 30(3)).

ODSPA, s. 25: After the request for an appeal, but before the SBT can make a decision, the SBT can direct the director to provide interim assistance "to an applicant or recipient if the tribunal is satisfied that the person will suffer financial hardship during the period needed for the tribunal to complete its review and give notice of its decision", up to a maximum as set out in section 66 of O. Reg. 222/98.

The *SPPA* does not apply to any proceeding of the SBT regarding interim assistance (s. 25(3)).

Look at the following:
• Appeal and Hearing Process Web page on the SBT website — Interim Assistance
• SBT website — Forms — Appeal Form
• SBT website — Practice Direction on Interim Assistance

E. PRE-HEARING CONFERENCE

The procedure used by the SBT for scheduling and conducting pre-hearing conferences is set out in "Practice Direction on Pre-Hearing Conferences". Pre-hearing conferences can be held at the request of a party or at the direction of the SBT (unless there are special or unusual circumstances to dispense). A pre-hearing conference request by a party must be made in writing, with reasons set out, and within 10 days of the filing of the appeal. Where an appeal raises a human rights issue or challenge, a pre-hearing conference is mandatory, and all parties must attend to discuss procedural matters prior to the hearing.

For the purposes of this Practice Direction, a pre-hearing conference is a meeting with all the parties conducted by an SBT member by way of one or a combination of telephone, video-conferencing, oral in-person session, or in writing. The purposes of the pre-hearing conferences are those set out in the provisions of the Direction and evidence is not to be presented. Once a pre-hearing conference is requested or directed, a Notice of Pre-Hearing Conference will be sent as soon as practicable to the parties, setting out the format(s) of the conference and its date, place, and time. Details about the choice of format and the matters that can be dealt with in the pre-hearing conference are set out in the Direction. The various outcomes of the pre-hearing conference are also detailed the Direction.

Look at the following:
• SBT website — Practice Direction on Pre-hearing Conferences

F. Human Rights Issue Or Challenge

The enabling legislation of the SBT does not have provisions dealing with human rights issues or challenges, so the procedures have been derived based on the 2006 SCC case of *Tranchemontagne v. Ontario (Director, Disability Support Program)*, as interpreted by the SBT and set out in "Practice Direction on Human Rights Issue or Challenge". In *Tranchemontagne v. Ontario (Director, Disability Support Program)*, 2006 SCC 14, the Supreme Court of Canada confirmed that the SBT has jurisdiction, which it cannot decline, to consider Ontario *Human Rights Code* ("*Code*") challenges to its governing legislation — the *Ontario Disability Support Program Act, 1997* and/or the *Ontario Works Act, 1997*. This case prompted the SBT to institute a two-stage procedure in this Practice Direction to deal with human rights issues and challenges raised under the *Code*.

All human rights issues or challenges before the SBT will follow the two-stage procedure prescribed in this Direction:

• Stage 1 hearing looks at the merits of the appeal.
• Stage 2 hearing considers the *Code* challenge if the appeal is not denied in Stage 1.

The first step for a party raising a human rights issue or challenge is to file a written Notice of the *Human Rights Code* Claim (Form 4) under R. 7.13 no later than 60 days prior to hearing the appeal with the SBT. (Form 4 requires, among other things, particulars of the challenge, the section(s) of the Ontario *Human Rights Code* (*Code*) relied upon, the desired remedy, and contact particulars of the party's representative, etc.). The SBT will write to the party to acknowledge receiving the Notice and, if more information is needed, direct the party to provide within 30 days. The SBT will send the written notice to the other parties within 10 days of receipt. A party who wishes to reply to such written notice must notify the SBT and send a copy of its intent to the Ministry of Community and Social Services, the Attorney General of the Province of Ontario, and the other parties within 30 days of receiving the written notice forwarded by the SBT. Where a party does not send a written notice of its intention to reply in the proper time, the SBT will assume that such party will not be participating in the human rights issue or challenge. As a general rule, the SBT will hold a pre-hearing conference to determine the procedure for the hearing of the challenge. In most cases, the SBT will address the human rights challenge or issue only after the main issue on the appeal has been heard if it is raised pursuant to these procedures. If the appeal of the main issue is granted, the human rights issue or challenge will not be dealt with.

If the SBT determines that, after receipt of a party's notice, the human rights issue or challenge is frivolous or vexatious, it may refuse to hear the claim. After notifying the party who raised the claim of its decision, the party must confirm whether the appeal on the merits should proceed. Any person seeking status to intervene in an appeal must submit a written request according to Rs. 7.16–7.17.

Look at the following:
• SBT website — Practice Direction on Human Rights Issue or Challenge

G. Hearing of the SBT

The procedures in respect of the actual hearing before the SBT are set out in the provisions of the *SPPA* and as set out in the website of the SBT. Following are specifics that occur after the appeal.

OWA
Within 60 days after it last receives evidence or submissions on the appeal (O. Reg. 134/98, ss. 78(1)), the SBT must deliver to the parties a written decision, with any of the following orders prescribed under section 31 of the *OWA*:
(a) deny the appeal,
(b) grant the appeal,
(c) grant the appeal in part, or
(d) refer the matter back to the administrator for reconsideration in accordance with any directions the SBT considers proper.

Such decision must include reasons for the decision and takes effect when it is made and, if it is appealed, continues in effect until a decision of the Divisional Court is made on appeal. Appeals can also be denied if the appellant, without reasonable cause, fails any of the circumstances listed in section 34 of the *OWA*: (i) to provide information within the required time; (ii) to attend the hearing, or (iii) to be available to be contacted for a hearing. The SBT's findings of fact shall be based exclusively on evidence admissible and facts of which notice may be taken under sections 15, 15.1, 15.2, and 16 of the *SPPA*, and the decision shall include the principal findings of fact and its conclusions based on those findings (ss. 78(2–3) of O. Reg. 134/98).

ODSPA
Within 60 days after it last receives evidence or submissions on the appeal (O. Reg. 222/98, ss. 67(1)), the SBT must deliver to the parties a written decision, with any of the following orders prescribed under section 26 of the *ODSPA*:
(a) deny the appeal,
(b) grant the appeal,

(c) grant the appeal in part, or

(d) refer the matter back to the director for reconsideration in accordance with any directions the SBT considers proper.

Such decision must include reasons for the decision, which takes effect when it is made and, if it is appealed, continues in effect until a decision of the Divisional Court is made on appeal. Pursuant to section 29 of the *ODSPA*, appeals can also be denied if the appellant, without reasonable cause, fails (i) to provide information within the required time; or (ii) to attend the hearing, or (iii) to be available to be contacted for a hearing. The SBT's findings of fact shall be based exclusively on evidence admissible and facts of which notice may be taken under sections 15, 15.1, 15.2, and 16 of the *SPPA*, and the decision shall include the principal findings of fact and its conclusions based on those findings (ss. 67(2–3) of O. Reg. 222/98).

Look at the following:
* Rule 7
* Appeal and Hearing Process on the SBT website — Step 4

H. Reconsideration

OWA: Section 79 of O. Reg. 134/98 details the process to ask the SBT to reconsider its decision on the appeal, including the timelines and other procedural matters.

ODSPA: Section 68 of O. Reg. 222/98 details the process to ask the SBT to reconsider its decision on the appeal, including the timelines and other procedural matters.

Look at the following:
* Rule 15
* Appeal and Hearing Process on the SBT website — Step 5
* SBT website — Practice Direction on Reconsideration Requests

I. Appeal or Judicial Review to Divisional Court

The procedures in respect of appeals and judicial review of an SBT decision are set out in the provisions of the *SPPA* and the *Judicial Review Procedure Act* and as set out in the website of the SBT. Following are specifics that occur after the decision of the SBT is sent to the parties:

* *OWA* — There is no privative clause preventing an appeal of the decision of the SBT: subsection 36(1) of the *OWA* states that "[t]he director and any party to a hearing may appeal the tribunal's decision to the divisional court on a question of law". *OWA*, section 36 and its O. Reg. 134/98, ss. 81–83 provide further information.

* *ODSPA* — There is no privative clause preventing an appeal of the decision of the SBT: subsection 31(1) of the *ODSPA* states that the "director and any party to a hearing may appeal the tribunal's decision to the divisional court on a question of law". Details of procedure are listed under the *ODSPA*, s. 31 and its O. Reg. 222/ 98, ss. 70–71.

Look at the following:
* Rule 16
* Appeal and Hearing Process on the SBT website — Step 5

Appendix 4.2
The Appeal Form[†]

Social Justice Tribunals Ontario
Providing fair and accessible dispute resolution
Social Benefits Tribunal

Appeal Form

Questions?

Toronto:
(416) 326-0978

Outside Toronto:
1-800-753-3895

Fax:
(416) 326-5135

Mail to:
Registrar
Social Benefits Tribunal
1075 Bay Street, 7th floor
Toronto, ON
M5S 2B1

Please attach copies of the following to this form:

- the original **Notice of Decision**

- your **request for an internal review** and

- the **Internal review decision** (if you received one).

Disponible en français.

Office Use Only

File number_____

Date post-marked _____

Before you can appeal to the Tribunal, you must request an internal review by the office that made the original decision. No appeal may be filed more than one year after the final decision.

1. General Information

○ Mr ○ Mrs ○ Ms ○ Miss

Last Name

First Name

Address

Apartment   Telephone

City   Postal Code

When were you born?   DD — MM — YYYY

Which office do you deal with?

○ Ontario Works office   ○ Ontario Disability office

Member / Case ID

Office name

Office address

Case worker's name

Case worker's telephone

If you did not request internal review, you may not appeal to the Tribunal.

2. Internal Review

What is the date of your original Notice of Decision?   DD — MM — YYYY

When did you make your request for an internal review?   DD — MM — YYYY

Did you receive an internal review decision?

○ Yes   ○ No

Page 1 of 4

[†] Source: SBT website, "Forms and Filing" <http://www.sjto.gov.on.ca/sbt/forms-filing/#form2>

Important: If you do not attend your hearing and fail to provide a reasonable explanation for your absence, your appeal will be denied. In addition, you will not be allowed to appeal a subsequent decision on the same issue for two years.

The Social Benefits Tribunal does not have the authority to review all social assistance decisions. We will advise you in writing of the reasons if your appeal cannot be heard.

You must file your appeal within 30 days of the end of the internal review period. If you do not do so, you must explain why you were late filing. The Tribunal may extend the 30 day time limit for filing this appeal, up to 1 year, if it is satisfied that there is a reasonable explanation for the delay.

3. Your Reasons for Appealing

What are you appealing?

○ Ontario Works   ○ Ontario Disability Support Program (disability, seniors or children with severe disabilities)

Why are you appealing? Check **all** the boxes that apply to you.

☐ I was refused assistance.   ☐ My assistance has been cancelled.

☐ My assistance has been reduced.   ☐ My assistance is on hold.

☐ I have an overpayment.   ☐ They say I am not disabled.

☐ The amount of my assistance is wrong.

What is the effective date of the decision you are appealing?   DD ☐ — MM ☐ — YYYY ☐

You **must** explain **what** you disagree with in the original decision and **why.**

Use the space below and attach additional pages if necessary.

Will you need any of the following services at the hearing?

☐ Interpreter: Language [   ]   Dialect [   ]

☐ Sign language interpreter   Physical or other accommodation to participate in the hearing. Please specify. [   ]

Signature _____   DD ☐ — MM ☐ — YYYY ☐

Print Form

This completes the appeal section. If you are experiencing financial hardship, see section 4 on Interim assistance.   Page 2 of 4

Interim assistance is financial help you may be eligible to receive while waiting for your appeal to be concluded.

The Tribunal may order that you receive interim assistance if you will experience financial hardship as a result of the original decision made by your local office. To assess your request for interim assistance, the Tribunal requires detailed financial information.

You will be notified in writing of the Tribunal's decision regarding interim assistance.

Note: If you lose your appeal, your interim assistance shall be assessed as an overpayment.

4. Application for Interim Assistance

Describe your household. How many people, including yourself, have you applied on behalf of?

Adults ☐   Children ☐

Check the box beside those sentences that best describe your situation

☐ I am looking for work.   ☐ I am in an employment assistance program.

☐ I am attending school   ☐ Full-time   ☐ Part-time

☐ High School   ☐ College   ☐ University   ☐ Other.

☐ I am under 18 and cannot live at home.

☐ I am working, but earn less than the Ontario Works entitlement.

Are you receiving any money at all? [▾]

If you live with your spouse, is he/she receiving any money? [▾]

If you or your spouse are receiving money, please provide details of your household income below. Include the amount you receive, when you last received it and how often it and how often you receive this income.

Type of Income	Amount	Date Last Received	Weekly, Monthly, or Other (Specify)
Example: Income A	**$100.00**	**June 1, 2011**	**Monthly**
Earnings from a job			
Vacation pay			
Ontario Works (OW)			
Ontario Disability Support Program (ODSP)			
Workplace Safety & Insurance Benefits (WSIB)			
Employment Insurance			
Canada Pension Plan			
Disability insurance (other than CPP, WSIB)			
Support payments			
Trust fund income			
Ontario Student Assistance Plan (OSAP)			
Rental/boarder income			
Borrowed money			
Foreign Pension			
Self-employment earnings			
Other 1 -			
Other 2 -			

Will you be receiving any money next month that you have not already listed?

What type? [   ]   Amount [   ]

Provide the details below of the assets you or any member of your household have.	
Bank accounts (personal and business)	
Stocks, bonds, GICs	
RSPs	
Land and property other than your home	
Other -	
How much money do you pay each month for:	
Rent	
Mortgage	
Property taxes	
Room and board	
Heat	
Electricity	
Water	
Food	
Other -	

Are you behind in any of your payments or unable to pay these expenses?

○ Yes   What expenses have you been late paying or unable to pay?

○ No   [   ]

Have you received an eviction notice or notice your electricity or other service will be shut off?

○ Yes   Provide details:

○ No   [   ]

Please provide any additional information that you feel the Tribunal should know regarding your financial circumstances.

[   ]

Signature _____   DD [ ] – MM [ ] – YYYY [ ]

The Social Benefits Tribunal collects the personal information requested on this form under the *Ontario Works Act, 1997* or the *Ontario Disability Support Program Act, 1997*. It will be used for the purpose of conducting the appeal and will be shared with the respondent. If you have any questions, please contact the FIPP representative at the Tribunal at 1-800-753-3895.

Print Form

Appendix 4.3
Application for Reconsideration[†]

 Social Benefits Tribunal

Application for Reconsideration

Questions?	1. General Information

Questions?

Toronto:
(416) 326-0978

Outside Toronto:
1-800-753-3895

Fax:
(416) 326-5135

Mail to:
Registrar
Social Benefits Tribunal
1075 Bay Street, 7th Floor
Toronto ON
M5S 2B1

Office Use Only
File number
Date post-marked

The Reconsideration Process

You have thirty (30) days after receiving the appeal decision to submit your application for reconsideration.

The Tribunal will advise you with sixty (60) days of receiving your request whether or not it will grant a reconsideration hearing.

Disponible en français

(10/98)

1. General Information

This application is to be used when you request the Social benefits Tribunal to reconsider a decision made on an appeal. Please complete all of the following sections. For more information on the reconsideration process, please see the side panels.

- Are you the appellant ☐ or the respondent ☐ ?
- The file number on the appeal decision is
- The date of the appeal decision is ____ / ____ / ____
  Day

2. Information about the Appellant

Mr ☐   Mrs ☐   Ms ☐   Miss ☐

LAST NAME_____

FIRST NAME _____

ADDRESS _____

APARTMENT_____ TELEPHONE (_____)_____

CITY _____ POSTAL CODE_____

• Appellant's date of birth is _____ / _____ / _____
                                  Day   Year   Month

3. Information about the Respondent

• The Respondent is an ☐ Ontario Works office or ☐ Ontario Disability office.

OFFICE NAME_____

OFFICE ADDRESS_____

CITY _____ POSTAL CODE_____

TELEPHONE (_____)_____

CONTACT _____

[†] Source: SBT website, "Forms and Filing" <http://www.sjto.gov.on.ca/sbt/forms-filing/#form2>

4. Request for Reconsideration

- Why should the Tribunal grant your request for a reconsideration hearing. Please give your reasons below. Attach additional pages if necessary.

_____
_____
_____
_____
_____
_____
_____
_____
_____
_____
_____
_____
_____
_____
_____
_____
_____
_____
_____
_____

You must send a copy of this application for reconsideration to those whose were parties to the original appeal decision.

Other parties may, within fifteen (15) days of receiving copies of this application for reconsideration, file a written submission with the Tribunal in response to this application.

If you have any questions about the collection of this information, please contact the Tribunal at 1-800-753-3895.

5. notice of Service

• Were there other parties to the original hearing other than the appellant and respondent?   No ☐   Yes ☐ Please provide the name(S):

_____

• I have served a copy of this application on the other parties by:

☐ Prepaid regular post to the last known address,

☐ Delivering it personally,

☐ Sending a facsimile (fax).

Signature:_____   Date:_____

Name (please print) _____

The Social Benefits Tribunal collects the personal information requested on this form under the _Ontario Works Act, 1997, S.O. 1997, c.25, Sched. A._ It will be used in deciding whether or not a reconsideration hearing will be granted and will become part of the Tribunal's file.

Assessment Review Board

WHAT THIS CHAPTER OFFERS

- The background of the Assessment Review Board (ARB)
- A discussion of the cluster of environment and land tribunals (ELTO) and its impact on the ARB
- Details and explanation of the enabling legislation relevant to the ARB
- Provisions of the *Statutory Powers Procedure Act* relevant to the ARB
- Concepts of public policy relevant to the ARB
- Specific rules and procedures for the ARB
- A walk-through of the ARB website
- Summaries of relevant cases and decisions highlighting the legal principle or issue in question
- A flow chart summarizing the procedural stages of an appeal before the ARB

LEARNING OBJECTIVES

After reading this chapter, the reader should be able to:

- state the legislation that governs the operation of the ARB
- research the ARB website for important information needed to understand the agency's practices and procedures and to represent a client properly before the ARB
- compare and prioritize the various sources of practice and procedure of the ARB
- apply the specific rules and procedures in a proceeding before, during, and after a hearing of the ARB
- argue the law before the ARB using appropriate legislation and case law

INTRODUCTION

The Assessment Review Board (ARB) is an Ontario statutorily created adjudicative agency. Its key function is to hear appeals on property assessment and classification. The ARB also deals with other complaints, such as school support designation and some property tax appeals. The ARB holds hearings across Ontario.

Readers should note that on the "Welcome to Assessment Review Board (ARB)" Web page, a video prepared by the ARB shows a sample hearing to provide people with an idea of what to expect.

The ARB website is accessed through the Environmental and Land Tribunals of Ontario website, <www.elto.gov.on.ca>. ELTO was formally designated as Ontario's first cluster of tribunals under the *Adjudicative Tribunals Accountability, Governance and Appointments Act 2009 (ATAGA)*, on April 7, 2010. A brief description of how this cluster formed is set out in the ARB Annual Report 2008–2009:

> In September 2006, the Ontario government appointed an Agency Cluster Facilitator to work with five tribunals in the municipal, environment and land-use planning sectors to find ways to improve services through cross-agency coordination of operations, administration and dispute resolution. The five tribunals included in the cluster were: the Assessment Review Board (ARB), the Board of Negotiation (BON), the Conservation Review Board (CRB), the Environmental Review Tribunal (ERT) and the Ontario Municipal Board (OMB).

The reader who wishes to understand the procedures and practices of the ARB from this date forward should also explore the ELTO website. There is a more thorough discussion of Ontario's clusters of tribunals, including the ELTO in the preamble to Part II.

OVERVIEW AND BACKGROUND

The 2006–2007 Annual Report for the ARB provides a succinct history and overview of the ARB and assessment in Ontario as follows:

> Property assessments have been conducted in what is now Ontario since 1793. In 1970, the province assumed the role of assessing property from municipalities and replaced the Courts of Revision with the Assessment Review Court (ARC). ARC was renamed the Assessment Review Board in 1983.
>
> With the enactment of the *Fair Municipal Finance Act, 1997*, the ARB became the province's sole adjudicative tribunal for property assessment complaints. The legislation reduced duplication and ensured that the Board was the final tribunal

of appeal for such complaints. Prior to 1998, ARB decisions could be appealed to the Ontario Municipal Board (OMB).

In 1998, an amendment to the *Assessment Review Board Act* gave the ARB the capacity to dismiss frivolous complaints. Decisions by the Board are final and binding, subject only to appeal to Divisional Court on questions of law when the Court grants leave to appeal. The Board also exercises the power to review its decisions.

The Board's jurisdiction and its authority are defined by the *Assessment Review Board Act*, the *Assessment Act*, the *Municipal Act, 2001*, the *City of Toronto Act, 2006*, the *Education Act* and the *Statutory Powers Procedure Act*.

Each of the statutes mentioned in the last sentence of the paragraphs just quoted have either been reviewed in the previous chapter on the *SPPA* or are discussed in the relevant sections later in this chapter.

There are four major participants in the property assessment system of Ontario:

1. The provincial government, through the Ministry of Finance, sets the laws regarding property assessment.
2. Municipalities are responsible for setting tax rates and collecting property taxes.
3. The Municipal Property Assessment Corporation (MPAC) assesses and classifies all properties in Ontario.
4. The Assessment Review Board (ARB) hears complaints filed by property owners if there is a dispute between a property owner and MPAC.

MPAC is a statutory, non-profit corporation created under the *Municipal Property Assessment Corporation Act, 1997*, and managed by a board composed largely of municipal representatives. It conducts property assessments throughout the province as well as assessment updates and other non-relevant activities.

According to the 2012–2013 annual report, the ARB has been carrying a caseload balance of approximately 90,000 in each of the last three fiscal years. In February 2012, the ARB introduced a revised strategy, prior to the start of the next four-year assessment cycle commencing in 2013, to expedite resolution of its outstanding caseload, particularly for non-residential cases. The result of this strategy is described in ELTO's 2014–2015 annual report:

> The ARB Streaming Strategy, which was previously developed in consultation with staff, members and stakeholders, continued to make excellent progress. The strategy was designed to

address the outstanding backlog of cases from previous assessment cycles and improve the ARB's ability to resolve new cases within the current 2013–2016 cycle. As of March 31, 2015, the total number of outstanding appeals was 66,000 on 24,000 properties. The ARB continues to see progress on the resolution of the backlog of appeals, resulting in an 80 per cent reduction in pre-2013 appeals.

ENABLING LEGISLATION

The jurisdiction and authority of the ARB are defined by the following legislation:

(i)   The *Assessment Review Board Act*, R.S.O. 1990, c. A.32, as amended (*ARBA*), establishes the ARB and also sets out a few procedural rules.

(ii) The *Assessment Act*, R.S.O. 1990, c. A.31, as amended.

(iii) The *Municipal Act, 2001*, S.O. 2001, c. 25, as amended.

(iv) The *Education Act*, R.S.O. 1990, c. E.2, as amended.

(v)   The *City of Toronto Act, 2006*, S.O. 2006, c. 11, Sched. A, as amended, gives jurisdiction to the ARB.

(vi) The *Provincial Land Tax Act, 2006* S.O. 2006, c. 33, Sched. Z.2, as amended.

(vii) The *Statutory Powers Procedure Act* (*SPPA*), which is a statute of general application, imposes minimum rules of procedure and ties the ARB Rules that have been published into the procedure.

(viii) *The Condominium Act, 1998*, S.O. 1998, c. 19.

All the legislation, except the *Statutory Powers Procedure Act*, which is discussed in Chapter 2, are examined as each relates to the ARB.

The *ARBA*

The *ARBA* replaced the previous statute in 1990 and continued the ARB (s. 2). Under section 3, the Lieutenant Governor in Council (the Ontario Cabinet) appoints the chair and vice-chairs and other members of the ARB. Only one member of the ARB is sufficient to constitute a quorum, and therefore there only has to be one member to adjudicate a hearing with all the jurisdiction and powers of the ARB (s. 5). Pursuant to section 6, a chair or vice-chair has power to assign, change, and prescribe duties to the members in various sittings of the ARB. The oath required to be taken by every member before entering her/his duties is set out in section 7. Under section 8.1, the ARB may set and charge fees, subject to the approval of the Attorney General, for proceedings under the *Assessment Act* and the *Municipal Act*, for furnishing copies of forms, notices, or documents filed with or issued by the ARB for other services provided by the ARB. Different kinds of complaints, applications, and appeals can be treated differently in fee setting, which is made available to the public usually by regulation (e.g., O. Reg. 290/07 sets out fees for some applications under the *City of Toronto Act*). The ARB can also waive or refund all or part of a fee charged in the appropriate circumstances. Further to section 8.2, the ARB may, on its own or at the motion of any party, dismiss a complaint or an appeal brought before it, without holding a hearing, as the ARB considers appropriate, on any of the following three grounds:

1. The ARB is of the opinion that the proceeding is frivolous or vexatious, is commenced in bad faith, or is commenced only for the purpose of delay.
2. The ARB is of the opinion that the reasons set out in the complaint or appeal do not disclose any apparent statutory ground on which it can make a decision.
3. The complainant or appellant has not responded to the ARB's request for further information within the time the ARB specified.

Before dismissing an appeal or complaint under any of these grounds, the ARB shall notify the appellant or complainant and give that person the opportunity to respond.

Pursuant to section 9, effective January 1, 2009, the chair of the ARB shall determine where the board sits to hear and decide all complaints relating to assessments. Finally, under section 12, the municipality where sittings of the ARB are held is required to provide a suitable room and other necessary accommodation for the ARB.

The *Assessment Act*

Definitions and Purpose

The ARB is defined as being the ARB under subsection 1(1) of the *ARBA*, which means that the *Assessment Act* does not create the ARB but only gives it jurisdiction. The Minister of Finance, under subsection 2(2), is given the authority to make regulations, which include resolving issues as to (i) whether land is in the farm property class or managed forests property class or (ii) whether land is conservation land (ss. 2(d.3) and (d.4), which are related to procedures to be used by the ARB). (The reader should keep up-to-date with the legislation if involved with the ARB or any tribunal.) The purpose of the *Assessment Act* is to set up a system to assess land value so that municipal (or realty) taxes can be determined. The assessment depends on such factors as the current value of the land (ss. 19(1)), the classification of the real property (s. 7), and the support of a specific type of school board (s. 16). The assessment is done by MPAC (as defined in ss. 1(1)), using factors and procedures set out under the assessment legislation, and includes classes of land exempt from taxation in order to produce an annual assessment roll within the time period set out in section 36 for each municipality and in accordance with section 14 for each locality and non-municipal territory.

School Support Designation

MPAC is also required under section 16 to provide an annual school support list. Under subsection 16(3), "[a]ny person may apply in a form approved by the Minister [of Finance] to the assessment corporation to have his or her name included or altered in the assessment roll as a supporter of a type of school board under the *Education Act*". A refusal by MPAC will require it to "inform the applicant in writing that the application is refused, that the school support of the applicant as designated on the list prepared under [s. 16(9)] will be confirmed on the notice of assessment to which the applicant is entitled under section 31 and that the applicant may, upon receipt of the notice of assessment, appeal the school support designation as confirmed by [MPAC] to the Assessment Review Board under section 40". Note also that subsection 16(10) states the following:

> Where an application under this section has been received by [MPAC] before the day fixed for the return of the roll but has not been considered by the corporation until after the delivery of the notice of assessment provided for in section 31, [MPAC] shall, if [it] refuses the application, inform the applicant in writing that the inclusion or amendment requested in the application is refused and that an appeal may be taken by appealing to the Assessment Review Board the applicant's school support designation as shown on the notice of assessment delivered under section 31 but, where [MPAC] approves the application, the corporation shall deliver to the applicant an amended notice of assessment.

Change of Information

If there is a change in the information required, as described in ss. 14(1), (1.1), or (1.2), but not reflected in the last assessment roll, MPAC shall deliver, in accordance with section 31 and in a form approved by the Minister of Finance, a notice of assessment with information required by subsection 31(1) to every person affected by such change. The notice of assessment shall be accompanied by an information notice and delivered by a certain date and in a certain manner, all in accordance with section 31.

Appeal under s. 36

The assessment roll is to be returned by MPAC to the municipality clerk (or similar person for non-municipal lands) on the date set out in subsection 36(2), although the date to return can be extended by MPAC under subsections 36(2) and (3). The timeline for the ARB to hear appeals, including complaints under section 33 (omitted assessments) and section 34 (supplementary assessments), for that assessment roll is set out in subsection 36(5) as being as soon as practicable after the return of the assessment roll. The last revised assessment roll is accomplished as set out in section 37; however, subsection 37(5) states that "[n]othing in this section deprives a person of a right of appeal provided for in this Act, which may be exercised and the appeal proceeded with in accordance with this Act, despite the fact that the assessment roll has become the last revised assessment roll".

Reconsideration by MPAC

Section 39.1 details the ability of a person who received, or would be entitled to receive, a notice of assessment to request MPAC to reconsider any matter that could form the basis of an appeal under subsection 40(1) or an application under s. 46, no later than March 31 of the taxation year in respect of which the request is made except for the first taxation year for a general assessment, which has a 120-day appeal window. The reconsideration request must be made within the time limits as set out in subsections 39.1(2) and (3) and must give the basis for the person's request and all the relevant facts (ss. 39.1(4)) that will be considered by MPAC (ss. 39.1(5)). Regulations regarding disclosure by both MPAC and the person requesting reconsideration can be made by the Minister of Finance (ss. 39.1(6)), but as of the time of writing, none has been published. Under subsection 39.1(7), MPAC shall mail to the requesting party the results of the reconsideration by either September 30 of the taxation year or November 30 of the taxation year if such extension is agreed upon. However, if the request for reconsideration relates to a notice of correction, the date to get the results is 180 days after the request is made (ss. 39.1(8)). In the case that MPAC and the requestor can settle, MPAC shall give notice of settlement to either the municipality clerk or the Minister of Finance as required (ss. 39.1(9)). The municipality or the Minister can object to the settlement under subsection 39.1(11), but the appeal must be made (i) to the ARB within 90 days after receiving notice of settlement, and (ii) on the basis that section 40 applies as if the assessment roll had been changed to reflect the settlement.

Appeal under s. 40

Specific details of an appeal to the ARB are covered under the various subsections of section 40. Under subsection (1)(a), any person may appeal to the ARB on the following bases:

(i) the current value of the person's land or another person's land is incorrect,

(ii) the person or another person was wrongly placed on or omitted from the assessment roll,

(iii) the person or another person was wrongly placed on or omitted from the roll in respect of school support,

(iv) the classification of the person's land or another person's land is incorrect, or

(v) for land, portions of which are in different classes of real property, the determination of the share of the value of the land that is attributable to each class is incorrect.

Another basis for appeal can be any ground that the Minister of Finance may prescribe, but as of the date of this writing, there is no regulation prescribing another basis. **Note that if a timely request for reconsideration is not made in respect of certain classes of property as set out in subsection 40(3), no appeal may be brought to the ARB**, except where there are extenuating circumstances as determined by the ARB (ss. 40(4)). A proviso for the 2017 and subsequent taxation years is set out in subsection 40(3.1). There are further end dates to appeal to the ARB, depending on specific circumstances as set out in subsections 40(5) to (8). Where the appellant is a person other than the person who was assessed, procedures are stated under subsection 40(9). Pursuant to subsection 40(10), upon receipt of an appeal, the ARB shall immediately send a copy to MPAC. The parties to the appeal are MPAC, the appellant(s) and the person whose assessment is the subject of the appeal, and the municipality in which the land is located, or the Minister of Finance if it is non-municipal land (ss. 40(11)). The ARB shall give at least 24 days' notice to all the parties to the hearing before the date of the hearing (ss. 40(12)). Regulations regarding disclosure by the parties to the appeal can be made by the Minister of Finance (ss. 40(13)), but none has been published to date; however, R. 56 of the ARB Rules of Practice and Procedure, to be discussed below, does discuss discovery.

The mechanisms for adding a party to the appeal are discussed in subsection 40(14), and the person whose property is the subject to the appeal is given the opportunity to make the closing statement at the hearing under subsection 40(15). Where the valuation is the ground for appeal, a recent amendment states that MPAC has the burden to prove the correctness of the current value (ss. 40(17)). However, if the appellant refuses (i) to give MPAC a reasonable opportunity to inspect the property under section 10 or (ii) to comply with a request for information and documentation under section 11, the burden of proving the correctness of the current value shall rest with the appellant (ss. 40(18)). It is possible that even if MPAC does not meet the burden, the ARB may have little choice but to confirm if the complainant fails to provide determinative evidence. Pursuant to subsection 40(19), after hearing the evidence and the submissions of the parties, the ARB shall determine the matter.

Once the decision has been made, the ARB shall immediately forward its decision to the municipality clerk under subsection 40(20), or the Minister of Finance under subsection 40(21), as the case may be, and such person "shall alter the assessment roll in accordance with the decisions of the [ARB] from which no further appeal is taken, indicate on the roll that the alteration has been made and complete the roll by totalling the amounts of the assessments in the roll and inserting the total". Subsection 40(22) states that the ARB, "as to all matters within its jurisdiction under this section, has authority to hear and determine all questions of law or of fact and a decision of the Board under this section is final and binding unless it is appealed under section 43.1". Some specific situations are dealt with in subsections 40(23) to 40(28).

Palpable Errors in Assessment Roll

The ARB is given authority, where there are palpable errors in the assessment roll, to correct the roll if no alteration in assessed values or classification of land is involved and, if there is such an alteration, to extend the time for bringing appeals and direct MPAC to be the appellant (s. 40.1).

Assessment Roll as Evidence

A certified copy of the assessment roll as evidence in a hearing is discussed in section 42 as follows:

> The following documents may be received in evidence by a court or tribunal, without proof of the signature of the person certifying the document and without production of the original of which the document purports to be a copy:

1. A document that is a copy of all or part of the assessment roll for a municipality, certified by the clerk of the municipality to be a true copy of it.
2. A document that is a copy of all or part of the assessment roll for non-municipal territory, certified by the Minister to be a true copy of it.

Stating a Case

Under section 43, the ARB may, upon application of any person or on its own motion, and upon such security (i.e., money to be put up) as it determines is necessary, "state a case in writing for the opinion of the Divisional Court upon any question that, in the opinion of the [ARB], is a question of law", and the Divisional Court shall hear and determine such stated case. This provision is used in very limited circumstances, and, if used, all the parties have to agree to pay their own costs and to indemnify the ARB.

Leave to Appeal to Divisional Court

Under section 43.1, an appeal from the ARB on a question of law lies upon the leave of appeal to the Divisional Court, and an application for leave to appeal shall be made within 30 days of the mailing of the decision by the ARB.

Powers of the ARB

Pursuant to subsection 44(1),

> Upon an appeal on any ground against an assessment, the [ARB] or court, as the case may be, may reopen the whole question of the assessment so that omissions from, or errors in the assessment roll may be corrected, and the amount for which the assessment should be made, and the person or persons who should be assessed therefor may be placed upon the roll, and if necessary the assessment roll, even if returned as finally revised, may be opened so as to make it correct in accordance with the findings made on appeal.

Also under subsection 44(3),

> in determining the value at which any land shall be assessed, the [ARB] shall,
> (a) determine the current value of the land; and
> (b) have reference to the value at which similar lands in the vicinity are assessed and adjust the assessment of the land to make it equitable with that of similar lands in the

vicinity if such an adjustment would result in a reduction of the assessment of the land.

Further Powers of the ARB

The powers of the ARB in respect of an appeal are stated in section 45:

> Upon an appeal with respect to an assessment, the Assessment Review Board may review the assessment and, for the purpose of the review, has all the powers and functions of the assessment corporation in making an assessment, determination or decision under this Act, and any assessment, determination or decision made on review by the Assessment Review Board shall be deemed to be an assessment, determination or decision of the assessment corporation and has the same force and effect.

Applications to the Superior Court of Justice

Applications to the Superior Court of Justice for certain situations are discussed in section 46 but note subsection 46(6): "Despite the fact that a question of the assessment of any person is pending before the Assessment Review Board, the judgment of the Superior Court of Justice or the Divisional Court shall be given effect to and is binding upon the Board." In other words, the decision of the Divisional Court will bind the ARB.

Limitation on Defences

Section 49 is the last section that involves ARB:

> No matter that could have been raised by way of appeal to the [ARB] or in a proceeding with respect to an assessment in a court within the times limited for bringing the appeal or proceeding under this Act shall be raised by way of defence in any proceeding brought by or on behalf of a municipality or, in the case of land in non-municipal territory, by the Minister.

The *Municipal Act*

All the situations involving the ARB under the *City of Toronto Act* are covered under the *Municipal Act*, which deals with the municipalities generally, thus including the municipality of Toronto.

Taxes on Eligible Property — Comparables

The first provision is section 331, which deals with ensuring taxes on eligible properties are levied at the same level as comparable properties (ss. 331(1)). The four steps the municipality is to use to determine the municipal and school taxes for eligible properties are set out in subsection 331(2) and in accordance with section 329. Under subsection 331(6), MPAC "shall identify six comparable properties with respect to an eligible property for the purposes of this section or, if there are fewer than six comparable properties, as many comparable properties as there are" and provide immediately the list of comparable properties to the municipality (ss. 331(8)) so that the city can determine the taxes in accordance with the section.

Pursuant to subsection 331(9), the municipality shall mail to the owner of each eligible property the list of the comparable properties and the determination made under the section with respect to that eligible property within 60 days after the date the list is received by the municipality. The owner is then given the right to complain to the ARB, as stated in subsection 331(11):

> The owner of an eligible property or the local municipality may, within 90 days of the mailing of information under subsection (9), complain to the Assessment Review Board in writing concerning the properties on the list and request that up to six alternative properties be used as comparable properties for the purposes of this section.

There is also a mechanism for the owner to complain to the ARB where MPAC could not provide a list of comparable properties under subsections 331(10) and (12). A complaint to the ARB under either scenario is to be treated, in accordance with subsection 331(13), as a complaint under section 40 of the *Assessment Act*. Appeals of decisions from the ARB to Divisional Court on questions of law (ss. 331(14)) are dealt with under section 43.1 of the *Assessment Act*. The authority granted to the ARB pursuant to subsection 331(15) is to either identify up to six comparable properties from among the comparable properties (situated in the same municipality as the subject property) proposed by the complainant or by MPAC, or to determine that there are no comparable properties. Once the ARB has made its decision, the municipality under subsection 331(18) shall determine the taxes for municipal and school purposes in accordance with the decision.

Dividing Land into Parcels and Apportioning Taxes

Section 356 involves decisions made by a municipal council in dividing land into parcels (ss. (1)(a)) and apportioning the taxes on application of either the municipal treasurer or the owner of the land (ss. (1)(b)). Within 14 days of the municipal council making its decision, pursuant to subsection (5), it shall give a notice to the applicant and/or owner of the decision and state the last date to appeal the decision; within 35 days after the decision, the applicant and/or owner may appeal the municipal council's decision with respect to the apportionment of taxes to the ARB (ss. (6)) by filing a notice of appeal with the registrar of the ARB. Under subsection (7), upon giving notice to the appellant and/or owner and the municipal treasurer, the ARB shall hear the appeal and apportion the taxes under subsection (1)(b). Since the municipality is also given the power, under subsection (8), to pass a by-law to delegate the authority to make the determination to apportion taxes directly, rather than going through the municipal council, in such case a certified copy of such by-law shall be forwarded to the registrar of the ARB and MPAC, as well as a copy of every application to which the by-law applies in accordance with subsection (9). **If you are dealing with a municipality under section 356, check to see if the municipality has passed the requisite by-law to determine if you should proceed to the municipal council or directly to the ARB. Note, the decision of the ARB with respect to subsection (1)(b) as well as the municipal council's decision with respect to subsections (1)(a) and (c) are final (ss. 356(10)), which means that this is a privative clause.** Copies of the decisions by the ARB and municipal council are to be forwarded to the municipal treasurer and MPAC under subsection (11), and the municipal treasurer, pursuant to subsection (12), shall immediately adjust the tax roll in accordance with the decisions made.

Cancellation, Reduction, or Refund of Taxes — s. 357 and s. 334

The ARB also reviews decisions that involve cancellation, reduction, or refund of taxes, as set out in subsection 357(1), including subsection (d.1), where the applicant is unable to pay taxes due to sickness or extreme poverty. On or before February 28 of the year following the year in which the application is made (ss. (3)), or other deadline per subsection (4), on application to and filed with the municipal treasurer by the owner of the land or another interested person, as set out in subsection (2), the municipality can cancel, reduce, or refund taxes on eight circumstances detailed in subsection (1). Municipal council can have a meeting, make its decision under subsection (5), give notice of its decision under subsection (6), and allow the applicant to appeal the decision to the ARB under subsection (7). It can also delegate the power to make a decision to the ARB by by-law under subsection (11). If a by-law is passed, a certified copy of that by-law shall be forwarded by municipal council to the registrar of the ARB and MPAC, as well as a copy of every application to which the by-law applies in accordance with subsection (12). **If you are dealing with a municipality under section 357, check to see if the municipality has passed the requisite by-law to determine if you should proceed to municipal council or directly to the ARB. Note that the decision of the ARB is final (ss. (17)), which means that this is a privative clause.** Copies of the decisions by the ARB and municipal council are to be forwarded to MPAC under subsection (18). Furthermore, note that under section 334 an application to the municipal treasurer for cancellation, reduction, or refund of taxes levied *with respect to the year in which the application is made* may be made by a person who was overcharged by reason of a gross or manifest error that is a clerical error — the transposition of figures, a typographical error, or similar type of error in the calculation of taxes, using the same procedure as set out in section 357.

Cancellation, Reduction, or Refund of Taxes — s. 358

On the other hand, taxes that were overcharged *in one or both of the two years preceding the year in which the application is made* and the overcharge was caused by a gross or manifest error in the preparation of the assessment roll that is clerical or factual in nature — including the transposition of figures and typographical errors or similar errors — but not an error in judgment in assessing the property are dealt with in section 358 rather than section 357. The application to the municipal treasurer to cancel, reduce, or refund the taxes can be made only pursuant to subsection (2) by the owner of the land or another interested person as set out in subsection 357(2). The timing to bring the application is set out in subsections (3) and (4), subject to a further restriction of no application if the circumstance of subsection (5) exists. Under subsection (6), the municipal treasurer is to send a copy of the application to MPAC and the registrar of the ARB. Municipal council can either have a hearing to decide the application pursuant to subsection (9) or pass a by-law delegating power to the ARB to hear the application directly under subsection (12).

Increase of Taxes — s. 359 and s. 337

Section 359 allows for an application to be made by the municipal treasurer for the municipality to increase taxes levied on land in the year the application is made to the extent of any undercharge caused by a gross or manifest error that is a clerical or factual error, including the transposition of figures, or a typographical or similar error, but not an error in judgment in assessing the land. The deadline for the application is set out in subsection (2.1), and the application cannot be made if the circumstance set out in subsection (2) occurs. Municipal council can either have a hearing to decide the application pursuant to subsection (3) or pass a by-law delegating power to the ARB to hear the application directly under subsection (8). **If you are dealing with a municipality under section 359, check to see if the municipality has passed the requisite by-law to determine if you should proceed to municipal council or directly to the ARB.** If there is no by-law, the municipal council holds a meeting on the application, gives notice of its decision under subsection (4), and allows the affected land owner to appeal the decision to the ARB under subsection (5).

As set out in section 337, where a person is undercharged taxes the procedure detailed in section 359 applies. **The decision of the ARB is final (ss. (11)), which means that this is a privative clause.**

Also note that if a calculation error as described in subsection 359.1(1) is identified by the treasurer who then submitted an application, the municipal council will hold a meeting under subsection 359.1(2). A notice to the treasurer and the affected party must be given within 14 days of decision (s. 359.1(3)); an appeal can be made, pursuant to subsection 359.1(4), to the ARB in accordance with subsections 359(5) to 359(7).

Rebates on Taxes Due to Vacant Portions of Property — s. 364

Section 364 deals with the procedure involving rebates on taxes to owners of properties in any of the commercial or industrial classes defined in subsection 308(1) that have vacant portions; that procedure ultimately can involve the ARB. Applications can be made for a rebate if the tax rebate program meets the six requirements enumerated in subsection (2). Within 120 days after the municipality mails to the applicant its determination of the rebate (ss. (14)), the applicant can make a written complaint to the ARB. The applicant can also file a complaint with the ARB if the municipality fails to make a determination 120 days after receiving the application (ss. (15)). The ARB shall determine the amount of the rebate under subsection (16). **Note that subsection (18) allows an appeal of the ARB decision on a question of law to the Divisional Court, and, therefore, there is no complete privative clause.**

If the municipality determines that a rebate, or any portion of the rebate, made under subsection (22) has been paid in error, the municipality, subject to the time limit set out in subsection (23), may notify the owner of the property on which the rebate was made of the amount of the overpayment. Upon so doing, the overpaid amount shall have priority lien status and shall be added to the tax roll. The owner of the property who was sent a notice of overpayment of the rebate has the right under subsection (24) to make written complaint to the ARB that the rebate was properly payable.

The *City of Toronto Act*

The *City of Toronto Act* is derived from the *Municipal Act*; therefore they are very similar, as the reader will discover when reviewing them.

Purpose

One of the purposes of the *City of Toronto Act* is to determine the appropriate levels of spending and taxation for the City of Toronto. In order to help with that determination, the legislation gives the right to complain or appeal many situations that establish the assessment roll and thereby help to decide the appropriate levels of municipal taxation. The forum for such complaints and appeals is often the ARB. The following are various provisions of the legislation that give authority or jurisdiction to the ARB.

Taxes on Eligible Property — Comparables

The first provision is section 294, which deals with ensuring that eligible property is taxed at the same level as comparable properties (ss. 294(1)). The four steps the City is to use to determine municipal and school taxes for eligible properties are set out in subsection 294(2) and in accordance with section 291. To ensure a fair tax level, MPAC is required to provide a list of *six* comparable properties with respect to an eligible property, or as many as there are if fewer than six are available (ss. 294(6)), to the City as soon as practicable (ss. 294(8)) so that the City can determine the taxes in accordance with the section. Pursuant to subsection 294(9), the City shall mail to the owner of each eligible property the list of the comparable properties and the determination made under the section with respect to that eligible property within 60 days after the date the list is received by the City. The owner is then given the right to complain to the ARB, as stated in subsection 294(11):

> The owner of an eligible property or the City may, within 90 days of the mailing of information under subsection (9), complain to the Assessment Review Board in writing concerning the properties on the list and request that up to six alternative properties be used as comparable properties for the purposes of this section.

There is also a mechanism for the owner to complain to the ARB where MPAC could not provide a list of comparable properties under subsections 294(11) and (12). A complaint to the ARB under either scenario is to be treated in accordance with subsection 294(13) as an appeal under section 40 of the *Assessment Act*. As stated under subsection 294(14), appeals of ARB decisions to the Divisional Court will be dealt with in accordance with section 43.1 of the *Assessment Act* (i.e., appeal on a question of law only, and leave to appeal must be made within 30 days of the mailing of the ARB decision). The authority granted to the ARB pursuant to subsection 294(15) is either to identify up to six comparable properties (in the City or Municipality of Toronto) from among the comparable properties proposed by the complainant or MPAC or to determine that there are no comparable properties. Once the ARB has made its decision, the City shall determine the taxes for municipal and school purposes in accordance with the decision, pursuant to subsection 294(18).

Dividing Land into Parcels and Apportioning Taxes

Section 322 involves city council dividing land into parcels and apportioning paid and unpaid taxes upon applications of either the city treasurer or the owner of the land, as described in subsection (1). Within 14 days of city council making its decision, city council, pursuant to subsection (4), shall give a notice to the applicant and/or owner of the decision and state the last date to appeal the decision. Within 35 days after the decision, the applicant and/or owner may appeal to the ARB city council's decision with respect to the apportionment of taxes (ss. (5)) by filing a notice of appeal with the registrar of the ARB. Under subsection (6), upon giving notice to the appellant(s) and/or owner(s) and the city treasurer, the ARB shall hear the appeal and confirm or re-apportion the taxes in accordance with subsection (1)(b).

Under subsection (7), the City is also given the power to pass a by-law to delegate the authority to make the determination to apportion taxes directly rather than going through city council. In accordance with subsection (8), a certified copy of such by-law shall be forwarded to the registrar of the ARB and MPAC, as well as a copy of every application to which the by-law applies. **A by-law had been passed, giving the ARB the power to accept (i) applications under section 322(1)(b) and (ii) appeals on decisions made by the council on applications of section 322(1)(b). The reader should look at it in detail if faced with this situation. Note that the decision of the ARB with respect to subsection (1)(b) and city council's decision with respect to subsections (1)(a) and (c) are final (ss. (9)), which means that this is a privative clause.** Under subsection (10), copies of the decisions by the ARB and city council are to be forwarded to the city treasurer and MPAC, and the city treasurer shall immediately adjust the tax roll in accordance with the decisions, pursuant to subsection (11).

Cancellation, Reduction, or Refund of Taxes — s. 323 and s. 297

Cancellation, reduction, or refund in taxes can also be granted by the City, upon receiving the application, in circumstances described in subsection 323(1), which include failure to pay taxes due to sickness or extreme poverty (subcl. (1)(e)). Except for applications made by the city treasurer, as set out in subsection (4), applications, made only by the land owner or interested persons prescribed in subsection (2), must be filed with the city treasurer on or before February 28 of the year following the year in which the application is made, as stated in subsection (3). Under subsection (5), on or before September 30 of the year following the year in which the application is made, city council must make a decision after holding a meeting allowing applicants to make representations to council. A notice of the meeting by mail must be sent to the applicants 14 days prior. Within 14 days after the decision is made, council must give notice of its decision and specify last day for appeal to the applicants, as required in subsection (6). The applicants, as stated in subsection (7), have 35 days to appeal the decision to the ARB by filing a notice of appeal with the ARB. Where no decision is made at the time set out in subsection (5), applicants can file an appeal to the ARB by October 21 of the year after the year for which the application was made (ss. (8)). The ARB is required to hear the appeal and make a decision that the council could have made (ss. (10)); and, in pursuant to subsection (9), a notice of the hearing is to be given 14 days prior.

Subsection (11) allows city council to pass a by-law to delegate to the ARB its powers and functions under subsections (1) to (5) concerning applications made under subsection (1). In accordance with subsection (12), if a by-law is passed, a certified copy of such by-law shall be forwarded by city council to the registrar of the ARB and MPAC, as well as a copy of every application to which the by-law applies. **There is such a by-law, and the reader should look at it in detail if faced with this situation. Subsection (17) is a privative clause as it declares the decision of the ARB is final.** Copies of the decisions by the ARB and city council are to be forwarded to MPAC, as required by subsection (18). Note that under section 297, a person who was overcharged taxes by reason of a gross or manifest error that is clerical or factual in nature can apply to the city treasurer for cancellation, reduction, or refund of taxes *levied in the year the application is made*, using the same procedure as set out in section 323.

Cancellation, Reduction, or Refund of Taxes — s. 325

Overcharges in taxes that were caused by a gross or manifest error in the preparation of the assessment roll that was clerical or factual in nature are dealt with under section 325, not section 323. Overcharge claims can include *one or both of the two years preceding the year in which the application is made*. Pursuant to subsection (2), only the owner of the land or persons listed in subsection 323(2) can make application to the city treasurer to cancel, reduce, or refund the overcharged taxes. The timing to bring the application is set out in subsections (3) and (4), subject to a restriction of no application for taxes levied in a year in which the assessment of the land is being appealed (ss. (5)). Under subsection (6), the city treasurer is to send a copy of the application to MPAC and the registrar of the ARB. According subsections (7) and (8), city council will not hear the application if (i) MPAC did not confirm the error referred to in the application, or (ii) the application is invalid under subsection (5). City council can either have a hearing to decide the application, pursuant to subsection (9), or pass a by-law delegating power to the ARB to hear the application directly, under subsection (11). **Note that there is such a by-law, and the reader should look at it in detail if faced with this situation. The decision of the ARB is final (ss. (14)), which means that this is a privative clause.**

Increase of Taxes — s. 326 and s. 300

Section 326 allows the City to increase taxes if there is an undercharge caused by a gross or manifest error that is clerical or factual. It does not apply to undercharge caused by an error in judgment in assessing the land.

According to subsection (1), the City, upon the city treasurer making an application, can increase the taxes levied on land in the year in which the application is made. The extent of increase is limited to the undercharge caused by the error. As stated in subsection (3), the last date for making the application is December 31 of the year following the year for which the application is made. No application can be made under the circumstance set out in subsection (2). Procedures for city council to hear and decide the application are provided under subsections (4) and (5). Applicants can appeal the city council's decision to the ARB, and procedures are set out in subsections (6) to (8). Under subsection (9), city council can delegate its power to hear and decide applications to the ARB by passing a by-law. Such a by-law does not exist as of 2014. **Subsection (12) is a privative clause, stating that the decision of the ARB under section 326 is final.**

The procedures detailed in this section also apply to a person who is undercharged taxes in accordance with section 300.

Rebates on Taxes Due to Vacant Portions of Property —
s. 331

Section 331 deals with vacancy tax rebates to owners of properties that are in the commercial or industrial classes defined in subsection 275(1). Applications for a rebate can be made if the tax
rebate program meets the six requirements enumerated in subsection
(2). Under subsection (14), the applicant can appeal to the ARB
within 120 days after the City mails to the applicant the determination of the rebate amount. According to subsection (15), the applicant can make written complaint to the ARB if the City fails to make
a determination within 120 days after receiving the application. The
ARB, under subsection (16), shall determine the amount of the
rebate. **Note that subsection (18) allows an appeal of the ARB
decision to the Divisional Court on a question of law; therefore, there is no complete privative clause.**

Subject to the time limit set out in subsection (23), subsection
(22) allows the City to rectify errors in the payment of a rebate
made under section 331 by notifying the owner of the property of
which the rebate was made of the overpaid amount. Upon notification, the overpaid amount will have priority lien status and will be
added to the tax roll. The property owner who was sent the notice of
overpayment of the rebate has the right under subsection (24) to
make written complaint to the ARB that the rebate was properly paid.
Section 40 of the *Assessment Act* applies to the complaints made
under subsections (14), (15), or (24), except that MPAC is not a
party to the complaint.

For a comparison of provisions of the *Municipal Act* and the *City
of Toronto Act, 2006*, see Table 5.1.

The *Education Act*

Under section 236, a person is allowed, on application to MPAC under
section 16 of the *Assessment Act*, to have his or her name included
or altered on the assessment roll as a supporter of a specific type of
school board. A similar provision is also found in the *Assessment Act*,
where subsection 16(3) states that any person can apply in a form
approved by the Minister of Finance to MPAC to have his or her name
included or altered in the assessment roll as a specific kind of school
supporter prescribed in section 257.4 of the *Education Act*. If MPAC
refuses the application, subsections 16(9) and (10) of the *Assessment Act* allow the applicants to appeal the ARB; the *Education Act* is
therefore connected to the ARB.

Table 5.1
Chart of Comparison of Provisions of
the *Municipal Act* and the *City of Toronto Act*, 2006 ("COTA")

Provisions of Acts Regarding ARB	The *Municipal Act*	COTA
Comparables (6 Prop.)	s. 333	s. 294
• By-Law	NO	NO
• Privative Clause	NO	NO
Dividing Land	356	322
• By-Law	YES	YES
• Privative Clause	YES	YES
Cancellation (Error in Judgement)	ss. 357 & 334	ss. 323 & 297
• By-Law	YES	YES
• Privative Clause	YES	YES
Cancellation (Typo)	358	325
• By-Law	YES	YES
• Privative Clause	YES	YES
Increase In Taxes	ss. 359 & 337	ss. 326 & 300
• By-Law	YES	YES
• Privative Clause	YES	YES
Rebates (Vacant Land)	s. 364	s. 331
• By-Law	NO	NO
• Privative Clause	NO	NO

The *Provincial Land Tax Act*

This Act deals with property tax on lands that are not under any municipal representations. An annual tax is levied in accordance with section 2 "in the amount determined under section 5 on land that is included in the tax roll for non-municipal territory and that, under the *Assessment Act*, is liable to assessment and taxation". Sections 8 and 9 of this Act give jurisdiction to the ARB to deal with appeals relating to applications for cancellation, refund, or objection to restoration of this tax. **Subsection 8(9) is a privative clause, stating that "[a] decision of the Board is final".**

The *Condominium Act*, 1998

This Act allows an amendment to a condominium corporation's by-laws regarding objecting to an assessment and the need to provide notice to the ARB under subsection 56(5) if some owners object to that change in the by-law authorizing such objection.

RELEVANT REGULATIONS

The review of regulations relevant to the procedures of the ARB (currently only some fees) was done along with the review of the enabling legislation above.

ENVIRONMENTAL AND LAND TRIBUNALS OF ONTARIO

(the tribunal cluster that includes the ARB)

As detailed in the preamble portion to this Part II, clusters of Ontario agencies started to occur in 2009, and the first cluster created was the ELTO, which included the ARB. The ELTO website was discussed in the same preamble and should be referred to as necessary.

PROCEDURES OF BOARD

The ARB has "RULES OF PRACTICE AND PROCEDURE" (the "ARB Rules") effective January 4, 2016, on its website on the Web page "Legislation and Rules", downloadable in Adobe pdf and MS Word formats. As noted in the ARB Rules, they were made under section 25.1 of the *SPPA*, which allows an agency to make its own rules. Currently, there are 146 rules. The ARB Rules refer to a number of forms, which can be located on the Web page "Forms". **The ARB Rules and the forms shall be discussed in summary fashion and in varying detail below, but the reader should only rely on her/his own reading and interpretation of both, and not rely on the author's.** Remember, the procedures in the enabling legislation also are applicable, as is the *SPPA*, where noted in the ARB Rules.

RULES

General (Rs. 1–6)

The ARB Rules are applicable to all proceedings before the ARB, and the forms referred to in the Rules are available on the Board's website (R. 1). There are definitions of words or terms used in the

ARB Rules (R. 6). Those definitions must be referenced when looking at the ARB Rules to fully understand their meaning. The ARB Rules are to be liberally interpreted to ensure the just, most expeditious, and least expensive determination of every proceeding on its merits. Also, the ARB may issue Practice Directions from time to time, which should also be consulted (R. 2). If the ARB Rules do not cover a procedure, the ARB may do what is necessary and permitted by law to decide a matter (R. 3). Substantial compliance with requirements in respect of content of forms, notices, and documents under ARB Rules or any Act is sufficient (R. 4). Rule 5 states that "[t]he parties must consent before the [ARB] can permit exceptions from procedural requirements contained in statutes or regulations."

Non-compliance with Rules and Orders (Rs. 7–8)

In the comments under the heading of this section of the Rules, it is stated that if "a party fails to comply with any Rule, order, direction, undertaking or request of the [ARB]; causes undue delay; does not attend a scheduled hearing event for which notice was issued or does not provide to the [ARB] or a party materials required as part of the proceeding, the [ARB] may make an order granting relief against the failure." If there has been a failure to comply, the aggrieved party should make a motion to the ARB; and in considering the motion, the ARB will usually consider the factors set out in the comments. The parties are to comply with the ARB Rules and Orders; if they do not, the ARB will determine the consequences of such non-compliance (R. 7). It is the parties' responsibility to report failure to comply to the ARB; what happens next, as set out in R. 8, depends on whether the matter is in the Direct Hearing Stream or the Standard Stream.

Representatives (Rs. 9–11)

A party may attend in person or by a representative. If the representative is not licensed by the LSUC, he or she must obtain a written authorization to so act, which the ARB may request at any time (R. 9). Notice to a representative is deemed to be given to the party who is the client of the representative (R. 10). Pursuant to R. 11, where a party or representative is in a hearing event, such person may be both advocate and witness in the Direct Hearing Stream unless otherwise ordered by the ARB. In the Standard Stream, no representative may be both advocate and witness unless the ARB orders otherwise. For a representative to appear in both roles, notice must be given to the other parties in accordance with this rule. Rule 11 does not apply to lawyers appearing as counsel.

Time (Rs. 12–15)

The Comments on the Time Requirements note that the ARB "**cannot extend a time given in a statute such as the *Assessment Act* except as set out in the Rules for late appeals. Therefore applications must be filed with the [ARB] at the <u>latest</u> on the day established in the appeals sections of the applicable legislation as the last day for appealing.**" The Comments then illustrate how the ARB computes time with an example. Unless otherwise stated, time is computed (i) under the ARB Rules or (ii) under the applicable law if in an ARB order (R. 12). The ARB may extend or reduce any time required in the ARB Rules or in an ARB order with any terms and conditions, either by motion or on its own initiative, and the ARB "may extend the time for filing a request for reconsideration with MPAC if in the [ARB]'s view, the circumstances set out in the request by the appellant, provide sufficient reasons" (R. 13). If written consent is given by all those to be served, time for delivery of a document may be extended or reduced (R. 14). Rule 15 details the wait time for proceedings in two circumstances: (i) in-person hearing, 30 minutes after the time set for commencement; and (ii) electronic hearing, 10 minutes after the time set for commencement. For non-attendance without reasonable cause, R. 15 also allows the ARB to proceed to determine or dismiss the matter.

Initiating Proceeding (Rs. 16–18)

As stated in R. 16, unless any statutes or the ARB Rules provide or the ARB directs otherwise, an appeal may be commenced by letter or an Appeal Form containing information and documents listed in the rule and the appropriate fee. Two exceptions to R. 16 are identified in R. 17: (i) persons filing appeals for many persons and/or many properties must file appeals in accordance with the directions of the ARB; and (ii) appeals under the *Provincial Land Tax Act, 2006*, the *Municipal Act, 2001*, and the *City of Toronto Act, 2006* are to be filed in accordance with the specific provisions provided in the rule. According to R. 18, unless the ARB directs otherwise, the ARB will not consider appeals if the appropriate fee has not been paid.

Screening of Appeals (Rs. 19–26)

The Comments on the Screening of Appeals identifies two types of screening: (i) administrative screening by staff, who may suspend an appeal application because of incomplete information; and (ii) adjudicative screening by ARB members, who may dismiss an appeal without a full hearing. Administrative screening is conducted by the ARB to determine the compliance with the six items set out in

R. 19. If the information submitted is incomplete, the ARB will stop processing the appeal and will only continue after the application is considered complete by the ARB's established requirements (R. 20). Before rejecting an incomplete application, the ARB will notify the party and provide an opportunity to respond within the time set out in the notification (R. 21). Under R. 22, the ARB may cancel the request for information if it is satisfied with the reason provided by the appellant. Once an incomplete appeal is amended, the amended appeal and further materials shall be provided to the other parties and the ARB (R. 23). If the appeal was corrected within the stated time, the appeal will be deemed properly filed on the day it was initially received (R. 24). According to R. 25, an ARB member may conduct an adjudicative screening using the four circumstances set out in the rule; if any of the four circumstances exists, the member may dismiss the appeal without a hearing. Before the dismissal, pursuant to R. 26, the ARB must notify the appellant and allow time for the appellant to respond. The appeal is dismissed only after the appellant fails to respond within the time stated in the notification.

Late Appeals (R. 27)

The ARB will consider a late appeal under the conditions set out in R. 27: (i) the appellant satisfies the ARB with an affidavit stating that the appeal was mailed within the time set out; or (ii) the appellant satisfies the ARB with an affidavit stating (a) that the notice under the appropriate legislation was not received by a certain date, and (b) the date that the appellant or representative became aware of the matter being appealed.

Notice (Rs. 28–29)

Notices under the ARB Rules or an ARB order are to be in writing unless otherwise directed by ARB (R. 28), and an affidavit must be filed at the beginning of the proceeding to prove that notice directed by the ARB was properly given (R. 29).

Special Notices (Rs. 30–33)

Special Notice by Party of Request for Higher Assessment and/or Higher Tax Rate Property Class (R. 30)

The requirements for notice where a party requests a change in property class to a class with a higher tax rate or an assessment that would result in a higher assessment than that fixed by the MPAC are set out in R. 30.

Notice after Statement(s) (R. 31)

If a party gives a notice of intention to request a higher assessment after he or she has already delivered a Statement of Issues or a Statement of Response in the proceeding, the notice would be treated as an amendment of document in the Standard Stream, and the rule regarding amendment of documents (i.e., R. 39) will apply.

Special Notice by MPAC to Shift Burden of Proof (Reverse Onus) (R. 32)

Pursuant to the non–co-operation section (s. 40(18)) of the *Assessment Act*, MPAC may request the ARB to make a finding to shift the burden of proof as to the correctness of the current value of land to the appellant. If such request is made, MPAC must give notice as required by R. 32. Written notice must be given to the other parties and filed with the ARB at least 21 days prior to the hearing in the Direct Hearing Stream. In the Standard Stream, notice is to be given in the Response to the Statement of Issues.

Special Notice of Issue Estoppel (R. 33)

If a party intends to raise issue estoppel at a hearing, written notice must be given to the other parties at least 21 days prior to the hearing in the Direct Hearing Stream; in the Standard Stream, notice is to be given in the Response to the Statement of Issues. (The Comments before R. 33 clarify what the ARB means by issue estoppel.)

Service (Rs. 34–38)

The six methods of service of notice or a document by one party on another party or person are set out in R. 34 and shall be sent to the persons identified in R. 35. The proof of service requirements are set out in R. 36. Any document served by fax or e-mail after 5:00 p.m. is deemed to have been served on the next business day (R. 37). If a document is more than 12 pages long, including cover page, it cannot be served by fax unless the person receiving it has given advance permission (R. 38).

Documents — Filing and Amendment (Rs. 39–44)

At any stage of a proceeding, documents served on parties and/or filed with the ARB can only be amended on motions in accordance with R. 39. According to R. 40, a party who seeks to amend a document by motion with leave of the board (R. 39(2)(c)) must give notice to all other parties in two circumstances: (i) if the matter is in the Standard Stream; or (ii) there is a Board order if the matter is in the Direct Hearing Stream. Rule 41 states the prerequisites for the ARB to grant an order for amendment of documents with leave of the board. In addition to all other requirements, two copies of each document must be filed with the ARB at the hearing, unless there is an ARB direction otherwise (R. 42). In respect of the Standard Stream, Statements or amended Statements of Issues or Response, as set out in R. 43, must be filed with the ARB at least 60 days prior to the pre-hearing conference or within 16 months after filing the appeal. In addition to any requirements of the ARB Rules, the ARB may direct the parties to exchange and file documents and submissions at any time upon a party's request or on its own initiative (R. 44).

Disclosure, Evidence, Experts and Discovery (Rs. 45–56)

The time limits, based on the Stream, for providing documentary evidence, exchange of materials in response, and disclosure of information prior to hearing are set out in R. 45; the ARB may refuse to accept the documents at the hearing if disclosure was not made within the given time. Under R. 45(1), MPAC is also required to disclose to the appellant and the municipality data and analysis that supports its assessment in 90 days after an appeal of the assessment is filed.

According to R. 46, in the Standard Stream, a request to admit a fact or document is permissible at any time, but a copy of the document for authentication must be served with the request if that document is not in the possession of the other party. A response to the request to admit must be done within 21 days after the request is served, and failure to respond in time or a response without specifically stating rejection or refusal of the request is deemed admitting the request according to R. 47.

The timelines and requirements in the Standard Stream for expert reports and calling of an expert witness without a report are stated in R. 48, as are the requirements of reply report under R. 50 and a supplemental report in R. 51. The duties imposed by expert witnesses are set out in R. 49.

Under R. 52, one copy of all written arguments must be provided to each panel member and to each party unless an ARB order provides otherwise. In accordance with R. 53, a person may examine and make copies of any document filed with the ARB or look at visual evidence, unless a statute or a court or ARB order provides otherwise. The ARB may order that any document filed be treated as confidential (R. 54). Upon request of the person filing it, the ARB may return the exhibit, but only 180 days after the ARB decision is issued or mailed, provided that there is no pending appellate review (R. 55).

The ARB may grant an order for discovery in a manner set out in clauses (a) to (g) of R. 56, where a party has requested by notice of motion, together with an affidavit detailing the efforts to obtain the desired information, why the information is needed, and the fact that the information has been refused or no answer has been received.

Motions (Rs. 57–64)

For an oral or electronic motion, the person who makes the motion must first obtain from the Board's Case Coordinator a hearing date. Once a date or permission is obtained, a notice of motion must be submitted, with an affidavit setting out a brief statement of the facts by the person swearing the affidavit, all in accordance with R. 57. Unless the ARB agrees to a lesser time, the notice of motion and all supporting documents must be served by the moving party at least 10 days before the oral or telephone conference call or such other times as set out in R. 58, and an affidavit of such service must also be filed with the ARB. A responding party must serve a notice of response if the party intends to use (i) other reasons/documents not provided or (ii) an affidavit as evidence, which must be attached with the notice along with a brief statement of facts (R. 59). Unless the ARB agrees to a lesser time, the notice of response must be served by the moving party on all parties at least five days before the hearing of the motion as set out in R. 60, and an affidavit of such service as well as two copies of the notice must be provided to the ARB member at the hearing.

Both the moving and responding parties can submit oral evidence at the hearing of the motion during an oral or electronic hearing if permission is requested from the ARB upon filing the motion or response (Rs. 61–62). A motion can be made at an oral hearing only if the need for it arises out of events in the hearing, and the procedures for the motion shall be ordered by the presiding member; but generally, if a moving party knows that a motion will be made, it should be served in accordance with Rs. 57–58 and should request that the ARB reduce the time required for service, if necessary (R. 63). Any person, other than the applicant and any person made a party by statute, who wishes to take part in a proceeding, either as a party or a participant, must comply with R. 64 by bringing a motion, servicing notice, with proof of service if required by the ARB.

Settlement before ARB Proceedings (Rs. 65–66)

Where the parties reach a settlement before any hearing is held, the ARB may hold a brief hearing into the terms of the settlement; the ARB may issue a decision approving it after compliance with the statutes is confirmed. Further, the parties must either appear at an in-person hearing or submit Minutes of Settlement to the ARB (R. 65). The form and contents of the Minutes of Settlement are set out in R. 66; requirement for signatures of all parties, except absent party at a hearing, is also noted in the rule.

Withdrawal of Appeals (Rs. 67–68)

In accordance with R. 67, an appellant may, by notice of withdrawal to the ARB and other parties, withdraw the appeal in all appeal cases except (i) a case that is under the *Assessment Act* where another party has given notice of intention to request a higher assessment and/or higher tax rate, or (ii) a case for which the hearing has commenced. Withdrawals of appeal under these two circumstances require a leave of the ARB, and R. 68 states the types of disposition by the ARB on motion to withdraw an appeal.

Compelling Attendance of Witness by Summons (Rs. 69–70)

A party who wishes to require a witness in Ontario to attend an oral or electronic hearing may serve a summons on such person. Summons will be issued after the ARB is satisfied that the requirements and conditions set out in R. 69 are met. A summons must be personally delivered on the witness, together with attendance money, at least five days before the time of attendance (R. 70).

Language of Proceedings (Rs. 71–76)

ARB proceedings may be conducted in English or French, or in both, and with sign language interpretation if requested (R. 71). A person who wants a hearing in French, or in both French and English, or who requires sign language interpretation, must notify the ARB at least 25 days before the hearing (R. 72). A person who needs interpretation services either for a language that is neither English nor French or for a non-recognized sign language in order to participate in the hearing will have to provide a qualified interpreter at his or her own expense (R. 73).

Under R. 74, a French language or bilingual proceeding shall be presided over by a bilingual member or panel. Where the ARB considers it necessary for the fair determination of the matter, English or French translation of the written evidence or submission could be provided upon request (R. 75). For French language or bilingual proceedings, decisions and written reasons by the ARB will be in English and French (R. 76).

Streaming (Rs. 77–79)

In the Comments prior to R. 77, there is a discussion of the two types of streams — the Direct Hearing Stream and the Standard Stream — along with what generally happens in each stream, and the factors used by the ARB in choosing the appropriate stream.

A matter can be scheduled by the ARB into (i) the Direct Hearing Stream or (ii) the Standard Stream (R. 77). An appeal that has completed the request for reconsideration with MPAC will be put in the Direct Hearing Stream (R. 78). As stated in R. 79, a change of the hearing stream can be done, but with different requirements: (i) transfer from the Standard Stream to Direct Hearing Stream can be made as of right within six months of filing the appeal; (ii) transfer from Direct Hearing Stream to Standard Stream requires a party bringing a motion before the ARB within 120 days after filing the appeal. The ARB can also at any time on its own motion transfer a matter if that will result in a speedier resolution.

Consolidation (Rs. 80–83)

Where the ARB considers that two or more matters are related in ways of facts, issues, questions of law or other reasons, it may take any of the three actions listed under R. 80. In accordance with R. 81, when two or more proceedings are consolidated, statutory procedural requirements, parties, and evidence of the original separate proceedings become part of the consolidated proceeding. As stated in R. 82, R. 81 does not apply if the proceedings are heard together but not consolidated. Under R. 83, the ARB can separate consolidated proceedings or matters heard together at any time for the reasons, including a party being unduly prejudiced, set out in the rule.

Pre-hearing Conferences (Rs. 84–92)

At the request of a party or on its own initiative, the ARB may direct the parties to take part in a pre-hearing conference, which can include events like settlement conferences or motions, in order to accomplish any of the items listed in R. 84. A pre-hearing conference for appeals in the Direct Hearing Stream is rare and is limited to one only under the conditions set out in R. 85: "One pre-hearing conference may be held in the Direct Hearing Stream if doing so is consistent with the intent of the Direct Hearing Stream, is proportionate to the issues under appeal and assists in an expeditious resolution of the appeal." The purpose of a pre-hearing conference in the Standard Stream, under R. 86(1), is to check on the status of the appeal, give direction, and approve the draft procedural order. In accordance with R. 86(2), there are requirements to be met prior to the pre-hearing and within six months of filing the appeal: (i) a request to MPAC to release assessment data must be made; and (ii) a Statement of Issues and Statement(s) of Response have been served.

Under R. 87, if the ARB receives neither a request for pre-hearing nor an approved Procedural Order within 18 months after the appeal is filed, the ARB will set a peremptory pre-hearing date and require that the parties accept a Procedural Order with benchmarks and processes designed to resolve the appeal(s) within two to three years.

As stated in R. 88, the ARB may provide the parties with a sample procedural order, and the parties are expected to meet prior to the pre-hearing conference to consider the matters set out in R. 84 so that a draft procedural order can be ready for the conference.

In accordance with R. 89, the applicant who requests a pre-hearing conference must serve the notice of pre-hearing from the ARB to all parties and must provide an affidavit of service to the ARB at the pre-hearing. Under R. 90, the ARB member may, at any time, conduct a procedural discussion or a pre-hearing conference and may convert from one to the other. The rule also states that parties to the pre-hearing are forewarned by the notice of pre-hearing to be prepared for a procedural and settlement conference. According to R. 91, the member conducting the pre-hearing conference will issue an order (i) deciding any of the matters considered in the conference or (ii) giving procedural directions for subsequent hearing events. Rule 92 has been removed.

Form of Statements (Rs. 93–94)

The Statements of Issues and Responses are intended to bring focus to matters in the Standard Stream. The minimum information required in these forms is listed in R. 93 and in accordance with four identified issues: (i) current value; (ii) equity in assessment under s. 44(3) of the *Assessment Act*; (iii) classification of property; and (iv) cancellation, reduction, or refund of taxes pursuant to ARB's authority under four statutes. The ARB, under R. 94, requires Statements of Issues and Responses to be filed with the ARB according to R. 43.

Adjournments (Rs. 95–97)

In the Comments prior to Adjournment Rules, the following is stated: "Hearing dates are fixed and will proceed as scheduled unless an adjournment is granted. The [ARB] expects parties to be ready for hearings and attend on time. ... Adjournments will not be granted automatically, even where parties consent." In accordance with R. 95, hearing event dates are fixed and the ARB will allow adjournment only on very few situations, such as preservation of fair hearing or unavoidable emergencies.

According to R. 96, the party requesting the adjournment must give notice to all parties and provide the ARB with a written submission and the supporting documents listed in the rule. This rule also states that the ARB may (i) address the request with all parties in an electronic or in-person hearing, or (ii) address the request on the hearing date. As set out in R. 97, upon the adjournment request, the ARB may (i) allow the request, with or without terms and conditions; (ii) deny the request; or (iii) make other appropriate order.

Mediation (Rs. 98–103; Rs. 104–107 have been removed)

In the Comments portion prior to the Mediation Rules, the following is stated: "Mediation is a form of consensual dispute resolution, in which the parties meet with [an ARB] Member (or someone else appointed by the [ARB]) as mediator or neutral third party (rather than as adjudicator). All present try to settle the dispute in an informal way. The [ARB] Member will attempt to identify the interests of each party, and explore possible settlement of the issues in an appeal." The Comments also mention that reference should be made to the ARB's Mediation Information Sheet.

Under R. 98, the ARB may direct, on its own initiative or at the request of the parties, the parties to participate in mediation, which may be in-person or by way of electronic conferencing, possibly with very short notice, such as by telephone.

The Board member who presides at the mediation in which one or more issues are not resolved shall not preside at the hearing unless ordered by the ARB and consented to by the parties.

According to R. 99, the ARB will evaluate the suitability of using mediation to resolve the issues based upon the criteria set out in the rule. The parties should provide consent to the ARB if it determines that a mediation should proceed. Upon receipt of consent, the ARB will set the date for the mediation and direct how notice of the mediation shall be given.

In accordance with R. 100, at least 21 days before the mediation date, unless otherwise ordered, the parties shall prepare and provide the ARB and the other parties with the documents listed.

According to R. 101, all contents of the mediation — documents created, anything said, settlement offer, and the notes made by the presiding person — are confidential and cannot be used in any proceeding unless the ARB approves and the party who created the document or offer consents.

How the mediation should be conducted and what powers and responsibilities the presiding person has are set out in R. 102.

Details of what is to be done with a partial resolution are set out in R. 103. Rules 104–107 have been removed.

Methods of Holding Hearing Events (Rs. 108–118)

The ARB can hold hearing events or any part of a hearing event orally (in person), electronically, or in written form in accordance with the *SPPA* and the ARB Rules.

Electronic Hearings (Rs. 108–113)

The ARB, as set out in R. 108, may hold a hearing event by teleconference or videoconference or other automated means to determine matters. In deciding whether to hold a hearing event by automated means, the ARB may consider relevant factors, including fairness and convenience, cost and efficiency, suitability and credibility, etc., as set out in R. 109. A party may object to an electronic hearing on grounds of significant prejudice in writing, 10 days prior to the hearing; the ARB may decide against the objection and confirm to hold the electronic hearing on the original date (Rs. 110–111).

Under R. 112, the ARB may direct the arrangements for the electronic hearing so that the integrity of the hearing process is protected. In accordance with R. 113, participants attending a videoconference from different locations are required to be clearly visible in the camera view, with minimum visual obstructions, throughout the hearing.

Written Hearings (Rs. 114–118)

The ARB may hold a written hearing in whole or in part unless a party files an objection within 10 days of the notice of hearing and satisfies the ARB that there is good reason for not doing so (R. 114). In determining whether to hold a written hearing, the ARB may look at any relevant factors, such as fairness and convenience to parties, cost and efficiency, agreed facts and evidence, number of legal issues, and necessity of oral testimony (R. 115). The party who objects to a written hearing must file and provide to other parties with a written objection containing the reasons in 10 days of the notice of hearing (R. 116). The requirements for submission and exchange of documents in a written hearing are set out in R. 117. As stated in R. 118, for a written hearing, affidavits are required for evidence and documents filed with the ARB, and evidence submitted in other form, or in electronic form, may be permitted by the ARB upon request.

Conduct of Proceedings (Rs. 119–127)

Hearing events, other than mediation events, of the ARB are open to the public unless the ARB determines that it is not possible or practical or that the matter should be heard in private (R. 119). Unless the ARB Rules or the appropriate legislation provide differently, the ARB may by order fix the procedure at a hearing event (R. 120).

At the start of the hearing, the ARB will confirm the name of the applicant, and the parties *must* confirm the information set out in R. 121 for each property and assessment that is the subject of the hearing. If a party is absent from the hearing event, such party cannot have any part of the event re-opened or recommenced without leave of the ARB (R. 122). Photographic, audio, and video recording of open hearings will be permitted only on the conditions that the ARB considers appropriate (R. 123).

Recording of a proceeding may be allowed upon request, which is to be placed as soon as the issue arises. The timing and person to ask for authorization, the right of the parties of the proceeding, and the criteria for the ARB to consider granting the request are set out in R. 124. Whether the ARB approves the recording request with or without conditions, the recording is subject to the conditions listed in R. 125. The ARB can withdraw permission to record if (i) any of the conditions listed in R. 125 or the conditions specifically set for this recording are not met; or (ii) the ARB cannot conduct a full and fair hearing in the circumstances (R. 126). Under R. 127, the ARB will permit a proceeding to be recorded by a qualified verbatim reporter, subject to the four listed conditions.

Board Decisions and Written Reasons (Rs. 128–129)

To receive written reasons for a decision, a request must be made, either at the conclusion of the hearing or in writing within 14 days of the hearing date; **a party who seeks a review of the decision with the ARB must have requested Written Reasons** (R. 128). According to R. 129, the ARB Registrar will issue a written decision, unless the ARB directs otherwise; and the decision is effective on the release date of the written decision, unless stated otherwise.

Correcting Minor Errors (Rs. 130–132)

The ARB can correct minor errors, such as typing errors or incorrect figures, in a decision or order on its own initiative or upon request, and such correction request is free of charge (R. 130). A correction or clarification request considered substantive by the ARB will be treated as a request for review (R. 131). As stated in R. 132, from the time the hearing is ended till the decision or requested written reasons are issued, notice to and consent from all parties to the hearing are required for any party who wishes to communicate directly with the presiding ARB member concerning the hearing.

Costs (Rs. 133–139)

According to R. 133, the ARB may, on its own initiative or upon request, order a party who has acted unreasonably, frivolously, vexatiously, or in bad faith to pay costs to the other party. A request for costs by a party must be made to the ARB at the end of the hearing event; otherwise, the party must file the request, with notice to all other parties to the proceeding, within 30 days of the issuance of the written decision or written reasons. The party making the request must satisfy the ARB that the requested costs meet the conditions set out in R. 134. As stated in R. 135, the request must include two documents: (i) an explanation of how Rs. 133, 134, and 137 have been met; and (ii) a summary statement providing a calculation of costs requested and their details. The procedures to make a response to the costs award are set out in R. 136. To determine whether a party has acted unreasonably, frivolously, vexatiously, or in bad faith, the ARB must consider all circumstances, including the four listed under R. 137; and if that is confirmed, the ARB may award costs, pursuant to R. 138, and the amount of costs awarded are subject to the provisions of R. 139.

Re-hearing (R. 140)

As stated in R. 140, the ARB will allow rehearing only in two rare situations: (i) if a Notice of Hearing was not issued or (ii) a party failed to attend a scheduled hearing because of circumstances beyond the control of the party.

Review of a Board Decision/Order (Rs. 141–146)

In the Comments portion prior to the Review Rules, the following is stated: "The [ARB] must be convinced from the written material submitted in an affidavit that it is possible that there was an error in the original decision or process. Review requests will not be successful if they merely attempt to provide the same evidence or reargue the matter. ... The [ARB] requires very good reasons for changing a final decision. It will not review a decision if in its view the basic conclusions will not change even though there is an error in the decision. If the reason for the request is 'new evidence,' the evidence must not have been available at the time of the hearing; the evidence must be credible, and material to the original result; the requester must act quickly upon becoming aware of it; and the prejudice to the requester must be far greater than the other parties' right to a final decision."

The types of decision that are ineligible for review are listed in R. 141(2). In accordance with R. 141(1), the ARB has (i) the power to review all or part of a decision and (ii) the power to confirm, vary, suspend, or cancel the decision, or to order a rehearing before a different member. Under R. 142, the ARB may refuse a request in three circumstances: (i) the request is not filed within the time limit, (ii) the request is incomplete, or (iii) same or similar request has been made by the same party.

In accordance with R. 143, a written request for review, containing the information and items set out in the rule, must be made to the Chair of the ARB within 30 days of the release of the ARB decision and copied to all parties. The possible actions that the ARB may take upon receiving the request are listed in R. 144. The ARB will consider reviewing a decision if the reasons provided in the request convince the ARB that one of the situations listed in R. 145 occurs. When the ARB grants a motion to argue the question or a re-hearing without a motion, there are specific procedures to follow, and they are set out in R. 146.

At the end of the ARB Rules, there are two appendices: Appendix "A" — Expert Duty Form, and Appendix "B" — ARB Sample Procedural Order.

PRACTICE DIRECTIONS

The following Practice Directions currently (as of early February 2016) appear on the ARB's website, on the Web page "Legislation and Rules"; all except Mediation are effective April 2, 2013, and are downloadable in Adobe pdf and in MS Word.

Practice Direction: Requests for Adjournment

"Adjournments, particularly at the last minute, are a significant impediment to fair and timely resolution of matters before the [ARB]." This Practice Direction provides guidance to parties regarding adjournments.

Practice Direction: Scheduling Pre-hearings and Hearings

"The Assessment Review Board is committed to delivering modern, fair, accessible, effective and timely dispute resolution services." Recognizing the importance of the parties' availability and readiness to attend hearings, directions are given under four categories: (i) Current Cases, with or without final hearing date set; (ii) Procedural Orders and Pre-hearings — Standard Stream; (iii) Transfers between Streams; and (iv) Hearing Notices and Timeframes.

Practice Direction: Case Management

This Practice Direction contains (i) transitional directions regarding case management under previous rules for 2008 or earlier cases, and (ii) directions on applying for case management and additional procedural requirements for 2013 Standard Streams appeals.

Practice Direction: Mediation

Effective January 4, 2016, this Practice Direction stresses the strong encouragement of the use of mediation by the ARB, explaining why mediation can lead to better results and reduce costs. The process that should be followed is in accordance with Rules 98–103 and is set out in this Practice Direction.

Also on the same Web page are an Expert Duty Form and a Sample Procedural Order.

FORMS

It is necessary to discuss the forms provided on both the ARB and MPAC websites that are relevant to the reader in context. As various forms are largely duplicated, only the first of the connected forms will be discussed in detail, plus a brief description of the related forms. As always, the reader should review all forms necessary to properly comply with the procedures for the particular complaint made under the fact situation and the appropriate legislation.

Request for Assessment Reconsideration by MPAC

> After each reassessment, MPAC sends property owners a Property Assessment Notice that shows the current value of the property as of the valuation date. After property owners have received their Property Assessment Notices, they may request that MPAC reconsider the assessed value of their property, if they believe it is incorrect. The procedure for requesting this reconsideration is described on the Property Assessment Notice itself.

How MPAC does assessments is summarily described in the document entitled "Resolving Property Assessment Concerns". The form to be used in requesting reconsideration of MPAC assessment is the Request for Reconsideration, with separate forms for both residential and non-residential property; all are available on MPAC's website. (See Appendix to this chapter for a Request for Reconsideration for residential property by MPAC.)

If MPAC agrees to change the assessment as a result of the reconsideration, there is no charge for such reconsideration and also no need to file an appeal with the ARB. However, if MPAC does not agree to change the assessment before the cut-off date for filing complaints with the ARB, an appeal may be filed with the ARB, along with the applicable filing fee, as stated on the ARB Web page entitled "Appeal Process". The Web page discusses (i) the procedure that leads to the appeal stage, (ii) how to file an appeal, and (iii) how to withdraw an appeal, using a Withdrawal Form accessible on that page. A series of useful definitions can also be found on the ARB website on the "Glossary" Web page.

The appeal forms used to get a matter before the ARB are dependent on the legislation and the sections of the legislation. The appeal forms for various pieces of legislation are accessible online through the Web page entitled "Filing an Appeal".

ARB Property Assessment Appeal Form

The appeal form is included in the Appendix to this chapter, along with instructions for filling it in.

The deadline for filing an Annual Assessment appeal is 90 calendar days from the mailing date on the RFR decision letter.

Appeal under the Municipal Act

The appeal forms, which also include instructions and a summary of how to prepare for a hearing event, are accessible on the ARB's website under the Web page entitled "Municipal Act Appeals". The forms for appeal under the *Municipal Act* are as follows:

* Application/Appeal — Apportionment — s. 356 (included in the Appendix to this chapter)
* Complaint — Comparables — s. 331
* Application/Appeal — Sickness or Poverty — s. 357
* Complaint — Vacant Unit Rebate — s. 364
* Application/Appeal — Cancel, Reduce, Refund — ss. 357, 358, 359
* Application/Appeal — Limitation of Taxes — ss. 334, 337

Check with the municipality where the assessment is in dispute to determine if, pursuant to the appropriate section of the *Municipal Act*, a by-law was passed that delegated responsibility to hear the matter directly to the ARB. If such a by-law exists, the form is an application; if there is no such by-law, the form is an appeal to the ARB after an unfavourable ruling by the municipal council.

Appeal under the City of Toronto Act, 2006

As the *City of Toronto Act, 2006* has many of the same provisions of the *Municipal Act*, the forms used under both are nearly identical. Set out below are the names of the forms used for assessment disputes in Toronto and found on the Web page "City of Toronto Act Appeals":

• Application/Appeal — Apportionment — s. 322 (See Appendix to this chapter)
• Complaint — Comparables — s. 294
• Application/Appeal — Sickness or Poverty — s. 323
• Complaint — Vacant Unit Rebate — s. 331
• Application/Appeal — Cancel, Reduce, Refund — ss. 323, 325, 326
• Application/Appeal — Limitation of Taxes — ss. 297, 300

Check with the City of Toronto to determine if, pursuant to the appropriate section of the *City of Toronto Act, 2006*, a by-law was passed that delegated responsibility to hear the matter directly to the ARB. If such a by-law exists, the form is an application; if there is no such by-law, the form is an appeal to the ARB after an unfavourable ruling by the Toronto council.

A narrative summary of the procedure — from complaint, application, and appeal stage to decision — appears on the ARB Web page entitled "Appeal Process". Although useful, reliance should be placed on the relevant sections of the enabling legislation and the ARB Rules for the precise and exact requirements and timelines.

Similarly, a narrative summary of the procedure from the decision stage to possible appeals appears on the Web page entitled "Decisions". Again, although useful, reliance should be placed on the relevant sections of the enabling legislation and the ARB Rules for the precise and exact requirements and timelines.

POLICIES

Due to the *Ontarians with Disabilities Act, 2001* (ODA) and the *Accessibility for Ontarians with Disabilities Act, 2005* (AODA), the cluster of tribunals under ELTO, including the ARB, have instituted an Accessibility Policy. The reader should review the Accessibility Policy if needed. There are "Vision Mission Values" statements for MPAC on its website, which is relevant in dealing with MPAC in the following areas: (i) the initial assessment, (ii) a request for reconsideration, and (iii) as an opposing party before the ARB.

EXPLANATORY LITERATURE FROM THE BOARD

The ARB website provides various useful online literature to assist the reader with the ARB's process.

1. "Your Guide to the Assessment Review Board" brochure, in both MS Word and pdf, under the Web page "Publications", describes in layman's terms the functions of the ARB and the various stages of the appeal process. (See Appendix 5.6.)

2. The *Preparing for your hearing at the ARB* pamphlet, found under "Brochures", explains the procedure of hearings before the ARB in layman's terms. (See Appendix 5.7.)

3. On the Web page entitled "Municipal Act Appeals" there is an "Information Sheet" that explains in layman's terms appeals under the *Municipal Act*. (See Appendix 5.8.)

4. On the Web page entitled "City of Toronto Act Appeals" there is an "Information Sheet" that explains in layman's terms appeals under the *City of Toronto Act*.

5. On the Web page entitled "Annual Reports & Statistics" are the Annual Reports for each of the years from 1999–2000 to 2009–2010. The Annual Reports contain that year's chair's message, the ARB overview, operations for that year, financial summary for the ARB and a listing including the original appointment dates of the members of the ARB. Starting in 2010–2011, the Web page begins to list the ELTO Annual Reports. The ELTO Annual Report includes most of the information previously provided in the ARB reports, and the newest ELTO Annual Report currently listed is for 2014–2015.

6. Information Sheet 3 discusses what one needs to know in filing an appeal with the ARB. Links to this Information Sheet are found on three different Web pages: "Filing an Appeal", "Brochures", and "Information Sheets".

7. There are electronic services available on the website to determine when a matter is being heard and its status upon providing certain information on the site.

8. Although it is not literature, there is a video of a sample ARB hearing that is worth a look.

RELEVANT CASES AND/OR DECISIONS

The cases and decisions discussed below are not meant to be exhaustive and are only those found in the spring of 2008. They should not be relied upon as legal opinion but are,

rather, the author's interpretation. The reader must continue to update and research cases and decisions, and case briefings should be done by the reader in any event.

Fourteen matters, including cases from the Ontario Court of Appeal (C.A.), the Divisional Court (Div. Ct.), and before one judge of the Superior Court of Justice (Sup. Ct. J.), as well as decisions of the ARB, are discussed in chronological order, with the oldest one first (unless the case is one in a series, in which case the discussion will begin with the lowest level court to the highest). The selection is intended to give the reader a sampling of how these cases and decisions have been decided and their relevance to the ARB. Not every case discussed is a ground-setting decision; however, the review should give the reader some idea of how the ARB and the courts have dealt with various procedural and substantive issues in the first decade of the 21st century.

Ambler v. Municipal Property Assessment Corp., Region No. 7

In the ARB decision of *Ambler v. Municipal Property Assessment Corp., Region No. 7*, [2005] O.A.R.B.D. No. 643, File No. 44733, Hearing No. 106795, Complaint Nos. 1661382, 1688295, 1734038, 1734061 (the *Ambler* ARB decision), the issue was whether the subject property should be classified entirely in the Industrial Property class or whether a portion of it should be classified in the Commercial Property class. Based on the facts and the legislation, specifically, subsection 5(2)(b) of O. Reg. 282/98, the ARB held that the classification should be entirely in the Industrial Property class. Leave to appeal the *Ambler* ARB decision was moved in *Ambler v. Municipal Property Assessment Corp., Region No. 7*, [2006] O.J. No. 2124, 24 M.P.L.R. (4th) 95, 148 A.C.W.S. (3d) 520, 2006 CarswellOnt 3258 (the *Ambler* leave case). In this 2006 motion hearing, the Superior Court of Justice looked at the facts and detailed what happened at the ARB hearing (which was more than what is discussed in the *Ambler* ARB decision). The judge held that in order for leave to appeal to be granted generally, the moving party must satisfy the court with the following:

(a) there is some reason to doubt the correctness of the Board's decision; and

(b) the point of law is of sufficient importance to merit the attention of the Divisional Court.

Municipal Property Assessment Corp. v. Minto Developments Inc., [2002] O.A.R.B.D. No. 253 leave to appeal to Div. Ct. granted, [2003] O.J. No. 404 (QL).

> *Ontario Property Assessment Corp. v. Praxair Canada Inc.*, [2001] O.A.R.B.D. No. 110, leave to appeal to Divisional Court granted, [2001] O.J. No. 2200 (Div. Ct.) (QL).
>
> *1098478 Ontario Ltd. v. Ontario Property Assessment Corp. Region No. 11*, [1999] O.A.R.B.D. No 129 (2001), leave to appeal to Div. Ct. granted, [2000] O.J. No. 2050 (QL).

Based on the submissions of both parties, the court held that there was doubt as to the correctness of the ARB decision on the following grounds:

> (a) [The ARB] dwelt on a section 5 analysis before dealing with the section 6 analysis [of O. Reg. 282/98]. In my view that ought to have been reversed and a different decision may have been made.
>
> (b) [The ARB] treated the two lessees as being one corporation. This is contrary to well established law on the subject. The fact that the companies had the same directors and officers[] does not necessarily clothe them with the same commercial interest.

The judge was also satisfied that the case dealt with important issues sufficient to warrant granting leave because the legislation was, at that time, relatively recent and should have had Div. Ct. jurisprudence. The *Ambler* ARB decision was appealed and heard at the Divisional Court in 2007: *Ambler v. Municipal Property Assessment Corp., Region No. 7*, [2007] O.J. No. 1672, 224 O.A.C. 54, 157 A.C.W.S. (3d) 18 (the *Ambler* Div. Ct. case). The court held that the ARB "erred in law in failing to interpret and apply s. 6(1) of O. Reg. 282/98 under the *Assessment Act*, R.S.O. 1990, c. A.31, to determine whether the portion of the building used by Swish fell within that provision". After reviewing the findings of fact of the ARB that Swish had no involvement in manufacturing, the court found the following:

> Given the Board's findings of fact, the Board erred in holding that the entire property fell within the industrial property class. Had the Board given proper consideration to the language of s. 6(1), the Board should have concluded that the portion of the property used by Swish fell within the commercial property class.

Based on this finding, the court allowed the appeal and, instead of referring the matter back to the ARB, used its power under section 44 of the *Assessment Act* to order the Swish portion of the property to be classified under the Commercial Property class.

Chong v. Municipal Property Assessment Corp., Region No. 14

Chong v. Municipal Property Assessment Corp., Region No. 14, [2005] O.A.R.B.D. No. 337, File No. 39783, Hearing No. 102993, Complaint Nos. 1716292, 1736933 (the *Chong* ARB decision) dealt with the issue of how nuisance factors on the property, such as a hydrant, a water main valve, a sewer grate at the bottom of the driveway, and a school sign on the other side of the driveway, affect the value of the property, and whether an adjustment should be made in the assessment. The ARB heard evidence from both parties about comparable properties, as the property value was assessed using the Sales Comparison Approach. The presiding member of the ARB also looked at the definition of "current value", as well as at subsection 19(1) and subsection 44(2) of the *Assessment Act*, and held that subsection 19(1), which states that assessment is based on current value, is paramount to subsection 44(2), which looks at values of similar properties. Based on that finding, the ARB concluded "that there is no better evidence of current value of a property than actual evidence of what a willing buyer paid to a willing seller for the subject property or comparable properties in the required time frame". After looking at comparable properties sold during the relevant period of time, the ARB confirmed the MPAC assessment:

> In this case, the Board looked for evidence to support the complainant's position that a series of nuisance factors negatively affect the value of his property. The Board must be persuaded that the nuisance has resulted in a loss of market value. However, it found none. The Board relies on the sales of similar properties in order to arrive at a value for a property that did not sell in the base year of 2003 or shoulder years of 2002 and 2004. The Board finds that the evidence does not support a finding that the assessment of the subject property is incorrect. The evidence of sales suggests the property is correctly assessed.

The homeowner made a motion for leave to appeal in *Chong v. Municipal Property Assessment Corp., Region No. 14*, [2006] O.J. No. 2126, 148 A.C.W.S. (3d) 514, to the Superior Court of Justice (the *Chong* leave case). An interesting preliminary matter was raised in the motion regarding whether the homeowner, who initially brought an application for judicial review of the *Chong* ARB decision, could then bring the motion for leave to appeal well after the 30-day requirement in the legislation. The application for judicial review failed for the following reason:

The full panel of the Divisional Court dismissed his application for judicial review on the basis that a statutory appeal route was available, and in the absence of exceptional circumstances, the full panel did not have discretion to hear this application.

Even though it could be argued that the homeowner should be estopped from bringing the motion for leave to appeal after his application for a judicial review failed, the judge found there was no prejudice that would accrue to the respondents should the motion be allowed to proceed and be heard. The homeowner stated that the ARB, "in arriving at its decision, broke laws, abused its statutory powers and ignored his concerns. He itemized a number of specific complaints in support of his position". The court noted that there can only be an appeal of the ARB decision on a question of law pursuant to section 43.1 of the *Assessment Act*:

> There is a 2-pronged test for granting leave to appeal being, first, whether there is some reason to doubt the correctness of the decision of the Board and, second, whether the decision involves a point of law of sufficient importance to merit the attention of the Divisional Court. (*Mullabrack Inc. v. Ontario Property Assessment Corp., Region No. 16*, [2001] O.J. No. 1047 (Div. Ct.).)

The court held that the test for granting leave had not been met as the motion does not raise a question of law.

> The Board is required to determine the correct current value after hearing the evidence and submissions of the parties. The reasons demonstrate that the Board heard the parties and that there was evidence upon which the Board could make its decision. In any event, the determination of the correctness of the current value is a question of fact. There is no appeal from factual determinations.

Arguments raised regarding bias of the presiding member of the ARB and an OMB decision not being followed were insufficient to support the motion, as was the refusal of the ARB to allow a recording of the hearing:

> There is no statutory or common-law requirement that the Board arrange to record the proceedings before it. Rule 105 of the Board's rules provides for the recording and transcription of the Board's proceedings. With leave of the Board, any party may arrange for a qualified verbatim reporter to attend at the [party's] own expense for the purpose of recording all testimony. Chong did not arrange for a qualified verbatim reporter

to attend at his expense, notwithstanding his stated intention that he wanted the proceedings recorded. He did not request leave from the Board to arrange for such a reporter to attend at his own expense.

Further allegations of negligence by the assessor and MPAC were considered without foundation. The motion was therefore dismissed.

Thousand Island Tax/Duty Free Store Ltd. v. Municipal Property Assessment Corp.

Thousand Island Tax/Duty Free Store Ltd. v. Municipal Property Assessment Corp., [2006] O.J. No. 924, 28 M.P.L.R. (4th) 92, 208 O.A.C. 78, 146 A.C.W.S. (3d) 588, 2006 CarswellOnt 1406 (the *Thousand Island* case) is a 2006 Div. Ct. case involving a stated case put to the court by the ARB under section 43 of the *Assessment Act* and is discussed here as an example of the practice of stating a case allowed by the legislation. The ARB is given the power under the legislation to frame questions of law for the court to answer and based upon the decision of the court to deal with complaints or applications/appeals before it. In this case, the ARB posed two questions to the court:

1. Does the use of the direct capitalization of income methodology (the "income method") in valuing duty free stores result in the valuation of the properties in question contrary to the general provisions of the Act which mandate only the valuation of real property as defined in sections 1 and 3 of the *Assessment Act*?
2. If the answer to (a) is yes, do ss. 3(2) and (3) of the *Assessment Act* preclude the use of the income method of valuation and mandate in its place the use of the depreciated replacement cost plus land methodology or any other specific method of valuation for duty free stores located on the land of a bridge or tunnel authority at an international crossing?

The court answered "no" to the first question, and therefore it did not answer the second question. In arriving at the decision, the court determined that the issue before it "is whether revenue solely attributable to the use of the bridge or tunnel can be considered in the assessment of the duty free stores". In looking at the relevant legislation, the court stated that there was no general provision directing the assessor to use any particular methodology in determining current value and, therefore, the appropriate method to determine current value is a question of fact for the ARB, pursuant to

Municipal Property Assessment Corporation v. Inmet Mining Corp., [2002] O.J. No. 3540 (Div. Ct.) at para. 14. The court held that the income approach taken by MPAC in respect of the facts was not appropriate.

UniRoyal Goodrich Holdings Inc. v. Municipal Property Assessment Corp., Region No. 21

UniRoyal Goodrich Holdings Inc. v. Municipal Property Assessment Corp., Region No. 21, [2006] O.A.R.B.D. No. 130, File No. 44880, Hearing No. 103266, Complaint Nos. 10911, 31291, 1196216, 1332431, 1413211, 1413212, 1413213, 1413214, 1426705, 1426706 (the *UniRoyal* ARB decision) focused on sections 33, 34, and 40 complaints under the *Assessment Act*. The issue before the ARB was the determination of the classification of certain warehouses and structures located on the specific property. The structures were classified as "Large Industrial Property", and the complainant wanted to change the classification to "Commercial Property" due to a change in O. Reg. 282/98 under sections 5, 6, and 14.

The ARB heard expert witnesses from both parties on the uses of the warehouses and the classifications under the regulation, as well as having a site visit of the structures. The ARB stated that inherent in the change to the regulation "is the issue of separation of any warehouse facilities vis-à-vis the manufacturing areas". The ARB found as a fact that the warehouses are separated from each other and from the manufacturing areas by a series of firewalls and then stated the following:

> The Board finds that because of the firewalls and the independent support walls that support the roofs of each of the warehouses and the manufacturing facility, each warehouse is a separate independent building from the other. This finding is supported by two definitions the Board was made aware of, the definition of "building" contained in the Ontario Building Code and the dictionary definition of "building". Subsection 5(2) of the Classification Reg., as amended, introduces the word "building" into the classification analysis but nowhere in the *Assessment Act* or supporting Regulations is there any attempt to define the word "building". The Board, therefore, adopts both the Ontario Building Code and the dictionary definition as a guideline in defining "building".

The ARB then continued with the following:

> The Board must also address the issue of "minimal linkage". The Board heard evidence from both sides on the issue of link-

age as it relates to the openings in the fire doors and the transfer of tires from the manufacturing plant to the warehouse area. The Board does not consider the linkage to be even minimal, given the fact that the fire doors are part of the firewall and an independent structure that separates three of the four warehouse areas and the manufacturing plant from each other. Based upon all of the evidence, the Board is satisfied that the four warehouses may possibly comply with the requirements set out in section 5 of the Classification Reg., and may be eligible to be classified in the Commercial Property Class.

To complete the determination of the proper classification, the Board must individually look at each separate area and determine if all of the requirements of section 5 have been met.

The ARB then looked at each warehouse in question in relation to the evidence relating to each and found that warehouses #3 and #4 were separate buildings, did not contain manufacturing, and therefore fit within the "Commercial Property Class". The ARB found warehouses #1 and #2 were one building, and although the "whitewall protectorant application" was not a manufacturing process, the "nailguard operation" was and therefore would be classified as "Large Industrial Property Class".

In this case, the ARB only made a determination of the property tax classes that apply to the warehouses for the years under complaint. The Board was advised at the hearing by the parties that they had reached an agreement on the current value of the property and the apportionment of the current value between the buildings and structures. The Board was aware that "Minutes of Settlement with respect to the total current value for each complaint and the apportionment of the value between the buildings and structures for each complaint either had [been] or would be executed." The apportionments were received from the parties and attached to the decision as Schedule "A".

MPAC made a motion for leave to appeal to the Superior Court of Justice in *UniRoyal Goodrich Holdings Inc. v. Municipal Property Assessment Corp., Region No. 21*, [2007] O.J. No. 1233, 156 A.C.W.S. (3d) 517 (the *UniRoyal* leave case). The grounds for the appeal were that the ARB erred in classifying warehouses #3 and #4 and the firewalls in the Commercial Property Class. The court started with the test for a leave case:

> The test on a motion for leave to appeal is twofold: is there good reason to doubt the correctness of the tribunal's decision and is there a question of law of sufficient importance to merit

the attention of the Divisional Court (*1098748 Ontario Ltd. v. Ontario Property Assessment Corporation, Region No. 11*, [2000] O.J. No. 2050 (Div. Ct.) at para. 22).

The judge looked at the evidence before the ARB and the interpretation of subsection 5(2) and said the determination was based largely on a finding of fact and the conclusion made by the presiding member was correct. As to the submission that the reasons of the ARB were inadequate, the court held that "the reasons are adequate and meet the requirements in *Gray v. Director of the Ontario Disability Support Program* (2002), 59 O.R. (3d) 364 (Ont. C.A.) (the *Gray* case). They deal with the issues, make appropriate findings of fact and explain the result". The court also stated that the ARB, in the classification of the firewalls, while not specifically requested by the parties, and although the ARB may have erred in not giving notice before dealing with the issue, was not doubted in the correctness of the classification. The motion was therefore dismissed.

Toronto (City) v. 28 Goldene Way

In the ARB decision of *Toronto (City) v. 28 Goldene Way*, [2007] O.A.R.B.D. No. 640, File No. 59346A, Hearing No. 130586, Application No. 1785420 (the *Goldene* decision), an application was made to the ARB under subsection 356(1) of the *Municipal Act* to apportion unpaid taxes for a tax year. The issues before the ARB were as follows:

1. Are there unpaid taxes for taxation year 2002 on the land which had roll number 1904-094-240-00200-0000 ("parent roll number")?
2. If there are unpaid taxes for taxation year 2002 on the parent roll number, should they be apportioned among the twenty-two subject parcels created out of the parent roll number ("child roll numbers"), in proportion to their relative value when the assessment roll for taxation year 2002 was returned, or in any other manner?

In this particular situation, the City of Toronto, through a by-law, delegated power to hear application in respect of apportionment claims under section 356 to the ARB to hear such a complaint, which is why this is an application and not an appeal to the ARB. The ARB found that there were taxes unpaid by the builder and that the builder defaulted in paying the taxes when selling various homes to the subsequent owners. The ARB recognized that the word "may" in subsection 359(1) means that the power to apportion the taxes is discretionary. In noting the problems in collecting the unpaid taxes from the builder and expressing sympathy to the subsequent owners, the ARB held "that it would be better to avoid the unpleasantness, uncertainties, delays and expense of such Court proceedings, by apportioning the unpaid taxes equitably among the 22 child roll numbers in proportion to their relative values as determined by MPAC".

Vadala v. Municipal Property Assessment Corp., Region No. 26

In *Vadala v. Municipal Property Assessment Corp., Region No. 26*, [2007] O.A.R.B.D. No. 727, File No. DM 195, Hearing No. 135021, Complaint Nos. 1699881, 1699882 (the *Vadala* decision), a motion for review was made under R. 114 of the ARB Rules, alleging that the ARB had acted outside its jurisdiction in the original decision. The *Vadala* decision is noted here as an example of a request for the ARB to reconsider its decision. The problem, which led to the request to review, hinged on whether the municipality, Lambton Shores, or the County of Lambton properly brought the complaint to the ARB. Although the property owners complained, two panels of the ARB increased the taxes and allowed the complainant to make the complaint. The ARB ruling on the motion for review denied the motion because, in working through the chain of events, it found that the county properly made the complaint (ratifying the actions of a delegate) and, therefore, that there was no issue of the ARB acting outside its jurisdiction in allowing the complaint to proceed.

Franklin Sandblasting and Painting Ltd. v. Municipal Property Assessment Corp., Region No. 25

In the ARB decision of *Franklin Sandblasting and Painting Ltd. v. Municipal Property Assessment Corp., Region No. 25*, [2007] O.A.R.B.D. No. 766, File No. 64051, Hearing No. 137218, Appeal No. 1713321 (the *Franklin Sandblasting* decision), the applicant made an appeal under section 357 of the *Municipal Act* regarding reduction of taxes. The property in question contained a structure with an office and a shop, of which 50% was destroyed by fire. The applicant rented other premises during the seven months that it took to rebuild and made application to city council to reduce the taxes. City council reduced the taxes for a lesser amount than was requested on the basis that the property being assessed at current value should be reduced but should not be zero as contended. The ARB justified its decision in denying the appeal in the following statement: "Taxes are calculated based on current value and it makes sense to the Board that any reduction and refund should be calculated based upon the change to the current value."

Rudell v. Municipal Property Assessment Corp., Region No. 25

In *Rudell v. Municipal Property Assessment Corp., Region No. 25*, [2007] O.A.R.B.D. No. 776, File No. 64303A, Hearing No. 138407 (the *Rudell* decision), complaints were made to the ARB regarding the proper assessment of nine properties on the Bruce Peninsula. MPAC produced a list of comparable properties for the ARB to look at and determine current value under sections 19 and 44 of the *Assessment Act*. The complainants used two ads in two newspapers as their comparable properties sold. The ARB stated the following finding:

> The Board does not agree with Mr. Rudell and Mr. Ross that the sale of the nine lots by the Town of South Bruce Peninsula to the current owners in July 2006 established the current value of the properties. The Board does not consider these municipal sales as valid indicators of current value.
>
> The Board finds that the one-day advertisement in the Toronto Star and two days advertisement in the Owen Sound Sun Times offered limited exposure to the market. Even with the municipal website advertising the properties, the Board finds that the properties were not exposed to the market for a reasonable amount of time.
>
> The Board is satisfied that the nine sales were sold under special circumstances. The Board finds that the sale prices paid for the nine lots are not comparable to any other evidenced sales or evidenced assessments in the vicinity.
>
> The onus is on the complainant to prove that the assessed values are incorrect. No evidence has been provided to show any other properties in the vicinity, other than the nine municipal sales, that have sold [at] or that are assessed as low as the 2006 sales prices, four of which are being appealed in this hearing.
>
> The Board finds that there is no evidence before it to suggest that a correction to the current value is required for the four appealed properties. Similar properties in the vicinity are all assessed at $20,500.

The complaints were dismissed, and the assessed values confirmed.

Municipal Property Assessment Corp. v. Cisco Systems Co.

In *Municipal Property Assessment Corp. v. Cisco Systems Co.*, [2008] O.J. No. 295, 42 M.P.L.R. (4th) 315, 233 O.A.C. 187, 164 A.C.W.S. (3d) 567, 2008 CarswellOnt 371 (the *Cisco* case), MPAC appealed to the court on questions of law set out in a consent order granting leave to appeal a decision of the ARB as follows:

> (i) Did the Board err in law in its interpretation of the meaning of the words "parcel" in the *Assessment Act* and in O. Reg. 282/98?
>
> (ii) Did the Board err in law in holding that two separate improved lots, on a registered plan of subdivision[,] can be combined as 'a single parcel' with a single roll number for purposes of s. 14 of O. Reg. 282/98?

The court looked at the facts of the subject properties and the classification given by the ARB as a "Large Industrial Property Class" based on its interpretation of sections 6 and 14 of O. Reg. 282/98 as well as the use of the word "parcel" in section 14 of the *Assessment Act*.

The court found that Ottawa is the only municipality in Ontario where the tax rate for "Large Industrial Property Class" is lower than the "Industrial Property Class", and the court believed that triggered the proceedings of the case. Since tax rates are set by the municipality, the court concluded that the tax rate is neutral when considering an assessable classification. The judge further answered the question whether the ARB had erred in law as follows:

> The [ARB] recognizes that the concept of occupation is an integral and important factor as to what constitutes a "parcel". From Section 14 of the *Act*, elements referable to the word "parcel" include a whole subdivision or a portion thereof or the whole or portion of a building in "separate occupation". From the regulation "parcel or a portion of a parcel of land" is used, with occupation to be by a single occupant and with square footage to exceed 125,000 square feet. The elements of single occupation and square footage are essential elements to determine the classification of a parcel or a portion of a parcel.

The court found that the decision of the ARB was correct and therefore did not err in law, and the appeal was dismissed.

St. George and St. Rueiss Coptic Orthodox Church v. Toronto (City)

The *St. George and St. Rueiss Coptic Orthodox Church v. Toronto (City)*, [2008] O.J. No. 1046 (the *St. George Church* case) is a leave to appeal case before the Superior Court of Justice. An application was made to the ARB pursuant to section 357 of the *Assessment Act*, requesting an exemption due to land being used in connection with "a place of worship". The ARB did not find the land exempt and also refused a request for a review. The focus of the court's decision was on the ARB's refusal to review. The request to review, made under ARB Rule 62.02(4)(b), included a statutory declaration, which was considered and discussed in refusing the request. The court found the following:

> For purposes of this motion, it is important to focus on the decision to refuse the Request for Review, rather than on the decision of the Original Board. That is often easier said than done because the decision to refuse the Request for Review derives from the Original Board decision. In this case, the Chair of the ARB made a fresh finding of fact and law on the point in issue in the application for leave.
>
> The threshold for finding that there is good reason to doubt the correctness of the decision to refuse the Request for Review is low. I need not conclude that the decision is wrong or even probably wrong.
>
> I am satisfied that there is good reason to doubt the correctness of the decision dated June 20, 2007 because of the absence in the decision of a reference to "land used in connection with" a place of worship. The focus on "place of worship" alone may be found to be an error of mixed fact and law. To the extent that that finding encompasses a question of law, that criterion has been met.

Based on the above finding, the court held that leave was granted to determine if the ARB in its decision to refuse the request for review "erred in law in finding that the land used by a Church for storage of Church property and for Church youth programs cannot be 'used in connection with' a 'place of worship' pursuant to s. 3(1)3(i) of the *Assessment Act*".

REVIEW QUESTIONS

1. What is the enabling legislation for the ARB?
2. Where would you find the practices and procedures of the ARB?
3. How does the *SPPA* apply to the ARB?
4. What do the privative clauses of the enabling legislation prevent and allow, and under what circumstances?
5. What is a stated case as discussed in the enabling legislation?
6. What rule(s) gives discretion and flexibility to the ARB in applying the ARB Rules?

7. What rule(s) deal with disclosure, and what is the result of insufficient disclosure?
8. What rule(s) deal with motions, and what is the appropriate procedure to have a motion dealt with by the ARB?
9. What is the difference between reconsideration before MPAC and a review of an ARB decision, and how is each accomplished?
10. What jurisdiction is the ARB given to reconsider a decision under the various procedures and practices of the ARB?
11. How do the various procedures and practices of the ARB deal with the ability to appear on behalf of a party before the ARB?
12. How do the various procedures and practices of the enabling legislation deal with appeals under each such statute?

EXERCISE

Based upon the facts of the *UniRoyal* ARB case discussed in the chapter, fill out appropriate form(s) to institute this matter currently before the ARB.

Appendix 5.1
Overview of Procedural Stages of a Matter Before the ARB

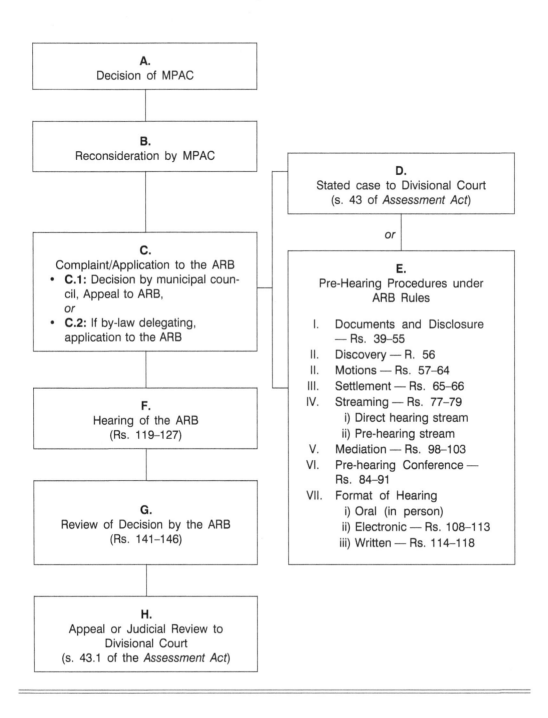

SUMMARY

A. Decision of MPAC

If decision by MPAC
- Send Notice of Assessment under section 31 of the *Assessment Act*
- Notice of Assessment to include school support designation under the *Education Act* and section 16 of the *Assessment Act*

Look at the following:
- *Assessment Act*, ss. 31, 36, 16
- *Education Act*, s. 257.6
- ARB website Web pages: "Introduction to Property Assessment" — "MPAC"; "Appeal Process"
- MPAC website, Web page: "Property Owners" — Property Assessment Notice of the year

B. Reconsideration by MPAC

Assessment Act, s. 39.1 — Ability of person to request MPAC to reconsider any matter relating to the assessment or classification of property under time limits under the section

Look at the following:
- *Assessment Act*, s. 39.1
- MPAC website Web pages on Request for Reconsideration: "Property Owners" — "Concerns about Your Assessed Value" and "Forms"
- ARB website Web page: "Appeal Process" — "Request for Reconsideration"

C. Complaint, Application/Appeal to the ARB

Assessment Act, s. 33 (Omitted Assessment) or s. 34 (Supplementary Assessment) — Complaint to ARB

Look at the following:
- ARB website Web page: "Appeal Process" — "Filing an Appeal"
- ARB website Web page: "Forms" — Assessment Appeal Form

Assessment Act, s. 40 — Complaint to ARB

Look at the following:
- ARB website Web page: "Appeal Process" — "Filing an Appeal"
- ARB website Web page: "Complaint Types" — Complaint Forms for section 40 — **Only available when complaints can be made under appropriate timeline.**
- ARB website Web page "Filing an Appeal"

Due to similarities in the legislation, the documents used for complaints, applications, and appeals are similar for the *Municipal Act* and the *City of Toronto Act*.

Municipal Act, s. 356 and *City of Toronto Act*, s. 322
Taxes on Eligible Property — Apportionment
- If no by-law, appeal from council to the ARB
- If by-law exists, application to ARB — Privative Clause

Look at the following:
- ARB website Web page: "Municipal Act Appeals" — Form "ARB-M1"
- ARB website Web page: "City of Toronto Acct Appeals" — Form "ARB-COTA1"
- ARB website Web page: "Filing an Appeal"

Municipal Act, s. 331 and *City of Toronto Act*, s. 294
Taxes on Eligible Property — Comparables
Complaint to the ARB → Appeal to Divisional Court

Look at the following
- ARB website Web page: "Municipal Act Appeals" — Form "ARB-M2"
- ARB website Web page: "City of Toronto Act Appeals" — Form "ARB-COTA2"
- ARB website Web page: "Filing an Appeal"

Municipal Act, s. 357 and *City of Toronto Act*, s. 323
Cancel, Reduce, Refund — Sickness or Poverty
- If no by-law, appeal from council to the ARB
- If by-law exists, application to ARB — Privative Clause

Look at the following:
- ARB website Web page: "Municipal Act Appeals" — Form "ARB-M3"
- ARB website Web page: "City of Toronto Act Appeals" — Form "ARB-COTA5"
- ARB website Web page: "Filing an Appeal"

Municipal Act, s. 364 and *City of Toronto Act*, s. 331
Increase in Taxes — Vacant Unit Rebate
Complaint to the ARB → Appeal to Divisional Court

Look at the following:
- ARB website Web page: "Municipal Act Appeals" — Form "ARB-M4"
- ARB website Web page: "City of Toronto Act Appeals" — Form "ARB-COTA4"
- ARB website Web page: "Filing an Appeal"

Municipal Act, ss. 357–359 and *City of Toronto Act*, ss. 323, 325, 326
Cancel, Reduce, Refund
- If no by-law, appeal from council to the ARB
- If by-law exists, application to ARB — Privative Clause

Look at the following:
- ARB website Web page: "Municipal Act Appeals" — Form "ARB-M5"
- ARB website Web page: "City of Toronto Act Appeals" — Form "ARB-COTA5"
- ARB website Web page: "Filing an Appeal"

Municipal Act, ss. 334, 337 and *City of Toronto Act*, ss. 297, 300
Limitation of Taxes
- If no by-law, appeal from council to the ARB
- If by-law exists, application to ARB — Privative Clause

Look at the following:
- ARB website Web page: "Municipal Act Appeals" — Form "ARB-M6"
- ARB website Web page: "City of Toronto Act Appeals" — Form "ARB-COTA6"
- ARB website Web page: "Filing an Appeal"

For *Municipal Act* Forms look at
- ARB website Web page: "Municipal Act Appeals" — Forms and Information Sheets

For *City of Toronto Act* Forms look at
- ARB website Web page: "City of Toronto Act appeals" — Forms and Information Sheets

For both
- ARB website Web page: "Appeal Process" — "Filing an Appeal"

All forms can be obtained indirectly through ARB website Web page: "Appeal Process" — "Filing an Appeal".

There are also e Services available on ARB website Web pages: "E Calendar", "E Status", and "E File". (Note: E File is not available for Municipal Act Appeals and City of Toronto Act Appeals.)

D. Stated Case to Divisional Court

Assessment Act, s. 43 — the ARB may, upon application of any person or on its own motion, and upon such security as it determines is necessary, "state a case in writing for the opinion of the Divisional Court upon any question that, in the opinion of the [ARB], is a question of law" and the Divisional Court shall hear and determine such stated case.

Look at the *Assessment Act*, s. 43

E. Pre-hearing Procedures under ARB Rules

    I. Documents and Disclosure — Rs. 39–55
    II. Discovery — R. 56
    III. Motions — Rs. 57–64
    IV. Settlement — Rs. 65–66
    V. Streaming — Rs. 77–83
        i) Direct Hearing Stream
        ii) Pre-hearing stream
    VI. Mediation — Rs. 98–103; Practice Direction: Mediation
    VII. Pre-hearing Conference
    VIII. Format of Hearing
        i) Oral (in person)
        ii) Electronic — Rs. 108–113
        iii) Written — Rs. 114–118

Look at the following:
- ARB website Web page: "Legislation and Rules" — Rules of Practice and Procedure
- ARB website Web page: "Appeal Process" — "Hearing Process"

F. Hearing of the ARB

- *ARBA*
- ARB Rules

Look at the following:
- ARB website Web page: "Legislation and Rules" — Rules of Practice and Procedure
- ARB website Web pages: "Appeal Process" — "Filing an Appeal"; "Hearing Process" — *How to Prepare for Your Hearing* pamphlet

G. Review of the Decision by ARB

ARB Rules — Rs. 146–152

Look at the following:
- ARB website Web page: "Appeal Process" — "Decisions"
- ARB website Web page: "Legislation and Rules" — Rules of Practice and Procedure

H. Appeal or Judicial Review to Divisional Court

The procedures in respect of appeals and judicial review of the decision of the ARB are set out in the provisions of the *SPPA* and the *Judicial Review Procedure Act* and as set out in the website of the ARB. Following are specifics that occur after the decision of the ARB is sent to the parties: *Assessment Act*, s. 43.1.

Look at the following:
- ARB website Web page: "Appeal Process" — "Decisions"
- ARB website Web page: "Legislation and Rules" — Rules of Practice and Procedure

Appendix 5.2
Request for Reconsideration by MPAC†

Filing a 2017 Request for Reconsideration (RfR):
What You Need to Know (Residential Properties)

MUNICIPAL
PROPERTY
ASSESSMENT
CORPORATION

Who is MPAC?

The Municipal Property Assessment Corporation (MPAC) is an independent, not-for-profit corporation funded by all Ontario municipalities. We are responsible for accurately assessing and classifying more than five million properties in Ontario in compliance with the *Assessment Act* and regulations established by the Government of Ontario.

What is a Request for Reconsideration (RfR)?

If you disagree with MPAC's assessment of your property's value and/or classification as of January 1, 2016, you can ask MPAC to review the assessment to make sure that it is right. This is called a Request for Reconsideration (RfR). You can make this request by completing and sending an RfR form to us. This request is free of charge.

What is the deadline to file an RfR for the 2017 property tax year?

Your deadline is printed on your Property Assessment Notice. If you have misplaced your 2016 Property Assessment Notice, please call us at 1 866 296-MPAC (6722). One of our customer service representatives can assist you.

We also look at these five factors, which account for 85% of your property's value:

- Location
- Living area
- Lot dimensions
- Age of the property
- Quality of construction

What information does MPAC need to reconsider my property's assessment?

Section 39.1 of the *Assessment Act* requires you to provide the reasons for your Request for Reconsideration. This includes sending us all key details about your property that we should know. We also compare your property's assessed value with sales and values of similar properties in your area.

How long does it take for MPAC to review my RfR?

Starting in 2016, property owners will have 120 days from the Issue Date on their Property Assessment Notice to file an RfR. The Issue Date and your unique RfR deadline are included on your Property Assessment Notice. MPAC will send you a letter with the results of our review within 180 days (or less) of when we get your request. Sometimes, we need more time (up to 60 more days) to reconsider a property assessment and complete our review. We will contact you if we need more time.

The Request for Reconsideration (RfR) Process

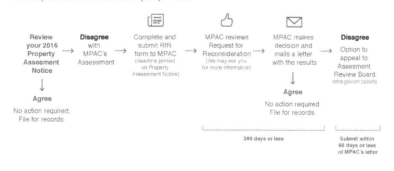

---

† MPAC website: Property Owners | Forms, <https://www.mpac.ca/PropertyOwners/Forms>. © MPAC.

Filing a 2017 Request for Reconsideration (RfR):
What You Need to Know (Residential Properties)

MUNICIPAL
PROPERTY
ASSESSMENT
CORPORATION

Ready to send your
Request for Reconsideration?

▼

 Online: aboutmyproperty.ca

OR

 mpac.ca/ContactUs

 Fax: 1 866 297-6703

 Mail: MPAC, PO Box 9808
Toronto ON M1S 5T9

How do I submit my completed RfR?

The fastest way to start the review of your property's assessment is to send MPAC your completed RfR form through aboutmyproperty.ca. While there are a number of factors that account for the assessment of a property, location is the most important one. As a result, comparing your assessment to similar properties in your area or neighbourhood will help you review your assessment. Log in to aboutmyproperty.ca with the Roll Number and Access Key found on page one of your Property Assessment Notice to compare your property to others in your neighbourhood. You can also use the interactive map to view and save your favourite properties, and download a detailed report to accompany your RfR submission. You may also send us your completed RfR form via mpac.ca/ContactUs, fax or mail.

Need more information?

If you need more information or help completing the RfR form, or have any accessibility needs, please contact us for assistance at 1 866 296-MPAC (6722) or TTY 1 877 889-MPAC (6722).

How does MPAC use the information in my completed RfR?

The information on the RfR form is collected under the authority of the *Assessment Act*. It will be used to reconsider your property's assessment. Please note that if your RfR is about eligibility for the farm property class, managed forests tax incentive program, or the conservation land tax incentive program, your request must be handled by the Ministry of Agriculture, Food and Rural Affairs, or the Ministry of Natural Resources and Forestry, in accordance with Ontario Regulation 282/98. When you file your RfR with MPAC, you authorize MPAC to transfer your request to the appropriate ministry for this purpose. Your privacy is protected under the *Municipal Freedom of Information and Protection of Privacy Act*.

Appealing to the Assessment Review Board (ARB)

You may also file an appeal of MPAC's assessment with the ARB. The ARB is an independent tribunal (decision-making body) of the Ontario Ministry of the Attorney General.

Please note that if your property, or a portion of it, is classified as **residential**, **farm** or **managed forests**, you must first file an RfR with MPAC before you are eligible to appeal to the ARB.

There is a time limit to submit an appeal to the ARB. It starts on the date that MPAC issues the results of your RfR, and ends after 90 days. The deadline for submitting an appeal to the ARB will be in the letter that MPAC sends you with the results of the RfR review. You can find more information about how to file an appeal, including forms and fees, at elto.gov.on.ca/arb.

Clear Form   **Print**

Request for Reconsideration
(For Residential Properties)
2017 Tax Year

Section 1: About your property

Roll Number (see page 1 of your Property Assessment Notice)

Property Address	
Municipality	
Owner 1 (Last Name, First Name)	Owner 2 (Last Name, First Name)
Company Name (if applicable)	Position/Title (if applicable)
Home Phone Number	Alternate Phone Number	E-mail Address

Tell us if we should send follow-up information about your RfR to a different mailing address than the property address:

Mailing Address

What is your property's value on January 1, 2016?
(Top of page 1 of Property Assessment Notice or
Amended Property Assessment Notice)

$

Section 2: Why MPAC should reconsider your property's assessed value

In the box below, please tell us why you are asking MPAC to reconsider your property's assessed value. Include details to
support your request. Take as much space as you need or use a second sheet of paper if you are not completing this form online.

Section 3: Your supporting documentation

Please tell us if you are including any documents or photographs with your RfR to support your request.

☐ Photos of this property

☐ Photos of similar properties

☐ Sale information for this property
and other similar properties

☐ Assessed value of similar properties

☐ Information supporting property
tax exemption under Section 3
of the *Assessment Act*

☐ Other documents, such
as municipal zoning records

Clear Form   **Print**

Section 4: Residential property data

Roll Number (see page 1 of your Property Assessment Notice)

☐☐ - ☐☐ - ☐☐☐ - ☐☐☐ - ☐☐☐☐☐ - ☐☐☐☐

For properties with a residential dwelling (not including condominium properties), please provide the following data to confirm the information that we have on file for your property.

Main Structure Details

Full Storeys	☑ 1 Storey ☐ 2 Storeys ☐ 3 Storeys	Total Area (sq. ft.) _____
Part Storeys	☐ ¼ Storey ☐ ½ Storey ☑ ¾ Storey	1st Floor (sq. ft.) _____
Design	☐ Back Split ☑ Side Split ☑ Raised Bungalow	2nd Floor (sq. ft.) _____
Full Bathrooms	☐ 1 ☑ 2 ☑ 3 ☑ 4 ☐ Other: _____	3rd Floor (sq. ft.) _____
Half Bathrooms (no tub or shower)	☐ 1 ☐ 2 ☐ 3 ☐ 4 ☐ Other: _____	Basement Area (sq. ft.) _____
Basement Finished Area	☐ ¼ Finished ☐ ½ Finished ☐ ¾ Finished ☐ Fully Finished ☐ Not Finished	
Basement Finished Type	☐ Recreation Room ☐ Multiple Room Finish ☐ Basement Apartment Completion date of finished basement: _____	
Basement Walkout	☐ Yes ☐ No	
Primary Heating System		
Fuel Source	☐ Oil ☐ Natural Gas ☐ Electric ☐ Propane ☐ Geo-Thermal ☐ Other: _____	
Heating Type	☐ Forced Air ☐ Radiant Electric ☐ Hot Water ☐ Gravity Furnace ☐ Heat Pump ☐ Pipeless Hot Air ☐ Pipeline Hot Air ☐ In-Floor Radiant ☐ No Central Heating ☐ Airtight Stove ☐ Other _____	
Central Air Conditioning	☐ Yes ☐ No	
Built-in Fireplaces	☐ 1 ☐ 2 ☐ 3 ☐ 4 ☐ Other: _____	
Sauna	☐ Yes ☐ No Length (ft): _____ Width (ft): _____ Height (ft): _____	
Hot Tub/Whirlpool Bath (separate from bathroom)	☐ Yes ☐ No sq. ft. of Hot Tub/Whirlpool Bath: _____	
Porches/Decks Please provide details on the size and type of porch/deck(s) below (e.g. 300 sq. ft. and 200 sq. ft. covered porch)	☐ N/A ☐ Uncovered (No Roof) ☐ Covered (Full Roof) ☐ Enclosed ☐ Enclosed (Insulated)	

Site Services

Water	☑ Municipal ☑ Private Well ☑ Shared Well ☑ Lake/River ☑ Other: _____
Sanitary	☑ Municipal ☑ Septic Bed ☑ Holding Tank
Hydro Available	☐ Yes ☐ No
Site Access	☐ Year Round ☐ Seasonal ☐ Private Road ☐ Water ☐ No Access ☐ Other: _____
Driveway/Parking	☐ Private ☐ Shared ☐ Rear Lane ☐ Other: _____

Clear Form | **Print**

Section 4: Residential property data (continued)

Roll Number (see page 1 of your Property Assessment Notice)

☐☐ - ☐☐☐ - ☐☐☐☐ - ☐☐☐☐ - ☐☐☐☐☐☐ - ☐☐☐☐☐

Additions & Renovations

Have there been any additions to your property?	☐ Yes ☐ No Addition sq. ft. (Exterior) _____ Addition Completion Date _____ **Addition Storeys** ☐ 1 Storey ☐ 2 Storeys ☐ 3 Storeys			
Have there been any improvements/alterations to the property since it was constructed?	**Interior**	**Completion Year**	**Exterior**	**Completion Year**
	Kitchen Modernization	_____	Exterior Cladding	_____
	Bathroom Modernization	_____	Roof Surface	_____
	Wiring Upgrade	_____	New Windows	_____
	New Heating System	_____	Foundation	_____
	Plumbing Upgrade	_____	Other: _____	_____
	Structural Changes	_____		
	Other: _____	_____		

Building permits
Have you been approved for a building permit for a new structure or a demolition in the last three years? ☐ Yes ☐ No
(If Yes, please provide details and completion date below)

Building permit details, comments and/or secondary structure information.
Please list any secondary structures (e.g. garages, sheds, in-ground pool) and any other relevant information about the property.

Section 5: Signature of owner

X	Date (dd/mm/yyyy)

MPAC collects the information on this form under the authority of the *Assessment Act*. We will use the information to reconsider your property assessment. If you have any questions about this information collection, please contact us at 1 866 296-6722. Your privacy is protected under the *Municipal Freedom of Information and Protection of Privacy Act*.

Section 6: Representative information

If you would like someone else to act for you while we review your Request for Reconsideration, please complete this section and provide a Letter of Authorization for that person. You may also use the Representative Authorization Form. It is available at mpac.ca or by calling us at 1 866 296-6722.

Please note that the *Law Society Act* specifies who can act as a representative for a property owner. Persons approved by the Law Society of Upper Canada to practice law or provide legal services in Ontario do not require Letters of Authorization.

Representative Name (Last Name, First Name)	LSUC License Number	Telephone

Appendix 5.3
ARB Property Assessment Appeal Instructions and Form[†]

Environment and Land Tribunals Ontario
ARB Property Assessment Appeal Form Instructions
Assessment Review Board, 655 Bay Street, Suite 1500, Toronto, Ontario M5G 1E5 **Phone:** (416) 212-6349 or 1-866-448-2248
Fax: (416) 314-3717 or 1-877-849-2066 **Website:** www.elto.gov.on.ca **E-mail:** assessment.review.board@ontario.ca

We are committed to providing services as set out in the Accessibility for Ontarians with Disabilities Act, 2005. If you have any accessibility needs, please contact our Accessibility Coordinator as soon as possible.

Before you fill in this form:

- Direct questions about your assessment to the Municipal Property Assessment Corporation (MPAC) at 1-866-296-6722
- Have your Property Assessment Notice from MPAC
- Have your Request for Reconsideration (RFR) and/or decision letter

- Be aware that only the **Superior Court of Justice** can hear appeals on exemptions from taxes
- File before your appeal deadline (see below)

Filing deadlines
If your property or a portion of it is classified as **residential, farm, managed forest or conservation land:**
1. File a RFR with MPAC or the Program Administrator first (by their deadline).
2. Your deadline to file with the ARB is **90 calendar days** from the mailing date on the RFR decision letter.

If your property is in **any other property class (i.e. commercial, industrial, etc.):**
1. You may file a RFR with MPAC **or** appeal directly to the ARB.
2. If you think the RFR decision is wrong, you may then file an appeal with the ARB. Your deadline to file with the ARB is 90 days from the mailing date on the RFR decision.
3. If you file directly with the ARB, your deadline to appeal is March 31 of the tax year for annual assessments or **90 calendar days** from the notice date for other types of assessments (i.e. Change or Amended Notice).

Part 1: Property Information and Classification

Provide the 19-digit property roll number (see MPAC notice) and the property address. Also fill in the roll number at the top of page 2 and 3 of the form in the space provided. Check the box indicating the classification of your property. Your property classification tells you the process for your appeal. If **any** part of your property is residential, farm, managed forest or conservation land, you must file a RFR with MPAC or the Program Administrator and receive an answer on your RFR before filing. If your property is **farm, managed forest or conservation land**, please fill out the Special Tax Class Form and attach it to this form. The Special Class Tax Form is available online or by calling the ARB. 'All other property classes' refer to properties that are commercial, industrial, etc.

Part 2: Appeal Information

Your Property Assessment Notice from MPAC tells you the type of assessment notice you have been sent and the tax years for your assessment. Read your notice carefully so that you use the correct type of appeal. If you received an Amended or Change notice please include **the effective date of taxation**. Also fill in the date and the appeal deadline date located on the RFR response letter you received from MPAC. If you have questions about your assessment notice, please contact MPAC at 1-866-296-6722 to help you.

Part 3: Appellant information

If there are two or more appellants or property owners, you only need to fill in one name. If you are not the property owner, also complete Part 5 of the appeal form. If you have chosen someone else to act on your behalf with regard to this appeal, also complete Part 6 of the appeal form. Sign your name where indicated. Choose the language you would like to communicate in by checking the box beside English or French.

AssmntAppeal   revised: April 2, 2013

[†] ARB Website: Forms <http://www.arb.gov.on.ca/english/Forms/ARBForms.html>. © Queen's Printer for Ontario, 2013.

Part 4: Reason(s) for Appeal

Check **only** the reason(s) that apply to your appeal. Refer to your notice from MPAC for your assessment value (the bolded valuation as of January 1st). The classification of your property is available on your notice from MPAC. For other appeal reasons, please refer to s. 40(1) of the Assessment Act. "Other" appeals must be under the jurisdiction of the Board. Arguments for your appeal will be heard at your hearing. For more information about property assessment appeals and property classification, see the Assessment Act and Ontario Regulation 282/98.

Part 5: Third Party Appeal Information

Only fill out this section if you are NOT the property owner. Include the name and address of the property owner. As a non-owner, you must appeal the assessment directly to the ARB first and may not file a RFR with MPAC. You must send a copy of the appeal form to the owner by the filing deadline. The appeal deadline is March 31 of the tax year for annual assessments, or 90 days from the notice date for other types of assessments. If the property owner is not sent a copy, your appeal will not be considered valid. Also write in the date you sent the property owner a copy of the appeal form.

Part 6: Representative Authorization

Representatives who are not licensed by the Law Society must confirm that they have written authorization. If you are the appellant filling out this form, complete this section, sign it and provide a copy to your representative. If you are the representative filling out this form, complete this section and make sure you have written authorization - signed by the appellant - to act on his or her behalf. Check the box indicating that written authorization has been provided.

Anyone representing someone before the ARB requires a legal licence, unless the person is not in the business of providing legal services and sometimes helps a friend or relative at no cost. For information on legal licensing please see the Law Society of Upper Canada's website www.lsuc.ca or call 416-947-3315 or 1-800-668-7380.

Part 7: How to File an Appeal

Use only ONE of the following options:

E File:	Fax to:	Mail or deliver to:
www.arb.gov.on.ca	(416) 314-3717 or toll-free	Assessment Review Board, 655 Bay Street
*Note: there is a $10	1-877-849-2066	Suite 1500 Toronto, Ontario M5G 1E5
discount if you E File		

If you are unsure whether you filed correctly and file more than once, please mark any additional submissions COPY to avoid duplicate charges. Due to the volume of appeals received by fax and mail, the Board does not confirm receipt of appeals by either method. E Filed appeals will receive an email acknowledging their appeal was received. Mailed and faxed appeals will receive an acknowledgment letter in the mail.

Part 8: Required Filing Fee

There are NO refunds of the filing fee, even if you settle with MPAC before your hearing date. The required filing fee is used to process your appeal. The fee payment information you include on this form is only used to process your appeal and will not be placed on file.

Residential, farm, managed forest or conservation land properties.................................$75* for each roll number
All other property classes..$150* for each roll number
*Note: there is a $10 discount if you E File at www.arb.gov.on.ca

Fill in the amount of the total fee submitted in the space provided. **E Filed or faxed** appeals can ONLY be paid by VISA, MasterCard or American Express. To pay by cheque or money order, you must send your appeal by mail. **Cheques and money orders** must be made payable to the **Minister of Finance.** Write the roll number on the front of the cheque or money order. Do not mail cash. If you are **filing in person**, you can pay by cash, cheque, money order, debit card or credit card. If a financial institution returns your cheque, an administration fee of $35 will apply.

After filing:

You will receive a Notice of Hearing by mail once your hearing date is scheduled. You may want to start preparing for your hearing. Read our information sheet called "Here's what you need to know about preparing for your ARB hearing" available on our website. For any questions about the appeal process please call Public Inquiry

AssmntAppeal   revised: April 2, 2013

316 | APPENDIX 5.3

Environment and Land Tribunals Ontario
ARB Property Assessment Appeal Form
Assessment Review Board, 655 Bay Street, Suite 1500, Toronto, Ontario M5G 1E5
Phone: (416) 212-6349or 1-866-448-2248 **Fax:** (416) 314-3717 or 1-877-849-2066
Website: www.elto.gov.on.ca **E-mail:** assessment.review.board@ontario.ca

Appeal #
Receipt #
Date Stamp
For office use only

Read the <u>Form Instructions</u> if you have questions about how to fill out this form.

- We are committed to providing services as set out in the Accessibility for Ontarians with Disabilities Act, 2005. If you have any accessibility needs, please contact our Accessibility Coordinator as soon as possible.
- Only the **Superior Court of Justice** can hear appeals on exemptions from taxes

Part 1: Property Information and Classification

Roll Number ☐☐☐☐ — ☐☐☐☐ — ☐☐☐☐ — ☐☐☐☐☐ — ☐☐☐☐   19-digit number on Property Assessment Notice

Street Address:_____Municipality:_____

☐ Residential - File a Request for Reconsideration (RFR) first.
☐ Farm, Managed Forest or Conservation Land - **See Special Tax Class Form**
☐ All other property classes - You may file directly with the ARB without a RFR OR you may file a RFR.

Part 2: Appeal Information

I received from MPAC this type of Property Assessment Notice (**see the top right corner of your Notice from MPAC**):

☐ Annual Property Assessment ☐ Property Assessment Change ☐ Amended Property Assessment

Tax year: _____ Effective date of taxation (only for **change and amended**): (D/M/Y) _____/_____/_____

Date of RFR decision letter (D/M/Y) _____/_____/_____ Appeal deadline: (D/M/Y)____/_____/_____

Part 3: Appellant Information

First name: _____Last name:_____

Company:_____Address:_____

City:_____Province:_____Postal code:_____Country (if not Canada):_____

Home #:_____Business #:_____Fax #: _____

Email:_____

Appellant (or Rep.) signature:_____

Roll Number ⬚⬚⬚⬚⬚—⬚⬚⬚⬚—⬚⬚⬚⬚—⬚⬚⬚⬚⬚⬚—⬚⬚⬚⬚

Part 3: Appellant Information Continued

Are you the owner of this property? ☐ yes ☐ no **If no, fill out Part 5 of this form** (and the rest of form.)

Do you have a representative?   ☐ yes ☐ no **If yes, fill out Part 6 of this form** (and the rest of form.)

I would like to communicate with the ARB in ☐ English **or** ☐ French

Are you filing as a municipality?   ☐ yes ☐ no

Part 4: Reason(s) for Appeal (Refer to Assessment Notice)

☐ **Assessment value is wrong** (If you checked "assessment value" as the appeal reason, fill in the information below.)

What is MPAC's assessment of the property? _____

What do you think the property assessment should be? _____

☐ **Property classification is wrong** (If you checked "property classification" as the appeal reason, fill in the information below.)

What is MPAC's current classification of your property? _____

What do you think your property classification should be? _____

Note: If your property is classified as a farm, managed forest or conservation land, fill in the Special Tax Class Form and attach to this completed form.

☐ **Other** - The assessment value or classification is wrong because:
*List reasons in the box provided, e.g. MPAC is missing/additional/inaccurate information about the property.

```



```

Roll Number ☐☐☐☐—☐☐☐—☐☐☐—☐☐☐☐—☐☐☐

Part 5: Third Party Appeal Information (Only fill out this section if you are NOT the property owner.)

As a non-owner, you must appeal to the ARB first. The appeal deadline is March 31 of the tax year for annual assessments, or 90 days from the notice date for other types of assessments. You must also send a copy of this appeal form to the property owner by the filing deadline.

Name of property owner: _____

Mailing address of above: _____

☐ Yes, I delivered/mailed a copy of this appeal form to the property owner on (D/M/Y): _____/_____/_____

Part 6: Representative Authorization (Only fill out this section if you have representation.)

Company name: _____ Name of representative: _____

Address: _____ Unit #:_____ City #_____

Province:_____Postal code:_____ Telephone #:_____

Fax #:_____Email address: _____

Representatives who are not licensed by the Law Society of Upper Canada must have written authorization and check the box below.
☐ I certify that I have written authorization from the appellant to act as a representative for this appeal and I understand that I may be asked to produce this authorization at any time. I understand that I can only be a representative if I qualify for an exemption under the rules of the Law Society of Upper Canada.

Part 7: How to File an Appeal

File your appeal using only ONE of the following options. If you are unsure whether you filed correctly and file more than once, please mark any additional submissions COPY to avoid duplicate charges.

Internet (Use the E File link. Credit card and email address required.)

www.arb.gov.on.ca

There is $10 discount if you E File. There is no discount if you use this form.

Mail*

Assessment Review Board
655 Bay Street, Suite 1500
Toronto, Ontario M5G 1E5

Fax*

Toronto Local: (416) 314-3717
Toll Free: 1-877-849-2066

In person

655 Bay Street, Suite 1500 (on Bay Street, north of Dundas Street)

*We do not immediately confirm receipt of appeal forms. For faxed appeals, keep a copy of the transmission report for your records. You will receive an acknowledgement letter after your appeal is processed.

Roll
Number

Part 8: Fee and Payment Information

The information in this section is confidential. It will **only be used to process your appeal** and will not be placed on file.

<u>**Fees**</u> *There are **no refunds** of the filing fee

Residential, farm, managed forest and conservation land properties......................$75* for each Roll Number
All other property classes...$150* for each Roll Number

Total fee submitted: $_____

<u>Payment Type</u>

☐ *Cheque or Money Order – make payable to the Minister of Finance and note roll number(s) on front

If a financial institution returns your cheque, or if you cancel or stop payment, an administrative fee of $35 will apply.

☐ Visa   or   ☐ MasterCard   or   ☐ American Express

Credit card #: _____Expiry date: _____/_____
                                                                                                                       month   year

Cardholder's name: _____

Cardholder's signature: _____Today's Date: (D/M/Y)_____/_____/_____

Personal information requested on this form is collected under section 40 of the Assessment Act. After an appeal is filed, all information relating to this appeal may become available to the public. For additional information, please contact an ARB public inquiry assistant at (416) 212-6349 or toll-free 1-866-448-2248. The Assessment Act is available at www.arb.gov.on.ca.

For office use only:

Fee received: $_____   ☐ Cash   ☐ Cheque   ☐ Money order   ☐ Credit card   ☐ Debit card

Verified by: _____

Appendix 5.4
Municipal Act Application/Appeal — Apportionment, s. 356[†]

Environment and Land Tribunals Ontario
Assessment Review Board, 655 Bay Street, Suite 1500, Toronto, Ontario M5G 1E5
Phone: (416) 212-6349 or 1-866-448-2248 **Fax:** (416) 314-3717 or 1-877-849-2066
Website: www.elto.gov.on.ca

MUNICIPAL ACT APPLICATION/APPEAL – APPORTIONMENT

Form and Instructions for filing a *Municipal Act, 2001* application/appeal with the
Assessment Review Board and information on how to prepare for your hearing event.

Please note: This form is for Municipal Act applications/appeals – Apportionment only. Do not use this form to file assessment complaints (sections 33, 34 or 40 of the *Assessment Act*). Do not use this form for any other applications, appeals and/or complaints under the *Municipal Act, 2001*. Different forms are available to file the other applications, appeals and complaints. Issues of tax exemption can only be addressed by the Superior Court of Justice.

Before Filing: Please contact the municipality where the property is located for information regarding the tax account and the application/appeal process. The ARB can only accept applications under section 356.(1)(b) where the municipality has passed a by-law that gives the ARB the same authority as municipal council to decide on Municipal Act applications. Before filing with the ARB, please ensure that the municipality has passed such a by-law.

Required Filing Fee: $25.00 for each roll number. Your application/appeal will not be accepted without the required filing fee.

Filing Deadline: Filing deadlines are established by legislation and cannot be waived by the ARB. Filing deadlines depend on the type of application or appeal you are making.

Important: Please attach to your appeal a copy of the supporting document requested in Part 2 of the appeal form. The ARB cannot determine if your appeal has been filed on time without the supporting document.

Accessibility: We are committed to providing services as set out in the Accessibility for Ontarians with Disabilities Act, 2005. If you have any accessibility needs, please contact our Accessibility Coordinator as soon as possible.

These descriptions are summarized – please refer to the *Municipal Act, 2001*.	
SECTION NUMBER AND APPLICATION/APPEAL REASON	**FILING DEADLINE**
356.(1)(b) To apportion taxes where land is assessed in a block. Filing for multiple taxation years is considered one application with one filing fee.	No deadline.
356.(6) Appeal a decision that the municipal council made on an application under section 356.(1)(b).	File within 35 days after Council makes its decision.

Instructions for filing a *Municipal Act, 2001* application/appeal with the Assessment Review Board

Part 1: Property Information

Please refer to your municipal property tax bill or property assessment notice when completing this section.

Roll Number: The roll number is a 19-digit number assigned to each property. Please ensure that this number is accurately recorded on each page of the application/appeal form.

Street Address and Property Description: Enter the municipal address of the property for which you are filing a Municipal Act application/appeal.

Municipality: Note the city, town or village in which the property is located.

Preferred Language: Check the appropriate box indicating your language preference for receiving ARB services, including hearings, notices and other public information materials.

[†] ARB website: Municipal Act Appeals <http://www.arb.gov.on.ca/english/ComplaintTypes/ComplaintProcess/MunicipalActAppeals/act_appeals.html>. © Queen's Printer for Ontario, 2013.

Part 2: Application/Appeal Information

Application/Appeal Reason:
Check the appropriate box to indicate the reason for your application/appeal. Check only one box. Continue moving to the right along the same row to complete the application/appeal. Application can be made under 356.(1)(b) for multiple taxation years.

The ARB can only accept applications under section 356.(1)(b) where the municipality has passed a by-law that gives the ARB the same authority as municipal council to decide on Municipal Act applications. Before filing with the ARB, please ensure that the municipality has passed such a by-law.

Taxation Year:
Write in the taxation year(s) that are the subject of your application(s)/appeal.

Supporting Documents:
Supporting documents are required by the Assessment Review Board to determine if your Municipal Act appeal has been filed within legislated deadlines. Check the appropriate box to indicate you have attached a copy of the supporting document to the appeal form.

If you do not have your supporting document, do not wait to file the appeal. **Filing deadlines are established by legislation and cannot be waived.** If you do not submit the required document with your appeal, the ARB will send you an Acknowledgement Letter requesting a copy of the required document.

Filing Deadline:
This is the last day a Municipal Act application/appeal can be filed with the Assessment Review Board. **Filing deadlines are established by legislation and cannot be waived.** Filing deadlines are not the same for all section numbers. It is important that you file your Municipal Act appeal by the deadline indicated for the section number. It will not be accepted after the deadline has passed.

MPAC's Statement of Relative Value:
Check the appropriate box to indicate if you have received a Statement of Relative Value produced by the Municipal Property Assessment Corporation (MPAC). If you have received the Statement of Relative Value, you must enclose a copy of the statement with your application/appeal form.

If you do not have a Statement of Relative Value, please record the name, mailing address and roll number for each of the current owners. The ARB requires this information as the legislation requires that the Board send Notices of Hearing to all parties.

Additional Pages:
If you require more room, please attach additional page(s) and check the box on the bottom line to indicate you have attached additional page(s).

Part 3: Applicant/Appellant Information

Representative:
Check the appropriate box to indicate if you have a representative to act on your behalf with regard to this application/appeal. If you have a representative, please complete Parts 3 and 4 of the form.

Owner:
Check the appropriate box to indicate if you are the owner of the property.

Contact Information:
Provide your contact information including name, address and telephone number(s).

You must notify the Assessment Review Board in writing of any change of address or telephone number.

Personal information requested on this form is collected under the various sections of the *Municipal Act, 2001*. After an application/appeal is filed, all information relating to this application may become available to the public. For additional information, please contact an ARB Public Inquiry Assistant at (416) 212-6349 or toll-free at 1-866-448-2248. The *Municipal Act, 2001* is available at www.elto.gov.on.ca.

Part 4: Representative Authorization

If you have chosen someone to act on your behalf, please provide their name, address, telephone number, fax number and e-mail address. You will need to sign this section and provide your representative with a copy of the form. If you provided a letter or another form of written authorization for your representative, please make sure the representative checked the box in this section confirming he or she received your written authorization.

Part 5: How to File an Application/Appeal

You can file your application/appeal in a number of ways. Please choose only ONE of the following filing options:

Mail it to: Assessment Review Board, 655 Bay Street, Suite 1500, Toronto, Ontario M5G 1E5

Fax it to: (416) 314-3717 or 1-877-849-2066 (toll free) (For faxing applications, appeals and complaints only.)

Deliver it in person to: 655 Bay Street, 15th Floor. (East side of Bay Street, north of Dundas)

Please file only ONCE. If you are unsure that your filing attempt was successful and resubmit, please mark any other submissions COPY to avoid duplicate charges.

You will receive an Acknowledgement Letter by mail once your application/appeal has been received by the ARB followed by a Notice of Hearing once your hearing has been scheduled.

Please note: Once you have filed your Municipal Act application/appeal, any additional correspondence with the ARB should be copied to all parties.

Part 6: Required Filing Fee

- **If you are faxing your Municipal Act application/appeal**, payment must be made by VISA, MasterCard or American Express, in Canadian funds. Please include your credit card number, expiry date, cardholder's name and the cardholder's signature.

- **If you are mailing your Municipal Act application/appeal**, payment can be made by credit card, cheque or money order, in Canadian funds, payable to the **Minister of Finance**. Please note the applicable roll number(s) on the front of the cheque or money order. **Please do not mail cash.** Please note that if a financial institution returns your cheque, an administration fee of $35 will apply.

- **If you are delivering your Municipal Act application/appeal in person,** payment can be made by cash, cheque, money order, debit card or credit card.

The filing fee is non-refundable. You will receive an **Acknowledgement Letter** in the mail once your application/appeal has been received, followed by a **Notice of Hearing** when your hearing has been scheduled. **The information you fill in under Required Filing Fee is confidential. It will only be used to process your application/appeal and will not be placed on file.**

How to Prepare for Your Hearing Event

1. Gather the information you require to support your case, including:
   - your initial application to the municipal council and any decision of the municipal council (if you are appealing a decision of municipal council);
   - your property tax bill;
   - any factual information, including documents that you require to support your case.

2. Contact the municipality to discuss your case.

3. Consider how you will present your case to the Board.
   - Decide which documents you will provide to the Board at the hearing.
     - Bring photocopies to the hearing of any documents you would like the Board to consider in support of your case. We suggest three copies of each document: one for the Board, one for the municipality, and one for you.
   - Decide whether you will require any witnesses other than yourself to give evidence at the hearing.
     - Contact your witnesses once you receive the Notice of Hearing to inform them of the hearing date, time and location.
     - If necessary, you can obtain a Summons to Witness from the Board's Registrar.
   - Consider whether there is any need for parties to exchange documents prior to the hearing.
     - Request from the municipality copies of any documents they will be relying on to support their position.
     - Prior to the hearing, consider providing the municipality with copies of the documents that you will be relying on at the hearing.

At this point, please remove the instructions (pages 1, 2 & 3) from the following application/appeal form and keep the information on how prepare for your hearing event.

MUNICIPAL ACT APPLICATION/APPEAL – APPORTIONMENT

Environment and Land Tribunals Ontario
Assessment Review Board, 655 Bay Street, Suite 1500, Toronto, Ontario M5G 1E5
Phone: (416) 212-6349 or 1-866-448-2248 **Fax**: (416) 314-3717 or 1-877-849-2066
Website: www.elto.gov.on.ca

Application/appeal #
Receipt #
Date Stamp
For office use only

Please note: This form is for Municipal Act applications/appeals – Apportionments only. Do not use this form to file assessment appeals (sections 33, 34 or 40 of the *Assessment Act*). Do not use this form for any other applications, appeals and/or complaints under the *Municipal Act, 2001*. Different forms are available to file the other applications, appeals and complaints. Issues of tax exemption can only be addressed by the Superior Court of Justice.

Before Filing: Please contact the municipality where the property is located for information regarding the tax account and the application/appeal process. The ARB can only accept applications under section 356.(1)(b) where the municipality has passed a by-law that gives the ARB the same authority as municipal council to decide on Municipal Act applications/appeals. Before filing with the ARB, please ensure that the municipality has passed such a by-law.

Required Filing Fee: $25.00 for each roll number. Your application/appeal will not be accepted without the required filing fee.

Filing Deadline: Filing deadlines are established by legislation and cannot be waived by the ARB. Filing deadlines depend on the type of application or appeal you are making. Please see Part 2 for the filing deadline.

Important: Please attach to this appeal form a copy of the supporting document requested in Part 2. The ARB cannot determine if your appeal has been filed on time without the supporting document.

Accessibility: We are committed to providing services as set out in the Accessibility for Ontarians with Disabilities Act, 2005. If you have any accessibility needs, please contact our Accessibility Coordinator as soon as possible.

Part 1: Property Information (Please print clearly)

Roll number:

```
[ ][ ][ ][ ]-[ ][ ][ ][ ]-[ ][ ][ ][ ][ ]-[ ][ ][ ][ ][ ]-[ ][ ][ ][ ]
```

PLEASE copy this roll number in the space provided at the top of every page of this form

Street address: _____

Municipality: _____

Please choose preferred language: ☐ English   ☐ French

Part 2: Application/Appeal Information

These descriptions are summarized – please refer to the *Municipal Act, 2001*.			
PLEASE CHECK ONLY ONE REASON FOR YOUR APPLICATION/APPEAL	**TAX YEAR(S) YOU ARE APPEALING**	**SUPPORTING DOCUMENT(S) YOU MUST ATTACH TO THIS APPLICATION/APPEAL FORM**	**FILING DEADLINE**
☐ Application: section 356.(1)(b) To apportion taxes where land is assessed in a block. Filing for multiple taxation years is considered one application with one filing fee. ☐ The municipality has passed a by-law delegating these applications to the ARB. If not, apply to the municipality instead.	_____ _____ _____ _____ _____	None	No deadline

OR

☐ Appeal: section 356.(6) Appeal a decision that the municipal council made about your application under section 356.(1)(b).	_____	Attach a copy of the decision you received from the municipality. ☐ I have attached a copy.	File within 35 days after council makes its decision.

AND (*Continue to next page to complete the Application/Appeal Information section.***)**

Roll Number: ☐☐☐☐ – ☐☐☐ – ☐☐☐ – ☐☐☐☐☐ – ☐☐☐☐

Part 2: Application/Appeal Information - Continued

Complete this section for applications under section 356.(1)(b) and appeals under section 356.(6).

I have received MPAC's Statement of Relative Value (check the correct answer below).

☐ Yes *If yes, you must enclose a copy of the statement with this application/appeal.*

☐ No *If no, you must include the names, mailing addresses and roll numbers of the new parcel owners (current owners).*

Owner's Name	Owner's Mailing Address	New Parcel Roll Number

If you require more room, please attach additional page(s). If you have attached additional pages, please check here. ☐

Roll Number: ☐☐☐☐☐—☐☐☐—☐☐☐—☐☐☐☐—☐☐☐

Part 3: Applicant/Appellant Information

Do you have a representative? ☐ Yes ☐ No *If yes, complete Parts 3 & 4.*

Are you the owner of the property? ☐ Yes ☐ No

Last name: _____ First name: _____

Company name (if applicable): _____

Mailing address: _____
Street address   Apt/Suite/Unit#   City

_____
Province   Country (if not Canada)   Postal Code

Business/other telephone #: _____ Home telephone #: _____

Fax #: _____ E-mail address: _____

Applicant/appellant signature: _____

Please note: You must notify the Assessment Review Board in writing of any change of address or telephone number.

Personal information requested on this form is collected under the various sections of the *Municipal Act, 2001.* After an application/appeal is filed, all information relating to this application/appeal may become available to the public. For additional information, please contact an ARB Public Inquiry Assistant at (416) 212-6349 or toll free at 1-866-448-2248. The *Municipal Act, 2001* is available at www.elto.gov.on.ca.

Part 4: Representative Authorization

I hereby authorize the named company and/or individual(s) to represent me:

Company name: _____

Last name: _____ First name: _____

Mailing address: _____
Street address   Apt/Suite/Unit#   City

_____
Province   Country (if not Canada)   Postal Code

Telephone #: _____ Fax #: _____

E-mail address: _____

Applicant/appellant signature: _____

Representatives who are NOT legal counsel **must** *confirm that they have* **written authorization** *by checking the box below.*

☐ I certify that I have written authorization from the complainant to act as a representative with respect to this complaint on his or her behalf and I understand that I may be asked to produce this authorization at any time.

Note: Anyone in Ontario providing legal services requires a licence, unless the group or individual is not captured by the Law Society Act or is exempt by a Law Society by-law. By-law 4 exempts persons who are not in the business of providing legal services and occasionally provide assistance to a friend or relative for no fee. For information on licensing please refer to the Law Society of Upper Canada's website www.lsuc.ca or call 416-947-3315 or 1-800-668-7380.

Roll Number: ☐☐☐☐–☐☐☐–☐☐☐–☐☐☐☐☐–☐☐☐☐

Part 5: How to File an Application/Appeal

File your application/appeal using only ONE of the following options:

Mail it to: Assessment Review Board, 655 Bay Street, Suite 1500, Toronto, Ontario M5G 1E5

Fax it to: (416) 314-3717 or 1-877-849-2066 (toll free) (For faxing applications, appeals and complaints only.)

Deliver it in person to: 655 Bay Street, 15th Floor. (East side of Bay Street, north of Dundas)

For additional information, call (416) 212-6349, (toll free) 1-866-448-2248 or visit our website: www.elto.gov.on.ca.

Please file your application/appeal only ONCE. If you are unsure that your filing attempt was successful and resubmit, please mark any other submissions COPY to avoid duplicate charges.

Part 6: Required Filing Fee

Total fee submitted: $_____ by: ☐ Cheque ☐ Money Order OR

Credit card: ☐ Visa ☐ MasterCard ☐ American Express

Credit card #: _____ Expiry date: _____/_____
                                                                        month   year
Cardholder's name: _____

Cardholder's signature: _____

- If you are **not** paying by credit card, the filing fee must be received by cheque or money order, in Canadian funds, payable to the **Minister of Finance.** Please note the applicable roll number(s) on the front of the cheque or money order. **Please do not send cash by mail**.
- If you are paying by VISA, MasterCard or American Express, **the Board will accept a faxed application/appeal with the full credit card information requested above.**
- **Please note that if a financial institution returns your cheque, an administrative fee of $35 will apply.**
- **The fee is non-refundable.**
- You will receive an **Acknowledgement Letter** followed by a **Notice of Hearing.**

The information you fill in under Required Filing Fee is confidential.
It will only be used to process your application/appeal and will not be placed on file.

For office use only:

Fee Received: $_____ ____ Cash ____ Cheque ____ Money order ____ Credit card

Verified by: _____

Appendix 5.5
City of Toronto Act Application/Appeal — Apportionment, s. 322[†]

Environment and Land Tribunals Ontario
Assessment Review Board, 655 Bay Street, Suite 1500, Toronto, Ontario M5G 1E5
Phone: (416) 212-6349 or 1-866-448-2248 **Fax:** (416) 314-3717 or 1-877-849-2066
Website: www.elto.gov.on.ca

CITY OF TORONTO ACT APPLICATION/APPEAL – APPORTIONMENT

Form and Instructions for filing a City of Toronto Act, 2006 application/appeal with the Assessment Review Board and information on how to prepare for your hearing event.

Please note: This form is for City of Toronto Act, 2006 applications/appeals – Apportionment only. Do not use this form to file assessment complaints (sections 33, 34 or 40 of the Assessment Act). Do not use this form for any other applications, appeals and/or complaints under the City of Toronto Act, 2006 or the Municipal Act, 2001. Different forms are available to file the other applications, appeals and complaints. Issues of tax exemption can only be addressed by the Superior Court of Justice.

Before Filing: Please contact the City for information regarding the tax account and the application/appeal process. The ARB can only accept applications under section 322.(1)(b) where the City has passed a by-law that gives the ARB the same authority as municipal council to decide on City of Toronto Act, 2006 applications. Before filing with the ARB, please ensure that the municipality has passed such a by-law.

Required Filing Fee: $25.00 for each roll number. Your application/appeal will not be accepted without the required filing fee.

Filing Deadline: Filing deadlines are established by legislation and cannot be waived by the ARB. Filing deadlines depend on the type of application or appeal you are making.

Important: Please attach to your appeal a copy of the supporting document requested in Part 2 of the appeal form. The ARB cannot determine if your appeal has been filed on time without the supporting document.

Accessibility: We are committed to providing services as set out in the Accessibility for Ontarians with Disabilities Act, 2005. If you have any accessibility needs, please contact our Accessibility Coordinator as soon as possible.

These descriptions are summarized – please refer to the City of Toronto Act, 2006.	
SECTION NUMBER AND APPLICATION/APPEAL REASON	FILING DEADLINE
322.(1)(b) To apportion taxes where land is assessed in a block. Note: Filing for multiple taxation years is considered one application with one filing fee.	No deadline.
322.(5) Appeal a decision that the municipal council made on an application under section 322 (1)(b).	File within 35 days after council makes its decision.

Instructions for filing a City of Toronto Act, 2006 application/appeal with the Assessment Review Board

Part 1: Property Information

Please refer to your municipal property tax bill or property assessment notice when completing this section.

Roll Number: The roll number is a 19-digit number assigned to each property. Please ensure that this number is accurately recorded on each page of the application/appeal form.

Street Address and Property Description: Enter the address of the property for which you are filing a City of Toronto Act, 2006 application/appeal.

Preferred Language: Check the appropriate box indicating your language preference for receiving ARB services, including hearings, notices and other public information materials.

[†] ARB website: City of Toronto Act Appeals <http://www.arb.gov.on.ca/english/Forms/ARBForms.html>. © Queen's Printer for Ontario, 2013.

328 | APPENDIX 5.5

Part 2: Application/Appeal Information

Application/Appeal Reason:
Check the appropriate box to indicate the reason for your application/appeal. Check only one box. Continue moving to the right along the same row to complete the application/appeal. Application can be made under 322.(1)(b) for multiple taxation years.

Taxation Year:
Write in the taxation year(s) that are the subject of your application(s)/appeal.

Supporting Documents:
Supporting documents are required by the Assessment Review Board to determine if your City of Toronto Act, 2006 appeal has been filed within legislated deadlines. Check the appropriate box to indicate you have attached a copy of the supporting document to the appeal form.

If you do not have a copy of your supporting document, do not wait to file the appeal. **Filing deadlines are established by legislation and cannot be waived.** If you do not submit the required document with your appeal, the ARB will send you an Acknowledgement Letter requesting a copy of the required document.

Filing Deadline:
This is the last day a City of Toronto Act, 2006 application/appeal can be filed with the Assessment Review Board. **Filing deadlines are established by legislation and cannot be waived.** Filing deadlines are not the same for all section numbers. It is important that you file your City of Toronto Act, 2006 application/appeal by the deadline indicated for the section number. It will not be accepted after the deadline has passed.

MPAC's Statement of Relative Value:
Check the appropriate box to indicate if you have received a Statement of Relative Value produced by the Municipal Property Assessment Corporation (MPAC). If you have received the Statement of Relative Value, you must enclose a copy of the statement with your application/appeal form.

If you do not have a Statement of Relative Value, please record the name, mailing address and roll number for each of the current owners. The ARB requires this information as the legislation requires that the Board send Notices of Hearing to all parties.

Additional Pages:
If you require more room, please attach additional page(s) and check the box on the bottom line to indicate you have attached additional page(s).

Part 3: Applicant/Appellant Information

Representative:
Check the appropriate box to indicate if you have a representative to act on your behalf with regard to this application/appeal. If you have a representative, please complete Parts 3 and 4 of the form.

Owner:
Check the appropriate box to indicate if you are the owner of the property.

Contact Information:
Provide your contact information including name, address and telephone number(s).

Please note: You must notify the Assessment Review Board in writing of any change of address or telephone number.

Personal information requested on this form is collected under the various sections of the City of Toronto Act, 2006. After an application/appeal is filed, all information relating to this application may become available to the public. For additional information, please contact an ARB Public Inquiry Assistant at (416) 212-6349 or toll free at 1-866-448-2248. The City of Toronto Act, 2006 is available at www.elto.gov.on.ca.

Part 4: Representative Authorization

If you have chosen someone to act on your behalf, please provide their name, address, telephone number, fax number and e-mail address. You will need to sign this section and provide your representative with a copy of the form. If you provided a letter or another form of written authorization for your representative, please make sure the representative checked the box in this section confirming he or she received your written authorization.

Part 5: How to File an Application/Appeal

You can file your application/appeal in a number of ways. Please choose only ONE of the following filing options:

Mail it to: Assessment Review Board, 655 Bay Street, Suite 1500, Toronto, Ontario M5G 1E5

Fax it to: **(416) 314-3717 or 1-877-849-2066** (toll free) (For faxing applications, appeals and complaints only.)

Deliver it in person to: 655 Bay Street, 15th Floor. (East side of Bay Street, north of Dundas.)

Please file only ONCE. If you are unsure that your filing attempt was successful and resubmit, please mark any other submissions COPY to avoid duplicate charges.

You will receive an Acknowledgement Letter by mail once your application/appeal has been received by the ARB followed by a Notice of Hearing once your hearing has been scheduled.

Please note: Once you have filed your City of Toronto Act, 2006 application/appeal, any additional correspondence with the ARB should be copied to all parties.

Part 6: Required Filing Fee

- *If you are faxing your City of Toronto Act, 2006 application/appeal*, payment must be made by VISA, MasterCard or American Express, in Canadian funds. Please include your credit card number, expiry date, cardholder's name and the cardholder's signature.

- *If you are mailing your City of Toronto Act, 2006 application/appeal*, payment can be made by credit card, cheque or money order, in Canadian funds, payable to the **Minister of Finance**. Please note the applicable roll number(s) on the front of the cheque or money order. **Please do not mail cash.** Please note that if a financial institution returns your cheque, an administration fee of $35 will apply.

- *If you are delivering your City of Toronto Act, 2006 application/appeal in person,* payment can be made by cash, cheque, money order, debit card or credit card.

The filing fee is non-refundable. You will receive an **Acknowledgement Letter** in the mail once your application/appeal has been received, followed by a **Notice of Hearing** when your hearing has been scheduled.

The information you fill in under Required Filing Fee is confidential. It will only be used to process your application/appeal and will not be placed on file.

For further information, please contact the Assessment Review Board at 416-212-6349,
toll free at 1-866-448-2248 or online at **www.elto.gov.on.ca**.

How to Prepare for Your Hearing Event

1. Gather the information you require to support your case, including:
   - your initial application to the municipal council and any decision of the municipal council (if you are appealing a decision of municipal council);
   - your property tax bill;
   - any factual information, including documents that you require to support your case.

2. Contact the municipality to discuss your case.

3. Consider how you will present your case to the Board.
   - Decide which documents you will provide to the Board at the hearing.
     - Bring photocopies to the hearing of any documents you would like the Board to consider in support of your case. We suggest three copies of each document: one for the Board, one for the municipality and one for you.
   - Decide whether you will require any witnesses other than yourself to give evidence at the hearing.
     - Contact your witnesses once you receive the Notice of Hearing to inform them of the hearing date, time and location.
     - If necessary, you can obtain a Summons to Witness from the Board's Registrar.
   - Consider whether there is any need for parties to exchange documents prior to the hearing.
     - Request from the municipality copies of any documents they will be relying on to support their position.
     - Prior to the hearing, consider providing the municipality with copies of the documents that you will be relying on at the hearing.

At this point, please remove the instructions (pages 1, 2 & 3) from the following application/appeal form and keep the information on how to prepare for your hearing event.

CITY OF TORONTO ACT APPLICATION/APPEAL – APPORTIONMENT

Ontario

Environment and Land Tribunals Ontario
Assessment Review Board, 655 Bay Street, Suite 1500, Toronto, Ontario M5G 1E5
Phone: (416) 212-6349 or 1-866-448-2248 **Fax:** (416) 314-3717 or 1-877-849-2066
Website: www.elto.gov.on.ca

Application/appeal #	
Receipt #	
Date Stamp	
	For office use only

Please note: This form is for City of Toronto Act, 2006 applications/appeals – Apportionment only. Do not use this form to file assessment complaints (sections 33, 34 or 40 of the Assessment Act). Do not use this form for any other applications, appeals and/or complaints under the City of Toronto Act, 2006 or the Municipal Act, 2001. Different forms are available to file the other applications, appeals and complaints. Issues of tax exemption can only be addressed by the Superior Court of Justice.

Before Filing: Please contact the City for information regarding the tax account and the application/appeal process. The Assessment Review Board (ARB) can only accept applications under section 322.(1)(b) where the municipality has passed a by-law that gives the ARB the same authority as municipal council to decide on City of Toronto Act, 2006 applications. Before filing with the ARB, please ensure that the municipality has passed such a by-law.

Required Filing Fee: $25.00 for each roll number. Your application/appeal will not be accepted without the required filing fee.

Filing Deadline: Filing deadlines are established by legislation and cannot be waived by the ARB. Filing deadlines depend on the type of application or appeal you are making. Please see Part 2 for the filing deadline.

Important: Please attach to this appeal form a copy of the supporting document requested in Part 2. The ARB cannot determine if your appeal has been filed on time without the supporting document.

Accessibility: We are committed to providing services as set out in the Accessibility for Ontarians with Disabilities Act, 2005. If you have any accessibility needs, please contact our Accessibility Coordinator as soon as possible

Part 1: Property Information (Please print clearly)

Roll number: ☐☐☐☐ - ☐☐☐☐ - ☐☐☐☐ - ☐☐☐☐ - ☐☐☐

PLEASE copy this roll number in the space provided at the top of every page of this form

Street address: _____

Municipality: **City of Toronto**

Please choose preferred language: ☐ English ☐ French

Part 2: Application/Appeal Information

These descriptions are summarized – please refer to the City of Toronto Act, 2006.			
PLEASE CHECK ONLY ONE REASON FOR YOUR APPLICATION/APPEAL	**TAX YEAR(S) YOU ARE APPEALING**	**SUPPORTING DOCUMENT(S) YOU MUST ATTACH TO THIS APPLICATION/APPEAL FORM**	**FILING DEADLINE**
☐ Application: section 322.(1)(b) To apportion taxes where land is assessed in a block. Note: Filing for multiple taxation years is considered one application with one filing fee. ☐ The municipality has passed a by-law delegating these applications to the ARB. If not, apply to the municipality instead.	_____ _____ _____ _____ _____	None	No deadline

OR

☐ Appeal: section 322.(5) Appeal a decision that the municipal council made on an application under section 322.(1)(b).	_____	Attach a copy of the decision you received from the municipality. ☐ I have attached a copy.	File within 35 days after council makes its decision.

Continue to next page to complete the Application/Appeal Information section.

ARB-COTA1 – 02.24.2010

Roll Number: ☐☐☐☐☐ – ☐☐☐ – ☐☐☐ – ☐☐☐☐ – ☐☐☐

Part 2: Application/Appeal Information - Continued

Complete this section for applications under section 322 (1)(b) and appeals under section 322 (5).

I have received MPAC's Statement of Relative Value (check the correct answer below).

☐ Yes *If yes, you must enclose a copy of the statement with this application/appeal.*

☐ No *If no, you must include the names, mailing addresses and roll numbers of the new parcel owners (current owners).*

Owner's Name	Owner's Mailing Address	New Parcel Roll Number

If you require more room, please attach additional page(s). If you have attached additional pages, please check here. ☐

Roll Number: ⬚⬚⬚⬚–⬚⬚⬚–⬚⬚⬚⬚–⬚⬚⬚⬚

Part 3: Applicant/Appellant Information

Do you have a representative? ☐ Yes ☐ No **If yes, complete Parts 3 & 4.**

Are you the owner of the property? ☐ Yes ☐ No

Last name: _____ First name: _____

Company name (if applicable): _____

Mailing address: _____
<table>
<tr><td>Street address</td><td>Apt/Suite/Unit#</td><td>City</td></tr>
</table>

<table>
<tr><td>Province</td><td>Country (if not Canada)</td><td>Postal Code</td></tr>
</table>

Business/other telephone #: _____ Home telephone #: _____

Fax #: _____ E-mail address: _____

Applicant/appellant signature: _____

   Please note: You must notify the Assessment Review Board in writing of any change of address or telephone numb er.

Personal information requested on this form is collected under the various sections of the City of Toronto Act, 2006. After an application/appeal is filed, all information relating to this application/appeal may become available to the public. For additional information, please contact an ARB Public Inquiry Assistant at (416) 212-6349or toll free at 1-866-448-2248. The City of Toronto Act, 2006 is available at www.elto.gov.on.ca.

Part 4: Representative Authorization

I hereby authorize the named company and/or individual(s) to represent me:

Company name: _____

Last name: _____ First name: _____

Mailing address: _____
<table>
<tr><td>Street address</td><td>Apt/Suite/Unit#</td><td>City</td></tr>
</table>

<table>
<tr><td>Province</td><td>Country (if not Canada)</td><td>Postal Code</td></tr>
</table>

Telephone #: _____ Fax #: _____

E-mail address: _____

Applicant/appellant signature: _____

*Representatives who are NOT legal counsel **must** confirm that they have **written authorization** by checking the box below.*

☐ I certify that I have written authorization from the complainant to act as a representative with respect to this complaint on his or her behalf and I understand that I may be asked to produce this authorization at any time.

Note: Anyone in Ontario providing legal services requires a licence, unless the group or individual is not captured by the Law Society Act or is exempt by a Law Society by-law. By-law 4 exempts persons who are not in the business of providing legal services and occasionally provide assistance to a friend or relative for no fee. For information on licensing please refe r to the Law Society of Upper Canada's website www.lsuc.ca or call 416-947-3315 or 1-800-668-7380.

Roll Number: ☐☐☐☐☐ - ☐☐☐ - ☐☐☐ - ☐☐☐☐☐ - ☐☐☐☐

Part 5: How to File an Application/Appeal

File your application/appeal using only ONE of the following options:

Mail it to: Assessment Review Board, 655 Bay Street, Suite 1500, Toronto, Ontario M5G 1E5

Fax it to: (416) 314-3717 or 1-877-849-2066 (toll free) (For faxing applications, appeals and complaints only.)

Deliver it in person to: 655 Bay Street, 15th Floor. (East side of Bay Street, north of Dundas)

For additional information, call (416) 212-6349, (toll free) 1-866-448-2248 or visit our website: www.elto.gov.on.ca.

Please file your application/appeal only ONCE. If you are unsure that your filing attempt was successful and resubmit, please mark any other submissions COPY to avoid duplicate charges.

Part 6: Required Filing Fee

Total fee submitted: $_____   by: ☐ Cheque   ☐ Money Order   OR

Credit card: ☐ Visa   ☐ MasterCard   ☐ American Express

Credit card #: _____   Expiry date: _____/_____
                                                                                                                    month   year

Cardholder's name: _____

Cardholder's signature: _____

- If you are **not** paying by credit card, the filing fee must be received by cheque or money order, in Canadian funds, payable to the **Minister of Finance.** Please note the applicable roll number(s) on the front of the cheque or money order. **Please do not send cash by mail.**
- If you are paying by VISA, MasterCard or American Express, **the Board will accept a faxed application/appeal with the full credit card information requested above.**
- **Please note that if a financial institution returns your cheque, an administrative fee of $35 will apply.**
- **The fee is non-refundable.**
- You will receive an **Acknowledgement Letter** followed by a **Notice of Hearing.**

The information you fill in under Required Filing Fee is confidential.
It will only be used to process your application/appeal and will not be placed on file.

For office use only:

Fee Received: $_____   ____ Cash   ____ Cheque   ____ Money order   ____ Credit card

Verified by: _____

Appendix 5.6
Your Guide to the ARB[†]

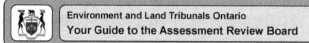

Environment and Land Tribunals Ontario
Your Guide to the Assessment Review Board

Contents	Pages

[†] ARB website: Publications <http://elto.gov.on.ca/wp-content/uploads/2015/08/ARB-Guide.pdf>. © Queen's Printer for Ontario, 2013.

Part I – Overview

About the Assessment Review Board

The Assessment Review Board (ARB) is an independent adjudicative tribunal that hears appeals about property assessments and classification. The ARB also deals with some Municipal Act and City of Toronto Act appeals. In a court-like setting, ARB Members hear appeals and makes decisions based on the law and the evidence presented at the hearing.

The ARB does not prepare or send out property assessment notices. The Municipal Property Assessment Corporation (MPAC) assesses all properties in Ontario.

ARB contact information:

The ARB 's address:
655 Bay Street, Suite 1500
Toronto, ON M5G 1E5

Website: www.elto.gov.on.ca
E-mail:
assessment.review.board@ontario.ca

To fax the ARB:
Toll Free: 1-877-849-2066 –
From Toronto: (416) 314-3717

To call the ARB:
Toll Free: 1-800-263-3237
From Toronto: (416) 314-6900

The ARB 's office hours:
Monday-Friday 8:30 a.m. – 5 p.m.
*Excluding statutory holidays

History

In 1970, the Province began issuing property assessments and replaced the Courts of Revision with the Assessment Review Court (ARC). ARC was renamed the Assessment Review Board (ARB) in 1983. When the Fair Municipal Finance Act, 1997, came into affect, the ARB became the Province's only adjudicative tribunal for property assessment appeals. Before 1998, ARB decisions could be appealed to the Ontario Municipal Board (OMB).

Decisions by the Board are final and binding, subject only to appeal to Divisional Court on a question of law when the Court grants leave to appeal. The Board also may review its decisions.

New legislation has been introduced for the 2009 tax year. This legislation introduced several changes to the assessment appeal process. This Guide has been produced to help you better understand some of the changes.

Jurisdiction

The Board's jurisdiction and its authority are defined by the Assessment Review Board Act, the Assessment Act, the Municipal Act, 2001, the City of Toronto Act, 2006, The Provincial Land Tax Act, 2006, the Education Act and the Statutory Powers Procedure Act.

ARB's Rules of Practice and Procedure

Made under section 25.1 of the Statutory Powers Procedure Act, the ARB's Rules of Practice and Procedure apply to all proceedings before the Assessment Review Board. It is recommended that any person who has dealings with the Board, review the Rules before attending a Board proceeding. The Rules can be viewed and printed from the ARB website free of charge. A hard copy of the Rules can be requested from the ARB's Public Inquiry office. There is a fee for a hard copy version of the rules.

Property assessment system in Ontario

The above diagram illustrates the major participants in the property assessment system of Ontario. The provincial government, through the Ministry of Finance, sets the laws on property assessment. Municipalities are responsible for setting tax rates and collecting property taxes. The Municipal Property Assessment Corporation (MPAC) assesses and classifies all properties in Ontario. When MPAC makes a decision about a property assessment that the owner does not agree with, the owner may file an appeal with the Assessment Review Board (ARB). MPAC and the ARB are two different organizations. The ARB process is described in this Guide.

Matters heard at the ARB

1. Assessment Act appeals
These appeals are made under sections 32, 33, 34 and 40 of the Assessment Act. Usually, reasons for these appeals include:

- A wrong property assessment (for example, if you believe your assessment is too high)
- A wrong property classification (for example, if you believe the current use of your land is not correctly classified)
- To correct factual errors in the assessment roll

2. Tax appeals
These appeals deal with the amount of taxes for a property. If the property is in the City of Toronto, the appeal is made under the City of Toronto Act, 2006. If the property is in any other municipality in the province, the appeal is made under Municipal Act, 2001. For properties outside of municipalities such as in unorganized territories, the appeal is made under the Provincial Land Tax Act, 2006. Usually, these appeals are against a decision made by the municipality about a tax

2

matter. In some cases, the municipality has passed a bylaw directing applications to be filed directly with the ARB. Ask your municipality about their process before filing with the ARB.

Part II – ARB Process

Filing assessment appeals

The Municipal Property Assessment Corporation (MPAC) assesses all properties in Ontario. MPAC is responsible for sending out the Property Assessment Notice. This notice tells you the assessed value of your property and your property class. **The process of filing an assessment appeal to the ARB depends on your property class.**

If your property, or a portion of it, is classified as **residential, farm*, conservation land* or managed forest***:
1) You MUST file a Request for Reconsideration (RFR) with MPAC first.
2) You MUST receive a RFR decision BEFORE filing an appeal with the ARB.
3) Your deadline to file with the ARB is 90 days from the mailing date of MPAC's Notice of Decision.

*Properties that are classed as farms, managed forests or conservation lands, may be eligible for special tax class programs. If you have issues with eligibility for these programs, you must first file a RFR with the Program Administrator. MPAC does NOT administer these programs. After you receive a RFR decision from the Program Administrator, you may appeal that decision to the ARB. See the ARB website for information on these property tax class programs.

If your property, or a portion of it, is classified as **any other property class:**
1) You may file a RFR with MPAC **or** you may file an appeal with the ARB.
2) If you file a RFR with MPAC first and do not agree with the RFR decision from MPAC, you may then file an appeal with the ARB. Your deadline to file with the ARB is 90 days from the mailing date on the RFR decision.
3) If you file with the ARB first, your deadline to file with the ARB is March 31 of the tax year.

If you are **not the property owner**, you must file your appeal with the ARB first and send a copy of the appeal form to the property owner by the filing deadline.

How to file your appeal

E File

You can file your appeal online using **E File** on the ARB website, www.elto.gov.on.ca. E Filing is a quick and easy way to file your ARB appeal. After you submit the online form, you will receive an e-mail confirming your appeal has been received. Processing time is also quicker since all the necessary information is automatically stored in the ARB's databse. You must have a credit card to file online. E Filed appeals receive a $10 discount to the filing fee.

Forms

If you are not E Filing your appeal, you may fill out a form and send it to the Board. This form is available on the ARB website (and at its office) and may be available through some MPAC offices, municipal offices and Government Information Centres.

Once the form has been filled out, you can send the form by fax or mail, or deliver it in person to the Assessment Review Board (see the beginning of this Guide for ARB contact information).

Filing Fees

There is a fee to file an ARB appeal. Please contact the Board or check the Board's website for the current fee amount.

Fees are payable by cheque, money order or major credit card (VISA, Master Card, American Express) and must be in Canadian funds. Cheques and money orders should be made payable to the "Minister of Finance" and should include the roll number of the property on the front of the cheque or money order. If hand-delivering an appeal, payment can also be made by cash or by debit. **There are no refunds of filing fees.**

Filing tax applications or appeals

To file a tax application or appeal, make sure to use the right form. The forms are available at ARB's offices and on the ARB website. The may also be available through some Government Information Centres and municipal offices.

These types of appeals can be sent to the Board via mail, fax or in person. Tax appeals cannot be E Filed. Filing fees for these types of appeals depend on the type of appeal being filed. The forms used for filing tax appeals indicate the correct filing fee. A listing of the ARB's filing fees may be found on the ARB website or by contacting the ARB.

After filing with the ARB

After filing your appeal, the ARB will send you an acknowledgment letter in the mail. If the appeal is E Filed, the acknowledgment of receipt is sent by e-mail immediately after submitting. A Notice of Hearing will be sent to you in the mail once your hearing date has been scheduled. Hearings are normally held in the municipality closest to the location of the property.

E Calendar

E Calendar allows you to search for ARB hearing dates on the website www.elto.gov.on.ca. Using E Calendar, you can view the hearings scheduled in a particular month and municipality. Only current information is available. Previous months hearing dates are not listed on E-Calendar.

E Status

E Status is a feature on the ARB website that allows you to find out the status of an appeal. Using the 19-digit roll number, you can view information such as the date, time and location of a hearing, as well as and what parties are involved in the hearing.

Adjournments

An adjournment is a delay of a hearing date. After receiving a Notice of Hearing, you should be prepared to attend the hearing. However, if you cannot attend, you may request that the hearing be adjourned (delayed) to a later date. Your request should:

- Be sent to the Board, in writing, as soon as you know an adjournment is needed;
- Include the reasons for the adjournment;
- Include proof that the other parties involved (i.e. MPAC and the municipality) agree to the adjournment.

Just sending your request to the Board does NOT mean that your hearing will be adjourned. The Board does not always grant adjournment requests. The Board will inform you of its decision on your request. You are expected to attend your hearing unless the Board informs you of any changes to your hearing date. Failure to show up for your hearing could result in your case being dismissed.

If you must make a last minute request to adjourn, please contact the Board right away to discuss your reasons. For more information about adjournments, please see the ARB's Rules of Practice and Procedure.

Withdrawals

To withdraw an ARB appeal, you must send a letter or fill out a withdrawal form and send it to the Board by fax, mail or e-mail. In the letter, include your name, address, the property roll number, and the reason for the withdrawal. A withdrawal form is available for download on the ARB website. After the withdrawal request is received the ARB will review it. If the request is granted, the Board will forward an acknowledgement of withdrawal to everyone involved in the matter and the file will be closed.

Case Managed Stream

If you did not file a Request for Reconsideration (RFR) with the Municipal Property Assessment Corporation (MPAC) and your property is above a certain assessed value, your appeal will be scheduled into the case managed stream. This process is meant to clarify issues and procedures before a full hearing of an appeal begins.

For more information about the case managed stream, please see the ARB's Rules of Practice and Procedure. The Rules are available on the Board's website.

Hearings

It is important that you come prepared to your ARB hearing. The hearing is your opportunity to explain why you think your property assessment is wrong. Although it is MPAC's responsibility to explain its valuation of your property, **you should still bring evidence to support your case**.

Appeals are usually called on a first come, first-served basis. When you arrive to the hearing, you must sign an attendance sheet. The order of the sign-in sheet is the order the appeals are called. Once your appeal is called, the hearing will usually follow the process outlined below.

5

1. MPAC will describe the property, explain how the assessment was made and present evidence.
2. You may question MPAC about their evidence.
3. You will have a chance to present your evidence and explain why you think the assessment is wrong.
4. MPAC may question you or any of your witnesses.
5. If the municipality is taking part in the hearing, its representative will also be given the opportunity to give evidence and question witnesses.
6. MPAC will summarize their case.
7. You will summarize your case.
8. MPAC will give their closing statement.
9. You will give your closing statement. As the appellant, you have the right to make the final closing statement.
10. The ARB Member gives an oral decision OR reserves the decision (meaning the Member will make the decision at a later date. In this case, an explanation of the decision called **Written Reasons** will be mailed to you.)
11. If you own a farm, managed forest or conservation land properties and are seeking a special tax classification, the ARB Member will refer the appeal for a further hearing. Your appeal is sent to the Agriculture Food Rural Affairs Appeals Tribunal (AFRAAT) if the property is a farm, or to the Mining and Lands Commissioner if the property is a managed forest or a conservation land.

For more information on hearings, please see the ARB's *Rules of Practice*.

PART III – Preparing for a hearing

Using a representative

When you come to the Board for your appeal, you can represent yourself or have someone else represent you. If you choose to have someone else represent you, you must provide the Board with your representative's name, address, telephone number, fax number and e-mail. ARB appeal forms include a section for collecting this information. It is your responsibility to make sure that the Board receives your authorization of representation before the hearing.

Note: anyone in Ontario providing legal services requires a licence, unless the person is not captured by the Law Society Act or is exempt by a Law Society by-law. By-law 4 exempts persons who are not in the business of providing legal services and occasionally provide assistance to a friend or relative for no fee. For information on licensing please refer to the Law Society of Upper Canada's website www.lsuc.ca or call 416-947-3315 or 1-800-668-7380.

Gathering Evidence

A hearing is **your** chance to explain **why you think your property assessment is wrong**. Your evidence and the evidence presented by the other parties will be used by the Board to **make a decision on your appeal**. Some examples of evidence that would be useful for you to bring are listed below (this is not an exclusive list, you may bring other evidence that you think would best support your case).

☐ Your property's location, lot size, square footage, number of stories and building age, amenities, condition, etc.

☐ Comparable properties' lot sizes, square footages, number of stories and building ages

☐ Sales information for your property and the comparable properties*

☐ Assessed values of your property and comparable properties

☐ Photographs of your property and comparable properties

* If current sales information is not available, the ARB may consider sales figures from other years.

It is important that ALL documents you plan to use as evidence be exchanged between parties AT LEAST 21 days before the hearing date. You must also make sure to bring **two extra** copies of all documents to the hearing.

These are some suggestions on where to find evidence to support your case:

- Through MPAC – call 1-866-296-6722 or visit online at www.mpac.ca
- Your municipal office (town hall or city hall)
- Land registry offices

See the ARB brochure "Preparing for your Hearing" for more information.

Part IV – After the Hearing

Decisions

At the Hearing

After all parties have had a chance to provide the Member with their evidence, the Member will summarize the evidence and give an oral decision. In some cases, the Member may need more time to consider the evidence and may reserve the decision to a later date. If the decision is reserved, a decision with Written Reasons will be mailed to the parties.

If an oral decision is given at the hearing, a written confirmation of the decision will be mailed to the parties after the hearing. If a request for Written Reasons is made, the decision will be sent with the Written Reasons.

Written Reasons

Any party may request Written Reasons for a Member's decision. Written Reasons outline why the Member made his or her decision. To request Written Reasons, you must ask for them at the hearing or make a request, in writing, to the Board within 14 days of the hearing date.

Review a Decision

The Board's Rules of Practice and Procedure provide guidelines for reviewing decisions. It is not an opportunity to rehear or reargue an appeal. For the Board to consider reviewing a decision, it may take into consideration:

- Whether a material error of law or fact was made, which, if corrected, would have a significant effect on the decision;
- Whether any other person has relied upon or acted on the decision; and
- Whether the rights of a party other than the requester will be prejudiced if the decision is changed.

To request a Review of Decision, a party must have requested Written Reasons for the decision. When you send in your request to the ARB for a review of your decision, you must include:
1.   A copy of the Written Reasons;
2.   An affidavit of the facts and reasons for your request;
3.   A $125 filing fee, per property (this fee is not refundable).

Appeal a Decision

A decision of the Board may be appealed to the Superior Court of Justice (Divisional Court) only on a question of law. To start the process of appealing, you must apply to the Court and seek leave to appeal. People usually consult legal counsel to explore this option.

Please Note

The information contained in this Guide is not intended as a substitute for legal or other advice, and in providing this information, the Assessment Review Board (ARB) assumes no responsibility for any errors or omissions and shall not be liable for any reliance placed on the information in this Guide. Additional information, including the ARB's Rules of Practice and Procedure, is available at www.elto.gov.on.ca, or by calling (416) 314-6900 or 1-800-263-3237.

The Assessment Review Board (ARB) is an independent adjudicative tribunal established by the Province of Ontario to hear appeals from persons who believe there is an error in the assessed value or classification of a property. The ARB, which operates under a variety of legislation including the Assessment Act, also deals with some types of property tax appeals under the Municipal Act and City of Toronto Act, 2006 and the Provincial Land Tax Act, 2006.

Produced by:
Assessment Review Board
655 Bay Street, Suite 1500, Toronto, ON M5G 1E5
Tel (416) 314-6900 or toll free 1-800-263-3237
Fax (416) 314-3717 or toll free 1-877-849-2066

Appendix 5.7
Preparing for Your Hearing at the ARB[†]

 Environment and Land Tribunals Ontario
Assessment Review Board   **Information Sheet 5**

Here's what you need to know about preparing for your hearing

This Information Sheet can be helpful to you if:
- You filed an appeal to the ARB and received an acknowledgment letter.
- You would like information on how to prepare for your ARB hearing.
- You would like information about the ARB hearing process.

If you have filed an ARB appeal, it is important that you prepare for your hearing. An ARB hearing is **your chance to explain why you think your property assessment from the Municipal Property Assessment Corporation (MPAC) is wrong**. This Information Sheet outlines what happens before your hearing, at your hearing and after your hearing.   If you have not yet appealed to the Board, please see our Information Sheet "***Here's what you need to know about filing your assessment appeal with the ARB***".

BEFORE YOUR HEARING

1. The ARB will send you a letter of acknowledgement for your appeal.
2. When scheduled, you will receive a Notice of Hearing telling you the date, time and location of your hearing.
3. You should begin to prepare for your hearing by collecting evidence to show why you think your property assessment from MPAC is wrong.

Why do I need to bring evidence to my hearing?

The ARB's decision on your appeal is based on **evidence and the law**. At the hearing, MPAC in most cases has the burden of proof to explain and defend their assessment of your property. However, **you should plan to explain why you think your assessment is wrong**. To support your case, you should bring evidence to your hearing.

What evidence should I bring to my hearing?

Listed here are some suggestions on the type of evidence you could bring to your hearing. You may also bring **any other evidence** that you think will best support your appeal.

Evidence about your property AND comparable properties could include:

- Assessed value
- Previous *sales information
- Location
- Lot size and square footage
- Number of stories
- Building age and condition
- Photographs
- Amenities

[†] ARB website: Information Sheet 5 <http://elto.gov.on.ca/wp-content/uploads/2015/12/ARB-InfoSheet5-PrepareForHearing.pdf>. © Queen's Printer for Ontario, 2013.

*Sales information should include property details (such as the ones listed above) and be as close to the valuation date as possible. For example, the valuation date for the tax years 2013-2016 is January 1, 2012. So your comparable properties' sales information should be from as close to January 1, 2012 as possible.

The Board requires that any documents you plan to use as evidence be exchanged among parties AT LEAST 21 days before the hearing date. Also, make sure to bring **two extra copies** of all documents to the hearing.

Where can I find the evidence I need to bring to my hearing?

Below are some suggestions on where to look for your evidence.

- MPAC – call 1-866-296-6722 or go online to www.mpac.ca
- Your municipal office (town hall or city hall)
- Land registry offices
- Local Realtor or Multiple Listing Service
- Accredited Appraisal Service

What if I can't make it to my hearing?

You should always be ready to attend your hearing, but if you or your representative cannot make it to the hearing, you must ask the Board for an adjournment (a delay). Your request should:

- Be sent to the Board, **in writing**, as soon as you know an adjournment is needed
- Include the reasons for the adjournment
- Include proof that the other parties involved (i.e. MPAC and the municipality) agree to the adjournment

The Board will let you know if your request is approved. **You are still expected to be at your hearing unless the Board approves the adjournment.** If you do not show up for your hearing, your appeal could be dismissed.

What if I change my mind and don't want to appeal?

You can always withdraw your appeal before the hearing. A withdrawal form is available on the ARB website or by calling the Board. Fill out the form and send it to the Board by mail, fax or e-mail. **There are no refunds of the filing fee.**

How do I find out if the hearing venue is easily accessible?

We are committed to providing services as set out in the Accessibility for Ontarians with Disabilities Act, 2005. If you have any accessibility needs, please contact our Accessibility Coordinator as soon as possible.

AT YOUR HEARING

1. When you arrive at the hearing venue, you should sign the attendance sheet.
2. The hearing starts when the ARB Member gives his or her opening remarks. These remarks briefly describe the Board, the law that applies to your assessment and the process for the day's hearing.
3. Appeals are called, usually in the order listed on the sign-in sheet.

Who will be at my hearing?

The people who participate in your hearing - also called parties – include you (or your representative), MPAC and the municipality. The municipality may choose not to participate in a hearing. An ARB Member presides over the hearing and makes the final decision. Hearings are normally open to the public and anyone may watch an ARB hearing.

Can I have an interpreter at my hearing?

Most ARB hearings are held in English. The ARB provides services in French on request, and can provide a sign language interpreter on request. If you would like to have someone at your hearing interpret for you in any other language, you may bring someone with you for that purpose.

What happens during my hearing?

Once your appeal is called, the hearing will usually follow the process outlined below:

1. MPAC will describe the property, explain how the assessment was made and present evidence.
2. You may question MPAC about their evidence.
3. You will have a chance to present your evidence and explain why you think the assessment is wrong.
4. MPAC may question you or any of your witnesses.
5. If the municipality is taking part in the hearing, its representative will also be given the opportunity to give evidence and question witnesses.
6. You will give your closing statement. As the property owner, you have the right to make the final closing statement.
7. The ARB Member may give an oral decision OR reserve the decision (meaning the Member will make the decision at a later date. In this case, an explanation of the decision called **Written Reasons** will be provided to you.)
8. If you own a farm, managed forest or conservation land properties and are seeking a special tax classification, the ARB Member will refer the appeal for a further hearing. Your appeal may be sent to the Agriculture Food Rural Affairs Appeals Tribunal (AFRAAT) if the property is a farm, or to the Ministry of Natural Resources and Forestry if the property is a managed forest or a conservation land.

For more information on hearings, please see the Board's *Rules of Practice*.

AFTER THE HEARING

1. A copy of the Board's decision on your appeal will be sent to you in the mail (usually the decision is also announced orally at the hearing).
2. You may request Written Reasons, which is a detailed explanation of how your decision was made, by writing to the Board within 14 days of your hearing. You may also ask for Written Reasons at the end of your hearing.
3. You will have a limited amount of time to dispute the decision, **and may do so only under very specific circumstances.**

What can I do if I disagree with the Board's decision?

You may, within 30 days of the release of Written Reasons, ask the ARB to review the decision. A review of an ARB decision is granted only under **very specific circumstances**. For the ARB to even consider a review, you must:

- Ask for **Written Reasons** within 14 days of your hearing date
- Submit a **non-refundable** $125 filing fee by cheque or money order, made payable to the Minister of Finance
- Submit an **affidavit** outlining the reasons for the request to review.

A decision of the Board may be appealed, within 30 days of its release, to the Superior Court of Justice (Divisional Court) **only on a question of law**. For more information on decision reviews and appeals, please read the ARB's Rules of Practice and Procedure, available on the ARB website.

How will the decision from the ARB affect my property assessment and taxes?

Copies of the ARB decision are also sent to MPAC and to the municipality. MPAC will issue a revised notice of phase-in calculations. The municipality is responsible for any changes to your property taxes resulting from the ARB decision. Please contact your municipality with any questions about your property taxes.

How do I contact the ARB?

Please review the ARB's website, **www.elto.gov.on.ca**, for more information about the ARB process. You can also contact the Board by:

Phone: (416) 212-6349 or toll free 1-866-448-2248 **Fax:** (416) 314-3717 or 1-800-849-2066
E-mail: assessment.review.board@ontario.ca
In person or by mail: 655 Bay street, 15th Floor, Toronto, ON M5G 1E5

Useful terms

Affidavit: A legal document containing written evidence that you swear to be true. It must be sworn and/or affirmed by a Notary Public or Commissioner.

Adjournment: To postpone or delay a hearing for another date.

Comparable Properties: These are properties in your neighbourhood that could be similar to your property. Some areas to compare for similarities are the location, lot size, living area, age and the quality of the property.

Current Value: This is, generally, the amount a willing buyer would pay a willing seller for a property.

Disclosure Rule: The Board expects that any documents you plan to use as evidence be exchanged between the parties AT LEAST 21 days before the hearing date.

MPAC: The Municipal Property Assessment Corporation is the organization that assesses and classifies properties in Ontario. MPAC and the ARB are two separate organizations. Questions about your assessment should be directed to MPAC at 1-866-296-6722.

Parties: These are the people/organizations that are involved in your appeal. Usually, the parties include you (or your representative), MPAC and the municipality.

Written Reasons: These explain how the ARB Member made his or her decision on your appeal. Written Reasons are only prepared on request or when the ARB Member reserves the decision for a later date.

A full glossary of useful ARB terms is on the ARB website, **www.elto.gov.on.ca**.

Please Note

The information contained in this sheet is not intended as a substitute for legal or other advice, and in providing this information, the Assessment Review Board (ARB) assumes no responsibility for any errors or omissions and shall not be liable for any reliance placed on the information in this sheet. Additional information, including the **ARB's Rules of Practice and Procedure**, is available at **www.elto.gov.on.ca**, or by calling (416) 212-6349 or toll free 1-866-448-2248.

The **Environment and Land Tribunals Ontario (ELTO)** includes the Assessment Review Board, Board of Negotiation, Conservation Review Board, Environmental Review Tribunal, Ontario Municipal Board, Niagara Escarpment Hearing Office and the Office of Consolidated Hearings. The Tribunals operate under specific legislative requirements and share resources and best practices. The Assessment Review Board hears appeals from persons who believe there is an error in the assessed value or classification of a property and also deals with some types of property tax appeals under the Municipal Act and City of Toronto Act. For more information contact us at:

Environment and Land Tribunals Ontario
655 Bay Street, Suite 1500, Toronto, ON M5G 1E5
Telephone: (416) 212-6349 or toll free: 1-866-448-2248
Website: **www.elto.gov.on.ca**

ISBN 0-7794-5789-X / © Queen's printer for Ontario, 2015

Disponible en français: Voici que vous devez savoir au sujet du remboursement de vos dépenses

Appendix 5.8
Information Sheet and FAQ on Municipal Act Appeals[†]

	Environment and Land Tribunals Ontario	
	Assessment Review Board	**Information Sheet 1**

Here's what you need to know about Municipal Act appeals

The ARB hears some appeals under the Municipal Act, 2001. These appeals deal with the **amount of the taxes** for a property. Usually, these appeals are against a decision made by the municipality about a tax matter.

What is the difference between a Municipal Act appeal and an assessment appeal?

A Municipal Act appeal deals with how the municipality calculates taxes for a specific property. It is made under the Municipal Act, 2001. An assessment appeal deals with your property assessment from the Municipal Property Assessment Corporation (MPAC). It is made under the Assessment Act.

How do I file a Municipal Act appeal with the Assessment Review Board (ARB)?

To file your appeal, follow the steps below.
1. Contact the municipality. Generally, Municipal Act applications are made to the municipality first. In some cases, the municipality has passed a bylaw directing applications to be filed directly with the ARB. Ask the municipality about their process before filing with the ARB.
2. Wait for a decision from the municipality on your Municipal Act application (in certain sections of the legislation you can also appeal to the Board if the municipality has not made a decision on your application within a specific amount of time.)
3. If you disagree with the decision the municipality made about your application, you may be able to appeal that decision to the ARB.
4. File your appeal using the correct appeal form as it provides specific information about filing fees and deadlines. These forms are available on the ARB website, **www.elto.gov.on.ca**.

After filling out the correct form, send it to the Board, **before the deadline**, along with the required filing fee.

- **By fax**: 416-314-3717 or 1-877-849-2066
- **By mail:** 655 Bay Street, 15th Floor, Toronto ON, M5G 1E5
- **In person:** 655 Bay Street, 15th Floor, Toronto (on Bay, north of Dundas)

Note: that to file an application for extreme poverty or illness you need to contact your municipality first.

What are the Board's filing fees?

The filing fees for Municipal Act appeals depend on the type of appeal you are filing. Check the appeal form for the correct filing fee, or contact the Board at (416) 212-6349 or 1-866-448-2248 for more information. There are no refunds of appeal filing fees.

[†] ARB website: Municipal Act Appeals <http://elto.gov.on.ca/arb/appeal-process/filing-an-appeal/municipal-act-appeals/>. © Queen's Printer for Ontario, 2013.

Is filing a Municipal Act appeal the only way to deal with this issue?

You can try contacting the municipality's finance or tax department.

Can anyone file a Municipal Act appeal?

The legislation and the type of appeal determine who can file a Municipal Act appeal. Please check the specific legislation.

What are the deadlines for filing Municipal Act appeals?

Filing deadlines for Municipal Act appeals are set by the legislation and cannot be waived. The deadlines are listed on the Municipal Act appeal forms.

What happens after I file my appeal with the Board?

The Board will send you a letter acknowledging that your appeal was received. If anything is missing from your appeal (i.e. supporting documents or filing fee), the Board will request the missing items in the letter. Supporting documents are needed to confirm the appeal was filed on time.

After the appeal is entered into the Board's system, a hearing event for your matter will be scheduled. You will receive a notice in the mail telling you the date, time and location of the hearing.

How do I prepare for my hearing?

The hearing is your chance to prove why you believe the municipality's decision was wrong. It is important that you back up your case with evidence. Types of evidence may include:

- Your initial application
- Any decisions made by the municipality
- Your tax bill
- Other factual information that supports your position

Do I have to be at my hearing?

Unless you have someone to represent you at a hearing, you must attend your hearing. If you do not attend, the Board may dismiss your appeal. If you know that you will be unable to attend, you must send the Board a request to adjourn the hearing. More information about adjournments is provided on the website.

What happens when my hearing is finished?

At the end of your hearing the ARB Member that heard your case may give an oral decision or the Member may reserve the decision for a later date. The decision will be sent to you in the mail. More information about decisions is provided on the website.

Please Note

The information contained in this sheet is not intended as a substitute for legal or other advice, and in providing this information, the Assessment Review Board (ARB) assumes no responsibility for any errors or omissions and shall not be liable for any reliance placed on the information in this sheet. Additional information, including the **ARB's Rules of Practice and Procedure**, is available at **www.elto.gov.on.ca**, or by calling (416) 212-6349 or toll free 1-866-448-2248.

The **Environment and Land Tribunals Ontario (ELTO)** includes the Assessment Review Board, Board of Negotiation, Conservation Review Board, Environmental Review Tribunal, Ontario Municipal Board, Niagara Escarpment Hearing Office and the Office of Consolidated Hearings. The Tribunals operate under specific legislative requirements and share resources and best practices. The Assessment Review Board hears appeals from persons who believe there is an error in the assessed value or classification of a property and also deals with some types of property tax appeals under the Municipal Act and City of Toronto Act. For more information contact us at:

Environment and Land Tribunals Ontario
655 Bay Street, Suite 1500, Toronto, ON M5G 1E5
Telephone: (416) 212-6349 or toll free: 1-866-448-2248
Website: **www.elto.gov.on.ca**

ISBN 0-7794-5789-X / © Queen's printer for Ontario, 2015

Disponible en français: Voici que vous devez savoir au sujet du report d'une audience (ajournements)

Human Rights Tribunal of Ontario

6

WHAT THIS CHAPTER OFFERS

- The background of the Human Rights Tribunal of Ontario (HRTO)
- A discussion of the Social Justice Tribunals Ontario (SJTO) and its impact on the HRTO
- Details and explanation of the enabling statutes and regulations relevant to the HRTO
- Provisions of the *Statutory Powers Procedure Act* relevant to the HRTO
- Concepts of public policy relevant to the HRTO and the Human Rights Legal Support Centre
- Specific rules and procedures for the HRTO
- A walk-through of the HRTO website
- Summaries of relevant cases and decisions highlighting legal principles or issues in question
- A flow chart summarizing the procedural stages of an appeal before the HRTO

LEARNING OBJECTIVES

After reading this chapter, the reader should be able to:

- state the legislation that governs the operation of the HRTO
- research the HRTO website for important information needed to understand the agency's practices and procedures and to represent a client properly before the HRTO
- compare and prioritize the various sources of practice and procedure of the HRTO

- apply the specific rules and procedures in a proceeding before, during, and after a hearing of the HRTO
- argue the law before the HRTO using appropriate legislation and case law

INTRODUCTION

The Human Rights Tribunal of Ontario (HRTO) is an independent adjudicative body. As of June 30, 2008, an individual who wants to make a discrimination claim will file an application at the HRTO. The HRTO, in addition to the courts and other Ontario tribunals, has jurisdiction to exercise the powers conferred under the Ontario *Human Rights Code*, R.S.O. 1990, c. H.19, as amended (*Code*), to be the decision-making body for all applications claiming a violation of human rights under the *Code*.

OVERVIEW AND BACKGROUND

On June 30, 2008, the scheme of making applications in respect of alleged breaches of the *Code* was changed from a system where complaints were made to the Human Rights Commission of Ontario (HRCO), which would investigate and then refer some complaints to the HRTO, to a system where any person could make application directly to the HRTO. On the home page of the HRTO website at the time of the change, the Chair of the HRTO notes that a major reason for the change is the fact that under the previous system "the enforcement procedures can be extremely time consuming and costly for the parties" and that the new system may change that. This reason for change continues to be the reason for the 2009 tribunal clustering.

The major changes brought in by the 2008 amended *Code* could be summarized as follows:

- Refocusing the role of the Ontario Human Rights Commission to working on public interests, such as systemic or root causes of discrimination
- Directing complaints to the Human Rights Tribunal of Ontario
- Creating the Human Rights Legal Support Centre to provide advice, support, and representation for some applicants

The Human Rights Legal Support Centre has its own website, and anyone making application to the HRTO should study its content. The Centre's services include legal assistance in filing an application at the HRTO and legal representation at mediations and hearings. It may provide opportunities for employment for paralegals and may also become a legal resource for persons claiming discrimination under the *Code*.

On August 9, 2010, the following notice appeared on the HRTO's "What's New" Web page:

> In December 2009, the *Adjudicative Tribunals Accountability, Governance and Appointments Act, 2009* received Royal Assent. The Act allows government to cluster tribunals and agencies with common stakeholders and related issues in order to improve public services.
>
> The clustering initiative promotes the best use of resources through cross-agency cooperation and coordination of operations and administration. It will also enhance consistency in tribunal practices, procedures and decision making.

This was the beginning of a cluster similar to the cluster of tribunals already formed that included the ARB, as set out in Chapter 5. That cluster, called the SJTO, has been in existence since 2010 and is discussed in the preamble to Part II of this text and also within this chapter.

On Friday, June 11, 2010, the Ontario Bar Association, Continuing Legal Education department held a seminar (one of a series of annual seminars) entitled "Ontario's Human Rights System: Keeping on Top of Key Developments", which the author attended. At the seminar, presenters such as then acting chair of the HRTO, David Wright, spoke. Many of the presented papers were included in the seminar binder and should be available from the Ontario Bar Association. Specifically, Mr. Wright provided figures for the number of hearings in the year before, and these figures appeared in the 2008/09 Annual Report posted on the website. Similar seminars have occurred at the Ontario Bar Association since the one referred to in this paragraph.

ENABLING LEGISLATION

The jurisdiction and authority of the HRTO are defined by the *Code* (which created the HRTO and sets out a few procedural rules), while the *Statutory Powers Procedure Act* is a statute of general application, which imposes minimum rules of procedure and ties the HRTO Rules that have been published into the process. Set out below is a discussion of the *Code*. In matters before the HRTO, other sections of the relevant enabling legislation are discussed and possibly interpreted; however, those sections are outside the purview of this book, other than as discussed in the selected decisions and cases in this chapter.

The *Code*

A broad overview of the *Code* is set out in the Applicant's Guide found on the "Guides & Forms" Web page of the HRTO website as follows:

> The Human Rights Code (the "Code") is an Ontario law that says that every person has the right:
> - to equal treatment in the five social areas named in the Code
> - to be free from discrimination or harassment on any of the listed grounds of discrimination named in the Code.
>
> The five social areas are:
> - Employment
> - Housing
> - Goods, Services and Facilities
> - Contracts
> - Membership in trade and vocational associations (such as unions)
>
> The grounds of discrimination are:
>
> 1. Race
> 2. Colour
> 3. Ancestry
> 4. Place of origin
> 5. Citizenship
> 6. Ethnic origin
> 7. Disability
> 8. Creed
> 9. Sex, including sexual harassment and pregnancy
> 10. Gender identity
> 11. Gender expression
> 12. Sexual orientation
> 13. Family status
> 14. Marital status
> 15. Age
> 16. Receipt of public assistance [**Note:** This ground applies **only** to claims about housing.]
> 17. Record of offences [**Note:** This ground applies **only** to claims about employment.]

[Note that numbers were substituted for the bullet points made in the original document for ease of reference.]

Gender identity (#10) and gender expression (#11) were new grounds for discrimination and harassment added by "Bill 33, *An Act to amend the Human Rights Code with respect to gender identity and gender expression"*, which came into force on June 19, 2012, and both apply to all five social areas.

The *Code* also has sections that prohibit the following:

- Discrimination because a person has a relationship, association, or other dealing with a person or persons who are identified by one of the grounds listed above. [This falls under Association.]
- Reprisal or threats of reprisal because a person has claimed rights or taken part in a proceeding under the *Code*.
- Reprisal or threats of reprisal because a person has refused to infringe on another's rights.
- Sexual solicitation or advances by a person who is in a position to give or deny a benefit.
- Reprisal or threats of reprisal for rejecting a sexual solicitation.

Keeping the Overview quoted above in mind, we shall look at specific provisions of the *Code*, especially those provisions relevant to the HRTO.

Preamble

The *Code*, in its preamble, states that "it is public policy in Ontario to recognize the dignity and worth of every person and to provide for equal rights and opportunities without discrimination that is contrary to law". The *Code* is the mechanism used to achieve such public policy.

Services

As stated in section 1, every person has a right to equal treatment with respect to services, goods, and facilities, without discrimination. See the first 15 grounds listed in the Overview discussed above (including the two new additional grounds).

Accommodation

Pursuant to subsection 2(1), every person has a right to equal treatment with respect to the occupancy of accommodation, without discrimination (see the first 16 grounds, including the two new additional grounds, listed in the Overview above). Under O. Reg. 290/98, landlords are entitled to request credit references and rental history information from a prospective tenant and to use such information in selecting or refusing the tenant without being in breach of the *Code*. Note that accommodation rights also include the freedom from harassment (i) by the landlord or agent of the landlord, or (ii) by an occupant of the same building, on the 15 grounds, including the two new additional grounds, identified in subsection 2(2). Further, in accordance with section 4, persons aged 16 or 17 who have withdrawn from parental control have accommodation rights and cannot be discriminated against even though they are aged less than 18. Sexual harassment is identified and dealt with in subsection 7(1), which declares that every person has the right to freedom from harassment because of his/her sex when obtaining housing.

Contracts

Under section 3, every person having legal capacity has a right to contract on equal terms without discrimination (see the first 15 grounds, including the two new additional grounds, listed earlier).

Employment

Section 5(1) states that every person has a right to equal treatment with respect to employment without discrimination (see the grounds listed earlier, including the two new additional grounds, except #16, which applies only to accommodation). Freedom from harassment in the workplace on all grounds, except sex, is also guaranteed under subsection 5(2). Sexual harassment in the workplace is dealt with under subsection 7(2), which states that every person has the right to freedom from harassment in the workplace because of his/her sex.

Vocational Associations

Pursuant to section 6, every person has a right to equal treatment with respect to membership in any trade union, trade or occupational association, or self-governing profession without discrimination on any of the first 15 grounds, including the two new additional grounds, listed in the Overview.

Sexual Solicitation

Freedom from unwelcome sexual solicitation or advances from a person "in a position to confer, grant or deny a benefit or advancement to" the complainant is set out in subsection 7(3)(a).

Reprisals and Infringement

Subsection 7(3)(b) and section 8 state the rights of a person (i) to be free from reprisal or threat of reprisal, (ii) to claim and enforce the right to freedom of reprisal, and (iii) to refuse to infringe on others' rights under the *Code*. Section 9 prohibits any infringement of rights protected under the *Code*.

Definitions
Under the definitions in sections 10 and 46, various words and terms used in the *Code* are defined.

Defences
The defence of reasonable and *bona fide* requirement, qualification, or factor is to exempt a claim of discrimination under sections 11 and 17 of the *Code*.

Special Program
The *Code*, under section 14, allows for preference or advantage created by special programs that are designed to (i) relieve hardship or economic disadvantage, (ii) promote equal opportunity for disadvantaged persons or groups, or (iii) help elimination of the infringement of rights. Note that under subsection 14(10), the HRTO may decide that a non–HRCO-designated program is a special program if the HRTO finds it meets the requirements of a special program under subsection 14(1).

Special Employment
Specific situations in employment listed in subsection 24(1) are not considered violations of the right to equal treatment with respect to employment. However, *bona fide* qualification under subsection 24(1)(b) can be exempted only if tribunals, including the HRTO, and courts are satisfied that reasonable accommodation cannot be achieved without undue hardship in accordance with requirements set out in subsections 24(2) and 24(3).

Discrimination in Employment under Government Contracts
According to section 26, compliance with section 5 of the *Code* is a deemed condition of any government contracts or grants and loans. If the HRTO finds a breach of condition, "the breach of condition is sufficient grounds for cancellation of the contract, grant, contribution, loan or guarantee and refusal to enter into any further contract with or make any further grant, contribution, loan or guarantee to the same person".

Policies by the HRCO
Pursuant to section 30, the HRCO may publish policies to provide guidance in the applications of Parts I and II.

Inquiries and Search Warrants

Under section 31, the HRCO may conduct an inquiry for the purpose of carrying out its functions prescribed by the *Code* if the Commission believes it is in the public interest to do so. The rest of the section sets out what happens on an inquiry and the powers of the HRCO. In conducting the inquiry, the HRCO can authorize a person to apply to a justice of the peace for a search warrant under section 31.1, and pursuant to section 31.2, evidence obtained on an inquiry under section 31 or section 31.1 may be used as evidence in a proceeding before the HRTO. The forms are prescribed under R.R.O. 1990, Reg. 642.

Composition and Recruitment of the HRTO

Section 32 confirms the continuation of the name of the tribunal and states the make-up, remuneration, and items regarding members and employees hiring process. Subsections 32(10) and 32(11) also notes that HRTO members/employees are exempted from giving testimony in proceedings not before the HRTO.

Applications to the HRTO

Although applications to the HRTO are supposed to be made within one year of the alleged infringing incident under both subsections 34(1) and (8), the HRTO can extend, by subsection 34(2), the time if it "is satisfied that the delay was incurred in good faith and no substantial prejudice will result to any person affected by the delay". The application to the HRTO shall be in the form approved by the HRTO (ss. 34(3)). Applications on behalf of another can be made pursuant to subsection 34(5), and such person making application can participate in the proceeding in accordance with the HRTO Rules (ss. 34(6)). Under subsection 34(11), a person cannot make an application to the HRTO if

(a) a civil proceeding has been commenced in a court in which the person is seeking an order under section 46.1 with respect to the alleged infringement and the proceeding has not been finally determined or withdrawn; or

(b) a court has finally determined the issue of whether the right has been infringed or the matter has been settled

and final determination will not be made unless the time for appealing expires and there is no appeal, pursuant to s. 34(12).

Applications by the HRCO

Section 35 states that the HRCO can make application to the HRTO for an order under section 45.3 if it believes that it is in the public interest to do so and that such order could provide the appropriate remedy. Under subsection 35(3), an application by the HRCO does not affect the right of others to make application under section 34 concerning the same matter. Further, unless the HRTO determines otherwise, s. 34 applications made by the HRCO and by an individual or organization regarding the same matter will be dealt with together in the same proceeding, as stated in subsection 35(4).

Parties

The rules for what persons are parties to an application to the HRTO under sections 34 and 35 are set out in section 36.

Intervention by the HRCO

As set out in section 37, the HRCO can intervene in s. 34 applications in two ways: (i) as an intervenor without consent of the applicant and subject to directions of the HRTO, or (ii) as a party to the application with the applicant's consent.

Powers of the HRTO

HRTO has full legal jurisdiction for all applications made under Part IV, as stated in section 39: "The Tribunal has the jurisdiction to exercise the powers conferred on it by or under this Act and to determine all questions of fact or law that arise in any application before it." Further, in accordance with section 40, the HRTO will adopt procedures and practices from its rules, or other sources available to it, to resolve applications in a fair, just, and expeditious manner. Section 41 permits liberal interpretation of Part IV of the *Code* and HRTO Rules, therefore giving the HRTO discretion over its own procedures and practices in handling applications before it.

The SPPA and the HRTO Rules

The provisions of the *SPPA* apply to proceedings before the HRTO. However, as stated in section 42, if there is a conflict, the *Code*, its regulations, and the HRTO Rules prevail. Under section 43(1), the HRTO is given the authority to make rules that govern its practice and procedure, and it has done so (see the HRTO Rules discussed below). According to subsection 43(2), the HRTO Rules must ensure that no HRTO proceedings will dispose application without (i) affording the parties an opportunity to make oral submissions in accordance with the rules, and (ii) giving written reasons. Other rule-making guidelines, including holding public consultation prior to making a rule, are enumerated in subsections 43(3)–43(7). As stipulated under subsection 43(8), non-compliance with the HRTO Rules by the HRTO does not automatically set aside an HRTO decision unless a substantial wrong was made and has affected the final disposition of the matter. However, if a party committed a non-compliance with the Rules, subsection 43(9) permits the HRTO to draw an adverse inference and to order the party to produce documents, evidence, or witnesses in accordance with subsection 43(3)(f).

HRTO Inquiry

Section 44 is similar to section 31 in that an inquiry can be ordered upon request of a party to the application, in this case by the HRTO, rather than the HRCO. However, HRTO inquiries are limited to evidence-seeking, as indicated in subsection 44(1)(a): "an inquiry is required in order to obtain evidence". Subsections 44(2)–(10) set out the scope of powers given to the person conducting the inquiry, which include warrantless entry, demand for documents, and questioning. Obstruction or interference with the exercise of any of these inquiry-related powers is prohibited under subsection 44(13). In accordance with subsections 44(11) and 44(14), the person conducting the inquiry is obligated to return seized items and to prepare a report and submit it to the HRTO and the parties to the application.

Deferral and Dismissal of an Application

Under section 45, the HRTO can defer an application in accordance with its rules. The HRTO may apply section 45.1 to dismiss an application, in whole or in part, in accordance with its rules if it is of the opinion that the substance of the application had been dealt with in another proceeding.

Orders of the HRTO on Applications under s. 34

If the HRTO determines that a party to an application has infringed upon another party's rights under Part I, the HRTO has the authority to make one or more orders, with or without request, directing the party who infringed on the right to (i) pay monetary compensation, (ii) make non-monetary restitution (e.g., public apologies), or (iii) perform an act (including future acts) that, in the opinion of the HRTO, promotes compliance with the *Code* (e.g., taking OHRC on-line training "Human Rights 101" course), all as set out in section 45.2.

Orders of the HRTO on Applications under s. 35

Upon confirming an infringement of right, the HRTO on an s. 35 application may make an order, with or without request, directing any party to the application to perform an act (including future acts) that, in the opinion of the HRTO, promotes compliance with the *Code*, as set out in section 45.3.

Matters Referred to the HRCO
Under section 45.4, the HRTO can refer any matters arising out of a proceeding to the HRCO if, in its opinion, they are matters of public interest or otherwise of interest to the HRCO, but the HRCO has the discretion to deal with such matters so referred.

HRCO Policies Considered by the HRTO
Under section 45.5, the HRTO may consider HRCO policies approved under section 30 in a proceeding, but the HRTO is required to consider such policies if a party to the proceeding or an intervenor requests that it do so.

Stated Case to Divisional Court
In any proceeding where the HRCO was a party or an intervenor and it believes the HRTO decision or order is not consistent with its policy under section 30, the HRCO may apply to the HRTO to have the case stated to the Divisional Court (ss. 45.6(1)). The details of stating a case to the Divisional Court, including but not limited to the parties to it and submissions by the HRTO, are set out in subsections 45.6(2)–(5). Unless it is ordered by the HRTO or the Divisional Court, a stating of a case does not automatically suspend the HRTO decision (ss. 45.6(6)).

Reconsideration by the HRTO
Any party to a proceeding before the HRTO may request that the HRTO reconsider its decision in accordance with the HRTO rules (ss. 45.7(1)). The HRTO can also reconsider its decision upon its own motion (ss. 45.7(2)). Note that, pursuant to subsection 45.6(7) with respect to a stated case, there is a time limit imposed for a reconsideration — within 30 days of receipt of the decision of the Divisional Court. Within that time limit, any party to the stated case proceeding may apply to the Tribunal for a reconsideration of the original HRTO decision or order in accordance with section 45.7.

Decisions of the HRTO are Final Except ...
Note that, in theory, there is a privative clause in section 45.8: "Subject to section 45.7 of this Act [stated case], section 21.1 of the *Statutory Powers Procedure Act* [correction of errors] and the Tribunal rules [which generally do not allow appeals to court], a decision of the Tribunal is final and not subject to appeal and shall not be altered or set aside in an application for judicial review or in any other proceeding unless the decision is patently unreasonable." This privative clause would not prevent judicial review.

Settlements

A settlement in writing and signed by the parties is binding on the parties, and the HRTO can make a consent order upon joint motion of the parties (ss. 45.9(1) and (2)). In the event there is a contravention of the settlement, the procedures for an HRTO order are detailed in subsections 45.9(3)–(8).

Human Rights Legal Support Centre

The Human Rights Legal Support Centre (HRLSC) is set up in section 45.11 as a corporation without share capital.

The objectives of the HRLSC are as follows:

(a) to establish and administer a cost-effective and efficient system for providing support services, including legal services, respecting applications to the Tribunal under Part IV;

(b) to establish policies and priorities for the provision of support services based on its financial resources.

The services to be provided by the HRLSC are as follows:

1. Advice and assistance, legal and otherwise, respecting the infringement of rights under Part I.
2. Legal services in relation to,
   i. the making of applications to the Tribunal under Part IV,
   ii. proceedings before the Tribunal under Part IV,
   iii. applications for judicial review arising from Tribunal proceedings,
   iv. stated case proceedings,
   v. the enforcement of Tribunal orders.
3. Such other services as may be prescribed by regulation.

General and Transitional Provisions

According to section 46.2, a person is guilty of an offence if he or she (i) contravenes section 9 or subsections 31(14), 31.1(8), or 44(13) of the *Code* or (ii) violates an order of the HRTO; and on conviction, he or she is liable to a fine to a maximum of $25,000. The *Code* prevails over any other legislation, as stated in subsection 47(2): "Where a provision in an Act or regulation purports to require or authorize conduct that is a contravention of Part I, this Act applies and prevails unless the Act or regulation specifically provides that it is to apply despite this Act." Finally, the transitional provisions of Part VI are applicable to situations as therein stated and should be examined if a situation comes within the parameters of those provisions.

SOCIAL JUSTICE TRIBUNALS OF ONTARIO
(the tribunal cluster that includes the HRTO)

As detailed in the preamble portion to this Part II, clusters of Ontario agencies started to occur in 2009, and the second cluster created was the SJTO that included the HRTO. In the SJTO website, there is a Web page entitled "Reports, Plans and Standards", which will be discussed later in this chapter, as well as a Web page entitled "SJTO Consultations", which provides links to proposed rules or policies, if any. As the mandate for clusters is to rationalize procedures and resources within the cluster, it is likely that more common practices will be developed for the SJTO, and the reader should continually review both the HRTO and SJTO websites to keep up to date.

The current SJTO Common Rules, which underwent a consultation period and became effective October 1, 2013, deal with adjudicative values and interpretive principles, specifically on such concepts as abuse of process, representatives and litigation guardians. Three Practice Directions also underwent consultation and became effective October 1, 2013: two are general and applicable to all tribunals in the cluster, while the third one is specific to the HRTO:

- Practice Direction on Representation deals with who can be a representative before any of the constituent tribunals making up the SJTO cluster and such representative's responsibilities.
- Practice Direction on Litigation Guardians "discusses how a person who does not have legal capacity can be a party to a case before the tribunals and boards of the Social Justice Tribunals Ontario ("tribunal") through a litigation guardian." It then discusses the possible need for litigation guardians for both minors and parties with mental capacity issues, and the naming and removal of a litigation guardian.
- Practice Direction on Filing Applications on Behalf of Another Person under Section 34(5) of the *Code*, appended to this chapter, provides general information on the procedure for such application.

All three Practice Directions, along with 14 other Practice Directions, can be found on the HRTO website as of February, 2016, while the first two are also available on the SJTO website and are in the Appendix to the Preamble to Part II.

RELEVANT REGULATIONS

Currently, there are two regulations made under the *Code*. Both are covered in the review of the enabling legislation above. The O. Reg. 290/98, relevant to the procedure of the HRTO, is covered under "Accommodation", and the R.R.O. 1990, Reg. 642, regarding the forms for search and entry warrants relevant to an HRCO inquiry, is covered under "Inquiries and Search Warrants".

PROCEDURES OF TRIBUNAL

The HRTO has "HRTO Rules of Procedure" (the HRTO Rules), effective May 10, 2016, on its Web page "Rules & Practice Directions", downloadable in Word. As noted earlier, the HRTO Rules were made under "the authority to make rules to govern its practices and procedures", stated in section 43 of the *Code*, and the HRTO Rules prevail if there is a conflict between provisions of the *SPPA* and the HRTO Rules, in accordance with subsection 42(2).

The HRTO Rules contains two parts: Part I lists the 10 SJTO Common Rules, and Part II contain the rules and a list of forms referenced in the rules that are specific to the HRTO. The forms referenced in the HRTO Rules, also referred to in various areas of the HRTO website, are available in the Web page "Forms and Filing".

The rules specific to the HRTO and the forms shall be discussed in summary fashion and in varying detail below, but the reader should rely only on her/his reading and interpretation of both rather than on the author. Please note that the procedures in the enabling legislation also are applicable, as are the *SPPA* and the *Code* where noted in the HRTO Rules.

RULES

SJTO Common Rules

The SJTO Common Rules in Part I provide general procedural rules that are applicable to all tribunals within the cluster. The Common Rules cover application and interpretation, discretion to exercise power, language of proceedings, requirement of courteous and respectful behaviour in proceeding, power to deal with abuse of process, and accommodation of *Code*-related needs, and they are summarized in the preamble to Part II of this text on pages 120–121.

HRTO-Specific Rules

The rules discussed below were made effective May 10, 2016.

General Rules (R. 1)

Practice directions may be issued by the Chair of the HRTO under R. 1.2. The forms, established by the HRTO, are not part of the HRTO Rules (R. 1.3). Fourteen words or phrases are defined in R. 1.4.

Numerous powers of the HRTO are listed in Rs. 1.6–1.7. Various methods, depending on the situation, to calculate time are set out in Rs. 1.8–1.10. Specific methods of communication with the HRTO, including the entitlement to do so in French and English, are detailed in Rs. 1.11–1.13.

The required contents for documents to be filed with the HRTO, except Forms 1–3, and how the filing is to occur are set out in Rs. 1.16–1.17. Documents by fax or e-mail received after 5:00 p.m. are deemed to be filed the next day (R. 1.19). The need to use a statement of delivery form to verify the delivery of all documents to the parties, except Forms 1–3, is stated in R. 1.20. When and how such a statement is to be filed is set out in R. 1.23. Various methods of delivery of documents are enumerated in R. 1.21, and the conditions of when the documents are deemed delivered are set out in R. 1.22.

Tribunal Proceedings (R. 3)

The obtaining of a witness summons and how it is to be delivered are set out in Rs. 3.1–3.2. Documents obtained in the proceedings can only be used in the proceeding, pursuant to R. 3.3. The HRTO can set dates for the proceedings with or without consultation of the parties (R. 3.4). Rule 3.5 states that the HRTO "may conduct hearings in person, in writing, by telephone, or by other electronic means, as it considers appropriate. However, no Application that is within the jurisdiction of the [HRTO] will be finally disposed of without affording the parties an opportunity to make oral submissions in accordance with these Rules". Under R. 3.7, the HRTO does not normally record or transcribe its proceedings, but if a recording does exist, it does not form part of the record in a judicial review situation.

Unless the HRTO determines otherwise, all proceedings are open to the public (R. 3.10), and written decisions are available to the public also (R. 3.12). The HRTO, however, may make an order to protect the confidentiality of personal or sensitive information (R. 3.11). In particular, the use of initials to identify a person in an HRTO decision is permitted under R. 3.11.1 to protect the identity of children.

The consequences of a party's not attending a hearing after giving notification are spelled out in R. 3.13. Rule 3.14 deals with who can file, as well as how and when to file, a request to intervene.

Notice of Constitutional Question (R. 4)

Rule 4.1 states the following:

> Where a party intends to question the constitutional validity or applicability of any law, regulation, by-law or rule or where a party claims a remedy under s. 24(1) of the *Charter of Rights*

and *Freedoms*, in relation to an act or omission of the Government of Canada or the Government of Ontario, a Notice of Constitutional Question must be delivered to the Attorneys General of Canada and Ontario and all other parties and filed with the Tribunal as soon as the circumstances requiring the notice become known and, in any event, at least (fifteen) 15 days before the question is to be argued.

Non-compliance with the Rules (R. 5)

The HRTO can do any of the enumerated acts in R. 5.5 if a respondent does not respond to a delivered application. Where a party seeks to present evidence or make submissions with respect to a fact or an issue not raised in any documents required under the HRTO Rules, the HRTO "may refuse to allow the party to present evidence or make submissions about the fact or issue unless satisfied that there would be no substantial prejudice and no undue delay to the proceedings" (R. 5.7).

Applications: ss. 34(1) and 34(5) of the Code (R. 6)

Rule 6.1 requires that applications under subsection 34(1) or 34(5) must be filed in Form 1, and if applicable, Form 4A, 4B, or 27. According R. 6.2, an application is considered complete only when the form(s) are completed with all contents requested, including facts that establish the discrimination claim. Applications determined by the HRTO as incomplete may be sent back or may be refused, as stated in R. 6.4. Once application is accepted for processing, it will be dealt with pursuant to Rs. 6.6 and 6.7. An application under subsection 34(5) shall, under R. 6.8, be filed with the signed consent (Form 27) of the person on whose behalf the application is brought.

Applications with Request to Defer Consideration (R. 7)

According to R. 7.1, an application under R. 6.1 can be made at the same time with a request to the HRTO to defer consideration of the application, permitted under R. 14, if there are other legal proceedings dealing with the same subject matter. Such a request of deferral must contain the material set out in R. 7.3. As noted in R. 7.2, the deferral request cannot be based on a legal proceeding that falls within the scope of s. 34(11) of the *Code*.

Response to Applications under ss. 34(1) and 34(5) of the Code (R. 8)

Rule 8.1 states as follows: "To respond to an Application under subsection 34(1) or subsection 34(5) of the *Code*, a Respondent must file a complete Response in Form 2 not later than 35 days after a copy of the Application was sent to the Respondent by the [HRTO]." The response must contain the material set out in R. 8.2; if it is not complete, it may be sent back for re-submission under R. 8.3. Where the respondent alleges the issues in dispute are the subject of an ongoing grievance or arbitration brought pursuant to a collective agreement, the respondent should respond in accordance with R. 8.2.1. A response accepted by the HRTO will be sent by the HRTO to the people and organizations listed in R. 8.4.

Reply (R. 9)

Form 3 must be used to reply to a response (R. 9.1) and may deal only with new matters raised in the response (R. 9.2). The delivery and filing of the reply are set out in R. 9.3.

Withdrawal of an Application (R. 10)

Except where the withdrawal forms part of a settlement, the applicant must deliver a completed Form 9 to the people and organizations listed in R. 10.1. Rule 10.3 states the following: "Where a Respondent or other person or organization receiving notice under Rule 10.1 wishes to respond to a Request to Withdraw, the response must be in Form 11, Response to Request, and must be filed no later than two days after the Request to Withdraw was delivered". A copy of the response must be delivered to those who received Form 9 before it is filed with the HRTO (R. 10.4).

Request to Intervene (R. 11)

Rule 11.1 states: "The [HRTO] may allow a person or organization to intervene in any case at any time on such terms as the [HRTO] may determine. The [HRTO] will determine the extent to which an intervenor will be permitted to participate in a proceeding". Such an intervention must be made by Form 5 (R. 11.2) and must comply with R. 11.3. Under R. 11.4, a party who wishes to respond to Form 5 must do so by Form 11. Intervention by the HRCO, with or without the consent of the applicant, can be accomplished in accordance with Rs. 11.6–11.13. Two rules, Rs. 11.14 and 11.15, adopted in May 2014, deal with intervention by a bargaining agent for a person who has filed an application about his/her employment. A bargaining agent who wishes to intervene in an application must file a Form 28 (R. 11.14); and to remove a bargaining agent as an intervenor, a request must be made in Form 10 in accordance with R. 19.

Commission Applications under s. 35 of the Code (R. 12)

Commission Applications under section 35 of the *Code* must be by Form 7, and a response to it by Form 8, followed by a case conference that will be convened, as set out in Rs. 12.1–12.5.

Dismissal of an Application Outside the HRTO's Jurisdiction (R. 13)

Rule 13.1 says the HRTO "may, on its own initiative or at the request of a Respondent, filed under Rule 19, dismiss part or all of an Application that is outside [its] jurisdiction". If the HRTO believes that an application is outside its jurisdiction, it shall issue a Notice of Intention to Dismiss the Application, in accordance with R. 13.2, and the HRTO shall deal with a dismissal under Rs. 13.3–13.5.

Deferral of an Application by the HRTO (R. 14)

According to R. 14.1, the HRTO "may defer consideration of an Application, on such terms as it may determine, on its own initiative, at the request of an Applicant under Rule 7, or at the request of any party"; but before deferring, it must give the parties notice of that intention and allow them the opportunity to make submissions, under R. 14.2. The HRTO may require a deferred application to proceed (i) upon request (Rs. 14.3 and 14.4), or (ii) on its own motion in appropriate circumstances (R. 14.5).

Mediation (R. 15)

At any time after the application is filed, mediation assistance may be offered by the HRTO or requested by a party (R. 15.1). The parties and their representatives must sign a confidentiality agreement before mediation starts (R. 15.2), and the HRTO may direct that a person with the authority to settle be present (R. 15.3). Everything disclosed in a mediation is confidential and can only be raised before the HRTO or in another proceeding, in accordance with R. 15.4. Rule 15.6 states the following about settlement:

> Where the terms of any settlement are in writing and signed by the parties the parties may request that the [HRTO] dispose of the matter in accordance with their agreement by filing a confirmation of settlement using Form 25 (Settlement). Parties may also ask the [HRTO] to issue a consent order in accordance with s. 45.9 of the *Code*. A completed Form 25 must be filed within ten (10) days of the date of the agreement.

Mediation-Adjudication with the Agreement of the Parties (R. 15A)

By written and signed mediation-adjudication agreement under R. 15A.2, the parties can agree that the HRTO member hearing the Application may act as a mediator, who can then continue to hear the matter as adjudicator (R. 15A.1).

Disclosure of Documents (R. 16)

No later than 21 days after the HRTO sends a confirmation of a hearing to the parties, each party must deliver to the other party documents, as detailed in R. 16.1, and a statement of delivery verifying that delivery must be filed. As set out in R. 16.2, unless otherwise ordered by the HRTO, at or before 45 days prior to the first scheduled day of the hearing, each party must deliver to the other party documents he or she relies upon. In addition to filing a statement of delivery verifying that delivery, R. 16.3 requires that each party also files such documents to the HRTO. Readers should note R. 16.4: "**No party may rely on or present any document not included on a document list and provided to other parties in accordance with Rule 16.1 and 16.2, and filed with the [HRTO] under Rule 16.3, except with the permission of the [HRTO].**"

Disclosure of Witnesses (R. 17)

Rules 17.1–17.4 require a witness list — including information detailed in Rs. 17.1–17.2 and, in the case of expert witnesses, the information under R. 17.3 — to be delivered and filed in the manner set out in R. 17.1. **If the witness list is not so filed and delivered, or if a witness is not listed in the delivered and filed material, the witness may not be presented at the hearing, except with the permission of the HRTO, as stated in R. 17.4.**

Case Assessment (R. 18)

Rule 18.1 states that the HRTO "may prepare and send the parties a Case Assessment Direction where it considers it appropriate. The Case Assessment Direction may address any matter that, in the opinion of the [HRTO], will facilitate the fair, just and expeditious resolution of the Application and may include directions made in accordance with any of its powers in Rules 1.6 and 1.7"; and the parties must be prepared to respond to any issues identified in such direction at the hearing, according to R. 18.2.

Request for an Order During Proceedings (R. 19)

Rule 19 involves what are normally called motions (whether prior to or in the hearing) but are referred to in the rule as "requests for an order during proceedings". The request can be made at any time during a proceeding by oral submission or in writing (R. 19.1). The written request, made by Form 10, is to be delivered and filed in accordance with R. 19.2 and must contain the enumerated items in R. 19.4. The response to the written request, made by Form 11, is to be delivered and filed in accordance with R. 19.5 and must contain the enumerated items in R. 19.6. As stated in R. 19.7, it is up to the HRTO to decide "whether a Request for Order will be heard in writing, in person, or electronically and, where necessary, will set a date for the hearing of the Request".

Summary Hearings (R. 19A)

Rule 19A.1 states as follows: "The [HRTO] may hold a summary hearing, on its own initiative or at the request of a party, on the question of whether an Application should be dismissed in whole or in part on the basis that there is no reasonable prospect that the Application or part of the Application will succeed". In summary hearings, Rs. 16 and 17, regarding disclosures, do not apply. Disclosure and witness statements are, however, included in the HRTO's directions on procedures the parties must take prior to the summary hearing (R. 19A.2). Where a party requests that an application be dismissed by a summary hearing, Form 26 shall be filed and delivered in accordance with R. 19A.3.

HRTO-Ordered Inquiries (R. 20)

Rule 20.1 states that a party may request an Order from the HRTO to appoint a person to conduct an inquiry under section 44(1) of the *Code*. A Request for a Tribunal-Ordered Inquiry must be made in Form 12, delivered to the other parties, and filed with the HRTO. The Request must be made promptly after the party becomes aware of the need for an inquiry. The contents of Form 12 are set out in R. 20.2. The response to the request is by Form 13 and is to be delivered and filed in accordance with R. 20.3, and it must contain complete submissions in support of the party's position, as stipulated in R. 20.4. Rule 20.6 states that the "person conducting an inquiry will prepare a written report and submit it to the [HRTO] and the parties in accordance with the terms of reference established by the [HRTO]". That written report can be evidence in the proceeding only if one of the conditions listed in R. 20.7 is met.

Expedited Proceedings (R. 21)

It is stated in R. 21.1 that an applicant may request the HRTO to deal with an application in an expeditious manner, based on circumstances that require urgent resolution to the disputed issues. A Request to Expedite an Application must be made in Form 14 and filed with the Application in accordance with Rules 6.1 or 24.1 and must meet the requirements set out in R. 21.2. A response to a request to expedite must be by Form 15 and must comply with R. 21.3.

Where the Substance of an Application Has Been Dealt with in Another Proceeding (R. 22)

The HRTO can dismiss an application if it has been appropriately dealt with in another proceeding, provided the parties can make oral submissions before the dismissal (Rs. 22.1–22.2).

Interim Remedies (R. 23)

An applicant, under R. 23.1, may request the HRTO to order an interim remedy in an application by submitting a Form 16 (Request for Interim Remedy). The Request for Interim Remedy must include the items set out in R. 23.3. The HRTO may grant the interim remedy if the requirements of R. 23.2 are met. A response to the request for an interim remedy must be in Form 17 and must comply with R. 23.4 and include the requirements set out in R. 23.5.

Contravention of Settlements (R. 24)

An application alleging contravention of a settlement must be by Form 18 (R. 24.1) and must comply with Rule 24.2 by answering all the questions in the form and including a copy of the settlement. A response to the application alleging contravention must be by Form 19 and be filed and delivered within the time set out in R. 24.3.

Request to Amend Clerical Errors (R. 25)

A correction of typographical or similar errors in the decision or order may be requested (i) by a party within 30 days from the date of a decision or order, or (ii) at any time by the HRTO (R. 25.1); and unless the Chair determines otherwise, the request should be considered by the panel that issued the original order or decision (R. 25.2).

Request for Reconsideration (R. 26)

Under R. 26.1, any "**party may request reconsideration of a final decision of the Tribunal within (thirty) 30 days from the date of the decision**", and such request shall be by Form 20

(R. 26.2) and contain the information required by R. 26.3. (Note that some flexibility regarding the 30 days deadline is provided in R. 26.5.1, which states, "A Request for Reconsideration made more than 30 days following the Decision will not be granted unless the Tribunal determines that the delay was incurred in good faith and no substantial prejudice will result to any person affected by the delay.") A party who is served with Form 20 responds only under direction to do so by the HRTO by Form 21, in accordance with R. 26.4. The HRTO will grant the request for reconsideration only if it is satisfied that one of the conditions listed in R. 26.5 exists. The HRTO will provide the parties with an opportunity to make submissions (R. 26.6), which, unless determined otherwise by the HRTO, shall be written (R. 26.7).

If a request for reconsideration is granted, the HRTO may make a decision based on the substance of the request without further submissions from the parties, or it may decide to have a rehearing for all or part of the matter (R. 26.8). The HRTO can also reconsider its decision on its own initiative (R. 26.9); and if a prehearing is decided, the procedure will allow parties to make submissions (R. 26.10).

Stated Case to Divisional Court (R. 27)

Rule 27.1 states that where the HRTO "has made a final decision or order in a proceeding in which the Commission was a party or intervenor, the Commission may, under section 45.6 of the *Code*, apply to the [HRTO] to have the [HRTO] state a case to the Divisional Court", and such application shall be by Form 22, in accordance with R. 27.2. The rest of Rule 27 (Rs. 27.3–27.6) relates to (i) parties both in support and in opposition to the HRCO's application, and (ii) the fact that the application is, in and of itself, a stay to a final decision or order, unless otherwise ordered by the HRTO or the court.

List of Forms Referred to in the Rules

The forms that are referred to in the HRTO Rules, including the new Form 28 for the new R. 11.14, effective in May 2014, are listed at the end of the HRTO Rules of Procedure. (See Exhibit 6.1 for the list of forms.)

PRACTICE DIRECTIONS

Practice Directions may be issued by the Chair of the HRTO under the HRTO Rules (R. 1.2). As of May 2016, there are 17 Practice Directions listed in the "Practice Directions" portion of the Web page under

EXHIBIT 6.1
Forms Used in HRTO Proceedings

Form	Title	Rule
1	Application	6
	Supplemental	
	• Form 1-A — Employment	
	• Form 1-B — Housing	
	• Form 1-C — Goods, Services, or Facilities	
	• Form 1-D — Contracts	
	• Form 1-E — Membership in a Vocational Association	
2	Response	8
3	Reply	9
4A	Litigation Guardian on Behalf of a Minor	A10
4B	Litigation Guardian: Mental Incapacity	A10
5	Request to Intervene	11
6	Notice of Commission Intervention (with Consent)	11
7	Application by Commission	12
8	Response to Commission Application	12
9	Request to Withdraw	10
10	Request for Order During Proceedings	19
11	Response to a Request for Order During Proceedings	19
12	Request for Tribunal-ordered Inquiry	20
13	Response to Request for Tribunal-ordered Inquiry	20
14	Request to Expedite Proceeding	21
15	Response to Request to Expedite Proceeding	21
16	Request for Interim Remedy	23
17	Response to Request for Interim Remedy	23
18	Application for Contravention of Settlement	24
19	Response to Application for Contravention of Settlement	24
20	Request for Reconsideration	26
21	Response to Request for Reconsideration	26
22	Commission Application to Request Stated Case	27
23	Statement of Delivery	1.23
24	Summons to Witness	3.1
25	Settlement	15
26	Request for Summary Hearing	19A
27	Application under Section 34(5) of the HRC on Behalf of Another Person	6
28	Notice of Intervention by Bargaining Agent	11.14
	Mediation/Adjudication Agreement	N/A
	Mediation Confidentiality Agreement	N/A

the Web link "Rules & Practice Directions". All these practice directions govern Part IV applications under the *Human Rights Code*.

Practice Direction on Requests for Language Interpretation

This Practice Direction states the following:

> Where a party requires language interpretation or sign language interpretation services in order to participate fully in a hearing (including a Case Resolution Conference), or mediation, and makes a request that the HRTO provide such services, the HRTO will provide for interpretation services to be available to the requesting party at the hearing and/or in the mediation conference.
>
> Requests for language interpretation or sign language interpretation services must be made to the Registrar as soon as possible and well in advance of a scheduled hearing or mediation.

Practice Direction on Reconsideration

The applicability of this Practice Direction is set out in the following:

> Parties may ask the HRTO to reconsider a final decision. The HRTO may also reconsider a decision on its own initiative where it considers it appropriate.
>
> Reconsideration is a discretionary remedy; there is no right to have a decision reconsidered by the HRTO. Reconsideration is not an appeal or an opportunity for a party to change the way it presented its case.

The procedure for the request for reconsideration is set out in this Practice Direction and Rule 26 of the HRTO Rules. In most cases, the adjudicator who heard the original matter, and is therefore in the best position to determine whether new issues or submissions are raised in the request, will be assigned to determine the reconsideration request.

The HRTO makes its decision on whether or not to grant a request for reconsideration based on the facts of the situation and on the criteria set out in the HRTO Rules (R. 26.5). Some examples for both granting and not granting the request are set out in the Practice Direction, and the courses of action may be taken by the HRTO, if a request for reconsideration is granted, are also discussed.

The option to challenge an HRTO decision through an application for judicial review to the Divisional Court is also briefly mentioned at the end of the Practice Direction.

Practice Direction on Recording Hearings

This Practice Direction was amended as of May 2013. In the amended Practice Direction, the HRTO outlines its approach, in general, to recording hearings. General direction is provided under four categories: General Practice on Recording, Recording as Accommodation for *Code*-related Needs, Self-recording and Transcription, and Use of a Court Reporter. (For details, the Practice Direction is included as Appendix 6.2 to this chapter.) This practice direction is provided for general information only and may vary where the HRTO deems appropriate.

Practice Direction on Hearings in Regional Centres

This Practice Direction was amended as of March 2013. In the direction, the HRTO outlines its approach, in general, to regional hearing centres:

> The HRTO is committed to making its hearings and mediations accessible. The HRTO will hold hearings in the following regional centres: Toronto; Hamilton; Kingston; London; North Bay; Ottawa; Sarnia; Sault Ste. Marie; St. Catharines; Sudbury; Timmins; Thunder Bay; and Windsor.
>
> The HRTO may hold hearings in locations other than the ones listed above in order to accommodate Code-related or other needs of the parties or their witnesses. Any request for a change in location should be in writing and made to the Registrar as soon as possible.

The HRTO may vary this approach where it deems appropriate.

Practice Direction on Representation

See the summary in the preamble to Part II on page 122.

Practice Direction on Applications on Behalf of Another Person Under s. 34(5) of the Code

In October 2013, instead of one Practice Direction covering both s. 34(1) and s. 34(5) Applications on Behalf of Another Person, two were introduced to deal with each application separately. This Practice Direction deals with applications made by a person or an organization on behalf of another person if that person has given consent (s. 34(5)). Note that the person or organization making the application is the applicant, while the person on whose behalf the application is made is the claimant. The claimant must be 18 or older and have the legal capacity to give consent. The Practice Direction points out that the claimant needs only the legal capacity to commence the application, to delegate power to pursue the application, and to terminate the application through a withdrawal (see *Kacan v. OPSEU*, 2010 HRTO 795). The consent (Form 27) must be filed with the application.

Practice Direction on Litigation Guardians
See the summary in the preamble to Part II on page 121.

Practice Direction on Electronic Filing by Licensed Representatives
Where an Application (Form 1) or a Response (Form 2) is filed electronically, by email or as a Smart Form, by the licensed representative (lawyer or licensed paralegal) of the applicant or respondent, the signature of the applicant or respondent is not required. By so filing, the representative undertakes that (i) he or she has the authorization to represent the client, and (ii) the client has reviewed the document and has confirmed the declaration set out in the Practice Direction in the form(s).

Practice Direction on Communicating with the HRTO
This Practice Direction provides general information as to how communication is to be done (i) between the HRTO and parties (or their representatives) to the proceeding, and (ii) between parties (or their representatives). Also discussed is how the HRTO will communicate its decisions. All written communications with the HRTO should be through the Registrar. Procedures for e-mail communication are set out. Finally, it is noted that "[c]ommunications that are unduly lengthy, repetitive or disrespectful of any other participant or the Tribunal may be rejected." (Note that at the top of the direction there is a reminder of the requirement of complete and accurate contact information in the Application and Response forms and the requirement to inform the HRTO and all other parties if there is a change.)

Practice Direction on Hearings before the HRTO
This Practice Direction provides information on how hearings, in general, as well as Case Resolution Conferences, and hearings in the Transitional Applications stream may be conducted. Procedural guidelines for summary hearings before the HRTO are provided in a another Practice Direction, which will be discussed below. It is noted that the "HRTO is committed to a process that is accessible; fair, just

and expeditious; responsive to the parties that appear before the HRTO; appropriate to the nature of the particular case; and, able to determine the merits of an application, considering the facts and the relevant legal principles." To achieve this, the HRTO adopts a flexible approach to hearings, taking into account the aforementioned core values. The principal objective of the process is always fair and timely, and the outcome must be based on the facts, the law, and the merits of the application.

A human rights application will proceed to a hearing if the parties to the application do not agree to mediation, or the mediation fails to produce a settlement. The HRTO will send the parties a Notice of the hearing. The procedures thereafter should follow what is stated in the Practice Direction until closer to the hearing date, when an HRTO adjudicator will decide whether to issue a Case Assessment Direction to assist the parties to prepare for the hearing after reviewing the documents and witness statements in the file. Some cases' Case Assessment Direction preparation may involve a case conference call with the parties. The examples given in the direction offer the reader an idea of the matters a Case Assessment Direction may deal with.

A hearing or Case Resolution Conference before the HRTO is a legal proceeding. The parties are expected to attend prepared and to present their case through evidence (witnesses and documents) and submissions. The role and powers of the adjudicator are also described.

Practice Direction on Naming Respondents

This Practice Direction provides guidance in naming respondents requested in section 3 of the Application (Form 1). An individual or organization should be named as a respondent only if the applicant believes that the individual or organization is legally responsible for the discrimination he or she experienced. Each respondent will receive the application and have the right to file and respond and to participate in the proceeding. To avoid delays caused by unnecessary respondents, applicants are advised to get legal advice and assistance from the HRLSC. Note that there is specific information about respondents that the applicant must provide the HRTO.

In this Practice Direction, specific discussion is given to (i) naming employees of an organization respondent; (ii) naming a union or employee association as a respondent; and (iii) naming Ontario government ministry or agency as a respondent.

Generally, it is not necessary to name an individual employee if the organization is already named as a respondent, and the HRTO, under R. 1.7(b), can remove a party. Exceptions, exist and two conditions that would justify naming an employee of an organization as a respondent are given. To name a union or association as a respondent, it must be proven that the union's or association's refusal to pursue a discrimination claim was based on discriminatory factors.

An Ontario government ministry or agency can be named as a respondent in an application heard by the HRTO. If this occurs, the ministry or agency must be named in a specific way. Examples of naming a ministry or agency were provided in this Practice Direction.

Human right claims against federal government or federally regulated activities cannot be heard by the HRTO jurisdiction. Rather, they fall within the jurisdiction of the Canadian Human Rights Commission (CHRC). For businesses conducting activities beyond Ontario, the line of jurisdiction becomes murky, and getting legal advice is recommended. Examples of federally regulated activities and interprovincial businesses are provided.

Practice Direction on Requests to Expedite an Application and Requests for an Interim Remedy

As noted in the beginning of this Practice Direction, the information applies to applications for expediting requests for an interim remedy filed under section 34 or 35 of the Ontario *Human Rights Code*.

Under HRTO Rules (R. 21), it is possible for an applicant to request to have his or her application heard earlier than allowed by normal timelines. However, these expedited hearing requests are granted only in *exceptional circumstances*:

> In its decisions, the HRTO has refused to grant requests to expedite unless the circumstances are truly urgent, requiring the resolution of the human rights dispute in a particularly rapid manner as compared with the time required to complete the HRTO's regular process (*Weerawardane v. 2152458 Ontario Ltd.*, 2008 HRTO 53 (CanLII)) or where refusal to expedite will render the remedy for the alleged human rights breach moot or unavailable (*Ebrahimi v. Durham District School Board*, 2009 HRTO 1062 (CanLII)).
>
> Except in the rarest of circumstances and without a compelling explanation, an applicant who has not filed the application promptly after identifying the alleged human rights breach will not be given the priority for HRTO resources of an expedited proceeding (*Kwan v. Hospital for Sick Children*, 2009 HRTO 621 (CanLII)).

Upon a decision to order an expedited proceeding, the HRTO will determine the changes that are necessary to its processes for that particular case. Changes to the processes may include abridgement of response, reply, and disclosure timelines and, where the parties consent to mediate, scheduling rapid mediation dates and/or setting early hearing dates.

The HRTO may also exercise its powers under the *Human Rights Code* and Rule 1.7 to direct the hearing process to ensure that a resolution will be made expeditiously. The HRTO reviews requests to expedite and may shorten the times for filing the Response to Request to Expedite (Form 15) in urgent circumstances.

The procedure for requesting an expedited procedure is set out in the Practice Direction, including Form 14, and possibly other forms to be filled out, and the contents thereof. Note that Form 14 "**must also include one or more declarations signed by persons with direct first-hand knowledge detailing all of the facts upon which the applicant relies in support of the Request to Expedite**." Information on declarations can be found in the "What is a Declaration?" section on the Web page.

A party to an application can seek an interim remedy, but the party must prove that the request meets all elements of the Rule, as clearly stated in the Tribunal's decision in *TA v. 60 Montclair*, 2009 HRTO 369 (CanLII). The Tribunal's decision to grant an interim remedy is based on whether the interim remedy is "necessary to facilitate and ensure the Tribunal is able to award a complete, appropriate and effective remedy at the end of a hearing, should a violation of the *Code* be found".

Declarations signed by persons with direct first-hand knowledge, detailing all of the facts, are also required to support the Request for an Interim Remedy.

Practice Direction on Scheduling of Hearings and Mediations, Rescheduling Requests, and Requests for Adjournments

This Practice Direction discusses approaches to balancing competing interests in scheduling and rescheduling mediation and hearings, as well as dealing with requests for adjournments. Note that the information in this Practice Direction also applies to s. 53(5) hearings and s. 53(3) Case Resolution Conferences in the Transitional Applications stream and that all references to "hearings" also apply to Case Resolution Conferences. This Practice Direction was amended as of January 2011; if needed, it, as well as all the Practice Directions, should be reviewed in detail for specifics and any other amendments in place as of the time of the review.

Practice Direction on Summary Hearing Requests

This Practice Direction deals with summary hearings under Rule 19A of the HRTO Rules. A summary hearing may be ordered upon the

HRTO's own initiative or a respondent's Request for Summary Hearing, and the decision is made only on the basis that there is no reasonable prospect that the application will succeed. While the HRTO can order a summary hearing at any time on its own initiative, it will not consider a Request for Summary Hearing unless the respondent has filed a complete Response.

The process, starting from (i) Respondent submitting the request, (ii) Applicant responding to the request, to (iii) what happens if the request is granted (e.g., Case Assessment Direction, when and how the Summary Hearing is held, etc.), is detailed in this Practice Direction.

Practice Direction on Intervention by a Bargaining Agent

This Practice Direction was introduced in April 2014, providing general guidelines on the approach to the new Rules 11.14 and 11.15. When a dispute arises in a workplace and the applicant is a member of a union or association (namely, "the bargaining agent"), the bargaining agent is presumed to have an interest in the dispute and, therefore, the right to participate in the application as an intervenor. The process for the bargaining agent to become an intervenor, including filing Form 28, is then discussed.

Practice Direction on Anonymization of HRTO Decisions

This Practice Direction, introduced in April 2014, discusses the HRTO's approach to balancing the principle of having an open and transparent justice system with the principle of maintaining the privacy interest of the participants (Rs. 3.10–3.12). Most of the HRTO proceedings are open to the public, and the decisions, including the names of the parties, are also available to the public. The HRTO may use initials in its decision under two circumstances: (i) it is necessary in order to protect the identity of underage parties to the proceeding; and (ii) there are significant consequences if the personal or sensitive information is exposed. Two HRTO cases were included to illustrate how the HRTO decide: *C.M. v. York Region District School Board* ("C.M."), 2009 HRTO 735, sets out two reasons why minors should be given special consideration; and in *Mancebo-Munoz v. NCO Financial Services Inc.*, 2013 HRTO 974, the HRTO gave the reason why naming participants is critical to the Canadian legal and human rights system: "It is important for there to be public scrutiny when respondents [are] found to have violated these rights and also when accusations of discrimination are made by applicants but not upheld. ...it is a serious matter to be accused of breaching the Code, which may also cause stress and stigma. Without good reasons for doing so, parties should not make or defend allegations from behind a veil of anonymity, assured that they will not be identified if they are found not credible, their allegations are rejected or they are held to have violated the Code."

Parties who want their initials, instead of their names, to be used in the HRTO decisions must file a Request for Order during Proceedings in accordance with R. 19. The HRTO will decide based on facts, applicable law, and submissions from both applicant and respondent of the request. Parties may also request other types of privacy protection (e.g., a publication ban); however, they are rarely granted because it contradicts the principle of open and transparent justice that the HRTO holds.

Practice Direction on Establishing a Regular Contact Person for an Organization

This Practice Direction, effective November 2015, sets out the process for a respondent organization to establish a regular contact for the HRTO to contact.

FORMS

There are currently 28 forms for applications to the HRTO (as listed in the HRTO Rules). They can be found on the "Forms and Filing" Web page. All the forms are downloadable in MS Word and Adobe pdf formats. Specific instructions are provided for the Application and Response forms, and both are offered in SmartForm.

Form 1 — Application under Part IV of the *Human Rights Code*

This form is the general application under section 34 of the *Code* and consists of two pages of information concerning filing a s. 34 application. (See Appendix to the chapter for a copy of the form.)

Supplemental Forms

Depending on which of the five areas of discrimination is alleged, in addition to Form 1, one of the Supplemental Forms also needs to be filled out and filed.

- Form 1-A — Employment
- Form 1-B — Housing
- Form 1-C — Goods, Services, or Facilities
- Form 1-D — Contracts
- Form 1-E — Membership in a Vocational Association

Note that there is no downloadable Form 1 on the website. There are five Application forms; each contains Form 1 and one of the five supplemental forms. In the event that the claim involves more than one social area, the applicant needs only to choose one Application, indicate other social area(s) in Question 6, and provide an explanation in Question 8.

Form 2 — Response
This form is a response to a Form 1 application. The first two pages provide information on filing a Response. (See Appendix to this chapter for this form.)

Other Forms
The other 26 forms listed at the end of the HRTO Rules should be completed and filed as required by the procedure. Two other ADR-related forms are also included in this list of "Forms and Guides" under the "Forms and Filing" Web page.

POLICIES
There are two policies listed on the HRTO website as of the date of writing, downloadable in both MS Word and Adobe pdf formats, and they can be accessed by the Web Link "Law, Rules & Policies" on the "Policies" Web page.

Policy on Accessibility and Accommodation
This policy is predicated on three guiding principles in making all HRTO services accessible:

- Services should be provided in a manner that respects the dignity and independence of members of the public.
- Services should be provided in a manner that fosters physical and functional access to the [HRTO's] processes and promotes the inclusion, and full participation of members of the public.
- All persons should be given equal opportunity to obtain, use and benefit from the Tribunal's services. Where required, individualized accommodation will be provided, short of undue hardship.

The HRTO "will promote equal access for all individuals including parties, witnesses and representatives, to fully participate in its processes, short of undue hardship". This policy applies to all HRTO public offices and all HRTO staff and members.

Requests for accommodation will be considered on an individualized basis and are to be made to the Registrar. The policy also discusses the services and facilities of the HRTO available to accommodate those that need such accommodation.

Policy on Public Complaints

This policy sets out how complaints about the HRTO's "services and/or conduct of an adjudicator or staff person are to be made and resolved" and details important information about (i) making a complaint when the HRTO will not deal with the complaint, and (ii) how a complaint is made.

EXPLANATORY LITERATURE FROM THE HRTO

Other than the documents already discussed, there are four guides that explain the Forms and processes of the new procedures before the HRTO on the Web page entitled "Forms and Filing": "Applicant's Guide", "Respondent's Guide", "Plain Language Guide", and "Guide to Preparing for a Hearing Before the HRTO" (all downloadable in MS Word and Adobe pdf formats). The reader may want to refer to the four guides to gain further insight into the procedures, as well as to the Web page "FAQ's" to see how the procedure is discussed broadly; however, a clear understanding of the HRTO Rules will probably benefit the reader more.

Before holding a hearing to decide an application, the HRTO will normally assist the parties to settle their issues through a mediation process. Under "Forms and Filing", there is "A Guide to Mediation at Human Rights Tribunal of Ontario", which provides a brief introduction to the mediation process and answers questions about what to expect at and how to best prepare for a typical HRTO mediation.

Direct access to decisions of the HRTO is no longer available on the HRTO website. HRTO Decisions are now accessible free of charge through the CanLII website. A direct link to "HRTO Decisions on CanLII" is provided on the "Decisions" Web page. Also posted on the Web page is a link to the archived decisions made by the Board of Inquiry from 1963–2002.

RELEVANT CASES AND/OR DECISIONS

The cases and decisions discussed below are not meant to be exhaustive and are only those found in July of 2008. The discussion reflects only the author's interpretation and should not be regarded as legal opinion. Readers should continue to

update and research new cases and decisions, and briefings must be done in all circumstances.

Thirteen matters, including cases before the Divisional Court (Div. Ct.) and before one judge of the Superior Court of Justice (Sup. Ct. J.), as well as decisions of the HRTO, shall be discussed in chronological order, with the oldest one first (unless the case is one in a series, which will be discussed starting with the lowest court) to give the reader a sampling of how these cases and decisions have been decided and their relevance to the HRTO. Not every case discussed is a precedent-setting decision; however, the review should give the reader some idea of how the HRTO and the courts have dealt with various procedural and substantive issues in the first decade of the 21st century.

Barker v. Famous Players, A Division of Viacom Canada Inc.

Barker v. Famous Players, A Division of Viacom Canada Inc., 2004 HRTO 10 (the *Barker* decision), is an interim decision, which is set out in a decision brief form, partly as an example of decision briefing for the reader.

PARTIES: Ontario Human Rights Commission (the "Commission")
Nancy Barker, Scott Simser and Gary Malkowski (the "Complainants")
Famous Players, A Division of Viacom Canada Inc. (the "Respondent")

WHERE FOUND: URL: http://www.canlii.org/en/on/onhrt/doc/2004/2004hrto10/2004hrto10.html

BACKGROUND (FACTS)

This matter arose as complaints were made to the Commission by the Complainants, alleging that their rights to equal treatment with respect to services, goods, and facilities without discrimination as required by the *Ontario Human Rights Code* (*Code*) had been infringed on by the Respondent; that is, by failing to provide captioning services in its movie theatres.

Motions, brought on consent, to combine the three matters and with respect to adjournment of the hearing dates scheduled for August 2004 were both granted. The motion brought by the Respondent to further postpone its disclosure obligations was granted based upon certain factual findings not relevant to this brief. The motion regarding Mr. Simser's amending his complaint to add a new allegation of reprisal was heard and ruled on in this decision. Mr. Simser submitted that a reprisal occurred based upon an e-mail sent by the public affairs department of the Respondent on February 21, 2003, which stated in part as follows: "Essentially the complainant is demanding we immediately install Rear Window Captioning on ALL of our 845 screens across Canada."

ISSUES

1. What is the meaning of reprisal as set out in section 8 of the *Code*?
2. Is the e-mail sent by the department of the Respondent, on its face, sufficient to give rise to the appearance of reprisal within the meaning of section 8 of the *Code* subject to any natural justice concerns?
3. If the second issue is answered in the affirmative, can Mr. Simser amend his Complaint to include the allegation of reprisal?

DECISION

For reasons set out in the decision, Mr. Simser's motion to amend the Complaint to include the allegation of reprisal was dismissed.

REASONS

The word "reprisal" is set out in section 8 of the *Code* in relation to a person being able to make a claim and enforce his or her rights under the *Code* without "reprisal". The adjudicator referred to the following judgments and decisions to help her interpret the meaning of reprisal as used in section 8. The Ont. C.A. case of *Entrop v. Imperial Oil Ltd. (No. 7)* (2000), 37 C.H.R.R. D/481 (the *Entrop* case), agreed with the predecessor board to the HRTO that reprisal is a deliberate, wilful, and reckless action in retaliation for the complainant filing the complaint. The Divisional Court judgment in *Jones v. Amway of Canada Ltd.* (2002), 159 O.A.C. 331 (the *Jones* case), agreed with the adjudicator of the predecessor board's decision, saying that "[a]lthough it is clear that in human rights law generally there is no need to prove an intent to discriminate, we have great difficulty appreciating how there can be a breach of section 8 without an intent to perpetrate the prohibited conduct".

The adjudicator agreed with the above and with the decision of *Ketola v. Alue Propane Inc. (No. 1)* (2002), 44 C.H.R.R. D/20 (the *Ketola* decision). She stated the following:

> The Tribunal believes that the right set out in section 8 stands apart from the other provisions within Part I of the *Code* for which intent is not required, because ... its purpose is to protect the assertion of human rights from collateral attack that would otherwise "gut" the *Code* and render it ineffectual.

Based on (i) the need for showing at least the intent to retaliate and (ii) the finding that the e-mail is not a reprisal but an attempt to lobby, the adjudicator concluded that there are insufficient facts to support the argument that there is a triable issue with respect to reprisal. The adjudicator further dismissed the motion as it would be against natural justice to require the Respondent to expend time and expense necessary to answer an allegation that is without a triable issue.

For a recent case on reprisal and natural justice concerns, see *Vasileski v. Canadian Union of Public Employees, Local 5167*, 2014 HRTO 697.

McEwan v. Commercial Bakeries Corp.

In *McEwan v. Commercial Bakeries Corp.*, [2004] O.H.R.T.D. No. 13, 2004 HRTO 13, File No. HR-0568-03 (the *McEwan* decision), an HRTO decision, the issues were related to preliminary motions for disclosure of certain medical records and witness statements made by the respondent. The complainant stated that his medical condition caused a disability, and the treatment by his employer in not accommodating him infringed on his right to equal treatment with respect to employment without discrimination. The adjudicator, in determining that some records should be disclosed and not others, first noted the duty to disclose and the relevance of medical records in matters before the courts and tribunals:

> Everyone owes a general duty to give evidence relevant to the matters in issue, so that the truth may be ascertained: *M.(A.) v. Ryan*, [1997] 1 S.C.R. 157. Moreover, at common law, the test for production is arguable relevance.
>
> Unlike the civil courts that follow the *Rules of Civil Procedure*, the Tribunal is not bound by any particular rule that mandates the production of medical records. Thus, while the courts must comply with *Rule* 31.10, and the case law that follows it, the Tribunal only looks to these sources for guidance where relevant.

After looking at the justification for the production of medical records in civil litigation matters, the adjudicator said the following about situations such as the one before her:

> In comparison, individuals who are found to be disabled within the meaning of the *Code* are seeking accommodation of their disabilities, rather than financial recovery for the causation of them. For the most part, since causation is not normally in issue, less medical information is required for human rights cases dealing with disability than for personal injury cases. How-

ever, where the existence of the disability is itself very much in issue, the Tribunal must engage in a balancing exercise.

Taking into account the case law in the matter, the adjudicator noted the balancing act that must be done in situations such as the one before her:

> As a matter of natural justice and fairness, the Tribunal must balance the general duty to require production of all relevant material in disability cases, where the disability itself is in dispute, so that Respondents have sufficient opportunity to advance their case, versus the invasion of the Complainant's privacy vis-à-vis his confidential conversations and private records with his physicians and psychological counsellors.

Finding that the medical records more than met the test of arguable relevance, the adjudicator ordered that those records be disclosed, but witness statements and lists should not be disclosed at that time when the respondent does not even know what witnesses would be called.

For more recent cases on how the HRTO deals with production of documents, see *Vetharaniyam v. Timothy J. Tallon Sales Inc.*, 2013 HRTO 1678, and *Labao v. Toronto Police Services Board*, 2013 HRTO 723.

Modi v. Paradise Fine Foods Ltd.

Modi v. Paradise Fine Foods Ltd., [2005] O.H.R.T.D. No. 225, 2005 HRTO 25, File No. HR-0569-03 (the *Modi* decision) dealt with the issue of the admissibility of character evidence in an HRTO hearing. In this situation, the complainant alleged that the respondent was acting in a discriminatory manner in serving the complainant. The respondent's defence was that he was not at the store when the alleged incident occurred. He wanted to call witnesses who would give evidence as to how he generally comported himself in the store. The adjudicator had to determine whether the respondent could call such witnesses and, after determining such evidence to be "character" evidence, stated the legal position regarding admissibility as follows:

> Character evidence is generally inadmissible in civil proceedings in Canada, and the [HRTO] (and its predecessor, the Ontario Board of Inquiry (Human Rights Code)) has applied that principle: *Rubio v. A-Voz Portuguese Canadian Newspaper Ltd.*, [1997] O.H.R.B.I.D. No. 10; *Chacko v. Transpharm Canada Inc. (c.o.b. Toronto Institute of Pharmaceutical Technology)*, [2001]

O.H.R.B.I.D. No. 11. In contrast, similar fact evidence is more readily admissible. Classification of the nature of the relevant evidence therefore tends to be critical.

In *Chacko*, M.A. McKellar states the situation simply and usefully:

> [11] The propositions underlying the so-called "similar fact rule" may be briefly stated. Generally speaking, evidence going to a party's character or reputation is not relevant and not admissible. In some circumstances, however, evidence that the party whose behaviour is now impugned has previously acted in a manner similar to that currently alleged is admissible. Whether such evidence is admissible is a discretionary decision, requiring the probative value of the evidence to be assessed against its prejudicial effect.

As the respondent in this situation stated that he was not there, the evidence from the witnesses would be character evidence and not admissible.

For more recent cases on how the HRTO deals with admissibility of character evidence, see *Garofalo v. Cavalier Hair Stylists Shop Inc.*, 2013 HRTO 170, and *Janes v. Wright*, 2012 HRTO 1621.

Smith v. Ontario (Human Rights Commission)

Smith v. Ontario (Human Rights Commission), [2005] O.J. No. 377, 195 O.A.C. 323, 38 C.C.E.L. (3d) 135, 136 A.C.W.S. (3d) 1106 (the *Smith* case), is a 2005 Div. Ct. case dealing with an appeal of an HRTO decision, which was set out in the *Code* prior to the 2008 amendments. (The HRTO decision is final and not subject to appeal, as prescribed in s. 45.8 of the current *Code*.) In the original case, the HRTO found that the complainant's race was not a factor in the decision to terminate employment; therefore, he was not entitled to compensation for lost wages. The HRTO also found that the poisoned workplace that existed was not wilful or reckless; therefore, the complainant was not entitled to compensation for mental anguish. As there is no longer a right to appeal HRTO decisions under the current *Code*, the Div. Ct. case finding of the standard of review is irrelevant to HRTO decisions. However, the case does state the law with respect to poisoned work environments in general and to the situation in the case:

> Where termination occurs within a poisoned work environment, a proper consideration of whether the termination was discriminatory requires that it be examined in the context of the poi-

soned work environment. See *Naraine v. Ford Motor Co. of Canada (No. 4)* (1996), 27 C.H.R.R. D/230 (Ont. Bd. Inq.) upheld [1999] O.J. No. 2530, 34 C.H.R.R. D/405 (Ont. Div. Ct.); *Moffatt v. Kinark Child and Family Services*, [1998] O.H.R.B.I.D. No. 19.

On this record, a finding that race was a factor is not only available, but in our view would have been made if the Tribunal had not assessed the evidence with a view to determining the existence of racial motivation, but had assessed the evidence to determine whether race was a factor in the termination.

We are all of the view that the appeal should be allowed and the decision of the Tribunal that race was not a factor is set aside.

The Divisional Court's approach in determining whether an action (in the *Smith* case, termination) is discriminatory by assessing whether, in the circumstances, a prohibited ground is a factor to the action, and not by looking for a discriminatory motive on the part of the respondents, was adopted by the adjudicator in *Saadi v. Audmax*, 2009 HRTO 1627.

Boodhram v. 2009158 Ontario Ltd. (c.o.b. A Buck or Two #324)

Boodhram v. 2009158 Ontario Ltd. (c.o.b. A Buck or Two #324), [2005] O.H.R.T.D. No. 54, 2005 HRTO 54, File No. HR-0976-05 (the *Boodhram* decision) is interesting because of its finding of the law with respect to an award for general damages for a breach of rights under the *Code*. In this case, the HRTO had a written hearing, for which the Respondents did not file submissions although they were properly served. The adjudicator found that the uncontradicted evidence showed discrimination in employment on a ground of disability — namely, an injury on the job for which the complainant was terminated — and then had to determine the appropriate compensation. In determining the general damages to award in the situation, the HRTO made the following statement:

> [The HRTO] and the Courts have recognized that there is an intrinsic value to the rights set out in the *Code* and a breach of those rights will merit the award of general damages. Jurisprudence also recognizes that general damage awards should not be set so low as to trivialize a breach of human rights. See: *Shelter Corp. v. Ontario (Human Rights Commission)* (2001), 39 C.H.R.R. D/111 (Div. Ct.) at paras. 43 and 44; *Gohm v.*

Domtar Inc. (No. 4) (1990), 12 C.H.R.R. D/161 at paras. 126–127 (Ont. Bd. of Inq.).

The Commission provided a number of cases in which general damage awards were made and which set out the criteria to be used in assessing the quantum of general damages. In the present case there was a single incident of discriminatory conduct and the behaviour of the Respondents does not appear to have been with particular malicious intent. Also, there was no evidence presented of mental anguish or distress, and the Commission did not seek damages in that regard. However, Ms. Boodhram's rights under the Code were violated and she is entitled to an award of general damages which recognizes the significance of those rights. Considering the facts of this case and the facts in the authorities provided by the Commissions, the Tribunal finds that the $5,000 sought is reasonable and appropriate. See: *Ontario (Human Rights Comm.) v. Ontario (Ministry of Health) (No. 2)* (1995), 24 C.H.R.R. D/250 (Ont. Bd. of Inq.) (total award of $7,000 for general damages); *Arias v. Desai* (2003), 45 C.H.R.R. D/308 (H.R.T.O.) (total general damages of $25,000); *Ketola v. Value Propane Inc. (No. 2)* (2002), 44 C.H.R.R. D/37 (Ont. Bd. of Inq.) (total general damages of $20,000); *deSousa v. Gauthier* (2002), 43 C.H.R.R. D/128 (Ont. Bd. of Inq.) (total award of $25,000 for general damages and mental anguish); *Baylis-Flannery v. DeWilde (No.2)* (2003), 48 C.H.R.R. D/197 (H.R.T.O.) (total general damages of $35,000).

[Note that the remedial provisions under the *Code* have been changed as of June 30, 2008. To get an idea how the HRTO awards remedies to damages under the amended *Code*, see *Lombardi v. Walton Enterprises*, 2012 HRTO 1675.]

York Advertising Ltd. v. Ontario (Human Rights Commission)

York Advertising Ltd. v. Ontario (Human Rights Commission), [2005] O.J. No. 1808, 197 O.A.C. 185, 139 A.C.W.S. (3d) 108, 55 C.H.R.R. D/308 (the *York* case) is a 2005 Div. Ct. case dealing with judicial review of a decision of the HRTO. The facts of the case are set out in the following paragraphs:

This proceeding arises out of a complaint filed by the respondent, Jane Doe (her pseudonym was substituted by the Tribunal for her proper surname), with the respondent, Ontario Human Rights Commission ("the Commission") in which she alleged that the applicants and the respondent, Hetherington, had infringed her right to equal treatment with respect to employment without discrimination based on her gender and her right to freedom from harassment in the workplace based on her gender. York was her employer and Murphy was York's data processing manager. Hetherington was formerly employed by York, but during the time frame covered by the complaints he provided services to York as an independent contractor through his company, the respondent Richland Marketing Inc. ("Richland").

At the Commission's invitation, York and Murphy agreed to mediate Doe's complaint. As a result of that mediation, York, Murphy and Doe entered into minutes of settlement which included a provision for a payment by York and Murphy to Doe. The minutes provided that the settlement was in full settlement of all claims by Doe against York and Murphy and recited that Doe had already executed a full and final release. The minutes also recited that the settlement did not constitute an admission by York and Murphy of any violation of the *Human Rights Code*, R.S.O. 1990, c. H.19 ("the *Code*").

That settlement was then approved by the Commission and thereby became final.

The HRCO referred Doe's complaint against Hetherington to the HRTO, and the decision made as a result thereof made findings against York, Richland, and Murphy, who then made application for judicial review of the decision because the HRTO "made various adverse findings of fact against York and Murphy and concluded that they too had violated various sections" of the *Code*. The court upheld the application for judicial review:

> The making of the adverse findings and conclusions against the applicants in the circumstances of this case constituted a violation of natural justice and due process.
>
> It is the applicants' position that it was not open to the Tribunal to expand its authority to inquire into issues beyond those referred to it by the Commission, namely, issues involving only Doe and Hetherington and that, by doing so, it exceeded its statutory jurisdiction. The Commission supports this position and the Tribunal opposes it. It is my view that the applicants' position is correct. The Tribunal's adverse findings and conclusions against the applicants reveal the over-reach by the Tribunal beyond what had been referred to it by the Commission in violation of the limits of its authority as set out in sections 36(1) and 39(1). By making findings and conclusions of wrongdoing against the applicants the Tribunal was, in effect, adjudi-

cating a complaint that had not been referred to it by the Commission.

The court provides the following to clarify its position:

> In the circumstances of this case, the applicants were entitled to assume that, once the terms of the settlement reached had been fully finalized, they could safely disengage themselves entirely from the complaints process without fear of being in jeopardy of being the subject of adverse findings and conclusions by the Tribunal. It would be incomprehensible, and contrary to law, that a statutory procedure for the resolution of human rights complaints in Ontario could lead to findings of wrongdoing against a party who had been released from the complaints process through a settlement, and who had no formal notice of the hearing, was not a party to it, and did not participate.

In *C.U. v. Blencowe*, 2013 HRTO 1667, the adjudicator, citing this case, excluded making any findings against two respondents who had settled with the Applicant and were no longer parties to the proceeding.

Metcalfe v. Papa Joe's Pizza & Chicken Inc.

Metcalfe v. Papa Joe's Pizza & Chicken Inc., [2005] O.H.R.T.D. No.46, 2005 HRTO 46, File No. HR-0595-04 and HR-0596-04 (the *Metcalfe* HRTO decision) involved an alleged discrimination based on sex and family status, and reprisal as the aftermath of a police investigation into the alleged sex discrimination. Believing the evidence of the complainants, the HRTO awarded damages in compensation, as well as ordered a number of public interest remedies. For a more recent case in which the HRTO ordered both monetary remedies and public interest remedies, see *Islam v. Big Inc.*, 2013 HRTO 2009.

Papa Joe's Pizza v. Ontario (Human Rights Commission)

Papa Joe's Pizza v. Ontario (Human Rights Commission), [2007] O.J. No. 2499, 225 O.A.C. 256, 59 C.C.E.L. (3d) 98, 158 A.C.W.S. (3d) 794, 2007 CarswellOnt. 4054 (the *Papa Joe's* case) is a 2007 Div. Ct. case appealing the *Metcalfe* HRTO decision. In deciding the case, the court held that the following three issues had to be decided:

1. Did the tribunal err in admitting similar fact evidence?
2. Did the reasons meet the minimum standard required to support the findings that Mr. Toufighjou violated the human rights of Ms. Metcalfe and Mr. Hoogerdijk?

3. Did the reasons meet the minimum standard required to support the compensations awards and public interest orders?

The court, throughout the decision, decried the lack of reasons given in the *Metcalfe* HRTO decision:

The reasons for the decision are sparse and, from the perspective of appellate review, leave a lot to be desired. The issue is whether those reasons are so inadequate and insufficient that they constitute a denial of natural justice based on procedural fairness. The duty to provide meaningful reasons is important.

In respect of the first issue regarding similar fact evidence, the court said the following:

Similar fact evidence in a case such as this is by its nature prejudicial. The issue is whether its probative value outweighs that prejudice. Though s. 15 of the *Statutory Powers Procedure Act*, R.S.O. 1990, c. S.22 relaxes the rules of evidence somewhat, caution is required.

Factors to consider in ruling on the admissibility of similar fact evidence in this case include:

(a) whether the evidence put forward does indeed involve similar facts;

(b) whether the evidence is put forward simply to cast doubt on Mr. Toufighjou's character, or to imply or establish his propensity [for] or predisposition towards committing such acts (in which case it should not be admitted); and

(c) whether the introduction of the evidence will confuse the issues by requiring the tribunal to engage in collateral issues beyond the subject matter of the complaint.

The court held that the similar fact evidence could be used in this case and that it was used properly for the following reasons:

The similar fact evidence went beyond mere propensity to commit a particular act or acts, or evidence of bad character. From the outset, this case was clearly a credibility contest between Ms. Metcalfe and Mr. Toufighjou. It is evident the tribunal member concluded the similar fact evidence would have probative value if it could assist him in determining credibility. ...

The tribunal member was cognizant of the correct legal test for the admission of the similar fact evidence, had the discretion to admit it, and reasonably exercised that discretion.

As to the issue of whether the reasons met the minimum standard required to support the finding, the court said they did:

> Once the tribunal member accepts the evidence of Ms. Metcalfe as truthful, it becomes the "clear and cogent" evidence required to support the findings against Mr. Toufighjou because there is no credible evidence to the contrary.

With respect to the reasons meeting the minimum standards required for the damages and public interest remedies ordered, the court said the reasons did not meet the minimum standard and then went on to modify the awards based on the reasons in the judgment.

Stephens v. Lynx Industries Inc.

Stephens v. Lynx Industries Inc., [2006] O.H.R.T.D. No. 33, 2006 HRTO 31, 58 C.H.R.R. D/274, File No. HR-0589-04 and HR-0590-04 (the *Stephens* decision) is an HRTO decision useful for its discussion as to when a tribunal can re-open or reconsider a decision. This case is not as relevant to the HRTO now because the HRTO Rules expressly give the HRTO authority to re-open a decision; the case was significant because there was no equivalent rule at the time. The HRCO made a motion to Divisional Court to ask the HRTO to re-open its decision where it awarded costs to the respondents and also named specific persons of the HRCO within the award. The HRCO said persons of the HRCO should not be specifically named. The court stated the three issues it had to determine in this case:

> The first deals with whether the Tribunal is *functus officio* at common law in this case. In particular, the questions to be addressed in relation to this issue are whether the Tribunal has the power to re-open its own hearings and, if so, whether this is a case in which this power should be exercised. The second is whether the Tribunal has jurisdiction to entertain this motion or whether the fact that the Commission has appealed to the Divisional Court prevents the Tribunal from all further actions in relation to this matter by virtue of the *Statutory Powers Procedure Act*, R.S.O. 1990, c. 22 (SPPA) ss. 25(1). The third is the discrete issue of whether the names of the Commission staff should be suppressed in this case.

The concept of *functus officio* was discussed first. This doctrine dictates that an agency is prevented from re-opening its decision because it has completed its hearing and no longer has jurisdiction, unless an exception to the doctrine exists, as stated by the court:

The common law doctrine of *functus officio* maintains that a final decision of a decision-making body cannot be re-opened except for very limited and exceptional reasons (*In re Nazaire Co.* (1879), 12 Ch.D. 88, *Paper Machinery Ltd. v. J.O. Ross Engineering Corp.*, [1934] S.C.R. 186). Originally created for the courts, the doctrine has extended to apply to administrative tribunals as well (*Chandler v. Alberta Association of Architects*, [1989] 2 S.C.R. 848; *Grier v. Metro International Trucks Ltd.* (1996), 28 O.R. (3d) 67 (Div. Ct) (*Grier*)). In the case of administrative tribunals, four exceptions to the *functus* doctrine justifying the re-opening of a decision can be discerned from the jurisprudence. These are situations in which:

(a) the power to re-open has been conferred on the tribunal by legislation (see e.g. *Grillas v. Minister of Manpower and Immigration*, [1972] S.C.R. 577)

(b) the tribunal has failed to dispose of an issue which is fairly raised by the proceedings and of which the tribunal is empowered by its enabling statute to dispose (see e.g. *Chandler, supra*)

(c) the tribunal has made a clerical error or error in expressing its manifest intention (see *In re Nazaire Co.* (1879), 12 Ch.D. 88, *Paper Machinery Ltd. v. J.O. Ross Engineering Corp.*, [1934] S.C.R. 186)

(d) the tribunal has made an error that renders its decision a nullity such as "a denial of natural justice which vitiate[s] the whole proceedings" (see *Chandler* at para. 25, *Ridge v. Baldwin*, [1964] A.C. 40 (H.L.)) or "a misapprehension of an important fact lying at the heart of the litigation" (*Grier, supra*) which may stem from its reliance on factual errors made by the parties (see e.g. *Grier, supra*; *Kingston (City) v. Ontario (Mining & Lands Commissioner)* (1977), 18 O.R. (2d) 166 (Div. Ct.)) (*Kingston*)).

As the HRTO, at that time, had no authority to re-open its case, either under its enabling legislation or its rules, the court had to find a denial of natural justice under the fourth exception to order the HRTO to re-open its decision. Based upon a finding of insufficient time for the HRCO to prepare for the issue of costs, the court found a denial of natural justice and granted the motion subject to the appeal that the HRCO filed on the decision to the court.

Although the HRTO is now given discretion to grant reconsideration, a quick survey of the results of reconsideration applications before the HRTO will tell the reader that it is a discretion rarely used.

Chornyj v. Trus Joist, a Division of Weyerhaeuser

Chornyj v. Trus Joist, a Division of Weyerhaeuser, 2006 HRTO 10, 49 C.C.E.L. (3d) 293, 2006 CarswellOnt. 2782, 56 C.H.H.R. D/96, File No. HR-0977-05 (the *Chornyj* HRTO decision) is an HRTO interim decision in which the respondents brought three motions, the key ones asking for either a dismissal or limiting of the complaint based upon an overview of the situation:

> This is a complaint brought under the *Human Rights Code*, R.S.O. 1990, c. H.19, as amended ("the *Code*"), alleging an infringement of sections 5(1) and 9. The Complaint was filed on or about May 29, 2003, and was referred to the Human Rights Tribunal of Ontario ("the Tribunal") on June 16, 2005. The case involves a challenge to a pre-employment drug testing policy and an allegation that a job offer made to the Complainant was improperly withdrawn as a result of a positive drug test.

In this matter, the complainant was hired for a job subject to drug testing. When the drug test was positive for marijuana, the job offer was revoked. Immediately after that, the complainant made a complaint of discrimination based upon a perceived disability. The HRTO found that the issues to be decided were as follows:

1. Does the Tribunal lack jurisdiction to deal with this Complaint and as a result, should the Complaint be dismissed without a hearing on the merits?
2. Should the Tribunal restrict the scope of the hearing to only the marijuana elements of the Respondent's pre-employment drug testing policy?

In looking at the first issue, the adjudicator set out the general legal principles regarding a motion to dismiss a case:

> In considering a motion to dismiss a case without a hearing, or to strike pleadings, or to otherwise narrow the inquiry into a complaint, it is important to bear in mind certain fundamental and well established principles of human rights law. Human rights tribunals and the Courts have long recognized the special "quasi-constitutional" status of human rights legislation. The *Code* must be interpreted and applied in a large, liberal and purposive manner. The approach to human rights adjudication should never be overly legalistic and technical, but rather should enhance accessibility and ensure that determinations are made on the true merits of the case. As the Court said in *Action Travail des Femmes v. Canadian National Railway Co.*,

[1987] 1 S.C.R. 1114, "[w]e should not search for ways and means to minimize those rights and to enfeeble their proper impact["] (at 1134). (See also: *Ontario Human Rights Commission et al. v. Simpsons-Sears Ltd. (O'Malley)*, [1985] 2 S.C.R. 536, at 546–547; *Toneguzzo v. Kimberly Clark*, [2005] O.H.R.T.D. No. 45, 2005 HRTO 45.)

It has been said that for a Respondent to succeed in having a complaint dismissed without a hearing, it must be "plain and obvious" that the complaint will fail. The Honourable Mr. Justice Peter Cory, sitting as a panel of this Tribunal[,] noted that the usual standard applied in civil proceedings for dismissal without a hearing[] ought to be even more rigorous in human rights cases:

> A stringent test must be met if this motion is to succeed. That is to say, it must be "plain and obvious" that the *Coroners Act* is consistent with the *Code* and the Complainants are certain to fail (see *Odhavji Estate v. Woodhouse*, [2003] 3 S.C.R. 263 at para. 15). It is indeed appropriate that this stringent test be applied to proceedings taken pursuant to the *Human Rights Code* which are frequently taken by individuals seeking to have their basic rights recognized and enforced ... (*Braithwaite v. Ontario (Chief Coroner)*, [2005] O.H.R.T.D. No. 31, 2005 HRTO 31 at para. 13)

He went on to say that the form and sufficiency of pleadings in a human rights case should not be scrutinized in the same manner as in civil proceedings. Rather, "complainants should simply be required to meet standards of basic fairness" (See: *Braithwaite, supra* at para 14. See also: *Toneguzzo, supra*).

The HRTO applied the legal principles and held that "[e]mployment is a social area covered by the *Code*. Disability (which includes perceived disability) is a ground of discrimination covered by the *Code*. The subject matter of the Complaint falls within the jurisdiction of the *Code* and the Tribunal". The adjudicator then stated that the alleged ground of discrimination deserved to be heard and not dismissed without a hearing. The adjudicator, in passing, stated what normally happens in a human rights case (or did happen at that time):

> In a typical human rights case, the Commission and the complainant will lead evidence to establish a *prima facie* case of discrimination. The onus then shifts to the respondent to provide a non-discriminatory explanation for its actions. The onus then shifts back to the Commission and complainant to prove

that the explanation is pretexual, that the real reason for the impugned action was tainted by discrimination. (See: *O'Malley*, *supra*)

Based on all of the above, the HRTO dismissed the motion.

For a more recent case on how the HRTO deals with a motion to dismiss an application for failure to show a *prima facie* case of discrimination, see *Delavalle v. Waterfront Inn (Sault) Ltd.*, 2013 HRTO 773. In this case, the adjudicator took a view similar to *Chornyj* and denied the Respondent's motion based on the broad definition of disability in the *Code*. The adjudicator did dismiss the Application, after considering the evidence as a whole and concluding that the Applicant failed to meet the onus of establishing that her disability and/or any perception of disability were factors of her discrimination.

Weyerhaeuser Co. (c.o.b. Trus Joist) v. Ontario (Human Rights Commission)

Weyerhaeuser Co. (c.o.b. Trus Joist) v. Ontario (Human Rights Commission), [2007] O.J. No. 640, 279 D.L.R. (4th) 480, 221 O.A.C. 245, [2007] CLLC para. 230-012, 156 A.C.W.S. (3d) 187 (the *Weyerhaeuser* case) is a 2007 Div. Ct. case dealing with judicial review of the *Chornyj* HRTO decision (discussed above). After recounting the facts and background of the case, the Divisional Court determined the standard of review to be applied in a HRTO decision, even an interim decision, as follows:

> The Ontario Court of Appeal in *Entrop v. Imperial Oil Ltd.* (2000), 50 O.R. (3d) 18 at paras. 42–43 (C.A.) [*Entrop*] outlined the applicable standards of review with respect to an appeal from a final decision of a Board of Inquiry (now the Tribunal). On a question of law the standard is correctness. On findings of fact and questions of mixed fact and law the standard is reasonableness *simpliciter*.
>
> In this case, however, there is no final decision. Rather, this is an application to judicially review an interim decision of the Tribunal. The *Code* does not provide a right of appeal from an interim decision of the Tribunal. In my opinion, this does not change the standards of review described in *Entrop*, *supra*. In *Dr. Q. v. College of Physicians and Surgeons of British Columbia*, [2003] 1 S.C.R. 226 at para. 27, the Supreme Court held that "silence [regarding a right of appeal] is neutral and does not imply a high standard of scrutiny". It follows that silence also does not imply a lower standard of scrutiny.

The standard of review in this case turns on the nature of the question before the Tribunal. I agree that Chornyj was not claiming he had a *Code*-protected right to lie. Chornyj claimed he was subject to discrimination in employment because of his recreational marijuana use. The alleged grounds of discrimination were disability and/or perceived disability. Therefore, there were two distinct issues before the Tribunal.

The first issue was whether a person who engages in recreational marijuana use can maintain a claim of discrimination on the ground of disability where that person admits he is not disabled by his marijuana use. This is a question of law subject to the correctness standard of review. The second issue was whether Weyerhaeuser's Standard is *prima facie* discriminatory on the ground of perceived disability because in effect it treated Chornyj as if he were disabled by drug dependency. This is a question of mixed fact and law subject to the reasonableness *simpliciter* standard of review.

The court then looked at the adjudicator's view of the matter depending on a perceived disability:

In *Quebec (Commission des droits de la personne et des droits de la jeunesse) v. Montreal (City); Quebec (Commission des droits de la personne et des droits de la jeunesse) v. Boisbriand (City)*, [2000] 1 S.C.R. 665 at para. 71 [*Boisbriand*], the Supreme Court concluded there is a subjective component of discrimination that protects individuals from discrimination on the ground of perceived disability.

The more difficult question is how a claimant can prove another party (for example, a prospective employer) "perceives" the claimant as having a disability. In *Boisbriand*, *supra* at paras. 76–84, the Supreme Court said that a multidimensional analysis is required. This approach was adopted by the Alberta Court of Queen's Bench in *Alberta (Human Rights and Citizenship Commission) v. Kellogg Brown & Root (Canada) Co.*, [2006] A.J. No. 583 at para. 89 (Q.B.) [*Kellogg*]. As *Kellogg* is similar in many respects to the case at bar it is instructive to examine it in more detail.

Kellogg involved a claim of discrimination by one Mr. Chiasson, a recreational marijuana user, who was terminated shortly after he began work with Kellogg, Root and Brown (Canada) Company ("KBR") because of a positive result in a pre-employment drug test. Under KBR's drug testing policy, the offer of employment was conditional on Chiasson's pre-employment drug test being negative. To assess whether Chiasson was subject to discrimination on the ground of perceived disability, S.L. Martin J. looked to evidence of actual subjective belief of Chiasson's drug dependency on the part of KBR and its employees, as well as the consequences of a positive drug test in KBR's drug testing policy.

S.L. Martin J. found there was evidence that KBR representatives and some of its employees subjectively believed Chiasson was drug dependent. Her Honour also found that the harsh consequence of a positive drug test prescribed by the drug testing policy (automatic dismissal) also indicated that KBR subjectively believed any person testing positive on a pre-employment drug test was a substance abuser. Taken together, she concluded Chiasson's dismissal was *prima facie* discriminatory on the ground of perceived disability: *Kellogg*, *supra* at paras. 90–94.

Applying the *Kellogg* analysis to this case, I conclude the Tribunal erred in finding that Chornyj had a tenable claim of discrimination on the ground of perceived disability, and therefore it was unreasonable that the Tribunal refused to dismiss his complaint.

Because a failed drug test, by the Weyerhaeuser's Standard, did not mean that an employee was automatically fired and that, in reality, many other steps would be taken to assist the employee, there was no tenable basis of the complainant's claim. The Divisional Court concluded that it was "plain and obvious" that the complainant could not succeed with the claim of discrimination based upon a perceived disability; therefore, the HRTO had no reasonable ground to refuse the respondent's motion to dismiss. The Divisional Court granted the application for judicial review and issued an order preventing the HRTO from hearing the matter.

Incorporated Synod of the Diocese of Toronto v. Ontario (Human Rights Commission)

Incorporated Synod of the Diocese of Toronto v. Ontario (Human Rights Commission), [2008] O.J. No. 1692 (the *Diocese* case) is a 2008 Div. Ct. case dealing with a judicial review application where the "applicants seek an order quashing the decision of the Commission referring the subject matter of the complaint to the Human Rights Tribunal of Ontario ('the Tribunal') and an order prohibiting the Tribunal from holding a hearing with respect to the complaint". This case involved the jurisdiction of the HRTO to hear the matter for two reasons:

(1) the relationship between the Incorporated Synod of the Diocese of Toronto ("the Diocese") and the complainant is not a "service" within the meaning of s. 1 of the *Ontario Human Rights Code* ("the *Code*"); and

(2) by virtue of the amendment of the complaint, the content of the investigating officer's case analysis, and concessions made by counsel for the Commission on this application, the "subject matter" of the complaint as referred to the Tribunal by the Commission has ceased to exist and there is nothing upon which the Tribunal can proceed.

Under the current legislation, the HRCO does not usually investigate and refers matters to the HRTO; this case, however, has an interesting discussion on what matters should be heard before the HRTO:

In our view, there is a clear jurisdictional issue raised as to whether the relationship between the Diocese and its postulants can be characterized as a "service" within the meaning of s. 1 of the *Code*. This is not a pure question of law. A proper analysis of the issue can only be done on a factual record establishing, for example, the nature of the relationship between the Diocese and those it accepts as postulants, the mutual obligations and expectations between them, what is provided to the postulants by the Diocese, the basis upon which things are provided to postulants, and the like. Those factual determinations are best made by the Tribunal, which would have the advantage of hearing live evidence on these issues if it thought it advisable. Also, the Tribunal has special expertise on issues of interpreting its home statute and the reviewing court would benefit from that opinion.

We are therefore of the view, that the preliminary jurisdictional issue is best decided in the first instance by the Tribunal. There is considerable jurisprudence supporting leaving such issues to be determined by the Tribunal except in the rarest of cases where it can be said that a proceeding before the Tribunal is "fatally flawed": *Re Roosma and Ford Motor Co.* (1988), 66 O.R. (2d) 18 (Div. Ct.); *Ontario College of Art v. Ontario (Human Rights Commission)* (1993), 11 O.R. (3d) 798 (Div. Ct.); *Ressel v. Board of Directors of Chiropractic*, [1990] O.J. No. 1715 (Div. Ct.). This is not one of those rare situations that would warrant the intervention of this Court at this stage.

In this particular case, the court held that applications would be dismissed, confirming that the HRTO had jurisdiction to hear the matter.

For a more recent case of judicial review application based on "jurisdiction of tribunal", see *City of Toronto v. The Dream Team*, 2012 ONSC 3904.

Smith v. Menzies Chrysler Inc.

Smith v. Menzies Chrysler Inc., [2008] O.H.R.T.D. No. 35, 2008 HRTO 37, File No. HR-1368-07 (the *Smith* HRTO interim decision) is an HRTO interim decision that dealt with four motions:

(a) a request for the adjudicator to recuse herself due to apprehension of bias,

(b) a request to examine the complainant's counsel,

(c) a request for an order to stay or dismiss the complaint because to proceed would constitute an abuse of process, and

(d) a request to examine the complainant.

The matter arose when William David Smith, the complainant, filed a complaint with the Ontario Human Rights Commission on December 14, 2006, alleging discrimination, harassment, and reprisal in employment on the basis of sex and sexual orientation. Further, in "March 2007, the complainant commenced a civil action in the Ontario Superior Court of Justice against the corporate respondent and personal respondent Graham alleging wrongful dismissal, infliction of mental harm, negligence, assault and conspiracy."

Dealing with each motion separately, there was a request for the adjudicator to recuse herself because of the situation that occurred at the initial conference call, where a counsel for one of the respondents made a humorous comment in terms of an allegation, upon which the adjudicator requested counsel to refrain from this type of humour. The allegation was that this action could be a reasonable apprehension of bias. The adjudicator stated the law in this area, which she did not find exist in the facts:

> As I noted in my oral ruling, the threshold test for reasonable apprehension of bias promulgated by de Grandpré J. in *Committee for Justice and Liberty v. National Energy Board*, [1978] 1 S.C.R. 369 is a high standard. The apprehension of bias must be both *reasonable* and *serious, supra* at 395. The test, at 394, is as follows:
>
> > [T]he apprehension of bias must be a reasonable one, held by reasonable and right minded persons, applying themselves to the question and obtaining thereon the

required information ... [T]hat test is "what would an informed person, viewing the matter realistically and practically — and having thought the matter through — conclude. Would he think it is more likely than not that the [decision-maker], whether consciously or unconsciously, would not decide fairly. The only concern articulated by the respondents as the basis for an apprehension of bias was my single request to Mr. Mack during the Initial Conference Call. Specifically, I asked Mr. Mack[] to refrain from joking about the allegations in the case. I note that Mr. Mack acceded to my request and no further discussion regarding this matter occurred.

Upon considering the above-noted test in the context of the exchange between Mr. Mack and myself, I concluded that the circumstances of the Initial Conference Call did not give rise to a reasonable apprehension of bias. I held that a reasonable person, viewing the matter realistically and having thought the matter through, would not perceive my direction to Mr. Mack reflected a lack of neutrality about the current dismissal motion or a predisposition towards the merits of the complaint. I concluded the alleged "disfavour" did not meet the threshold necessary to support disqualification for a reasonable apprehension of bias. Accordingly, the motion to recuse for apprehension of bias was dismissed.

I add that, in certain circumstances like this case, a simple request by an adjudicator to counsel to refrain from a particular line of humour is consistent with the Vice-Chair's responsibilities to foster an atmosphere conducive to a judicial process and respectful of, and sensitive to, the human rights issues that come before the Tribunal. Although Tribunal hearings can be less formal and legalistic, particularly with respect to rules of evidence, so as to promote accessibility, flexibility and expeditiousness, a relaxed tone to the proceedings does not diminish the seriousness of the rights, responsibilities and defences provided under the *Code*. A human rights hearing is a legal proceeding and it is critical that all parties, including counsel or representatives, maintain a level of decorum fitting the quasi-judicial nature of the process and necessary for the orderly administration of the Tribunal hearing.

In terms of the request to examine the complainant's counsel due to the "unusual" strategy of having instituted both a human rights complaint and a civil action, the HRTO held that the law of solicitor–client privilege trumps the request:

In *Pritchard v. Ontario (Human Rights Commission)*, [2004] 1
S.C.R. 809 at para. 16, Major J., on behalf of the Supreme
Court of Canada, described solicitor–client privilege as
"all-encompassing" and held that it applies to a broad range of
communications between lawyer and client "... as long as the
communication falls within the usual and ordinary scope of the
professional relationship". The Court confirmed that solicitor–
client privilege is "nearly absolute" and that "exceptions to it
will be rare", at para. 18.

The respondents seek to examine complainant's counsel in
order to explore Mr. McKeever's alleged pattern of pursuing
both human rights and civil claims. The respondents have prof-
fered no other purpose or rationale for a line of examination
that will necessarily intrude upon solicitor–client privilege. I
find the contention that Mr. McKeever routinely advises his clients to seek human rights and civil recourse does not address
the question of whether the continuance of this proceeding
would amount to an abuse of the Tribunal's process, and conse-
quently does not justify an incursion into areas sedulously protected by solicitor–client privilege. I further note that sections
5.4(2) and 15(2)(a) of the *Statutory Powers Procedure Act*,
R.S.O. 1990, c. S.22 (*SPPA*), bar an order for disclosure or
admission of privileged information.

With regard to the motion to stay or dismiss the complaint based
upon abuse of process, the adjudicator dealt with all the foundations
of such alleged abuse and dismissed each one. Regarding abuse of
process due to duplicative proceedings, the adjudicator noted that
the human rights complaint and the civil action involved different
parties, different legal issues, and different remedies; she then noted
the case law in the area:

I note that since 2003 there have been competing lines of
authority with respect to these issues and all parties referred to
various decisions which either mentioned or distinguished
McKelvey [*McKelvey v. D'Ercole* (2003), 32 C.C.E.L. (3d) 119
(Ont. S.C.J.)]. I further note the outcome in the 2005 decision
of *Schmidt v. Elko Properties Ltd.*, *supra*. In that case, the
employer defendant was unsuccessful in seeking a stay of a
wrongful dismissal action pending determination of the plaintiff's human rights complaint. Leave to appeal was denied by
Justice Hambly of the Superior Court, who commented, at
para. 9, that "... the absolute statement of Justice Echlin in
McKelvey, *supra*, that an employee cannot pursue a claim before

the Human Rights Commission and a civil action based on the same facts goes too far. It is not supported by the case law".

Lastly, although the respondents' submissions raised but did not squarely address the doctrine of *res judicata* and issue estoppel, I have considered the general concepts in arriving at this decision, and in particular the analysis of the principles in *Ford Motor Co. of Canada v. Ontario (Human Rights Commission)*, [2001] O.J. No. 4937 (Ont. C.A.), and the authorities cited therein. I find the first branch of the doctrine of *res judicata*, known as issue estoppel, is not applicable to the case at hand. The present situation does not satisfy the three criteria explained in *Ford Motor Co.*, *supra*, at para. 63: (i) the civil lawsuit is still in its early stages and there is no final decision; (ii) the parties are not the same; and (iii) nor are the issues and questions to be determined by this Tribunal the same.

In the circumstances of this case, I do not find the pursuit of both a human rights complaint and civil action amount[s] to an abuse of process. The respondents' "duplication" argument fails to recognize that Clark Menzies, Mark Lyons and the Commission are not parties in the civil proceeding and that there are distinct interests, issues and remedies that are pertinent to each of these participants and specific to the human rights process. I echo the suggestion of other decision-makers that the parties can prevent relitigation and double recovery by ensuring the second judicial body is fully informed about any findings and awards made by the first, see *Farris v. Stanbach Ontario Inc.*, [2004] O.J. No. 1227 (Sup. Ct. J.) and *Schmidt, supra*.

The arguments suggesting abuse of process due to undue prejudice and bad faith were also addressed and found wanting (or absent).

As to the final motion of examining the complainant, the HRTO held that such examination should be part of the hearing itself.

For a recent HRTO case on "abuse of process", see *Killeen v. Soncin Construction*, 2013 HRTO 350.

REVIEW QUESTIONS

1. What is the enabling legislation for the HRTO?
2. Where would you find the practices and procedures of the HRTO?
3. List five grounds (or groups) protected under the *Code* from being discriminated against or harassed.
4. Pursuant to the *Code*, how does the SPPA apply to the HRTO?

5. What does the privative clause of the *Code* related to the HRTO prevent and allow, and under what circumstances?
6. What is a stated case as discussed in the *Code* and the HRTO Rules?
7. What Rule(s) give discretion and flexibility to the HRTO in applying the HRTO Rules?
8. What Rules deal with Form 1, Form 2, and Form 3?
9. What Rule(s) deal with disclosure, and what is the result of insufficient disclosure?
10. What Rule(s) deal with motions, and what is the appropriate procedure to have a motion dealt with by the HRTO?
11. What jurisdiction is the HRTO given to reconsider a decision under the various procedures and practices of the HRTO?
12. How do the various procedures and practices of the HRTO deal with the ability to appear on behalf of a party before the HRTO?
13. How do the various procedures and practices of the HRTO deal with giving access to persons before the HRTO and dealing with their needs?

EXERCISE

Based upon the facts of the *Barker* case briefed in the chapter, fill out the form(s) to institute this matter currently before the HRTO.

Appendix 6.1
Overview of Procedural Stages of a Matter Before the HRTO

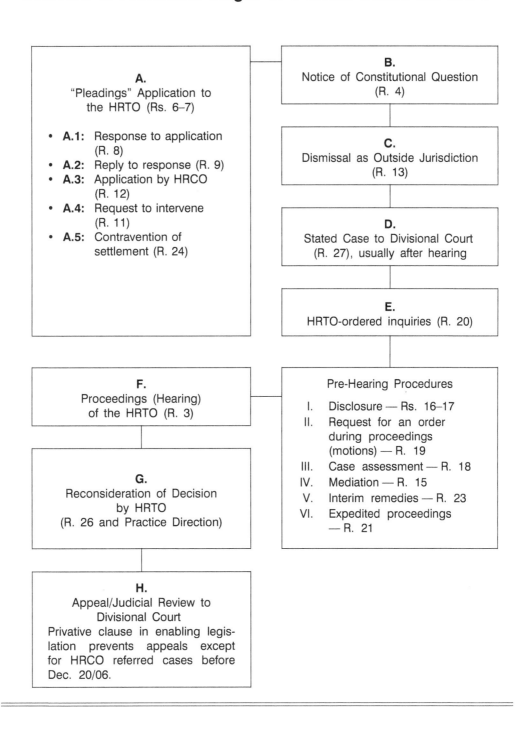

A.
"Pleadings" Application to
the HRTO (Rs. 6–7)

- **A.1:** Response to application
  (R. 8)
- **A.2:** Reply to response (R. 9)
- **A.3:** Application by HRCO
  (R. 12)
- **A.4:** Request to intervene
  (R. 11)
- **A.5:** Contravention of
  settlement (R. 24)

B.
Notice of Constitutional Question
(R. 4)

C.
Dismissal as Outside Jurisdiction
(R. 13)

D.
Stated Case to Divisional Court
(R. 27), usually after hearing

E.
HRTO-ordered inquiries (R. 20)

F.
Proceedings (Hearing)
of the HRTO (R. 3)

G.
Reconsideration of Decision
by HRTO
(R. 26 and Practice Direction)

H.
Appeal/Judicial Review to
Divisional Court
Privative clause in enabling legislation prevents appeals except for HRCO referred cases before Dec. 20/06.

Pre-Hearing Procedures

I. Disclosure — Rs. 16–17
II. Request for an order during proceedings (motions) — R. 19
III. Case assessment — R. 18
IV. Mediation — R. 15
V. Interim remedies — R. 23
VI. Expedited proceedings — R. 21

Appendix 6.2
Practice Direction on Recording Hearings†
Effective May 2013

The Human Rights Tribunal of Ontario (the HRTO) has developed the following approach to recording hearings. The procedure outlined below provides general information only. It is not a rule within the meaning of the HRTO's Rules of Procedure. The HRTO may vary the approach to recording hearings where appropriate.

General Practice on Recording
The HRTO does not normally record or transcribe its proceedings, but may record a proceeding at its own discretion. It has been recognized that transcription and recording of hearings may make proceedings more formal and expensive in administrative tribunals. Recordings may lengthen proceedings if parties ask to replay evidence. Adjudicators often travel and hold hearings in various locations without staff to assist them, so equipment problems may arise and it is impossible to guarantee a quality recording. Therefore, many tribunals including the HRTO do not record or transcribe their proceedings.

Recording as Accommodation for *Code*-related Needs
The HRTO will record a hearing when it is necessary to accommodate the needs of the panel, a party or a representative under the *Human Rights Code*. Please contact the Registrar as soon as possible if you require accommodation.

Self-recording and Transcription
If a party wishes to record a hearing to supplement his or her notes, he or she must get the permission of the panel and provide a copy of any recording or transcription to the other parties and the HRTO (on a USB device or CD). Such recordings or transcriptions do not form part of the HRTO's record of proceedings, including the record filed in court in respect of any application for judicial review. The recording or transcription may not be publicized or used for any purpose other than in the proceeding before the Tribunal.

Use of a Court Reporter
The HRTO may permit a party to have a court reporter record the hearing at the party's expense, upon request and at its discretion. This practice is discouraged because court reporters may lead to more formality, cause delay and many parties lack the financial resources to obtain a court reporter or order a transcript.

When a court reporter is permitted, to ensure that all parties and the tribunal member have the ability to access the transcript, the party that has obtained the court reporter must normally have transcripts produced and provide copies to the Tribunal and the other parties at its own expense. The HRTO may waive this requirement, or make directions about the date the transcript must be produced. The official transcript will normally be considered part of the HRTO's record of proceedings and be included in the record filed in court in respect of any application for judicial review.

---

† Source: HRTO website, "Rules and Practice Directions", <http://www.sjto.gov.on.ca/documents/hrto/Practice%20Directions/Recording%20Hearings.html>.

Appendix 6.3
Application under s. 34 of the *Code* (Form 1)[†]

Ontario

Human Rights Tribunal of Ontario

Application under Section 34 of the *Human Rights Code* (Form 1)

(Disponible en français)

www.hrto.ca

How to Apply to the Human Rights Tribunal of Ontario

Before you start:

1. Read the questions and answers below to find out if the Human Rights Tribunal of Ontario (the Tribunal) has the ability to deal with your Application.

2. Download and read the **Applicant's Guide** from the Tribunal's web site **www.hrto.ca**. If you need a paper copy or accessible format, contact us:

    Human Rights Tribunal of Ontario
    655 Bay Street, 14th floor
    Toronto, Ontario
    M7A 2A3
    Phone: 416-326-1312   Toll-free: 1-866-598-0322
    Fax: 416-326-2199   Toll-free: 1-866-355-6099
    TTY: 416-326-2027   Toll-free: 1-866-607-1240
    Email: HRTO.Registrar@ontario.ca
    Website: www.hrto.ca

    The Tribunal has other guides and practice directions to help all parties to an Application understand the process Download copies from the Tribunal's website or contact us.

3. Complete each section of this Application form. As you fill out each section, refer to the instructions in the Applicant's Guide.

Getting help with your application

For free legal assistance with the application process, contact the **Human Rights Legal Support Centre.** Website: www.hrlsc.on.ca, Mail: 180 Dundas Street West, 8th floor, Toronto, ON M7A 0A1, Tel: 416-597-4900, Toll-free 1-866-625-5179, Fax: 416-597-4901, Toll-free 1-866-625-5180, TTY 416-597-4903, Toll-free 1-866-612-8627.

Questions About Filing an Application with the Tribunal

The following questions and answers are provided for general information. They should not be taken as legal advice or a determination of how the Tribunal will decide any particular application. For legal advice and assistance, contact the **Human Rights Legal Support Centre.**

Who can file an Application with the Tribunal?

You can file an Application if you believe you experienced discrimination or harassment in one of the five areas covered by the Ontario Human Rights Code (the Code). The Code lists a number of grounds for claiming discrimination and harassment. To find out if you have grounds for your complaint under the Code, read the Applicant's Guide.

What is the time limit for filing an Application?

You can file an Application up to one year after you experienced discrimination or harassment. If there was a series of events, you can file up to one year after the last event. In some cases, the Tribunal may extend this time.

October 4, 2012   Form 1 - Page 1 of 14

[†]   Source: HRTO website <http://www.hrto.ca/>

Ontario

Human Rights Tribunal of Ontario

Application under Section 34 of the Human Rights Code (Form 1)

The discrimination happened outside Ontario. Can I still apply?

In most cases, no. To find out about exceptions, contact the **Human Rights Legal Support Centre**.

My complaint is against a federal government department, agency, or a federally regulated business or service. Should I apply to the Tribunal?

No. Contact the Canadian Human Rights Commission. Web: **http://www.chrc-ccdp.ca**. Mail: 344 Slater Street, 8th Floor, Ottawa, Ontario K1A 1E1. Phone: (613) 995-1151. Toll-free: 1-888-214-1090. TTY: 1-888-643-3304. Fax: (613) 996-9661.

Should I use this form if I am applying because a previous human rights settlement has been breached?

No. If you settled a previous human rights application and the respondent did not comply with the settlement agreement, use the special application called **Application for Contravention of Settlement, Form 18**. For a paper copy, contact the Tribunal.

Can I file this Application if I am dealing with or have dealt with these facts or issues in another proceeding?

The Code has special rules depending on what the other proceeding is and at what stage the other proceeding is at. **Read the** Applicant's Guide **and get legal advice, if:**

1. You are currently involved in, or were previously involved in a civil court action based on the same facts and asked for a human rights remedy; **or**

2. You have ever filed a complaint with the Ontario Human Rights Commission based on the same subject matter; **or**

3. You are currently involved in, or were previously involved in another proceeding (for example, union grievance) based on the same facts.

How do I file an Application on behalf of another person?

To file an application on behalf of another person, you must complete and file this Application (Form 1) as well one other form:

- Form 4A if you are filing on behalf of a minor;
- Form 4B if you are filing on behalf of a mentally incompetent person; or
- Form 27 for all other situations where you are filing on behalf of someone else.

When completing this Application, you must check the box in Question 1 that indicates you are filing an Application on Behalf of Another Person. You must provide your name and contact information in Question 1.

The completed Form 4A, Form 4B or Form 27 can be attached to your Application or sent to the Tribunal separately by mail, fax or email. If sent separately, it must be sent within **five (5) days** following the filing of your Application.

For more information on applications on behalf of another person, please see the following Practice Directions:

- Practice Direction on filing application on behalf of another person under section 34(5) of the Code
- Practice Direction on Litigation Guardians before Social Justice Tribunals Ontario

Note: If you are a lawyer or other legal representative providing representation to the applicant, do not use the Form 4A, Form 4B or Form 27. Your details should be provided in section 3, "Representative Contact Information," of this Application (Form 1).

Learn more
To find out more about human rights in Ontario, visit **www.ohrc.on.ca** or phone 1-800-387-9080.

Ontario

Human Rights Tribunal of Ontario

Application under Section 34 of the Human Rights Code (Form 1)

Instructions: Complete all parts of this form, using the **Applicant's Guide** for help. If your form is not complete, the Tribunal may return it to you. This will slow down the application process. At the end of this form, you will be required to read and agree to a declaration that the information in your Application is complete and accurate (if you are a lawyer or legal representative assisting an applicant with this Form 1, please see the **Practice Direction On Electronic Filing of Applications and Responses By Licensed Representatives**).

Contact Information for the Applicant

1. Personal Contact Information

☐ Check here if you are filing an Application on Behalf of Another Person. **Note**: you must *also* complete a Form 4A, Form 4B or Form 27, whichever is applicable, see Instructions above.

Please give us your personal contact information. This information will be shared with the respondent(s) and all correspondence from the Tribunal and the respondent(s) will go here. If you do not want the Tribunal to share this contact information, **you should complete section 2, below, but you must still provide your personal contact information for the Tribunal's records.**

*First Name	Middle Name	*Last Name

Street #	Street Name	Apt/Suite

City/Town	Province	Postal Code	Email
	Ontario		

Daytime Phone (e.g. 999-999-9999)	Cell Phone (e.g. 999-999-9999)	Fax (e.g. 999-999-9999)	TTY (e.g. 999-999-9999)

What is the best way to send information to you?
(If you check email, you are consenting to delivery of documents by email)   ○ Mail   ○ Email   ○ Fax

Ontario

Human Rights Tribunal of Ontario

2. Alternative Contact Information

If you want the Tribunal and respondent(s) to contact you through another person, you must provide contact information for that person below. You should fill this section out if it will be difficult for the Tribunal to reach you at the address above or if you want the Tribunal to keep your contact information private. **If you complete this section, all of your correspondence will be sent to you in care of your Alternative Contact.**

First (or Given) Name	Middle Name	Last (or Family) Name

Street #	Street Name	Apt/Suite

City/Town	Province	Postal Code	Email
	Ontario ▼		

Daytime Phone (i.e. 999-999-9999)	Cell Phone (i.e. 999-999-9999)	Fax (i.e. 999-999-9999)	TTY (i.e. 999-999-9999)

What is the best way to send information to you at your alternative contact?
(If you check email, you are consenting to delivery of documents by email)   ○ Mail   ○ Email   ○ Fax

3. Representative Contact Information

Complete this section only if you are authorizing a lawyer or another Representative to act for you.

☐ I authorize the named organization and/or person to represent me

My representative is:

☐ Lawyer	LSUC#	
☐ Paralegal	LSUC#	
☐ Legal Support Centre		
☐ Other- please specify the Nature of Exemption from licensing requirements in the text below:		

Nature of Exemption (e.g. family member, unpaid friend)

Ontario

Human Rights Tribunal of Ontario

Please choose the type of Representative: ○ A) Organizational Representative ○ B) Individual Representative

A) Organizational Representative

Full Name of Representative Organization

Name of the Contact Person from the Organization

First (or Given) Name	Last (or Family) Name	

Street #	Street Name	Apt/Suite

City/Town	Province Ontario	Postal Code	Email

Daytime Phone (i.e. 999-999-9999)	Cell Phone (i.e. 999-999-9999)	Fax (i.e. 999-999-9999)	TTY (i.e. 999-999-9999)

What is the best way to send information to your representative?
(If you check email, you are consenting to delivery of documents by email)   ○ Mail   ○ Email   ○ Fax

Contact Information for the Respondent(s)

4. Respondent Contact Information

Provide the name and contact information for any respondent against which you are filing this Application.

Please choose the type of respondent: ○ A) Organization Respondent   ○ B) Individual Respondent

A) Organization Respondent

Name the organization you believe discriminated against you. You should also indicate the contact person
from the organization to whom correspondence can be addressed.

Ontario

Human Rights Tribunal of Ontario

Full Name of Organization

Name of the Contact Person from the Organization

First (or Given) Name	Last (or Family) Name	Title

Street #	Street Name		Apt/Suite

City/Town	Province	Postal Code	Email
	Ontario ▼		

Daytime Phone (i.e. 999-999-9999)	Cell Phone (i.e. 999-999-9999)	Fax (i.e. 999-999-9999)	TTY (i.e. 999-999-9999)

Are there any additional respondents? ○ Yes   ○ No

Grounds of Discrimination

5. Grounds Claimed

The Ontario Human Rights Code lists the following grounds of discrimination or harassment. Put an "X" in the box beside each ground that you believe applies to your Application. You can check more than one box.

☐ Race
☐ Colour
☐ Ancestry
☐ Place of Origin
☐ Citizenship
☐ Ethnic Origin
☐ Disability
☐ Creed
☐ Sex, Including Sexual Harassment and Pregnancy
☐ Sexual Solicitation or Advances
☐ Sexual Orientation
☐ Gender Identity
☐ Gender Expression
☐ Family Status
☐ Marital Status

Ontario

Human Rights Tribunal of Ontario

☐ Age

☐ Receipt of Public Assistance (Note: This ground applies only to claims about Housing)

☐ Record of Offences (Note: This ground applies only to claims about Employment)

☐ Association with a Person Identified by a Ground Listed Above

☐ Reprisal or Threat of Reprisal

Areas of Discrimination under the Code

6. Area of Alleged Discrimination

The Ontario *Human Rights Code* prohibits discrimination in five areas. Put an "X" in the box beside the area where you believe you have experienced discrimination (choose one). Read the Applicant's Guide for more information on each area.

○ **Employment (Complete Form 1-A)**

○ **Housing (Complete Form 1-B)**

○ **Goods, Services and Facilities (Complete Form 1-C)**

○ **Contracts (Complete Form 1-D)**

○ **Membership in a Vocational Association (Complete Form 1-E)**

Does your Application involve discrimination in other areas? ○ Yes   ○ No

If "Yes", put an "X" in the box beside any other area where you believe you experienced discrimination:

☐ Employment   ☐ Housing   ☐ Goods, Services or Facilities   ☐ Contracts   ☐ Vocational Association

Facts that Support Your Application

7. Location and Date (see Applicant's Guide)

Please answer the following questions.

a) *Did these events happen in Ontario?	○ Yes	○ No
b) In what city/town?		
c) *What was the date of the last event? (dd/mm/yyyy)		
d) If you are applying more than one year from the last event, please explain why:		

Ontario

Human Rights Tribunal of Ontario

8. What Happened

*In the space below, describe each event you believe was discriminatory.

For each event, be sure to say:
- **What** happened
- **Who** was involved
- **When** it happened (day, month, year)
- **Where** it happened

Be as complete and accurate as possible. Be sure to give details of every incident of discrimination you want to raise in the hearing.

The Effect on You

9. How the Events You Described Affected You

*Tell us how the events you described affected you. What was the effect (e.g. were there financial, social, emotional or mental health, or any other)?

The Remedy

10. The Remedy You are Asking For (see Applicant's Guide)

Put an "X" in the box beside each type of remedy you are asking the Tribunal to order. Explain why you are asking for this remedy in the space below.

☐ Monetary Compensation	Enter the Total Amount $

Explain below how you calculated this amount:

Ontario

Human Rights Tribunal of Ontario

☐ **Non-Monetary Remedy-Explain below:**

☐ **Remedy for Future Compliance (Public Interest Remedy)-Explain below:**

Mediation

11. Choosing Mediation to Resolve Your Application

Mediation is one of the ways the Tribunal tries to resolve disputes. It is a less formal process than a hearing.
Mediation can only happen if both parties agree to it. A Tribunal Member will be assigned to mediate your Application. The Member will meet with you to talk about your Application. The Member will also meet with the respondent(s) and will try to work out a solution that both sides can accept. If Mediation does not settle all the issues, a hearing will still take place and a different Member will be assigned to hear the case. Mediation is confidential.

Do you agree to try mediation?   ☐ **Yes**

Other Legal Proceedings

12. Civil Court Action (see Applicant's Guide)

Note: If you answer "Yes" to any of these questions, you must send a copy of the statement of claim that started the court action.

*a) Has there been a court action based on the same facts as this Application?	○ Yes (Answer 12b)	○ No (Go to 13)

13. Complaint Filed with the Ontario Human Rights Commission (see Applicant's Guide)

Note: If you answer "Yes", you must attach a copy of the complaint.

***Have you ever filed a complaint with the Commission based on the same facts as this Application?	○ Yes	○ No

Ontario

Human Rights Tribunal of Ontario

14. Other Proceeding - in Progress (see Applicant's Guide)

Note: If you answer "Yes" to question "14a" you must attach a copy of the document that started the other proceeding.

*a) Are the facts of this Application part of another proceeding that is still in progress?	○ Yes (Answer 14b) ○ No (Go to 15)

b) Describe the other proceeding:

☐ A union grievance	Name of Union:	
☐ A claim before another board, tribunal or agency	Name of board, tribunal, or agency:	
☐ Other	Explain what the other proceeding is:	

*c) Are you asking the Tribunal to defer (postpone) your Application until the other proceeding is completed?	○ Yes ○ No

15. Other Proceeding - Completed (see Applicant's Guide)

Note: If you answer is "Yes" to question "15a" you must attach a copy of the document that started the other proceeding and a copy of the decision from the other proceeding.

*a) Were the facts of this Application part of some other proceeding that is now completed?	○ Yes (Answer Question 15b) ○ No (Go to 16)

b) Describe the other proceeding:

Ontario

Human Rights Tribunal of Ontario

☐ A union grievance	Name of Union:	
☐ A claim before another board, tribunal or agency	Name of board, tribunal, or agency:	
☐ Other	Explain what the other proceeding is:	

c) Explain why you believe the other proceeding did not appropriately deal with the substance of this Application.

Documents that Support this Application

16. Important Documents You Have

If you have documents that are important to your Application, list them here. List only the most important. Indicate whether the document is privileged. See the Applicant's Guide.
Note: You are not required to send copies of these documents at this time. However, if you decide to attach copies of the documents you list below to your Application they will be sent to the other parties to the Application along with your Application.

Document Name	Why It is Important to My Application

Add more Documents

Ontario

Human Rights Tribunal of Ontario

17. Important Documents the Respondent(s) Have

If you believe the respondent(s) have documents that you do not have that are important to your Application, list them here. List only the most important.

Document Name	Why It is Important To My Application	Name of Respondent Who Has It

Add more Documents

18. Important Documents Another Person or Organization Has

If you believe another person or organization has documents that you do not have that are important your Application, list them here. List only the most important.

Document Name	Why it is Important to my Application	Name of Person or Organization who has it

Add more Documents

Confidential List of Witnesses

19. Witnesses

Please list the witnesses that you intend to rely on in the hearing. **Note:** The Tribunal will not send this list to the respondent(s). (**see** Applicants Guide)

Name of Witness	Why This Witness Is Important To My Application

Ontario

Human Rights Tribunal of Ontario

	Add more Witnesses

Other Important Information

20. Other Important Information the Tribunal Should Know

Is there any other important information you would like to share with the Tribunal?

Checklist of Required Documents

22. Other Documents from Questions 12 to 15

Confirm whether you are sending the Tribunal any of the following documents:

☐ A copy of a statement of claim (from Question 12)

☐ A copy of a complaint filed with the Ontario Human Rights Commission (from Question 13)

☐ A copy of a document that started another proceeding based on these facts (from Question 14 or 15)

☐ A copy of a decision from another proceeding based on these facts (from Question 15)

Ontario

Human Rights Tribunal of Ontario

Declaration and Signature

23. Declaration and Signature

Instructions: Do not sign your Application until you are sure that you understand what you are declaring here.

Declaration:
To the best of my knowledge, the information in my Application is complete and accurate.

I understand that information about my Application can become public at an open hearing, in a written decision, or in other ways determined by Tribunal policies that balance transparency in the justice system and privacy interests of participants.

I understand that the Tribunal must provide a copy of my Application to the Ontario Human Rights Commission on request.

I understand that the Tribunal may be required to release information requested under the Freedom of Information and Protection of Privacy Act (FIPPA).

I understand that the Tribunal makes all of its Decisions and Case Assessment Directions available to the public, including the media on request, and that the Tribunal also makes its decisions available to the public on the websites of the Canadian Legal Information Institute (www.CanLii.org). I also understand that the Tribunal may issue decisions that protect the identity of an applicant, a respondent or a witness in certain circumstances.

*Signature Date (dd/mm/yyyy)

☐ *Please check this box if you are filing your Application electronically. This represents your signature. You must fill out the date, above.

Accommodation Required

If you require accommodation of Code-related needs please contact the Registrar at:
Email: HRTO.Registrar@ontario.ca
Phone: 416-326-1519   Toll-free: 1-866-598-0322
Fax: 416-326-2199   Toll-free: 1-866-355-6099
TTY: 416-326-2027   Toll-free: 1-866-607-1240

Note: Only file your Application <u>once</u>. If the Tribunal receives your application more than once, it will only accept the first Application Form received.

| Submit to HRTO | Print Form |

Appendix 6.4
Response to an Application under s. 34 of the *Code* (Form 2)[†]

Ontario

Human Rights Tribunal of Ontario

Response to an Application under Section 34 of the *Human Rights Code* (Form 2)

(Disponible en français)

www.hrto.ca

How to Respond to an Application Where You Are Named as a Respondent

Use this form if you have been named as a respondent in a human rights application under section 34 of the *Human Rights Code*.

If you fail to respond to the Application, you may be deemed to have accepted all of the allegations in the Application, and the Tribunal may proceed without further notice to you.

Before you start:

1. Read the questions and answers below.

2. Download and read the Respondent's Guide from the Tribunal's website www.hrto.ca.
   If you need a paper copy or accessible format contact us at:

Human Rights Tribunal of Ontario	Phone: 416-326-1312	Toll-free: 1-866-598-0322
655 Bay Street, 14th floor	Fax: 416-326-2199	Toll-free: 1-866-355-6099
Toronto, Ontario M7A 2A3	TTY: 416-326-2027	Toll-free: 1-866-607-1240
	Emai: hrto.registrar@ontario.ca	
	Website: www.hrto.ca	

The Tribunal has other guides and practice directions to help all parties to an Application understand the process. Download copies from the Tribunal's website or contact us.

3. Complete each section of the Response form that applies to you. As you fill out each section, refer to the instructions in the **Respondent's Guide**.

Questions about Responding to an Application

The following questions and answers are provided for general information. They should not be taken as legal advice or a determination of how the Tribunal will decide any particular application.

What happens if I fail to complete a Response Form?

You may be deemed to have accepted all the allegations. The Tribunal may deal with the Application without any further notice to you.

What is the time limit for responding?

Respondents must file a completed Response form no later than **thirty-five (35) days** after the Tribunal sends them a copy of the Application. The cover letter from the Tribunal gives you the exact date.

Are there defences to discrimination under the *Human Rights Code*?

Yes, there are some defences and exemptions in the *Code*. Please see the **Respondent's Guide.** If you believe one of these applies, please explain how when you fill out the Response form.

01/05/11

Form 2 - Page 1 of 15

[†] Source: HRTO Website <http://www.hrto.ca/>

Ontario

Human Rights Tribunal of Ontario

Response to an Application under Section 34 of the *Human Rights Code* (Form 2)

Can the Tribunal deal with an application where the facts and issues have been dealt with or are being dealt with in another proceeding?

The *Code* has special rules depending on what the other proceeding is and at what stage the other proceeding is at. Read the **Respondent's Guide** and get legal advice if:

1. You are currently involved in, or were previously involved in a civil action based on the same facts and the applicant asked for a human rights remedy; **or**
2. A complaint was ever filed with the Ontario Human Rights Commission based on the same subject matter; **or**
3. You are currently involved in, or were previously involved in another proceeding (for example, a union grievance based on the same facts.

You must file a Response even if you believe that the Tribunal should defer the the Application or that the Application is outside the jurisdiction of the Tribunal, except where you allege the issues in dispute fall within exclusive federal jurisdiction.

Learn more

To find out more about human rights in Ontario, visit www.ohrc.on.ca or phone 1-800-387-9080.

Ontario

Human Rights Tribunal of Ontario

Response to an Application under Section 34 of the *Human Rights Code* (Form 2)

Note: Complete all parts of this form, using the **Respondent's Guide** for help. If your form is not complete, the Tribunal may return it to you. At the end of this form, you will be required to read and agree to a declaration that the information in your Response is complete and accurate (if you are a lawyer or legal representative assisting a respondent with this Form 2, please see the **Practice Direction On Electronic Filing of Applications and Responses By Licensed Representatives**).

Respondents must file a completed Response form no later than **thirty-five (35) days** after the Tribunal sends them a copy of the Application. The cover letter from the Tribunal gives you the exact date.

Tribunal File Number	

Contact Information for the Respondent

Respondent Contact Information

Please choose the type of Respondent: ○ Organization Respondent   ○ Individual Respondent

1. Respondent Contact Information - Organization

Contact information for a responding organization, such as a corporation, association, or group. Please complete both this section and Question 3.

Full Name of Organization

Organization Type:
○ Corporation
○ Partnership
○ Sole proprietorship
○ Unincorporated business/organization
○ Other (specify):

Ontario

Human Rights Tribunal of Ontario

Response to an Application under Section 34 of the *Human Rights Code* (Form 2)

Name of the person within this organization who is authorized to negotiate and bind the organization with respect to this Application.

First (or Given) Name	Last (or Family) Name	Title

Street #	Street Name		Apt/Suite

City/Town	Province	Postal Code	Email

Daytime Phone	Cell Phone	Fax	TTY

What is the best way to send information to you?
(If you check email, you are consenting to delivery of documents by email)   ○ Mail   ○ Email   ○ Fax

Is this Response being filed on behalf of any other respondent? ○ Yes   ○ No

3. Representative Contact Information

Complete this Section only if you are authorizing a lawyer or other Representative to act for you.

☐ **I authorize the organization and/or person named below to represent me.**

My representative is:

☐ Lawyer	LSUC #	
☐ Paralegal	LSUC #	

☐ Other- please specify the Nature of Exemption from licensing requirements in the text box below:
(e.g. Unpaid family member or friend)

For further information, see the Tribunal's Policy on Representation before the HRTO at www.hrto.ca.

Ontario

Human Rights Tribunal of Ontario

Response to an Application under Section 34 of the *Human Rights Code* (Form 2)

First (or Given) Name

Last (or Family) Name

Organization (if applicable)

Street #	Street Name		Apt/Suite

City/Town	Province	Postal Code	Email

Daytime Phone	Cell Phone	Fax	TTY

What is the best way to send information to your representative?
(If you check email, you are consenting to delivery of documents by email)   ○ Mail   ○ Email   ○ Fax

Contact Information - Additional Respondent(s) and Affected Person(s)

Please complete this selection if you believe another person or organization should be named as a respondent or given notice as an affected person(s).

4. Contact Information - Additional Respondent

If there is another organization or person who is not already named as a respondent on the Application form and who you believe should be named as a respondent, provide their contact information here. See the Tribunal's **Practice Direction on Naming Respondents** for more information on how to correctly name a potential respondent.

Please choose the type of respondent: ○ Organization Respondent   ○ Individual Respondent

Additional Respondent Contact Information - Organization

Full Name of Organization

Ontario

Human Rights Tribunal of Ontario

Response to an Application under Section 34 of the *Human Rights Code* (Form 2)

Name of Contact Person from the Organization

First (or Given) Name	Last (or Family) Name	Title

Street #	Street Name	Apt/Suite

City/Town	Province	Postal Code	Email

Daytime Phone	Cell Phone	Fax	TTY

Add Another Respondent

5. Contact Information - Affected Person

If there is any other organization (such as a union or occupational association responsible for collective bargaining) or person who is not already named as an affected person on the Application form and who might be affected by this Application to the Tribunal, provide their contact information here.

Please choose the type of affected person: ○ Organization   ○ Contact

Affected Person Contact Information - Organization

Full Name of Organization

Name of Contact Person from the Organization

First (or Given) Name	Last (or Family) Name	Title

Ontario

Human Rights Tribunal of Ontario

Response to an Application under Section 34 of the *Human Rights Code* (Form 2)

Street #	Street Name		Apt/Suite

City/Town	Province	Postal Code	Email

Daytime Phone	Cell Phone	Fax	TTY

Add Another Affected Party

Request for Early Dismissal of the Application

6. Request for Dismissal - without Full Response

Complete this section only if you are requesting that the Tribunal dismiss the Application because one of the four situations below applies. Put an "X" in the box that applies. Please see the **Respondent's Guide.**

I request that the Tribunal dismiss this Application because:

☐ A claim based on the same facts has been filed in civil court, requesting a remedy based on the alleged human rights violation. (Attach a copy of the statement of claim and the court decision, if any. Include all your submissions in support of your request to dismiss the Application on this basis. The Tribunal may decide your request based only on your submissions.)

☐ A complaint was filed with the Ontario Human Rights Commission based on the same, or substantially the same, facts as this Application. (Attach a copy of the complaint and the decision, if any. Include all your submissions in support of your request to dismiss the Application on this basis. The Tribunal may decide your request based only on your submissions.)

☐ The applicant signed a full and final release with respect to the same matter. (Attach a copy of the release. Include all your submissions in support of your request to dismiss the Application on this basis. The Tribunal may decide your request based only on your submissions.)

☐ The issues in the Application are within exclusive federal jurisdiction. (Include all your submissions in support of your request to dismiss the Application on this basis. The Tribunal may decide your request based only on your submissions.)

Note: If you put an "X" in any of the boxes above, go to Question 20. Except in these four situations, or as otherwise directed by the Tribunal, requests to dismiss an Application will not be considered without a complete response.

Ontario

Human Rights Tribunal of Ontario

Response to an Application under Section 34 of the *Human Rights Code* (Form 2)

7. Request for Dismissal under s. 45.1 of the Code - with Full Response

Complete this section only if you are requesting that the Tribunal dismiss the Application because another proceeding has in whole or in part appropriately dealt with the substance of the Application. Put an "X" below if you are making this request. Please see the **Respondent's Guide.**

a) ☐ I request that the Tribunal dismiss the Application because another proceeding has in whole or in part appropriately dealt with the substance of the Application. (Attach a copy of the decision)

b) Please name the other proceeding:

c) Explain why you believe the other proceeding has in whole or in part appropriately dealt with the substance of the Application.

Note: You must complete the entire Response form and attach a copy of the document that started the proceeding and a copy of the decision.

Request to Defer the Application

8. Request to Defer

Complete this section only if the facts of the Application are part of another proceeding that is still in progress.

a) Describe the other proceeding:

☐ A union grievance	Name of Union:	

Ontario

Human Rights Tribunal of Ontario

Response to an Application under Section 34 of the *Human Rights Code* (Form 2)

☐ A claim before another board, tribunal or agency	Name a board, tribunal, or agency:	
☐ Other	Explain what the other proceeding is:	

b) Are you asking the Tribunal to defer (postpone) the Application until the other proceeding is completed? (Attach a copy of the document that started the other proceeding)	○ Yes	○ No

Responding to the Allegations in the Application

9. Responding to the Allegations

Please summarize the facts and defences that support your Response to this Application. See the **Respondent's Guide.**

Please include as part of your response:
- any submissions you make that the Application is outside the Tribunal's jurisdiction;
- what allegations in the Application you agree with;
- what allegations in the Application you disagree with;
- any additional facts that you intend to rely on; and
- any defences that you intend to rely on.

10. Exemptions

Complete this section only if you are relying on one of the exemptions found in the *Code*. See the **Respondent's Guide.**

a) What exemption in the *Code* do you believe applies to this Application?

Ontario

Human Rights Tribunal of Ontario

Response to an Application under Section 34 of the *Human Rights Code* (Form 2)

b) Please explain why you believe the exemption applies:

11. Knowledge of the Events

a) When and how did you first become aware of the events described in the Application?

b) How did you respond and what was the outcome?

12. Disability and Employment

Complete this section only if the applicant alleges that they experienced discrimination in employment on the ground of disability. See **Respondent's Guide**.

a) Did you know about the applicant's particular needs before seeing the Application? ○ Yes ○ No

b) What are the requirements (essential job duties) of the position in question?

Ontario

Human Rights Tribunal of Ontario

Response to an Application under Section 34 of the *Human Rights Code* (Form 2)

c) Do you have a written policy, job description or other documentation that describes the requirements of the job?	○ Yes	○ No
d) Was the applicant unable to perform the requirements of the job because of their disability?	○ Yes	○ No (Go to 13)

Note: If you said "Yes" to Question 12c, you must attach a copy of the policy, job description or other document that describes the requirements of the job.

Questions About Internal Human Rights Policies

13. Internal Human Rights Policies

Complete this section only if the respondent is an organization. Please see the **Respondent's Guide**.

a) Do you have a policy related to the type of discrimination alleged in the Application?	○ Yes	○ No
b) Do you have a complaint process to deal with discrimination and harassment?	○ Yes	○ No (Go to 14)

Note: You must attach a copy of the policy, complaint process, or the document that started the complaint, and the decision, if any.

Mediation

14. Choosing Mediation to Resolve the Application

Mediation is one of the ways the Tribunal tries to resolve disputes. It is a less formal process than a hearing. Mediation can only happen if both parties agree to it. A Tribunal Member will be assigned to mediate the Application. The Member will meet with you to talk about your Response. The Member will also meet with the applicant and will try to work out a solution that both sides can accept. If Mediation does not settle all the issues, a hearing will still take place and a different Member will be assigned to hear the case. Mediation is confidential.

Do you agree to try mediation? ☐ Yes

Ontario

Human Rights Tribunal of Ontario

Response to an Application under Section 34 of the *Human Rights Code* (Form 2)

Documents that Support Your Response

15. Important Documents You Have

If you have documents that are important to your Response, list them here. List only the most important. Indicate whether the document is privileged. Please see the **Respondent's Guide**.

Note: You are not required to send copies of your documents at this time. However, if you decide to attach copies of the documents you list below to your Response, they will be sent to the other parties to the Application along with your Response.

Document Name	Why It Is Important To My Response

Add more Documents

16. Important Documents the Applicant Has

If you believe the applicant has documents that are important to your Response, that you do not have, list them here. List only the most important.

Document Name	Why It Is Important To My Response

Add more Documents

17. Important Documents Another Person or Organization Has

If you believe another person or organization has documents that are important to your Response, that you do not have, list them here. List only the most important.

Document Name	Why It Is Important To My Response	Name of Person or Organization Who Has It

---

Ontario

Human Rights Tribunal of Ontario

Response to an Application under Section 34 of the *Human Rights Code* (Form 2)

Add more Documents

Confidential List of Witnesses

18. Witnesses

Please list the witnesses that you intend to rely on in the hearing. **Note:** The Tribunal will not send this list to the applicant. See the **Respondent's Guide**

Name of Witness	Why This Witness Is Important To My Response

Add more Witnesses

Other Important Information

19. Other Important Information the Tribunal Should Know

Is there any other important information you would like to share with the Tribunal?

Ontario

Human Rights Tribunal of Ontario

Response to an Application under Section 34 of the *Human Rights Code* (Form 2)

Checklist of Required Documents

20. Documents from Questions 6 to 13

Put an "X" in the box beside the documents that you are required to send with your Response. Put the Tribunal File Number on each document.

☐ Copy of a statement of claim and the Court decision, if any (from Question 6)

☐ Copy of a complaint filed with the Ontario Human Rights Commission and decision, if any (from Question 6)

☐ Copy of a full and final release that the applicant signed dealing with same matter (from Question 6)

☐ Submissions in support of a Request for Dismissal without Full Response (under Question 6)

☐ Copy of a decision from another type of proceeding that appropriately dealt with the substance of the Application (from Question 7)

☐ Copy of a document that started another type of proceeding based on the same facts (from Question 7 & 8)

☐ Copy of the policy, job description or other document that describes the requirements of the job (from Question 12)

☐ Copy of your organization's policy on discrimination or harassment relevant to this Application (from Question 13)

☐ Copy of your organization's complaints process relevant to this Application (from Question 13)

☐ Copy of the applicant's internal complaint (from Question 13)

☐ Copy of the decision from the internal complaint process (from Question 13)

Ontario

Human Rights Tribunal of Ontario

Response to an Application under Section 34 of the *Human Rights Code* (Form 2)

Declaration and Signature

21. Declaration and Signature

Instructions: Do not sign your Response until you are sure that you understand what you are declaring here.

Declaration:

To the best of my knowledge, the information in my Response is complete and accurate.

I understand that information about my Response can become public at an open hearing, in a written decision, or in other ways determined by Tribunal policies that balance transparency in the justice system and privacy interests of participants.

I understand that the Tribunal must provide a copy of my Response and any attached documents to the Ontario Human Rights Commission on request.

I understand that the Tribunal may be required to release information requested under the Freedom of Information and Protection of Privacy Act (FIPPA).

I understand that the Tribunal makes all of its Decisions and Case Assessment Directions available to the public, including the media on request, and that the Tribunal also makes its decisions available to the public on the websites of the Canadian Legal Information Institute (www.CanLii.org). I also understand that the Tribunal may issue decisions that protect the identity of an applicant, a respondent or a witness in certain circumstances.

Signature Date (dd/mm/yyyy)

Please check this box if you are filing your response electronically. This represents your signature. You must fill out the date, above.

Accommodation Required

If you require accommodation of *Code* related needs please contact the Registrar at HRTO.Registrar@ontario.ca or

Phone: 416-326-1312 Toll-free: 1-866-598-0322
Fax: 416-326-2199 Toll-free: 1-866-355-6099
TTY: 416-326-2027 Toll-free: 1-866-607-1240

Note: Only submit your Response once. If the Tribunal receives this Response more than once, it will only accept the first Response Form received.

Submit to HRTO	Print Form

7

WHAT THIS CHAPTER OFFERS

- The background of the Licence Appeal Tribunal (LAT)
- A discussion of the cluster of the Safety, Licensing Appeals and Standards Tribunals (SLASTO), and its impact on the LAT
- Details and explanations of the enabling legislation relevant to the LAT, specifically focusing on the new, as of April 1, 2016, portion of the LAT related to Automobile Accident Benefits Service (AABS)
- Concepts of public policy relevant to the AABS of the LAT
- Specific rules and procedures relevant to the AABS of the LAT
- A walk-through of the SLASTO, LAT, and AABS websites
- A proposed flow chart from the LAT dealing with what was called Automobile Insurance Dispute Resolution Services (AIDRS) and is now AABS

LEARNING OBJECTIVES

After reading this chapter, the reader should be able to:

- state the legislation that governs the operation of the LAT, especially the AABS portion of the LAT
- research the SLASTO, LAT, and AABS websites for important information needed to understand the agency's practices and procedures in respect of AABS and to represent a client properly before the AABS portion of the LAT
- apply the specific rules and procedures in a proceeding before, during, and after a hearing on the AABS portion of the LAT

INTRODUCTION

What the Licence Appeal Tribunal is and does are clearly described and explained on its website Home Page:

> The Licence Appeal Tribunal (LAT) is an adjudicative tribunal that is part of Safety, Licensing Appeals and Standards Tribunals Ontario (SLASTO).
>
> LAT's mandate is to provide a fair, impartial and efficient way to appeal decisions concerning compensation claims and licensing activities regulated by several ministries of the provincial government.
>
> The Tribunal receives appeals, conducts hearings, resolves disputes, and makes decisions on a wide variety of matters, with the most common cases involving liquor licences, new home warranty claims, medical suspension of driver's licences, impoundment of motor vehicles and regulation of various occupations and businesses.
>
> Effective April 1, 2016, the Tribunal will begin accepting applications to the new Automobile Accident Benefits Service (AABS) system that aims to quickly resolve disagreements between individuals and insurance companies about accident benefits.
>
> Also in 2016, the Tribunal is taking adjudicative responsibility for beer-in-grocery-store licensing appeals, as well as appeals relating to horse racing licences.
>
> The Tribunal is subject to the rules of natural justice and the requirements of the *Statutory Powers Procedure Act*. The members appointed to the Tribunal conduct fair, efficient and impartial hearings during which they consider all evidence presented and make a decision with written reasons. Most Tribunal decisions are subject to appeal to the Superior Court of Justice (Divisional Court). All Tribunal proceedings are subject to judicial review under the *Judicial Review Procedure Act*. LAT decisions are posted to CanLII.

One of the areas the LAT deals with involves resolving disputes between claimants and insurance companies in respect of claims for personal injuries. Unlike its predecessor, the FSCO DRG, the LAT AABS involves hearings before the tribunal. Considering there were over 100,000 collisions that resulted in fatalities and/or injuries each year between 1995–2014, the need for paralegals to represent clients in this area is high. Therefore, it is important for this book to examine the practices and procedures of the AABS even though it has just begun to operate on April 1, 2016. The materials examined below, including the quotes, are largely taken from the SLASTO, LAT, and AABS websites.

OVERVIEW AND BACKGROUND

In the 2014 Budget, the Ontario government announced a series of auto insurance reforms, including the transformation of the Auto Insurance Dispute Resolution System and its transfer to the Licence Appeal Tribunal (LAT), an adjudicative tribunal within the Safety, Licensing Appeals and Standards Tribunals Ontario (SLASTO) cluster.

The background regarding the shift from the DRS at FSCO to the AABS as part of the LAT is set out in the "Auto Insurance Dispute Resolution System (AIDRS) — Transformation Project Status Update" (found on the "What's New" Web page from the SLASTO website):

> In August 2013, the Honourable J. Douglas Cunningham, a former Superior Court judge, was appointed to conduct a review of the Ontario auto insurance dispute resolution system.
>
> In February 2014, he delivered the 'Ontario Automobile Insurance Dispute Resolution System Review' Final Report. Mr. Cunningham's recommendations sought to return the dispute resolution system to its originating principles. (See Exhibit 1 for a complete list of the final recommendations.)
>
> Bill 15, the *Fighting Fraud and Reducing Automobile Insurance Rates Act, 2014*, S.O. 2014, c. 9 ("Bill 15"), is the government's response to these recommendations. Bill 15 was introduced by the Minister of Finance in July 2014 and received Royal Assent on November 20, 2014.
>
> Bill 15 amended the *Insurance Act* to set out a new system for disputes about entitlement to or amount of benefits under the *Statutory Accident Benefits Schedule* (SABS — a regulation made under the *Insurance Act*). Many of these changes will be implemented by the creation of a new process at the Licence Appeal Tribunal (LAT).
>
> The amendments contained in Bill 15 are anticipated to be brought into force on April 1, 2016 and LAT will begin accepting cases on that date. ...

What's New in the New Process?

Bill 15 amended the *Insurance Act* to set up a new framework for SABS disputes resolution process that must be used at the LAT. The most significant differences between the new LAT process and the FSCO process are that in the former

- there is no mandatory mediation; and
- adjudication before the LAT is the ONLY means of resolving a SABS dispute. (Claimants are still able to attempt to settle disputes privately.)

EXHIBIT 1
Cunningham Recommendations Status Report

Recommendation #	Responsibility	Status
1. A new DRS should be established as a public sector administrative tribunal reporting to the responsible minister.	MAG	LAT is selected as the public sector administrative tribunal responsible for adjudicating SABS disputes pursuant to the *Insurance Act*. By April 1, 2016. In-progress.
2. Arbitrators should be appointed by order-in-council on the recommendation of the responsible minister.	MAG/ SLASTO/ LAT	LAT adjudicators are OIC appointees (i.e., Cabinet approves appointments). OIC Recruitment for additional LAT adjudicators in progress
3. Tendered contracts should be established with one or more private-sector dispute resolution service providers to address fluctuations in demand for services.	MAG/ SLASTO/ LAT	LAT will be managing the fluctuation in demand for services through the recruitment of a significant number of Part Time Order-In-Council Appointees.
4. Mediation services should be enhanced and continue to be a mandatory step in the DRS, but now as part of a settlement meeting.	N/A	There will be no mandatory "mediation" at LAT. but case conferences with trained LAT adjudicators will focus on achieving early resolution.
5. The person conducting the settlement meeting should not also conduct the arbitration between the same parties.	MAG/ SLASTO/ LAT	Provided for in the *Statutory Powers Procedure Act* and LAT Rules.
6. Statutory timelines and sanctions regarding settlement meetings, arbitration hearings and the release of arbitration decisions should be created.	MOF/ MAG/ SLASTO/ LAT	No statutory timelines for new LAT applications set out in Bill 15 amendments. LAT will manage timeline requirements.
7. The policy of no application fees for claimants at the settlement meeting stage should be continued.	MAG/ SLASTO	$100 application fee to be charged. This will be a fee set by LAT, approved by the Attorney General.
8. A claimant or insurer who abuses the process should be required to pay all or part of	MAG/ SLASTO	Parties who abuse the process will be subject to cost awards. *Continues....*

Exhibit 1 continued

Recommendation #	Responsibility	Status
the settlement meeting and arbitration fees of the other party. A party should not be able to claim costs in arbitration if they refused a settlement offer that is more favourable than the amount ordered by the arbitrator.		
9. The option of initiating a court proceeding instead of arbitration should be eliminated when the parties are unable to reach a settlement.	MAG/ MOF	Bill 15 eliminates the option of proceeding to court at first instance without first having the dispute heard at LAT.
10. Arbitration decisions should continue to be published.	LAT	All Decisions will be posted on CanLII.
11. An arbitration decision should provide guidance but not be binding on other disputes.	MAG/LAT	LAT and other adjudicative tribunals are not bound by precedent in the same way as the courts. While the Tribunal will strive for consistency and predictability, each decision will be made on the merits of the case before it.
12. The government should continue to use binding Superintendent's Guidelines incorporated by reference into the SABS to provide stakeholders and adjudicators with direction as required.	MOF	MOF has policy responsibility for the Insurance Act and SABS Regulation. LAT adjudicators bound to apply the regulation.
13. The current pre-arbitration meetings and neutral evaluation should be combined into a new settlement meeting.	MAG/ MOF	Bill 15 eliminates these steps. LAT adjudicators will focus on early resolution at the case conference.
14. Settlement meetings should be conducted by video conferencing rather than by telephone in cases where it is not feasible for the parties to meet in person.	LAT	Four channels for hearing; written, telephone, video, in-person.

Continues....

Exhibit 1 continued

Recommendation #	Responsibility	Status
15. Fees should be established for settlement meetings and the different streams of arbitration. Settlement meeting and arbitration fees should be reduced where the parties settle in advance.	MOF/LAT	LAT proposes a $100 application fee.
16. An adjournment fee should be established, which could be charged to the party requesting an adjournment in the absence of exceptional circumstances.	MAG/LAT	Requests for adjournment could be addressed by cost awards when appropriate.
17. The settlement of future medical and rehabilitation benefits should be prohibited until two years after the date of the accident.	MOF	Currently the SABS establish a one-year limit.
18. Experts should be required to certify their duty to the tribunal and to provide fair, objective and non-partisan evidence. Arbitrators should ignore evidence that is not fair, objective or non-partisan and, in such instances, the expert should not receive compensation for appearing as a witness.	LAT/ SLASTO	Provision requiring experts to provide fair, objective and non-partisan evidence is in revised LAT rules.
19. Each insurer should establish an internal review process and be required to inform a claimant how to access it following a benefit denial.	Insurance Sector/ MOF	MOF expected to consult with insurance sector in 2016.
20. Each insurer will determine how their internal review process is to be structured, but must provide a claimant with a written response that includes the outcome of the review and reasons for the company's decision within 30 days of the claimant's request.	Insurance Sector/ MOF	MOF expected to consult with insurance sector in 2016.

Continues....

Exhibit 1 continued

Recommendation #	Responsibility	Status
21. The Superintendent should collect utilization statistics from each insurer. A review should be conducted within two years to determine whether the internal review process leads to fewer disputes.	Insurance Sector/ MOF	MOF expected to consult with insurance sector in 2016.
22. Settlement meeting applications should be reviewed by the tribunal's registrar, who will determine if the parties are ready to proceed to a settlement meeting. The application should only be accepted once all outstanding issues have been addressed. The registrar or an arbitrator should be able to consolidate applications involving the same claimant and insurer.	LAT	Cases will be managed by case management officers, and LAT rules provide for the combining of cases.
23. The tribunal should develop an electronic filing system to expedite the filing of settlement meeting and arbitration applications.	MAG/LAT	E-filing is a year one goal of the new case management solution.
24. Following an unsuccessful settlement meeting and the filing of an arbitration application, the arbitrator should inform the parties whether it will take the form of a paper review, an expedited in-person hearing or a full in-person hearing.	MAG/LAT	The new LAT process allows the adjudicator to make a decision on the type of hearing at the end of the case conference.
25. Arbitration hearings should be conducted as paper reviews in cases where there are $10,000 or less of medical and rehabilitation benefits in dispute, or where the dispute involves a determination as to whether the claimant's injuries meet the minor injury definition.	MAG/LAT	Written Hearings have been established in the program design. An adjudicator will exercise his or her discretion to determine the format of a hearing.

Continues....

Exhibit 1 continued

Recommendation #	Responsibility	Status
26. Arbitration hearings should be conducted as an expedited in-person hearing in cases that do not qualify as either a paper review or full in-person hearing. This determination should be made by an arbitrator and not subject to appeal.	MAG/LAT	The adjudicator will exercise his or her discretion to determine the format of a hearing.
27. Arbitration hearings should be conducted as full in-person hearings for disputes involving catastrophic impairment determinations and whether the claimant still qualifies for 24-hour attendant care or income replacement benefits beyond 104 weeks.	MAG/LAT	The adjudicator will exercise his or her discretion to determine for the format of a hearing. Guidelines will provide that these types of disputes would be full in-person hearings.
28. Appeals of arbitration hearing decisions should be heard by a single judge of the Ontario Superior Court of Justice on a question of law.	MAG	Pursuant to provision of the *Licence Appeal Tribunal Act, 1999*, appeals to the Divisional Court (a branch of the Superior Court) will be allowed on issue of law alone.

Source: SLASTO website, "What's New — Auto Insurance Dispute Resolution (AIDRS) — Transformation Project Status Update", pages 11–16. Online: <www.slasto.gov.on.ca/en/Pages/What's-New.aspx>. [Edited.]

- LAT Order in Council (OIC) appointees appointed by Cabinet will be the adjudicators. (A total of 24 new full-time and part-time adjudicators have been appointed as of May 31, 2016.)
- There are no provisions for applying to court at first instance for SABS disputes.
- There is no right of appeal except for a reconsideration option with the Executive Chair of SLASTO in exceptional circumstances, or appeals to the Divisional Court on a question of law alone.

As stated in the Update, "all of these changes are government policy choices set out in Bill 15 and LAT/SLASTO and MAG are delivering the new process within this legislative policy framework."

Other changes introduced in this new process include the following:

- Simplified and fillable new application forms and responses are used, with a one-year goal to allow electronic filing and fee payment.

- Case conferences and hearings will be scheduled on shorter timelines: 45 days to case conference, followed by 60 days to hearing.

- Prior to the case conference, parties are required to submit case conference briefs that fully canvas settlement and list witnesses and evidence. Settlement offers will be exchanged at the case conference stage.

- For cases that cannot be resolved at case conference stage, the adjudicator will determine the hearing type, with input from the parties, based on three standard hearing types: written, electronic or in-person. In-person hearings are reserved for the most serious cases. The vast majority of cases are expected to be completed within six months.

- Under the new process, expert report and expert opinion evidence must be filed with an "Acknowledgement of Expert's Duty" form signed by the expert, acknowledging the expert's duty to the tribunal to give fair, objective and non-partisan evidence.

ENABLING LEGISLATION

The LAT was created by the *Licence Appeal Tribunal Act, 1999*, S.O. 1999, c. 12, Sched. G, to appeal decisions of various Ontario ministries. The key provisions of the *Licence Appeal Tribunal Act, 1999* are summarized as follows:

Section 2(1) establishes the LAT, and under s. 3(1) it has the power to hold hearings and perform other duties assigned to it by legislation. Under s. 6, the LAT "may make rules establishing procedures for hearings held by the [LAT] and the rights of parties to the hearings including, (a) rules requiring that, despite any other Act, parties shall submit disagreements to mechanisms of alternate dispute resolution that are set out in the rules before they are entitled to a hearing before the [LAT] on the subject matter of the disagreement; and (b) rules applicable if a member of the [LAT] conducting a hearing is unable to continue to conduct the hearing for any reason." Under s. 6(6), "[a] rule made under this section does not prevail over any provision of this or any other Act, or a regulation made under this or any other Act, that sets out requirements for procedures for hearings held by the [LAT] or rights of parties to the hearings." Section 8 allows the LAT to make an order of costs as it considers appropriate in the circumstances where the LAT is satisfied that the application for the hearing before the LAT is frivolous or vexatious. Appeals of the decision of the LAT under various statutes, including the *Insurance Act*, are set out in s. 11. Pursuant to s. 11(3) and specifically for the *Insurance Act* under s. 11(6), appeals are to the Divisional Court and on questions of law only.

Over time, more areas have been added to the jurisdiction of the LAT; as of April 1, 2016, 31 statutes, set out in the next section, give the LAT jurisdiction to hear a variety of matters.

The LAT conducts proceedings under statutes as set out below, including, as of April 1, 2016, AABS disputes under the *Insurance Act*:

- *Accessibility for Ontarians with Disabilities Act, 2005*, S.O. 2005, c. 11
- *Alcohol and Gaming Regulation and Public Protection Act, 1996*, S.O. 1996, c. 26, Sched.
- *Bailiffs Act*, R.S.O. 1990, c. B.2
- *Board of Funeral Services Act*, R.S.O. 1990, c. F.36
- *Building Code Act, 1992*, S.O. 1992, c. 23, O. Reg. 332/12 (Division C, Part 3)
- *Child Care and Early Years Act, 2014*, S.O. 2014, c. 11, Sched. 1
- *Child and Family Services Act*, R.S.O. 1990, c. C.11
- *Collection and Debt Settlement Services Act*, R.S.O. 1990, c. C.14

- *Consumer Protection Act, 2002*, S.O. 2002, c. 30, Sched. A
- *Consumer Reporting Act*, R.S.O. 1990, c. C.33
- *Discriminatory Business Practices Act*, R.S.O. 1990, c. D.12
- *Film Classification Act, 2005*, S.O. 2005, c. 17
- *Funeral, Burial and Cremation Services Act, 2002*, S.O. 2002, c. 33
- *Gaming Control Act, 1992*, S.O. 1992, c. 24
- *Highway Traffic Act*, R.S.O. 1990, c. H.8
    - Subclause 32(5)(b)(i) — Medical (MED)
    - Subsection 47(1) — Medical (MED) and Commercial Vehicle Operator's Registration (CVOR)
    - Subsections 17(2), (3) — Commercial Vehicle Operation's Registration (CVOR)
    - Subsection 48.3(2) — Administrative Driver's Licence Suspension (ADLS)
    - Section 82.1 — Commercial Vehicle Impoundment and Suspension (CVIS)
    - Subsection 95(1) — Motor Vehicle Inspection Licence (GAR)
    - Subsection 55.1(3) — Motor Vehicle Impoundment (MVIA)
- *Horse Racing Licence Act, 2015*, S.O. 2015, c. 38, Sched. 9
- *Insurance Act*, R.S.O. 1990, c. I.8
- *Intercountry Adoption Act, 1998*, S.O. 1998, c. 29
- *Liquor Control Act*, R.S.O. 1990, c. L.18
- *Liquor Licence Act*, R.S.O. 1990, c. L.19
- *Motor Vehicle Dealers Act, 2002*, S.O. 2002, c. 30, Sched. B
- *Ontario New Home Warranties Plan Act, 1990*, R.S.O. 1990, c. O.31
- *Paperback and Periodical Distributors Act*, R.S.O. 1990, c. P.1
- *Payday Loans Act, 2008*, S.O. 2008, c. 9
- *Post-Secondary Education Choice and Excellence Act, 2000*, S.O. 2000, c. 36, Sched., O. Reg. 279/02
- *Private Career Colleges Act, 2005*, S.O. 2005, c. 28, Sched. L
- *Private Security and Investigative Services Act, 2005*, S.O. 2005, c. 34
- *Real Estate and Business Brokers Act, 2002*, S.O. 2002, c. 30, Sched. C
- *Retirement Homes Act, 2010*, S.O. 2010, c. 11
- *Travel Industry Act, 2002*, S.O. 2002, c. 30, Sched. D
- *Vintners Quality Alliance Act, 1999*, S.O. 1999, c. 3

The focus of this chapter is on AABS, so the only other enabling legislation to be discussed in this chapter will be the *Insurance Act*. Further, the procedures and rules for hearings other than AABS matters are found on the LAT website on the Web pages "Information Sheets", "Forms", the FAQ, and the "Rules of Practice" (some of which will be discussed in the section with the Rules and the AABS). The LAT has decided to keep the AABS material separate from the other enabling statutes to avoid confusion, which is why the AABS Web pages were set up separately (entered into from the SLASTO website) from the LAT website.

The *Insurance Act* relevant to AABS

In order to understand the changeover from resolving matters under FSCO's Dispute Resolution Services to resolving matters under the AABS component of the LAT, the two versions (pre- and post-April 1, 2016 amendments) of the legislation are discussed below. The reader should also note that while new matters are now handled by the AABS component of the LAT, matters that were properly filed with FSCO on or before April 1, 2016, will continue at FSCO; therefore, the legislation below will remain relevant during the transition period.

The Insurance Act — Prior to April 1, 2016

STATUTORY ACCIDENT BENEFITS

Motor vehicle liability policy owners are entitled to statutory accident benefits under 268(1) of the *Insurance Act*:

> Every contract evidenced by a motor vehicle liability policy, including every such contract in force when the *Statutory Accident Benefits Schedule* is made or amended, shall be deemed to provide for the statutory accident benefits set out in the *Schedule* and any amendments to the *Schedule*, subject to the terms, conditions, provisions, exclusions and limits set out in that *Schedule*.

The insurer is liable to pay under the *Statutory Accident Benefits Schedule* (SABS) (s. 268(3)). Subsection 268(2) sets out the rules in determining, in various situations, who is liable to pay statutory accident benefits to both occupants and non-occupants connected to the motor vehicle accident. In most situations, one of the insurance companies involved, as determined by the rules, will be liable; however, the Motor Vehicle Accident Claims Fund can be liable as a last resort. The rules dealing with recourse to more than one insurer are set out in subsections 268(4–5.2).

If a dispute arises that needs to be resolved, remember subsection 268(8), which ensures that the claimant is receiving the benefits required by the SABS, notwithstanding the dispute:

> Where the *Statutory Accident Benefits Schedule* provides that the insurer will pay a particular statutory accident benefit pending resolution of any dispute between the insurer and an insured, the insurer shall pay the benefit until the dispute is resolved.

Section 268.3 requires that guidelines made in respect of the SABS, including subsection 268.3(1), which states that the "[s]uperintendent may issue guidelines on the interpretation and operation of the *Statutory Accident Benefits Schedule* or any provision of that *Schedule*", shall be considered in any determination involving the interpretation of the SABS.

CLAIMS FOR BENEFITS

Section 273(1) states a claimant's obligation to inform:

> Where any person makes a claim for damages in respect of bodily injury or death sustained by the person or any other person while driving or being carried in or upon or entering or getting onto or alighting from or as a result of being struck by an automobile, the claimant shall furnish the person against whom the claim is made full particulars of all insurance available to the claimant under contracts falling within the scope of section 268.

The claimant shall also include the details required by subsection 273(2).

DISPUTE RESOLUTION IN RESPECT OF STATUTORY ACCIDENT BENEFITS

The various services available through the DRG are set out in sections 279–288 of the *Insurance Act*. Disputes arising from a person's entitlement to statutory accident benefits give a party the "right to mediate, litigate, appeal or apply to vary an order as provided in sections 280 to 284" (s. 279(2)) and are resolved by those sections and by the SABS; they cannot be opted out of, except as detailed in the SABS. Note that for the purposes of sections 279–284, an "insured person" includes a person making a claim for death benefits or funeral expenses under the SABS. Both orders and interim orders can be made by the Director of Arbitrations or arbitrators appointed by the Director (ss. 279(3–4)). The representative of a party to any of the dispute resolution services must have the authority to bind his or her party, or else the service may be adjourned, with or without conditions (s. 279(5)).

MEDIATION

Under subsection 280(1), either the insured person or the insurer may refer to a mediator (who shall be appointed by the Director promptly (s. 280(3))) any issue regarding entitlement or the amount under the SABS (s. 280(1)) by filing with FSCO an application for the appointment of a mediator (s. 280(2)).

There is a time limit for the matters in dispute to be settled by the mediator (s. 280(4)), which is prescribed in O. Reg. 403/96, s. 51, as being within two years of the date of refusal by the insurer to pay the amounts claimed (s. 51(1)). In the event that mediation fails, a court proceeding "may be commenced within 90 days after the mediator reports to the parties under subsection 280(8) of the Act or within 30 days after the person performing the evaluation provides a report to the parties under section 280.1 of the Act, whichever is later." The time limit to complete the mediation can be extended by agreement of the parties (s. 280(5)).

The mediator must notify the parties forthwith if the mediator believes that the mediation will fail (s. 280(6)). The mediation is also considered to have failed, in addition to the notice given by the mediator, if the agreed time for mediation has expired and no settlement is reached (s. 280(7)). If the mediation fails, the mediator must prepare and give the parties a report containing the following items as set out in subsection 280(8):

(a) the insurer's last offer and a description of the remaining issues in dispute
(b) a list of outstanding materials, requested but not yet provided, that are necessary for a settlement discussion
(c) a recommendation as to whether the issues should be referred for an evaluation under section 280.1

Under subsection 280(9), the mediator's report may also be given to a person performing a neutral evaluation under section 280.1 or to an arbitrator conducting an arbitration under section 282.

NEUTRAL EVALUATION

A neutral evaluation of the probable outcome of a court proceeding or an arbitration under section 282 can be requested by the parties jointly or by the mediator, as stated in subsection 280.1(1):

> If mediation fails, the parties jointly or the mediator who conducted the mediation may, for the purpose of assisting in the resolution of the issues in dispute, refer the issues in dispute to a person appointed by the Director for an evaluation of the probable outcome of a proceeding in court or an arbitration under section 282.

Such evaluator shall be appointed promptly by the Director (s. 280.1(2)) and shall be provided by the parties with all the information requested (s. 280.1(3)). Such evaluator shall provide to the parties an oral opinion and a written report in accordance with subsection 280.1(4). The evaluator may give the written report to an arbitrator conducting an arbitration under section 282 (s. 280.1(5)).

ALTERNATIVES IF MEDIATION FAILS
Under subsection 281(1), the insured person may either "bring a proceeding in a court of competent jurisdiction" or refer the matter to an arbitrator appointed by the Director or a private arbitrator appointed by both parties to resolve the matter, provided that the steps in sections 280 and 280.1 have taken place first (s. 281(2)). Pursuant to section 281.1, a similar time limit as set out in subsection 280(4) is applicable to the commencement of the alternatives under subsection 280(1).

ARBITRATION
The *Arbitrations Act, 1991*, does not apply to arbitrations under section 282 pursuant to subsection 282(16). An insured person seeking arbitration under section 282 shall file an application for the appointment of an arbitrator with FSCO (s. 282(1)), and the Director shall ensure the appointment of such arbitrator promptly (s. 282(2)).

Whether the issues are raised by the insured person or the insurer, all issues in dispute shall be determined by the arbitrator (s. 282(3)). The arbitrator shall conduct the arbitration following the procedures and within the time limits set out in the regulations (s. 282(4)). If the arbitrator finds that the insurer unreasonably delayed or withheld payments that are to be made in accordance with the SABS, he or she can make a special award to the insured in accordance with subsection 282(10). In addition, under certain criteria set out in the regulations, the arbitrator can award the insured person or the insurer all or part of the expenses incurred in respect of an arbitration proceeding as prescribed in the regulations (s. 282(11)). The arbitrator can also make an interim award of expenses at any time during the arbitration (s. 282(11.1)).

The arbitrator can award expenses required to be paid by a party and direct that the representative of such party be personally responsible to pay any or all of such expenses if (i) the arbitrator is satisfied that any of the three criteria set out in this subsection occurred (s. 282(11.2)), and (ii) the representative has been given reasonable opportunity to make representations to the arbitrator (s. 282(11.4)). Note that subsection 282(11.2) does not apply to a lawyer: "Clause (11.2)(a) does not apply to a barrister or solicitor acting in the usual course of the practice of law" (s. 282(11.3)).

Under subsection 282(12), if a party believes the arbitrator is biased, he or she may apply to the Director for a new arbitrator, but it will be the Director who determines the issue.

Immediately after making a decision, the arbitrator shall deliver to the parties and the Director a copy of the decision and the reasons (s. 282(13)).

APPEAL AGAINST ARBITRATION ORDER

According to subsection 283(1), a party to an arbitration under section 282 may appeal the arbitrator's order on a question of law. A written appeal shall be made to the Director and shall be delivered to FSCO within 30 days after the date of the arbitrator's order (s. 283(2)). However, the Director, under subsection 283(3), can extend the time to request an appeal if he or she is satisfied that there are reasonable grounds for granting the extension.

The nature of the appeal and the powers of the Director on such appeal are set out in subsections 283(4) and (5), respectively. The appeal does not stay the order of the arbitrator unless the Director declares otherwise (s. 283(6)). Furthermore, the Director can, under subsection 283(8), allow intervenors to make submissions on issues of law arising in an appeal.

APPLICATION FOR VARIATION OF DIRECTOR'S OR ARBITRATOR'S ORDER

Any party under subsection 284(1) may apply to the Director to vary or revoke an order made by the Director or by an arbitrator appointed by the Director. The Director may decide the matter, return the matter to the same arbitrator, or assign it to some other arbitrator (s. 284(2)). The variation requested under this section may be granted under the following circumstances (s. 284(3)):

- If the person doing so considers it advisable to do so
- If there is a material change in the circumstance of the insured
- If there is new evidence available
- If there is an error in the order

The order of variation can be prospective or retroactive under subsection 284(4). **Also note subsection 284(5), which states that subsections 282(11) to (11.2) apply, with necessary modifications, to applications under this section.**

REPRESENTATION OF PARTIES

Under subsection 284.1(1), a party to a proceeding under sections 279–284 shall not be represented by a "person for compensation except in accordance with the regulations and subject to such terms and conditions as may be specified in the regulations". But such restriction does not apply to lawyers: "[Section 284.1] does not apply to a barrister or solicitor acting in the usual course of the practice of law." The regulation, R.R.O. 1990, Reg. 664, as amended in section 18, also exempts, for the purposes of subsection 398(1) of the *Insurance Act*, anyone licensed by the Law Society of Upper Canada to be a representative of a person making a claim under the SABS. Further, O. Reg. 7/00, as amended, in subsection 3(4)(b), exempts persons licensed by the Law Society of Upper Canada for the purposes of subsection 438(1) of the *Insurance Act* to be a representative of a person making a claim under the SABS.

STATED CASE AND OTHER MATTERS

Under section 285, the Director "may state a case in writing for the opinion of the Divisional Court upon any question that, in his or her opinion, is a question of law" which the Divisional Court shall hear.

MISCELLANEOUS PROVISIONS

A Director-appointed arbitrator of an order that is under appeal cannot revoke or vary that order or make a new order to replace that order (s. 286).

Insurers cannot unilaterally reduce benefits in any circumstances after an order is issued by the Director or by a Director-appointed arbitrator, as stated in section 287:

> An insurer shall not, after an order of the Director or of an arbitrator appointed by the Director, reduce benefits to an insured person on the basis of an alleged change of circumstances, alleged new evidence or an alleged error, unless the insured person agrees or unless the Director or an arbitrator so orders in a variation or appeal proceeding under section 283 or 284.

If the Director detects unfair or deceptive business practices of an insurer in the arbitration orders review process, the Director can recommend an investigation of such insurer to the Superintendent:

> **288.** The Director shall review arbitration orders and may recommend to the Superintendent that the Superintendent investigate the business practices of an insurer if the Director is of the opinion that any one or more arbitrations or appeals from arbitrations reveal unfair or deceptive business practices.

PROHIBITION AGAINST PUBLIC ADJUSTERS OF MOTOR ACCIDENT CLAIMS

Section 398(1), by way of the regulations, previously exempted SABS representatives, who were licensed by FSCO, but it now states:

> ... no person shall, on the person's own behalf or on behalf of another person, directly or indirectly,

(a) solicit the right to negotiate, or negotiate or attempt to negotiate, for compensation, the settlement of a claim for loss or damage arising out of a motor vehicle accident resulting from bodily injury to or death of any person or damage to property on behalf of a claimant; or

(b) hold himself, herself or itself out as an adjuster, investigator, consultant or otherwise as an adviser, on behalf of any person having a claim against an insured or an insurer for which indemnity is provided by a motor vehicle liability policy, including a claim for Statutory Accident Benefits.

Note that the SABS can be handled by a licensed paralegal. For supervised staff at law firms, they also require a licence from the LSUC to represent claimants in the dispute resolution process at FSCO.

UNFAIR DECEPTIVE ACTS AND PRACTICES IN THE BUSINESS OF INSURANCE

Part XVIII of the *Insurance Act* deals with unfair or deceptive acts or practices contrary to the statute (ss. 438–439) as prescribed in the regulations, including actions described in O. Reg. 7/00, as amended. As noted in that regulation, persons licensed by the Law Society of Upper Canada are, as of May 1, 2008, not in breach of such provision merely based on representing a person for compensation.

The Insurance Act — Effective April 1, 2016

The *Insurance Act* was amended, effective on April 1, 2016, to allow for disputes involving automobile accident benefits to be resolved by bringing the matter before the AABS branch of the LAT.

The following are key provisions of the *Insurance Act* related to automobile accident benefits, disputes, and the LAT.

Section 275 was amended as follows:

Note: On April 1, 2016, the day named by proclamation of the Lieutenant Governor, subsection (5) is repealed and the following substituted:

Stay of arbitration

(5) No arbitration hearing shall be held with respect to indemnification under this section if, in respect of the incident for which indemnification is sought, any of the insurers and an insured are parties to a proceeding before the Licence Appeal Tribunal under section 280 or to an appeal from such a proceeding.

Sections 279–288 are amended as follows:

Definitions

279. For the purposes of sections 280 to 283,

"insured person" includes a person who is claiming funeral expenses or a death benefit under the *Statutory Accident Benefits Schedule*;

"Licence Appeal Tribunal" means the Licence Appeal Tribunal established under the *Licence Appeal Tribunal Act, 1999*.

Resolution of disputes

280.(1) This section applies with respect to the resolution of disputes in respect of an insured person's entitlement to statutory accident benefits or in respect of the amount of statutory accident benefits to which an insured person is entitled.

Application to Tribunal

(2) The insured person or the insurer may apply to the Licence Appeal Tribunal to resolve a dispute described in subsection (1).

Limit on court proceedings

(3) No person may bring a proceeding in any court with respect to a dispute described in subsection (1), other than an appeal from a decision of the Licence Appeal Tribunal or an application for judicial review.

Resolution in accordance with Schedule

(4) The dispute shall be resolved in accordance with the *Statutory Accident Benefits Schedule*.

Orders, powers and duties

(5) The regulations may provide for and govern the orders and interim orders that the Licence Appeal Tribunal may make and may provide for and govern the powers and duties that the Licence Appeal Tribunal shall have for the purposes of conducting the proceeding.

Orders for costs, other amounts

(6) Without limiting what else the regulations may provide for and govern, the regulations may provide for and govern the following:

1. Orders, including interim orders, to pay costs, including orders requiring a person representing a party to pay costs personally.

2. Orders, including interim orders, to pay amounts even if those amounts are not costs or amounts to which a party is entitled under the *Statutory Accident Benefits Schedule*.

Note: On April 1, 2016, the day named by proclamation of the Lieutenant Governor, section 280.1 is repealed.

Protection of benefits after Tribunal resolution

281.(1) After the Licence Appeal Tribunal issues a decision, the insurer shall not reduce benefits to the insured person on the basis of an alleged change of circumstances, alleged new evidence or an alleged error except as provided under this section.

When benefits may be reduced

(2) The insurer may reduce benefits if,

(a) the insured person agrees;

(b) the insurer is authorized to do so as a result of a successful appeal of the Licence Appeal Tribunal's decision; or

(c) the insurer is authorized to do so by the Licence Appeal Tribunal.

Note: On April 1, 2016, the day named by proclamation of the Lieutenant Governor, section 281.1 is repealed.

Assessment of dispute resolution costs

282.(1) The Lieutenant Governor in Council may, in accordance with the regulations, assess all insurers that have issued motor vehicle liability policies in Ontario for expenses and expenditures of the Licence Appeal Tribunal relating to disputes described in subsection 280 (1).

Same

(2) If an assessment is made under subsection (1), the share of a particular insurer shall be determined in the manner prescribed by regulation, which may take into account the degree of usage made of the Licence Appeal Tribunal that is specified in the regulations.

Same, fees received

(3) In setting an assessment under subsection (1), the Lieutenant Governor in Council shall take into account the fees received from insurers and insured persons in respect of disputes described in subsection 280 (1).

Insurer's duty to pay

(4) An insurer shall pay the amount assessed against it.

Same

(5) If an insurer fails to pay an assessment made under subsection (1), the Superintendent may suspend or cancel the insurer's licence.

Same

(6) The Superintendent may revive the licence of an insurer whose licence was suspended or cancelled under subsection (5) if the insurer pays all amounts owing by the insurer under this section.

Transition — regulations

283.(1) The Lieutenant Governor in Council may make regulations,

(a) providing for transitional matters in connection with the resolution of disputes described in subsection (2);

(b) governing when a dispute arises and when it is finally determined for the purposes of clause (2) (a);

(c) providing for transitional matters in connection with the coming into force of the following provisions:

(i) Sections 1 to 10, subsections 11 (1) to (4) and (6) to (8) and sections 13 and 14, of Schedule 3 of the *Fighting Fraud and Reducing Automobile Insurance Rates Act, 2014*, which amend this Act.

(ii) Sections 1 to 4 of Schedule 5 of the *Fighting Fraud and Reducing Automobile Insurance Rates Act, 2014*, which amend the *Financial Services Commission of Ontario Act, 1997*.

(iii) Section 7 of Schedule 5 of the *Fighting Fraud and Reducing Automobile Insurance Rates Act, 2014*, which amends the *Motor Vehicle Accident Claims Act*.

Unresolved prior disputes

(2) The disputes referred to in clause (1) (a) are disputes that,

(a) arise before the transition date but are not finally determined before that date; and

(b) are in respect of an insured person's entitlement to statutory accident benefits or in respect of the amount of statutory accident benefits to which the insured person is entitled.

Regulations relating to disputes

(3) Without limiting what regulations may be made under clause (1) (a), the regulations under that clause may,

(a) provide that sections 279 to 282 do not apply or apply with such modifications as the regulations may specify;

(b) provide that sections 279 to 287 as those sections read immediately before being repealed by section 14 of Schedule 3 to the *Fighting Fraud and Reducing Automobile Insurance Rates Act, 2014* apply with such modifications as the regulations may specify;

(c) provide for other provisions of this Act, as those provisions read immediately before being amended or repealed by a provision of Schedule 3 to the *Fighting Fraud and Reducing Automobile Insurance Rates Act, 2014*, to apply with such modifications as the regulations may specify;

(d) provide for the continuation of,

(i) the office of the director of arbitrations appointed under section 6 as that section read immediately before being repealed by section 2 of Schedule 3 to the *Fighting Fraud and Reducing Automobile Insurance Rates Act, 2014*,

(ii) arbitrators appointed under section 8 as that section read immediately before being repealed by section 4 of Schedule 3 to the *Fighting Fraud and Reducing Automobile Insurance Rates Act, 2014*, and

(iii) mediators appointed under section 9 as that section read immediately before being repealed by section 5 of Schedule 3 to the *Fighting Fraud and Reducing Automobile Insurance Rates Act, 2014*;

(e) provide for the continuation of the powers and duties that any of the officials referred to in clause (d) had before the transition date to be exercised by the officials continued by regulations made under clause (d) or to be exercised by other persons or bodies specified in the regulations.

Other regulations

(4) Without limiting what regulations may be made under clause (1) (c), the regulations under that clause may,

(a) if the regulations made under clause (1) (a) provide for the continuation of the office of the director of arbitrations appointed under section 6 as that section read immediately before being repealed by section 2 of Schedule 3 to the *Fighting Fraud and Reducing Automobile Insurance Rates Act, 2014*, provide for that official to continue to be a member of the Financial Services Commission of Ontario, despite subsection 2 (2) of the *Financial Services Commission of Ontario Act, 1997*;

    (b)   govern how section 25 of the *Financial Services Commission of Ontario Act, 1997* applies in respect of assessments that cover expenses and expenditures relating to disputes described in subsection (2);

    (c)   modify the application of clause 6 (2) (b) of the *Motor Vehicle Accident Claims Act* with respect to disputes described in subsection (2).

Transition date

    (5) In this section,

"transition date" means the date on which this section (as re-enacted by section 14 of Schedule 3 to the *Fighting Fraud and Reducing Automobile Insurance Rates Act, 2014*) comes into force.

RELEVANT REGULATIONS

The regulations that are relevant or have provisions relevant to AABS include O. Reg. 403/96; O. Reg. 34/10; R.R.O. 1990, Reg. 664; and O. Reg. 7/00.

O. Reg. 403/96 and O. Reg. 34/10

Currently there are three SABS regulations (O. Reg. 776/93, O. Reg. 403/96, and O. Reg. 34/10) governing accidents occurred in three different periods. The SABS, O. Reg. 403/96, details benefits available for accidents on or after November 1, 1996 but before September 1, 2010, as follows:

- Income replacement benefit — Part II
- Non-earner benefit — Part III
- Caregiver benefit — Part IV
- Medical, rehabilitation, and attendant care benefits and case manager services — Part V
- Payment of other expenses — Part VI
- Death and funeral benefit — Part VII
- Optional benefits — Part VIII

    The procedures for claiming benefits are detailed in Part X of the regulation.

    The current SABS (effective September 1, 2010), O. Reg. 34/10, came into force for any matters arising from and after such date. The

O. Reg. 34/10 has many of the same provisions as the previous SABS, including the following:

- Income replacement, non-earner and caregiver benefits — Part II
- Medical, rehabilitation, and attendant care benefits (which include case manager services) — Part III
- Payment of other expenses — Part IV
- Death and funeral benefits — Part V
- Optional benefits — Part VI

The procedures for claiming benefits are detailed in Part VII of the regulation. (Note: To determine the current law, the reader should closely examine such regulation.)

R.R.O. 1990, Reg. 664 and O. Reg. 7/00

These two regulations have provisions that relate to representatives for SABS claimants.

Under section 18 of R.R.O. 1990, Reg. 664 (Automobile Insurance), public adjusters authorized by the Law Society of Upper Canada are exempted from the section 398 prohibition in the *Insurance Act*:

> A person who is authorized to provide legal services in Ontario pursuant to the *Law Society Act* is exempt from subsection 398(1) of the *Insurance Act* in respect of a claim for benefits under the Statutory Accident Benefits Schedule.

O. Reg. 7/00, which deals with unfair or deceptive acts or practices, stated in subsection 3(4) that acts or practices prescribed as unfair or deceptive in section 3 (except failure to disclose a conflict of interest under para. 6 of s. 3(2)) do not apply to persons licensed by the Law Society of Upper Canada acting as representatives of an SABS claimant:

> This section does not apply to a lawyer or paralegal with respect to activities that constitute practising law or providing legal services, as the case may be, as authorized under the *Law Society Act*. However, paragraph 6 of subsection (2) applies at all times with respect to lawyers and paralegals.

Amendments to the Regulations as of April 1, 2016

R.R.O. 1990, Reg. 664

On April 1, 2016, the day section 14 of Schedule 3 to the *Fighting Fraud and Reducing Automobile Insurance Rates Act, 2014* came into force, and various provisions of the Regulation are revoked and the following substituted (last amended, O. Reg. 43/16):

SETTLEMENTS — STATUTORY ACCIDENT BENEFITS

9.1 ...

(4) A description of the consequences of the settlement on the benefits described under paragraph 2 including,

    i. a statement of the restrictions contained in the settlement on the insured person's right to apply to the Licence Appeal Tribunal under subsection 280 (2) of the Act or appeal from a decision of the Licence Appeal Tribunal,

  iii. a statement that the insured person may not apply to the Licence Appeal Tribunal under subsection 280 (2) of the Act with respect to benefits that were the subject of a settlement or a purported settlement unless the insured person has returned the money received as consideration for the settlement.

...

(8) No person may apply to the Licence Appeal Tribunal under subsection 280 (2) of the Act with respect to benefits that were the subject of a settlement or a purported settlement unless the person has returned the money received as consideration for the settlement.

...

(10) A restriction in a settlement on an insured person's right to apply to the Licence Appeal Tribunal under subsection 280 (2) of the Act or appeal from a decision of the Licence Appeal Tribunal is void unless the insurer complied with subsections (2) and (3) and one of the following conditions is satisfied:

    1. The settlement is entered into on or after the first anniversary of the day of the accident that gave rise to the claim.

    2. Before entering into the settlement,

        i. the insured applied to the Licence Appeal Tribunal under subsection 280 (2) of the Act, and

       ii. if there were applicable rules or procedures of the Licence Appeal Tribunal in respect of case conferences at the time of the settlement, a case conference was held in accordance with the rules or procedures."

As of April 1, 2016, the following section 10 came into force:

DISPUTE RESOLUTION (SECTION 280 OF THE ACT)

10. If the Licence Appeal Tribunal finds that an insurer has unreasonably withheld or delayed payments, the Licence Appeal

> Tribunal, in addition to awarding the benefits and interest to which an insured person is entitled under the Statutory Accident Benefits Schedule, may award a lump sum of up to 50 per cent of the amount to which the person was entitled at the time of the award together with interest on all amounts then owing to the insured (including unpaid interest) at the rate of 2 per cent per month, compounded monthly, from the time the benefits first became payable under the Schedule.

As of April 1, 2016, transition provisions, sections 19–25, came into force and the schedule detailing the Dispute Resolution Expenses under what was s. 282(11) of the *Insurance Act* was revoked.

O. Reg 34/10, Statutory Accident Benefits Schedule
According to section 3(8),

> If in a dispute described in subsection 280 (1) of the Act, the Licence Appeal Tribunal finds that an expense was not incurred because the insurer unreasonably withheld or delayed payment of a benefit in respect of the expense, the Licence Appeal Tribunal may, for the purpose of determining an insured person's entitlement to the benefit, deem the expense to have been incurred.

Section 39(1) states that the insurer gives the insured person a notice informing the insured person that the insurer will pay the expenses without submission of a treatment and assessment plan under section 38. Under subsection 39(2)(d), if the notice was given under s. 39(1), "the insurer shall, if there is a dispute described in subsection 280 (1) of the Act about whether for the purpose of subsection 15 (1) or 16 (3) an expense described in the notice is reasonable or necessary, pay the expense pending resolution of the dispute."

Section 55 came into force on April 1, 2016, as follows:

> *Restriction on proceedings*
>
> **55.**(1) Subject to subsection (2), an insured person shall not apply to the Licence Appeal Tribunal under subsection 280 (2) of the Act if any of the following circumstances exist:
>
> 1. The insured person has not notified the insurer of the circumstances giving rise to a claim for a benefit or has not submitted an application for the benefit within the times prescribed by this Regulation.
>
> 2. The insurer has provided the insured person with notice in accordance with this Regulation that it requires an

examination under section 44, but the insured person has not complied with that section.

3. The issue in dispute relates to the insurer's denial of liability to pay an amount under an invoice on the grounds that,

   i. the insurer requested information from a provider under subsection 46.2 (1), and

   ii. the insurer is unable, acting reasonably, to determine its liability for the amount payable under the invoice because the provider has not complied with the request in whole or in part.

(2) The Licence Appeal Tribunal may permit an insured person to apply despite paragraph 2 or 3 of subsection (1).

(3) The Licence Appeal Tribunal may impose terms and conditions on a permission granted under subsection (2)."

Section 56 came into force on April 1, 2016, as follows:

Time limit for proceedings

56. An application under subsection 280 (2) of the Act in respect of a benefit shall be commenced within two years after the insurer's refusal to pay the amount claimed.

Amendments regarding what body disputes end up in, and the time restrictions similar to those in the current SABS regulation, can also be found in previous SABS regulations.

SAFETY, LICENSING APPEALS AND STANDARDS TRIBUNALS ONTARIO
(the tribunal cluster that includes the LAT)

As detailed in the preamble portion to this Part II, SLASTO is discussed.

CHANGES TO AUTOMOBILE INSURANCE DISPUTE RESOLUTION PROCESS

As stated in subsection 268(1) of the *Insurance Act*, a person involved in a motor vehicle accident in Ontario is entitled to make a claim for benefits under the SABS to one's own insurance company (on a no-fault basis). If the claimant or the insurance company disagrees about the entitlement or the amount of the benefits, either may apply to FSCO's DRG branch (before April 1, 2016) or AABS of the LAT (beginning April 1, 2016), except for the following reasons:

- Claims for damages due to pain and suffering
- Claims for damages to the claimant's automobile or other property
- Decisions on who was at fault in the accident
- Resolutions of disputes between insurers about which company is responsible for the claimant's claim

Under FSCO's DRG, the process begins with an application for mediation, and claimants can go to arbitration or commence a lawsuit if mediation fails. Under LAT's AABS, the option to commence a lawsuit is eliminated. Parties to a disputed claim will participate in a case conference to attempt for a settlement. If a settlement cannot be reached, the matter will go to an arbitration hearing. As mentioned before, hearing decisions can only be appealed on two grounds: the decision contains a legal mistake or the party requests a judicial review.

KEY LAT RULES FOR AABS

Unlike other clusters, SLASTO, as of May 2016, does not have a set of common rules applicable to all the tribunals in the clusters. AABS currently does not have its own Rules of Procedures. Rather, AABS will follow the LAT Rules of Practice and Procedures, which include specific Rules for AABS. Below are some key LAT Rules relevant for AABS, effective April 1, 2016:

Rule 1: General
This section includes rules that establish a broad view of the Rules as to conflict and effective date.

AUTHORITY FOR RULES
The LAT Rules are made pursuant to s. 25.1 of the *SPPA* and pursuant to s. 6 of the *Licence Appeal Act, 1999*.

CONFLICT
Statute or regulation prevails over the Rules when in conflict.

Rule 2: Definitions
Below are the definitions key to SABS Disputes:

- "Appeal" also means an "Automobile Accident Benefits Service Claim" (Rule 2.1).

- "Automobile Accident Benefits Service Claim" is defined as an application to the LAT according to s. 280(2) of the *Insurance Act* seeking resolution of a dispute involving SABS (Rule 2.3).
- "Representative" is a person representing a party and is authorized under the *Law Society Act* to do so (Rule 2.19).
- "Statutory Accident Benefits Schedule (SABS)" means O. Reg. 34/10, as revised and any previous versions (Rule 2.23).

Rule 3: General

As prescribed in "3.1 Liberal Interpretation", the LAT Rules will be broadly interpreted to (i) facilitate fair, open, and accessible process; (ii) allow effective participation by all parties; and (iii) ensure efficient, proportional, and timely resolution of the merits of the proceeding before the LAT.

Rule 9: Disclosure

According to Rule 9.1,

> [the LAT] may at any stage in a proceeding, including prior to a case conference, order any party to provide such further particulars or disclosure as the Tribunal considers necessary for a full and satisfactory understanding of the issues in the proceeding.

In accordance with Rule 9.2, "Mandatory Disclosure",

> [a] party to a hearing shall, at least 10 days before the hearing, or at any other time ordered by the Tribunal or undertaken by the party:
> (a) Disclose to the other parties the existence of every document and anything else the party intends to present as evidence at the hearing;
> (b) Disclose a list of witnesses whom the party may call to give evidence at the hearing and a brief description of each witness' anticipated testimony; and
> (c) Serve a copy of the documents, numbered consecutively, on the other parties.

Rule 12: Format of Hearings and Case Conferences

The formats that are available for LAT proceedings are prescribed in Rule 12.1 Hearing or Case Conference May Be Oral or Written:

> In accordance with applicable provisions of the SPPA, the [LAT] may hold a hearing or case conference in any of the following formats as it considers appropriate:

(a) In-person;

(b) Electronic;

(c) Written; or

(d) Any combination of the above.

Rule 14: Case Conferences

Under Rule 14.2, the scope of subject matters that can be considered in a case conference is described:

> The [LAT] may on its own initiative, or in response to a party's written request, direct the parties to participate in a case conference to consider:
>
> (a) The settlement of any or all of the issues;
>
> (b) Facts or evidence that may be agreed upon;
>
> (c) The identification, clarification, simplification and narrowing of the issues and whether further particulars are required;
>
> (d) The identification of parties and other interested persons, adding parties, and the scope of each party's or person's participation at the hearing;
>
> (e) Disclosure and the exchange of documents, including witness statements and expert reports;
>
> (f) The dates by which any steps in the proceeding are to be taken or begun;
>
> (g) The estimated length of the hearing, including setting hearing dates;
>
> (h) Requirements for interpreters;
>
> (i) French-language or bilingual proceedings;
>
> (j) *Human Rights Code* or accessibility accommodation;
>
> (k) Motions, provided parties have complied with the requirements of this Rule and Rule 15, or otherwise on consent of the parties or Order of the {LAT]; or
>
> (l) Any other matter that may assist in a fair and efficient resolution of the issues in the proceeding.

Rule 18: Reconsideration of a LAT Decision

Under Rule 18.1, "Request for Reconsideration", the Executive Chair of SLASTO may on his or her own initiative or on a request, which is made within **21 days** of the date of the decision, reconsider the decision. A request for reconsideration must be served on all parties and contains the items set out in the rule.

Rule 18.2, "Criteria for Granting Reconsideration", sets out the conditions for reconsideration:

> A request for reconsideration will not be granted unless the Executive Chair is satisfied that one or more of the following criteria are met:

(a) The Tribunal acted outside its jurisdiction or violated the rules of natural justice or procedural fairness;

(b) The Tribunal made a significant error of law or fact such that the Tribunal would likely have reached a different decision;

(c) The Tribunal heard false or misleading evidence from a party or witness, which was discovered only after the hearing and would have affected the result; or

(d) There is new evidence that could not have reasonably been obtained earlier and would have affected the result.

Rule 18.4, "Outcome after Granting a Request for Reconsideration", lists the possible results of a reconsideration request:

> Upon consideration of a request for reconsideration, the Executive Chair may:
> (a) Dismiss the request; or
> (b) After providing all parties [with] an opportunity to make submissions,
>   (i) Confirm, vary, or cancel the decision or order; or
>   (ii) Order a rehearing on all or part of the matter.

Rule 19: Costs

According to Rule 19.1, a request for costs can be made only if the other party is acting unreasonably, frivolously, vexatiously, or in bad faith:

> 19.1 COST REQUESTS
>
> Where a party believes that another party in a proceeding has acted unreasonably, frivolously, vexatiously, or in bad faith, that party may make a request to the [LAT] for costs.

Rule 20: AABS Applications

Rule 20 details the process of AABS. Generally, LAT Rules apply to the AABS claims. However, when a LAT rule contradicts or varies from Rule 20, Rule 20 prevails.

> 20.1 APPLICATION OF THIS RULE
>
> Rule 20 applies to AABS Claims pursuant to the *Insurance Act* only. All other [LAT] rules also apply to AABS Claims except to the extent varied or negated by this Rule.

> 20.2 RESPONSE TO AABS CLAIM
>
> A response to an AABS Claim shall be provided by a respondent, in the form specified by the [LAT], within 10 business

days of the respondent having been served with the AABS Claim, or within such other period as may be specified by the [LAT].

20.3 RESPONSE TO AABS CLAIM MUST DETAIL JURISDICTIONAL ISSUES

A response to an AABS Claim must clearly detail any jurisdictional issues that the respondent seeks to have considered by the [LAT].

20.4 AABS CASE CONFERENCE SUMMARY

Each party shall file an AABS Case Conference Summary, in such form as may be required by the Tribunal, with the [LAT] at least 10 days before a scheduled Case Conference. An AABS Case Conference Summary shall include:

(a) A list of key documents in the party's possession which he or she intends to use in a hearing;

(b) Verification that the documents listed in (a) have been disclosed and have been provided to the other parties;

(c) A list of key documents that the party intends to seek from other parties pursuant to the disclosure rules set out at Rule 9;

(d) A list of any information the party is seeking from non-parties and requests for issuance of summonses;

(e) The party's preference of hearing type with reasons for the preference;

(f) A list of anticipated witnesses, including expert witnesses, that the party intends to call at a hearing in electronic or in-person format and a brief description of each witness' anticipated testimony;

(g) An explanation of the necessity of calling more than two expert witnesses to provide opinion evidence, if a party seeks to call more than two such experts; and

(h) Details of the most recent settlement offer that is open for acceptance.

20.5 COMBINING AABS CLAIMS

Where two or more AABS Claims have been made involving the same parties or the same accident, the [LAT] may:

(a) Combine the Claims;

(b) Schedule any case conferences to take place simultaneously; or

(c) Combine any hearings on consent of the parties.

20.6 INTERPRETER TO BE ARRANGED AT [LAT]'S
 EXPENSE

Where a party gives notice pursuant to Rule 4.2 regarding the
need for an interpreter, the [LAT] shall arrange for an interpreter at the [LAT]'s expense, despite Rule 4.2.

PROCEDURES FOR AABS

The procedures for AABS are set out in the amended legislation and
the Rules set out above, as well as in the AABS website. As all of this
has occurred effective April 1, 2016, it is recommended that the
reader checks out the legislation and the SLASTO, LAT, and AABS
websites prior to being involved with AABS to discover any changes
or amendments likely to occur.

For a quick understanding of the AABS process, the reader is
recommended to review "AABS Questions & Answers" (dated January
2016). The information document is provided in both html and pdf
format and is located in SLASTO's "What's New" Web page, under
Public Information Sessions.

The Q&A are divided into five categories:

• Applications
• Case Conferences
• Timelines
• Hearings
• Other

Below is a summary of the key points made in this document
(a full version is included as an appendix to this chapter).

The New Application Process

A dispute arises when an insurance company denies a policy
holder's claim to a Statutory Accident Benefit. [If the dispute
cannot be resolved through negotiation, the claimant completes
an "Application by an Injured Person" form] (an online fillable
form), provides a copy to the insurance company, and sends it
to the LAT, along with the $100 application fee and a certifi-
cate of service form.

The Application Response Process

[A mandatory case conference is scheduled with a LAT adjudicator about 45 days after (i) receiving the insurance company's

response (i.e., within 10 days), or (ii) the date for sending a response has passed.]

The expectation is that the total process must be completed within 6 months. There will be a period of transition when participants adjust to the new timelines. The AABS performance measurement is that 90% of cases will be completed within 180 days, recognizing that exceptional cases may take much longer because of the complexity of the issues or evidence.

To meet these timelines, there is limited flexibility in dates set by the service.

Case Conferences: Dates and Formats

[Case conference dates are selected] with anticipated dates being about 45 days from the date the response is received or due. Parties will have an option to reschedule within strict parameters. [If a party cannot make the selected date,] three alternate dates that are acceptable to all parties that fall within 30 days of the originally scheduled case conference date can be proposed, and the tribunal will select an adjournment date.

The typical case conference will be held on the phone and will be scheduled for one hour. However, the tribunal has the ability to use discretion and be flexible. If there are language or accessibility requirements, the case conference may be conducted in-person. The scheduled length of a case conference may also be flexible depending on the issue and the probability of settlement. Parties are expected to call the tribunal in advance and explain the circumstances[,] and additional time may be scheduled.

Case Conferences: Adjudicator

The primary aim of the case conference is to settle the dispute. Case conferences are a key tool to achieve early resolution. It is highly encouraged that clients and representatives with the authorization to settle attend the case conferences.

The adjudicator will also assess the dispute and inform both parties of the likely decision, should the case proceed to a hearing (before a different adjudicator).

The case conference adjudicator will also make decisions about the hearing: will it be held in person or on the phone or by video; how evidence is to be submitted; if any adjournments are required due to outstanding evidence; etc. The goal is to schedule a hearing, if required, within 60 days of the case conference. Case conference adjudicators can also deal with preliminary issues like jurisdiction, limitation periods, etc., and make final decisions.

[The adjudicator that facilitates the case conference will not be the same adjudicator that presides at the hearing, and settlement discussions will not be shared with the adjudicator who conducts the hearing.]

The tribunal process is not as formal as the court process. There are not formal 'motions' and 'cross motions'. Matters can be discussed at the case conference. Adjudicators can make orders. If more evidence is needed, a timeline will be set for the receipt of information that adjudicators will need to make a decision, in writing or by phone.

Hearings

There are three hearing formats:

1. Written, in which the parties rely on documents, affidavits and written argument;
2. Electronic, which can be teleconference or video-conference; and
3. In-person.

In addition, a hearing can use any combination of these formats. For example, the case conference adjudicator could order that evidence of experts be provided by affidavits, but the injured party can speak directly to the adjudicator in an electronic or in-person format. When deciding on the hearing format, adjudicators will consider whether accessibility or language interpretation is required.

The administrative justice scheme is more flexible and less legalistic than civil proceedings before a court. If an adjudicator provides for cross–examination, it will take place, but there is not a "right" [of cross–examination on affidavits].

Cost Recovery from Vexatious Appeals

There is not cost recovery to the insurers. However, there are cost provisions in the Rules for certain frivolous or vexatious behaviour before the Tribunal.

PRACTICE DIRECTIONS OF AABS

Currently there are no practice directions in the website. The reader is encouraged to check the site from time to time for new developments.

FORMS

There are five AABS-specific forms:

- Application by an Injured Person
- Application by an Insurance Company
- Response by an Injured Person
- Response by an Insurance Company
- Representing Minors and Mentally Incapable Persons

Other forms may be required during the application process. The ones generally used at the LAT, six of them, are listed:

- Certificate of Service
- Declaration of Representative
- Notice of Motion
- Summons of Witness
- Notice of Withdrawal
- Request for an Adjournment
- Acknowledgment of Expert's Duty

All of these forms can be downloaded via the "Forms" under "Forms, Filing Methods and Serving Documents" Web link.

EXPLANATORY LITERATURE FROM THE AABS

The AABS website provides various useful online literature to assist the reader with the AABS process.

The Application and Hearing Process Web Link

Under this Web, a wealth of information on this new AABS process can be found.

Before you File an AABS Application

On this Web page, it is stated that any application with AABS must be filed within two years from the date the insurance company denies policy benefits. Three steps are proposed that may be taken before filing an application with AABS. The Web page also notes who can apply to AABS as follows:

> The person injured by the accident or an insurance company can apply to AABS if there is a disagreement about the injured person's entitlement to accident benefits or the amount of benefits that should be paid, and this dispute cannot be settled.

If an insurance company believes an individual has been paid too much under their policy, the company can file an AABS application to have the money returned.

AABS does not hear disputes about:
• damages for pain and suffering;
• damage to cars or other property;
• who was at fault in the accident; and
• which insurer is responsible for your claim.

When can an AABS application be made?

If an insurance company denies or stops paying benefits to an insured person, they must provide written notice of this decision that includes the reason(s) for their decision, to you.

Filing an Application

On this Web page, the four steps of the AABS application are described:

1. Complete an AABS application form;
2. Send a copy of the application form to the other party (this is called 'serving' the other party);
3. Complete an AABS Certificate of Service form to explain how you have sent the copy of the application to the other party; and
4. Send the application form and the Certificate of Service form to AABS and pay the AABS application fee.

Note that the fee to file the application with AABS is $100 and is non-refundable once AABS has confirmed that it can go ahead with the claim.

Processing AABS Application

It is stated on this Web page that AABS may request further information so that the application is complete, and once complete it will issue a file number, at which time AABS will contact the other party by sending a Notice of Application and ask for a response.

Filing a Response

On this Web page the reader can find advice on how a responding party responds to an application, which is set out in three steps: Complete the appropriate response form; send a copy of the completed form to the other party; and provide a Certificate of Service and the completed Response Form to the AABS.

Case Conferences

The "Case Conferences" Web page details the goals, schedule, participants, and disclosures required in the mandatory case conference and the involvement of the Case Management Officer (CMO, a staff member of AABS). The case conference is led by an AABS adjudicator. The Web page ends with a description of what happens at a Case Conference:

> Most case conferences will be on the phone, The AABS adjudicator leads the case conference[,] which is informal and confidential. The adjudicator will have read the Case Conference Summary Forms and the offers to settle. The adjudicator will try to narrow the differences between the parties by asking questions and explaining how the SABS have been applied in other cases that were similar. Sometimes, the adjudicator may meet individually with just the claimant or just the insurance company, as a way of encouraging a settlement. If you and the insurance company cannot settle the case, the adjudicator may make decisions and give you instructions to prepare for a hearing. The adjudicator[] has the power to end the case at the case conference if it does not fall within the legal responsibility of AABS. The adjudicator can also order one or both parties to complete steps, exchange information or pay costs.
>
> The discussions are not recorded, and the adjudicator will not let the next adjudicator know about your confidential discussions. The only documents that go forward to the next adjudicator are those documents that both parties may agree to send forward, and any orders by the adjudicator to direct how the hearing will be held, or to decide any preliminary issues. The adjudicator that leads the hearing won't be the same one who leads the case conference.

Hearings

The "Hearings" Web page details the schedule and who the participants are at a hearing. A hearing will only be held if the mandatory case conference does not result in an agreement. The date of the hearing will be within 60–90 days after the case conference, and the details about the hearing will be sent by the CMO to the parties. "After the end of a hearing, the hearing adjudicator will make a final decision about the case, which will usually be sent to the parties later as a written decision. The [LAT] decisions are legally binding and must be followed by both the claimant and the insurance company." The Web page then sets out in layman's terms the roles of the adjudicator and the parties, discusses evidence and witnesses, and explains how original documents are used in a hearing.

Resolve the Dispute

This Web page details how settlements are to be done:

> The case can be settled by agreement at any time after one year has passed since the application. If one year has not passed, you will need to go to the case conference first. To settle a case, you and the other party will sign a document, with your representative, if any, and that document will end the case. If you reach a settlement during a case conference or hearing, tell the adjudicator[,] and they will let the CMO know the case is settled. You can provide a copy of the settlement document to the adjudicator.
>
> If the settlement of a case is reached between the parties directly and does not happen at the case conference or the hearing, one of the parties needs to write to AABS and copy the other party. This written notice must include:
> - Date;
> - AABS File Number;
> - A statement that the case has been settled; and
> - A request that the file be closed because the case was settled.

Withdrawing an Application

Any party to an AABS case can elect to end the case before a settlement has been reached: By completing the AABS the Notice of Withdrawal form and sending it to AABS and the other party, the party has withdrawn his or her application and will no longer have a right to an AABS hearing.

Orders

The Web page states that the adjudicator's orders, whenever made, are legally binding; and if not obeyed, the order can be registered with the Superior Court of Justice and become enforceable as an order of the court.

Reconsideration

The condition and process to request a reconsideration are described in this Web page. A party can ask AABS to reconsider the LAT decision within 21 days of the decision, all in accordance with Rule 18 of the LAT Rules of Practice and Procedures.

Appeals

AABS decisions can only be appealed on the ground of a legal mistake. The Web page discusses appeals as well as judicial review.

It states that appeals can be requested within 30 days of the date the decision is released on a question of "legal mistake" to Divisional Court. It also notes that in limited circumstances, judicial review to Divisional Court may also be available.

The FAQs

To understand how a tribunal works, FAQs is always a good source of information. The SLASTO — AABS — FAQs Web page currently gives three commonly asked questions, with answers to each:

1. Do I need a legal representative or paralegal?
2. Where can I get AABS forms?
3. Can I go to court to settle an auto insurance benefits dispute?

News

Currently, the page is displaying the announcement of AABS accepting applications starting April 1, 2016, and the items that are necessary to understand or compile to get ready for the process: Rules of Practice, Forms, and Applicable Regulations. In addition, the Web page contains the following:

• Proposed regulation for assessing costs against the insurance industry
• Sample of Case Conference Summary

Note: The last item is provided for reference purpose.

Laws, Rules, Guidelines and Decisions

On this Web Page, the reader can find out what legislations, regulations, and rules govern the AABS process.

The "Legislations and Regulations" Web page discusses key sections of the *Insurance Act* relevant to AABS and provides links to the Act and five other related statutes on the E-Laws website. There are also links to relevant regulations under the *Insurance Act*.

The "Rules" Web page links the New Rules of the LAT effective April 1, 2016, in both pdf and html.

Through the "Accessing Decisions" page, the public is advised that they can obtain decisions with reasons once the decision becomes available. On the Web page, it is stated that decisions of the AABS adjudicator will likely be written and given later after the hearing, and decisions will be published on the CanLII website.

RELEVANT CASES AND/OR DECISIONS

As the AABS portion of the LAT only became effective as of April 1, 2016, there are no decisions to summarize as of the time of writing on May 1, 2016. Please note the admonition given by the LAT, found on the Public Sessions AABS questions and answers January 2016, listed under the SLASTO's "What's New" Web page:

> Q: Can case law from FSCO be brought before LAT?
>
> A: Tribunals are not bound by decisions of other tribunals. LAT adjudicators will be making their own independent decisions although they will, of course, be bound by the courts' binding interpretations of the SABS and other relevant law.

REVIEW QUESTIONS

1. What is the enabling legislation for the LAT?
2. Where would you find the practices and procedures of the LAT?
3. How does the *SPPA* apply to the LAT?
4. What is SLASTO, and how is the LAT involved in it?
5. Why was the AABS portion of the LAT created, and why does it have a website separate from that of the LAT?
6. What Rule(s) gives discretion and flexibility to the LAT in applying the LAT Rules?
7. What Rules apply specifically to AABS?
8. What Rule(s) deal with disclosure, and what is the result of insufficient disclosure?
9. What Rule(s) deal with motions, and what is the appropriate procedure to have a motion dealt with by the LAT?
10. What jurisdiction is the LAT given to reconsider a decision?
11. What is the procedure, in summary fashion, if there is a dispute between the insured party and the insurer arising from statutory accident benefits being claimed pursuant to an automobile accident in Ontario?
12. What is the application fee to start the AABS component of the LAT, and when does it become non-refundable?
13. What powers does the AABS adjudicator have in a Case Conference, and what will such an adjudicator likely do in the Case Conference?

EXERCISE

Compare the previous mechanisms and procedures in place prior to April 1, 2016, for the DRS through FSCO to the current AABS component to the LAT. Discuss how well the new procedures of AABS meet the recommendations —set out in the chart in the "Overview and Background" section of this chapter — made by the Honourable J. Douglas Cunningham in the *Ontario Automobile Insurance Dispute Resolution System Review Final Report*. As of the date of this question being drafted, there are no completed matters using AABS, so discussion will be in a vacuum; however, as of May 2017, there will be actual matters through the process to make the discussion more factual.

Appendix 7.1
The AIDRS (now AABS) High Level Process Design[†]

† Source: SLASTO, "What's New", <http://www.slasto.gov.on.ca/en/Pages/WHAT'S-NEW.aspx>. [Note: AIRDS has become AABS.]

SUMMARY

A. Application/Response

Insurance Act, s. 280

Timelines — No later than 2 years after accidents

Look at the following:
* *Insurance Act*, ss. 268, 268.3, 273, 279, 257.6
* *SABS Regulation* — O. Reg. 403/96, as amended
* *Automobile Insurance Regulation* — O. Reg. 664, as amended
* AABS website, Web page, "Filing an Application"

B. Schedule Case Conference

Insurance Act, s. 280

Timelines — 45–60 days

Look at the following:
* Forms A and B on "Forms" Web Page
* AABS website, Web page, "Case Conferences"
* Rule 14

C. Hearing

Insurance Act, s. 280

Timelines — 75–150 days

Look at the Following:
* AABS website, Web page, "Hearings"

D. Decision

Insurance Act, s. 280

Timelines — From 30 to 90 days, depending on the format of the hearing

Look at the following:
* AABS website, Web page, "Decisions"
* CanLII

E. Reconsideration of a Decision

Rule 18

Timelines — within 21 days of the date of the decision

Look at the following:
* AABS website, Web page: "Reconsideration"

F. Appeals to Divisional Court

Insurance Act, s. 288(5)

Timelines — Within 30 days of the date the AABS releases its decision

Look at the following:
* AABS website, Web page "Appeals"
* Guide to Appeals in Divisional Court

Appendix 7.2
AABS Questions and Answers[†]

| Safety, Licensing Appeals and
Standards Tribunals Ontario
Licence Appeal Tribunal | Tribunaux de la sécurité, des appels en
matière de permis et des normes Ontario
Tribunal d'appel en matière de permis | |

Ontario

<u>Automobile Accident Benefits Service (AABS)</u>
<u>Questions and Answers</u>

<u>Applications:</u>

Q: What is the new application process?

A: A dispute arises when an insurance company denies a policy holder's claim to a Statutory Accident Benefit.

If through negotiation, the dispute cannot be resolved, the claimant completes an Application by an Injured Person (an online fillable form), provides a copy to the insurance company and sends it to the Licence Appeal Tribunal, along with the $100 application fee and a certificate of service form.

After the LAT has reviewed the form and entered it into the case management system, the system will send a letter to the insurer asking for a response to be filed within 10 days of the date of the letter.

Q: Is there a filing/application fee?

A: Yes. $100

Q: Is the internal review process at the insurance company required?

A: No. An internal review process within insurance companies is a recommendation from the Cunningham report, but the Ministry of Finance will work with companies on this policy issue, and this is not required for April 1, 2016.

Q: What is the fee for insurance companies?

A: The cost to the insurance company is determined by an assessment regulation under the *Insurance Act*. A draft of the regulation is available on the government's regulatory registry at:
http://www.ontariocanada.com/registry/quickSearch.do?searchType=current.

The system will be weighted and the insurance companies will pay a portion of the costs based on how far the case moves through the system. All fees collected from claimants will be applied against the costs of the system, and only the outstanding costs will be assessed against companies.

[†]   Source: FSCO Website <www.fsco.gov.on.ca>

Safety, Licensing Appeals and
Standards Tribunals Ontario
Licence Appeal Tribunal

Tribunaux de la sécurité, des appels en
matière de permis et des normes Ontario
Tribunal d'appel en matière de permis

Ontario

Application response process:

Q: Is a response expected by the insurance company?

A: Yes. The tribunal contacts the respondent insurance company and requests a
      completed Response by an Insurance Company within 10 days.

      A mandatory case conference is scheduled with a LAT adjudicator about 45 days
      after the response is received, or the date for sending a response has passed.

Q: How flexible are timelines? (i.e. 45 days from the response to the case
      conference and 60 days from the case conference to a hearing).

A: The expectation is that the total process must be completed within 6 months.
      There will be a period of transition when participants adjust to the new timelines.
      The AABS performance measurement is that 90% of cases will be completed
      within 180 days, recognizing that exceptional case may take much longer
      because of the complexity of the issues or evidence.

      To meet these timelines, there is limited flexibility in dates set by the service.

Case Conferences:

Q: How will Case Conference dates be chosen?

A: The tribunal will select dates with anticipated dates being about 45 days from the
      date the response is received or due. Parties will have an option to reschedule
      within strict parameters.

Q: What if one cannot make the case conference date?

A: Three alternate dates that are acceptable to all parties that fall within 30 days of
      the originally scheduled case conference date can be proposed, and the tribunal
      will select an adjournment date.

Q: Will case conferences be held in-person?

A: The typical case conference will be held on the phone and will be scheduled for
      one hour. However, the tribunal has the ability to use discretion and be flexible.
      If there are language or accessibility requirements, the case conference may be
      conducted in-person. The scheduled length of a case conference may also be

Safety, Licensing Appeals and
Standards Tribunals Ontario
Licence Appeal Tribunal

Tribunaux de la sécurité, des appels en
matière de permis et des normes Ontario
Tribunal d'appel en matière de permis

Ontario

flexible depending on the issue and the probability of settlement. Parties are expected to call the tribunal in advance and explain the circumstances and additional time may be scheduled.

Q: What is the case conference summary form?

A: The system's case management officer will send a draft case conference summary form to each party that is pre-populated based on information provided to date. Parties will verify the information, complete the form and return it to the tribunal no later than 10 days prior to the scheduled case conference. The case management officer will put this material before the adjudicator facilitating the case conference.

The summary also asks for a copy of the latest outstanding offer to settle from each party.

Q: Does each party file a case conference summary form? Are case conference summary forms filed with the case management officer?

A: Yes, each party completes a separate case conference summary which is filed with the case management officer. The case management officer will put this material before the adjudicator facilitating the case conference. The case management officer also uses the summaries to provide a preliminary hearing stream recommendation to the case conference adjudicator.

Q: What is the purpose of the case conference?

A: The primary aim of the case conference is to settle the dispute. Case conferences are a key tool to achieve early resolution. It is highly encouraged that clients and representatives with the authorization to settle attend the case conferences.

The adjudicator will also assess the dispute and inform both parties of the likely decision, should the case proceed to a hearing (before a different adjudicator).

The case conference adjudicator will also make decisions about the hearing: will it be held in person or on the phone or by video; how evidence is to be submitted; if any adjournments are required due to to outstanding evidence etc. The goal is to schedule a hearing, if required, within 60 days of the case conference. Case conference adjudicators can also deal with preliminary issues like jurisdiction, limitation periods etc. and make final decisions

Safety, Licensing Appeals and
Standards Tribunals Ontario
Licence Appeal Tribunal

Tribunaux de la sécurité, des appels en
matière de permis et des normes Ontario
Tribunal d'appel en matière de permis

Ontario

Q: Will the adjudicator that facilitates the case conference be the same adjudicator that presides at the hearing?

A: No. The adjudicators will be different. Settlement discussions will not be shared with the adjudicator who conducts the hearing.

Q: Are interim motions to be made at the case conference?

A: The tribunal process is not as formal as the court process. There are not formal 'motions' and 'cross motions'. Matters can be discussed at the case conference. Adjudicators can make orders. If more evidence is needed, a timeline will be set for the receipt of information that adjudicators will need to make a decision, in writing or by phone.

Timelines:

Q: How flexible are timelines? (i.e. 45 days to a case conference and 60 days to hearing)

A: The expectation is that the total process must be completed within 6 months. There will be a period of transition when participants adjust to the new timelines. The service's performance measurement is that 90% of cases will be completed within 180 days, recognizing that exceptional case may take much longer because of the complexity of the issues or evidence.

To meet these timelines, there is limited flexibility in dates set by the service.

Q: What are the repercussions if timelines are not met?

A: Adjudicators are independent and have many tools available to them (e.g. cost orders, procedural orders etc.). Everyone benefits if cases which are not complex are resolved quickly, so that more complex case can get the attention they need.

Q: Are delays resulting from third party productions subject to the same timelines?

A: There may be flexibility in these circumstances, but LAT will do all it can to facilitate early disclosure. If you anticipate delay as a result of third party production, let the case conference adjudicator know.

Q: Is there a separate process for each benefit over which there is a dispute?

Safety, Licensing Appeals and
Standards Tribunals Ontario
Licence Appeal Tribunal

Tribunaux de la sécurité, des appels en
matière de permis et des normes Ontario
Tribunal d'appel en matière de permis

Ontario

A: Adjudicators will have the ability to combine and separate disputes. But most disputes will combine outstanding issues, and if another issue arises after the application is filed, parties can ask for it to be added at the case conference.

Q: How will this new system impact self-represented parties?

A: The forms are simple and can be filled out online. Electronic filing is a goal within the first year of operation.

One of the goals of the mandatory case conference is to educate the parties about the process and the expected outcome of a hearing. The goal is to settle as early as possible.

Q: Will there be an entirely new forms process?

A: Yes. There will be new electronic forms that will eventually make e-filing simpler and make the process more user-friendly.

Q: Is there a timeline already in place regarding the exchange of documents and expert reports or is that discussed during the case conference?

A: The case conference adjudicator will address the timelines for any further exchange of documents and information.

Hearings:

Q: What format will hearings take?

A: There are three hearing formats:

1. Written, in which the parties rely on documents, affidavits and written argument;
2. Electronic, which can be teleconference or videoconference; and
3. In-person.

In addition, a hearing can use any combination of these formats. For example, the case conference adjudicator could order that evidence of experts be provided by affidavits, but the injured party can speak directly to the adjudicator in an electronic or in-person format. When deciding on the hearing format, adjudicators will consider whether accessibility or language interpretation is required.

Safety, Licensing Appeals and
Standards Tribunals Ontario
Licence Appeal Tribunal

Tribunaux de la sécurité, des appels en
matière de permis et des normes Ontario
Tribunal d'appel en matière de permis

Ontario

Q: Is there a right of cross-examination on affidavits?

A: The administrative justice scheme is more flexible and less legalistic than civil proceedings before a court. If an adjudicator provides for cross –examination, it will take place, but there is not a "right".

Q: Will hearings only be held in Toronto?

A: No. Recruitment is underway for adjudicators in several communities across the province.

Q: Can a tribunal decision be appealed?

A: An amendment to the *Licence Appeal Tribunal Act* comes into effect when Bill 15 is proclaimed so that an appeal can be on a question of law only. The appeal is to the Divisional Court. The FSCO internal appeal process is not part of the new LAT system.

Other:

Q: Is there a complaints process?

A: Yes, there is an existing tribunal complaints process.

Q: How are OICs for the LAT adjudicators being recruited?

A: Through the Public Appointments Secretariat. An ad was posted from Aug-Sept. 2015; it was published in Ontario Reports, and it was sent out to legal organizations.

   Approximately 600 applications were received. The interview process is now underway. Any additional recruitment will follow the same process.

Q: What happens to files that are with FSCO on April 1, 2016?

A: There are currently three streams of dispute resolution at FSCO: mediation, arbitration and appeals.

   On April 1, 2016, if mediation has been completed, but the arbitration process has not begun, a party can apply to LAT and begin the new process.

   If you already have an arbitration case number at FSCO, the case remains at FSCO. Existing cases will not be transferred from FSCO to LAT.

Safety, Licensing Appeals and
Standards Tribunals Ontario
Licence Appeal Tribunal

Tribunaux de la sécurité, des appels en
matière de permis et des normes Ontario
Tribunal d'appel en matière de permis

Ontario

Q: Justice Cunningham had specific criteria for streaming based on monetary value? Under the new system, does the adjudicator at case conference have discretion to select a streaming type?

A: The case conference adjudicator will determine the hearing type (or stream). The decision will be based on the complexity of the case, but also on the needs of the parties.

Q: Will LAT conduct more information sessions about the new system?

A: LAT is planning to hold detailed information sessions for administrative staff who will be filling out forms, interacting with LAT staff on behalf of applicants and respondents.

       These will be held in mid-late March and in April. Dates will be communicated via the email list.

Q: Is there an enforcement mechanism regarding timelines of decision issuance?

A: Member management. If a timeline will not be met, the parties will be notified. For the system to work and to make continued improvements, it is important for parties to provide feedback on any issues they experience and areas that are working.

Q: Can case law from FSCO be brought before LAT?

A: Tribunals are not bound by decisions of other tribunals. LAT adjudicators will be making their own independent decisions although they will, of course, be bound by the courts' binding interpretations of the SABS and other relevant law.

Q: What is the difference between Duty Vice Chairs, Vice Chairs and Members?

A: Adjudicators can either be Members or Vice Chairs. Duty Vice Chairs are the senior adjudicators 'on-call'. All adjudicators dedicated to this work are specially trained.

Q: Is there an ability to recover cost assessments to the insurers from vexatious appeals?

A: No. There is not cost recovery to the insurers. However, there are cost provisions in the Rules for certain frivolous or vexatious behaviour before the Tribunal.

Appendix 7.3
AABS Application by an Injured Person[†]

Automobile Accident Benefits Service
Licence Appeal Tribunal

Ontario

Application by an Injured Person for Auto Insurance Dispute Resolution under the *Insurance Act*

Important Information

- You must complete all sections of this form and attach additional information and/or documents as required.
- You must send a copy of this application to the Insurance Company or the Insurance Company's Representative (if known).
- On this form the Injured Person is referred to as "the Claimant".
- The processing of an application could be delayed if information or documents are missing.

Fields marked with an asterisk (*) are mandatory.

Claimant Information

I am making this application: *

☐ By Myself ☐ With a Representative

Claimant Name

Last Name *	First Name *	Middle Initial

Claimant Mailing Address

Unit Number	Street Number *	Street Name *	PO Box

City/Town *	Province/State *	Postal/Zip Code *

Country *

One of the following fields must be completed daytime phone, alternate phone or email address: *

Daytime Phone	Ext.	Alternate Phone	Ext.	Fax Number

Email Address

Date of Birth (yyyy/mm/dd) *	Gender: * ☐ Male ☐ Female ☐ Other Gender Identity

Preferred Language: *

☐ English ☐ French ☐ Other

What is your preferred method of communication with the Tribunal? *

☐ Email ☐ Fax ☐ Regular Mail ☐ Phone ☐ Through My Representative

Note: If you check email you are consenting to the delivery of communications and some documents by email. However, applications and responses are currently **only accepted** via fax, regular mail or delivery.

Is the Claimant under 18 years old? * ☐ Yes ☐ No	Is the Claimant mentally incapable? * ☐ Yes ☐ No

Accommodation, Language and Location Requests

1. Do you or any witness(es) require accommodation under the Ontario Human Rights Code to participate in a Tribunal hearing?

☐ Yes ☐ No

2. Do you want the dispute resolution proceedings (e.g. case conference and hearings) to be conducted in French?

☐ Yes ☐ No

3. Do you or any witness(es) require language interpretation services?

☐ Yes ☐ No

0457E (2016/03) © Queen's Printer for Ontario, 2016 Disponible en français Page 1 of 6

Print Form Save Draft Save Final Clear Form

[†] Source: SLASTO — AABS, "Forms, Filing Methods and Serving Documents" — Forms, <http://www.slasto.gov.on.ca/en/AABS/Pages/Forms.aspx>

4. Would you like the hearing to be conducted outside the Greater Toronto Area?

☐ Yes   ☐ No

About the Accident

What was the date of the accident? * (yyyy/mm/dd)

Where did the accident take place?

Unit Number	Street Number	Street Name

City/Town	Province/State	Postal/Zip Code

Country

Intersection

Insurance Company Information

Insurance Company Name *

Claim Representative Name (if known)

Last Name	First Name	Middle Initial

Claim Number *	Policy Number *

Policy Holder Name

Last Name	First Name	Middle Initial

General Information

1. Did the Claimant notify the Insurance Company of the circumstances giving rise to a claim? *

☐ Yes   ☐ No

2. Did the Claimant submit an application within the times set out by the Statutory Accident Benefits Schedule (SABS)? *

☐ Yes   ☐ No

3. Was the claim for benefits denied by the Insurance Company? *

☐ Yes   ☐ No

4. Did the Claimant and the Insurance Company attempt to resolve the claim through the Insurance Company's internal dispute resolution process? *

☐ Yes   ☐ No

5. Was the Claimant provided with notice by the Insurance Company that it requires an examination? *

☐ Yes   ☐ No

6. Did the Insurance Company deny payment of an invoiced amount because a service provider has not responded to a request for information from the Insurance Company? *

☐ Yes   ☐ No

Issues in Dispute

Does this claim involve optional benefits? *

☐ Yes   ☐ No

Does this claim involve catastrophic impairment? *

☐ Yes   ☐ No

Provide a **full** description of the accident benefits that are in dispute.

☐ Income Replacement

Print Form   Save Draft   Save Final   Clear Form

☐ Non-Earner

☐ Caregiver Benefits

☐ Attendant Care Benefits

☐ Medical Benefits

☐ Rehabilitation Benefits

☐ Case Manager Services Benefits

☐ Other Expenses

☐ Death Benefits

☐ Funeral Expenses

☐ Other Disputes

☐ Interest

Print Form   Save Draft   Save Final   Clear Form

Documents List (This section **must** be completed) *

It is expected that the Claimant and the Insurance Company have exchanged key documents prior to the filing of an Application.

List key documents in your possession to which you will refer in the dispute process. Identify the type of document (letter, medical report, tax return), the name of the writer or issuing institution and the date of the document.

List key documents not currently in your possession, which you intend to get from other sources (such as employers, doctors, Revenue Canada) for use in the dispute process. You should also include any documents requested from the Insurance Company (such as surveillance evidence, a summary of benefits paid) which have not yet been provided. Wherever possible, identify the type of document (letter, medical report, tax return), the name of the writer or issuing institution and the date of the document.

Print Form   Save Draft   Save Final   Clear Form

Acknowledgement

Read carefully then check each box to confirm the statement and sign and date the form.

☐ I have completed all pages of this form and attached all the required documentation. *

☐ I certify that all information in the Application and attachments is true and complete. *

☐ If applicable, I authorize the respondent insurance company to release all medical reports and information relating to the issues in dispute to the Automobile Accident Benefits Service, Licence Appeal Tribunal. I realize that information filed with this Application will be given to the other party in this dispute.

☐ I have served a copy of all the above pages of this form and all additional attached documents to the Insurance Company or the Insurance Company's representative. I have attached a completed 'Certificate of Service' to this form as proof of service of the documents on the Insurance Company. (Blank 'Certificate of Service' forms are available on the Tribunal's website at www.slasto.gov.on.ca/en/AABS) *

☐ I have completed the 'Payment Information' section on the final page of this form and am submitting payment for my claim in an acceptable format. (Do not serve a copy of the payment page to the Insurance Company. Your payment information should only be provided to the Tribunal.) *

Claimant

Print Name *	Signature *	Date (yyyy/mm/dd) *

The Licence Appeal Tribunal collects the personal information requested on this form under section 3 of the *Licence Appeal Tribunal Act, 1999* and under the *Insurance Act*. This information will be used in the dispute resolution process for accident benefits. After an appeal is filed, all information may become available to the public. Any questions about this collection may be directed to the Licence Appeal Tribunal at (416) 314-4260 or toll-free at 1 (800) 255-2214.

Send the completed form to the Licence Appeal Tribunal at the address noted below. Keep an additional copy of the completed form for yourself.

Mail your form to:

Automobile Accident Benefits Service (AABS)
Licence Appeal Tribunal (LAT)
77 Wellesley St. W.
Box 250
Toronto ON M7A1N3

Fax your form to:

Automobile Accident Benefits Service (AABS)
Licence Appeal Tribunal (LAT)
416-325-1060
1-844-618-2566

Deliver your form in-person to:

Licence Appeal Tribunal
20 Dundas St. W., Suite 530
Toronto ON M5G 2C2

For additional information, please visit the Automobile Accident Benefits Service website at: www.slasto.gov.on.ca/en/AABS or call the Licence Appeal Tribunal at 416-314-4260 or toll-free at 1-800-255-2214. If you are using a TTY device you can call us at 416-916-0548 or TTY toll-free at 1-844-403-5906.

[Print Form]   [Save Draft]   [Save Final]   [Clear Form]

This page is not part of your disclosure to the other parties. **Submit this page to the Tribunal only.**

Payment Information

- Payment of $100 must be submitted with this form in one of the acceptable formats below.
- The filing fee is per application.
- Money Orders, Bank Drafts and Certified Cheques must be made payable to the Minister of Finance.

Acceptable Methods of Payment:

If you are filing your appeal ...	You must pay by ...
by fax	credit card
by mail or courier	credit card certified cheque money order bank draft
in person at the Tribunal office	credit card certified cheque money order bank draft debit card

I am paying my $100 filing fee by:

☐ Certified Cheque ☐ Money Order ☐ Bank Draft ☐ Debit Card ☐ Credit Card [1]

[1] If you are paying by credit card, you must provide the following information:

☐ MasterCard ☐ American Express ☐ Visa

Expiry Date (yyyy/mm)	Credit Card Number	Cardholder Name (as it appears on card)

Signature

For Licence Appeal Tribunal Office Use Only:

Tribunal File No.	Date Appeal and Fee Processed

Print Form   Save Draft   Save Final   Clear Form

Appendix 7.4
AABS Application by an Insurance Company†

Automobile Accident Benefits Service
Licence Appeal Tribunal

Ontario

**Application by an Insurance
Company for Auto Insurance Dispute
Resolution under the *Insurance Act***

Important Information

- You must complete all sections of this form and attach additional information and/or documents as required.
- The Insurance Company must send a copy of this application to the Claimant and the Claimant's Representative.
- On this form the Injured Person is referred to as "the Claimant".
- The processing of an application could be delayed if information or documents are missing.

Fields marked with an asterisk (*) are mandatory.

Insurance Company Information

Who is making this application? *

☐ Insurance Company   ☐ Insurance Company's Representative

Insurance Company Name *

Claim Representative Name

Last Name	First Name	Middle Initial
Claim Number *	Policy Number *	

Policy Holder Name

Last Name *	First Name *	Middle Initial

Accommodation, Language and Location Requests

1. Do you or any witness(es) require accommodation under the Ontario Human Rights Code to participate in a Tribunal hearing?

☐ Yes   ☐ No

2. Do you want the dispute resolution proceedings (e.g. case conference and hearings) to be conducted in French?

☐ Yes   ☐ No

3. Do you or any witness(es) require language interpretation services?

☐ Yes   ☐ No

4. Would you like the hearing to be conducted outside the Greater Toronto Area?

☐ Yes   ☐ No

About the Accident

What was the date of the accident? * (yyyy/mm/dd)

Where did the accident take place?

Unit Number	Street Number	Street Name
City/Town	Province/State	Postal/Zip Code
Country		
Intersection		

Claimant Information (as known)

Claimant Name

| Print Form | Save Draft | Save Final | Clear Form |

---

† Source: SLASTO — AABS, "Forms, Filing Methods and Serving Documents" — Forms, <http://www.slasto.gov.on.ca/en/AABS/Pages/Forms.aspx>

Last Name *	First Name *	Middle Initial

Mailing Address

Unit Number	Street Number *	Street Name *	PO Box

City/Town *	Province/State *	Postal/Zip Code *

Country *

Daytime Phone	Ext.	Alternate Phone	Ext.	Fax Number

Email Address

Date of Birth (yyyy/mm/dd)

General Information

1. Did the Claimant notify the Insurance Company of the circumstances giving rise to a claim? *

☐ Yes ☐ No

2. Did the Claimant submit an application within the times set out by the Statutory Accident Benefits Schedule (SABS)? *

☐ Yes ☐ No

3. Did the Claimant and the Insurance Company attempt to resolve the claim through the Insurance Company's internal dispute resolution process? *

☐ Yes ☐ No

4. Was the Claimant provided with notice by the Insurance Company that it requires an examination? *

☐ Yes ☐ No

5. Did the Insurance Company deny payment of an invoiced amount because a service provider has not responded to a request for information from the Insurance Company? *

☐ Yes ☐ No

Issues in Dispute

Does this claim involve optional benefits? *

☐ Yes ☐ No

Does this claim involve catastrophic impairment? *

☐ Yes ☐ No

Provide a **full** description of the accident benefits that you are seeking repayment for:

☐ Income Replacement

☐ Non-Earner

☐ Caregiver Benefits

☐ Attendant Care Benefits

☐ Medical Benefits

☐ Rehabilitation Benefits

☐ Case Manager Services Benefits

☐ Other Expenses

☐ Death Benefits

☐ Funeral Expenses

☐ Other Disputes

☐ Interest

Print Form   Save Draft   Save Final

Clear Form

Documents List (This section **must** be completed) *

It is expected that the Claimant and the Insurance Company have exchanged key documents prior to the filing of an Application.

List key documents in the Insurance Company's possession to which you will refer in the dispute process. Identify the type of document (letter, medical report, tax return), the name of the writer or issuing institution and the date of the document.

List key documents not currently in the Insurance Company's possession, which you intend to get from other sources (such as employers, doctors, Revenue Canada) for use in the dispute process. You should also include any documents requested from the Claimant (such as financial or employment records) which have not yet been provided. Wherever possible, identify the type of document (letter, medical report, tax return), the name of the writer or issuing institution and the date of the document.

Print Form   Save Draft   Save Final   Clear Form

Acknowledgement

Read carefully then check each box to confirm the statement and sign and date the form.

☐ I have completed all pages of this form and attached all the required documentation. *

☐ I certify that all information in the Application and attachments is true and complete. *

☐ I have served a copy of all the above pages of this form and all additional attached documents to the Claimant and the Claimant's representative. I have attached a completed 'Certificate of Service' to this form as proof of service of the documents on the Insurance Company. (Blank 'Certificate of Service' forms are available on the Tribunal's website at www.slasto.gov.on.ca/en/AABS) *

☐ I have completed the 'Payment Information' section on the final page of this form and am submitting payment for my claim in an acceptable format. (Do not serve a copy of the payment page to the Claimant. Your payment information should only be provided to the Tribunal.) *

Insurer

Print Name *	Signature *	Date (yyyy/mm/dd) *

The Licence Appeal Tribunal collects the personal information requested on this form under section 3 of the *Licence Appeal Tribunal Act, 1999* and under the *Insurance Act*. This information will be used in the dispute resolution process for accident benefits. After an appeal is filed, all information may become available to the public. Any questions about this collection may be directed to the Licence Appeal Tribunal at (416) 314-4260 or toll-free at 1 (800) 255-2214.

Send the completed form to the Licence Appeal Tribunal at the address noted below. Keep an additional copy of the completed form for yourself.

Mail your form to:

Automobile Accident Benefits Service (AABS)
Licence Appeal Tribunal (LAT)
77 Wellesley St. W.
Box 250
Toronto ON M7A1N3

Fax your form to:

Automobile Accident Benefits Service (AABS)
Licence Appeal Tribunal (LAT)
416-325-1060
1-844-618-2566

Deliver your form in-person to:

Licence Appeal Tribunal
20 Dundas St. W., Suite 530
Toronto ON M5G 2C2

For additional information, please visit the Automobile Accident Benefits Service website at: www.slasto.gov.on.ca/en/AABS or call the Licence Appeal Tribunal at 416-314-4260 or toll-free at 1-800-255-2214. If you are using a TTY device you can call us at 416-916-0548 or TTY toll-free at 1-844-403-5906.

Print Form   Save Draft   Save Final   Clear Form

This page is not part of your disclosure to the other parties. **Submit this page to the Tribunal only.**

Payment Information

- Payment of $100 must be submitted with this form in one of the acceptable formats below.
- The filing fee is per application.
- Money Orders, Bank Drafts and Certified Cheques must be made payable to the Minister of Finance.

Acceptable Methods of Payment:

If you are filing your appeal ...	You must pay by ...
by fax	credit card
by mail or courier	credit card certified cheque money order bank draft
in person at the Tribunal office	credit card certified cheque money order bank draft debit card

I am paying my $100 filing fee by:

☐ Certified Cheque ☐ Money Order ☐ Bank Draft ☐ Debit Card ☐ Credit Card [1]

[1] If you are paying by credit card, you must provide the following information:

☐ MasterCard ☐ American Express ☐ Visa

Expiry Date (yyyy/mm)	Credit Card Number	Cardholder Name (as it appears on card)

Signature

For Licence Appeal Tribunal Office Use Only:

Tribunal File No.	Date Appeal and Fee Processed

Print Form   Save Draft   Save Final   Clear Form

Appendix 7.5
AABS Response by an Insurance Company[†]

Automobile Accident Benefits Service
Licence Appeal Tribunal

Ontario

Response by an Insurance Company to an Injured Person's Application for Auto Insurance Dispute Resolution under the *Insurance Act*

Important Information

- Provide a full response to any issues raised by the Claimant that you wish to dispute.
- Attach additional information and/or documents as required.
- The Insurance Company must send a copy of this Response to the Claimant and the Claimant's Representative.
- On this form the Injured Person is referred to as the "Claimant".

Fields marked with an asterisk (*) are mandatory.

Response to Tribunal File Number * _____

Insurance Company Information

Who is making this response? *

☐ Insurance Company   ☐ Insurance Company's Representative

Insurance Company Name *

Claim Representative Name

Last Name	First Name	Middle Initial
Claim Number *	Policy Number *	

Policy Holder Name

Last Name *	First Name *	Middle Initial

Accommodation, Language and Location Requests

1. Do you or any witness(es) require accommodation under the Ontario Human Rights Code to participate in a Tribunal hearing?

☐ Yes   ☐ No

2. Do you want the dispute resolution proceedings (e.g. case conference and hearings) to be conducted in French?

☐ Yes   ☐ No

3. Do you or any witness(es) require language interpretation services?

☐ Yes   ☐ No

4. Would you like the hearing to be conducted outside the Greater Toronto Area?

☐ Yes   ☐ No

Response

Provide a full response to the matters raised by the Claimant about the accident benefits that are in dispute with reference to the paragraph numbers in the claim. You may also identify new issues you wish to raise.

☐ Income Replacement

☐ Non-Earner

☐ Caregiver Benefits

☐ Attendant Care Benefits

☐ Medical Benefits

☐ Rehabilitation Benefits

0456E (2016/03)   © Queen's Printer for Ontario, 2016   Disponible en français   Page 1 of 4

[Print Form]   [Save Draft]   [Save Final]   [Clear Form]

[†] Source: SLASTO — AABS, "Forms, Filing Methods and Serving Documents" — Forms, <http://www.slasto.gov.on.ca/en/AABS/Pages/Forms.aspx>

- [ ] Case Manager Services Benefits
- [ ] Other Expenses
- [ ] Death Benefits
- [ ] Funeral Expenses
- [ ] Other Disputes
- [ ] Claim for Repayment
- [ ] Interest

Print Form   Save Draft   Save Final   Clear Form

Documents List (This section **must** be completed) *

It is expected that the Claimant and the Insurance Company have exchanged key documents prior to the filing of an Application.

List key documents in the Insurance Company's possession to which you will refer in the dispute process. Identify the type of document (letter, medical report, tax return), the name of the writer or issuing institution and the date of the document.

List key documents not currently in the Insurance Company's possession, which you intend to get from other sources (such as employers, doctors, Revenue Canada) for use in the dispute process. You should also include any documents requested from the Claimant (such as financial or employment records) which have not yet been provided. Wherever possible, identify the type of document (letter, medical report, tax return), the name of the writer or issuing institution and the date of the document.

Print Form   Save Draft   Save Final   Clear Form

Acknowledgement

Read carefully then check each box to confirm the statement and sign and date the form.

☐ I have completed all pages of this form and attached all the required documentation. *

☐ I certify that all information in the Response and attachments is true and complete. *

☐ I have served a copy of all the above pages of this form and all additional attached documents to the Claimant and the Claimant's representative. I have attached a completed 'Certificate of Service' to this form as proof of service of the documents on the Insurance Company. (Blank 'Certificate of Service' forms are available on the Tribunal's website at www.slasto.gov.on.ca/en/AABS) *

Insurer

Print Name *	Signature *	Date (yyyy/mm/dd) *

The Licence Appeal Tribunal collects the personal information requested on this form under section 3 of the *Licence Appeal Tribunal Act, 1999* and under the *Insurance Act*. This information will be used in the dispute resolution process for accident benefits. After an appeal is filed, all information may become available to the public. Any questions about this collection may be directed to the Licence Appeal Tribunal at (416) 314-4260 or toll-free at 1 (800) 255-2214.

Send the completed form to the Licence Appeal Tribunal at the address noted below. Keep an additional copy of the completed form for yourself.

Mail your form to:

Automobile Accident Benefits Service (AABS)
Licence Appeal Tribunal (LAT)
77 Wellesley St. W.
Box 250
Toronto ON M7A1N3

Fax your form to:

Automobile Accident Benefits Service (AABS)
Licence Appeal Tribunal (LAT)
416-325-1060
1-844-618-2566

Deliver your form in-person to:

Licence Appeal Tribunal
20 Dundas St. W., Suite 530
Toronto ON M5G 2C2

For additional information, please visit the Automobile Accident Benefits Service website at: www.slasto.gov.on.ca/en/AABS or call the Licence Appeal Tribunal at 416-314-4260 or toll-free at 1-800-255-2214. If you are using a TTY device you can call us at 416-916-0548 or TTY toll-free at 1-844-403-5906.

Print Form   Save Draft   Save Final   Clear Form

Appendix 7.6
AABS Response by an Injured Person†

Automobile Accident Benefits Service
Licence Appeal Tribunal

Ontario

Response by Injured Person regarding Insurance Company's Application for Auto Insurance Dispute Resolution under the *Insurance Act*

Important Information

- Provide a full response to any issues raised by the Insurance Company that you wish to dispute.
- Attach additional information and/or documents as required.
- You must send a copy of this Response to the Insurance Company or the Insurance Company's representative (if known).
- On this form the Injured Person is referred to as "the Claimant".

Fields marked with an asterisk (*) are mandatory.

Response to Tribunal File Number * _____

Claimant Information

I am responding: *

☐ By Myself   ☐ With a Representative

Claimant Name

Last Name *	First Name *	Middle Initial

Claimant Mailing Address

Unit Number	Street Number *	Street Name *	PO Box

City/Town *	Province/State *	Postal/Zip Code *

Country * ☐

One of the following fields must be completed daytime phone, alternate phone or email address: *

Daytime Phone	Ext.	Alternate Phone	Ext.	Fax Number

Email Address

Date of Birth (yyyy/mm/dd) *	Gender: * ☐ Male ☐ Female ☐ Other Gender Identity

Preferred Language: *

☐ English ☐ French ☐ Other

What is your preferred method of communication with the Tribunal? *

☐ Email ☐ Fax ☐ Regular Mail ☐ Phone ☐ Through My Representative

Note: If you check email you are consenting to the delivery of communications and some documents by email. However, applications and responses are currently **only accepted** via fax, regular mail or delivery.

Is the Claimant under 18 years old? * ☐ Yes ☐ No	Is the Claimant mentally incapable? * ☐ Yes ☐ No

Accommodation, Language and Location Requests

1. Do you or any witness(es) require accommodation under the Ontario Human Rights Code to participate in a Tribunal hearing?

☐ Yes ☐ No

Print Form   Save Draft   Save Final   Clear Form

---

† Source: SLASTO — AABS, "Forms, Filing Methods and Serving Documents" — Forms, <http://www.slasto.gov.on.ca/en/AABS/Pages/Forms.aspx>

2. Do you want the dispute resolution proceedings (e.g. case conference and hearings) to be conducted in French?

☐ Yes ☐ No

3. Do you or any witness(es) require language interpretation services?

☐ Yes ☐ No

4. Would you like the hearing to be conducted outside the Greater Toronto Area?

☐ Yes ☐ No

Response

Provide a full response to the matters raised by the Insurance Company about the accident benefits that are in dispute with reference to the paragraph numbers in the claim. You may also identify new issues you wish to raise.

☐ Income Replacement

☐ Non-Earner

☐ Caregiver Benefits

☐ Attendant Care Benefits

☐ Medical Benefits

☐ Rehabilitation Benefits

☐ Case Manager Services Benefits

☐ Other Expenses

☐ Death Benefits

☐ Funeral Expenses

☐ Other Disputes

☐ Claim for Repayment

☐ Interest

Print Form   Save Draft   Save Final   Clear Form

Documents List (This section **must** be completed) *

It is expected that the Claimant and the Insurance Company have exchanged key documents prior to the filing of an Application.

List key documents in your possession to which you will refer in the dispute process. Identify the type of document (letter, medical report, tax return), the name of the writer or issuing institution and the date of the document.

List key documents not currently in your possession, which you intend to get from other sources (such as employers, doctors, Revenue Canada) for use in the dispute process. You should also include any documents requested from the Insurance Company (such as surveillance evidence, a summary of benefits paid) which have not yet been provided. Wherever possible, identify the type of document (letter, medical report, tax return), the name of the writer or issuing institution and the date of the document.

Print Form   Save Draft   Save Final   Clear Form

Acknowledgement

Read carefully then check each box to confirm the statement and sign and date the form.

☐ I have completed all pages of this form and attached all the required documentation. *

☐ I certify that all information in the Response and attachments is true and complete. *

☐ If applicable, I authorize the respondent insurance company to release all medical reports and information relating to the issues in dispute to the Automobile Accident Benefits Service, Licence Appeal Tribunal. I realize that information filed with this Response will be given to the other party in this dispute.

☐ I have served a copy of all the above pages of this form and all additional attached documents to the Insurance Company or the Insurance Company's representative. I have attached a completed 'Certificate of Service' to this form as proof of service of the documents on the Insurance Company. (Blank 'Certificate of Service' forms are available on the Tribunal's website at www.slasto.gov.on.ca/en/AABS) *

Claimant

Print Name *	Signature *	Date (yyyy/mm/dd) *

The Licence Appeal Tribunal collects the personal information requested on this form under section 3 of the *Licence Appeal Tribunal Act, 1999* and under the *Insurance Act*. This information will be used in the dispute resolution process for accident benefits. After an appeal is filed, all information may become available to the public. Any questions about this collection may be directed to the Licence Appeal Tribunal at (416) 314-4260 or toll-free at 1 (800) 255-2214.

Send the completed form to the Licence Appeal Tribunal at the address noted below. Keep an additional copy of the completed form for yourself.

Mail your form to:

Automobile Accident Benefits Service (AABS)
Licence Appeal Tribunal (LAT)
77 Wellesley St. W.
Box 250
Toronto ON M7A1N3

Fax your form to:

Automobile Accident Benefits Service (AABS)
Licence Appeal Tribunal (LAT)
416-325-1060
1-844-618-2566

Deliver your form in-person to:

Licence Appeal Tribunal
20 Dundas St. W., Suite 530
Toronto ON M5G 2C2

For additional information, please visit the Automobile Accident Benefits Service website at: www.slasto.gov.on.ca/en/AABS or call the Licence Appeal Tribunal at 416-314-4260 or toll-free at 1-800-255-2214. If you are using a TTY device you can call us at 416-916-0548 or TTY toll-free at 1-844-403-5906.

Print Form   Save Draft   Save Final   Clear Form

Appendix 7.7
AABS Case Conference Summary[†]

Safety, Licensing Appeals and
Standards Tribunals Ontario
**Automobile Accident Benefits
Service**

Licence Appeal Tribunal
Mailing Address: 77 Wellesley St. W.,
Box 250, Toronto ON M7A 1N3
In-Person Service: 20 Dundas St. W.,
Suite 530, Toronto ON M5G 2C2
Tel.:   416-314-4260
         1-800-255-2214
TTY: 416-916-0548
         1-844-403-5906
Fax: 416-325-1060
         1-844-618-2566
Website: www.slasto.gov.on.ca/en/AABS

Tribunaux de la sécurité, des appels en
matière de permis et des normes Ontario
**Service d'aide relative aux indemnités
d'accident automobile**

Tribunal d'appel en matière de permis
Adresse postale : 77, rue Wellesley Ouest,
Boîte n° 250, Toronto ON M7A 1N3
Adresse municipale : 20, rue Dundas Ouest,
Bureau 530, Toronto ON M5G 2C2
Tél. :   416 314-4260
         1 800 255-2214
ATS :   416 916-0548
         1 844 403-5906
Téléc. : 416 325-1060
         1 844 618-2566
Site Web : www.slasto.gov.on.ca/fr/AABS

Ontario

AABS Case Conference Summary (Automobile Accident Benefits Service under the *Insurance Act*)

IMPORTANT INFORMATION

- You must complete all sections of this form.
- The case conference could be delayed if information or documents requested by the Tribunal are not included.
- On this form the Injured Person is referred to as "the Claimant".
- An "AABS Application" is an application to the Tribunal pursuant to s. 280(2) of the Insurance Act seeking resolution of a dispute involving statutory automobile accident benefits claims under the Insurance Act and the Statutory Accident Benefits Schedule.
- Rule 20.4 of the Tribunal's rules of procedure requires that both the applicant and respondent file an AABS Case Conference Summary at least 10 days before the scheduled case conference.

Tribunal File Number: *<Tribunal File Number>*

Date of Scheduled Case Conference: *<Case Conference Date>*

You are the: *<Claimant> <Insurer>*

Name and Contact Information:

<Last Name   First Name   Middle Initial

Address: Street No. and Name, Unit No.

| City | Province/State | Postal Code/ Zip |
| Code | | |

Country

| Email | Phone Number: | Fax Number:> |

Representative's Name and Contact Information (if represented):

| <Last Name | First Name | Middle Initial |

Address: Street No. and Name, Unit No.

| City | Province/State | Postal Code/ Zip |
| Code | | |

Country

| Email (required) | Phone Number: | Fax Number:> |

Complete Parts 1 and 2 below and submit this document to the Tribunal at least 10 days before the scheduled Case Conference. Provide a copy of this form to all other parties in the case at the same time as you submit it to the Tribunal.

If you fail to comply with the Tribunal's Rules of Practice with respect to disclosure or inspection of documents or things, or list of witnesses, you may not rely on the document or thing as evidence, or call the witnesses to give evidence without the consent of the Tribunal. Please refer to Rule 9 and Rule 10 of the Tribunal's Rules of Practice for more information.

PART I

| Jurisdictional Issues/Motions | Describe in detail any jurisdictional issue you will raise at the case conference. |
| | List any motions you want to be decided at the case conference and attach the motion material. |

Disclosure	List and summarize the contents of each key document intended for use at hearing:
	Were these key documents provided to the other party? Yes or No? If Yes, date provided:
	List of key documents still required from the other party and not yet received:
	List of key documents still required from non-parties and not yet received:
	List of who you will summon:

Witnesses	List of proposed witnesses (other than expert witnesses) and summary of what they will speak to:
	List of expert witnesses to provide opinion evidence and the issue each expert will address:
	If calling more than two expert witnesses, you must explain why more than two are necessary:
Most Recent Settlement Offer (if any)	Attach a copy of the most recent settlement offer that is open for acceptance.

PART II

I, _____, certify that the information set forth above
is accurate and complete as of this date.

_____   _____
Signature   Date

Send the completed Case Conference Summary to the Licence Appeal Tribunal at the
address noted below. Keep a copy of the original Case Conference Summary for
yourself. Provide a copy of this form to all other parties in the case at the same time as
you submit it to the Tribunal.

You may mail your Case Conference Summary to:

Automobile Accident Benefits Service (AABS)
Licence Appeal Tribunal (LAT)
77 Wellesley St. W.
Box 250
Toronto, ON, M7A1N3

You may also fax your Case Conference Summary to:

Automobile Accident Benefits Service (AABS)
Licence Appeal Tribunal (LAT)
416-325-1060
1-844-618-2566

For additional information, please visit the Automobile Accident Benefits Service
website at: www.slasto.gov.on.ca/en/AABS or call the Licence Appeal Tribunal at (416)
314-4260 or toll-free at 1 (800) 255-2214. If you are using a TTY device you can call the
Tribunal at 416-916-0548 or TTY toll-free at 1-844-403-5906.

The Licence Appeal Tribunal collects the personal information requested on this form
under section 3 of the *Licence Appeal Tribunal Act, 1999* and under the *Insurance Act.*
This information will be used in the dispute resolution process for accident benefits.
After an appeal is filed, all information may become available to the public. Any
questions about this collection may be directed to the Licence Appeal Tribunal at (416)
314-4260 or toll-free at 1 (800) 255-2214.

Part III

Selected Federal Agency

How to Deal with a Federal Tribunal

This part discusses a selected federal tribunal under the following topics:

- Overview and Background
- Enabling Legislation, including statute(s) and any appropriate regulation(s)
- Relevant Regulation(s), if any (in addition to those discussed in Enabling Legislation)
- Tribunal Procedures:
  - Rules
  - Practice Directions
  - Forms
- Policies
- Explanatory Literature of the Tribunal
- Relevant Cases and/or Decisions

The selected tribunal shall be discussed as applicable to paralegals representing clients at those agencies.

The material being discussed will primarily be from the tribunal itself as posted on its own website, which shall be referenced extensively, as well as from the websites of the appropriate government departments dealing with the tribunal. **Note that the Ontario statute, the *Statutory Powers Procedure Act* (*SPPA*), does not apply to federal agencies.** The "Relevant Cases and/or Decisions" contains cases and decisions that can be found on the tribunal website and/or from research online or at most law libraries. Paralegals are not lawyers, but to be a good advocate and to best represent a client, paralegals need to find, understand, and use cases and/or decisions in their work. Further research over and above what is found in this book must always be done by the paralegal in preparing to appear before any tribunal.

The website reviewed and the research done for this edition occurred in the summer of 2010 with a follow-up in May 2016. As the law constantly changes, it is important that paralegals review the tribunal's website and research the matter that they are involved in. All selected tribunal websites are reviewed systematically here. This systematic review approach can be applied to other tribunals that are not explored here.

In respect of federal agencies, there is no statute of general application such as the Ontario *SPPA*. The rules and procedures imposed on these agencies arise from the following sources:

- What is set out in their enabling legislation
- The rules and practice directions (or notes) of each agency
- The rules of natural justice (or procedural fairness) derived from case law and the *Charter*, as discussed in the opening chapter of this book as applied by decision and case law
- Other relevant statutes

One federal statute relevant to all federal agencies, unless specifically excluded under its enabling legislation, is the *Federal Courts Act*, R.S.C., 1985, c. F-7, as amended (*FCA*). This statute allows for judicial review to the Federal Court — Trial Division or the Federal Court of Appeal.

The sections of the *FCA* that are relevant to the jurisdiction of the Federal Court — Trial Division to hear applications for judicial review of a federal agency are as follows:

EXTRAORDINARY REMEDIES, FEDERAL TRIBUNALS

18.(1) Subject to section 28, the Federal Court has exclusive original jurisdiction

(a) to issue an injunction, writ of *certiorari*, writ of prohibition, writ of *mandamus* or writ of *quo warranto*, or grant declaratory relief, against any federal board, commission or other tribunal; and

(b) to hear and determine any application or other proceeding for relief in the nature of relief contemplated by paragraph (a), including any proceeding brought against the Attorney General of Canada, to obtain relief against a federal board, commission or other tribunal.

Extraordinary remedies, members of Canadian Forces

(2) The Federal Court has exclusive original jurisdiction to hear and determine every application for a writ of *habeas corpus ad subjiciendum*, writ of *certiorari*, writ of prohibition or writ of *mandamus* in relation to any member of the Canadian Forces serving outside Canada.

Remedies to be obtained on application

(3) The remedies provided for in subsections (1) and (2) may be obtained only on an application for judicial review made under section 18.1.

APPLICATION FOR JUDICIAL REVIEW

18.1(1) An application for judicial review may be made by the Attorney General of Canada or by anyone directly affected by the matter in respect of which relief is sought.

Time limitation

(2) An application for judicial review in respect of a decision or an order of a federal board, commission or other tribunal shall be made within 30 days after the time the decision or order was first communicated by the federal board, commission or other tribunal to the office of the Deputy Attorney General of Canada or to the party directly affected by it, or within any further time that a judge of the Federal Court may fix or allow before or after the end of those 30 days.

Powers of Federal Court

(3) On an application for judicial review, the Federal Court may

(a) order a federal board, commission or other tribunal to do any act or thing it has unlawfully failed or refused to do or has unreasonably delayed in doing; or

(b) declare invalid or unlawful, or quash, set aside or set aside and refer back for determination in accordance with such directions as it considers to be appropriate, prohibit or restrain, a decision, order, act or proceeding of a federal board, commission or other tribunal.

Grounds of review

(4) The Federal Court may grant relief under subsection (3) if it is satisfied that the federal board, commission or other tribunal

(a) acted without jurisdiction, acted beyond its jurisdiction or refused to exercise its jurisdiction;

(b) failed to observe a principle of natural justice, procedural fairness or other procedure that it was required by law to observe;

(c) erred in law in making a decision or an order, whether or not the error appears on the face of the record;

(d) based its decision or order on an erroneous finding of fact that it made in a perverse or capricious manner or without regard for the material before it;

(e) acted, or failed to act, by reason of fraud or perjured evidence; or

(f) acted in any other way that was contrary to law.

Defect in form or technical irregularity

(5) If the sole ground for relief established on an application for judicial review is a defect in form or a technical irregularity, the Federal Court may

(a) refuse the relief if it finds that no substantial wrong or miscarriage of justice has occurred; and

(b) in the case of a defect in form or a technical irregularity in a decision or an order, make an order validating the decision or order, to have effect from any time and on any terms that it considers appropriate.

INTERIM ORDERS

18.2 On an application for judicial review, the Federal Court may make any interim orders that it considers appropriate pending the final disposition of the application.

REFERENCE BY FEDERAL TRIBUNAL

18.3(1) A federal board, commission or other tribunal may at any stage of its proceedings refer any question or issue of law, of jurisdiction or of practice and procedure to the Federal Court for hearing and determination.

Reference by Attorney General of Canada

(2) The Attorney General of Canada may, at any stage of the proceedings of a federal board, commission or other tribunal, other than a service tribunal within the meaning of the *National Defence Act*, refer any question or issue of the constitutional validity, applicability or operability of an Act of Parliament or of regulations made under an Act of Parliament to the Federal Court for hearing and determination.

HEARINGS IN SUMMARY WAY

18.4(1) Subject to subsection (2), an application or reference to the Federal Court under any of sections 18.1 to 18.3 shall be heard and determined without delay and in a summary way.

Exception

(2) The Federal Court may, if it considers it appropriate, direct that an application for judicial review be treated and proceeded with as an action.

EXCEPTION TO SECTIONS 18 AND 18.1

18.5 Despite sections 18 and 18.1, if an Act of Parliament expressly provides for an appeal to the Federal Court, the Federal Court of Appeal, the Supreme Court of Canada, the Court Martial Appeal Court, the Tax Court of Canada, the Governor in Council or the Treasury Board from a decision or an order of a federal board, commission or other tribunal made by or in the course of proceedings before that board, commission or tribunal, that decision or order is not, to the extent that it may be so appealed, subject to review or to be restrained, prohibited, removed, set aside or otherwise dealt with, except in accordance with that Act.

In summary, an application for judicial review for a prerogative writ or other remedies, as discussed in the first chapter of the book, can be made in accordance with the provisions of sections 18 and 18.1–18.4, provided that if legislation allows for an appeal, then such matter is not subject to judicial review except as detailed in such legislation.

The jurisdiction of the Federal Court — Trial Division to hear an application for judicial review is also affected by section 28 of the *FCA*, which gives sole jurisdiction to the Federal Court of Appeal to hear an application for judicial review in the following circumstances:

JUDICIAL REVIEW

28.(1) The Federal Court of Appeal has jurisdiction to hear and determine applications for judicial review made in respect of any of the following federal boards, commissions or other tribunals:

(a) the Board of Arbitration established by the *Canada Agricultural Products Act*;

(b) the Review Tribunal established by the *Canada Agricultural Products Act*;

(b.1) the Conflict of Interest and Ethics Commissioner appointed under section 81 of the *Parliament of Canada Act*;

(c) the Canadian Radio-television and Telecommunications Commission established by the *Canadian Radio-television and Telecommunications Commission Act*;

(d) [Repealed, 2012, c. 19, s. 272]

(e) the Canadian International Trade Tribunal established by the *Canadian International Trade Tribunal Act*;

(f) the National Energy Board established by the *National Energy Board Act*;

(g) the Governor in Council, when the Governor in Council makes an order under subsection 54(1) of the *National Energy Board Act*;

(g) the Appeal Division of the Social Security Tribunal established under section 44 of the *Department of Employment and Social Development Act*, unless the decision is made under subsection 57(2) or section 58 of that Act or relates to an appeal brought under subsection 53(3) of that Act or an appeal respecting a decision relating to further time to make a request under subsection 52(2) of that Act, section 81 of the *Canada Pension Plan*, section 27.1 of the *Old Age Security Act* or section 112 of the *Employment Insurance Act*;

(h) the Canada Industrial Relations Board established by the *Canada Labour Code*;

(i) the Public Service Labour Relations and Employment Board that is established by subsection 4(1) of the *Public Service Labour Relations and Employment Board Act*;

(i.1) adjudicators as defined in subsection 2(1) of the *Public Service Labour Relations Act*;

(j) the Copyright Board established by the *Copyright Act*;

(k) the Canadian Transportation Agency established by the *Canada Transportation Act*;

(l) [Repealed, 2002, c. 8, s. 35]

(m) [Repealed, 2012, c. 19, s. 272]

(n) the Competition Tribunal established by the *Competition Tribunal Act*;

(o) assessors appointed under the *Canada Deposit Insurance Corporation Act*;

(p) [Repealed, 2012, c. 19, s. 572]

(q) the Public Servants Disclosure Protection Tribunal established by the *Public Servants Disclosure Protection Act*; and

(r) the Specific Claims Tribunal established by the *Specific Claims Tribunal Act*.

Sections apply

(2) Sections 18 to 18.5, except subsection 18.4(2), apply, with any modifications that the circumstances require, in respect of any matter within the jurisdiction of the Federal Court of Appeal under subsection (1) and, when they apply, a reference to the Federal Court shall be read as a reference to the Federal Court of Appeal.

Federal Court deprived of jurisdiction

(3) If the Federal Court of Appeal has jurisdiction to hear and determine a matter, the Federal Court has no jurisdiction to entertain any proceeding in respect of that matter.

Canadian Human Rights Tribunal

8

WHAT THIS CHAPTER OFFERS

- The background of the Canadian Human Rights Tribunal (CHRT)
- A discussion of the Canadian Human Rights Commission
- Details and explanation of the enabling statutes and regulations relevant to the CHRT
- Specific rules and procedures for the CHRT
- A walk-through of the CHRT website
- Summaries of relevant cases and decisions, highlighting legal principle(s) or issue(s) in question
- A flow chart summarizing the procedural stages of an appeal to the CHRT

LEARNING OBJECTIVES

After reading this chapter, the reader should be able to:

- understand how to research any federal agency by exploring its website to find the important information needed to understand the agency's practices and procedures and how a paralegal would properly represent a client before such an agency by doing so with the Canadian Human Rights Tribunal (CHRT)
- document the background of the CHRT
- detail and explain the provisions of the enabling legislation relevant to the CHRT
- elaborate on various concepts of public policy relevant to the CHRT and the relevant sections of the *Federal Courts Act* (*FCA*)
- compare and prioritize the various sources of practice and procedure of the CHRT
- identify the specific rules and procedures for the CHRT and how they would be applied in a proceeding before, during, and after a hearing of the CHRT

- review and explain the procedures and practices of the CHRT by way of a flow chart and key forms and documents available on the CHRT website
- assess how the relevant provisions invoked by the duty to act fairly apply to the CHRT
- outline the various explanatory literature available on the CHRT website to assist the paralegal to understand the CHRT and better represent the client
- appreciate the need to find decisions and/or cases in order to understand and argue the law before the CHRT
- illustrate and discuss principles that flow from the various cases and decisions as they relate to the CHRT

INTRODUCTION

The Canadian Human Rights Tribunal (the CHRT or Tribunal) is an independent, adjudicative body. It hears matters referred to it by the Canadian Human Rights Commission (the CHRC or Commission) on issues arising "through the fair-minded and equitable interpretation and enforcement of the *Canadian Human Rights Act* and the *Employment Equity Act*", as stated on the CHRT website, <www.chrt-tcdp.gc.ca>, to help ensure an environment free from discrimination. The Tribunal was originally created by the federal Parliament in 1977 to "apply the *Canadian Human Rights Act* [(the "*CHRA*")] based on the evidence presented and on the case law". The *CHRA* confers jurisdiction on the CHRT only to deal with federally regulated matters. The recent listing of current status of the CHRT is set out in the following paragraphs in the "History of the Canadian Human Rights Tribunal" Web page:

> On November 1, 2014, through the coming into force of the *Administrative Tribunals Support Service of Canada Act* (*ATSSCA*), the Government of Canada consolidated the provision of support services to eleven administrative tribunals — including the CHRT — into a single organization, the Administrative Tribunals Support Service of Canada (ATSSC). The CHRT ceased to exist as a public service organization, but continued as an adjudicative body. All staff formerly employed by the CHRT became employees of the ATSSC, and either continued to serve the CHRT directly through the CHRT Secretariat, or commenced serving all eleven tribunals as part of the ATSSC corporate services team. That said, the adjudicative role and authority of the CHRT Members remain unchanged: Through the pooling of support services, the establishment of ATSSC strengthens the independence of the CHRT, without affecting the mandate of the CHRT. Proceedings continue to be initiated, managed, heard and decided in accordance with the *CHRA* and existing CHRT procedures. ...
>
> The CHRT remains a quasi-judicial body with a statutory mandate to apply and interpret the *CHRA*. Under this legislation, the CHRT shall fairly and expeditiously inquire into complaints of discrimination that have been referred by the Commission. If, at the conclusion of the inquiry, the CHRT Member presiding over the case finds that the complaint is substantiated, that Member may make an order against the person found to have engaged in a discriminatory practice.

In 1996 the *Employment Equity Act* (*EEA*) was proclaimed, and the Tribunal was given the responsibilities to adjudicate complaints under the Act, which regulates employers with more than 100 employees. The *EEA* also stipulates that the CHRT operate as Employment Equity Review Tribunal, which are assembled as needed from members of the CHRT. The Employment Equity Review Tribunal will be briefly discussed in the "Enabling Legislation" section, but the focus of this chapter shall be on the practices and procedures of the CHRT.

OVERVIEW AND BACKGROUND

As of June 1998, the CHRT officially became a separate agency from the CHRC. However, the process still starts with the CHRC's receiving and investigating complaints and then referring matters to the CHRT, as described on the Web page, "Chairperson Message", on the CHRT website:

> The Canadian Human Rights Tribunal is a quasi-judicial body that inquires into complaints of discrimination referred to it by the Canadian Human Rights Commission and decides whether the conduct alleged in the complaint is a discriminatory practice within the meaning of the *Canadian Human Rights Act*. The Tribunal can also review directions and assessments made under the *Employment Equity Act*.
>
> The Tribunal operates pursuant to the *Canadian Human Rights Act*, which aims to give effect to the principle that all individuals should have an equal opportunity to live their lives unhindered by discriminatory practices based on race, national or ethnic origin, colour, religion, age, sex (including pregnancy), marital status, family status, sexual orientation, disability (including drug dependency) or pardoned criminal conviction.
>
> The *Act* applies to federally regulated employers and service providers, including: federal government departments and agencies, federal Crown corporations, chartered banks, airlines, shipping and inter-provincial trucking companies, telecommunications and broadcasting organizations, and as well as First Nations governments as well as federally regulated Aboriginal organizations.

Once a matter is referred, the CHRT will hold a public hearing to inquire about the complaints of discrimination. The Chairperson will assign one or three members, selected among the Chairperson, Vice-Chairperson, and 13 other full- or part-time members, to hear each case. The panel (containing one or three members) will decide whether discrimination has occurred, based on the evidence presented and on the law. If the panel hearing the case concludes that discrimination has occurred, it will decide on the appropriate remedy and how to prevent similar cases of discrimination in the future.

The administrative functions of the CHRT are carried out by the Registry staff. The Registrar and staff of the Tribunal plan, organize, and direct the Tribunal's operations, but their activities are entirely separate from the decision-making process. The staff plan and arrange hearings, provide administrative support to members to carry out their duties, and act as a liaison between the parties and the members of a hearing.

For each hearing, there is a Registry Officer assigned to it, and the officer is deemed an "officer of the court" responsible to the Tribunal. Under the direction of the Tribunal, the officers manage the logistical support services necessary for the hearings they are assigned. Officers can also provide advice and guidance to the members, counsel, and parties on Tribunal practices, such as media coverage, scheduling of witnesses, and future hearing dates. During a hearing, the Registry Officer also receives and files documents on behalf of the Tribunal, administers the oath, records a brief summary of the proceedings, and drafts orders under the specific direction of the Tribunal. Not only a liaison between the members and the parties in a case, the officer also serves as a liaison between the public and media.

ENABLING LEGISLATION

Although the jurisdiction and authority of the CHRT are defined by the *CHRA*, which creates the CHRT and sets out a few procedural rules, the *Federal Courts Act* (*FCA*), as a statute of general application, deals with appeals and judicial review from the decisions of the CHRT and ties the CHRT Rules that have been published into the process. (The relevant sections of *FCA* on the CHRT operation are discussed in the preamble to Part III). Below is a discussion of the *CHRA*. In matters before the CHRT, other sections of the relevant enabling legislation and a quick review of the *EEA* may be discussed and, possibly, interpreted; however, such sections are outside the purview of this book and are discussed only in the decisions and cases.

The *CHRA*

A quick overview of the *CHRA* related to prohibited grounds of discrimination can be found in the FAQ section under "About the CHRT" in the CHRT website. In summary, as set out in section 3, the *CHRA* prohibits discrimination on the following grounds:

1. race
2. national or ethnic origin
3. colour

4. religion
5. age
6. sex (e.g., pay equity, harassment, which also applies to all other grounds, pregnancy, and childbirth)
7. marital status
8. family status
9. sexual orientation
10. disability (e.g., mental/physical disability, disfigurement, past or present, alcohol or drug dependence)
11. conviction that has been pardoned

If one or more of these prohibited grounds of discrimination occur, resulting in a denial of goods, services, facilities, accommodation, employment, membership in an employee organization, or receipt of equal wages, a complaint about a "discriminatory practice" can be made. Subject to certain exceptions, complaints can also be filed against the infliction of harassment or retaliation.

The complaint process generally involves a complaint to the Commission, which appoints a person to investigate. The person would provide a report, and the matter would be dismissed or a conciliator might be appointed to try to settle. If settlement is not achieved or if the Commission decides to directly refer the matter to the CHRT, a hearing will be held and a decision shall be made, all in accordance with the CHRT Rules. An appeal or an application for judicial review of the Tribunal's decision can be made to the Federal Court.

Keeping the overview set out above in mind, we shall look at specific provisions of the *CHRA*, especially those provisions relevant to the CHRT.

Purpose

Section 2 states that "all individuals should have an opportunity equal with other individuals to make for themselves the lives that they are able and wish to have and to have their needs accommodated, consistent with their duties and obligations as members of society, without being hindered in or prevented from doing so by discriminatory practices". The *CHRA* is the mechanism used to achieve such public policy and within federal authority.

Part I — Proscribed Discrimination

PROHIBITED GROUNDS OF DISCRIMINATION AND DISCRIMINATORY PRACTICES

Stated in section 3 are the prohibited grounds of discrimination, which are shown above in the overview. A discriminatory practice may include a practice based on one or more prohibited grounds of discrimination (s. 3.1) or on the effect of a combination of the prohibited grounds. If the results of such discriminatory practice fall within the description of sections 5–14.1, the practice may be the subject of a complaint under Part III (s. 4).

DENIAL OF GOOD, SERVICE, FACILITY, OR ACCOMMODATION
Pursuant to section 5, it is a discriminatory practice to deny, to deny access to, or "to differentiate adversely in relation to any individual" with regard to their access to, any good, service, facility, or accommodation customarily available to the general public on a prohibited ground of discrimination.

DENIAL OF COMMERCIAL PREMISES OR RESIDENTIAL ACCOMMODATION
Under section 6, it is a discriminatory practice to deny or to differentiate adversely an individual occupancy of any commercial premises or residential accommodation on a prohibited ground of discrimination.

EMPLOYMENT
Section 7 states that it is a discriminatory practice, whether directly or indirectly, "(a) to refuse to employ or continue to employ any individual, or (b) in the course of employment, to differentiate adversely in relation to an employee, on a prohibited ground of discrimination". Under section 8, an employment application or advertisement or any inquiry "that expresses or implies any limitation, specification or preference based on a prohibited ground of discrimination" is a discriminatory practice.

EMPLOYEE ORGANIZATIONS
Pursuant to section 9, it is a discriminatory practice to exclude an individual from full membership in an employee organization or do anything that adversely affects the status of the individual's membership in such organization. A company practice or policy "that deprives or tends to deprive an individual or class of individuals of any employment opportunities on a prohibited ground of discrimination" is a discriminatory practice under section 10.

EQUAL WAGES
Setting or keeping differences in wages between male and female employees doing work of equal value in the same establishment is a discriminatory practice, as detailed in section 11.

PUBLICATION OF DISCRIMINATORY NOTICES
Displaying or publishing materials that express or imply discrimination, or that intend to discriminate, or that incite or intend to incite

discrimination are deemed discriminatory practices. This concept is addressed in section 12.

HATE MESSAGES

It was a discriminatory practice under section 13 for a person or persons to communicate by telephone or electronically "any matter that is likely to expose a person or persons to hatred or contempt by reason of the fact that that person or those persons are identifiable on the basis of a prohibited ground of discrimination". **This section was repealed in 2013.**

HARASSMENT (INCLUDING SEXUAL HARASSMENT)

In providing the services set out in sections 5–7, it is a discriminatory practice per section 14 to harass (including sexually harass) an individual on a prohibited ground of discrimination.

RETALIATION

Under section 14.1, retaliation against a complainant of discriminatory practice is itself a discriminatory practice.

DEFENCES

Various exceptions and defences defining actions that are considered not discriminatory practices are detailed in section 15, and specific programs designed to prevent discrimination or lessen disadvantages suffered by a group by favouring such group are not a discriminatory practice as stated in section 16.

Part II — Canadian Human Rights Commission

POWERS, DUTIES AND FUNCTIONS OF THE CHRC

The broad duties of the CHRC, in addition to dealing with complaints of discriminatory practices under Part III, are set out pursuant to section 27.

Part III — Discriminatory Practices and General Provisions

COMPLAINTS

Under subsection 40(1), but subject to subsections (5) and (7), an individual or a group who under reasonable grounds believes that a person is engaging in or has engaged in a discriminatory practice can file a complaint with the Commission. The complaint must be in a form that is acceptable to the Commission. The Commission can initiate a complaint under subsection 40(3) if it believes someone is engaged in a discriminatory practice.

COMMISSION TO DEAL WITH COMPLAINTS

The CHRC is to deal with any complaint filed with it under section 40 except complaints that fall within the five situations set out in subsection 41(1).

NOTICE

Under subsection 42(1), if the CHRC decides not to proceed with a complaint, the CHRC must notify the complainant, in writing, of its decision and provide the reason behind its decision.

INVESTIGATOR

Section 43(1) states that the CHRC may designate an "investigator" to investigate a complaint. Various powers are given to the investigator, which are detailed in subsections 43(2.1)–43(3).

REPORT

As soon as possible after the conclusion of the investigation, the investigator shall submit to the CHRC a report of the investigation's findings (s. 44(1)). Upon receipt of the report, the CHRC can take one of the following actions:

(a)   Refer the complainant to the proper authority if the CHRC is satisfied that the complaint fits within subsection 44(2).
(b)   Refer the complaint to the Chairperson of the CHRT to institute an inquiry if the CHRC is satisfied that the complaint fits within subsection 44(3)(a)
(c)   Dismiss the complaint if the CHRC is satisfied that the complaint fits within subsection 44(3)(b).

Once the CHRC decides on its course of action, it must notify the complainant and any other person pursuant to subsection 44(4) of its action.

CONCILIATOR

The CHRC may, in accordance with section 47, appoint a conciliator to try bring about a settlement of the complaint.

REFERRAL OF A SETTLEMENT TO THE CHRC

Under subsection 48(1), a settlement made between the parties after a complaint has been filed with the CHRC but before a CHRT hearing must be referred to the CHRC for approval.

ESTABLISHMENT OF THE CHRT

Under section 48.1, the CHRT is established and the qualifications, appointment, and make-up of the Tribunal are set out.

TERM OF OFFICE

Section 48.2 deals with the term of office and reappointment of the members of the CHRT.

CONDUCT OF PROCEEDINGS

The CHRT shall conduct proceedings before it "as informally and expeditiously as the requirements of natural justice and the rules of procedure allow" (s. 48.9(1)). The Chairperson of the CHRT may make rules of procedure governing the practice and procedure before the CHRT, which include the following:

(a) the giving of notices to parties;
(b) the addition of parties and interested persons to the proceedings;
(c) the summoning of witnesses;
(d) the production and service of documents;
(e) discovery proceedings;
(f) pre-hearing conferences;
(g) the introduction of evidence;
(h) time limits within which hearings must be held and decisions must be made;
(i) awards of interest.

REQUEST FOR INQUIRY

Section 49(1) states that, any time after the filing of a complaint, the Commission can request the Chairperson of the Tribunal to institute an inquiry into the complaint if the Commission deems an inquiry is warranted. In accordance with subsection 49(2), the Chairperson may assign one member or a panel of three members to hear the inquiry. A copy of the rules of procedure shall be made available to the parties involved, pursuant to subsection 49(4).

CONDUCT OF THE INQUIRY

After notice of an inquiry is given to the Commission and the parties involved in the complaint, the hearing member or panel shall inquire into the complaint. All parties should be given sufficient time and opportunity to appear at the inquiry and to present evidence and make representation.

> **50**(1) After due notice to the Commission, the complainant, the person against whom the complaint was made and, at the discretion of the member or panel conducting the inquiry, any other interested party, the member or panel shall inquire into the complaint and shall give all parties to whom notice has been given a full and ample opportunity, in person or through counsel, to appear at the inquiry, present evidence and make representations.

Sections 50(2)–(3) grant various powers to the member or panel appointed to hear the inquiry, including the power to determine all questions of law and fact (s. 50(2)). However, the power is also limited: "[s. 50(4)] The member or panel may not admit or accept as evidence anything that would be inadmissible in a court by reason of any privilege under the law of evidence."

DUTY OF THE CHRC ON APPEARING
If the CHRC decides to participate at a hearing, it must take a position of representing the public interest (s. 51): "In appearing at a hearing, presenting evidence and making representations, the Commission shall adopt such position as, in its opinion, is in the public interest having regard to the nature of the complaint."

HEARINGS TO BE PUBLIC EXCEPTION
An inquiry by the CHRT is to be public, but the member or panel conducting the inquiry may, on application, make an order to ensure the confidentiality of the inquiry. The measure not to hold a public inquiry can be taken only if the member or panel anticipates that one of the four risks set out in subsection 52(1) may occur.

COMPLAINT DISMISSED
If the complaint is concluded to be not substantiated by the inquiry, the member or the panel must dismiss the complaint (s. 53(1)).

COMPLAINT SUBSTANTIATED
If the inquiry concludes that the complaint is substantiated, the member or panel may make an order against the person found guilty of discriminatory practice using any of the actions listed in subsection 53(2) that are considered appropriate:

> (a) that the person cease the discriminatory practice and take measures, in consultation with the Commission on the general purposes of the measures, to redress the practice or to prevent the same or a similar practice from occurring in future, including
> > (i) the adoption of a special program, plan or arrangement referred to in subsection 16(1), or
> > (ii) making an application for approval and implementing a plan under section 17;
> (b) that the person make available to the victim of the discriminatory practice, on the first reasonable occasion, the rights, opportunities or privileges that are being or were denied the victim as a result of the practice;

(c) that the person compensate the victim for any or all of the wages that the victim was deprived of and for any expenses incurred by the victim as a result of the discriminatory practice;

(d) that the person compensate the victim for any or all additional costs of obtaining alternative goods, services, facilities or accommodation and for any expenses incurred by the victim as a result of the discriminatory practice; and

(e) that the person compensate the victim, by an amount not exceeding twenty thousand dollars, for any pain and suffering that the victim experienced as a result of the discriminatory practice.

The member or panel, under subsection 53(3), can also award special compensation of an amount not to exceed $20,000 to the victim if the discriminatory practice was committed wilfully or recklessly. An award for compensation may, subject to the Rules of the CHRT, include an award for interest at a rate and for a period considered appropriate.

INTIMIDATION OR DISCRIMINATION

Section 59 states that "[n]o person shall threaten, intimidate or discriminate against an individual because that individual has made a complaint or given evidence or assisted in any way in respect of the initiation or prosecution of a complaint or other proceeding under this Part, or because that individual proposes to do so".

The *EEA*

As stated in section 2, this legislation was enacted "to achieve equality in the workplace so that no person shall be denied employment opportunities or benefits for reasons unrelated to ability and, in the fulfilment of that goal, to correct the conditions of disadvantage in employment experienced by women, aboriginal peoples, persons with disabilities and members of visible minorities by giving effect to the principle that employment equity means more than treating persons in the same way but also requires special measures and the accommodation of differences." The CHRC is given a large role in determining if inequality exists and in making orders to correct such inequality. If an inquiry is required under the *EEA*, the Employment Equity Review Tribunal (the EERT) shall be established to hear the matter. The members of the EERT are appointed from the CHRT.

It is unlikely that paralegals will appear before the EERT, so this chapter shall not discuss the agency further. For further information, the reader should examine the *EEA* in greater detail.

RELEVANT REGULATIONS

The *Human Rights Tribunal Appeal Regulations*, SOR/80-394, is the only regulation in force at the time of writing that is relevant to the CHRT; and it deals with notice and the forms to be used to appeal a decision or order of the CHRT.

PROCEDURES OF TRIBUNAL

The Canadian Human Rights Tribunal Rules of Procedure (the CHRT Rules) can be found, in html, on the CHRT website on "Procedures > Rules of Procedures" and, in pdf format, under "Operations > Standards Forms and Templates" (rules applicable to complaints referred to the tribunal after April 30, 2004). The rules of procedures were made under the authority given by section 48.9 of the *CHRA*: "the authority to make rules to govern its practices and procedures". The Rules contain nine main rules and some transitional provisions. **The CHRT Rules and amendments and other similar provisions, such as the "Mediation Procedures", are discussed in a summary fashion and in varying detail. The reader, therefore, should rely only on her/his own reading and interpretation of both the rules and the forms.** Keep in mind that the procedures in the enabling legislation and other relevant legislation, such as the *FCA*, are also applicable.

RULES

Purpose, Interpretation (R. 1)
The three main purposes of the CHRT Rules are stated in R. 1(1):

> These Rules are enacted to ensure that
> (a) all parties to an inquiry have the full and ample opportunity to be heard;
> (b) arguments and evidence be disclosed and presented in a timely and efficient manner; and
> (c) all proceedings before the Tribunal be conducted as informally and expeditiously as possible.

Both Rs. 1(2) and (4) give much flexibility to the panel in charge of the matter to apply the CHRT Rules liberally or even to dispense with compliance with any rule to advance the purposes of the rules.

Service, Filing (R. 2)
R. 2(1) states that "[u]nless otherwise stipulated, all written communications made under the Rules shall be served on all parties and

filed with the Registry". Methods of service and proof of each type of service are set out in Rs. 2(2) and (3), respectively, and the method of filing to the Registry is laid out in R. 2(4). The language of all documents filed and served is detailed in R. 2(5).

Motions, Adjournments (R. 3)

All motions, including those for adjournments, are to be made by Notice of Motion in accordance with R. 3(1). Upon receipt of the Notice of Motion, the panel shall and/or may take the following action under R. 3(2):

(a) shall ensure that the other parties are granted an opportunity to respond;

(b) may direct the time, manner and form of any response;

(c) may direct the making of argument and the presentation of evidence by all parties, including the time, manner and form thereof;

(d) shall dispose of the motion as it sees fit.

Administrative Information (R. 4)

Rule 4(1) sets out the requirements of Form 1, to be prepared by the CHRC based on its current knowledge or belief and to accompany a request by the CHRC to the CHRT to institute an inquiry. As it is a form to be prepared by the CHRC, there is no Form 1 on the CHRT website. Under R. 4(2), the Registrar of the CHRT may request further information from a party by questionnaire, which must be completed and filed as directed.

Case Conferences (R. 5)

Pursuant to R. 5(1), a case conference held either in person or by telephone may be scheduled "to resolve matters of an administrative or procedural nature in respect of the inquiry". Any matters or motions to be raised will be by Notice of Motion per R. 5(2). Six obligations or powers given to the panel at the case conference are detailed in R. 5(3).

Statement of Particulars, Disclosure, Production (R. 6)

Rule 6(1) requires the service and filing, within a time fixed by the panel, of a Statement of Particulars detailing key information about the case:

- the material facts
- the position on the legal issues

- the relief sought
- two lists of documents in the party's possession where privilege is (list #1) and is not (list #2) claimed related to the case
- a list of all witnesses, together with a summary of the anticipated testimony

A reply to the respondent's Statement of Particulars shall be prepared, served, and filed by the complainant and the CHRC in the two situations set out in R. 6(2). Within the time fixed by the panel, each party shall serve and file a report in respect of any expert witnesses such party intends to call, containing the information set out in R. 6(3). Under R. 6(4), each party shall provide other parties with a copy of the documents for which privilege is not claimed, as set out in the party's Statement of Particulars. Such documents shall not be filed with the CHRT. Each party shall provide such additional disclosure and production as is necessary for either of the two reasons set out in R. 6(5).

Book of Authorities (R. 7)

Under R. 7, a party may serve and file a book of authorities containing copies of the statutory provisions, case law, and other legal authorities (with the relevant provisions highlighted) that a party intends to refer to, provided that if a case or decision referred to is included in the CHRT Book of Jurisprudence, only the excerpt relied upon has to be included.

Addition of Parties and Interested Parties (R. 8)

Rule 8 allows for the addition of parties and for the recognition of interested parties by motion as detailed in the sub-rules of such rule.

Hearing, Evidence (R. 9)

The usual hours of the hearing, unless otherwise directed by the panel, are stated in R. 9(1). Under R. 9(2), a party that requires special arrangements or an interpreter for the hearing shall notify the Registrar as soon as possible. **Except by leave of the panel or the need to lead evidence in reply, items, such as issue, witness, relief, document or report, not disclosed in the Statement of Particulars and/or produced as required, all as detailed in R. 6, shall not be raised, called, or introduced, as stated in R. 9(3)**. A party can, under R. 9(5), bring a motion for an order to examine a person, who is unable to attend a hearing, as directed by the panel under R. 9(6). A party intending to challenge the constitutional validity, applicability, or operability of a legislation before the panel must serve notice in accordance with section 57 of the *FCA* and Form 69 of the *Federal Court Rules* pursuant to R. 9(7). As per R. 9(8), the hearing may proceed even though a party fails to appear before the panel, provided the panel is satisfied that such party received proper notice of the hearing. The panel, under R. 9(9), may order the exclusion of witnesses except in the situations set out in R. 9(10), and there shall be no communication with the excluded witness as detailed in R. 9(11). Unless the panel orders otherwise, the rate and accrual of any interest awarded shall be in accordance with R. 9(12).

EVALUATIVE MEDIATION PROCEDURES

The CHRT published document, "Evaluative Mediation Procedures", effective December 10, 2010, can be found, in html, on the CHRT website, under "Mediation Procedures" (through Site Map). Mediation is optional to the parties to a CHRT proceeding. The Evaluative Mediation Procedures document is meant to explain the mediation process so that the parties involved can decide if mediation would help and, if so, to help them prepare for it.

The document first explains that mediation is a process to help the parties explore settlement possibilities and then details how the mediation process works in the CHRT. The mediators are members of the CHRT who are trained in mediation. Once mediating a matter that proceeds to a hearing, that mediating member will not be an adjudicator on that case, nor can he or she divulge to the adjudicator(s) any information learned in the mediation.

A mediation will occur, on neutral ground, as soon as it is practical after the matter is referred to the CHRT, and it tends to be a short, confidential, and voluntary process. After discussing what information should be provided to the mediator, the document indicates that persons who can make decisions to settle should attend the session. Special needs will be accommodated with best efforts during the mediation. Even if settlement is not reached in the mediation, efforts should be made to resolve or narrow issues and to agree upon facts so that the hearing time can be shortened. A sample "Terms and Conditions of Evaluative Mediation" form is attached as an appendix to the document.

MEDIATION-ADJUDICATION (MED-ADJ)

The CHRT published document, "Consent and Request for Mediation-Adjudication" form can be found, in pdf format, on the CHRT website, under the "Mediation-Adjudication (Med-Adj)" Web page. Where mediation fails to result in a settlement, parties may request that the Tribunal Member who conducted the mediation preside over the hearing.

BOOK OF JURISPRUDENCE

This document, referred to in R. 7(3) of the Tribunal Rules, effective March 13, 2001, can be found, in pdf format, on the CHRT website, under "Procedures". The document consists of a list of 39 cases with citation. This list is sorted by case name. These are important cases in matters before the CHRT.

PRACTICE NOTES

Practice notes may be issued by the CHRT, and as of May 2016, there are three practice notes, which can be found, in html format as listed, on the CHRT website, under "Procedures" under the following names: "PRACTICE NOTE No. 1" re Timeliness of Hearings and Decisions; "PRACTICE NOTE No. 2" re Representation of Parties by Non-Lawyers; and "PRACTICE NOTE No. 3" re Pre-Hearing Case Management Process.

Practice Note No. 1

This practice note is dated October 22, 2007. There are two reasons for this practice note:

1. Section 48.9(1) of the *CHRA* requires that proceedings before the CHRT shall be conducted as expeditiously as the rules of procedure allow.

2. Five key observations were made by the court in *Nova Scotia Construction Safety Association v. Nova Scotia Human Rights Commission*, 2006 NSCA 63. Of particular interest is the fifth observation: "that there is a public interest in having complaints of discrimination dealt with expeditiously", which was also stated in the case of *Bell Canada v. C.E.P.* (1997), 31 C.H.R.R. D/65.

For these two reasons, the practice note states that "all participants in *CHRA* inquiries are reminded of their obligation to assist in the timely completion of the hearing and deliberation process" and the intent of the CHRT "to release decisions as often as possible within a four month time frame".

Practice Note No. 2

Due to the importance of this practice note to the readers, the practice note will be reproduced in full as Appendix 8.3.

Practice Note No. 3

This practice note sets out time periods and procedures regarding the pre-hearing case management process: from the Initial Letter from the CHRT to Commission File, to Statement of Particulars, to Disclosure of Documents, to First Case Management Conference Call, to Identification and Anticipated Testimony of Proposed Witnesses, to Expert Witness Reports, and to a possible Second Case Management Conference Call. Refer to the practice note for specific details.

FORMS

There are no mandated forms on the CHRT website.

POLICIES

There are no policies on the CHRT website.

EXPLANATORY LITERATURE OF THE TRIBUNAL

Other than the documents already discussed, on the CHRT website there is a downloadable guide that explains the mechanisms of the procedures before the CHRT, entitled "A Guide to Understanding The Canadian Human Rights Tribunal". Included in the appendix to this chapter is an edited version of the guide to the CHRT process, which gives great details of the usual processes of the CHRT.

On the CHRT website there is a link to the Annual Reports of the CHRT, which, as of the time of writing, had reports from 1998 to 2015. Below is a summary of what the Annual Report contains, with specific references to the 2015 Annual Report:

> The report starts with the Chairperson's Message, setting out the purposes of administrative tribunals, especially those like the CHRT, that involve high stakes and the need to make decisions that are transparent, justifiable and intelligible. The Chairperson also makes reference to the Administrative Tribunal Support Service of Canada, which is designed to bring together greater efficiencies and economies to 11 different federal tribunals. The

Annual Report then discusses what the CHRT does, and how it works, and shows a chart of the parties before the CHRT and the avenues of judicial review and appeal, which appears as the last appendix to this chapter.

The Annual Report next discusses the CHRT caseload by trend analysis and statistics and explores the then current operating environment of the CHRT, following with an overview of the CHRT activities. Next is an examination of what the report calls "tribunal decisions or rulings that were particularly significant in their impact": *Tanner v. Gambler First Nation*, 2015 CHRT 19; *Moffat v. Davey Cartage Co. (1973) Ltd.*, 2015 CHRT 5; *Tabor v. Millbrook First Nation*, 2015 CHRT 9; *Cawson v. Air Canada*, 2015 CHRT 17. Each of the four cases includes a "Results For Canadians" section summarizing the impact of the case. The report finishes with biographies of the members of the CHRT.

On the CHRT website, there is direct access to decisions of the CHRT by title, using the search engine.

On the "A Guide to Understanding The Canadian Human Rights Tribunal" Web page, there is a long narrative discussing the *CHRA*, the CHRT, Mediation, Mediation-Adjudication, Pre-Hearing Case Management, the Hearing, the Decision, and possible Judicial Review procedures, all written in plain language. Although not legally binding, it is meant to make the law and procedures more accessible to the general public.

RELEVANT CASES AND/OR DECISIONS

The cases and decisions discussed below are not meant to be exhaustive and are only those found as of the summer of 2010. The discussion reflects only the author's interpretation and should not be regarded as legal opinion. Readers should continue to update and research on new cases and decisions, and briefing must be done in any event.

Fourteen matters, including cases before the Federal Court (Fed. Ct.), the Federal Court of Appeal (the Fed. C.A.), and before the Supreme Court of Canada (SCC), as well as decisions of the CHRT, shall be discussed in chronological order, with the oldest one first (unless the case is one in a series, which will be discussed starting with the lowest court) so as to give the reader a sampling of how these cases and decisions have been decided and their relevance to the CHRT. Not every case discussed is a ground-setting decision;

however, the review should give the reader some idea of how the CHRT and the courts have dealt with various procedural and substantive issues in the first decade of the 21st century.

Thompson v. Rivtow Marine Limited

Thompson v. Rivtow Marine Limited, 2001 CanLII 38323, (2001), 43 C.H.R.R. 502 (the *Thompson* decision), involved a motion requesting the CHRT to decline to deal with a complaint of alleged discrimination due to the complainant not being allowed to come back to work after a medical leave of absence. The motion was made because the complainant's union filed a grievance on his behalf, citing the respondent's failure to rehire the complainant. The respondent argued that the CHRT should therefore defer to the grievance arbitration process. If the CHRT did not decline, the respondent requested that the CHRT be bound by the ruling of the arbitration process pursuant to a legal concept known as "issue estoppel".

On the question of deference, the CHRT stated the following:

> There is no doubt that workplace disputes at the Federal level give rise to numerous potential avenues of redress. It is by no means uncommon for matters underlying a human rights complaint to also be the subject of a grievance arbitration, or proceedings under statutes such as the *Canada Labour Code*, Worker's Compensation legislation or the *Employment Insurance Act*. These multiple avenues of redress are the source of much concern, and have been the subject of comment in several recent studies.
>
> A review of the *Canadian Human Rights Act* discloses that Parliament was alive to this concern. Indeed, the *Act* specifically contemplates consideration of whether a matter might best be dealt with in another forum at two different points in the complaints process. In each case, however, the determination of whether the matter should be referred elsewhere is a decision for the Canadian Human Rights Commission, and not for the Tribunal.
>
> Once a complaint is referred to the Tribunal, Section 49(2) of the *Act* provides that the Chairperson of the Tribunal shall institute an inquiry.... According to Section 50(1) of the *Act*, upon due notice being given to the parties, the member or members assigned to the case shall inquire into the complaint. In light of the mandatory nature of this language, and having regard to the structure of the legislative scheme as a whole, I do not think that it is open to the Tribunal to simply decline to deal with a complaint on the basis that, in the Tribunal's view, the matter might better be dealt with elsewhere.

While the Tribunal may not have any jurisdiction to refuse to hear a case altogether, as master of its own procedure, it clearly has the power to determine when the hearing will take place. The issue of whether this hearing should be adjourned in light of the pending arbitration will be dealt with further on in this ruling.

In respect of "issue estoppel", the CHRT first set out the three elements necessary to give rise to "issue estoppel":

i) The same question is being decided in each proceeding;
ii) The decision which raises the issue estoppel is a final decision; and
iii) The parties to the two proceedings are the same parties or their privies.

After reviewing the first two elements, the CHRT concluded that the parties are not the same in both hearings:

A review of the *Canadian Human Rights Act* makes it clear that both the Commission and Mr. Thompson are parties to the complaint under the *Act*. The Commission does not represent Mr. Thompson; rather, the responsibility of the Commission is to represent the public interest. This is reflective of the quasi-constitutional nature of the rights guaranteed by the *Act*. In my view, a finding that the Commission is a privy of a complainant would be contrary to the policy considerations underlying the *Act*. Such a conclusion would result in the ability of the Canadian Human Rights Commission to take positions that it believes are in the public interest being inhibited by findings made in the context of other proceedings, proceedings of which the Commission would likely have had no notice and no opportunity to participate in.

Finally, on the request of an adjournment of the CHRT hearing pending the grievance arbitration, the CHRT held that since complaints of discrimination should be held expeditiously, no adjournment would be granted.

Hujdic v. Air Canada

In *Hujdic v. Air Canada*, 2001 CanLII 25845 (the *Hujdic* decision), the respondent made a motion for a stay of the proceedings due to the possible appeal of a case to determine if there was a reasonable apprehension of institutional bias of the CHRT. The case in question was *Bell Canada v. CTEA, Femmes Action and Canadian Human Rights Commission* (Bell Canada) before the Trial Division of the Federal Court. In *Bell Canada*, Madam Justice Tremblay-Lamer found that the CHRT was not an institutionally independent and impartial body due to the fact that the CHRC has the power to issue guidelines binding upon the Tribunal. Tremblay-Lamer J. also concluded that the independence of the Tribunal was compromised by requiring the Tribunal Chairperson's approval for members of the Tribunal to complete cases after the expiry of their appointments. As a consequence, Tremblay-Lamer J. ordered that there be no further proceedings in the Bell Canada matter until such time as the problems that she identified with the statutory regime were corrected. That case was overturned by the Federal Court of Appeal, and Bell Canada's application for leave to appeal to the Supreme Court of Canada was pending at the time of that decision. The CHRT held that the Federal Court of Appeal decision was binding and therefore should be applied. As to the respondent's request for a stay to await a possible appeal, the CHRT stated that there was no evidence of irreparable harm if the matter proceeded, and therefore the motion was dismissed.

Desormeaux v. Ottawa–Carleton Regional Transit

The decision of *Desormeaux v. Ottawa–Carleton Regional Transit*, 2003 CHRT 2, (2003), 46 C.H.R.R. 1 (the *Desormeaux* decision), reached the Supreme Court of Canada through an application for judicial review and subsequent appeals. In the original hearing, the complainant claimed discrimination due to disability by the employer because of the termination for chronic innocent absenteeism arising from medical issues. The CHRT found that there was a *prima facie* case of discrimination on the basis of a disability based on the evidence of her doctor regarding migraines and that she was terminated due to her medical condition. The *prima facie* case shifted the onus onto the respondent "to establish that attending work on a regular and reliable basis is a *bona fide* occupational requirement for a bus operator". The CHRT held that there was a duty on the employer to accommodate, and after reviewing the facts and the case law the CHRT stated the reason for its decision as follows:

> The law regarding the duties of employer and employee in relation to accommodation is clear: it is the responsibility of the disabled employee to bring the facts relating to the discrimination to her employer's attention. Through the efforts of Mr. Vye, Ms. Desormeaux did this. It is not up to the employee to originate a solution — that is the responsibility of the employer. In these circumstances, I am satisfied that Ms. Desormeaux fulfilled her duty to facilitate the search for accommodation.

Based on the findings, the CHRT found that the respondent had to comply with a number of orders to grant the complainant relief.

There was an application for judicial review of the *Desormeaux* decision to the Federal Court, and a judgment was reached, in conjunction with a similar matter against the same employer, in *City of Ottawa v. Canada (Human Rights Commission)*, [2004] F.C.J. No. 2172, [2004] A.C.F. no. 2172, 2004 FC 1778, 2004 CF 1778, 267 F.T.R. 216, [2005] CLLC para. 230-019, 136 A.C.W.S. (3d) 338 (the *Desormeaux* Fed. Ct. case). After reviewing the evidence and the parties' submissions, the judge first addressed the standard of review by stating the following:

> Applying the guidance provided by the Supreme Court in *Pushpanathan*, [1998] 1 S.C.R. 982, and more recently in *Baker v. Canada (Minister of Citizenship and Immigration)*, [1999] 2 S.C.R. 817, I am satisfied that the standard of review of decisions of the Tribunal in this matter is correctness in respect of questions of law, reasonableness simpliciter in respect of questions of mixed law and fact, and patent unreasonableness in respect of "fact-finding and adjudication in a human rights context". On the facts of this matter, I find the standard of review of questions of law and questions of fact-finding and adjudication in a human rights context by the Tribunal not to have been modified by recent decisions of the Supreme Court of Canada or of the Federal Court Trial Division regarding the pragmatic and functional approach to the determination of standard of review. **[Author's Note: The case law currently states that there are only two standards of review, correctness and reasonableness, not three. See *Dunsmuir v. New Brunswick*, [2008] 1 S.C.R. 190, 2008 SCC 9 (the *Dunsmuir* case), where the majority stated that there are only two standards of review by the courts judicially reviewing a decision of an agency: correctness and reasonableness.]**

In respect of the raised issue of issue estoppel, the court did not have to address the matter, as the court determined that the judicial review on this matter should have been within 30 days after the decision of the CHRT on a preliminary motion and not the final motion; therefore, it was made too late.

The judge then examined whether the CHRT erred on the issue of whether the *prima facie* discrimination was proven. After examining some possible problems with the findings of the CHRT, the judge found as follows:

> In the case of Ms. Desormeaux, I conclude that the Tribunal's finding that she suffered from a disability was unreasonable

based upon the evidence. Dr. Meehan was qualified as an expert in family medicine, not as a neurologist. Accordingly, I find that the Tribunal's reliance on her evidence was in error to the extent that her evidence exceeded the legitimate purpose for which her expert testimony was receivable: see *R. v. Reid* (2003), 65 O.R. (3d) 723 at 736. I conclude that there is no prima facie case for the employer to answer as I am not satisfied that there is properly admissible evidence to support a finding of disability. The application for judicial review will be allowed in respect to Ms. Desormeaux.

Desormeaux appealed this judgment to the Federal Court of Appeal: *Desormeaux v. Ottawa (City)*, 2005 FCA 311, (2005), 54 C.H.R.R. 462 (the *Desormeaux* Fed. C.A. case). After reviewing the history of the matter, the court first held that the issue estoppel argument was not time barred and could be raised in the appeal. The Federal Court of Appeal, however, found the CHRT's consideration of the matter legally unimpeachable, "in that two of the three elements required for issue estoppel — that is, same question and same parties — had not been established (following the test set out in *Danyluk v. Ainsworth Technologies Inc.*, 2001 SCC 44 (CanLII), [2001] 2 S.C.R. 460 at para. 25, citing *Angle v. Canada (Minister of National Revenue)*, 1974 CanLII 168 (S.C.C.), [1975] 2 S.C.R. 248 at 254, per Dickson, J)". As a result, the court further concluded there was no need to consider the scope of the residuary discretion residing in the Tribunal on the estoppel issue.

The court then addressed the matter of whether the *prima facie* discrimination was proven. The court disagreed with the judge in the *Desormeaux* Fed. Ct. case, where it was found that there was proof of *prima facie* discrimination, and stated as follows:

> [T]his conclusion was incorrect. Whether the standard of review for this mixed question of law and fact was reasonableness or patent unreasonableness, the Tribunal's decision on this issue was clearly one that deserved considerable deference. As the Supreme Court established in *Granovsky v. Canada*, 2000 SCC 28 (CanLII), [2000] 1 S.C.R. 703 at para. 34 and in *City of Montreal, supra*, at para. 71, disability in a legal sense consists of a physical or mental impairment, which results in a functional limitation or is associated with a perception of impairment. In light of this test, there was evidence before the Tribunal upon which it could reasonably find that there was a disability because of the headaches, whether they were migraine headaches, migraine/tension headaches or some other type of severe headache condition. The Report of Dr. Rabinovitch did

not really conflict with the evidence of Dr. Meehan; it may have been less forceful and more tentative, but, in any event, the Tribunal was persuaded on all of the evidence that there was disability on the basis of the headaches. The Tribunal's conclusion was certainly a reasonable one based on all the evidence and should not have been upset on judicial review.

On the matter of the comparator group, the Applications Judge found that the wrong comparator group was identified by the Tribunal; in any event, however, the error furnished no basis for judicial intervention, since the standard of review was reasonableness. On appeal, Counsel correctly devoted very little attention to this issue. Whichever comparator group was chosen, the conclusion that there was differentiation established in the treatment of the complainant would not be affected.

Hence, *prima facie* discrimination being established, it was necessary to determine whether OC Transpo's standard of reasonable and regular attendance was a *bona fide* occupational requirement (BFOR). As the Tribunal correctly stated, the applicable three-stage test was set out in *British Columbia (Public Service Employee Relations Commission) v. BCGSEU*, 1999 CanLII 652 (S.C.C.), [1999] 3 S.C.R. 3 at para. 54 ["*Meiorin*"]. To qualify as a BFOR, the employer must show that the standard was (1) adopted for a purpose rationally connected to the performance of the job; (2) adopted pursuant to an honest and good-faith belief; and (3) is reasonably necessary to the accomplishment of the legitimate work-related purpose. A standard is considered "reasonably necessary" if the employer can demonstrate that it is impossible to accommodate individual employees sharing the characteristics of the claimant without imposing undue hardship on the employer.

The court agreed with the CHRT, holding that the BFOR test was not met as there was no reasonable necessity found and that the employer should have accommodated the employee, but did not. [Note: The Fed. Ct. case did not address this issue as it stopped once it concluded there was no *prima facie* discrimination.] Although the employer advanced the argument that the employee did not specially request that her disability be accommodated, the court found the following:

The Tribunal correctly stated (at para. 110) the law on this question: the employee has a duty to bring to the attention of the employer the facts relating to discrimination, and to facilitate the search for accommodation, but the duty to originate a solution remains with the employer (*Central Okanagan School*

> *District No. 23 v. Renaud*, 1992 CanLII 81 (S.C.C.), [1992] 2
> S.C.R. 970 at 994–95). The Tribunal found that there was suffi-
> cient discussion with the employer on this issue to fulfill Ms.
> Desormeaux's duty of notification and facilitation with respect
> to accommodation (see Tribunal's findings at paras. 29 and
> 109–110). I am not persuaded that there was any error made
> by the Tribunal on this issue, let alone an unreasonable or
> patently unreasonable error.

Based on the foregoing, the court allowed the appeal and rein-
stated the CHRT decision.

There was one final attempt to appeal to the Supreme Court of
Canada, but the application for leave to appeal was dismissed:
[2005] S.C.C.A. No. 534 (the *Desormeaux* SCC case).

Canada (Attorney General) v. Brown

Canada (Attorney General) v. Brown, 2005 FC 1683, [2005] F.C.J.
No. 2124, [2005] A.C.F. no 2124, 2005 CF 1683, 284 F.T.R. 291, 144
A.C.W.S. (3d) 922, 58 C.H.R.R. D/482 (the *Brown* Fed. Ct. case),
was an application for judicial review to set aside a decision of
the CHRT. The complainant was represented at the CHRT hearing by
a non-lawyer, and after the complaint of discrimination was found
substantiated, the CHRT awarded legal costs to the complainant's
representative. The key parts of the decision were summarized by
the Federal Court as follows:

> Regarding the Tribunal's jurisdiction to award costs, the Tribu-
> nal concluded that the power to award costs cannot be found
> in the Act. The Tribunal held that its jurisdiction derives more
> from its broad and quasi-constitutional mandate under the Act
> than from the literal wording of the Act. The Tribunal found
> that the Act's mandate gives the Tribunal all the incidental
> powers to protect the viability of the remedies under the Act.
> The Tribunal also found that the cumulative effect of subsec-
> tion 53(2) in relation to personal remedies is Parliament's
> express intention to make a victim of discrimination whole.
> Therefore, the Tribunal has the power to order the payment of
> costs in order to preserve the damages awarded and, as a
> result, allow a victim of discrimination to an effective remedy.
> The Tribunal concluded that the Respondent was entitled to
> reasonable costs but was not entitled to claim the entirety of
> her legal costs because the principle of *restitutio in integrum*
> applies only to damages and not to costs.
>
> With respect to the Applicant's arguments based on subsec-
> tion 50(1) of the Act that Mr. Finding was not entitled to rep-

resent the Respondent, the Tribunal observed that Mr. Finding represented the Respondent throughout the hearing with the full knowledge of the Applicant who did not object to his participation until the final submissions. The Tribunal also noted the position taken by the Applicant that Mr. Finding had contravened the *British Columbia Legal Profession Act*, R.S.B.C. 1998, c. 9 in doing so. The Tribunal commented that whether subsection 50(1) of the Act permits non-lawyers to represent complainants at Tribunal hearings is a live issue for the Tribunal but it should be resolved in a case where it has been properly addressed. Similarly, the question of whether a non-lawyer representative appearing before the Tribunal is practising law contrary to the governing provincial legislation should be dealt with in a case where the matter is properly raised at the outset of the process.

On the question of whether the fees of a lay representative are recoverable, the Tribunal simply noted the parties' positions on the matter. The Applicant argued that there is no authority under the Act to award costs for the services of a lay representative. The Respondent argued that there was no reason to distinguish between representatives who are lawyers and those who are not, and suggested that the Tribunal should follow the approach of the British Columbia Labour Relations Board in *Graham (Re)*, [2000] B.C.L.R.B.D. No. 1, in which the Board recognized that the fees of non-lawyer representatives should be recoverable.

The court stated that the issue to be determined was "whether the Tribunal erred in law and in fact in awarding costs to the Respondent for 'legal and representation fees' of a non-lawyer". The court first looked at the standard of review of the CHRT decision and found that since "the determinative issue raises a question of mixed fact and law, the decision will be reviewed on a standard of reasonableness". The court held that subsection 50(1) of the *CHRA* in the English version uses the word "counsel" but in the French version uses the word "advocat", and the court stated the following:

> In *R. v. Mac*, [2002] 1 S.C.R. 856 at 857, Justice Bastarache held that where the words of one version of bilingual legislation may give rise to an ambiguity, the Court should first look at the other version to ascertain whether its meaning is plain and unequivocal. Where the ambiguity in one version is resolved by the clear and unambiguous language of the other version, there is no need to consider other rules of statutory interpretation.

> In the present case, the French text is clear and unambiguous. Accordingly, I conclude that the term "counsel" in the English version means "lawyer" and excludes non-lawyers. However, this does not end the matter.

The next submission on the matter examined was the SCC case of *Law Society of British Columbia v. Mangat*, [2001] 3 S.C.R. 113, where the court found that the case stands for the following authority:

> The Supreme Court of Canada concluded that there was a conflict between the two statutes. Sections 30 and 69(1) of the *Immigration Act* expressly authorized non-lawyers to appear before the tribunal for a fee but the *Legal Profession Act* prohibited non-lawyers from engaging in the practice of law for a fee. The Court found that it was impossible to comply with both statutes without frustrating Parliament's purpose. The Court concluded that where there is a conflict between two statutes the principle of paramountcy applies and, in that case, the *Immigration Act* prevailed over the *Legal Profession Act*.

The court distinguished the case from the *Mangat* case because, it stated, there was no conflict here.

> Unlike the *Immigration Act*, the Act does not contain a statutory provision authorizing non-lawyers to appear for a fee before the Tribunal or a provision in relation to expenses for such representation. Again without deciding the issue, even if the Tribunal has the implied jurisdiction to award costs to a successful complainant under the Act, Parliament has not expressly authorized non-lawyers to appear for a fee before the Tribunal in the legislation. On the other hand, the *Legal Profession Act* clearly prohibits non-lawyers from appearing as counsel or advocate for a fee. In this case, the *Legal Profession Act* prevails.

The finding was therefore that the CHRT did err in awarding fees and costs and that part of the decision was set aside. **[Author's Note: Does the amendment to the *Legal Profession Act* to license paralegals change how this case would be decided?]**

Goodwin v. Birkett

The CHRT decision of *Goodwin v. Birkett*, 2004 CHRT 29, [2004] C.H.R.D. No. 17, [2004] D.C.D.P. No 17, 2004 TCDP 29 (the *Goodwin* decision), led to judicial review and then an appeal in the Federal

Court, all from a complaint of sexual harassment. In recounting the facts, the CHRT found that the complainant's evidence of the sexual harassment was credible over the respondent's testimony after noting what sexual harassment is as follows:

> Sexual harassment is broadly defined as unwelcome conduct of a sexual nature that detrimentally affects the work environment or leads to adverse job-related consequences for the victims of harassment. Sexual harassment in the workplace attacks the dignity and self-respect of the victim, both as an employee and as a human being. (*Janzen v. Platy Enterprises Inc.*, [1989] 1 S.C.R. 1252)

Based upon the evidence and the definition set out above, the CHRT found as follows:

> I am also satisfied that his behaviour that night constituted sexual harassment. His conduct was unwelcome, of a sexual nature and detrimentally affected her work environment. She was no longer comfortable working at the same workplace with the Respondent, which was one of the factors in her decision to resign from PMCL. While the incident occurred during a single evening, the Respondent's conduct was severe enough to create a hostile working environment by the measure of any reasonable person (See *Canada (HRC) v. Canada (Armed Forces) and Franke* (1999), 34 C.H.R.R. D/140 at paras. 29–50 (F.C.T.D.)).
>
> I therefore find that the Respondent discriminated against the Complainant by sexually harassing her. The complaint is substantiated.

In so finding, the CHRT then determined what relief should be granted to the complainant and stated the following:

> Taking these circumstances into account, and considering the prevailing case law with respect to non-pecuniary damages involving harassment (see e.g., *Bushey v. Sharma*, 2003 CHRT 21; *Woiden v. Lynn (No.2)* (2002), 43 C.H.R.R. D/296 (C.H.R.T.)), I am satisfied that both of the Complainant's claims are more than justified. The Respondent is ordered to pay the Complainant the sum of $2,500 in compensation for her pain and suffering (s. 53(2)e)), and the sum of $2,500 in special compensation (s. 53(3)). Simple interest shall be payable on both of the monetary awards, to be calculated on a yearly basis, at a rate equivalent to the Bank Rate (Monthly series)

set by the Bank of Canada. The interest will run from August 29, 1999.

The Complainant has also requested that the Respondent be ordered to provide her with a letter of apology. In *Canada (Attorney-General) v. Stevenson*, 2003 FCT 341, the Federal Court found that the *Act* does not empower Tribunals to make such orders. The Complainant's request for a letter of apology is therefore denied.

The respondent made an application for judicial review to the Federal Court: *Birkett v. Canada (Human Rights Commission)*, 2007 FC 428, (2007), 312 F.T.R. 71 (the *Goodwin* Fed. Ct. case). The respondent submitted that there was no evidence for the CHRT to make its findings and that there were a number of breaches of the rules of natural justice and procedural fairness, including a claim of a reasonable apprehension of bias at the hearing. The court first looked at the standard of review and stated the following:

> As always, a prime issue is the degree of deference the Court owes the Tribunal. As noted by Mr. Justice Gibson in *International Longshore & Warehouse Union (Marine Section), Local 400 v. Oster (T.D.)*, 2001 FCT 1115 (CanLII), 2001 FCT 1115, 2001 FCT 1115 (CanLII), [2002] 2 F.C. 430, and the cases cited therein, the Canadian Human Rights Tribunal has superior expertise when it comes to fact finding and adjudication in a human rights context. He concluded that the standard of review in respect of questions of law was correctness, reasonableness *simpliciter* in respect of questions of mixed law and fact, and patent unreasonableness in respect of fact finding. There is nothing in the subsequent decisions of the Supreme Court in *Dr. Q. v. College of Physicians and Surgeons of British Columbia*, 2003 SCC 19 (CanLII), [2003] 1 S.C.R. 226 and *Law Society of New Brunswick v. Ryan*, 2003 SCC 20 (CanLII), [2003] 1 S.C.R. 247, to put the *Oster* decision into question when it comes to the pragmatic and functional approach to judicial review in this context. However, natural justice and procedural fairness are another matter all together. The Court owes the Tribunal no deference (*C.U.P.E. v. Ontario (Minister of Labour)*, 2003 SCC 29 (CanLII), 2003 SCC 29, 2003 SCC 29 (CanLII), [2003] 1 S.C.R. 539 and *Canada (Attorney General) v. Sketchley*, 2005 FCA 404 (CanLII), 2005 FCA 404).

The court then looked at the transcript, which covered the whole two-day hearing and stated that "the Chair was scrupulously fair and helpful to both parties". After looking at specific situations in the hearing, the court found that the hearing was fair, and then it looked to the evidence:

> What it comes down to then is credibility. One point seized upon by the Chair was that Ms. Goodwin testified clearly that there had been two beds in the room and that she had removed her suitcase and clothing from one so that Mr. Birkett could sit on it. Mr. Birkett's memory was vague. He suggested at first that there was only one bed and then allowed that he might be wrong. Findings of fact are not to be disturbed unless patently unreasonable.
>
> As noted by Mr. Justice Evans in *Cepeda-Gutierrez et al. v. Canada (Minister of Citizenship and Immigration)* 1998 CanLII 8667 (F.C.), (1998), 157 F.T.R. 35 at paragraph 14:
>
> > It is well established that s. 18.1(4)(d) of the **Federal Court Act** does not authorize the court to substitute its view of the facts for that of the Board, which has the benefit not only of seeing and hearing the witnesses, but also of the expertise of its members in assessing evidence relating to facts that are within their area of specialized expertise. In addition, and more generally, considerations of the efficient allocation of decision-making resources between administrative agencies and the courts strongly indicate that the role to be played in fact-finding by the court on an application for judicial review should be merely residual. Thus, in order to attract judicial intervention under s. 18.1(4)(d), the applicant must satisfy the court, not only that the Board made a palpably erroneous finding of material fact, but also that the finding was made "without regard to the evidence" ...

In dismissing the application for judicial review, the court found as follows:

> In my opinion, the application of the Tribunal's findings of fact to the law was a mixed question. The Tribunal was entitled to deference on a reasonableness *simpliciter* standard. It was not unreasonable for the Tribunal to conclude that Mr. Birkett's conduct was unwelcome, of a sexual nature and detrimentally affected Ms. Goodwin's work environment. She was no longer comfortable working at the same workplace as him which was one of the factors leading to her resignation.
>
> Finally on the question of double jeopardy, which the respondent characterizes as issue estoppel, Ms. Goodwin was

entitled in law to avail herself of the *Canadian Human Rights Act* regardless of whether Mr. Birkett's employer conducted an inquiry into the issue or not (see *Tweten v. RTL Robinson Enterprises Ltd.*, [2004] C.H.R.D. No. 14 (QL)).

The matter was then appealed to the Federal Court of Appeal: *Birkett v. Canada (Human Rights Commission)*, 2008 FCA 127, [2008] F.C.J. No. 537, 165 A.C.W.S. (3d) 504 (the *Goodwin* Fed. C.A. case). As noted by the appellate court, the appeal from the Fed. Ct. decision "was limited to the issue of procedural fairness as the finding as to the characterization of the conduct giving rise to the complaint was not appealed". One of the matters examined was the fact that the CHRT did not allow the respondent to call and question the complainant's ex-husband.

The appellate court held as follows:

> The appellant now says that he was not allowed to call the complainant's ex-husband and that in addition to the evidence already described, the latter would have testified as to her general character. The application judge noted that the Tribunal had found that the complainant had not put her character in issue: see paragraph 24 of his reasons. Leaving aside that the decision not to call the complainant's ex-husband was made with the appellant's apparent consent, the fact remains that, since the complainant did not put her character in issue, it would have been improper to allow evidence of general character in any event: see *R. v. Beland*, [1987] 2 S.C.R. 398. While administrative tribunals are not bound by the strict rules of evidence, they ought, nonetheless, to be especially careful when an attempt is made to refute an allegation of a sexual misconduct by evidence of the victim's character. We find no error in the application judge's disposition of this question. As for the issue of the complainant's willingness to call the police, the relevant facts were admitted and the appellant was free to make what he could of them.

In conclusion, the appellate court found no errors were made and dismissed the appeal.

Yarinder Brar and the Royal Canadian Mounted Police

This is a group of cases that involved Yarinder Brar and the Royal Canadian Mounted Police (RCMP), with the CHRT interim decision, *Brar v. R.C.M.P.*, 2007 CHRT 12 (the *Brar* decision), related to a joint motion made by the parties in which the CHRT ordered, *inter alia*, the following:

[1] The Respondent's motion to clarify the nature and scope of the complaint which will be the subject matter of the inquiry before the Tribunal is disposed of on the basis that the Complainant will be allowed to make the allegations as set out in paragraphs 33–52, but excluding paragraphs 51(b), (f) and (h), of his Statement of Particulars dated June 23, 2006 and call evidence relating to those allegations, without precluding the Respondent from objecting to any of these allegations, or any of the witnesses coming forward to support these allegations on the basis of prejudice or other objections.

[2] The Respondent's motion for an order prohibiting the Complainant from calling certain witnesses is dismissed, without prejudice to the Respondent to argue the relevance of the evidence, the timeliness of the evidence, any prejudice of the evidence, or the fact that the evidence should be subject to immunity, in context of the hearing.

[3] The Respondent's motion for an order limiting the ambit of the testimony to be given by certain other witnesses is dismissed, without prejudice to object at the time of the hearing when these witnesses appear.

The respondent made application to judicially review the interlocutory orders to the Federal Court, *Canada (A.G.) v. Brar*, 2007 FC 1268, [2007] F.C.J. No. 1629, 162 A.C.W.S. (3d) 643 (the *Brar* Fed. Ct. case). The court looked at the CHRT's orders and stated the following:

In his oral decision, the Tribunal Chairperson explained the basis for his decision, observing that:

[T]he reason I made this decision is because it is my view that there is a link between the allegations that I am allowing the Complainant to pursue and the complaint. Having come to this conclusion, this is not to preclude, once the hearing has started, and in the context, and more fulsome evidence — this does not preclude the Respondent from objecting to any of these allegations going forward, or any of the witnesses coming forward to support these allegations on the basis of relevance, or on the basis of prejudice, or whatever other objection the Respondent may seek to put forward at the time of the hearing.

As I said, I am reluctant to eliminate allegations in a Statement of Particulars or put into a Statement of Claim, unless it is apparent that there is no relevance, or that they have absolutely nothing to do with the facts alleged in the complaint.

While a number of matters were dealt with at the case management conference, this application is restricted to challenging the Tribunal's refusal to limit the ambit of Sgt. Brar's complaint. At this point in time, the RCMP does not take issue with the Tribunal's decision not to limit the list of witnesses, their testimony, or the RCMP's disclosure obligations.

While the Attorney General has raised several issues, I am satisfied that the question of prematurity is dispositive of the matter.

The court then looked at the matter of the judicial review of interlocutory orders:

As a general rule, in the absence of special circumstances, interlocutory rulings made by administrative tribunals should not be challenged until the tribunal has rendered its final decision: see, for example, *Sherman v. Canada (Customs and Revenue Agency)*, [2006] F.C.J. No. 912, 2006 FC 715 at para. 39, *Zündel v. Canada (Human Rights Commission)*, [2000] 4 F.C. 255, 256 N.R. 125 (C.A.), at para. 10 and *Szczecka v. Canada (Minister of Employment and Immigration)*, [1993] F.C.J. No. 934, 116 D.L.R. (4th) 333 at 335.

There are a number of reasons why this is so, including the fact that the application may be rendered moot by the ultimate outcome of the case, and the risk of the fragmentation of the process, with the accompanying costs and delays. Also of concern is the absence of a full record at the preliminary stage, with the resultant inability to see how the ruling actually played out in the ultimate determination of the case. There is also the possibility that the tribunal may end up modifying its original ruling as the hearing unfolds.

The fact that an issue may arguably relate to the tribunal's jurisdiction does not automatically justify immediate judicial review: see *Air Canada v. Lorenz*, [2000] 1 F.C. 494 para. 13. See also Brown and Evans, *Judicial Review of Administrative Action in Canada* (Toronto: Canvasback Publishing, 1998), at 3: 4100.

Many of the underlying policy concerns which support the principle that interlocutory decisions of inferior tribunals should not ordinarily be subject to immediate judicial review arise in this case.

In particular, it is clear that the ruling of the Tribunal Chairperson did not finally determine the scope of the hearing to be held before the Canadian Human Rights Tribunal. Indeed, the Chairperson was very careful to reserve the final decision in this regard to the Tribunal member ultimately dealing with the merits of Sgt. Brar's complaint.

That is, the Chairperson specifically preserved the right of the RCMP to object to particular post-complaint allegations being advanced by Sgt. Brar on whatever basis it deemed appropriate, deferring the final determination of the scope of the hearing to the hearing on the merits.

In dismissing the application for judicial review, the court found the following:

The fact that the hearing into Sgt. Brar's complaint may be shortened by an immediate ruling from this Court is not determinative. In this regard, I note that in the *Lorenz* case, Justice Evans declined to entertain an application to judicially review a decision regarding an allegation of bias, preferring to wait until the Board had rendered its final decision. This notwithstanding the fact that there were several weeks of hearing left to go, which would have been invalidated, had the allegations of bias ultimately been sustained.

Moreover, as was the case in *Lorenz*, I am of the view that the possibility of waste in this case is mitigated by the fact that it is not plain and obvious that the Tribunal is without jurisdiction to entertain the allegations in issue.

Powell v. United Parcel Service Canada Ltd.

In *Powell v. United Parcel Service Canada Ltd.*, 2008 CHRT 43 (the *Powell* decision), the respondent made a motion to confirm an "alleged" settlement of the complainant's human rights complaint and bring the matter before the CHRT to a close. The respondent claims that a settlement was reached by the parties after the matter was referred to the CHRT by the Commission, but then the complainant, after changing counsel, refused to sign either the proposed minutes of settlement or the release. The respondent therefore brought the motion to confirm settlement upon which the CHRT ruled in this matter. It was first noted that according "to section 48 of the *Act*, settlements of any complaints that are reached before the commencement of a hearing must be referred to the Commission for approval or rejection". As to the meaning of section 48 and what occurred in this matter, the CHRT stated the following:

Prior to the commencement of the hearing, no complaint can be settled without Commission approval. The Federal Court pointed out in *Loyer v. Air Canada*, 2006 FC 1172 (CanLII), 2006 FC 1172 at para. 87, that:

> There has been little judicial consideration of section 48 of the *Canadian Human Rights Act*. However, when the section is read in context, consistent with the aims of the Act as a whole, and <u>in light of the public interest mandate of the Canadian Human Rights Commission, it is clear that the section is there to ensure that the Commissioners themselves have input into settlements</u>, so as to ensure that the remedial goals of the Act are adequately addressed in the resolution of individual complaints. [emphasis added]

> Under s. 48, there is no option made available to the parties to choose whether or not to submit the settlement to the Commission. In the English rendering of the section, it is stated that the settlement "shall be referred to the Commission". In the French rendering, the parties "present" the terms of the settlement for approval by the Commission. This requirement is consistent with the finding in *Loyer* that the section exists to ensure that the Commissioners have an input into settlements to make certain that the remedial goals of the *Act* are adequately addressed in the resolution of the individual complaints. Without such input, there can be no settlement.

> There is no indication that the Commission has either explicitly or tacitly approved the alleged settlement between Ms. Powell and UPS. Absent such approval, it cannot be said that there exists a settlement bringing about an end to the Tribunal's inquiry into the complaint.

The respondent then argued that there was no need for the Commission to approve the settlement as the matter was not prior to the commencement of the hearing; steps such as the case management process and the motion being heard indicated that the CHRT had embarked on the hearing process. The CHRT found the following in respect of that position:

> While the *Act* refers to a "hearing" and an "inquiry", there is no mention made anywhere of a "hearing process". The Federal Court considered these two terms ("hearing" and "inquiry") in *Canada (Canadian Human Rights Commission) v. Canada Post Corp.*, 2004 FC 81 (CanLII), 2004 FC 81 at para. 17. The Court pointed out that s. 50 of the *Act* makes reference to each of these expressions separately, and treats them as distinct notions. The Court was sitting in review of a ruling by the Tribunal on a preliminary motion that the respondent had

filed seeking the dismissal of the complaint prior to the start of the hearing into the merits of the complaint. The Commission had argued that the Tribunal was required to conduct the hearing before dismissing the complaint and that the motion was therefore premature. The Court disagreed. It concluded that although, according to s. 50, a Tribunal must conduct an "inquiry" into every complaint referred to it, there is no requirement that there be a "hearing" in every case. The motion to dismiss was thus not premature.

I take it, therefore, from the Court's finding, that the meaning to be assigned to the term "hearing" is the conduct of the actual hearing into the merits of the complaint itself. It does not encompass any preceding activity, including preliminary motions that the Tribunal may entertain in order to "clear the procedural underbrush" (*Canada Post* at para. 14), such as the motion to dismiss that had been brought in that case.

The motion was therefore dismissed.

Zhou v. National Research Council et al.

In *Zhou v. National Research Council et al.*, 2009 CHRT 11 (the *Zhou* decision), the complainant made an application to adjourn a scheduled hearing due to newly retained counsel needing time to prepare. The request was for three months, but the CHRT granted a two-week adjournment with the following reasons:

[The] Tribunal must weigh the goal of resolving human rights complaints in a timely manner against the requirement to be fair to all parties and to provide them with a full and ample opportunity to present their case (*Leger v. Canadian National Railway Company*, Interim Ruling, November 26, 1999 (CHRT); stay application dismissed [2000] F.C.J. 243 (T.D.)).

A two week adjournment in the present case will give counsel 5 weeks to prepare. There is, therefore, enough time to prepare so that the Complainant's right to a fair hearing is not compromised.

Moreover, it must be noted that on October 3, 2008, all of the parties agreed to set down four weeks for a hearing in April and May of the following year. Dr. Zhou had ample time to seek counsel or the assistance of his bargaining agent. However, it was not until March 18, 2009, a month before the commencement of the hearing, that the Tribunal was informed that counsel had been retained to represent Dr. Zhou.

Translation services for the hearing have been booked and confirmed. The hearing rooms have been reserved. Staffing

2

resources have been allocated. Other cases that could have been set for hearing during this time period were not set down for that time.

The Tribunal must run an efficient hearing system in order to achieve its legislative mandate to hear and resolve complaints expeditiously (s. 48.9(1) of the CHRA; *Canada Post Corporation v. PSAC and the CHRC*, 2008 FC 223 at para. 274; *Nova Scotia Construction Safety Association, Collins and Kelly v. Nova Scotia Human Rights Commission and Davison*, 2006 NSCA 63 at para. 76). A hearing requires the dedication of considerable financial and human resources. Those resources cannot be reallocated without significant disruption to the whole system, especially at this stage in the process. Such disruptions have an impact on the timeliness not only of the present case, but also of other cases in the system. For those reasons, an adjournment is granted only in cases where proceeding will clearly have an impact on the fairness of the hearing.

REVIEW QUESTIONS

1. What is the enabling legislation for the CHRT?
2. Where would you find the practices and procedures of the CHRT?
3. List five grounds (or groups) protected under the *Human Rights Act* from being discriminated against or harassed.
4. Pursuant to the *CHRA*, how does the duty to act fairly apply to the CHRT?
5. What does the privative clause of the *FCA* related to the CHRT prevent and allow, and under what circumstances?
6. What rule(s) gives discretion and flexibility to the CHRT in applying the CHRT Rules?
7. What rule(s) deal with disclosure, and what is the result of insufficient disclosure?
8. What rule(s) deal with motions, and what is the appropriate procedure to have a motion dealt with by the CHRT?
9. What jurisdiction is the CHRT given to reconsider a decision under the various procedures and practices of the CHRT?
10. How do the various procedures and practices of the CHRT deal with mediation before the CHRT?
11. How do the various procedures and practices of the CHRT deal with giving access to persons before the CHRT and dealing with their needs?

EXERCISE

Based upon the facts of the *Desormeaux* decision briefed in the chapter, summarize the steps this matter took before the CHRT to its decision and then briefly discuss how it got to the court system.

Appendix 8.1
Overview of Procedural Stages of a Complaint under the *CHRA*

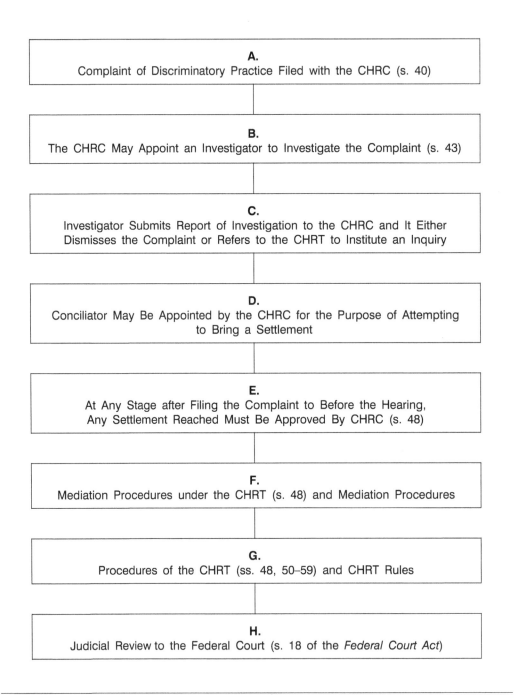

A.
Complaint of Discriminatory Practice Filed with the CHRC (s. 40)

B.
The CHRC May Appoint an Investigator to Investigate the Complaint (s. 43)

C.
Investigator Submits Report of Investigation to the CHRC and It Either Dismisses the Complaint or Refers to the CHRT to Institute an Inquiry

D.
Conciliator May Be Appointed by the CHRC for the Purpose of Attempting to Bring a Settlement

E.
At Any Stage after Filing the Complaint to Before the Hearing, Any Settlement Reached Must Be Approved By CHRC (s. 48)

F.
Mediation Procedures under the CHRT (s. 48) and Mediation Procedures

G.
Procedures of the CHRT (ss. 48, 50–59) and CHRT Rules

H.
Judicial Review to the Federal Court (s. 18 of the *Federal Court Act*)

Appendix 8.2
Excerpts from the CHRT's Guide to the Tribunal Process[†]

A GUIDE TO
UNDERSTANDING
THE CANADIAN HUMAN
RIGHTS TRIBUNAL

1

[†] Source: CHRT Website, "Guide to CHRT", <http://www.chrt-tcdp.gc.ca/procedures/practice-notes-en.html#>.

TABLE OF CONTENTS

1. ABOUT THIS GUIDE

This Guide is intended to help the participants in a human rights case understand what happens once a complaint of discrimination is referred to the Canadian Human Rights Tribunal. In this document, the *Canadian Human Rights Act* and the Canadian Human Rights Tribunal are described in plain language to make the law, and the processes and procedures surrounding the law, more accessible to the general public.

PLEASE NOTE: this guide is not a legal document and is for illustrative purposes only. Any reference to the *Canadian Human Rights Act* is not an authoritative interpretation. Nothing in this document should be taken as legal advice.

The Tribunal would like to acknowledge and thank its stakeholders for providing valuable input and feedback on the Tribunal's practices during the 2011 national stakeholder consultations. This Guide incorporates much of the feedback and suggestions received during those consultations.

Reference Documents

This Guide should be read together with, and makes reference to, the following documents:

- *Canadian Human Rights Act*

    o For a copy of the *Canadian Human Rights Act* visit http://laws-lois.justice.gc.ca/eng/acts/H-6/index.html.

- *Canadian Human Rights Tribunal Rules of Procedure*

    o For a copy of the *Canadian Human Rights Tribunal Rules of Procedure* visit http://www.chrt-tcdp.gc.ca/NS/about-apropos/trp-rpt-eng.asp

5

3. THE CANADIAN HUMAN RIGHTS TRIBUNAL

A. Role

The Tribunal's role is much like that of a court. It hears evidence and witnesses about complaints of discrimination; decides whether discrimination has occurred; and, if so, determines an appropriate remedy.

B. Jurisdiction

The Tribunal can only hear complaints of discrimination filed against federally regulated employers and service providers. These include:

- federal government departments, agencies and Crown corporations (including the Canadian Forces and the RCMP)

- chartered banks

- airlines

- television and radio stations

- interprovincial communications and telephone companies

- interprovincial transportation companies

- First Nations governments and some other First Nations organizations

C. Members

The Tribunal is composed of a full-time Chairperson and Vice-Chairperson, and up to 13 full or part-time Members who are appointed for terms up to five years.

When a case is referred to the Tribunal, the Chairperson assigns either one or, in certain cases, three Members to hear the case.

Short biographies of the Chairperson, Vice-Chairperson and Members are available on the Tribunal's Web site (http://chrt-tcdp.gc.ca/NS/about-apropos/cb-lp-eng.asp).

D. Separate & Independent from the Canadian Human Rights Commission

The Tribunal and Commission are separate and independent institutions, each with their own role in the human rights complaint process.

The Canadian Human Rights Commission is the first point of contact for registering a complaint under the *Canadian Human Rights Act*. The Commission has the authority to investigatediscrimination complaints and, if it finds the complaint warranted, it refers the case to the Tribunal for a Hearing.

As mentioned above, the Tribunal's role is then to hear witnesses and other evidence about the referred complaint; and, decide whether discrimination has occurred.

The Commission may, if it decides to participate in the Hearing,present evidence and make argumentsbefore the Tribunal regarding discrimination complaints. The duty of the Commission when it appears before the Tribunal is to represent the public interest. However, the Commission is not required to participate in every Tribunal case.

Please Note: All documentation and argument a party wishes to present to the Tribunal, including any documents already filed with the Commission,should be filed again as part of the Statement of Particulars (see part 4.5(A) below) and served on the other parties (see part 4.5(E)(I) below).

- For more information on the Commission visit http://www.chrc-ccdp.gc.ca/.

4. THE COMPLAINT RESOLUTION PROCESS

4.1 Complaint Resolution Process Diagram

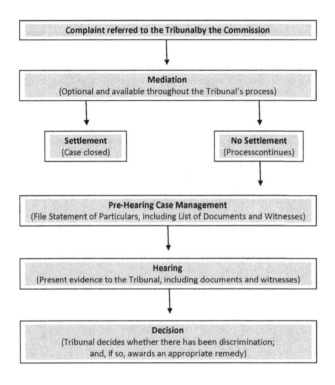

4.6 Hearing

A Hearing is where the parties to the complaint are given the opportunity to present their evidence, witnesses and argument to the Tribunal (see Rule 9). The objective of the Hearing is to allow the Tribunal to hear the merits of the case so it can decide whether discrimination has occurred. If you are the person alleging discrimination, the Hearing is your chance to establish why you believe you were discriminated against. If you are the person accused of discrimination, the Hearing is your chance to rebut the complaint and/or establish why the discrimination was justified.

How long will the Hearing last?

The length of the Hearing depends on the complexity of the case and the number of witnesses. The average length of a Hearing before the Tribunal is 5 days. Usually, the Hearing is held from 9:30 a.m. to 5:00 p.m. with a break in the morning, a break for lunch and a break in the afternoon.

Where will the Hearing be held?

The Tribunal generally holds Hearings in a location that minimizes, to the extent possible, the travel costs of parties and witnesses. The location is often a public building such as a hotel or conference centre. In larger cities, it is not uncommon for Hearings to be held in a federal courthouse and, in Ottawa, there are dedicated Tribunal Hearing rooms that are used.

A. Preparing for the Hearing

I.   Witnesses

Subpoena(s)

It is possible that a witness does not wish to appear before the Tribunal, or needs a legal document to justify his or her absence from work. A subpoena is a legal document that orders a person to appear at the Hearing as a witness. It may also require that person to bring to the Hearing any documents or items that he or she owns or has control over that relate to the complaint.

A subpoena can be requested from the Tribunal. If the Tribunal grants the request to subpoena a witness, it will provide a signed subpoena, which the party must then arrange to have served on the witness.

Witnesses are also entitled to be paid for their time before the Tribunal by the party who calls them to the Hearing (see s. 50(6) of the *Act*). The Registry Officer assigned to the case will provide important information on paying witness fees when requesting a subpoena.

It is not necessary to serve a subpoena and pay witness fees if the witness is willing and able to appear without a subpoena. In many cases, witnesses appear voluntarily, without a subpoena or the payment of fees.

Oath or affirmation

A witness testifying before the Tribunal is asked to take an oath or make an affirmation.

An oath is a solemn appeal to God, or a revered person, or object such as a holy book, in witness of a promise to speak the truth.

A solemn affirmation is the equivalent to an oath for those witnesses who do not have religious beliefs, or do not wish to refer to them.

Prior to the Hearing, a party should ask each of their witnesses whether they wish to take an oath or affirmation before providing their testimony. If a witness wishes to take an oath on a holy book, or object, they are asked to bring the holy book or object of their choosing.

At the beginning of the Hearing, each party will be asked to complete a Record of Appearance indicating the type of oath or affirmation each of their witnesses wishes to take before they testify.

II.   Copies of Documents& Book of Authorities

Prior to the Hearing, the Tribunal will send a letter to the parties explaining the Tribunal's procedures on the filing of Exhibits and Books of Authorities at the Hearing.

An exhibit is any document, picture or object put forward as evidence at the Hearing. Not every document that was disclosed will necessarily become an exhibit at the Hearing. At the disclosure stage, parties are showing each other all the documents in their possession that are potentially relevant to the case.   At the Hearing, parties introduce as exhibits only those documents they believe are necessary to support their case. In so doing, parties can introduce as exhibits documents that were disclosed by the opposing party.

However,   the   Tribunal   cannotreceive   as   exhibits   documents   that   are privileged.Furthermore, if a document was not previously disclosed by one of the parties, the Tribunal may refuse to receive that document as an exhibit (see Rule 9(3)(c)).

A Book of Authorities contains copies of the case law and legislation a party will use to argue its case before the Tribunal. The sections of case law and/or legislation that support the party's argument should be highlighted in the Book of Authorities.

The Tribunal's letter will ask each party to prepare a set number of copies of all the exhibits and case law they plan to file with the Tribunal. Usually, the Tribunal asks for six (6) copies of each exhibit and Book of Authorities (one for the Tribunal Member; one for the official record; one for the witness; one for the Commission; one for the opposing party; and, one for the party filing the document for use during the Hearing).

III.   Accommodation of special needs

The Tribunal is committed to making the Hearing process as accessible as possible for all participants: the parties, witnesses, counsel, other representatives and observers. Anyone who requires accommodation of special needs for the Hearing should notify the Registry Officer assigned to the case as early as possible.

While the Tribunal tries to respect the privacy of individuals seeking accommodation of special needs, where those accommodations could affect the rights of other participants to the Hearing, those other participants may have to be notified of the request and given an opportunity to speak to it. Ultimately, the decision on the request for special needs accommodation will be made by the Member presiding over the Hearing.

B. At the Hearing

I.Who is there and where do they sit?

Several people may be present at the Hearing. They may include the Complainant, the Respondent, their respective lawyers, the lawyer for the Canadian Human Rights Commission, any other interested parties, and the witnesses that will be testifying (however, see Rule 9(9), 9(10) and 9(11)).

Also present will be the Registry Officer and the Member or Members of the Tribunal who will hear the case.

The Hearing is also open to the public and anything said in the Hearingis public. Therefore, journalists and members of the public may also be present in the Hearing room. In certain exceptional circumstances however, the Tribunal may decide to put into place measures to ensure the confidentiality of the Hearing (see s. 52(1) of the *Act*).

A typical Hearing room will have the following layout:

Tribunal Member(s)		
Registry Officer		Witness (could be on the other side of the Registry Officer, depending on the room's configuration)
Complainant (and lawyer)	Commission (lawyer)	Respondent (and lawyer)
Extra seating (for interested parties, assistants to lawyers, etc.)		
Public Seating		

II.   Record of appearance

Upon arrival at the Hearing, the Registry Officer will ask each party to complete a Record of Appearance. On the form, a party must state their name and address, the witnesses they will call and whether they will testify under oath or affirmation.

III.   Introductions

Once all the parties have filled in and returned their Record of Appearance forms, the Registry Officer will call the Hearing to order, introduce the Tribunal Member or Members hearing the case, and ask the parties to introduce themselves.

The normal order for introductions is: the Complainant, the Commission, the Respondent and any interested parties. The parties and their lawyers each take turns standing up and introducing themselves.

For example, the Complainant in a case may introduce themselves as follows: "Good morning, my name is Sofia Li and I am the Complainant in this matter".

IV.   Opening statements

After introductions, all parties are asked if they would like to make an Opening Statement. An Opening Statement is a summary of what that party intends to prove during the Hearing. In an Opening Statement, a party will describe the facts they intend to prove and the evidence they will present to prove these facts. Opening Statements may also briefly refer to the main legal principles that a party feels are relevant to the case.

The Complainant usually goes first, followed by the Canadian Human Rights Commission(if participating) and then the Respondent. Any of the parties can decide not to give an Opening Statement. Or, a party may decide to give their Opening Statement later, when it is their turn to present their case.

V.   Witness testimony

When opening statements are completed, the Tribunal Member will invite the Complainant to call its first witness.When the Complainant has finished calling all of its witnesses and presenting their evidence, it is then followed by the Commission, should it be participating in the inquiry.

In certain circumstances, the Commission may call its witnesses before the Complainant.

The Complainant and the Commission call all their witnesses and provide all of their evidence before the Respondent is invited to call his or her witnesses and make his or her case.

Each party is given an opportunity to ask each witness questions. This process is called "Examination". There are three different kinds of Examination: Direct examination, Cross-examination and Re-examination.

Questioning your witnesses& putting forward documents ("Direct Examination")

Asking questions of a witness you called to the Hearing is referred to as direct examination or examination in chief. The purpose of direct examination is to provide the Tribunal with evidence of the facts that make up your case.

Direct examination is also the time to put forward documents in support of your case. Generally, each document must be identified by a witness before they will be accepted into evidence by the Tribunal.

In some cases, the Complainant or Respondent may not be represented by a lawyer, but will want to provide witness testimony. In that situation, a party can testify without having someone ask them questions. They simply present theirtestimony from the witness box and state the facts as they understand them.While the party is giving evidence on the stand, they are not expected at the same time to provide argument. Later on, once all witnesses have been heard from, they will have an opportunity to convince the Tribunal that there is, based on their interpretation of the facts and law, a particular conclusion that should be reached (see Final Argument section below).

At the direct examination stage, a party is required to put all their intended evidence theyare planning to present before the Tribunal. This should include evidence in support of their relief sought. It is improper to deliberately hold back known evidence for the purposes of attempting to introduce it later in the Hearing.

Questioning the other party's witnesses ("Cross-examination")

Asking questions of a witness who was called by an opposing party, after that party has questioned that witness, is referred to as cross-examination. There are two purposes for cross-examination: to cast doubt on the truth or accuracy of what the witness has said and to flush out additional information that will support your side of the story. Generally, all witnesses who present evidence under direct examination are subject to cross-examination by the other side.

During direct examination by the opposing party of the opposing party's witnesses, it is advisable to make notes of the points you would like to askthose witnesses in cross-examination. It is not advisable to make the cross-examination simply repeat the direct examination.

Re-questioning your witness("Re-examination")

Asking additional questions of the witness you called, after the other parties have cross-examined that witness, is referred to as re-examination. Re-examination is usually allowed only to clarify or explain new issues that came up during cross-examination.

VI.   Reply

After the Respondent's witnesses have been examined, cross-examined and re-examined, the Commission and Complainant may be given an opportunity to present evidence in reply toanynew evidence introduced by the Respondent that was not covered during the Complainant's or Commission's direct evidence.

Reply evidence cannot relate to a new issue, and must relate to an issue raised in the Respondent's case. Also, reply evidence cannot be presented without the express permission of the Tribunal.

VII.   Final argument

When all of the evidence has been presented, each party is given an opportunity to present a Final Argument. This is a chance for each party to explain what facts they believe have been proven by the evidence, and why. This is also a chance for each party to explain why they feel the evidence as a whole either supports a finding of discrimination or not within the meaning of the *Canadian Human Rights Act*. Final Argument is not the time for introducing additional evidence; rather, during Final Argument parties refer to evidence that was presented earlier.

The Final Arguments of the Canadian Human Rights Commission and the Complainant also include a description of the remedy they seek, together with a recap of the evidence that supports this request.

The Respondent's Final Argument summarizes his or her answer to the complaint. It revisits evidence he or she feels tends to support its view of the facts, and explains why those facts do not support the conclusion that discrimination occurred or why they fail to demonstrate that the requested remedy is appropriate.

Final Argument also gives each party an opportunity to refer to the *Canadian Human Rights Act* or any other statute, as well as case law in support of their case (Book of Authorities).

4.7   Decision

Following a Hearing, the Tribunal will issue a decision explaining its reasons for finding that the complaint has or has not been substantiated. If a complaint is substantiated, the decision may also order a remedy to rectify the discrimination.

The Tribunal tries to release a decision within four months of hearing the complaint, but more complex cases may take longer.

4.8   Judicial Review

If a party disagrees with the Tribunal's decision, it can ask the Federal Court of Canada to review it. This is done by filing an application for judicial review with the Federal Court of Canada within 30 days after the time the decision was first communicated by the Tribunal to the parties.

- For more information on the Federal Court of Canada visit http://cas-ncr-nter03.cas-satj.gc.ca/portal/page/portal/fc_cf_en/Index

5. FOR MORE INFORMATION

For more information about the Tribunal, visit the website at www.chrt-tcdp.gc.ca or contact the Tribunal at:

Canadian Human Rights Tribunal
160 Elgin Street, 11th Floor
Ottawa, Ontario
K1A 1J4

Telephone: (613) 995-1707

TTY: (613) 947-1070

Fax: (613) 995-3484

E-mail: registrar-greffier@chrt-tcdp.gc.ca

6. OTHER RESOURCES

- For a glossary defining commonly used Tribunal terms please visit: http://chrt-tcdp.gc.ca/NS/about-apropos/g-eng.asp

- To search or browse the full text of Tribunal decisions please visit: http://decisions.chrt-tcdp.gc.ca/chrt-tcdp/en/nav.do\

- To search or browse the full text of court decisions and other provincial human rights tribunal decisions please visit: http://www.canlii.org/

- To search and browse legislation please visit: http://laws.justice.gc.ca/eng/

- To access the Bank Rate (monthly series) please visit:http://www.bankofcanada.ca/rates/interest-rates/canadian-interest-rates (Seeabove: 4.5 A. III – Interest)

Appendix 8.3
The CHRT's Practice Note No. 2[†]

PRACTICE NOTE

CANADIAN HUMAN RIGHTS TRIBUNAL PRACTICE NOTE No. 2

12 June 2009

RE: Representation of Parties by Non-Lawyers

1. On occasion, parties to the inquiry process are represented by non-lawyers.

2. The Tribunal expects non-lawyer representatives to accept the obligations of participating in the inquiry process by:
    a. treating the Members and staff of the Tribunal, as well as the other participants in the inquiry process, with courtesy and respect;
    b. obtaining a clear written authorization from the party they are representing which sets out the terms and conditions of their mandate;
    c. being well informed of the case and the position of the party they are representing;
    d. being available for conference calls, hearings and other events scheduled by the presiding Member;
    e. complying with any time limits set by the Tribunal, as well as any other directions or orders given by the Tribunal;
    f. complying with the Tribunal's Rules of Procedure, except where the rules require the services of a lawyer;
    g. fulfilling any undertakings given to the Tribunal or to another party, including confidentiality undertakings;
    h. refraining from any activity that would undermine the proper administration of justice, such as knowingly presenting false or misleading evidence, failing to disclose the existence of relevant documents or dissuading a witness from giving evidence.

[†] Source: CHRT website, "Procedures > Practice Notes", <http://www.chrt-tcdp.gc.ca/procedures/practice-notes-en.html#2>

3. Non-lawyer representatives do not have the same representative responsibilities and rights as lawyers in the Tribunal inquiry process. In some instances, the law, or the Tribunal rules, authorize only lawyers to accomplish certain acts, (such as proof of service by a solicitor's certificate under rule 2(3)). Non-lawyers who choose to represent parties before the Tribunal must do so in full knowledge and acceptance of these limitations.

4. Finally, it should be noted that the Tribunal Member presiding over the inquiry retains the authority to limit or exclude the participation of non-lawyer representatives where the Member has formed the opinion that such participation, for example, is likely to hinder, rather than facilitate, the inquiry process.

Appendix 8.4
Parties before the Tribunal and Avenues of Judicial Review and Appeal[†]

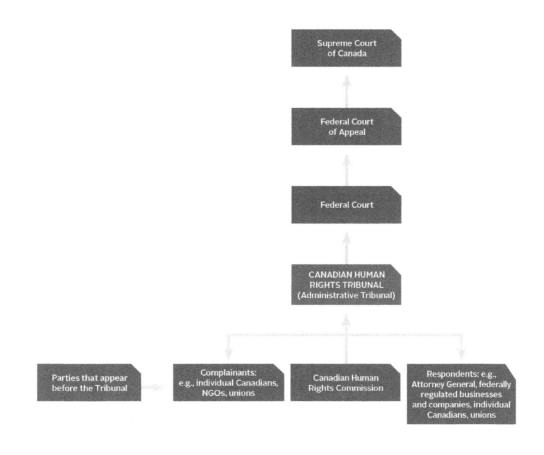

† Source: *Canadian Human Rights Tribunal Annual Report 2015*, p. 6, online: <http://www.chrt-tcdp.gc.ca/transparency/reports/documents/annual-reports/2015-en.pdf>

Appendix 8.5
Tribunal Inquiry Process and Judicial Review[†]

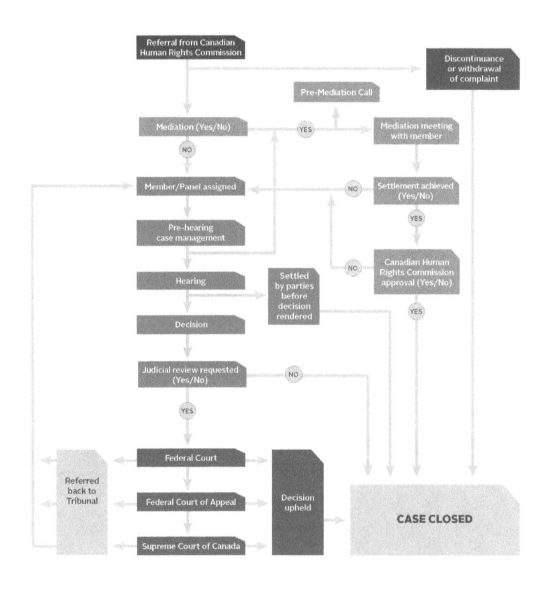

[†] Source: *Canadian Human Rights Tribunal Annual Report 2015*, p. 7, online: <http://www.chrt-tcdp.gc.ca/ transparency/reports/documents/annual-reports/2015-en.pdf>